The Book of
Women's Firsts

The
Book of
Women's
Firsts

Phyllis J. Read
Bernard L. Witlieb

BREAKTHROUGH

ACHIEVEMENTS

OF ALMOST 1,000

AMERICAN WOMEN

RANDOM HOUSE
New York

Library of Congress Cataloging-in-Publication Data

Read, Phyllis J.
The book of women's firsts: breakthrough achievements of almost
1,000 American women/by Phyllis J. Read and Bernard L. Witlieb.
p.   cm.
Includes index.
ISBN 0-679-40975-0.—ISBN 0-679-74280-8 (pbk.)
1. Women—United States—Biography.   2. Success—United States—
Miscellanea.   3. World records—Miscellanea.   4. Women—United
States—Societies and clubs—History.   I. Witlieb, Bernard, 1939-   .
II. Title.
CT3260.R428   1992
920.72′0973—dc20   92-16872

Book design by Levavi & Levavi

Manufactured in the United States of America

1 2 3 4 5 6 7 8 9

First Edition

New York   Toronto   London   Sydney   Auckland

To the memory of Dora Sue Murrell Gibbs, my mother and greatest friend, who provided a powerful and enduring model of a strong and independent woman . . .

and to Don Read, my husband, who has been the most constant positive and loving influence in my life.

Phyllis J. Read

To the memories of Saul Albin and Rose and Jack Rothman.

Bernard L. Witlieb

ACKNOWLEDGMENTS

I wish to thank a special group of friends, all strong, successful women, for adding joy and richness to my life: Mary Baughan, Bunny (Benita) Dolin, Marcia Dunne, Julie Skurdenis, Dorothy Taylor, and Ellen Witlieb.

And four men who provided crucial support and guidance at important moments in my life: Vernon L. Gibbs, my brother; Sheldon Grebstein, former English professor, now president of the State University of New York at Purchase, who encouraged me to become a writer and to major in English; John I. Gray, my first flight instructor; and Carl Polowczyk, Dean of Academic Affairs at Bronx Community College of The City University of New York, valuable mentor and colleague.

Phyllis J. Read

Love and respect to the women in my family whose lives have been models of self-sufficiency and courage: my mother, Sadie Witlieb; my daughter, Rachel; my sister, Rhoda Albin; my sisters-in-law, Carole Lapidus and Laurie Rothman; and my nieces, Lisa Radimer and Marie Albin.

Above all, I have been blessed by the love and strengths of my wife, Ellen Witlieb.

Bernard L. Witlieb

In this large undertaking, we relied upon the help of many people. Although their numbers are too great to permit naming them all here, we hope they will accept our heartfelt gratitude.

We thank Charlotte L. Mayerson and Judy Johnson, our editors at Random House, for their valuable assistance and hard work. Special thanks to Susan Banks, Jennifer Friedman, Leni Glauber, Judith Reinfeld, Penny Wolff, and

Nancy Zachary, the expert reference librarians of the Scarsdale, New York, Public Library; Sam Daniel and Maja Keech, reference specialists, Prints and Photo Division, Library of Congress; the staff in the reference units of the National Archives; the staff in the manuscript division of the Library of Congress; James Hoffman and Terence A. Johnson, Schomburg Center for Research in Black Culture, The New York Public Library; and Paul Feys, Director, International Student House, Washington, D.C.

Special thanks also to Roderick D. Hibben; Meredith M. Layer, senior vice-president of Public Responsibility, American Express Company, and former board member of the New York Women's Forum; Barbara Martineau, Woods Hole Oceanographic Institution; Peggy Silhanek, Director of Development, J. B. Speed Art Museum, Louisville, Kentucky; and Carole Zavin.

Special acknowledgment to Irwin and Roberta Berger; Pat Camarinos; Heather Corbalis; Patricia Patrick Cornett; Emily Dais; Jack Giordano; Neil Grill; David and Harvey Hoffman; Patricia Ray Lanier; Sonia Olivero; Michele Peate; Cheryl Quinn; Réka Souwapawong; Jacqueline Stuchin-Paprin; and Andy Witlieb.

We thank the following people who were especially helpful in our search for information and photographs:

Joanna Adamus, NASA; Tracey Allen, the Royal Air Force, High Wycombe, England; Ricki Bar-Zeev, The American Physical Society; Michele Boden and Judy Burns, Charles Scribner's Sons; Joanna Cerreta and Ann Shumard, The National Portrait Gallery; Wendy Cooper and Simon Matthews, Bruce Coleman, Ltd., Uxbridge, Middlesex, England; Carolyn Davis, Marguerite Higgins Collection, Special Collections Department, Syracuse University; Ann Marie Deane, Nestlé Chocolate; Peter Elliott, the Royal Air Force Museum, Hendon, London, England; George Gill, president and publisher, *The Courier-Journal,* and Mary Jane Stinson, his assistant; Christina L. Gimbel, The National Museum of Women in the Arts; April Goebel, National Geographic Society; Marie-Helene Gold, Schlesinger Library, Radcliffe College; Joyce Goulait, Photographic Services, Smithsonian Institution; Jennifer Greenfeld, U.S.A. Weekend; Araina Heath, Sophia Smith Collection, Smith College; Florence Howe, founder, The Feminist Press; Robert Ieva and Martin Skrocki, U.S. Merchant Marine Academy; Pat Jones, Indy 500 Photos; Rosa Lamas, Fundacion Angel Ramos, Inc.; Margery S. Long, Walter P. Reuther Library, Wayne State University; Robin McElheny, Harvard University Archives; Susan McElrath, Bethune Museum and Archives, Washington, D.C.; Northwood Institute, Midland, Michigan, for its Distinguished Woman Awards; Cheryl Orlick, the Albright-Knox Art Gallery; Charla Prager and Sara Pritchard, American Association of Cost Engineers; Susan Prickett, Raymond James & Associates; Jody Randazzo

Awards; Jan Smiley, University of Missouri Press; Steven Smith, American Institute of Chemical Engineers; Linda Souyack, Daily Racing Form; Andrea Swinhart, Walt Disney Studios; Vicki A. Tanner, Arlington National Cemetery; Tony Terry, Churchill Downs; Marjorie Tinkerton, *San Gabriel Valley Tribune*; Suzanne Trimel, Office of Public Information, Columbia University; Raymond Wald; Claudia Stone Weissberg, The Pulitzer Prizes; Judith Witham, The Evangelical and Reformed Historical Society; New York Public Relations Office, World Council of Churches.

Our gratitude to Gloria Steinem, inspirational leader; to the members of the Women's History Month Committee of Bronx Community College: Carrie Ashby, Connie DeYorgi, Joyce Einson, Alice Fuller, Sharlene Hoberman, Ellen Hoist, J. Jeuchter, Evelyn Kish, Dolores Magnotta, Marilyn Russell, Carin Savage, Ann Smith, and Louise Squitieri; and to Lilia Melani, CUNY Women's Coalition.

PICTURE CREDITS

Cover: *(top)* **Abigail Smith Adams** From original painting by Gilbert Stuart, Prints and Photographs Division, Library of Congress; *(middle)* **Sandra Day O'Connor** By permission of the Public Information Office of the U.S. Supreme Court; *(bottom)* **Sally Ride** NASA; **5, Abigail Smith Adams** From original painting by Gilbert Stuart, Prints and Photographs Division, Library of Congress; **9, Jane Addams** Sophia Smith Collection, Smith College, Northampton, Massachusetts; **12, Women's Air Derby** Smithsonian Institution, Washington, D.C., SI photo number 79-10578; **20, Mary Anderson** Prints and Photographs Division, Library of Congress; **40, Clara Barton** Sophia Smith Collection, Smith College, Northampton, Massachusetts; **50, Mary McLeod Bethune** Bethune Museum and Archives, Inc.; **53, Shirley Temple Black** Prints and Photographs Division, Library of Congress; **56, "The New Costume Polka"** Lithograph by J. Queen, 1851, Prints and Photographs Division, Library of Congress; **61, Evangeline Booth** Prints and Photographs Division, Library of Congress; **72, Olympia Brown** Engraving by J. C. Buttre of photo by C. D. Mosher, Prints and Photographs Division, Library of Congress; **73, Virginia Mae Brown** Prints and Photographs Division, Library of Congress; **74, Pearl Buck** Clara Sipprell Collection, Department of Special Collections, Syracuse University Library, Syracuse, New York; **77, Dorothy V. Bush** Prints and Photographs Division, Library of Congress; **86, Carrie Chapman Catt** Prints and Photographs Division, Library of Congress; **95, Jacqueline Cochran** Smithsonian Institution, Washington, D.C., SI photo number 72-6627; **98, Bessie Coleman** Schomburg Center for Research in Black Culture, The New York Public Library, Astor, Lenox and Tilden Foundations; **114, Daughters of the American Revolution National Board of Management** Prints and Photographs Division, Library of Congress; **130, Amelia Earhart** Smithsonian Institution, Washington, D.C., SI photo number A43033-C; **134, Elsie Eaves** Charles Leon, compliments of American Association of Cost Engineers; **136, Marian Wright Edelman** Rich Reinhard, compliments of Children's Defense Fund; **138, Gertrude Ederle** Prints and Photographs Division, Library of Congress; **140, Amy Eilberg** Photography by Nyki Wals-Kundynmahl; **145, "Election Day" cartoon** Prints and Photographs Division, Library of Congress; **151, Rebecca Felton** Photo by National Photo Company, November 20, 1922, Prints and Photographs Division, Library of Congress; **152, Ma Ferguson** Prints and Photographs Division, Library of Congress; **157, Anna L. Fisher** NASA; **163, Dian Fossey** R I M Campbell; **165, Lucinda Franks** Columbia University, New York, New York; **171, Juliane Gallina** U.S. Naval Academy; **174, Janet Gaynor** In "State Fair," 1933, Courtesy of 20th Century–Fox; **182, Katharine Meyer Graham** Prints and Photographs Division, Library of Congress; **184, Ella Grasso** Prints and Photographs Division, Library of Congress; **188, Janet Guthrie** IMS photo by Ron McQueeney; **189, Helene Hahn** Compliments of Walt Disney Pictures; **195, Patricia Roberts Harris** Prints and Photographs Division, Library of Congress; **203, Marguerite Higgins** Marguerite Higgins Collection, Department of Special Collections, Syracuse University Library, Syracuse, New York; **203, Carla Anderson Hills** Official photo; **204, Tina (Argentina) Hills** Personal photo; **208, Oveta Culp Hobby** Photo by Harris & Ewing; **211, Wilhelmina Cole Holladay** Personal photo; **214, Grace Hopper** Official U.S. Navy photograph by James S. Davis; **216, Harriet Hosmer** Schlesinger Library, Radcliffe College, Cambridge, Massachusetts; **218, Julia Ward Howe** Prints and Photographs Division, Library of Congress; **219, Lady Clerks** Wood engraving in *Harper's Weekly*, February 18, 1865, Prints and Photographs Division, Library of Congress; **220, Winifred Huck** Photo by National Photo Co., February 15, 1923, Prints and Photographs Division, Library of Congress; **222, Anne M. Hutchinson** Boston Athenaeum; **223, Ada Louise Huxtable** Columbia University, New York, New York; **229, Anna M. Jarvis** Gutenhunst photo, 1909, Prints and Photographs Division, Library of Congress; **230, "Marinettes"** Photo by Harris & Ewing, Prints and Photographs Division, Library of Congress; **233, Dorothy Jurney** Personal photo; **234, "Studies in Expression when Women Are Jurors"** Wash drawing by Charles Dana Gibson for *Life*, October 23, 1912, Prints and Photographs Division, Library of Congress; **237, Laura Keene** Prints and Photographs Division, Library of Congress; **237, National Women's Trade Union League** Prints and Photographs Division, Library of Congress; **243, Susan Goodman Komen and Nancy Goodman Brinker** Personal photo; **244, Juanita Morris Kreps** Prints and Photographs Division, Library of Congress; **247, Harriet Lane (Johnston)** Drawing by Rosenmeyer in *Ladies Home Journal*, May, 1901, Prints and Photographs Division, Library of Congress; **248, Julia Lathrop** Photo by Harris & Ewing, Prints and Photographs Division, Library of Congress; **249, Florence B. Lawrence** Scene from the Biograph film "Resurrection," 1909, produced by D. W. Griffith, Prints and Photographs Division, Library of Congress; **253, Mary Todd Lincoln** Photo by Brady, 1861, Prints and Photographs Division, Library of Congress; **254, Anne Morrow Lindbergh** Prints and Photographs Division, Library of Congress; **256, Mary Livermore** Copyright 1901 by J. E. Purdy, Boston, Prints and Photographs Division, Library of Congress; **257, Belva Ann Lockwood** Prints and Photographs Division, Library of Congress; **263, Lucky (Joy) Lucas** Personal photo; **264, Shannon W. Lucid** NASA; **277, Molly Pitcher (Mary McCauley)** Lithograph by Currier & Ives, 1876, Prints and Photographs Division, Library of Congress; **281, Anita N. McGee** Photo by Clinedinst, c. 1904, Prints and Photographs Division, Library of Congress; **282, Mary McGrory** Columbia University, New York, New York; **299, Ellie Moore** Personal photo; **300, Esther Morris** Prints and Photographs Division, Library of Congress; **302, Lucretia Coffin Mott** Sophia Smith Collection, Smith College, Northampton, Massachusetts; **315, Eleanor Holmes Norton** Personal photo; **317, Mary Norton** Photo by National Photo Co., Prints and Photographs Division, Library of Congress; **318, Antonia Novello** *(left)* Compliments of the Surgeon General's Office; *(right)* Photo by Molly Roberts; **321, Early Telephone Exchange—Women Operators** A. I. Kener illustration for *Harper's New Monthly Magazine*, October 1896, Prints and Photographs Division, Library of Congress; **322, Annie Oakley** Copyright Richard K. Fox, 1899, Prints and Photographs Division, Library of Congress; **323, Sandra Day O'Connor** Copyright National Geographic Society; **325, Kitty O'Neil** Personal photo; **327, Ruth Bryan Owen** Prints and Photographs Division, Library of Congress; **330, Maud Park** Prints and Photographs Division, Library of Congress; **333, Alice Paul** Copyright Underwood & Underwood, Prints and Photographs Division, Library of Congress; **338, Ellen F. Pendleton** Portrait by G. B. Abell, 1911, Prints and Photographs Division, Library of Congress; **340, Frances Perkins** Archives of Labor and Urban Affairs, Wayne State University, Detroit, Michigan; **342, Esther Peterson** Personal photo; **347, Mary Pickford** A still from the movie "King Brings Molly'o to His Home," 1915, Prints and Photographs Division, Library of Congress; **349, Pocahontas** Photograph of a painting by W. R. Leigh, c. 1943, Prints and Photographs Division, Library of Congress; **353, Harriet Quimby** Smithsonian Institution, Washington, D.C., SI photo number A43515; **357, Shulamit Ran** Columbia University, New York, New York;

360, Jeannette Rankin Matzene, Chicago, 1917, Prints and Photographs Division, Library of Congress; **361, Vinnie Ream** Prints and Photographs Division, Library of Congress; **364, Judith A. Resnick** NASA; **370, Sally K. Ride** NASA; **371, Aileen Riggin** Prints and Photographs Division, Library of Congress; **374, Betty (Elizabeth) Robinson** Prints and Photographs Division, Library of Congress; **379, Eleanor Roosevelt** *(left)* Prints and Photographs Division, Library of Congress; *(right)* Photo by United Press, Prints and Photographs Division, Library of Congress; **384, Wilma Rudolph** Schomburg Center for Research in Black Culture, The New York Public Library, Astor, Lenox and Tilden Foundations; **387, Ruth St. Denis** Photo by Alice Boughton, Prints and Photographs Division, Library of Congress; **389, Deborah Sampson** Engraving by H. Mann, 1797, Prints and Photographs Division, Library of Congress; **391, Margaret Sanger** Prints and Photographs Division, Library of Congress; **396, Arlette Schweitzer** Personal photo; **397, Blanche Scott** Prints and Photographs Division, Library of Congress; **399, Margaret Rhea Seddon** NASA; **402, Elizabeth Ann Bayley Seton** Lithograph by John Penniman, 1817–50, Prints and Photographs Division, Library of Congress; **406, Anna Shaw** Starting on last parade before suffrage was won in New York State, Prints and Photographs Division, Library of Congress; **410, Hazel Brannon Smith** Columbia University, New York, New York; **411, Margaret Chase Smith** Photo 1943, Prints and Photographs Division, Library of Congress; **425, Marjorie and Katherine Stinson**, Smithsonian Institution, Washington, D.C., SI photo number A5532-A; **429, Kathryn D. Sullivan** NASA; **430, Mary Surratt** Wood engraving after sketch, from *Frank Leslie's Illustrated Newspaper,* May 27, 1865, Prints and Photographs Division, Library of Congress; **431, Carol Sutton** Reprinted with permission from *The Courier-Journal;* **436, Marion Talley** Prints and Photographs Division, Library of Congress; **437, Ida Tarbell** Robertson Studio, Muskogee, Prints and Photographs Division, Library of Congress; **438, Anne E. Taylor** Prints and Photographs Division, Library of Congress; **441, Helen A. Thomas** United Press International; **448, Janet Graeme Travell** Prints and Photographs Division, Library of Congress; **449, Women's Triathlon** Compliments of Danskin; **451, Harriet Tubman** Schomburg Center for Research in Black Culture, The New York Public Library, Astor, Lenox and Tilden Foundations; **454, Julia Gardiner Tyler** Photo by Franceco Auelli, in the White House, before 1864, Prints and Photographs Division, Library of Congress; **461, Venita VanCaspel** Personal photo; **466, Lillian Wald** Underwood & Underwood, Prints and Photographs Division, Library of Congress; **467, Maggie Walker** Schomburg Center for Research in Black Culture, The New York Public Library, Astor, Lenox and Tilden Foundations; **472, Martha Washington** Prints and Photographs Division, Library of Congress; **473, Mary Ball Washington** Attributed to Robert Edge Pine (c. 1730–88), Prints and Photographs Division, Library of Congress; **476, Mae West** Prints and Photographs Division, Library of Congress; **477, Edith Wharton** Gessford, New York, compliments of Charles Scribner's Sons; **482, Emma Willard** Prints and Photographs Division, Library of Congress; **484, Sarah Williamson** On election day, May, 1991, John Melingagio, Boys Town; **485, Helen Wills** Prints and Photographs Division, Library of Congress; **488, Suffragette Night Paraders** Prints and Photographs Division, Library of Congress; **493, Victoria Chaflin Woodhull** Engraving by J. C. Buttre, from Brady photo, Prints and Photographs Division, Library of Congress; **497, Patience Lovell Wright** Etching, *The London Magazine,* November, 1775, Prints and Photographs Division, Library of Congress; **498, C. S. Wu** Columbia University, New York, New York; **502, Babe Didrikson Zaharias** Photo July 1954, Prints and Photographs Division, Library of Congress; **503, Ellen Taaffe Zwilich** Columbia University, New York, New York.

INTRODUCTION

This book of first achievements of women in the United States, its territories, and pre-Revolutionary colonies is a celebration—an open-ended, ongoing, expanding work-in-progress, a record of lives and events unfolding as well as of those already finished and recorded.

The women celebrated here did what no woman before was known to have done in the United States. Their lives were lived and their achievements realized in every era of U.S. history from the late sixteenth century Roanoke plantation to the present time, as the twentieth century records its final events. After all this time and history, this book can only be a bare-bones record of the women of this country who were the first to erect milestones of human endeavor. More often than not, they paid dearly for their achievements. Too frequently their accomplishments were derided, ignored, or forgotten.

It is difficult to single out individual stories for special attention. A common thread, especially in the early days of U.S. history but extending to the present as well, is the litany of incredible obstacles—known or inferred—faced by these pioneers. Some of the most difficult involved the social ostracism, scorn, and calumny heaped upon these women of the avant-garde. It is difficult to imagine or to underestimate the price many of these women paid in the currency of loneliness, self-doubt, ridicule, and insult. They were often considered to be in flagrant violation of the laws, written and unwritten, of God and man. Many were jailed for their beliefs and activities. They were seen to be violating the natural order, the way "everyone" knew things were supposed to be. They persevered against odds that should have been overwhelming—and they triumphed.

Our approach to this book has been serious, but not solemn. Included in this montage of first achievers are women whose accomplishments are frivolous, outrageous, and comic, as well as those that are impressive in serious contexts. The women celebrated here include senators and scientists, explorers and physicians, jockeys, movie stuntwomen, and vaudeville performers. We hope the reader will be impressed with the former, delighted with the latter, and applaud all with equal gusto. The fields in which these pioneering women recorded their "firsts" create their own alphabet from artists and astronauts through yachtswomen and zoologists. Here also are counterfeiters, murderers, spies, the first woman to survive going over Niagara Falls in a barrel, and the woman who gave birth to her own grandchildren.

The individual entries are not exhaustive; some of them are quite sketchy. We hope the stories here will inspire readers to go out and learn more about the individual women— maybe to write much-deserved biographies of some of them.

There are almost certainly some omissions. In selecting women for inclusion in this book, we encountered numerous obstacles. Since the activities of women were, more often than not, considered to be of little significance, many of their feats went unnoticed or unpublished in books or the mass media. (To see how little that has changed, just follow the obituary page of major daily newspapers for a few weeks. Unless the life span for women has suddenly taken a quantum leap, it's clear that—as the newspapers see things—very few women of notable achievement ever die. In the obituary notices, the ratio of women to men is probably no greater than one in twenty. And many days go by when there is not a single woman whose passing is deemed worthy of a column-inch.)

For many of the women who appear in this book, vital statistics are missing or hard to come by. In some cases the women married, or remarried, and their histories were subsumed under their husbands' names.

There is also a geographical imbalance of sorts in this book that is a function of the way the country was settled—east to west. We particularly regret the scarceness of Native American women and African-American women. In the case of Native American women, the absence of written languages often dooms their stories to obscurity. We are told, for example, that women of certain Native American tribes were responsible for the design and construction of dwellings. It is likely, therefore, that the first woman architect was a Native American. Similarly, the stories of many African-American women, who for generations were forbidden by law to read and write, are lost in the darkness of slavery and prejudice.

The catalog of first achievements filled this book to its planned size and overflowed. Numerous women whose stories deserve to appear here had to be left out because the text had grown too long. In any case, there is no such thing as a "complete" or finite list—and that is reason for rejoicing.

While we hope the book will be seen and used by many readers as a reference, it should be viewed equally as an ongoing tribute—a monument to the U.S. women, especially the unsung and unheard of, living and dead, who have been groundbreakers, pathfinders, and marchers in the vanguard of progress toward equal status, equal treatment, and equal place in the annals of humankind.

The Book of
Women's Firsts

Emma Abbott

First woman to form an opera company (1878).

Born Chicago, Illinois, 1850; died 1891.

Abbott, who made her professional debut in New York City in 1871, and her English debut in 1876, formed her company—the Emma Abbott English Opera Company—in 1878. The company, presenting shortened versions of contemporary operas, ran until December, 1890, one month before her death.

Grace Abbott

First woman to serve as an unofficial U.S. delegate to the League of Nations (1922).

Born Grand Island, Nebraska, November 17, 1878; died Chicago, Illinois, June 19, 1939.

Since the United States was never an official member of the League of Nations, Abbott served as an unofficial delegate to the organization's Advisory Committee on Traffic in Women and Children from 1922 to 1934. (The function of the committee was to formulate international policy on trade in women and children for illegal labor and immoral practices.)

Abbott earned a Ph.B. degree from Grand Island College in 1898, then taught high school. In 1908, as a resident of Hull House (Chicago, Illinois), the first settlement house in the United States, she began a career as a social worker, serving as the first president of the Immigrants' Protective League. In 1909 Abbott earned an M.A. degree in political science from the University of Chicago (Illinois). In 1917 at the invitation of Julia Lathrop (see entry), she joined the staff of the federal Children's Bureau; she also published a book, *The Immigrant and the Community*. Between 1919 and 1921 Abbott was the first to hold the post of director of the Illinois State Immigrants' Commission. From 1921 to 1934 she was head of the Children's Bureau, which opened 3,000 child health and prenatal care centers throughout the United States.

In 1934 Abbott was named professor of public welfare at the School of Social Service Administration, University of Chicago, and from 1934 to 1939 she was editor of *Social Service Review*.

Margaret Abbott

First person to win the Olympic gold medal in golf (1900).

Dates unknown.

The Olympic golf event, held in Paris, France, was a onetime event. Abbott, a citizen of Chicago, Illinois, who was an art student living in Paris, won the nine-hole event with a score of forty-seven, two strokes better than the Swiss representative, Polly Whittier.

In 1902 Abbott married Finley Peter Dunne, the satirist who created "Mr. Dooley." He died in 1936, with Abbott and four children surviving him.

Simonne Abboud

First woman in recent history to serve as a crew member on a U.S. cargo ship (1971).

Born France, c. 1930.

Abboud, who immigrated to the United States in 1959, became a crew member on board *American Astro-naut,* a U.S. Lines freighter in 1971. Called a "mess man," she set five tables in the crew's mess quarters, serving food and cleaning up after meals. The only woman member of a forty-man crew, she earned $352 a month and was assigned to a private cabin with a private bath.

Abboud had worked aboard passenger ships since 1958. Among her positions was that of steward aboard Moore-McCormack cruise ships sailing to Central America.

According to the National Maritime Union, Coast Guard officials, and veteran sea personnel, there was no recollection of any other woman having sailed on a U.S. freighter.

Paula Ackerman

First woman to perform a rabbi's function (1951).

Born c. 1894.

When her husband, rabbi of a Reform congregation in Meridian, Mississippi, died, Ackerman was named by the trustees to serve in his place until a "regular" rabbi was selected. The 100-member congregation was Temple Beth Israel, second largest Jewish community in Mississippi. Ackerman served for several months as the congregation's spiritual leader, with all the authority and duties of a rabbi.

Phyllis Ackerman

First woman to do sports commentary for a professional basketball team (1974).

Born c. 1940.

Competing with 179 applicants, Ackerman, a schoolteacher with no previous television experience, was chosen in 1974 by a local Indiana station to do the color commentary for the Indiana Pacers, then a team in the American Basketball Association.

Abigail Smith Adams

First wife of a U.S. president to live in the original White House—the president's house on the Potomac (1800).

Born Weymouth, Massachusetts, November 11 (Old Style), 1744; died

Braintree (now Quincy), Massachusetts, 1818.

Abigail Smith married John Adams on October 25, 1764. He became president in 1797, and three years later the couple moved into the original White House, although the structure was not yet finished.

Annette Abbott Adams

First woman to hold office as U.S. assistant attorney general (1920); first to be U.S. district attorney (1918); first to be assistant U.S. attorney (1914).

Born Prattville, California, 1877; died Sacramento, California, 1956.

After graduating from the State Normal School, Chico, California, in 1897, Adams taught school. She returned to college at the University of California–Berkeley, receiving a bachelor of letters degree in 1904, then resumed her teaching career at Alturas High School, Alturas, California, where from 1907 to 1910 she served as principal.

At the University of California–Berkeley again, she earned a J.D. degree in 1912—the only woman in her graduating class. Adams became active in Democratic politics: in 1912 she was president of the Woman's State Democratic Club of California—in support of Woodrow Wilson.

In 1914 Adams was named federal prosecutor for the Northern District of California—the first woman to hold the post. In 1918 she became special U.S. attorney in San Francisco, and was promoted in June, 1920, to assistant attorney general in Washington, D.C. Her job was to oversee prosecution of violators of the Volstead Act—the 1919 act of Congress providing for federal enforcement of the Eighteenth Amendment, the Prohibition amendment.

Her first job, however, under U.S. Attorney General A. Mitchell Palmer was to try to round up women's votes for Mitchell's bid for the Democratic presidential nomination at the San Francisco national convention. Adams also made her own bid—for the vice-presidential nomination. She received one vote for president, on the thirty-seventh ballot.

In 1921 Adams left public service, going back into private practice in California. She continued to be an active participant in Democratic politics.

President Franklin D. Roosevelt asked Adams to serve as assistant special counsel under California Supreme Court Judge John Preston to handle the prosecution of two government cases (1935). In one of them, *U.S.* v. *Standard Oil*, Adams won a $7 million judgment.

The following year, Adams was elected to head the National Pro-Roosevelt Association of Woman Lawyers.

Entering the political arena again, Adams was elected in November, 1944, to a twelve-year term on the California Third District Court of Appeals. For ten of those twelve years, Adams was presiding judge—the first woman to hold such a high-ranking judicial position in California.

In 1950 she sat on the California Supreme Court to hear a single case, again earning the distinction of first woman to occupy such a position.

Clara Adams

First woman to fly from South America to North America (1931); first paying American woman passenger aboard the **Graf Zeppelin** *on its homeward flight from Lakehurst, New Jersey, to Friedrichshafen, Germany (1928).*

Born c. 1899.

In 1914 Adams, of Tannersville, Pennsylvania, made her first flight as a passenger in a Thomas flying boat, a seaplane built by Thomas Brothers Aeroplane Company, at Fort Eustis, Florida.

The dirigible flight, which left Lakehurst at 1:55 A.M. on Monday, October 29, 1928, lasted about sixty-five hours. Adams was the only woman among the twenty-five passengers.

Her record-setting South America–North America flight originated in Rio de Janeiro, Brazil, making stops in Miami, Florida, Charleston, South Carolina, Norfolk, Virginia, and New York City. There were forty passengers in the giant Dornier DO-X flying boat that followed the Pan American World Airways route on its July flight.

Adams also set a globe-circling record as a passenger, traveling for sixteen days, nineteen hours, and four minutes on a commercial flight that left Port Washington, Long Island, on June 28, 1939, and landed at the Newark, New Jersey, airport on July 15, 1939. The flight was two days faster than the previous around-the-world record set in 1936. An inveterate passenger, she was also the first woman aboard the China Clipper on its inaugural flight from San Francisco to Manila in 1936.

Fae Margaret Adams

First woman doctor to receive a regular commission in the United States Army (1953).

Born 1918.

Adams, of San Jose, California, earned her M.D. degree at the Medical College of the University of Pennsylvania (Philadelphia). She was commissioned a first lieutenant and was a reserve medical officer in the

Women's Army Corps. After her military service, Adams opened an obstetrics and gynecology practice in Albuquerque, New Mexico. At the time of this writing, she was retired.

Hannah Adams

First woman to become a professional writer (1784).

Born Medfield, Massachusetts, October 2, 1755; died Brookline, Massachusetts, December 15, 1831.

When she was a child, Adams read and memorized many of the works of poets such as Pope and Milton. Following in the footsteps of her father, a distant cousin of President John Adams, she became a voracious reader. When her father went bankrupt in 1772, Hannah, then only seventeen, was forced to support herself. After following some of the traditional routes for women at that time—making lace and tutoring—she decided to pursue writing as her career. She was a tireless researcher in the field of religious sects and decided to create an impartial history of all creeds and religions. Under the pen name H. A. Adams, she wrote *An Alphabetical Compendium of Various Sects,* her first work, sold by subscription in 1784.

In 1799 Adams published a second major book, *A Summary History of New England*. At the time she embarked on this project, there were few existing works on the history of New England. Other historical writers had concentrated on Massachusetts alone. Later, she produced an abridged version of the history for schoolchildren—*An Abridgement of the History of New England*. The publisher of the book went bankrupt, so she earned nothing from that book.

In 1812 Adams published another book titled *History of the Jews*. It sold well, as did her previous books. It was also one of the few books by an American writer to be reprinted in England at that time. Another work, *Letters on the Gospels,* was published in 1824.

Harriet Chalmers Adams

Organizer and first president of the Society of Women Geographers (1925).

Born Stockton, California, October 22, 1875; died Nice, France, July 17, 1937.

In 1925 Adams organized and became the first president of the Society of Women Geographers, an organization formed to support the aims and careers of professional woman geographers by providing information exchange and news of job opportunities.

Adams was also the first woman

outsider to visit many Central and South American regions, beginning her trips there around 1900. She wrote regularly for *National Geographic* magazine and was a fellow of the Royal Geographical Society of London.

Marian Hooper Adams

First woman to gain recognition for portrait photography (c. 1883).

Born Boston, Massachusetts, September 13, 1843; died Washington, D.C., December 6, 1885.

Adams made photographic portraits of statesman John Hay and historian George Bancroft that were highly praised. She was the wife of historian and novelist Henry Adams; they were married in 1872.

Sharon Sites Adams

First woman to complete a solo sail across the Pacific Ocean (1969).

Born c. 1930.

Sailing a thirty-one-foot ketch, Adams left Yokohama, Japan, on May 12, 1969, and arrived in San Diego, California, on July 25, 1969, covering the distance of approximately 5,620 miles in seventy-four days, seventeen hours, and fifteen minutes.

Perry Miller Adato

*First woman to win an award
from the Directors Guild of
America (1977).*

Born Yonkers, New York, date unknown.

Adato won her first Directors Guild of America award for her television documentary *Georgia O'Keeffe* (1977), shown on the Public Television network. The work was also selected for exhibition at one of the London Film Festivals.

She studied at the Marshalov School of Drama (New York, New York) and the New School for Social Research (New York, New York). In 1984 Adato was awarded an honorary doctorate (L.H.D.) by Illinois Wesleyan University (Bloomington).

In the 1950s and 1960s, Adato worked as organizer and director of the Film Advertising Center in New York City; film consultant and researcher for Columbia Broadcasting System in New York City; associate producer and eventually producer and director of cultural documentary films for the national production division of WNET—the Public Broadcasting System station in New York City.

Many of Adato's documentaries feature well-known writers and artists, such as Gertrude Stein, Dylan Thomas, Mary Cassatt, Louise Nevelson, and Pablo Picasso. Her features on Carl Sandburg (*Echoes and Silences,* 1982) and Eugene O'Neill (*Eugene O'Neill: A Glory of Ghosts,* 1986) also won Directors Guild of America awards.

Jane Addams

*First woman to receive the Nobel
Peace Prize (1931).*

Born Cedarville, Illinois, September 6, 1860; died Chicago, Illinois, May 21, 1935.

Addams won the Peace Prize in 1931 for her lifetime of dedication to the cause of peace and justice for all. She shared the prize with Nicholas Murray Butler.

She is credited with many other first achievements by a woman: first to organize and chair a Women's Peace party in the United States (1915); first to make a nominating

speech at a national political convention (1912); first head (1911) of the National Federation of Settlements, an organization she served until she died; first to receive an honorary degree from Yale University (New Haven, Connecticut) (1910); first to be elected president of the National Conference of Charities and Correction (later known as the National Conference of Social Work) (1909).

Addams graduated from Rockford College (Rockford, Illinois) in 1882. The following year she studied at the Woman's Medical College of Pennsylvania (Philadelphia), where she became unhappy after realizing that medicine was not the right career choice for her. She then spent two years traveling in Europe before returning to Baltimore, Maryland. In 1887 she and Ellen Gates Starr, a Rockford College classmate, traveled to Europe, where they observed the work of a settlement house in London, England. In 1889 Addams, assisted by Starr, founded the first major settlement house in the country, Chicago's Hull House, which became the model for settlement houses throughout the United States. The settlement house generated programs of education in childcare, English, the fine arts, health education, and nursery and playground supervision. The program also provided recreational opportunities for Chicago's immigrant families. Among the settlement workers who lived at Hull House were Julia Lathrop (see entry) and Sophonisba Breckinridge (see entry).

Along with Emily Greene Balch (1867–1961), who was to win the Nobel Peace Prize in 1946, she founded the Women's International League for Peace and Freedom in 1915.

Addams, an intrepid crusader for peace and social justice, helped found the American Civil Liberties Union in 1920, and served on its national committee for ten years.

Democracy and Social Ethics (1902), *Twenty Years at Hull House* (1910), *Peace and Bread in Time of War* (1922), and *The Second Twenty Years at Hull House* (1930) are four of the major works she wrote.

Addams was elected to the Hall of Fame for Great Americans, Bronx Community College (Bronx, New York) of the City University of New York in 1965. Her bust, displayed in the Hall of Fame, was sculpted by Granville W. Carter in 1968.

Sparky (Billy) Adels

Only woman licensed as a ship radio operator (1950).

Dates unknown.

Adels, whose home is San Francisco, California, was licensed as a ship radio operator in the U.S. Merchant Marines in 1950. She had been at sea since 1944.

Agriculture Training School, Women's

First agricultural training school to be established exclusively for women (1911).

In 1911 Alva Belmont (see entry) donated 200 acres of land that she owned in Hempstead, Long Island, New York, to be used as a training farm and school of agriculture for women. The first class of twenty students was selected from 630 applicants; they were taught by Laura D. Williams, a farmer. The students, aged sixteen and over, also took classes in cooking and housekeeping. They were paid an allowance that was increased in proportion to the income generated by their work on the training farm.

Caroline Leonetti Ahmanson

One of the first two women appointed to serve as chair of a Federal Reserve regional bank (1981) (see also Jean A. Crockett).

Born San Francisco, California, 1918.

Ahmanson was appointed in 1981 for a one-year term as chair of the Federal Reserve Bank of San Francisco, Twelfth District, after having chaired the Los Angeles branch of the Federal Reserve Bank of San Fran-

cisco from 1978 until 1979. (Prior to 1981 women had chaired some of the branch banks in each of the twelve regional districts.)

She is the chair and executive officer of Caroline Leonetti Ltd., Hollywood, California, a charm school that she founded in 1957. Between February and September of 1963, she made several appearances on "The Art Linkletter Show," offering beauty commentary.

Ahmanson, the widow of Howard F. Ahmanson, one of the United States's wealthiest philanthropists, has received many awards. Among them are the Certificate of Merit from the Council of the City of Los Angeles, the Distinguished Women's Award from the Northwood Institute, Midland, Michigan (1978), and a Special Service Award from the Federation of Youth Clubs, resulting from her work with teenagers.

Air Derby, Women's *(see also Marvel Crosson, Phoebe Fairgrave Omlie, and Louise McPhetridge Thaden)*

First cross-country women's air derby (1929).

The first cross-country women's air derby began on August 18, 1929. Twenty pilots competed, eighteen from the United States. The race began at Clover Field, Santa Monica, California, and finished at Cleveland Municipal Airport, Cleveland, Ohio, a

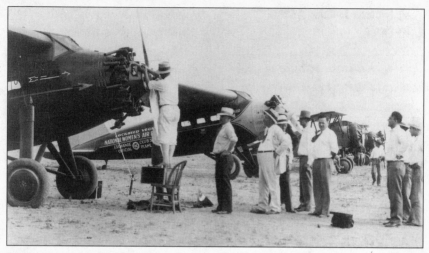

Women's Air Derby—Earhart's plane is in foreground

distance of 2,350 miles. The race, often called the Powder Puff Derby, took a week to complete. The pilots flew solo and no mechanics were allowed in the planes.

Louise McPhetridge Thaden, from Pittsburgh, Pennsylvania, came in first in the heavier-plane class, having finished the cross-country race in twenty hours, nineteen minutes, ten seconds. She collected $2,500 of the $9,850 prize. Phoebe Fairgrave Omlie, from Memphis, Tennessee, won in the lighter-plane division; her time was twenty-four hours, twelve minutes. Omlie and runners-up in both plane divisions split the remaining prize money.

Amelia Earhart (see entry) was a contestant, as was Ruth Nichols (see entry). Fifteen of the pilots, sometimes called Sweethearts of the Air, Flying Flappers, or Petticoat Pilots,

finished the race. One of the U.S. fliers, Marvel Crosson, who held the women's pilot altitude record at the time, parachuted from her disabled plane while flying over Arizona. She died when the parachute failed to open.

Air Force Academy *(see United States Air Force Academy)*

Air Force Pilots *(see United States Air Force Pilots)*

Jane Aitken

First woman to print the Bible in the United States (1808).

Born Paisley, Scotland, 1764; died Philadelphia, Pennsylvania, 1832.

Aitken arrived in Philadelphia, Pennsylvania, in 1771. Her father, Robert Aitken, was a bookbinder who published in 1782 the first English Bible in the United States.

After her father died in 1802, she took over his business. During the next ten years she published over sixty books, including the four-volume Thomson Bible. (Translated by Charles Thomson, it was the first English translation of the Septuagint, the Greek version of the Hebrew Scriptures.)

Aitken's business failed in 1813.

Toshiko Akiyoshi

The only woman in the history of jazz to have composed and arranged an entire library of music (1974).

Born Ryoyo, Manchuria, China, December 18, 1929.

Akiyoshi, a jazz pianist, arrived in the United States in 1956. Having developed an interest in jazz while living in Japan in the 1940s, she studied music at Berklee College of Music (Boston, Massachusetts), from which she graduated in 1959. She encountered both racial and sexual prejudice when she played in clubs wearing a kimono. She said that people were amazed to see an Asian woman playing jazz.

In the 1970s she was a force for the revival and modernization of the "big band" tradition. She composed and arranged a collection of pieces and then, along with her husband, saxophonist Lew Tabackin, hired her own sixteen-piece band to perform them. The first album of compositions from her jazz library, *Kogun,* was cut in 1974. In 1976 Japan's *Swing Journal* chose her album *Insights* as the best jazz album of the year, and in 1977 Akiyoshi was voted leader of the number one big band by its readers. During the same period, she also received two Grammy nominations for her recordings. Akiyoshi was a participant in the first Women's Jazz Festival, in Kansas City, Missouri, in 1978 (see entry), and for four consecutive years (1978–81) was named Best Arranger, Best Band by *down beat,* a U.S. jazz magazine. Since 1984, Akiyoshi has led her own orchestra, Toshiko Akiyoshi's New York Jazz Orchestra.

The only woman in the history of jazz to have composed and arranged an entire library of music, Akiyoshi writes compositions that often deal with social themes and reflect her Asian background as well. One work, "Tales of a Courtesan," is intended to express the unpleasant life of an Asian courtesan. "For three centuries under the shoguns," Akiyoshi says, "poor families had to sell their daughters into slavery. Though some courtesans were highly educated, they had no freedom; attempted escape meant punishment by death. My music expresses the contrast between the superficially luxurious life of some of these women and the tragic denial of human rights they suffered."

Tenley Albright

First woman to win the World Amateur Figure Skating Championship crown (1953); first to win the gold medal at the Winter Olympics (1956); first to be named to the U.S. Olympic Committee (1976).

Born Boston, Massachusetts, July 18, 1935.

Despite an attack of polio that threatened her skating career when she was eleven, Albright persisted, and won her first U.S. championship in 1952. She held the title until she retired in 1956 to attend Harvard University Medical School, Cambridge, Massachusetts. The university made her retirement a condition of admission.

A graduate of Radcliffe College, Cambridge, Massachusetts, Albright received her M.D. degree from Harvard in 1961 and became a practicing surgeon in Boston, Massachusetts. She was awarded honorary doctorates of science by Hobart and William Smith Colleges, Geneva, New York (1965), and by Russell Sage College, Troy, New York (1975). The first woman to be a member of the Harvard University Hall of Fame, Albright was also admitted to the Ice Skating Hall of Fame (1974), the U.S. Figure Skating Hall of Fame (1976), and the Olympic Hall of Fame (1988).

Lucy Maclay Alexander

First woman to receive the Distinguished Service Medal of the U.S. Department of Agriculture (1950).

Dates unknown.

A Maryland native, Alexander was honored with the award "for outstanding achievement in applying fundamental scientific principles to meat and poultry cooking." During World War II, as an employee of the U.S. Bureau of Home Nutrition and Home Economics, she experimented with and developed recipes for preparing the less tender cuts of meat that were available to the U.S. population under wartime rationing.

Florence Ellinwood Allen

First woman on the U.S. Court of Appeals (1934); first on the Ohio Supreme Court (1922); first on any general court (1920) (see also Genevieve Cline).

Born Salt Lake City, Utah, March 23, 1884; died Waite Hill, Ohio, September 12, 1966.

Allen, whose mother, Corinne Marie Tuckerman, was the first student admitted to Smith College in Northampton, Massachusetts, graduated Phi Beta Kappa from Western Reserve University, Cleveland, Ohio, in 1904. Her father was a professor of classical languages there. Under his tutelage, she had become proficient in Greek and Latin by the time she was seven.

From 1906 to 1909, Allen was music critic for the Cleveland *Plain Dealer*. After a nerve injury forced her to abandon hopes of a career in music, she went to the University of Chicago Law School, leaving before she completed her studies in order to work with immigrants in New York City (1910). When she arrived in New York, Allen enrolled in New York University Law School, where in 1913 she graduated second in her class.

In 1914 Allen opened a law office in Cleveland, Ohio; she also became an advocate for women's rights,

doing much of the legal work for the Woman's Suffrage party. She was named assistant county prosecutor in Cuyahoga County, Ohio, in 1919. Other first accomplishments in Ohio include being the first woman to preside at a first-degree murder trial, and the first woman to sentence a convicted felon to death.

In 1920, after ratification of the Nineteenth Amendment, which established that men and women have equal rights to vote, Allen ran in a nonpartisan election for common pleas court judge and won against nine male opponents. Her next electoral victory came in 1922, when a large majority of the electorate placed her on the Ohio Supreme Court. She was reelected to that seat in 1928.

President Franklin D. Roosevelt appointed Allen to the Sixth Circuit Court of Appeals, Cincinnati—covering Ohio, Michigan, Kentucky, and Tennessee—in 1934, a position she held until her retirement in 1959. During her tenure on that court, she was one of the judges who upheld the decision affirming that the power granted to the Tennessee Valley Authority was constitutional. At her retirement, Allen held the position of senior judge.

During her lifetime, Allen was awarded twenty-five honorary degrees, and New York University honored her with its 1960–61 Gallatin Award. The award goes to an outstanding alumna who has "made a contribution of lasting significance to society."

Allen published her autobiography—*To Do Justly*—in 1965.

Gracie (Grace Ethel Cecile Rosalie) Allen

First film actress to have a movie named after her—The Gracie Allen Murder Case *(1939).*

Born San Francisco, California, July 26, 1895; died Hollywood, California, August 27, 1964.

Daughter of a vaudeville song-and-dance man, Allen made her first stage appearance when she was six years old. She left school at fourteen and for the next few years did solo acts and acts with her sisters.

In 1922 Allen met George Burns, and they agreed to become a team. Their story is that it happened by accident. Burns's team of Burns & Lorraine was breaking up, and a friend of Allen's suggested that she get together with Billy Lorraine, adding that Burns was awful. Allen talked to Burns by mistake, and by the time she discovered that he wasn't Lorraine, they had agreed to form a comedy team called "The Lamb Chops."

The account ends with Allen walking away from Burns saying, "Goodby, Mr. Lorraine."

Allen and Burns were married in 1926. "The Lamb Chops" toured the United States and Europe under the longest contract that had been written in vaudeville at the time. In 1930 Allen signed her first movie contract and proceeded to make *The Big Broadcast* (1932); *College Humor* (1933); and *Love in Bloom* (1935). During that same year, she did a fifteen-week run on BBC radio and also appeared in radio guest spots with Guy Lombardo, Eddie Cantor, and Rudy Vallee.

Allen and Burns launched their radio show, "The Adventures of Gracie," on the Columbia Broadcasting System in 1932. Allen played a daffy, off-the-wall-but-lovable character, and Burns was her straight man.

In 1939 Allen made *The Gracie Allen Murder Case,* a film based on characters created by novelist S. S. Van Dine. Allen, playing herself in a role in which she helps detective Philo Vance solve the murder of an escaping convict, appeared without George Burns.

The comedy team switched to the National Broadcasting Company in 1945, returning to CBS with their network television series in 1950.

Poor health forced Allen's retirement in 1958.

Sadie Allen

First woman in a woman-man team to successfully ride through the Niagara Falls rapids in a barrel (1886) (see also Anna E. Taylor).

Born c. 1868.

Allen, an eighteen-year-old from Buffalo, New York, made the trip with partner George Hazlett on November 28, 1886. In a barrel weighted with 500 pounds of sand, they began the descent of the rapids at the Maid of the Mist landing at 2:00 P.M. About two hours later, after passing through some whirlpool rapids, they floated into an eddy near the Canadian shore, which suddenly swept them back into the whirlpool. Realizing that they were in danger, a keeper of the Canadian Whirlpool Park threw them a rope and pulled the barrel to shore at 4:45 P.M. Allen and Hazlett suffered only slight bruises.

Amateur Athletic Union

Women were first admitted to the Amateur Athletic Union in 1923. They were accepted in the sports of basketball, gymnastics, handball, swimming, and track and field.

Fanny Baker Ames

Cofounder of the first visiting social worker service in the United States (1873).

Born Canandaigua, New York, 1840; died Barnstable, Massachusetts, 1931.

Along with her husband, Charles G. Ames, Fanny Baker Ames founded the Relief Society of Germantown, Pennsylvania, where her husband headed a Unitarian congregation. The society afforded the first opportunity for "social workers"—actually volunteer women—to visit the urban poor and report on needy cases.

Ames and her husband also helped found the Philadelphia Society for Organizing Charity in 1878, and her ideas led to the founding of the Women's Auxiliary Conference of the Unitarian Church in 1880.

Ames attended Antioch College, Yellow Springs, Ohio, for one year and subsequently taught in the Cincinnati, Ohio, public schools. In 1890 she became the first female factory inspector in Massachusetts.

Bette B. Anderson

First woman to be appointed undersecretary of the Treasury (1977).

Born c. 1929.

In 1960 Anderson was made assistant cashier at the Citizens and Southern Bank in Atlanta, Georgia; she was the first woman officer of Citizens and Southern.

She attended the Stonier Graduate School of Banking of Rutgers University (New Brunswick, New Jersey) and graduated in 1975. The title of her thesis was "Women in Bank Management: A Changing Pattern of Development."

In 1976 Anderson was elected president of the 17,000-member National Association of Bank Women.

A year later President Jimmy Carter appointed Anderson undersecretary of the Treasury. At that time, she was vice president of the credit administration department of the Citizens and Southern Bank in Savannah, Georgia.

Anderson joined the board of directors of International Telephone and Telegraph (ITT) in 1981 and the board of directors of the Hartford Insurance Group in 1985.

(Helen) Eugenie Moore Anderson

First woman to hold the rank of ambassador (1949); first to sign a nation-to-nation treaty (1951).

Born Adair, Iowa, May 26, 1909. Anderson received her college education at Stephens College (Columbia, Missouri), Simpson College (Indianola, Iowa), and Carleton College (Northfield, Minnesota) between 1926 and 1930. In 1930 she married John P. Anderson and took up residence in Red Wing, Minnesota, where, as a Democrat, she became active in state politics. She was named to the Democratic National Committee in 1948.

As a reward for her vigorous campaigning for his election, President Harry S. Truman named Anderson ambassador to Denmark in 1949 (see Ruth Bryan Owen). She held that post until 1953, when Dwight D. Eisenhower became president. While she was ambassador, Anderson signed, in 1951, a treaty between the United States and Denmark announcing agreements of friendship, commerce, and navigation. She was the first woman to sign such a treaty.

From 1955 to 1960 Anderson served as chair of the Minnesota Commission for Fair Employment Practices. In 1962, President John F. Kennedy named her U.S. envoy to Bulgaria, making her the first woman ambassador to a Communist nation. She left that post in 1964; the following year she became the U.S. representative on the Trusteeship Council of the United Nations, where she served until 1968.

Anderson was special assistant to the Secretary of State from 1968 to 1972. From 1973 until her retirement she served as a member of the Commission on the Future of Minnesota.

Mary Anderson

First director of the Women's Bureau of the U.S. Department of Labor (1920).

Born Lidköping, Sweden, August 27, 1872; died Washington, D.C., January 29, 1964.

In 1918 Anderson was serving on the staff of Mary van Kleeck, a friend who headed a woman's branch in the Ordnance Department of the U.S. Army. Van Kleeck then became director of the Women in Industry Service of the National Defense in the U.S. Department of Labor, and she appointed Anderson assistant director. When van Kleeck resigned in 1919, Anderson was made director. A year later, Congress converted the Women in Industry Service into a permanent Women's Bureau of the Labor Department, and Democratic President Woodrow Wilson appointed Anderson its director. Later, Republican President Warren G. Harding reappointed her, and she remained with the bureau until her retirement in 1944.

Anderson began life in the United States as an immigrant in 1889, washing dishes in a Michigan boardinghouse for lumberjacks. She was paid two dollars a week plus board.

In 1892 she took a job as a stitcher in a Chicago shoe factory and worked at a stitching machine for the next eighteen years.

In 1899 Anderson and a number of her female coworkers joined the International Boot and Shoe Workers Union. The following year, she was elected president of the women stitchers' Local 94 and its delegate to the Chicago Federation of Labor.

From 1906 to 1919 Anderson served as a member of her union's national executive board. In 1911 she left the shoe factory to become a salaried organizer for the Women's Trade Union League, the position she held when she joined Mary van Kleeck's staff.

President Franklin D. Roosevelt sent Anderson to the International Labor Organization in 1933 as chief of the U.S. delegation.

During her tenure with the Women's Bureau at the Department of Labor, Anderson was largely responsible for seeing that women were covered by the federal minimum wage and hour law.

At the age of ninety, Anderson was honored by the U.S. Department of Labor with its Award of Merit for her contributions to the "welfare of the wage earners in the United States."

She published her autobiography, *Women at Work,* in 1951.

Mary Anderson with delegates of Convention of Knights of Labor

Barbara Andrews

First woman to be ordained as a minister in the American Lutheran Church (1970).

Born c. 1934; died 1978.

Andrews began her ministry in 1970 at a church in Minneapolis, Minnesota.

A paraplegic confined to a wheelchair, she was unable to escape from a fire caused by defective wiring in a table lamp. At the time of her death, Andrews was acting pastor of Resurrection Lutheran Church, Detroit, Michigan.

Ethel Andrus

Founder and first president of the American Association of Retired Persons (AARP) (1958); founder and first president of the National Retired Teachers Association (NRTA) (1947).

Born San Francisco, California, 1884; died Long Beach, California, 1967.

When Ethel Andrus retired in 1944 from a career of over forty years as a public school teacher and principal, her retirement pay was about sixty dollars per month. To improve the lot of and restore dignity to former teachers, she worked for better retirement pay and health insurance for retirees. This activity led to her founding of the NRTA in 1947.

In 1956 the association sponsored the first U.S. health insurance plan for people over sixty-five. The AARP, founded by Andrus soon thereafter, extended this insurance coverage to all retired persons over fifty-five and added other benefits to the package.

Andrus grew up in Chicago, Illinois, graduating from the University of Chicago in 1903. From 1903 to 1910 she taught at Lewis Institute (now the Illinois Institute of Technology, Chicago) and worked at settlement houses.

In 1910 she returned to her native California, where she worked at Abraham Lincoln High School in Los Angeles, moving through the ranks from teacher to principal. During her years at Abraham Lincoln, she also earned an M.A. (1926) and a Ph.D. (1930) from the University of Southern California (Los Angeles).

Andrus was named National Teacher of the Year in 1954 by the International Senior League. In 1961 she was made a member of the national advisory committee for the White House Conference on Aging. She also served on the advisory board of the American Association of Homes for the Aged. In 1963 Andrus established the Institute of Life Long Learning for retirees. She was also a founder and editor of *Modern Maturity,* the magazine of AARP.

Susan B. Anthony

Cofounder of the National Woman Suffrage Association (NWSA)— the first U.S. woman's suffrage organization (1869); first woman to be depicted on a U.S. coin (1979).

Born Adams, Massachusetts, February 15, 1820; died Rochester, New York, March 13, 1906.

An aggressive worker for women's rights, temperance, and abolition, Anthony, along with Elizabeth Cady Stanton (see entry), formed the National Woman Suffrage Association (NWSA) in May, 1869. Stanton became the president of the organization, "a movement controlled and defined by women."

Anthony, who had been brought up in the Quaker tradition, taught in a Quaker seminary in New Rochelle, New York, and headed the women's department at Canajoharie Academy (Canajoharie, New York) from 1846 to 1849. In 1852 she established the Woman's New York State Temperance Society, the first such society formed by and for women. Elizabeth Cady Stanton was its first president.

A staunch advocate of abolition, Anthony worked with leading abolitionists, including Frederick Douglass, Wendell Phillips, and William Lloyd Garrison. She became a prominent New York leader in Garrison's American Anti-Slavery Society, based in New England (1856).

At the same time, Anthony was campaigning in New York State against the unequal treatment of women. By 1860 she succeeded in establishing the liberalization of laws regarding married women's property rights.

After the Civil War, she lobbied for changing the Fourteenth Amendment to include voting rights for women and blacks, and in 1866 she became the corresponding secretary of the newly formed American Equal Rights Association. In 1872 she and twelve other women suffragists were arrested when they tried to vote in the presidential election in Rochester, New York, as a means of testing the suffrage rights guaranteed in the Fourteenth Amendment. Anthony, who cast one vote, was convicted and a fine was imposed. The case was dropped, however, in spite of her refusal to pay the fine. During the next twenty years, Anthony lectured and crusaded for suffrage.

In 1868 she had become the publisher of *Revolution,* a suffrage periodical, of which Elizabeth Cady Stanton was editor. When the periodical went into debt in 1870, Anthony traveled across the country giving lectures to ease the paper's financial burden.

The National Woman Suffrage Association had been established early in 1869. Later in the year, as a result of disputes concerning strategies for the movement, Lucy Stone (see entry) left the NWSA, establishing the American Woman Suffrage Association (AWSA). In 1890 the two suffrage associations merged, forming a new organization called the National American Woman Suffrage Association (see Woman Suffrage Associations). Anthony succeeded Stanton as president in 1892, retiring in 1900.

Anthony, who worked for various reforms for nearly fifty years, was the head of the 1904 U.S. delegation to the International Council of Women, of which she had been a principal founder.

History of Woman Suffrage, a four-volume work which she wrote with Stanton and Matilda Gage, was published one volume per year in 1881, 1882, 1886, and 1902.

Anthony was elected to the Hall of Fame for Great Americans at Bronx Community College (Bronx, New York) of the City University of New York in 1950. In 1952 her bust, sculpted by Brenda Putnam, was added to the Hall of Fame.

In 1979 the U.S. government issued a silver dollar with her image on it.

Antioch College

First nonsectarian college to grant women absolutely equal rights with men (1852).

Antioch College (Yellow Springs, Ohio), chartered in 1852, had three women in its first graduating class (1857). Jane Andrews (1833–87) was the first student to register in the fall, 1853.

Constance M. K. Applebee

Introduced field hockey to the United States (1901).

Born Chigwell, England, 1874; died New Milton, Hampshire, England, January 26, 1981.

Applebee, of the British College of Physical Education, came to the United States in 1901 to take a course in anthropometry—the measurement of the human body. She mounted the first demonstration of field hockey in Cambridge, Massachusetts, in a courtyard adjacent to the Harvard University gymnasium. She then arranged a series of exhibition matches at some prominent women's colleges—Bryn Mawr, Mount Holyoke, Radcliffe, Smith, Vassar, and Wellesley.

She formed a team in Philadel-phia, Pennsylvania, and in 1920 took them to England—where they lost eight out of ten matches. Their application to participate in the 1920 Olympic Games in Antwerp was rejected.

Countess Geraldine Apponyi

First woman of United States descent to become a queen (1938).

Born Hungary, 1915.

Apponyi, daughter of Gladys Stewart Girrault of New York City and Count Julius Nagi-Apponyi of Hungary, became queen when she married King Zog I of Albania (1895–1961) on April 27, 1938. A countess sans fortune, she had been working just prior to their marriage as a sales clerk in the souvenir shop of the Budapest National Museum, where she earned a modest salary.

In 1939 the royal pair and their two-day-old son fled invading Italian forces, residing in England and Egypt during World War II. After the war, the new Communist regime in Albania deposed King Zog in absentia (1946), and the family eventually took up residence in France.

After the king's death in 1961, Countess Geraldine translated his memoirs from Albanian into French.

Goody Armitage

Reportedly the first woman in the colonies to be an innkeeper (1643).

Dates unknown.

Armitage was granted permission by the General Court of Massachusetts to "keepe the ordinary [a meal served to the public at a fixed price], but not to drawe wine."

Anne L. Armstrong

First woman to be national cochair of the Republican party (1971–73); first to deliver the keynote speech at a major party's national convention (1972); first to have full cabinet status as counselor to the president (1972).

Born New Orleans, Louisiana, December 27, 1927.

Armstrong attended the Foxcroft School in Middle, Virginia, where she was valedictorian of her 1945 class. In 1949 she graduated Phi Beta Kappa from Vassar College, Poughkeepsie, New York, with majors in English and journalism. Armstrong first participated in politics as a worker in the 1948 campaign of President Harry S. Truman. By the next presidential election, however, she had defected to the Republican ranks and supported the candidacy of Dwight D. Eisenhower.

By 1956, Armstrong, married with five children, began to get involved in Republican politics in Texas and at the national level. After holding a number of executive positions in the Texas Republican organization, she went to the Republican national conventions in 1964 and 1968 as a delegate and platform committee member. She served as Texas's Republican national committeewoman from 1968 to 1973; in 1971, with Senator Robert Dole of Kansas and Thomas B. Evans, she was cochair of the Republican National Committee, where she was a supporter of the Equal Rights Amendment.

President Richard M. Nixon named her counselor to the president with full cabinet status in 1972. While serving in that post, Armstrong founded the first Office of Women's Programs in the White House. She resigned in 1974, becoming one of the last to call for President Nixon's resignation in the wake of the Watergate scandal.

After leaving the White House, Armstrong served on the boards of directors of several major U.S. corporations, including General Motors and American Express. In 1976/77 she was ambassador to Great Britain, and subsequent to that she served as chair of the Advisory Board Center for Strategic and International Studies and chair of the president's Foreign Intelligence Advisory Board. From 1978 to 1990 she was a member of the board of overseers of the Hoover Institute, and in 1980 was co-chair of the Reagan-Bush presidential campaign.

In 1986 Armstrong was named to the Texas Women's Hall of Fame, and in 1987 she was awarded the Presidential Medal of Freedom.

Margaret Arnstein

First woman to win the Rockefeller Public Service Award (1965).

Born New York, New York, October 27, 1904; died New Haven, Connecticut, October 8, 1972.

Niece of New York Governor Herbert H. Lehman, Arnstein graduated from Smith College, Northampton, Massachusetts, in 1925, and from New York City's Presbyterian Hospital School of Nursing in 1927. After serving as a public health nurse in Westchester County, New York, she earned a master of public health degree from Johns Hopkins University, Baltimore, Maryland, in 1934.

After a period as professor of public health nursing at the University of Minnesota (Minneapolis), Arnstein became a New York State nursing

officer before joining the U.S. Public Health Service in 1946.

From 1957 to 1964 she was chief of Public Health Service nursing. In 1965 she was named to the new position of senior nursing advisor for the International Health Office of the U.S. Surgeon General's office.

In 1967 Arnstein was appointed dean of the Yale University Nursing School, New Haven, Connecticut.

With Gaylord Anderson and Mary Lester, she wrote a book called *Communicable Disease Control*, published in 1941.

Dorothy Arzner

First woman to direct sound films (1929).

Born San Francisco, California, January 3, 1900; died La Quinta, California, October 1, 1979.

Arzner's father had a small café in Hollywood, California, and her first encounters with people in the movie business came there. After her college years at the University of Southern California (Los Angeles) were cut short by World War I, she went to work as a stenographer for William de Mille of Famous Players. Promoted to script clerk, then film cutter, then editor, she first impressed directors with her editing of *Blood and Sand* (1922), starring Rudolph Valentino.

Arzner's first directing opportunity came from Paramount Pictures, when she was selected to direct *Fashions for Women* (1927). The film won her a first prize for directing at the London International Festival of Women's Films. She also directed *Ten Modern Commandments* and *Get Your Man* (both 1927), and *Manhattan Cocktail* (1928), before she was assigned to direct Paramount's first sound film: *The Wild Party* (1929).

During the 1930s, Arzner—the only woman director of the period—directed fourteen sound films, including *Merrily We Go to Hell* (1932), with Fredric March and Sylvia Sidney; *Christopher Strong* (1933), with Katharine Hepburn; *Nana* (1934), with Anna Sten; and *The Bride Wore Red* (1937), with Joan Crawford. Her last commercial film, completed in 1943, was *First Comes Courage,* with Merle Oberon. Her films frequently portrayed strong women in unconventional roles.

From 1943 to 1945 Arzner made Women's Army Corps training films for the U.S. Army. In the years following the war, she periodically taught film courses at the University of California–Los Angeles and made occasional commercials.

In 1972 *The Wild Party* was shown at the first International Festival of Women's Films, and the second IFWF presented a retrospective of her work. In 1975, when she was seventy-five years old, the Directors Guild of America organized "A Tribute to Dorothy Arzner" in Los Angeles.

Juanita Ashcraft

First woman to be named assistant secretary of the U.S. Air Force (1976).

Born c. 1921.

The post—assistant secretary for manpower and reserve affairs—to which Ashcraft was appointed by President Gerald Ford, is the highest civilian appointive post ever given to a woman in the U.S. Air Force.

Prior to the air force appointment, Ashcraft was on the California State Employment Board for ten years. She was also an assistant appointments secretary to California Governor Ronald Reagan. From 1970 to 1976 she was a member of the California governor's commission on executive salaries.

Sarah Byrd Askew

First person to design a bookmobile (1920).

Born 1877; died 1942.
Recognizing the need to make li-

brary books and services available to rural communities, shut-ins, and other people without access to lending libraries, Askew—a librarian in Burlington County, New Jersey—designed a bookmobile (a traveling lending library, usually mounted on a small truck or trailer) to serve her local area. She was also the first person to receive an honorary degree from the New Jersey College for Women (later Douglass College, now Rutgers University, New Brunswick) (1930).

Nan Jane Aspinall

First woman to ride across the United States alone on horseback (1910).

Dates unknown.

Aspinall left San Francisco, California, on September 1, 1910, covering over 4,500 miles in 301 days (108 actual travel days), and arrived in New York City on July 8, 1911. She carried a letter from the mayor of San Francisco, California, to the mayor of New York City.

Caroline Schermerhorn Astor

First woman to determine the Four Hundred in New York society (1888).

Born New York, New York, September 22, 1830; died New York, New York, October 30, 1908.

At her annual January ball, Astor invited the Four Hundred, the cream of high society. (The term was coined by Ward McAllister, who is also credited with "snob" and "bon vivant.") Acknowledged as the queen of that social stratum, Astor was an absolute dictator. According to one story, she was put on the social defensive on only one occasion: Alva Belmont (see entry) held a festive ball and invited all of those in the Astors' social stratosphere—all but the Astors themselves. When they launched clandestine inquiries into the matter, Belmont is reported to have said that she could not invite people who had never called on her. The Astors called—and they got their invitation to the ball.

In 1902 Astor extended her social orbit to include Newport, Rhode Island.

Gertrude Atherton

First woman to be president of the National Academy of Literature (1934).

Born San Francisco, California, 1857; died San Francisco, California, 1948.

Atherton wrote about sixty books of

fiction and nonfiction—many of them about California. Her first bestseller, *The Conqueror* (1902),was about Alexander Hamilton. Her most successful bestseller was *Black Oxen* (1923), a novel about a middle-aged woman whose sex glands were revitalized by X rays, permitting her to re-enter the world as a new and different woman.

Active in Allied causes during World War I, Atherton was awarded three decorations by France, including the Légion d'Honneur (1925).

Her autobiography, *Adventures of a Novelist,* was published in 1932. In 1934 Atherton was named president of the National Academy of Literature (now defunct), an organization parallel to the National Academy of Science and founded as an equivalent to the royal academies of France and England.

Atherton donated a collection of her manuscripts and other memorabilia to the Library of Congress in 1943, at the library's request.

At the age of eighty-nine Atherton wrote *My San Francisco,* her reminiscences about the city and its history.

Eudora Clark Atkinson

First woman to be superintendent of the first state reformatory for women (1877).

Dates unknown.

She headed the Reformatory Prison for Women in Sherborn (now Framingham), Massachusetts. In 1911 it was renamed the Reformatory for Women.

Helen Atwater

First woman to be full-time editor of the Journal of Home Economics *(1923).*

Born Somerville, Massachusetts, May 29, 1876; died Washington, D.C., June 26, 1947.

Atwater graduated from Smith College, Northampton, Massachusetts, in 1897. Her father was a professor specializing in food chemistry, and she worked as his assistant until he died in 1907.

From 1909 to 1923 she was on the staff of the Office of Home Economics in the U.S. Department of Agriculture. In 1923 Atwater went to work for the *Journal of Home Economics,* a publication of the American Home Economics Association for which she had written over the years. She edited the *Journal* until her retirement in 1941.

Atwater was part of the White House Conference on Child Health and Protection in 1930, and in 1942 served as chair of the Committee on

Hygiene in Housing of the American Public Health Association.

The year after her death, the American Home Economics Association established the Helen Atwater International Fellowship Award.

Axis Sally (Mildred E. Gillars)

First woman to be convicted of wartime treason for broadcasting Nazi propaganda in World War II (1949).

Born Portland, Maine, 1900; died Columbus, Ohio, June 25, 1988.

Gillars attended college at Ohio Wesleyan University (Delaware, Ohio) from 1918 to 1923 but did not graduate. She traveled to Germany where, in 1940—at the urging of her German lover—she took a job as a radio broadcaster, broadcasting Nazi propaganda to American and Allied troops in Europe and North Africa, where she was known as Axis Sally.

She was paid the highest salary of all of Germany's broadcasters; her programs often began, "Hello, gang. Throw down those little old guns and toddle off home. There's no getting the Germans down."

After the war, in 1946, U.S. officials found Gillars living in the cellar of a bombed-out building in Frankfurt am Main. She was returned to the United States in 1948 and tried for treason. Found guilty on March 10, 1949, she was sentenced to thirty years in prison and fined $10,000. After serving twelve years in the Federal Reformatory for Women at Alderson, West Virginia, she was released in 1961.

After her release from prison, she taught kindergarten, and in 1973 she returned to college to complete a bachelor's degree in speech.

Harriet Hubbard Ayer

First woman to make a fortune in the cosmetics industry.

Born Chicago, Illinois, 1849; died 1903.

After her twenty-one-year marriage to wealthy Chicago-born businessman Herbert C. Ayer ended in 1886, Ayer began to manufacture and sell a facial cream that, according to her claims, had been discovered in Paris and used by Mme. Récamier—a famous beauty of Napoleon's day. Ayer put Récamier's name on the label with her own, and she used extensive newspaper advertising to sell the product.

After losing control of her company in 1896, she wrote a column in the New York *World* in which she dispensed beauty advice, and in 1899 she published a bestseller: *Harriet Hubbard Ayer's Book: A Complete and Authentic Treatise on the Laws of Health and Beauty.*

Ayer was a graduate of the Convent of the Sacred Heart, Chicago, Illinois.

Anne Ayres

First woman to be consecrated as an Episcopal sister (1845); founder of the first U.S. Episcopal sisterhood (1852).

Born London, England, January 3, 1816; died New York, New York, February 9, 1896.

Ayres came to the United States in 1836. After becoming an Episcopal sister, she founded the Sisterhood of the Holy Communion, attached to the Church of the Holy Communion in New York City (see also Harriet Cannon). Ayres, as Sister Anne, was named first sister.

The members of the order did not take lifetime vows; instead, they contracted a three-year, renewable term of service, pledging not to marry during their term of duty. Instead of a nun's habit, they wore a form of secular dress.

In 1858 Ayres was house mother (administrator of nursing and household matters) of the newly constructed St. Luke's Hospital in New York City. In 1867, her book *Evangelical Sisterhoods* was published.

Mary Andrews Ayres

First woman elected director of the American Association of Advertising Agencies (1971).

Dates unknown.

Ayres, one of a small number of women to reach the top of the ladder on the business rather than the creative side of advertising, became director of the American Association of Advertising Agencies, a fifty-four-year-old organization, in 1971.

In 1967 Ayres was senior vice president at Sullivan, Stauffer, Colwell & Bayles, Inc. A year later she became executive vice president. She was responsible for as much as $16 million in billings each year. In the late 1960s there were only three women board members in the top twenty advertising agencies. She was the only woman in account services at Sullivan, Stauffer, Colwell & Bayles. By 1977, however, about one-third of the account staff was female.

Delia Salter Bacon

First person to claim that Francis Bacon wrote the works attributed to William Shakespeare (1856).

Born Tallmadge, Ohio, February 2, 1811; died Hartford, Connecticut, September 2, 1859.

Bacon contended that the works of Shakespeare were the products of a radical group led by Francis Bacon. She presented her ideas in an article, "William Shakespeare and His Plays: An Inquiry Concerning Them," which appeared in *Putnam's Monthly Magazine* in January, 1856. She then wrote a book on the subject titled *The Philosophy of the Plays of Shakespeare Unfolded* (1857). Her ideas were ignored or dismissed.

Bacon attended Catharine Beecher's Hartford Female Academy in Connecticut for one year (1825). She taught school from 1826 to 1832. In 1831 she began writing sentimental fiction and plays. She also lectured and gave dramatic readings. Following the publication of her Shakespeare book and its negative reception, Bacon became insane.

Mabel Bacon

First woman to take part in a power boat race (1910).

Dates unknown.

Bacon and her husband, members of the Kennebec Yacht Club in Maine, raced their 46½-foot cabin cruiser in a race to Hamilton, Bermuda, from June 25 to June 29, 1910. They finished the 670-mile course in second place. During the course, Mabel Bacon, one of a crew of three, took her regular turn at the wheel.

Mary Bacon (Anderson)

First woman jockey to win 100 races (1970); part of the first all-woman daily double (1974).

Born Chicago, Illinois, 1948; died Fort Worth, Texas, June 8, 1991.

A rider in horse shows and other equestrian events from the time she was a young girl, Bacon began her professional racing career in the United States in the 1960s, and rode her first winner on June 5, 1969, at the Finger Lakes track, Canandaigua, New York. She won her one hundredth race on June 30, 1970, at Thistledown racetrack in Cleveland, Ohio, riding a horse called California Lassie, becoming the first woman jockey to achieve such a feat. In her lifetime she rode in 3,526 races, which included 286 wins, 310 seconds, and 323 thirds; her winnings amounted to $1 million.

At Aqueduct racetrack (New York, New York) on November 1, 1974, Bacon and Canadian jockey Joan Phipps won the first all-woman daily double: Phipps, riding Chick'n Lou, won the first race, and Bacon, atop Princess M.L., won the second. A two-dollar daily-double bet won $72.40.

Bacon won blue ribbons in showing and dressage, then began racing as an amateur in England. After Kathy Kusner (see entry) successfully went to court in her fight for a jockey's license, Bacon took the opportunity to secure her own license.

Her racing career was marked by injuries and other mishaps. In October, 1969, she was kidnapped at knife-point by a stablehand, but managed to escape uninjured. In 1979 Bacon was injured in a starting-gate mishap; she was awarded $3 million in damages in a subsequent law suit. At Golden Gate Fields track, Albany, California, she was hurt in a

fall that left her in a coma for eight days. According to her second husband, Jeff Anderson, she never fully recovered. Her racing days were finally ended by cancer, which ultimately left her too weak to ride. Severely depressed by her inability to race, Bacon committed suicide on June 8, 1991.

Her husband arranged for her ashes to be scattered in a ceremony at Belmont Park, Elmont, Long Island, New York.

Sarah Bagley

First woman to be a telegraph operator (1846); first to be a union leader (1845–46).

Possibly born Meredith, New Hampshire, date unknown.

Bagley, who began work in 1836 at a Lowell, Massachusetts, cotton mill, was later employed by the Lowell office of the New York & Boston Magnetic Telephone Company. By 1847 she was promoted to superintendent of the telegraph office.

In 1845 Bagley was instrumental in forming the Female Labor Reform Association of Lowell, Massachusetts. Initially, five women had met in December, 1844, to discuss strategy for achieving a ten-hour day. By May, 1845, they had over 600 members, and Bagley had been elected president. She collected over 2,000 signatures on a petition that was sent to the Massachusetts state legislature, asking for a ten-hour day and investigation of working conditions in the mills. The petition was rejected by both houses of the legislature.

After the failed attempt before the Massachusetts legislature, Bagley organized branches of the union at other Massachusetts locations and in New Hampshire. In 1846 she was named delegate to the National Industrial Congress, and the same year was elected vice president of the Lowell Union of Associationists. Later, Bagley published *Factory Tracts,* and became the chief editor of *Voice of Industry*—both prolabor publications.

Elizabeth Bailey

First woman to serve on the Civil Aeronautics Board (CAB) (1977); first to head a major graduate business school (1983).

Born New York, New York, November 26, 1938.

Bailey, an economist, filled an unexpired term on the Civil Aeronautics Board (1977), then served a full term, which expired on December 31, 1983. The Civil Aeronautics Board was established to promote and regulate the civil air transport industry in the United States.

As an economist, she has been an associate professor of economics at New York University (1973–77) and

has held several positions at Bell Labs, culminating in her heading the economics research department there. She was named dean of the Graduate School of Industrial Administration at Carnegie Mellon University, Pittsburgh, Pennsylvania, in 1983. Bailey has also been a member of the board of directors of Honeywell, Philip Morris, CSX Corporation, and Natwest Bancorp. She was a trustee of Princeton University, Princeton, New Jersey, (1978–82) and joined the board of trustees of Presbyterian University Hospital in 1984. Bailey was also a founding member of the Harbor School for Learning Disabilities.

After earning a B.A. degree magna cum laude from Radcliffe College, Cambridge Massachusetts (1960), and an M.S. degree from Stevens Institute of Technology, Hoboken, New Jersey (1966), she went on to earn a Ph.D. from Princeton University in 1972.

Florence Merriam Bailey

First woman to be a fellow of the American Ornithologists' Union (1929).

Born Locust Grove, New York, August 8, 1863; died Washington, D.C., September 22, 1948.

In 1885 Bailey became the first woman to be an associate member of the American Ornithologists' Union.

In 1908 the chickadee was named in her honor: *farus gambeli baileyae*. She published *Birds of New Mexico* in 1928, which won her the AOU's Brewster Medal (1931). She was the first woman to receive this award.

Bailey attended Smith College, Northampton, Massachusetts, as a special student for four years, leaving in 1886 without a degree. (The college granted her a bachelor's degree in 1921.) She married Vernon Bailey, and together they explored the western and southwestern United States, writing about the birds they identified and discovered there. She also wrote *Birds through an Opera Glass* (1889), a children's book, and *Birds of Village and Field* (1898), one of the first U.S. bird guides to achieve wide popularity.

Bailey's brother, Clinton Hart, was the first chief of the U.S. Biological Survey.

Belle Baker

First person to host a radio variety program from a moving train (1932).

Born New York, New York, c. 1895; died Los Angeles, California, April 28, 1957.

Baker, a torch singer with a deep resonant voice, hosted a radio variety program from the B & O train that ran throughout the state of Maryland. The broadcast from the train was a way of demonstrating the mobility and versatility of radio broadcasting.

A performer from the vaudeville era, she was also known for her renditions of comedy songs. She appeared at the Palace Theater in New York City when she was only twenty. She had star billing, sharing the program with actress Sarah Bernhardt.

In 1926 she had top billing in Rodgers and Hart's *Betsy*. Also starring in the Ziegfield Follies, she introduced Irving Berlin's "Blue Skies."

Baker was among the stars at the first anniversary of the return of vaudeville to the Palace Theater in 1950, and in 1955 she was honored on the television show, "This Is Your Life."

Helen Balliser

One of the first two women to serve as ambulance doctors (1914) (see also Ana Tjohnlands).

Dates unknown.

Balliser and Tjohnlands passed the Cornell Medical School (New York, New York) examinations, which qualified them to serve as Bellevue Hospital ambulance doctors. They served in that function for eighteen months.

Ann Bancroft

First woman to walk to the North Pole (1986).

Born St. Paul, Minnesota, 1955. Bancroft was a member of the Will Steger International Polar Expedition. The team walked, skied, and pushed dog sleds, traveling 1,000 miles in fifty-five days. They walked from Ward Hunt Island, Canada, to the North Pole. This was the first dogsled team to make the trip over the polar ice, with no outside assistance, since Robert Peary and his team made the trek in 1909.

Bancroft, who earned a B.S. degree in physical education at the University of Oregon, Eugene, was a teacher of physical education and taught the physically handicapped in Minnesota. She gave up her teaching job and moved to Baffin Island, Canada, to train, along with other members of the expedition, in dog sledding in preparation for the long and difficult trip.

At the beginning of the trek, there were eight members of the team and forty-nine dogs. Their typical day lasted about twelve hours, during which they broke camp, prepared their sleds, took care of their dogs, and set up trails, most of the time in −70°F weather. Along the way, Bancroft fell into open freezing waters, but the team quickly pulled her out. She dried out in a tent that was pitched immediately. One other member of the team was injured and one was frostbitten. Both were flown out along with twenty-eight of the sled dogs. It had been prearranged that the dogs would be flown out. Only six members of the team and twenty-one dogs completed the expedition.

After the expedition, Bancroft moved to Sunfish Lake, Minnesota.

Bar Association, Women's National

First national women's group to promote the interest of women lawyers (1899).

In 1899 a group of women practicing law in Connecticut, New Jersey, and New York City met in the office of Edith Griswold. Griswold, a former schoolteacher, was practicing patent law in New York City at the time. The group formed the Women Lawyers' Club, which nine years later was renamed the Women Lawyers' Association (WLA). Griswold served as president of the WLA from 1912 until 1914.

In 1923 the constitution of the organization was changed to resemble that of the American Bar Association.

Theda Bara

First movie star to wear eye makeup (1914).

Born Cincinnati, Ohio, July 20, 1885; died Los Angeles, California, April 7, 1955.

In 1914 cosmetics tycoon Helena Rubenstein invented eye makeup for Theda Bara as a means of establishing a market for a new cosmetic product.

Bara, born Theodosia Goodman, attended the University of Cincinnati (Cincinnati, Ohio) from 1903 to 1905, then went to New York to pursue a career on the stage. Her debut came in 1908 in *The Devil,* written by Ferenc Molnar.

In 1914 director Frank Powell offered her the lead in *A Fool There Was,* a silent movie (1915) based on a play inspired by Rudyard Kipling's poem "The Vampire." The movie gave rise to the expression *vamp*—a woman who entices, then brings about the ruin of honorable but helpless men.

In 1917 she legally changed her name to Bara for the movies. Between 1915 and 1920 she made about forty films, but her acting career then declined, in part because of overly repetitive roles. There were some notable departures, however, particularly her role of Esmeralda in *The Darling of Paris,* based on Victor Hugo's novel *The Hunchback of Notre Dame.* Her last film was *Madame Mystery,* a short comedy co-directed by comedian Stan Laurel. Bara did a parody of the vamp that had made her famous.

Barbers, First Women

Following a day-long debate at its annual convention (1924), the Journeymen Barbers International Union voted to admit women. Women had sought membership in the union for fifteen years prior to the vote.

(Elizabeth) Jane Rucker Hadley Barkley

First woman to marry a vice president while he was in office (1949).

Born Keytesville, Ohio, 1911; died Washington, D.C., September 6, 1964.

Educated in Europe, Jane Barkley married her first husband when she was nineteen and became a widow at thirty-four. After his death in 1945, she was a secretary at George Washington University (Washington, D.C.).

In 1949 Barkley met Vice President Alben W. Barkley, seventy-eight years old, and married him in St. Louis, Missouri, in November of that year. Alben Barkley, a Democrat from Kentucky, served with President Harry S. Truman, and afterwards returned to the U.S. Senate. He died in 1956.

Jane Barkley wrote *I Married the Veep* in 1958.

Kate Barnard

First woman in the United States voted into statewide elective office by an all-male electorate (1907).

Born Geneva, Nebraska, May 23, 1875; died Oklahoma City, Oklahoma, February 23, 1930.

Barnard was elected Oklahoma commissioner of charities and corrections in 1907, defeating her Republican opponent by over 35,000 votes. She amassed more votes than any other candidate for state office in that election. Barnard ran for a second term and won reelection in 1910.

After attending St. Joseph's parochial school in Oklahoma City, Oklahoma, Barnard became a teacher in rural schools (1892–95). She then left teaching, trained as a stenographer at Oklahoma City Business College (c. 1902), and first entered the world of politics when she was hired as clerk and stenographer by the Democratic party in the Oklahoma territorial legislature. She also wrote articles for the *Daily Oklahoman,* notably a series describing the life of the poor in Oklahoma City (1904/5). She headed campaigns to furnish food, shelter, clothing, and medical attention for needy people, and was instrumental in organizing them into a federal labor union, chartered by the American Federation of Labor (AFL).

As an elected official and labor activist, Barnard fought for pension benefits for laborers' widows, attacked the blacklisting of union members, opposed the use of convict labor, and battled those who attempted to defraud Native Americans.

During her second term, she suffered a nervous breakdown due to the pressures of a heavy workload and aggressive opponents. In 1914 Barnard retired from politics. She then managed family real estate and fought against the ravages of a severe skin disease.

Jhane Barnes

First woman to win the Coty Award for menswear (1980).

Born Baltimore, Maryland, March 4, 1954.

Barnes won the Coty Award at the thirty-eighth annual presentation; it was the first time that an award was offered for menswear. Voting by editors and fashion writers across the country took place by mail. Her two strongest competitors were men: Alan Flusser and Don Polley.

Designing is Barnes's forte. She began designing menswear in the 1970s, at a very young age. She fashioned men's clothing without buttons, cuffs, and sometimes without lapels. Since 1976 Barnes has been the major designer and president of her own firm, Jhane Barnes, Inc., located in New York City, whose annual retail sales reached $20 million in 1988.

She has received the Product Design Award of the Institute of Business Designers and *Contract* magazine from 1983 to 1986. At the time of this writing, Barnes is still designing and marketing menswear.

Pancho (Florence) Lowe Barnes

First woman to be a stunt pilot in motion pictures (1929); first to fly from Los Angeles, California, to Mexico City, Mexico (1930).

Born Pasadena, California, 1901; died Boron, California, 1975.

Barnes was the daughter of a wealthy Pasadena family that suffered severe losses in the Great Depression of the thirties.

She flew in the first Women's Air Derby (see entry) in 1929. She was in first place in the second stage of the race, but damaged her plane in a landing and was compelled to withdraw.

Her first air stunts came in Howard Hughes's 1929 movie *Hell's Angels*. The following year, she set a new women's speed record of 196.19 miles per hour.

In 1930 Barnes flew from Los Angeles, California, to Mexico City, Mexico, becoming the first woman pilot to fly that route. She took her mechanic on the sightseeing trip, made in easy stages.

In 1931 Barnes chaired a transcontinental race for women. More than fifty planes competed, and the race was completed without a mishap. In 1934 she and other women pilots formed a flying group for providing emergency assistance in disasters. In one demonstration of their skill, they dropped a crate of eggs from an altitude of 7,000 feet without breaking a single one.

Later, she ran a resort ranch on property adjoining Edwards Air Force Base in California. In 1953 she brought a $300,000 suit against Brig. Gen. J. S. Holtoner, commanding officer of the base, charging that he had threatened to bomb her ranch in order to further the government's plan of enlarging the base by acquiring her property. Barnes had purchased the eighty-acre ranch in 1933.

Nora Stanton Barney *(see Nora Stanton)*

Barbara Olive Barnwell

First woman to receive the U.S. Navy–Marine Corps medal for heroism (1953).

Dates unknown.

Barnwell, a staff sergeant from Pittsburgh, Pennsylvania, and a member of the U.S. Marine Reserve, saved a soldier from drowning in 1952.

Rose Tyler Barrett

First woman to be a city manager (c. 1920).

Born XYZ Ranch, Spink County, South Dakota, 1889.

About 1920 Barrett became city manager of Warrenton, Oregon, at the mouth of the Columbia River. (The other city administrators included a mayor and three commissioners.) As city manager, she was head of a corporate entity with a capital worth of $3 million, over 1,100 employees, and a monthly payroll of $45,000.

Barrett, who had only a fifth-grade education, was married at nineteen and widowed before she was twenty-four. Then living in Portland, Oregon, she went to night school to learn commercial law. She opened a real estate business and began investing in land at Warrenton, Oregon, speculating that the city's location and fresh-water harbor augured a bright future. Barrett was proved right: railroad and shipping terminals began to appear in Warrenton, and in 1918 she went to Montana farmers and convinced them that they would realize larger profits by shipping their goods to Warrenton. She became a wealthy woman.

In 1924 Ida Tarbell (see entry) said of Barrett's accomplishment that it was "one of the most remarkable pieces of constructive work ever accomplished."

Emily Dunning Barringer *(see Emily Dunning)*

(Katharine) Isabel Hayes Barrows

First woman to work for the U.S. State Department (1868); first to be a stenographer for congressional committees (1870–71).

Born Iras, Vermont, 1845; died Croton-on-Hudson, New York, 1913.

Her husband, Samuel Barrows, was the stenographic secretary to

Secretary of State William H. Seward in the summer of 1868. When he became ill, Barrows took his place. That same year she enrolled in the Woman's Medical College of the New York Infirmary for Women and Children (New York, New York), and the following year she went to Vienna, Austria, to study for a specialty in ophthalmology. She returned to the United States to open a private medical practice and teach at Howard University (Washington, D.C.).

A number of years later, Barrows's husband became a Unitarian minister, and she became the editor of the *Christian Register*, a Unitarian weekly. From 1884 to 1904 she served as reporter and editor for the National Conference of Charities and Correction; her interest in prison reform was a driving force for the remainder of her life.

Clara (Clarissa) Barton

Founder of the American Red Cross (1881).

Born Oxford, Massachusetts, December 25, 1821; died Glen Echo, Maryland, April 12, 1912.

Barton began work as a schoolteacher when she was fifteen. She founded a public school in New Jersey—one of the first in the state—in 1852, but resigned in 1854 when a man was placed in the school as her superior.

She went to work in the U.S. Patent Office as a clerk and copyist, copying documents submitted in support of patent applications. In a short time, she was promoted to the position of confidential clerk to the superintendent of patents—a job with the status and salary of a male.

With the outbreak of the Civil War, Barton first served the troops as an unpaid nurse, then was appointed superintendent of the Department of Nurses of the Army of the James. Seeking greater public support, she encouraged women's service organizations to prepare and contribute bandages, foodstuffs, etc., which—with permission from U.S. Surgeon General Hitchcock—she personally delivered to the front.

Between 1866 and 1868, Barton

traveled extensively, giving over 300 lectures about her experiences as a nurse and organizer of medical and morale services for Union Army soldiers during the Civil War. In 1868 she suffered a nervous breakdown; she convalesced in England. While in Europe, she discovered the International Committee of the Red Cross, founded in Geneva, Switzerland, in 1843. Barton joined forces with that organization, working to set up military hospitals during the Franco-Prussian War of 1870–71.

After returning to the United States in 1873, Barton planned at least a partial retirement; when the Russo-Turkish War broke out in 1877, however, it spurred her campaign to organize the Red Cross in the United States. She was named the first president of the American Red Cross, serving in that post until 1904.

Florence Bascom

First woman to be elected a fellow of the Geological Society of America (1894); first to receive an appointment to the U.S. Geological Survey (1896).

Born Williamstown, Massachusetts, July 14, 1862; died Northhampton, Massachusetts, June 18, 1945.

Bascom earned the first Ph.D. degree awarded to a woman by Johns Hopkins University in Baltimore, Maryland (1893). Prior to that, she attended the University of Wisconsin (Madison), earning a B.S. degree in 1882, an M.S. degree in 1884, and an A.M. degree in 1887. Her father, John Bascom, was president of the university when Florence attended.

Florence Bascom taught at Ohio State University (Columbus) from 1893 to 1895. She then moved to the science department at Bryn Mawr College, Bryn Mawr, Pennsylvania, where she taught from 1895 to 1928, moving through the ranks from lecturer to full professor (1906).

In 1896 Bascom was appointed assistant geologist with the U.S. Geological Survey and was later appointed geologist. She served as associate editor of the *American Geologist* from 1896 to 1903, and in 1930 was elected vice president of the Geological Society of America.

Basketball, Women's

Women first played basketball at Smith College (Northampton, Massachusetts) in 1892.

The game was introduced by Senda Berenson (see entry), director of physical education at Smith. She drew up the first official rules for women's basketball in 1899.

The first women's intercollegiate

basketball game was held on April 4, 1896, at Berkeley, California. The women's team from the University of California–Berkeley played the women's team from Stanford University. Male spectators were barred.

Basketball Conference, Inc., All-American Girls'

First basketball league for girls on a national scale (1974).

The league started in East Greenwich, Rhode Island, with two divisions: seniors (ages fourteen and fifteen) and juniors (ages twelve and thirteen). Shortly after its inauguration, more than twenty states began to explore the establishment of affiliated leagues.

Vietta M. Bates

First enlisted woman to be sworn into the regular U.S. Army (1949).

Dates unknown.

Bates enlisted in the Women's Auxiliary Army Corps (WAAC) in March, 1945. Legislation was passed in June, 1949, which made the WAAC part of the regular army. Thus, Bates was sworn into the Women's Army Corps (WAC) on July 8, 1949. She was then assigned to duty with the Military District of Washington, D.C.

Anne Bauchens

First woman to receive an Academy Award for film editing (1940); first person to receive the American Cinema Editors' Achievement Award (ACE) (1952).

Born St. Louis, Missouri, February 2, 1881; died Woodland Hills, California, May 7, 1967.

Winning an Oscar for editing the 1940 film *North West Mounted Police,* Bauchens went on to win an ACE for *The Greatest Show on Earth* (1952), which also won her another Oscar nomination. She also received Oscar nominations for *Cleopatra* (1934) and *The Ten Commandments* (1956).

Originally a switchboard operator at the *St. Louis Post-Dispatch* and later secretary to William C. de Mille, Bauchens went to Hollywood with de Mille and created the job of script clerk—the production secretary who logs all of the film shots. De Mille recommended her as film editor for *You Can't Have Everything* (1918), which she co-edited with Cecil B. De-Mille. Between 1918 and 1959 she edited Cecil DeMille's last forty films.

Ann Baumgartner

First woman to fly a jet plane (1944).

Born c. 1923.

Formerly a journalist, the twenty-one-year-old Women's Auxiliary Ferrying Service (WAFS) pilot flew a YP-59, the United States' first experimental jet. She reached 350 miles per hour and an altitude of 35,000 feet at Wright Field, Dayton, Ohio, in October, 1944.

Blanche Bayliss

First woman to star in a feature film (1894).

Dates unknown.

Bayliss starred in a short skit called *Miss Jerry,* the first Magic Lantern feature film, made at Carbon Studio, New York City. (A "magic lantern" was an early device for projecting pictures by means of a candle and shuttered lens that provided the illusion of movement.) (See also Florence Bridgewood Lawrence.)

Amy Marcy Cheney (Mrs. H. H. A.) Beach

First woman composer to have a symphonic musical work performed (1896); founder and first president of the Association of American Women Composers (1926).

Born Henniker, New Hampshire, September 5, 1867; died New York, New York, December 27, 1944.

Beach had already written numerous choral, orchestral, and chamber works when she composed her *Gaelic Symphony* in 1896. It was first performed by the Boston Symphony, Emil Paur, conductor, in October of the same year.

Beach made her debut as a concert pianist in Boston, Massachusetts, in 1883. Two years later she was married, and thereafter she concentrated on composition—for which she had no formal training.

For Beach 1892 was a banner year. On May 1 her composition, *Festival Jubilate,* written to celebrate the opening of the Women's Building at the World Columbian Exposition, was performed by a special Columbian Exposition orchestra of 120 members, conducted by Theodore Thomas. The same year, the Handel and Haydn Society, the oldest choral group in the United States, performed her Mass in E-flat with the Boston Symphony, marking the first time that chorus had ever performed a work by a woman. Beach was also the first woman whose music was performed by the New York Philharmonic Society. The society, under the direction of Walter Damrosch, presented her concert aria, *Eilende Wolken,* in the winter of 1892. Mrs. Carl Alves sang the aria.

From 1922 to 1914 she toured Europe playing her own compositions in concert performances.

In 1928 the University of New

Hampshire awarded Beach an honorary master of arts degree.

Beach continued to write until she was well advanced in years, composing her opus 150—a trio for piano, violin, and cello—in 1938, when she was over seventy.

Florence Beaumont

First woman to immolate herself as an antiwar protest (1967).

Born La Puente, California, c. 1912; died Los Angeles, California, October 15, 1967.

On October 15, 1967, Beaumont, a fifty-five-year-old citizen of La Puente, California, stood in front of the Federal Building in Los Angeles, doused her clothing with gasoline, and set herself on fire with a match. She took her life in protest against United States participation in the war in Vietnam.

Audrey P. Beck

First woman president of the American Society of Planning Officials (1976).

Born Brooklyn, New York, c. 1911; died Willington, Connecticut, March 11, 1983.

Beck, assistant minority leader for the Democrats in the Connecticut House of Representatives in 1973, became the first woman president of the American Society of Planning Officials three years later. In that capacity she presided over meetings and delivered the annual keynote address.

She was elected to the Connecticut senate, where she became the assistant majority leader for fiscal affairs in that chamber (1983). She was serving her fourth term in the senate when she apparently committed suicide on March 11, 1983.

Dorothy Jacobs Bellanca

First woman to be elected to the executive board of the Amalgamated Clothing Workers of America (ACWA) (1914); first to be a full-time organizer for the ACWA (1917).

Born Zemel, Latvia, August 10, 1894; died New York, New York, August 16, 1946.

As a young child, Bellanca immigrated to the United States with her family in 1900. Scarcely into her teens, she went to work in a garment factory, sewing buttonholes by hand. Along with other female teenage co-workers, she founded a local of the United Garment Workers of America (c. 1908), and within two years Bellanca was named to lead it. After persuading most of the males who operated the buttonhole machines to join her union, she took the local into the recently founded ACWA.

In the 1930s Bellanca was a member of New York City's Committee on Unemployment, and in 1938 she was named to the U.S. Department of Labor's Advisory Committee on Maternal and Child Welfare.

Bellanca made an unsuccessful run for Congress in 1938.

Alva Smith Belmont

Founder and first president of the Political Equality Association (1909).

Born Mobile, Alabama, January 17, 1853; died Paris, France, January 26, 1933.

Belmont was a recognized authority on architecture, and some of the most magnificent homes in the United States were built under her supervision. One of them, the French Gothic Beacon Towers of Sands Point, Long Island, New York, was bought by Mrs. William Randolph Hearst.

Belmont was educated in France, where her family had moved after the Civil War. In 1874 she married William K. Vanderbilt, and one of his gifts to her was the renowned Marble House of Newport, Rhode Island—a house that in 1892 reportedly cost $2 million to build and another $7 million to furnish and decorate. Three years later, the couple was divorced,

and the following year she married Oliver H. P. Belmont (1896).

Belmont became known for her concern about, and activities on behalf of, less fortunate people. She worked to improve hospitals, abolish child labor, improve sanitary conditions for women, and expedite the enactment of woman suffrage laws.

In 1909 she founded and became the first president of the Political Equality Association. Belmont established the first agricultural training school for women (1911) (see entry) and organized free soup kitchens for women (1915). She also wrote, in 1915, an operetta called *Melinda and Her Sisters* to raise money for advancing the cause of suffrage. The operetta, starring Marie Dressler, earned $8,000.

Belmont joined and became a member of the executive board of the Congressional Union, founded by Alice Paul (see entry) and Lucy Burns to lobby for passage of the national suffrage amendment. After Belmont organized the National Women's Party Convention (1915), she donated a mansion in Washington, D.C., to serve as party headquarters. She was elected party president in 1921, and twice won reelection.

After the suffrage amendment was passed and ratified, Belmont continued to work for true equality for women, concentrating on such issues as legal equality and equality in the workplace. In 1926 Belmont and

Paul led a group of delegates from the National Woman's party to a convention of the International Woman Suffrage Alliance, in Paris, France.

Alice Bennett

Probably the first woman to be a superintendent at a state hospital for the insane (1880).

Born Wrentham, Massachusetts, 1851; died 1925.

Superintendent of the women's section at the Pennsylvania State Hospital for the Insane (Norristown, Pennsylvania), Bennett introduced occupational therapy and advanced nonrestraint methods. She resigned as superintendent in 1886.

Bennett earned an M.D. degree from the Woman's Medical College of Pennsylvania (Philadelphia) in 1876. She remained at Woman's College as a demonstrator of anatomy for four years. She then earned a Ph.D. degree in anatomy from the University of Pennsylvania (Philadelphia) in 1880—the first woman to get a Ph.D. degree from that university.

Elizabeth H. Bennett

First woman to have a successful Caesarean operation (1794).

Dates unknown.
Bennett's husband, Dr. Jessee

Bennett, performed the procedure, using laudanum as an anesthetic.

Joan Benoit (Samuelson)

First woman to win an Olympic marathon (1984).

Born Cape Elizabeth, Maine, May 16, 1957.

Benoit won the women's marathon (26 miles, 385 yards) the first time it was held as an Olympic event in 1984, running the distance in a time of 2 hours, 24 minutes, 52 seconds. She had led the race after the first 14 minutes, defeating perennial rival Grete Waitz, the great Norwegian distance runner, and finishing 400 meters ahead of the second-place runner.

She had begun distance running as a teenager in 1973 to rebuild muscles weakened by a skiing accident. In 1979, the year she graduated as a history and environmental studies major from Bowdoin College (Brunswick, Maine), Benoit was the women's winner in the Boston Marathon—the second time she had entered a marathon. She won it again in 1983, setting a world record time of 2 hours, 22 minutes, 43 seconds.

Benoit did not run another marathon until the Olympic trials in May, 1984, less than three weeks after she had undergone arthroscopic surgery.

A year after her Olympic victory, she won the Chicago Marathon.

During her running career, Benoit set U.S. records for the 10-kilometer, half-marathon, 10-mile, and 25-kilometer distances. She has garnered numerous awards, including the Women's Sports Foundation Sportswoman of the Year award, shared with Olympic gymnast Mary Lou Retton (1984); the James E. Sullivan Award for outstanding amateur athlete of the year (1986); and the Abibe Bikila Award for contributions to long-distance running (1986).

In 1987 Benoit published her autobiography—*Running Tide*.

Senda Berenson

The person who established the rules for girls' basketball (1892).

Born Butrimonys, Lithuania, March 19, 1868; died Santa Barbara, California, February 16, 1954.

Berenson was born Senda Valvrojenski, but when she and her family immigrated to Boston, Massachusetts, in 1875, they changed their name to Berenson. Senda attended the Boston Normal School of Gymnastics (Boston, Massachusetts) from 1890 to 1892, then got a teaching job at Smith College (Northampton, Massachusetts). It was there that she developed a set of basketball rules for women.

According to Berenson's rules of the game, players could dribble only three times and could hold the ball for no more than three seconds. These rules were the standard ones for seventy years.

In 1905 Berenson, sister of the art collector and critic Bernard Berenson, was appointed chair of the basketball rules committee of the American Association for the Advent of Physical Education, the forerunner of the National Association for Girls and Women in Sports. She served on the committee until 1917.

In 1911 Berenson became the director of physical education at a private girls' school, where she remained until 1921.

Lena (Edith) Berg

First U.S. woman to ride in a plane in another country (1908) (see also Mrs. Ralph Henry Van Deman).

Born Aledo, Illinois; died March 1, 1931.

On October 7, 1908, Berg flew with Wilbur Wright during a promotional exhibition to demonstrate the reliability of the Wright plane for licensing in France. The flight lasted two minutes and three seconds; they flew at an altitude of fifty feet over the Hunaudières racetrack in Le Mans, France. The plane was tethered to a

48

rock by a wire. Berg's husband, Hart O. Berg, was European business manager for the Wright brothers.

Aline Bernstein *(born Hazel Frankau)*

First woman to be a major professional theatrical designer (mid-1920s); first to be a member of the United Scenic Art Union (AFL) (1926).

Born New York, New York, December 22, 1882; died New York, New York, September 7, 1955.

From 1915 through the early 1930s, Bernstein designed scenery and costumes for the Neighborhood Playhouse of the Henry Street Settlement, New York City. In 1925 she did memorable work for the Theatre Guild and executed her famous designs for the first U.S. production of *The Dybbuk,* by Shloyme Zanvl Rappoport (S. Ansky).

Bernstein applied in 1924 for membership in the Brotherhood of Painters, Decorators and Paperhangers, Local 829, of the American Federation of Labor (AFL). She was turned down then and on subsequent occasions, but in 1926 was finally admitted as the first woman member. The set designers eventually seceded from this union and formed the United Scenic Art Union of the AFL.

For the next two decades, Bernstein worked as resident designer for Eva Le Gallienne's Civic Repertory Theatre in New York City. She designed the costumes and scenery for five Lillian Hellman plays and went to Hollywood to design two movie epics for RKO—*She* and *The Last Days of Pompeii* (both 1935). She was also instrumental in the establishment of the Museum of Costume Art, later the Costume Institute of the Metropolitan Museum of Art, New York City.

After spending most of the 1940s as a costume design instructor at Vassar College, Poughkeepsie, New York, Bernstein designed the costumes for the opera *Regina,* based on Lillian Hellman's play *The Little Foxes,* winning a Tony Award for her accomplishments (1949).

Bernstein was born Hazel Frankau, but her mother changed her name to Aline. She studied at Hunter College and the New York School for Applied Design, both in New York City. Married in her early twenties, she had two children.

Between 1925 and 1930 Bernstein had a famous love affair with novelist Thomas Wolfe, whose character Esther Jack, in *The Web and the Rock* (1939) and *You Can't Go Home Again* (1940), was based on her. She herself also wrote short stories and novels; her novel *The Journey Down* (1938) was inspired by Thomas Wolfe's early days in New York City.

Joanne Bethune

First person to direct a nursery school (1827).

Born Fort Niagara, Canada, 1770; died New York, New York, July 28, 1860.

As a disciple of the Swiss educator Johann Heinrich Pestalozzi, Bethune established the Infant School Society in the United States. She immediately set up the first free school for infants in New York City (1827), and eight more schools followed in short order.

The mission of the schools was to free working-class parents from some of the burden of child care; they were open to children aged eighteen months to five years. The schools established by the society lasted for just over a decade.

Daughter of Isabella M. Graham, Bethune had moved with her family to New York City in 1789. She taught in her mother's successful school, then in 1806 organized the Orphan Asylum Society in New York City. In 1816 Bethune founded the Female Union Society for the Promotion of Sabbath-Schools—the schools were attended by 8,000 children from city-wide churches of all faiths.

Louise Bethune (Blanchard)

First woman to gain prominence as a professional architect (1881); first to be elected a member of the American Institute of Architects (1888); first to be named a fellow of the organization (1889).

Born Waterloo, New York, July 21, 1856; died New York, New York, December 18, 1913.

After she graduated from high school, Bethune became a draftsman in an architect's office (1876). In 1881 she married Robert Bethune, and together they opened an office in Buffalo, New York, in 1888. She designed many buildings—schools, factories, hotels, housing developments, residences, a bank—including the Hotel Lafayette in Buffalo. A music store that she designed in Buffalo was one of the country's first structures with a steel frame and poured concrete slabs.

In March, 1891, Bethune's article titled "Women of Architecture" was published in *Inland Architect and News Record*. She had become a well-known architect by the time she declined to compete in the World's Columbian Exposition in Chicago, 1892–93, which celebrated the 400th anniversary of Columbus's voyage. She claimed that she had not been offered a fair honorarium.

Mary McLeod Bethune

First woman to establish a secondary school that became a four-year accredited college (1904); founder of the National Council of Negro Women (1935).

Born Mayesville, South Carolina, July 10, 1875; died Daytona Beach, Florida, May 18, 1955.

Born on a plantation where she picked cotton, Bethune walked ten miles each day to attend school—an experience that later impelled her to open a school for black children.

In 1893 she graduated from Scotia Seminary (now Barber-Scotia College) in Concord, North Carolina, a Presbyterian school for black girls. Determined to become a missionary in Africa, she attended the Moody Bible Institute, Chicago, Illinois, and

graduated in 1895. When she applied to become a missionary, however, the Presbyterian Mission said there were no openings for blacks. Thus, in 1895 she began her career as a teacher.

Bethune worked diligently to fund and build her own school, which reportedly she financed with her own small savings. In 1904 she opened the Daytona Normal and Industrial Institute in Daytona Beach, Florida. Her son and five girls became the first students. By 1923 the faculty and staff had grown to twenty-five, and there were 300 girl students. That year, with the help of the Board of Education for Negroes of the Methodist Episcopal Church, the school merged with Cookman Institute (Jacksonville, Florida) and became coeducational. In 1929 the school was renamed Bethune-Cookman College. In 1943 the fully accredited college awarded its first four-year degrees.

After several years as president of the college, Bethune stepped down in 1942 in order to raise funds for its support. Through these efforts she met such influential people as Eleanor Roosevelt (see entry), who assisted her in raising money. After tremendous success as a fund-raiser, she resumed her position as president of the college in 1946, retiring as president emeritus the following year.

Bethune was the first black woman to become a presidential adviser when Franklin Delano Roosevelt, thirty-second president of the United States, placed her in charge of Negro Affairs of the National Youth Administration in 1936 and appointed her director of the Division of Negro Affairs in 1939, where she served until 1944. She also advised the secretary of war on the selection of officer candidates for the Women's Army Auxiliary Corps (WAAC), established in 1942.

Bethune, who was president of the Association for the Study of Negro Life and History from 1936 to 1951, also served as vice president of the National Association for the Advancement of Colored People (NAACP) from 1940 to 1955. She later became vice president of the National Urban League.

For many years, Bethune was also active in associations for black women. From 1917 until 1924 she was president of the Florida Federation of Colored Women, and from 1924 to 1928 was president of the National Association of Colored Women. In 1935 she founded the National Council of Negro Women (NCNW), formed by uniting major national black women's associations. President of the NCNW from its founding in 1935 until 1949, she represented the organization at the founding conference of the United Nations, held in San Francisco, California, in 1945. Today, the NCNW serves several million people.

Isabel Bevier

First woman to establish a home economics laboratory on a college campus (1908); first person to use a thermometer for meat cooking (1907).

Born Plymouth, Ohio, November 14, 1860; died Urbana, Illinois, March 17, 1942.

Bevier studied the chemistry of foods and sanitary chemistry at Western Reserve University (Cleveland, Ohio) and at the Massachusetts Institute of Technology (Cambridge). In 1900 she was named head of the newly named, reorganized Department of Household Science at the University of Illinois (Urbana). The department focused on food, clothing, and shelter, refusing to offer sewing and dressmaking courses.

In 1910 Bevier became the second president of the American Home Economics Association, serving until 1915, and in 1921 she became the chair of the department of home economics at the University of California–Los Angeles. She held that position for two years, then returned to the University of Illinois, where the home economics building was named in her honor in 1928.

Bevier had earned a Ph.B. degree from the University of Wooster (Wooster, Ohio) in 1885, and a master's degree in Latin and German, also from the University of Wooster, in 1888. From 1888 to 1897 she was professor of natural sciences at the Pennsylvania College for Women in Pittsburgh.

Alice McLellan Birney

Founder and first president of the Parent-Teacher Association (PTA) (1897).

Born Marietta, Georgia, October 19, 1858; died Chevy Chase, Maryland, December 20, 1907.

Originally called the National Congress of Mothers, then the National Congress of Parents and Teachers, the PTA had its beginnings in 1897, when 2,000 women met at a "mothers' congress" in Washington, D.C., and founded the National Congress of Mothers. The organization's purpose, in Birney's words, was to make the nation "recognize the supreme importance of the child." The major goal of the PTA was to unite the forces of home, school, and community in behalf of children and young people. Previously a child welfare worker, Birney was named the first president. Within two years, membership had grown to 50,000 mothers.

Birney resigned in 1902 because of poor health. She then wrote a book, *Childhood,* about child rearing. In 1908, the year following her death, the organization she founded was renamed the Parent-Teacher Association.

She had attended Mt. Holyoke Seminary, South Hadley, Massachusetts, for one year (1875).

Emily Bissell

First person to battle tuberculosis through the sale of Christmas seals (1907).

Born Wilmington, Delaware, 1861; died Wilmington, Delaware, March 8, 1948.

Bissell was the first person outside the medical profession to be awarded the Trudeau Medal of the National Tuberculosis Association (1942). She was also honored in 1980 by the issuing of a U.S. stamp (fifteen cents) bearing her likeness.

The idea of selling a Christmas stamp to fight tuberculosis was first conceived by a postal clerk in Denmark. Immensely successful from the beginning, the idea spread to Iceland and Sweden, and Jacob Riis, the Danish-born journalist and reformer, publicized the practice in the United States.

After reading an article by Riis about the stamps, Bissell designed a seal surrounded by a holly wreath and the words "Merry Christmas." Borrowing forty dollars with which to print 50,000 penny seals, Bissell netted $3,000 on her first campaign.

She then persuaded the American Red Cross to mount a nationwide campaign and sale in 1907. The seals had the Red Cross symbol on them.

From 1889 onward, Bissell played a role in many Delaware charities, including the first public playground and the first free kindergarten in Wilmington. She also organized the Delaware state chapter of the American Red Cross.

Shirley Temple Black

First woman to be chief of protocol for the president of the United States (1976).

Born Santa Monica, California, April 23, 1928.

President Gerald Ford appointed Black chief of protocol. Her function was to appear at diplomatic parties, make speeches, and serve on committees.

She had made an unsuccessful bid for a seat in Congress in 1967. However, after she had demonstrated her talents as a successful Republican fund-raiser, President Richard Nixon named her a United States representative to the United Nations (1969). She served from 1974 to 1976 as United States ambassador to Ghana, and from 1989 to 1992 as ambassador to Czechoslovakia.

As a child, Black was a major movie star and is believed to have earned $5 million over the course of her career. Between 1935 and 1938 she was the biggest box-office draw in Hollywood. Once she reached adolescence, however, her star began to dim, and she abandoned the movies in 1949. Among her major films were *Stand Up and Cheer* (1934), which made her a star; *Little Miss Marker* (1934); and *Now and Forever* (1934).

The Academy of Motion Picture Arts and Sciences awarded Black a special Oscar as "the outstanding personality of 1934."

Winifred Sweet Black (Bonfils)

First woman reporter to cover a prizefight (c. 1903).

Born Chilton, Wisconsin, October 14, 1863; died San Francisco, California, May 25, 1936.

Black, whose pen name was Annie Laurie, was a reporter for the *San Francisco Examiner* from 1890 to

1895. She was known for the stunts she pulled to get stories. For example, in 1892 she got an interview with President Benjamin Harrison by hiding under a table aboard his campaign train; in 1900 she covered the tidal wave that struck Galveston, Texas, by slipping through police lines disguised as a boy. She wrote, too, about the 1906 San Francisco earthquake and the 1907 New York trial of Harry Thaw for the murder of prominent architect Stanford White. (Black and three other women reporters were dubbed "sob sisters" at this trial.)

Black covered World War I in Europe for the *Examiner*, writing a regular column until it ended. At her death in 1936, *Examiner* owner William Randolph Hearst had her body laid in state in the rotunda of the city hall in San Francisco.

Antoinette Brown Blackwell *(see Antoinette Brown)*

Elizabeth Blackwell

First woman to receive a medical degree (1849).

Born Counterslip, near Bristol, England, February 3, 1821; died Hastings, Sussex, England, May 31, 1910.

The Blackwell family immigrated to the United States when Elizabeth was eleven. She was educated well by private tutors. Later, when her family experienced financial difficulties, she and other family members opened a private school in Cincinnati, Ohio (1938). In 1942 she left Cincinnati to teach school in Kentucky and the Carolinas. While teaching, she studied medicine privately, using the medical books of practicing physicians.

In 1847 Blackwell went to Philadelphia, where she gained the sponsorship of two Quaker physicians, but she was refused entry to several medical colleges. Determined not to be defeated, Blackwell continued to study medicine privately, while she continued her search for a college that would admit her. Geneva Medical College (Geneva, New York) finally enrolled her in 1847, but it was rumored that the male students accepted her application thinking that it was a joke. In 1849 she graduated from Geneva, becoming the first woman in the United States to earn a medical degree.

Blackwell's struggle was not over, however. After interning at St. Bartholomew's Hospital in England and taking a course in midwifery in Paris, France, in August, 1851 she returned to the United States, where hospitals refused to hire her because she was a woman. In 1853 she opened a tiny clinic in a slum district of New York City. (The first woman to practice medicine in the United States was Harriot Kezia Hunt, see entry.) Later, two other women doctors joined her at the clinic: Blackwell's sister, Emily, and Marie E. Zakrzewska. Blackwell had helped both women be admitted to the medical department of Western Reserve College (Cleveland, Ohio), where they received their medical degrees. The practice grew, and attempts at fund-raising were successful. By 1857 the three physicians had a large practice and enough money to expand the clinic. They moved to Greenwich Village, New York City, and opened the New York Infirmary for Women and Children.

One of Blackwell's longtime dreams had been to establish a medical college of high standards. In 1868 her dream was realized with the opening of the Woman's Medical College of the New York Infirmary. She instituted entrance examinations, a variety of medical courses, and the offering of clinical experience as part of the college's program. The medical college remained open until 1899.

In 1869 Blackwell moved to England, where she lived until her death in 1910.

(Carol) Blaze Blazejowski

First woman athlete to win the Margaret Wade Trophy for best woman collegiate basketball player in the nation (1978).

Born Cranford, New Jersey, c. 1957.

Blazejowski, a 5'10" star of her basketball team at Montclair State College (Upper Montclair, New Jersey), where she scored a total of 3,199 points, won the Margaret Wade Trophy in 1978, the first time it was ever awarded. At Madison Square Garden (New York City) she set a record of fifty-two points in a single game.

She played amateur basketball after college in order to qualify for the 1980 Olympics, but the United States boycotted the Olympics that year. She then signed with the New Jersey Gems. In 1984 she signed with the New York club of the newly organized Women's American Basketball Association.

Blazejowski is a fellow player of Nancy Lieberman (see entry), who was the second woman athlete to win the Wade Trophy. They both acquired some of their basketball techniques by playing in the streets and on playgrounds. According to Blazejowski, "Playing street ball really helps your game. Playing the black style . . . gives us an advantage."

Amelia Jenks Bloomer

Publisher and editor of the first prominent women's rights newspaper (1849).

Born Homer, New York, May 27, 1818; died Council Bluffs, Iowa, December 30, 1894.

"The New Costume Polka," dedicated to Lydia Bloomer

Bloomer was educated both at home and in local schools in Homer, New York, where she grew up. When she was seventeen she taught school for one term in Clyde, New York. She then tutored privately and worked as a governess in Waterloo, New York.

In 1840 Amelia married Dexter C. Bloomer, a Quaker newspaper editor from Seneca Falls, New York. Soon after their marriage she began writing articles for various publications. She also joined the newly formed Ladies' Temperance Society.

In 1849 she established a newspaper for women: the *Lily*. The first newspaper to be edited entirely by a woman, it featured articles on women's rights and temperance issues. The paper quickly gained a widespread reputation for its writing—one of its regular contributors was Elizabeth Cady Stanton (see entry)—and for hiring women as typesetters.

In the winter of 1850–51 Elizabeth Smith Miller (see entry) visited Bloomer and her cousin, Elizabeth C. Stanton, in Seneca Falls, dressed in fully gathered Turkish style pantaloons worn under a short skirt. Bloomer was delighted with the costume and promoted it in her newspaper. After her articles on women's wear and the pantaloon outfit appeared in the *Lily*, other newspapers across the country followed suit, publishing articles giving credit to Bloomer for the outfit. Although Miller was the first woman to wear the clothes, "Bloomer Costume" became the popular term.

Bloomer began a lecturing career in 1852, while continuing to edit the *Lily*. She and her husband moved from Seneca Falls to Mount Vernon, Ohio, in 1853. However, she continued to publish the newspaper until 1856; she sold it after the couple moved to Council Bluffs, Iowa.

During the Civil War, Bloomer organized and worked with the Soldiers' Aid Society of Council Bluffs. Following the war, during the early 1870s, she continued her campaign on behalf of women's rights, working successfully for state legislation that substantially increased the property rights of married women. She carried the torch for women's rights and social reform until her death in 1894.

Susan E. Blow

First woman to open and teach in a United States public kindergarten (1873) (see also Elizabeth Palmer Peabody).

Born Carondelet (now St. Louis), Missouri, June 7, 1843; died New York, New York, March 26, 1916.

Having traveled in Europe and observed the kindergarten methods used in Germany, Blow returned to her home in St. Louis, Missouri, and convinced the superintendent of schools there to let her open a kindergarten. The first United States public kindergarten was at the Des Peres School in St. Louis. The following year she opened the first training school for kindergarten teachers, and by 1880 all the schools in St. Louis included kindergartens. She received no salary for her innovative work.

Blow was educated privately and traveled extensively, first with her father, who was a congressman, and later alone.

In 1889 she moved east; she lived in Boston, Massachusetts, and in New York City. From 1905 until 1909 she lectured at Teachers College, Columbia University, New York, New York.

Nellie Bly *(pseudonym of Elizabeth Cochrane Seaman)*

First woman to circle the globe alone in seventy-two days, six hours, eleven minutes, and fourteen seconds in competition with a fictional character (1889–90).

Born Cochran's Mills, Pennsylvania, May 5, 1865; died New York, New York, January 27, 1922.

In 1889 Bly decided to challenge the eighty-day round-the-world record of the fictional Phileas Fogg from Jules Verne's *Around the World in Eighty Days*. Her trip started on November 14, 1889, when she sailed from Hoboken, New Jersey, and ended on January 25, 1890, when she arrived in New York City by train from Chicago. Her actual (elapsed) travel time was fifty-six days, twelve hours, forty-one minutes. The trip itself took seventy-two days. Using commercial transportation for every leg of her journey, Bly traveled by steamship, train, rickshaw, and sampan.

Bly's real name was Elizabeth Cochrane Seaman; she took the pen name Nellie Bly—inspired by Stephen Foster's song "Nellie Bly"—after she got her first newspaper job on the *Pittsburgh Dispatch* in 1885. She had gotten the job after writing an angry letter to the newspaper opposing its editorial stand against woman suffrage.

Later, Bly reported for the New York *World* and became famous for her exposés of the appalling conditions in insane asylums, jails, and sweatshops. She also published a book, *Ten Days in a Mad-House,* in 1887.

Helen Francesca Franzolin Boehm

First woman to have a Vatican museum named in her honor (1992); first to be honored by investiture into the Sovereign Order of Cyprus (1977).

Born Brooklyn, New York, date unknown.

Helen Franzolin married Edward M. Boehm, a porcelain artist, in 1944. They became partners in a porcelain studio in Trenton, New Jersey. After her husband's death in 1969, she became chair of the Boehm porcelain studios.

In 1969, at the request of President Richard M. Nixon, she decorated the Oval Room of the White House with a collection of Boehm porcelain. In 1972 President Nixon presented her *Bird of Peace,* a sculpture of mute swans, to Chairman Mao Zedong and the People's Republic of China. Boehm porcelain was shown in a major Russian exhibit, and a Boehm porcelain bald eagle, given to the U.S.S.R. by the United States, is in the Hermitage museum, in Leningrad.

Boehm was honored by the Order of Cyprus in 1977 because of her international achievements in the field of arts.

At the Vatican Museum on June 19, 1992, the Gregorian Etruscan Museum was dedicated in honor of Edward M. Boehm and Helen Franzolin Boehm, recognizing their outstanding service in the arts and to mankind. It was the first time in 500 years that a museum in the Vatican had been named for a person other than a pope, royalty, or nobility. Pope John Paul II also conferred upon Boehm the medal "Pro Ecclesia et Pontifice" for her support of the Vatican museum.

Louise Bogan

First woman to be appointed by the Library of Congress as consultant in poetry in English (1945).

Born Livermore Falls, Maine, August 11, 1897; died New York, New York, February 4, 1970.

The office, the nearest U.S. equivalent to the British position of poet laureate, was created in 1937 and first filled by Joseph Auslander, poetry editor of the *North American Re-*

view. Bogan was the fourth person to occupy the office.

Bogan, who attended the Girls' Latin School, Boston, Massachusetts; Mount St. Mary's Academy, Manchester, New Hampshire; and the University of Boston, was first published in the *New Republic*. She won *Poetry* magazine's John Leed Memorial Prize in 1930, and was awarded Guggenheim Fellowships in 1933 and 1937.

Bogan also won the Bollingen Prize in Poetry (shared with Leonie Adams) (1955); The Academy of American Poets Award, including a $5,000 prize (1959); and $10,000 from the National Endowment for the Arts as one of five "distinguished senior writers" in the United States (1967). In 1965 she was elected to membership in the American Academy of Arts and Letters.

Described by poet Theodore Roethke as a poet with strong affinities to Thomas Campion, the Elizabethans, and the metaphysical poets, Bogan worked primarily in traditional, lyrical verse forms. Among her works are *Body of This Death* (1923); *Dark Summer* (1929); *The Sleeping Fury* (1937); *Collected Poems, 1923 to 1953* (1954); *The Blue Estuaries* (1968); *Achievement in American Poetry, 1900 to 1950* (criticism, 1951); *What the Woman Lived* (letters, 1974); and *Journey Around My Room* (autobiography, 1981).

Boilermakers' Union

First women members (1942).

As the result of an urgent need for workers in a huge shipbuilding program in 1942, the executive council of the International Brotherhood of Boilermakers, Iron Shipbuilders and Helpers, a union of the American Federation of Labor (AFL), issued an edict opening the union to women.

Lin Bolen

First woman to become head of daytime programming at a major television network (1972).

Born Benton, Illinois, 1941.

Bolen, who re-created radio dramas with paper dolls when she was ten, got her start in television producing commercials in her early twenties. She was hired in 1972 by NBC in its prime-time programming department in Los Angeles. After five months, she asked to be moved to New York as head of daytime programming—and got the job, which made her the highest-ranking woman at any network. Bolen was in charge of twelve shows at NBC, from 10 A.M. until 4 P.M. Within two and one-half years, the network's daytime programming was number one in ratings for the first time.

Known for expanding soap operas to one hour from thirty minutes, Bolen was also an avid backer of game shows, making substantial increases in the amounts of the cash prizes.

In 1976 she left NBC to form her own production company—Lin Bolen Productions. Bolen is generally believed to be the inspiration for the Faye Dunaway character in the movie *Network*.

Bolen won a national baton twirling championship at the age of fourteen. After high school she attended City College of New York, majoring in advertising—but did not complete a degree.

Bolen's father was a United Mine Workers labor organizer. Her sister, Marilyn, was said to be the first woman stockbroker on the floor of the exchange in St. Louis, Missouri.

Elizabeth Patterson Bonaparte

First U.S. woman to marry European royalty (1803).

Born Baltimore, Maryland, February 6, 1785; died Baltimore, Maryland, April 4, 1879.

Elizabeth Patterson married Jerome Bonaparte, youngest brother of Napoleon, in Baltimore in 1803. Napoleon arranged for a declaration of nullity in 1806, and Jerome Bonaparte married Princess Catherine of Württemberg in 1807. Patterson obtained a Baltimore divorce in 1813. Her son by Jerome Bonaparte, born July 7, 1805, remained in the United States.

Carrie Jacobs Bond

First woman to be a major popular songwriter.

Born Janesville, Wisconsin, August 11, 1862; died Hollywood, California, December 28, 1946.

Among her songs were "I Love You Truly" (1901) and "A Perfect Day" (1910). "A Perfect Day" sold 5 million copies in about ten years.

Writing in the sentimental mode that characterized much nineteenth-century song, Bond produced over 400 songs—about 170 of which were published.

Marie Bonfanti

First woman to be a musical comedy star (1866).

Born Milan, Italy, c. 1847; died New York, New York, January 25, 1921.

A ballerina by training, Bonfanti made her stage debut in 1866 as the star of *The Black Crook*, which has often been called the first musical comedy. The play ran in New York City until 1868.

Bonfanti performed in plays and in ballet sequences of grand operas throughout the United States until 1887. From 1894 to 1916 she was affiliated with a ballet school in New York City.

Winifred Bonfils (see Winifred Sweet Black)

Gertrude Bonnin

Founder and first president of the National Council of American Indians (1926).

Born Yankton, South Dakota, 1876; died Washington, D.C., January 26, 1938.

After attending Earlham College, Richmond, Indiana, from 1895 to 1897, Bonnin was a teacher for two years at the Carlisle Indian School in Carlisle, Pennsylvania. She wrote *Old Indian Legends* (1901) and *American Indian Stories* (1921).

Bonnin joined the Society of American Indians (1911–20), the first reform organization whose membership and management was limited exclusively to people of Native American blood. In 1916 she became its secretary.

In 1926 Bonnin founded and became president of the National Council of American Indians—a post she held until her death in 1938. The council was a reform group and was successor to the Society of American Indians.

Evangeline Booth

First woman to be commander of the Salvation Army in the United States (1904); first to receive its Distinguished Service Medal (1919).

Born London, England, December 25, 1865; died Hartsdale, New York, July 17, 1950.

Booth was the daughter of Catherine and Sir William Booth, cofounders of the Salvation Army (1865). She came to the United States in 1896 when her brother, the leader of the Salvation Army in the United States, resigned in protest against their father's absolute rule. Booth served as commander of the Salvation Army in the United States from 1904 to 1934,

when she was named general of the International Salvation Army, serving in this post until 1939.

Booth became a United States citizen in 1923. Under her leadership, the Salvation Army expanded its evangelical efforts, social services, and emergency disaster relief. (See also Maud Booth.)

Maud Booth

Cofounder of the Salvation Army in the United States (1887); cofounder of Volunteers of America (1896).

Born Limpsfield, Surrey, England, 1865; died Great Neck, New York, August 26, 1948.

Booth came to the United States in 1887 with her husband, Ballington Booth (son of Gen. William Booth) to supervise the Salvation Army in the United States. In 1895 they became United States citizens.

When Booth and her husband disagreed with Gen. Booth's policy of absolute and centralized control, he ordered their resignation (1896). They then founded the Volunteers of America, a purely American organization that, unlike the Salvation Army, elected its commander in chief.

Booth focused her attention on rehabilitation of prisoners through religion, via the Volunteer Prison League. The league established group homes for the families of prisoners and provided employment for ex-convicts. (See also Evangeline Booth.)

Deborah Borda

First woman to be executive director of a major U.S. symphony orchestra (1989).

Born c. 1949.

A former violist who trained at the Royal College of Music, England, Borda was named executive director of the Detroit Symphony (Detroit, Michigan) in 1989. For eight years she had been with the San Francisco Symphony Orchestra (San Francisco, California), where she became general manager. From 1986 to 1988 she was director of the St. Paul Chamber Orchestra (St. Paul, Minnesota).

In 1990 Borda was named president of the Minnesota Orchestra. In September, 1991, she became managing director of the New York Philharmonic (New York, New York), where her duties included labor negotiations, budget planning and management, marketing and ticket sales, and collaboration with the orchestra's board of directors on the organizations's long-range artistic and financial goals and strategy.

Bowling

First sanctioned women's bowling tournament (1917).

The tournament was sponsored by the Women's International Bowling Congress, which was organized in St. Louis, Missouri, in 1916 and incorporated in 1919. Its founders included Ellen Kelly, Gertrude Dornblasser, and Catherine Menne. The first sanctioned tournament took place in 1917, with 100 women participating. M. Koester won in the individual player high school age group, bowling an average of 162.

Boycotters

First women to boycott a product (1770).

In 1770 the Daughters of Liberty of the New England Colonies vowed not to drink tea imported from Great Britain until after the Revenue Act was repealed.

Anna Callender Brackett

First woman to be principal of a normal school (1863).

Born Boston, Massachusetts, 1836; died Summit, New Jersey, March 18, 1911.

After graduation from State Normal School, Framingham, Massachusetts, in 1856, Brackett taught and served as assistant principal in a number of schools. In 1863 she was named principal of the St. Louis Normal School (St. Louis, Missouri), where she remained until her resignation in 1872.

Brackett then opened a private school for girls, which practiced advanced teaching methods. There was no grading or written examinations, and she did not believe in punishment.

In 1874 Brackett edited a symposium published as *The Education of American Girls,* and in 1893 she was the editor of *Woman and the Higher Education.* She retired in 1895.

Amy Bradley

First woman to supervise a public school system (1869).

Born East Vassalboro, Maine, 1823; died Wilmington, North Carolina, January 15, 1904.

Bradley, who educated herself, began teaching at the age of fifteen. When she was twenty-one, she was named principal of a grammar school in Gardiner, Maine.

When health problems forced her to move to San José, Costa Rica, she opened an English school there. Bradley returned to the United States, and early in the Civil War she was named superintendent of a brigade hospital. Later, she headed hospital ships.

In 1862 the U.S. Sanitary Commission appointed her matron of a new institution in Washington, D.C. She was subsequently assigned to a convalescent camp near Alexandria, Virginia.

When the Civil War ended, Bradley moved to Wilmington, North Carolina, where she organized a school for poor white children. More schools were added, and in 1869 she was named superintendent of the system.

Bradley opened Tileston Normal School in Wilmington in 1872 to train local women for the teaching profession. She retired in 1891.

(Mary) Molly Brant

Probably the first woman to spy against the United States (1777).

Born c. 1736, New York State; died Kingston, Ontario, Canada, April 16, 1796.

During the American Revolution, Brant informed the British of patriot movements before the battle of Oriskany.

Brant was the consort, or common-law wife, of Sir William Johnson, superintendent of Indian affairs for the northern colonies from 1759 until his death in 1774. She bore him nine children, referred to in his will as "natural" children by his "house-

keeper," despite widespread rumors of an Indian marriage ceremony. The will, however, was generous to Brant and their children, providing them with large tracts of land. The family moved to a farm near Canajoharie, New York, in the Mohawk Valley.

Her brother, Joseph, was one of the most noted Iroquois warriors of the American Revolution, and her son, Peter Johnson, captured Ethan Allen during the fighting at Montreal, Canada.

After her spying was discovered, Brant took refuge with relatives among the Six Nations, using her considerable influence and political ties to keep the Cayugas and Senecas loyal to the British forces.

In 1783, after the war ended, she moved to Ontario, Canada, where she lived out her life, receiving an annual pension of £100 from the British government in recognition of her assistance during the war.

E. Lucy Braun

First woman to be president of the Ecological Society of America (1950).

Born Cincinnati, Ohio, April 19, 1889; died Mt. Washington, Ohio, March 5, 1971.

Also the first woman to be president of the Ohio Academy of Science (1933–34), Braun was a career professor of botany and plant ecology at the University of Cincinnati, Cincinnati, Ohio. She was a teaching assistant from 1910 to 1917, then a professor until her retirement in 1948.

Her publications include the authoritative *Deciduous Forests of Eastern North America* (1950). She was also the editor of *Wild Flower,* the magazine of the Wild Flower Preservation Society.

In 1952 Braun was awarded the Mary Soper Pope Medal for her outstanding achievements in botany.

Mary Breckinridge

Founder of the Frontier Nursing Service (1928).

Born Memphis, Tennessee, 1881; died Hyden, Kentucky, 1965.

Daughter of a U.S. congressman from Arkansas and granddaughter of John Cabell Breckinridge, vice president under President James Buchanan, Mary Breckinridge launched a campaign to bring medical services to isolated mountain families. Her campaign began in 1925 in Leslie County in the mountains of southeastern Kentucky. Known as the Kentucky Committee for Mothers and Children, it evolved into the Frontier Nursing Service and then into the American Association of Nurse-Midwives. Her midwives traveled through the hills on horseback, fording or if necessary swimming across rivers and streams. By significantly lowering the death rate associated with childbirth, Breckinridge and her associates quickly demonstrated the value of the nurse-midwife function.

Breckinridge assisted in the establishment of the Hyden, Kentucky, hospital on the slopes of Thousand Sticks Mountain in 1928, and in 1939 she established the Frontier Graduate School of Midwifery. At her death in 1965, the Frontier Nursing Service—modeled after an organization founded by Sir Leslie MacKenzie to care for Scottish mothers and babies—had an annual budget of $350,000, twenty-nine nurses, and twenty-seven beds in the Hyden Hospital. During her tenure, Breckinridge's nurse-midwives had handled over 15,000 maternity cases.

She was educated in Switzerland and at Keuka College, Keuka Park, New York. A 1910 graduate of the St. Luke's Hospital School of Nursing in New York City, she spent the early part of her nursing career in the United States and Europe. In 1925 she joined the Midwives Institute of London, England.

Breckinridge received the Harmon Fanton Prize for public health work in 1926. In 1961 the National League of Nursing presented her with its highest distinction, the Mary Adelaide Nutting (see entry) Award for Distinguished Service.

Sophonisba Preston Breckinridge

First woman to be a delegate to the Pan-American Congress (1933).

Born Lexington, Kentucky, April 1, 1866; died Chicago, Illinois, July 30, 1948.

Breckinridge was also the first Kentucky woman to pass the bar examination, and the first woman to receive a Ph.D. degree in political science from the University of Chicago (Chicago, Illinois).

After graduating from Wellesley College (Wellesley, Massachusetts) in 1888, she taught high school mathematics in Washington, D.C., until 1894, when she returned to Kentucky to study law. She was admitted to the bar, but her practice did not prosper, so she moved on to the University of Chicago, where she received her Ph.D. degree in political science in 1901. Just three years later, she earned the J.D. degree from the University of Chicago Law School.

In 1904 Breckinridge began teaching at the University of Chicago, initially in the department of household administration. In 1907 she became a resident of Hull House, the first major U.S. settlement house, and spent part of each year there for the next thirteen years. (See also Jane Addams.) She also began to teach at the Chicago School of Civics and Phi-

lanthropy in 1907, becoming head of its research department and dean. In 1920, as a result of her influence, the school became the University of Chicago's Graduate School of Social Service Administration, with Breckinridge as professor and assistant dean of women.

Breckinridge helped organize and became the first secretary of Chicago's Immigrants' Protective League (1908); she also helped organize and became the secretary of the Women's Peace party (1915).

Her books include *The Modern Household* (with Marion Talbot, 1912); *The Delinquent Child and the Home* (with Edith Abbot, 1912); *Truancy and Non-Attendance in the Chicago Schools* (1917); *Public Welfare Administration* (1927); and *The Family and the State* (1934).

Margaret Brent

First woman to demand the vote (1647 [Old Style]/1648 [New Style]).

Born Gloucester, England, c. 1601; died Westmoreland County, Virginia, c. 1671.

In 1638 Brent immigrated to Maryland with her sister, Mary, purchasing seventy acres of land in St. Mary's City, then capital of the colony. Four years later she acquired 1,000 acres on Kent Island from her brother Giles.

Brent was named executor for Governor Leonard Calvert in 1647. She applied to the state assembly of Maryland, demanding two votes—one as a freeholder of land, the other as an executor, or landowner's attorney. Her request to vote as a freeholder was denied, although a male freeholder would automatically have been entitled to the vote. She was, however, granted a vote as Governor Calvert's attorney, but she was not seated in the assembly.

Maryland ended the right of female attorneys to represent clients in the 1650s, but other colonies continued to allow the practice. Brent moved to Virginia in 1651, probably to avoid the Protestant-Catholic struggles in Maryland. She helped develop the colony and encouraged the immigration of many settlers. In Virginia, as the wealthy niece of Lord Baltimore, she was the ruling woman of a large manor, speculating on land and acting as agent and attorney for her brothers.

Lucy Brewer

First woman marine (1812).

Dates unknown.

Brewer, alias George Baker (later Louisa Baker), concealed her sex when she enlisted in the marines. She served aboard the U.S.S. *Constitution* in its winning battle against the British frigate *Guerriere* on Au-

gust 19, 1812. The *Constitution*, which had left port seventeen days earlier to avoid being blockaded, encountered the *Guerriere* about 750 miles east of Boston, Massachusetts. (See also Opha M. Johnson.)

Margaret A. Brewer

First woman to achieve the rank of U.S. Marine Corps (USMC) brigadier general (1978).

Born Lansing, Michigan, c. 1930.

Brewer, a graduate of the University of Michigan (Ann Arbor), served at the Marine Corps Development and Education Command at Quantico, Virginia. In 1972 she became the seventh and last director of the Women Marines. With 2,000 women under her command, she remained director until the service group was disbanded in 1977.

Brewer became director of information at the U.S. Marine Corps headquarters in Washington, D.C. In 1978 she was named brigadier general. The USMC was the last of the armed services to promote a woman to the rank of general.

Laura Dewey Bridgman

First blind, deaf mute to receive a formal education (1837).

Born Etna, New Hampshire, December 21, 1829; died Boston, Massachusetts, May 24, 1889.

Bridgman attended the Perkins Institution, a school for the blind in Boston, Massachusetts, directed by Dr. Samuel Gridley Howe. The teaching technique involved marking common objects with raised letters. After learning to "read" in this manner, Bridgman learned to communicate with other people by tapping a manual alphabet into their hands.

Her formal education ended when she was twenty, but from the time she was twenty-three she spent the rest of her life at Perkins Institution, living with her family only in the summers.

Emily Edson Briggs

First woman to go regularly to the White House for news (1861); first president of the Women's National Press Association (1882).

Born Burton, Ohio, September 14, 1830; died Washington, D.C., July 3, 1910.

Wife of John R. Briggs, Jr., assistant clerk of the U.S. House of Representatives (appointed 1861), Emily Briggs wrote an article for the *Washington Chronicle* countering charges that the women who were being hired for the first time as government clerks were inefficient. The owner of the *Washington Chronicle* was John W. Forney—who was also clerk of the House. Forney hired Briggs to write a daily column for another of his papers, the *Philadelphia Press*. She worked as a reporter and columnist for the two papers from 1861 to 1882.

Briggs and her husband had known Abraham Lincoln in the Midwest, and she went with her husband to the White House during the Civil War. In addition to newsgathering, she also wrote feature articles about Mrs. Lincoln. In 1882 Briggs became the first president of the Women's National Press Association, an organization formed to support the aims and careers of professional women reporters.

Briggs was among the first women admitted to the congressional press gallery and reportedly the first woman to use the telegraph for spot news. She was also known for the "Olivia" letters she wrote for the newspapers—Olivia being her pen name. The letters, which dealt with contemporary political and social issues, were published in book form in 1906.

Elizabeth Knight Britton

First person to propose the creation of the New York Botanical Garden (1891).

Born New York, New York, January 9, 1858; died Bronx, New York, February 25, 1934.

The New York Botanical Garden was incorporated in 1891; Britton's husband, Nathaniel, was named its first director-in-chief (1896). Inspired by the Royal Botanic Gardens of Kew, England, the New York installation was noted for its systematic displays of botany, ecology, and horticulture and for its botanical education programs.

Britton graduated from New York City's Normal College (later Hunter College) in 1875. For the next eight years she served on the staff of the college as a critic-teacher, evaluating the work of students in the model school. From 1883 to 1885 she was an assistant in the natural science department. In 1883 she wrote her first scientific paper—the first of approximately 350 papers she would write during the course of her lifetime.

In 1885 Britton married Nathaniel Britton, an assistant in the geology department at Columbia College (New York, New York), and accompanied him on almost all of his botanical expeditions to the Caribbean. She was a principal founder of the Sullivant Moss Society (known as the American Bryological Society after 1949), serving as its president from 1916 to 1919. She also cofounded the Wild Flower Preservation Society of America in 1902 and became the organization's secretary and treasurer.

Fifteen species of plants and a moss genus *(Bryobrittonia)* were named after her, and after her husband's death a double mountain peak in Luquillo National Park, Puerto Rico, was named Mount Britton.

(Georgia) Tiny Broadwick

First woman to free-fall parachute from an airplane (1913).

Born c. 1895.

On June 21, 1913, Broadwick made three jumps from an airplane with a static line that automatically pulled the release cord on her parachute. On her fourth jump, the static line was hooked briefly by the tail of the plane. To avoid a possible recurrence, Broadwick cut the static line on her fifth jump and pulled the parachute release cord herself. The plane, flying at thirty miles per hour, was at an altitude of 1,000 feet. Broadwick fell about 100 feet, pulled the rip cord, and the eleven-pound silk parachute dropped her safely into a barley field.

Broadwick's jump at Griffith field in Los Angeles was part of a U.S. Army test of an eleven-foot parachute, called a "life boat," invented by Glenn Martin, the plane's pilot.

Antoinette Brown (Blackwell)

First woman to be ordained as a minister of a Protestant denomination (1853).

Born Henrietta, New York, May 20, 1825; died Elizabeth, New Jersey, November 5, 1921.

A committed scholar, Brown studied throughout her lifetime. She attended Oberlin College (Oberlin, Ohio), finishing her literary course in 1847, then a theological course in 1850. The college refused to award her a degree because she was a woman. (Twenty-eight years later, she received the degree.) While at Oberlin, she became friends with abolitionist and suffragist Lucy Stone (see entry).

On September 15, 1853, Brown was ordained minister of the First Congregational Church of Butler and Savannah, New York, thus becoming the first woman to be ordained by a nationally recognized denomination. Within a short time, however, it became apparent that she had serious theological differences with her congregation, and she withdrew as minister of that church in 1854. She subsequently became a Unitarian.

Brown spent a year doing volunteer work in the slums and prisons of New York City. She studied the causes of mental and social disorder; her studies led to a series of articles for Horace Greeley's *New York Tribune.*

In 1856 she married Samuel Blackwell, a brother of Elizabeth Blackwell (see entry) and brother of the husband of Lucy Stone.

A mother of six daughters, she wrote ten books, including *Studies in General Science* (1869), a philosophical work on religion and science; *The Island Neighbors* (1871), a novel; and *The Sexes throughout Nature* (1875), a work presenting the thesis that Darwin's male perspective limited his understanding of the roles of the sexes. Her last book was published when she was ninety-three.

Also a strong supporter of the woman suffrage movement, Brown gave lectures around the country and wrote articles for the *Woman's Journal,* edited by Lucy Stone, president of the American Woman Suffrage Association (see Woman Suffrage Associations), and her husband Henry Blackwell. Antoinette Brown was able to exercise her newly won right to vote for the first time in 1920—at the age of ninety-five.

Brown continued her participation in religious activities, and from 1908 until her death served as pastor emeritus of All Souls Unitarian Church, Elizabeth, New Jersey.

Mrs. Charles S. Brown

Winner of the first national women's golf tournament (1895).

Dates unknown.

The first national women's golf tournament (unofficial) was held at Meadowbrook Hunt Club, near Hempstead, Long Island, New York. An amateur, Brown shot 132 for eighteen holes. Competing in a field of thirteen, she won by two strokes over N. C. Sargeant.

Brown, who represented the Shinnecock Hills Long Island Golf Club at the tournament, won the U.S. Women's Amateur Championship the same year.

Ellie (Eleanor) Durall Brown *(see Ellie (Eleanor) Durall (Brown) Moore)*

Hallie Quinn Brown

Cofounder of the Colored Woman's League of Washington, D.C. (1893); first woman to campaign for office at the general conference of the African Methodist Episcopal Church (1900).

Born Pittsburgh, Pennsylvania, March 10, 1850; died Wilberforce, Ohio, September 16, 1949.

After she graduated from Wilberforce University (Wilberforce, Ohio) in 1873 with a B.S. degree, Brown's career in education led her to positions as a teacher, principal, dean, and professor of elocution at Wilberforce (1893, 1900–03).

The Colored Woman's League was the forerunner of the National Association of Colored Women; Brown was its president from 1920 to 1924.

In 1895 she spoke at the convention of the World's Woman's Christian Temperance Union, and in 1924 she was a speaker at the Republican National Convention in Cleveland, Ohio.

Mary Babnick Brown

First woman to have her hair used in a bombsight (1942).

Born c. 1907.

Brown's hair, donated to the war effort in response to an advertisement, was thirty-four inches long when she submitted it for experimental use as the crosshairs in a new aiming device, the Norden bombsight. Human hair was sought because of its adaptability to extremes of temperature, humidity, and altitude.

The bombsight, used in the B-17 Flying Fortresses, B-24 Liberators, and B-29 Super Fortresses, was a carefully guarded military secret. Plane crews were instructed to detonate explosives attached to the bombsights if their plane was at risk of falling into enemy hands.

Olympia Brown

First woman to be ordained as a minister by the full authority of her denomination (1863).

Born Prairie Ronde, Michigan, January 5, 1835; died Baltimore, Maryland, October 23, 1926.

A member of the Northern Universalists, a Protestant denomination, Brown was ordained at their association meeting in Malone, New York, and her first pastorate was in Weymouth, Massachusetts.

Brown graduated with a B.A. degree from Antioch College (Yellow Springs, Ohio) in 1860, then from the theological school of St. Lawrence University (Canton, New York) in 1863. The woman who most inspired and influenced her life was Antoinette Brown (Blackwell) (see entry).

In 1866 Brown became a charter member of the American Equal

Rights Association. She was pastor of a church in Racine, Wisconsin, when she was elected president of the Woman Suffrage Association—a position she held from 1884 to 1912. She resigned her pastorate in 1887 to devote all of her energies to the cause of woman's suffrage.

Rachel F. Brown

First woman to receive the Pioneer Chemist Award from the American Institute of Chemists (1975).

Born Springfield, Massachusetts, 1898; died Albany, New York, January 14, 1980.

Brown became a chemist for the New York State Department of Health in 1926, where she discovered a vaccine for pneumonia, one which is still being administered to the elderly and infirm. She received the department's award for distinguished service at her retirement in 1968.

In 1950, along with Elizabeth Hazer, she isolated the first antifungal antibiotic effective against fungus diseases of the mouth, ear, and intestines, which was called nystatin (named for the New York State laboratories). Brown and Hazer donated their income from the antibiotic to research—half to the Research Corporation of New York, which supports institutional research, and half to research in the biological sciences under the direction of a committee.

Brown, who earned an M.S. degree from the University of Chicago (Chicago, Illinois) and a Ph.D. degree from Mount Holyoke (South Hadley, Massachusetts) in 1924, received the Rhoda Benham Award of the Medical Mycological Society of the Americas in 1975.

Virginia Mae Brown

First woman to be head of an independent federal administrative agency (1969); first to serve on the Interstate Commerce Commission (ICC) (1964); first to be a state insurance commissioner (1961).

Born Pliny, Virginia, 1923; died Charleston, West Virginia, February 24, 1991.

A lawyer by profession, Brown was also the first woman to be executive secretary to the Judicial Council of West Virginia (1944–52); first to be a West Virginia assistant attorney general (1952–61); and first to be a member of the West Virginia Public Service Commission (1962).

President Lyndon B. Johnson appointed Brown to the ICC on May 25, 1964, as one of eleven members. She served on the ICC from 1964 to 1979 and headed the commission for the 1969/70 year.

Brown graduated from the University of West Virginia (Morgantown) in 1945 and from the University of West Virginia School of Law in 1947.

Ruth Bryan *(see Ruth Bryan Owen)*

Alice Gertrude Bryant

One of the first two women to be admitted to the American College of Surgeons (ACS) (1914).

Born Boston, Massachusetts, c. 1862; died Boston, Massachusetts, July 25, 1942.

Bryant and Florence West Duckering (see entry) became the first two women members of the ACS in 1914, the second year the college was in existence. They were among approximately 1,000 candidates to be admitted that year.

Bryant graduated from Vassar College (Poughkeepsie, New York) in 1885 and the Woman's Medical College of the New York Infirmary in 1890.

A specialist in the ear, nose, and throat, Bryant invented the tonsil-separator (a device used by surgeons to separate the tonsils from the tonsil bed), tongue depressor, and bone-gripping forceps (a type of pliers used to stabilize broken bones while a screw or plate is inserted to repair a fracture).

A former engineering student at Massachusetts Institute of Technology (Cambridge, Massachusetts), she was also a researcher in heating and ventilation.

During her lifetime, Bryant was a member of some fifty-six scientific and humanitarian associations.

Bryn Mawr College

First women's college to offer graduate programs (1885).

Bryn Mawr College (Bryn Mawr, Pennsylvania) offered graduate programs from the time it first opened in 1885.

Pearl Sydenstricker Buck

First woman to win a Nobel Prize in literature (1935).

Born Hillsboro, West Virginia,

June 26, 1892; died Danby, Vermont, March 6, 1975.

Buck, who wrote over a hundred books—including more than forty novels—and countless speeches, articles, and scripts of various kinds during her lifetime, gained literary prominence as a popularizer of Chinese culture.

She first went to China as an infant with her Presbyterian missionary parents. They left China to escape the Boxer Rebellion in 1900, and Buck, then eight, returned to the United States. In 1914 she received a B.A. degree from Randolph-Macon Woman's College, Lynchburg, Virginia; she then returned to China.

In 1917 she married John Buck, a U.S. agricultural expert in China. After earning a master's degree in English at Cornell University, Ithaca, New York, Pearl Buck went back to China to teach English literature at the University of Nanking (1921), where her husband was head of the farm management department. She taught at National Southeastern University, China, from 1925 to 1927 and at Chung-Yang University from 1928 to 1930.

Her first novel, *East Wind, West Wind*, was published in 1930. The next one, *The Good Earth*, a Pulitzer Prize winner, was at the top of the bestseller list for many months, ultimately selling over 2 million copies. The book was the basis for a Broadway play and a movie, and it was translated into more than thirty languages.

The Mother, Buck's 1934 novel, ventured into new territories with its depictions of childbirth and abortion. The later novels, although less popular with the critics, continued to enjoy popular success.

Divorced from John Buck in 1935, she married Richard Walsh, a publisher, and remained in the United States.

During World War II, Buck supported the Allied cause by supplying information guides to Asia and writing propaganda plays for radio. She also published, with her husband, *Asia Magazine* (1941–46).

Other works by Buck include: *Dragon Seed* (1942), dealing with Japan's vicious treatment of China; five novels set in the United States under the pen name John Sedges (1945–53); and *The Child Who Never*

Grew, a book relating her experiences with a retarded daughter.

Buck founded Welcome House, Inc., an adoption agency for Asian-American children, in 1949.

From 1958 to 1965 Buck was president of the Authors' Guild, Inc.

(Flora) Elizabeth Burchenal

Founder and head of the American Folk Dance Society (1916).

Born Richmond, Indiana, c. 1876; died Brooklyn, New York, November 21, 1959.

In 1903 Burchenal became a faculty member at Teachers College of Columbia University, New York, New York. Her objective was to see dance incorporated into the physical education curriculum. As inspector of athletics for the New York Department of Education, Burchenal introduced folk dancing into the public school curriculum, organizing mammoth folk festivals that attracted as many as 10,000 schoolchildren to Central Park.

Burchenal also traveled throughout the United States, Canada, and Europe, proselytizing for the cause of folk dance. After World War I, she worked with the War Workers Community Service as a special national representative, trying to ameliorate racial and ethnic tensions through the creation of cultural, recreational, and social programs.

In 1928 Burchenal was sent as a delegate to Prague, Czechoslovakia, where the League of Nations was mounting the first International Congress of Folk Arts.

The following year the American Folk Dance Society, which she had founded in 1916, became a division of the National Committee of Folk Arts (NCFA). Burchenal was named to head the new NCFA, a position she held until shortly before her death.

Burchenal had earned an A.B. degree from Earlham College, Richmond, Indiana (1896), and a diploma from Dr. Sargent's College of Physical Education (later part of Boston University, Boston, Massachusetts) (1908). In 1943 Boston University awarded her an honorary doctor of science degree.

In her lifetime, Burchenal wrote numerous articles and fifteen books on folk dancing. She established the Archive of American Folk Dance and was a fellow of the American Academy of Physical Education.

Celia C. Burleigh

First woman ordained as a minister in the Unitarian Church (1871).

Born c. 1827; died Syracuse, New York, July 27, 1875.

Following her ordination in 1871, Burleigh was a minister at a parish in Brooklyn, Connecticut. She resigned around 1873 because of poor health. A woman suffrage advocate and preacher, at one time she was president of the Woman's Club in Brooklyn, Connecticut.

Theo (Theodosia) Burr

One of the two women to be mentioned in the first New York Times *crossword puzzle, February 15, 1942.*

Born Albany, New York, June 21, 1783; disappeared at sea in the Atlantic, January, 1813.

Burr was known for her unfaltering love and adoration of her father, Aaron Burr, vice president of the United States under President Thomas Jefferson. Her name, Theo, was the answer to the crossword puzzle clue, "Aaron Burr's daughter"; the other woman whose name was the answer to a clue was Amelia Earhart (see entry).

Burr grew up in New York City, where her private education was overseen by her father, a brilliant lawyer and omnivorous reader. Reading such works as Mary Wollstonecraft's *A Vindication of the Rights of Women* helped persuade him that the education of a young woman should be equal to that of a young man.

Thus, he closely supervised the tutors who educated his only living daughter.

After the death of her mother in 1794, Theo took over the role of social organizer at the Burr family estate. She married Joseph Alston, who became the governor of South Carolina in the same year her father became vice president of the United States (1801).

Aaron Burr, who had dueled with Alexander Hamilton, exiled himself in Europe after he was indicted, but acquitted, for treason (1807). While he was living there, he and Theo corresponded a great deal. After he returned to the United States and was living in New York, she sailed from Charleston, South Carolina, to visit him there. The ship and its passengers disappeared in the Atlantic Ocean in January, 1813.

Anne Burras

First woman of the Virginia Colonies to have her wedding recorded (1609).

Dates unknown.

Burras, one of the first women colonists, arrived in 1608. She was a maid to "Mistress Forrest" when she married John Laydon in 1609.

Dorothy V. Bush

First woman to be an officer for either major national political party (1944).

Born Baldwyn, Mississippi, December 8, 1916; died Naples, Florida, December 21, 1991.

As secretary of the national Democratic party, Bush called the roll of the states at the national nominating conventions and kept the vote count for presidential nominees. She performed this function under ten presidents of the United States and seventeen chairs of the Democratic party. She offered her resignation to each new party chair, but each time it was rejected. She resigned her post in 1989.

Bush was a graduate of the Missis-

sippi State College for Women, Columbus, Mississippi (1937), where she majored in secretarial studies. After graduation, she worked as an executive secretary for the Tennessee Coal and Iron Division of the U.S. Steel Corporation (1937–40).

Business Owners, Women

First association of women business owners (1972).

The Association of Women Business Owners was founded in 1972 by thirteen entrepreneurs from Washington, D.C.: Anne Banville, Ann Barker, Kathleen Bowers, Denise Cavanaugh, Dorothy Cook, Susan Eisenberg, Daisy Fields, Josephine Gibson, Susan Hagar, Mary King, Kathy Kraemer, Jinx Melia, and Gillian Nixon.

The organization expanded and in 1974 was called the National Association of Women Business Owners.

The first executive director was Helene C. Bloom in 1977.

Mary Peck Butterworth

Probably the first woman to be charged with counterfeiting in the United States (c. 1716).

Born Rehoboth, Massachusetts, 1686; died Rehoboth, Massachusetts, February 7, 1775.

In 1715 Rhode Island issued five-pound notes of credit. Butterworth, with the help of Hannah Peck and about a dozen cohorts in Rehoboth, Massachusetts (then Plymouth Colony), allegedly counterfeited the notes by transferring the image from a piece of muslin to clean paper. Since her process did not involve the use of copper plates and therefore left no tangible evidence, Butterworth was freed and the charges were dropped.

Frances Xavier Cabrini

First person to be named a saint of the Roman Catholic church (1946).

Born Sant'Angelo Lodugiano, Lombardy, Italy, July 15, 1850; died Chicago, Illinois, December 22, 1917.

In 1868 Cabrini graduated from the Daughters of the Sacred Heart, a convent school in Arluno, Italy, with a teacher's license. After graduating with honors, she assumed a nun's habit and took her religious vows in 1877 without joining any formal order.

In 1880 she founded and was named superior of a new order: the Missionary Sisters of the Sacred Heart. She was assigned to take care of an orphanage in Codogno, Italy. By 1887 the order had seven convents, and in 1888 it was approved and formally recognized by the Vatican.

Pope Leo XIII sent Mother Cabrini to the United States in 1889 to work among poor Italian immigrants. In 1889 a mass was offered for the first time in her order's first American motherhouse. After a few months, during which she opened a school, Cabrini went to Italy to oversee the convents. She returned to the United States in 1890. In the next few years she founded a convent, school, and orphanage in New Orleans, set up a hospital in New York City, and established convents in Europe, South and Central America, eventually establishing sixty-seven houses—one for each year of her life.

Her order reached Denver, Colorado (1902); Seattle, Washington (1903); and Los Angeles, California (1905). She became a naturalized U.S. citizen in 1909. In 1910 Cabrini was made superior general of her order for life.

Her canonization process began in 1928, and on July 7, 1946, Cabrini was declared a saint.

Calendar, Nude

First nude calendar in the world (1913).

The calendar, which displayed a reproduction of the painting *Septem-*

ber Morn, by the French artist Paul Chabas (1869–1937), created quite a controversy. The League of Decency and other groups forced shop owners to remove the calendars from their windows, whereas *The New York Times* wrote editorials against such censorship.

Mary Whiton Calkins

First woman elected president of the American Psychological Association (1905); the first elected president of the American Philosophical Association (1918).

Born Hartford, Connecticut, March 30, 1863; died Newton, Massachusetts, February 26, 1930.

Author of *The Persistent Problems of Philosophy* (1907), Calkins was a graduate of Smith College (Northampton, Massachusetts), where she majored in classics and philosophy. She was awarded an L.H.D. degree from Columbia University (New York, New York) in 1909, and an LL.D. degree from Smith College in 1910. Calkins completed all requirements for the Ph.D. degree at Harvard University (Cambridge, Massachusetts) in 1895, but she was denied the degree—even though philosopher William James praised her performance at the oral examination.

Calkins began her teaching career as a tutor in Greek at Wellesley College (Wellesley, Massachusetts), progressing through the ranks as an instructor and researcher in philosophy and psychology. She established an experimental psychology laboratory at Wellesley in 1891—the first at a women's college and one of the first in the United States. Calkins was eventually named full professor and chair of the department of mental philosophy at Wellesley, holding that post until her retirement in 1929.

Her primary field of interest was metaphysics. She called her own doctrine "personalistic absolutism," defined by the belief that the universe—and therefore whatever is "real"—exists in the mind and is, for that reason, personal.

Camp Fire Girls

First national nonsectarian interracial organization for girls (1910).

In 1910 Charlotte Vetter Gulick (see entry) and her husband, Luther Halsey Gulick, along with William Chauncey Langdon founded the Camp Fire Girls, the first national nonsectarian, interracial organization for girls. The organization emphasizes character development and the importance of good mental and physical health generated by participation in indoor and outdoor activities.

The first encampment, called WoHeLo (Work, Health, Love), held in Maine, was attended by seventeen girls. The theme for the event was Native American lore and ceremonials.

By the mid-1980s, the organization for girls aged seven to eighteen had approximately 400 local councils and more than 600,000 members.

The organization, now called Camp Fire, today has more than a half million members, both boys and girls.

Maude B. Campbell

First woman to fly on a commercial airline as a paying customer (1926).

Dates unknown.

On June 10, 1926, Campbell paid $180 to fly in an open cockpit biplane round trip from Salt Lake City, Utah, to Los Angeles, California. The trip took about seven hours each way. Campbell, the only passenger on the two-seater biplane, said that she was given a parachute and emergency instructions: jump, count to ten, and pull the rip cord.

In 1976, on the flight's fiftieth anniversary, a Salute to Pioneer Pilots banquet was held to commemorate the event. Campbell, a retired secretary, traveled from Los Angeles to Washington, D.C., for the banquet.

Annie Jump Cannon

First person to systematically classify the heavens (1918); first woman to receive an honorary doctorate from Oxford University, Oxford, England (1925); first to be awarded the Draper Gold Medal of the National Academy of Sciences (1931); first to receive an honorary doctorate in astronomy from the University of Groningen, Netherlands (1921).

Born Dover, Delaware, December 11, 1863; died Cambridge, Massachusetts, April 13, 1941.

An honorary member of the Royal Astronomical Society in England (1914) and one of the few women elected as an honorary member of the American Philosophical Society (1925), Cannon classified more stars during her lifetime—about 400,000—than any person had ever done before.

Cannon was an astronomer at the Harvard College Observatory, Cambridge, Massachusetts, from 1896 until her retirement in 1940. Classifying stellar bodies according to their temperatures, she published *The Henry Draper Catalogue* (1918–24), which classified the spectra of all stars from the North Pole to the South Pole. Stellar spectra study is the study of the characteristics of stars that are revealed when their light is photographed through a refracting prism. (See also Williamina Stevens Fleming.) Between 1925 and 1949 she published *The Henry Draper Extension,* which classified the faint stars. The two catalogs represented a total of about 350,000 stars. In addition to establishing the basic sequence of stellar spectra, Cannon discovered about 300 long-period variable stars. (A long-period variable star is one whose light intensity varies in a regular pattern that requires several years to complete.)

Educated at Wellesley College (Wellesley, Massachusetts) and Radcliffe College (Cambridge, Massachusetts), Cannon was appointed curator of astronomical photographs at the Harvard College Observatory in 1911; in 1938 she was appointed William Cranch Bord Astronomer at Harvard University.

Dyan Cannon *(born Samille Diane Friesen)*

First woman nominated for Academy Awards as both director (1977) and actress (1979).

Born Tacoma, Washington, January 4, 1939.

Cannon received an Academy Award nomination for director of the best short film, *Number One* (1976), which she wrote and produced as well. She was also nominated for the Academy Award for best supporting actress in *Heaven Can Wait* (1978).

She received the New York Film Critics' Award for best supporting actress of 1969 for her role in *Bob and Carol and Ted and Alice,* for which she also received an Academy Award nomination.

Cannon, who made her film debut in *The Rise and Fall of Legs Diamond* (1960), attended the University of Washington (Seattle) and studied acting with Sanford Meisner at the Neighborhood Theater (New York, New York).

Harriet Starr Cannon

First woman superior of the first Episcopal religious community in the United States (1865).

Born Charleston, South Carolina, May 7, 1823; died Peekskill, New York, April 5, 1896.

Cannon established the Community of St. Mary in New York City in 1865. This was the first new community to be officially established by an Episcopal bishop since the sixteenth century, when the English monasteries were dissolved.

Cannon began her vocation as a probationer with the Episcopal Sisterhood of Holy Communion, organized by Anne Ayres (see entry), in New York City. Accepted as a full member in 1857, she worked as a nurse in St. Luke's Hospital, which was operated by the sisterhood.

As a result of a dispute with the sisterhood over Cannon's insistence that the organization be more traditionally monastic, Cannon and three other women left and established the Community of St. Mary. Their projects included management of the House of Mercy, a refuge for young women who had become prostitutes. The community also established orphanages, homes for homeless women and children, hospitals, and convent schools.

Hattie Wyatt Caraway

First woman elected to the U.S. Senate (1932); first to preside over Senate sessions (1932); first to conduct Senate hearings; first to chair a Senate committee; first to be president pro tem of the Senate (1943); first woman member of Congress to endorse the Equal Rights Amendment (1943).

Born Bakerville, Tennessee, February 1, 1878; died Falls Church, Virginia, December 21, 1950.

Wife of Arkansas Democratic Senator Thaddeus C. Caraway, Hattie Caraway was appointed to fill her husband's seat after his death in 1931. In January, 1932, she won without opposition a special election to serve the balance of her husband's term—through March, 1933. At the time of her appointment, she promised the governor of Arkansas that she would retire at the end of her husband's uncompleted term. She changed her mind, however, and surprised the Arkansas politicians by announcing, in May, 1932, her decision to run for reelection. Supported by Senator Huey Long of Louisiana, Caraway won the primary election with a vote tally equal to that of her six opponents combined and was elected to a full six-year term.

Some of her favorite legislative causes included populist, anti–big-business measures, farm relief, anti-isolationism, the New Deal, flood control, anti-lobby legislation, and safety in commercial aviation. She chaired the Senate Committee on Enrolled Bills from the Seventy-third to the Seventy-eighth Congress, and in 1940 was a cosponsor of the proposed Equal Rights Amendment. Her Senate career ended in 1944 when she was defeated in the Arkansas primary election by William Fulbright.

Caraway served on the Federal Employees' Compensation Commission (later the Bureau of Employees' Compensation) in 1945/46, and on the Employees' Compensation Appeals Board from 1946 to 1950.

She received a B.A. degree from Dickson Normal School (Dickson, Tennessee), in 1896.

Eva Carey

First woman to hold an administrative office in the Protestant Episcopal Church in the United States (1921).

Dates unknown.

The annual Diocesan Convention, held in Boston, Massachusetts (1921), elected Carey a member of the Bishop's Council. Her election was made possible by an amendment passed at the previous convention, which opened membership to women as laymen in administrative affairs of the church.

Anna Ella Carroll

Possibly the first woman military adviser to a president (Abraham Lincoln, 1861).

Born Pocomoke City, Maryland, August 29, 1815; died Washington, D.C., February 19, 1893.

Carroll claimed that she was responsible for General Grant's strategy of traveling up the Tennessee River—rather than the Mississippi—in order to attack the Confederacy. She told of meeting, by chance, a riverboat pilot who told her that the Tennessee would provide better access to the heart of the Confederate states than would the Mississippi. She persuaded him to put his reasons in writing, and submitted her version to Assistant Secretary of War Thomas A. Scott. Scott forwarded the suggestion to his superiors, including President Lincoln, and in 1862 General Grant moved up the Tennessee River.

In 1868 Carroll claimed the strategy had been her own idea, and from 1870 to 1884 she submitted claims to Congress for payment. In response, the government maintained that the invasion from the Tennessee River had been proposed independently of Carroll in 1861, and that General Grant had acted on his own—not at the orders of anyone in Washington.

Daughter of Thomas Carroll, onetime governor of Maryland, Anna Carroll left home in 1837. In 1854 she delivered and distributed printed versions of anti-Catholic lectures in Baltimore. She also campaigned for the election of President Millard Fillmore (1856). When the Civil War started, Carroll wrote pamphlets that supported Lincoln and the Union, but she was also an anti-abolitionist who argued that the U.S. Congress had no power to emancipate the slaves of the South.

Ann Shaw Carter

First woman to get a helicopter rating (1947).

Born Brooklyn, New York, December 5, 1922.

Carter received her helicopter rating at the Westchester County Airport, Westchester, New York, on June 9, 1947. She was one of the first thirteen members of the Whirly Girls (see entry), the first association of woman helicopter pilots (1955). She also has a commercial license and a seaplane rating.

Carter, who had polio when she was a child, attended Ms. Thomas's Girls School, Fairfield, Connecticut, and Bryn Mawr College, Bryn Mawr, Pennsylvania. She was a member of the Women's Army Service Pilots group (WASP) and now resides in Fairfield, Connecticut.

Maybelle Addington Carter

First person to use a guitar technique called the "Carter lick" (c. 1925); member of the first group to be inducted into the Country Music Foundation's Hall of Fame (1970).

Born Nickelsville, Virginia, May 10, 1909; died Madison, Tennessee, October 23, 1978.

Carter, known as the "First Lady of Country Music," along with her brother-in-law A.P. and his wife, Sarah, comprised the original Carter Family group. She moved to Maces Springs, Tennessee, in 1926, after marrying Ezra "Eck" Carter. She was the first person to use the "Carter lick" (also called "church lick"), a method of guitar playing in which the thumb picks out the melody while the other fingers brush the treble strings in rhythm. This innovative technique changed the role of the guitar in country music from an accompanying instrument to a lead one.

The original Carter Family is reportedly the first group to record a country music album. At a studio on State Street in Bristol, Tennessee, they completed six recordings between August 1 and August 4, 1927: "Bury Me Under a Weeping Willow"; "Poor Orphan Child"; "The Storms Are on the Ocean"; "Log Cabin by the Sea"; "Single Girl, Married Girl"; and "Wandering Boy." The most popular recording the group ever made was "Wildwood Flower," which sold more than 1 million copies.

The original group disbanded in 1943. Carter, who was known for her unique Autoharp licks as well as her rich alto voice, formed a new group with her three daughters, Anita, June (who married country singer Johnny

Cash), and Helen. The group was known as Mother Maybelle and the Carter Sisters.

Adelaide Case

First woman appointed to full professorial rank in an Episcopal or Anglican seminary (1941).

Born St. Louis, Missouri, 1887; died Boston, Massachusetts, June 19, 1948.

Author of *Liberal Christianity and Religious Education,* Case was named professor of Christian education at the Episcopal Theological School, Cambridge, Massachusetts; she held the position until her death.

Case received an A.B. degree from Bryn Mawr College, Bryn Mawr, Pennsylvania, in 1908, and an A.M. and doctorate in religious education from Teachers College of Columbia University, New York, New York. She was appointed to professorial rank at the Episcopal Theological School in 1935 and became the chair of her department in 1941.

Carrie Lane Chapman Catt

First woman to call for establishment of the League of Women Voters (1919).

Born Ripon, Wisconsin, January 9, 1859; died New Rochelle, New York, March 9, 1947.

Catt attended Iowa State College (Ames), graduating with a B.S. in November, 1880. The following year she became principal of Mason City (Iowa) High School, and in 1883 was named superintendent of schools— an unusually high educational position for a woman.

In February, 1885, she married Leo Chapman, owner and editor of the *Mason City Republican,* and became assistant editor. Her husband died of typhoid in 1886. She moved to Charles City, Iowa, joined the Iowa Woman Suffrage Association, and in 1890 went as Iowa delegate to the new National American Woman Suffrage Association (see Woman Suffrage Associations).

After her marriage to George William Catt, head of a construction company, in 1890, she lived with him in Seattle, then after 1892 in New York City. An interesting sidelight of their marriage was a contract they signed stipulating that she would have two months each spring and fall for suffrage work. (George Catt also believed in the cause of woman suffrage.) Catt became an effective public speaker, and so impressed her colleagues in the suffrage movement that when Susan B. Anthony (see entry) retired in 1900 as president of the NAWSA she chose Catt as her successor. Catt resigned from the position in 1904 because of her husband's ill health.

Catt died in 1905, leaving his wife financially independent. She began to work full time for the movement, and in 1915 was named president of NAWSA once again.

In 1918, strongly influenced by Catt, President Woodrow Wilson led his party in demanding a suffrage amendment. Catt led the battle, and when the amendment was finally ratified on August 26, 1920, it was generally agreed that Catt, more than any other woman except Susan B. Anthony, was responsible for winning the vote for women.

From 1902 to 1923 Catt also worked for worldwide woman suffrage, particularly in the International Women Suffrage Alliance. In 1919 she had called for the establishment of a League of Women Voters in states where women had already won the franchise. She also became an activist in the cause of world peace, serving as chair from 1925 to 1932 on the Committee on the Cause and Cure of War.

Catt was awarded honorary degrees from the University of Wyoming (first state to give women the vote), Iowa State College, Smith College, and Moravian College. She received the American Hebrew medal for her work on behalf of German Jewish refugees (1933) and a citation of honor by President Franklin Roosevelt (1936). In 1947 the League of Women Voters established the Carrie Chapman Catt Memorial Foundation to help women around the world who had recently been granted the vote understand the democratic process.

Jane Champlin

First woman to die in a plane crash under military conditions (1943).

Born St. Louis, Missouri, date unknown; died Westbrook, Texas, 1943.

A Women's Auxiliary Ferrying Squadron pilot, she died with her instructor on a night training flight near Westbrook, Texas, on June 7, 1943, after the engine of her BT-13 caught fire in the air.

She had been a secretary for the Railway Express Agency.

Augusta Chapin

First woman to serve on the council of the Universalist Church (1870); believed to be the first to be granted an honorary doctorate (1893).

Born Lakeville, New York, 1836; died New York, New York, June 30, 1905.

Chapin enrolled at Olivet College (Olivet, Michigan) in 1852, and became interested in theology. She received a degree and then began preaching as an itinerant minister in 1856. In 1863 she was ordained by the Universalists, holding pastorates and continuing her itinerant ministry.

She became a charter member of Sorosis (see entry) in 1865, and in 1873 was made a member of the first executive committee of the Association for the Advancement of Women. After being granted an honorary doctor of divinity degree by Lombard University (Galesburg, Illinois) in 1893, Chapin belatedly received an A.M. degree from the University of Michigan (Ann Arbor)—which had previously denied her admission because of her gender.

Pamela Chelgren

First woman to join the National Oceanic and Atmospheric Administration Corps (1972); first to be appointed field operations officer (1977).

Born c. 1949.

Chelgren, of Port Orchard, Washington, was a lieutenant in the National Oceanic and Atmospheric Administration Corps, the smallest of the seven U.S. uniformed services.

Her appointment to field operations officer in 1977 put Chelgren in the highest shipboard position ever held by a woman in the U.S. uniformed services. She was field operations officer aboard the hydrographic survey ship U.S.S. *Pierce.*

Lydia Maria Francis Child

Founder of the first U.S. periodical for children (1826); possibly the first person to write an antislavery book (1833).

Born Medford, Massachusetts, February 11, 1802; died Wayland, Massachusetts, October 20, 1880.

One of the first U.S. women of literary distinction, Child (born Lydia Maria Francis) began publication of her bimonthly *Juvenile Miscellany* in 1826. She is probably best known for her antislavery book, *An Appeal in Favor of That Class of Americans Called Africans,* an important abolitionist work that helped attract some important U.S. figures to the antislavery cause. With its suggestions that African-Americans be educated, its attacks on segregation, miscegenation laws, and unequal employment opportunities, the book was considered outrageous by much of Child's contemporary society. It created a furor in Boston. Child was banned from the Boston Athenaeum and shunned by society. Sales of her other books were hurt severely, and in 1834 the *Juvenile Miscellany* went under.

She continued to write abolitionist books and pamphlets and also published, in 1836, *Philothea,* a romantic novel for which she is probably best known.

In 1840 William Lloyd Garrison took over the American Anti-Slavery Society; he named Child to the executive committee, and the following year she went to New York City to become editor of the *National Anti-Slavery Standard,* the society's weekly publication.

After some abolitionists, including Garrison, became unhappy with the *Standard* for being too genteel and moderate in its views, Child left in 1843. She had been supplementing her *Standard* salary by writing columns for the Boston *Courier;* she now collected those pieces and published them as *Letters from New York (1843–45);* the collection was immensely successful and went through eleven editions between 1845 and 1879.

When John Brown was imprisoned after the Harper's Ferry raid in 1860, Child offered to minister to him in prison. Her offer was strongly denounced by the wife of Senator James M. Mason of Virginia, author of the Fugitive Slave Act. Child's reply was a long pamphlet condemning the system of slavery; it sold over 300,000 copies in the North. To Mrs. Mason's assertion that southern white women were kind and helpful to slave women in childbirth, Child replied: "In New England, too, 'the pangs of maternity' . . . meet with the requisite assistance; and here at the North, after we have helped the mothers, *we do not sell the babies.*"

Later in her life, Child published other books *Incidents in the Life of a Slave Girl* (1861); *The Freedmen's Book* (1865); *Romance of the Republic* (1867); *An Appeal for the Indians* (1868); and *Aspirations of the World* (1878).

When she died at seventy-eight of heart disease, John Greenleaf Whittier recited a memorial poem at her funeral.

Laura Blears Ching

First woman to compete against men in an international surfing contest (1973).

Born c. 1951.

The international surfing contest, in which Ching competed against thirty professional and amateur male surfers, took place in Oahu, Hawaii, in 1973. A twenty-two-year-old resident of Honolulu, she had been named Hawaii's top woman surfer twice, and had won the women's international surfing championship at Makaha Beach, Hawaii, in 1972.

Ellen Church

First airline stewardess (1930).

Born near Cresco, Iowa, c. 1905.

It was Church's idea to have stewardesses on airlines, and she suggested it to the manager of the San Francisco (California) office of Boeing Air Transport, predecessor of United Airlines. On May 15, 1930, Church became the first stewardess on a flight from Cheyenne, Wyoming, to Oakland, California. One passenger was Herbert Hoover, Jr., the president's son. The unpressurized Boeing-80, flying 150 miles per hour at 12,000 feet, carried fifteen passengers, a pilot, copilot, and one stewardess.

A registered nurse herself, Church—who had grown up as a farm girl near Cresco, Iowa—selected seven other registered nurses as stewardess-trainees: Margaret Arnott, Jessie Carter, Ellis Crawford, Harriet Fry, Alva Johnson, Inez Keller, and Cornelia Peterman. (For the next twelve years, all stewardesses were required to be registered nurses.) None of the original group stayed on the job for more than two years.

Candidates were required to weigh no more than 115 pounds. Their uniform included a flowing cape and a "shower-cap-like" hat. Their duties included carrying luggage, cleaning the cabin, serving cold box lunches and pouring coffee, caring for passengers in emergencies, bolting down seats, joining a bucket brigade to fuel planes, and pushing planes into hangars.

After a year and a half, Church left Boeing Air Transport because of injuries suffered in an automobile accident. She later served in the Army Nurse Corps and as administrator of the Union Hospital School of Nursing, Terre Haute, Indiana.

Conchita (Verrill) Cintrón

First U.S. woman to become a bullfighter in Spain (1949).

Born Chile, 1922.

Since Cintrón, born Consuela, was the daughter of U.S. citizens, she was registered as a U.S. citizen, even though she was born in Chile and grew up in Brazil. She made her first appearance as a *torera* at a bullfight in Mexico when she was only fifteen. During her thirteen-year career as a *rejoneadora* (mounted bullfighter), she slew 800 bulls and was gored only twice.

In 1949 Cintrón defied the law by dismounting and executing passes at a bull during a bullfight in Spain. She was arrested but pardoned immediately when the crowd demanded her release. She left the ring, retired to Lisbon, and never returned. (In South America it was popular for young women to fight bulls, but France, Portugal, and Spain resisted it.)

In 1951 she married and retired from bullfighting.

Georgia Neese Clark

First woman to be treasurer of the United States (1949).

Born Richland, Kansas, January 27, 1900.

A 1921 graduate of Washburn College (now Washburn University), Topeka, Kansas, with a B.A. degree in economics, Clark went to New York City to pursue an acting career, which lasted until 1930. She returned to Kansas, where she assisted her father with his businesses and became involved in Democratic politics. In 1936 she was elected to the Democratic National Committee, and in 1937, after her father's death, she became president of the Richland State Bank.

Clark campaigned for the nomination and election of Harry S. Truman in 1948. A year later President Truman appointed her U.S. treasurer. She became the first of a succession of women to fill the post. Clark left the Treasury post in 1953 and returned to Kansas.

Edith Clarke

First woman elected fellow of the American Institute of Electrical Engineers (1948).

Born Howard County, Maryland, February 10, 1883; died Olney, Maryland, October 29, 1959.

Clarke was reportedly the first women to address the American Institute of Electrical Engineers (AIEE) when she spoke at its convention in New York City in February, 1926. Her topic was "Steady-State Stability in Transmission Systems." In 1940 Clarke, Vivien Kellems, and Mabel McFerran Rockwell, were the only three women members of the AIEE, whose membership numbered 17,000. Her most significant work was simplifying and increasing the accuracy of mathematical computations involving electrical power transmission lines.

Clarke was elected a fellow of the AIEE in 1948. At that time she was a professor of electrical engineering at the University of Texas (Austin), where she taught until 1959.

She earned an A.B. degree in math and astronomy from Vassar College (Poughkeepsie, New York) in 1908. Following her graduation, she taught for three years in California and West Virginia. During the 1911/12 school year, she took civil engineering courses at the University of Wisconsin (Madison). She worked for American Telephone and Telegraph (AT&T) from 1912 to 1918, where her work largely consisted of solving mathematical equations. In 1919 Clarke earned an M.S. degree in electrical engineering from the Massachusetts Institute of Technology (Cambridge), becoming the first woman to do so.

She worked for General Electric for nearly three decades after joining the company in 1919. During that period, however, she took a leave and was visiting professor of physics at Istanbul Woman's College in Turkey (1920).

A writer of many articles, two of which received AIEE prizes, Clarke received the Society of Women Engineers' Achievement Award in 1954.

Julia Clarke

First woman to die in an airplane accident (1912).

Born Chicago, Illinois, date unknown; died Springfield, Illinois, June 17, 1912.

Clarke, making her first flight in a Curtiss biplane at the Illinois State Fairgrounds, Springfield, on June 17, 1912, crashed into a tree at forty miles per hour; her plane turned over on its back. Clarke had learned to fly in San Diego, California, after her interest in aviation was piqued by the International Aviation Meet in Chicago in August, 1911. She was the third American woman to get a pilot's license. (See also Bessie Coleman.)

Two weeks before the fatal flight, officials in Milwaukee had refused her permission to fly, deeming her plane unsafe. It was then overhauled and considered airworthy for the Springfield flight.

Mary Clarke

First woman to be named to the rank of major general in the U.S. Army (June, 1978).

Born Rochester, New York, December 3, 1924.

Clarke was the last commander of the Woman's Army Corps (WAC); when the WAC was dissolved and made a part of the regular army in 1978, she was promoted to major general and reassigned as commander of the U.S. Army Military Police and Chemical School Training Center at Fort McClellan, Alabama. The same year she received a doctorate in military science from Norwich University (Northfield, Vermont). In 1980 Clarke was named director of human resources development for the Office of the Deputy Chief of Staff for personnel, Washington, D.C., where she served until she retired in October, 1981, at age fifty-six, after serving in the army for thirty-six years—the longest army career of any woman. In 1984 she was made a member of the Defense Advisory Committee on Women in the Services, a position she still holds at the time of this writing.

Clarke had enlisted in the WAC in World War II, expecting to serve for the war's duration plus six months, but decided to stay because a male commander had said it was unlikely she could survive the demanding officers training program.

Emeline Horton Cleveland

First woman to be a professional ovariotomist (one who performs surgery on ovaries) (1875); possibly the first to perform major surgery (1875).

Born Ashford, Connecticut, September 22, 1829; died Philadelphia, Pennsylvania, December 8, 1878.

An 1853 graduate of Oberlin College, Oberlin, Ohio, Cleveland earned her M.D. degree from the Female (later Woman's) Medical College of Pennsylvania (Philadelphia). The following year she became a demonstrator in anatomy at the college, and in 1857 was named chair of the department of anatomy and histology.

Cleveland received a diploma from the School of Obstetrics of the Maternité of Paris in 1861, returning to the United States as the chief resident of the newly chartered Woman's Hospital of Philadelphia. She held this post for seven years.

From 1872 until 1874 she was dean of the Woman's Medical College. Throughout her years as professor and hospital administrator Cleveland maintained her private practice, and in 1875 she performed several successful operations at the Woman's Hospital to remove ovarian tumors—probably the first performed by a woman.

She died in 1878 of tuberculosis.

Ruth Cleveland

First and only president's daughter to have a candy bar named after her (1921).

Born New York, New York, October 3, 1891; died Princeton, New Jersey, January 7, 1904.

Cleveland was known to the nation as "Baby Ruth" while she lived in the White House. Capitalizing on the popularity of Baby Ruth, the Curtiss Candy Company decided to change the name of its chocolate nut roll candy bar from Kandy Kake to Baby Ruth. The trademark for the candy was patterned after an 1893 medallion that pictures President Grover Cleveland, Mrs. Cleveland, and "Baby Ruth."

Genevieve Cline

First woman to be appointed as a U.S. federal judge (1928) (see also Florence Ellinwood Allen); first woman to be appointed an appraiser of merchandise at a large city port (1922).

Born Warren, Ohio, c. 1879; died Cleveland, Ohio, 1959.

President Calvin Coolidge appointed Cline, and on May 25, 1928, she was confirmed to the U.S. Customs Court. She served in the Customs Court for twenty-five years, until her retirement in 1953.

Cline went to Cleveland Spencerian College, Cleveland, Ohio, to gain some stenographic skills (c. 1896). After working for a few years, she entered Oberlin College, Oberlin, Ohio, in 1905, where she took a one-year business program. Upon completion of the program she worked for her brother, John A. Cline, a lawyer from Ohio who was a prosecutor at that time. In 1921 she earned an LL.B. degree from Baldwin-Wallace Law School, Berea, Ohio, where she read law. A Republican, Cline was involved in politics throughout her school years.

President Warren Harding appointed her to the post of appraiser of merchandise at the port of Cleveland, where she was responsible for appraising merchandise shipped from foreign ports. She served in that position from 1922 until 1928.

Cline was the vice president of the Ohio branch of the National Association of Women Lawyers (1927).

Coast Guard Academy *(see United States Coast Guard Academy)*

Jerrie (Geraldyn) Cobb

First woman to pass qualification tests and be recommended for astronaut duties (1960).

Born Norman, Oklahoma, March 5, 1931.

Cobb took the qualification tests, consisting of seventy-five exams, between February 15 and February 21, 1960—the same tests that had been administered to male astronaut candidates.

In 1962 she urged Vice President Johnson to name her the first female astronaut. On July 16, 1963, she was one of three women among seventy-one military pilots recommended for astronaut service. The National Aeronautics and Space Administration rejected them, however; at that time, NASA was apparently interested in determining whether women could survive in space and was not ready to accept them as astronauts.

Cobb, daughter of a U.S. Air Force lieutenant colonel who taught her to fly a biplane when she was twelve, earned her private pilot rating in

1947 when she was sixteen. On her eighteenth birthday she added commercial pilot and flight instructor ratings and began to teach at an aviation school. For several years she flew charter flights, pipeline patrol, and crop-dusting jobs. In 1952 she was the only woman working as an international ferry pilot.

Cobb set several new world records for women pilots:

- long-distance nonstop record: over 1,500 miles from Guatemala City, Guatemala, to Oklahoma City, Oklahoma (1957)
- altitude record: 30,361 feet (1957), 37,010 feet (1960)
- world speed record for C-1.d. planes: 226.148 miles per hour (1954)

In 1959 Cobb was named Woman of the Year in Aviation. She remained active in aviation throughout her life. In 1983 she was operator and pilot for an air cargo service between Florida and South America.

Jacqueline Cochran

First woman to break the sound barrier (1953); first to enter the Bendix Transcontinental Air Race (1935); first to be president of the renowned Fédération Aéronautique Internationale (1958).

Born Pensacola, Florida, c. 1910; died Indio, California, 1980.

The premier female aviator of her lifetime, Jacqueline Cochran took her first flying lesson at the age of twenty-two. Three years later she entered the Bendix race, and in 1938 she took the trophy.

In her life she set over 200 flying records, including a new altitude record—55,253 feet in 1961—and the woman's world speed record—1,429 miles per hour in an F-104G Super Starjet in 1964. She was the first woman to be awarded the Claude B. Harmon Trophy for contributions to world aviation (1937). She also won the award in 1938, 1939, 1946, 1950, and 1953. She was director of the Women's Air Force Service Pilots (see entry), consisting of 1,000 women who served in transport planes in World War II. In 1971 Cochran was the only living woman elected to the U.S. Aviation Hall of Fame. The first civilian awarded the Distinguished Service Medal by the United States, she was similarly honored by the governments of France, Spain, Turkey, China, and Thailand.

The adopted daughter of a poor couple, Cochran went to work in a sawmill as an eight-year-old. She soon left home, supporting herself in a variety of jobs as a beauty operator and cosmetician. In 1932 she learned to fly and earned her pilot's license in three weeks. Since she could barely read and write at that time, she took the pilot's exam orally.

The following year, Cochran opened a beauty parlor in Chicago and a beauty products lab in New York City—the beginning of what was to become a large and successful business for her. She married millionaire Floyd Odlum in 1936.

After World War II began in Europe, with civil aviators grounded, she persuaded General Henry "Hap" Arnold to let her fly a U.S. bomber to England—although there were such strenuous objections from military pilots that Cochran was required to relinquish the controls for takeoff and landing (1941). In 1942 the British invited her to bring a group of U.S. women fliers to join the Air Transport Auxiliary of the Royal Air Force; Cochran was named honorary flight-captain.

When she returned to the United States, Nancy Love (see entry) was organizing the Women's Auxiliary Ferrying Squadron, and Cochran drew up a training program for women with fewer than 500 hours of flying time experience, which had been the original prerequisite. In 1943 the Women's Auxiliary Ferrying Squadron merged with the Women's Air Force Service Pilots (WASPs), retaining the name of the latter group. Cochran was named director of women pilots.

At the end of World War II, Cochran was awarded the Distinguished Service Medal, which was usually reserved for the armed forces. She was present at the Japanese surrender ceremonies aboard the U.S.S. *Missouri*, became the first woman to land in Japan, then continued a prestigious around-the-world tour. She met with Madame Chiang Kai-shek and Mao Zedong in China, visited the Buchenwald concentration camp in Germany, and attended the Nazi war crime trials in Nuremberg, Germany.

In May, 1953, flying a Canadian Sabre jet, she flew faster than Mach 1, the speed of sound, three times in six hours of flying, breaking three men's records.

Cochran made an unsuccessful

bid for political office in 1956 when she ran as a Republican candidate for a seat in the House of Representatives.

Continuing her record-breaking flying career, she became the first woman to fly at Mach 2 in an A3J plane in 1960, and the first to pilot a jet in a transatlantic flight—New Orleans, Louisiana, to Hanover, Germany, 1962. In 1964 she broke the women's speed record by flying 1,429 miles per hour.

Cochran served in the U.S. Air Force Reserve, retiring in 1970 as a colonel. She also headed a cosmetics firm, and twice was named Woman of the Year in Business.

Jane Colden

Probably the first woman botanist in the United States (c. 1750).

Born New York, New York, 1724; died New York, New York, March 10, 1766.

Colden used the classification system developed by Carl Linnaeus, the Swedish botanist. By 1757 she had produced a detailed catalog of over 300 local plants. Her father, Cadwallader Colden, was the acting governor of the New York colony at various times. He had strong interests in botany and the physical sciences.

Bessie Coleman

First U.S. woman to earn an international pilot's license (1921).

Born Atlanta, Texas, January 26, 1893; died Jacksonville, Florida, April 30, 1926.

Also the world's first licensed black pilot, Coleman was inspired by Eugene Jacques Bullard, a black American who flew with the French in World War I. She was not allowed to learn to fly in the United States because of her color, so she learned French in order to take flying lessons in Europe. Her opportunity came near the close of the war when she went to France with a Red Cross unit attached to a French flying squadron. She prevailed upon the French pilots to teach her, and in 1921 she was licensed by the Fédération Aéronautique Internationale.

The Texas native flew the largest plane ever piloted by a woman at Staaken Airfield, near Berlin, Germany, in June, 1922. The plane was a German L.F.G. powered by a 220-horsepower Benz engine. Later that summer she flew a Dornier flying boat at Friedrichshafen, Germany.

After her return to the United States in August, 1922, Coleman traveled across the country giving lectures and flying demonstrations,

hoping to gather support for a U.S. flight school for U.S. blacks. On September 3, 1922, flying an American plane for the first time, Coleman made three short flights as part of an exhibition honoring the Fifteenth (Negro) Infantry Regiment of the New York National Guard. The exhibition also featured a successful parachute jump by an officer of the Negro Improvement Association of New York.

She was the twelfth of thirteen children born to sharecropper parents. She earned her pilot's license in ten months and returned to the United States as a celebrity. Her dream of a flying school for blacks was unfulfilled because she died when hurled from the open cockpit of her airplane during a flying exhibition at Jacksonville, Florida, on April 30, 1926.

Colorado

Colorado was the first state in the United States where men voted at the polls to give women the vote (1893).

Ada Comstock (Notestein)

First president of the American Association of University Women (AAUW) (1921); first woman to be dean of Smith College (Northampton, Massachusetts) (1912); first full-time president of Radcliffe College (Cambridge, Massachusetts) (1923–43).

Born Moorhead, Minnesota, December 11, 1876; died New Haven, Connecticut, December 12, 1973.

Comstock attended the University of Minnesota (Minneapolis) from

1892 to 1894, then completed her studies and graduated Phi Beta Kappa with a B.L. degree from Smith College (1897). After earning an A.M. degree in English, history, and education at Columbia University (New York, New York) (1899), she went to the University of Minnesota (Minneapolis), where from 1900 to 1912 she moved through the ranks to become a full professor of rhetoric and oratory as well as a dean—the only woman administrator in the university.

Comstock was named president of the American Association of University Women in 1921, when it was formed by the merger of the Association of Collegiate Alumnae and the Southern Association of College Women. The AAUW promotes the advancement of women on college and university faculties through advocacy and an emphasis on lifelong learning. It engages in lobbying, presents awards, and promotes research. Comstock served as the association's president until 1923.

During her tenure as president of Radcliffe College, Comstock brought about a much closer working relationship with Harvard University.

In 1929 President Herbert Hoover named Comstock to the eleven-member Wickersham Commission to study law enforcement problems—especially those stemming from Prohibition. The only woman on the commission, she voted in favor of *modifying*—not repealing—the Eighteenth Amendment.

Prior to World War II, Comstock was chair of the International Relations Department of the AAUW, urging United States intervention against totalitarian aggressors.

In 1941, as a member of the National Committee for Planned Parenthood, she led their fund-raising activities.

Elenor Conn

First person to fly a hot-air balloon over the North Pole (1980).

Dates unknown.

A previous attempt to fly a hot-air balloon over the North Pole was made in conjunction with the Andrée Expedition of 1897, but it ended in tragedy. Conn's was the first successful flight in this century.

Maureen Connolly

First woman to win the grand slam of tennis (1953); youngest woman ever to win the national junior championship of tennis (1949).

Born San Diego, California, September 17, 1934; died Dallas, Texas, June 21, 1969.

Connolly, whose first love was horseback riding, began playing tennis as a southpaw, but her coach instructed her to play right-handed. Her typical practice schedule involved three hours of practice with her coach each day, seven days a week. After five years of play, she won the national junior championship, the youngest woman ever to win it. The media responded well to her and nicknamed her "Little Mo."

As a member of the Wightman Cup team, Connolly did not lose a single match between 1951 and 1954. In 1952, after winning the Wimbledon championship in England, she went on to win the Australian, French, and U.S. tennis championships, and thus became the first woman to win the grand slam. She won three Wimbledon titles and two French titles before she retired from tournament play in 1954 after injuring herself in a horseback-riding accident. After her recovery, she taught tennis, wrote a sports column for the *San Diego Union,* and acted as a promoter for a sporting goods company.

She was named Woman of the Year for three consecutive years (1952–54) by an Associated Press sportswriters' poll and was inducted into the International Tennis Hall of Fame in 1968.

Harriet Maxwell Converse

First white woman to become a Native American chief (1891).

Born Elmira, New York, 1836; died New York, New York, November 18, 1903.

Converse and her husband's first contact with the Seneca Nation came in 1881 when they met General Ely S. Parker, a Seneca Indian who had served in the administration of President Ulysses S. Grant as commissioner of Indian affairs. (He was also a successful securities investor.) Converse then visited the Cattaraugus, New York, reservation of the Seneca Nation. In 1884 she wrote an ode called "The Ho-dé-no-saunee: The Confederacy of the Iroquois," and in 1885 was adopted into the Snipe Clan (a subtribal family group within the Seneca Nation).

Becoming active in the Native American cause, Converse lobbied successfully against a New York State bill to break up the reservations and distribute the land among individual tribe members (1891). In recognition of this and other activities in behalf of the Six Nations (the Cayuga, Mohawk, Onondaga, Oneida, Seneca, and Tuscarora nations, all of whom spoke dialects of the Iroquois language)—including Converse's donation of her collection of Native American artifacts to museums—the Council of the Seneca Nation formally made her a member in 1891, confirming her in the name of the dead wife of a former chief. On September 18, 1891, Converse was named honorary chief of the Six Nations at Tonawanda, New York.

Cordelia E. Cook

First to woman to receive the Bronze Star (1944); first to win two decorations in World War II (1944).

Born Fort Thomas, Kentucky, date unknown.

Cook, a first lieutenant in the Army Nurse Corps, was nursing wounded soldiers when her field hospital in Italy was bombed in 1943. She continued to carry out her hospital duties at the field hospital from November, 1943, until January, 1944, for which she received the Bronze Star for meritorious service.

Cook was wounded by artillery fire in January, 1944. For her wounds, she was awarded the Purple Heart.

She graduated from the Christ Hospital School of Nursing (Cincinnati, Ohio) in 1940 and married Harold E. Fillmore, a captain in the U.S. Army.

Sarah Ingersoll Cooper

First president of the International Kindergarten Union (1892).

Born Cazenovia, New York, December 12, 1835; died San Francisco, California, December 10, 1896.

In 1854 Cooper graduated from the Troy Female Seminary (Troy, New York), which was founded by Emma Willard (see entry). She moved with her family to California in 1864 because of her poor health. She taught a Sunday school class in a Presbyterian church in San Francisco, but in 1881 she was put on trial by the congregation because she refused to accept the doctrines of infant damnation and everlasting punishment. At her request she was expelled from the congregation, and she joined the Congregational Church—taking her Bible class with her.

Her work with this Bible class motivated her interest in kindergarten education, and in 1879 she founded one in San Francisco. Within six years, Cooper was the unsalaried director and superintendent of about forty kindergartens.

Margaret Corbin

First woman to assume the role of soldier in the American Revolution (1776); probably the first to receive a soldier's pension (1779).

Born Franklin County, Pennsylvania, November 12, 1751; died Westchester County, New York, c. 1801.

Corbin stepped in and filled the post of her husband, John, a cannoneer killed in the battle of Fort Washington, New York. She herself then suffered a permanently disabling injury when her arm was struck by three grapeshots.

In 1779 the Supreme Council of Pennsylvania voted her a relief payment of thirty dollars, and the Continental Congress ruled that she was entitled to half a soldier's regular disability pay for life (or the duration of the disability). She also received a clothing allowance.

Corbin is believed to be the "Captain Molly" who lived near West Point and Highland Falls, New York, until her death (see Mary McCauley). (She was dubbed "Captain" as a consequence of her Revolutionary War service, and "Molly" was apparently her nickname.) In order to receive her benefits, she enrolled in the Invalid Regiment for wounded veterans and remained in the regiment until it was disbanded in 1783.

Gerty Radnitz Cori

First U.S. woman to win the Nobel Prize for physiology or medicine (1947).

Born Prague, part of the Austro-Hungarian Empire (later Czechoslovakia), August 15, 1896; died St. Louis, Missouri, October 26, 1957.

After she and her husband, Carl Cori, worked for several years in the area of pharmacology and biochemistry, they shared the Nobel Prize with Bernardo Houssay of Argentina. They received the prize because of several discoveries, including the synthesis of glycogen in the test tube.

As a young woman, Gerty Radnitz received an M.D. degree from the medical school of the German University of Prague, Ferdinand University, in 1920. She met her husband at the university and married him the same year she received her degree.

The Coris immigrated to the United States in 1922, where they both began work at the New York Institute for the Study of Malignant Diseases (later called Roswell Park Memorial Institute), Buffalo, New York. They became naturalized citizens of the United States in 1928. Three years later they took positions at the Washington University School of Medicine, St. Louis, Missouri. Carl became the chair of the pharmacology department, but because of an anti-nepotism rule at the medical school, Gerty could not get a regular faculty appointment. Instead, she was given a research position in the same department, at a substantially lower salary.

The year she shared the Nobel Prize, she also became a professor of biochemistry. Her field of specialization was carbohydrate metabolism, especially the specific chemical reactions occurring in the process and the enzymes resulting from it.

In 1952 the Coris made the first report on a specific hereditary metabolic disease that is due to a deficiency of a specific enzyme.

Although she suffered for several years from myelofibrosis, a rare disease of the bone marrow, Cori continued her work until she died.

Lucia Marie Cormier

One of the first two women to run in an all-woman U.S. Senate election (1960) (see also Margaret Chase Smith).

Born Rumford, Maine, c. 1912.

Cormier was elected to the Maine House of Representatives in 1947; this was the first of her six victories in state elections. In 1960 she became the Democratic minority leader in the Maine legislature, the first woman of either party in the state to be a floor leader. In 1956 she was a Democratic national committeewoman and supported Averell Harriman in his unsuccessful campaign for the presidential nomination.

She challenged Senator Margaret Chase Smith in 1960. Smith won by a landslide, garnering more than sixty percent of the votes.

Cormier earned a B.A. degree from College of St. Elizabeth (Convent Station, New Jersey) and an M.A. degree in French from Columbia University (New York, New York). She taught Spanish and French at Stephens High School in Rumford, Maine, where she was head of the modern languages department. She also ran a bookstore there.

Juliet Corson

Founder of what is believed to be the first cooking school in the United States (1876).

Born Roxbury, Massachusetts, January 14, 1841; died New York, New York, June 18, 1897.

Privately educated, Juliet Corson became a writer for newspapers and magazines. In 1874 she gave cooking lectures at the Free Training School for Women in New York City while a chef demonstrated. She opened the

New York Cooking School in 1876; it was an instant success.

In 1877 Corson wrote her *Cooking Manual* and, in response to an economic crisis in the United States, she also wrote a pamphlet titled *Fifteen Cent Dinners for Families of Six*. The pamphlet's popularity led to a lecturing career for Corson, and she became a consultant on founding and funding schools similar to her own.

Phoebe Couzins

Reportedly the first woman to serve as a U.S. marshal (1887).

Born St. Louis, Missouri, c. 1839; died St. Louis, Missouri, December 6, 1913.

Daughter of U.S. Marshal John Couzins, Phoebe stepped into her father's position when he died, remaining in the office for two years.

In 1868 Couzins applied and was admitted to Washington University School of Law, St. Louis, Missouri. She received her degree in 1871, becoming the first woman to receive a law degree there. She was admitted to the bar in several states but never practiced. Instead, she became prominent in the suffrage movement, lecturing and traveling across the country with Susan B. Anthony (see entry). However, in 1897 she renounced the suffrage movement, apparently because she had been retained as a congressional lobbyist by the United Brewers' Association, which opposed restrictions on alcohol. Since the causes of woman suffrage and temperance were often linked, she had to disavow suffrage.

Gene Cox

First female page in the U.S. House of Representatives (1939).

Born c. 1925.

Daughter of Representative Edward E. Cox (Democrat from Georgia), Cox was thirteen years old when she served as page. She worked only one day, the first day of the Seventy-sixth Congress, January 3, 1939. She earned four dollars for running errands for a total of three hours. The next page, who worked on a regular basis, was Felda Looper of Heavener, Oklahoma. She was appointed in 1973 at the age of eighteen.

COYOTE

First organization for women prostitutes (1973).

The organization—Call Off Your Old Tired Ethics—had as its main purpose the protection of prostitutes and ex-prostitutes. The membership was made up of prostitutes, ex-prostitutes, lawyers, and various service providers. Headquartered in San Francisco, California, the organization sought legalization of prostitution, protection against arrest, and proper legal representation in case of arrest.

Minnie D. Craig

First woman to be elected speaker of a state house of representatives (1933).

Born Maine, date unknown.

Craig, a Republican who had served in the North Dakota state assembly for ten years, was the Republican national committeewoman from 1928 to 1932. She was elected speaker of the North Dakota House of Representatives after a caucus was held by the Nonpartisan League. She served from January 3, 1933, to March 31, 1933.

Jane Todd Crawford

First woman to have an ovariotomy (1809).

Born c. 1764; died c. 1842.

The procedure, involving a surgical incision into an ovary to remove an ovarian tumor, was performed without anesthetic by Dr. Ephraim McDowell in Danville, Kentucky, in 1809. Crawford lived for thirty-three years after the operation.

Hannah Mather Crocker

First woman to write a feminist tract (1818); the first matron of a Masonic Lodge (1778).

Born Boston, Massachusetts, June 27, 1752; died Roxbury, Massachusetts, 1829.

Crocker was the daughter of a minister and the granddaughter of clergyman Cotton Mather. Although she came from a family of educated people, there is no evidence that she received much in the way of formal education.

In 1778 Crocker and a group of friends who had been studying languages together organized a women's Masonic Lodge, over which she presided. The group was made up of the wives of men who were Masons.

She wrote several pieces about the women's lodge, all clearly aimed at a female audience. They were published as a compilation, *A Series of Letters on Free Masonry*, in 1815.

In 1818 she published the tract *Observations on the Real Rights of Women*, which contended that the female mind has powers equal to that of the male, that women have the capacity to judge and act for themselves, and that under Christianity the sexes share equally in divine grace.

Lucretia Crocker

First nonscientist elected to the American Association for the Advancement of Science (1880).

Born Barnstable, Massachusetts, December 31, 1829; died Boston, Massachusetts, October 9, 1886.

Crocker attended the State Normal School in West Newton, Massachusetts, graduating in 1850. She stayed on at the school as a teacher of natural science, geography, and mathematics until, suffering from ill health, she resigned in 1854.

After her health improved in 1857, she took a teaching position at Antioch College in Yellow Springs, Ohio, where she was a professor of mathematics and astronomy. She resigned from that position in 1859 and went to Boston, where she became involved in various aspects of education. She taught botany, served on the boards of educational associations and committees, and wrote science books and textbooks. With a former pupil, she wrote a geography textbook, *Our World* (1864), and published *Methods of Teaching Geography: Notes on Lessons* (1883).

From 1873 until 1877 Crocker headed the science department of the Society to Encourage Studies at Home, a correspondence school based in Boston, Massachusetts. In 1880 she was made a member of the American Association for the Advancement of Science in recognition of her development of a successful science curriculum in the Boston schools. She also served on the Boston school committee; among the innovations during her term was the introduction of such courses as zoology and mineralogy into the curriculum.

Jean A. Crockett

One of the first two women appointed to the chair of the Regional Federal Reserve Bank (1981) (see also Caroline Leonetti Ahmanson).

Born Tucson, Arizona, c. 1919.

Crockett was appointed in 1981 to serve a one-year term as chair of the Regional Federal Reserve Bank in Philadelphia, Pennsylvania; the term began on January 1, 1982. She had been a member of the board of the bank since 1977.

Before coming to the Federal Reserve Bank, Crockett was a professor of economics and chair of the finance department at the Wharton School, University of Pennsylvania (Philadelphia).

Crockett received B.A., M.A., and Ph.D. degrees in economics from the

University of Chicago (Chicago, Illinois). She then earned a Ph.D. degree in math from the University of Colorado (Boulder).

Caresse Crosby *(born Mary Phelps Jacob)*

First person to patent a brassiere (1914).

Born New York, New York, 1892; died Rome, Italy, 1970.

In November, 1914, Crosby patented what was called a "backless brassiere," made from two handkerchiefs and ribbon sewn together. She sold her patent to Warner Brothers Corset Company of Bridgeport, Connecticut for $1,500. Although the value of the patent was later estimated to be $15 million, Crosby did not receive any additional payment.

An heiress, she and her second husband, Harry Crosby, founded the Black Sun Press (Paris, France) in 1927. They published avant-garde writing by such authors as Hart Crane, James Joyce, D. H. Lawrence, Ezra Pound, and Gertrude Stein. During the 1930s they published Crosby Continental Editions, introducing to Europeans much of the work of such writers as Kay Boyle, William Faulkner, and Ernest Hemingway.

In 1953 Crosby wrote her autobiography, *The Passionate Years*, in which she professes to have been the first U.S. Girl Scout, and to have been indirectly responsible for the founding of Alcoholics Anonymous. (It is not likely that either claim was true, since the history and founders of both organizations are well documented.)

Marvel Crosson

First woman to die in a cross-country women's air derby (1929).

Born Warsaw, Indiana, 1904; died Wellton, Arizona, August 18, 1929.

Crosson was flying in the first of the derbies (see also Women's Air Derby), which began at Santa Monica, California, on August 18, 1929, when her plane—a TravelAir Speedwing Chaparral biplane—became disabled near Wellton, Arizona. She jumped from the plane, but her parachute failed to open—possibly because she was too close to the ground. There were questions, never resolved, about whether her plane had been tampered with or was inadequately maintained.

Crosson had held the women's altitude record of 23,996 feet, which she set in a monoplane near Inglewood, California.

She had begun flying when she and her brother Joe bought surplus airplanes and rebuilt a "Jennie," a type of early aircraft flown by such pilots as Charles Lindbergh. She soloed for the first time in 1923, then became a stunt flyer. She and Joe founded an air transport company for flying cargo to Alaska; she was frequently the pilot on these trips.

Julie Croteau

First woman to play on a men's college varsity baseball team (1989).

Born c. 1971.

Croteau, first baseman for St. Mary's College, St. Mary's City, Maryland—a Division III college of the National Collegiate Athletic Association—played her inaugural game on March 17, 1989, against Spring Garden College, Philadelphia, Pennsylvania. The 5'8", 130-pound, eighteen-year-old played five innings, handling six fielding opportunities without error. She got no hits for three times at bat, grounding out each time instead. Her team lost to Spring Garden, 4–1.

While at high school in Manassas, Virginia, Croteau filed a lawsuit against the school because she was rejected by the varsity baseball team after she had already played three years of junior varsity. She lost the suit.

The summer following high school, Croteau played semiprofessional baseball for the Fredericksburg, Virginia, Giants of the Virginia Baseball League. She hit consistently enough to be platooned at first base.

Diane Crump

First woman to ride in a parimutuel race in North America (1969); first to ride in a Kentucky Derby (1970).

Born Connecticut, 1949.

Crump's first mount in a parimutuel race was Bridle 'N Bit, at Hialeah Park (Hialeah, Florida), February 7, 1969. The horse finished tenth in a twelve-horse field. Her first victory came just six weeks later on March 20, 1969, at Gulfstream Park (Hallandale, Florida). In May, 1970 she became the first woman jockey to ride in a Kentucky Derby, appearing in the Churchill Downs (Louisville) classic aboard Fathom, who finished fifteenth in a field of seventeen. The second woman to ride in a Derby was Patricia Cooksey in 1984, who finished eleventh on So Vague. Cooksey was also the first woman to ride in the Preakness, at Pimlico racetrack (Baltimore, Maryland), finishing sixth on Tajawa in 1985.

In her seventeen-year career as a jockey, Crump compiled a record of 1,614 starts, with 235 victories, 204 seconds, and 203 thirds. Her total earnings were $1,262,640. After retiring in 1986, she became a trainer. Crump was seriously injured on February 1, 1989, when a horse she was training at her Virginia farm fell on her. She suffered a broken left leg and ankle, broken ribs, and a concussion. After her injuries healed, however, Crump returned to training.

Women have been increasingly prominent in horse racing in the twentieth century. The first woman owner of a Kentucky Derby winner, Elwood, was Mrs. C. E. Durnell, in 1904. The first woman to train a Kentucky Derby horse was Mary Hirsch (see entry); the horse, No Sir, ran thirteenth in the 1937 Derby.

The first woman to ride three winners in one day at Churchill Downs was apprentice jockey Melinda Spickard, whose accomplishment came on June 9, 1981.

At the time of this writing, the all-time victory and earnings leader among women jockeys is Julie Krone, who rode in the 1992 Derby, finishing fourteenth on Static Ride.

Alma Cummings (born Alma Stappenback)

First person to win the first U.S. dance marathon (1923).

Born San Antonio, Texas, c. 1891.

Cummings danced in a marathon at the Audubon Ballroom in New York City from March 31 to April 1, 1923. Wearing out six partners, she stayed on her feet for twenty-seven hours, setting a new world record.

Herself a dance instructor at the ballroom, she danced the fox trot, one-step, and waltz during the competition. To maintain her energy, she ate fruit and nuts and drank near beer (low-alcohol beer, typically 3.2 percent). Cummings ascribed her success in the competition to her nine-year vegetarian diet.

Marian Cummings

First woman to receive a commercial pilot's license (1932).

Born Seattle, Washington, c. 1892; died Greenwich, Connecticut, June 16, 1984.

Cummings was a corporate pilot for her husband's law firm, located in New York City. During World War II, she was a captain in the Civil Air Patrol and a ferry pilot in the Army Air Corps.

Kate Richards O'Hare Cunningham

First woman to join the International Order of Machinists (1894).

Born near Ada, Kansas, March 26, 1877; died Benicia, California, January 10, 1948.

In 1894 Cunningham became a machinist apprentice to her father and joined the International Order of

Machinists, becoming the first woman to join the union.

At one time she planned to become a minister. She lost her faith, however, and took up the cause of socialism. While attending a training school for Socialists, she met and married Francis O'Hare (1902). She wrote a Socialist novel, *What Happened to Dan* (1904), which was widely read. In 1912 she and her husband became editors of the *National Rip-Saw*, a socialist weekly that was later called *Social Revolution*.

Cunningham traveled across the country in 1917, making speeches protesting U.S. participation in World War I. Some phraseology from her speeches was used as evidence against her, and she was convicted of violating the Espionage Act. In 1919 she was sentenced to five years in prison. With the help of the Socialists, she had her sentence commuted in 1920, and President Calvin Coolidge finally granted her full pardon.

After her release from prison, she took up prison reform. One of her main targets was the prison contract-labor scheme. (Under the practice of contract prison labor, common in many states in the nineteenth century, private companies maintained prisons and/or prisoners, usually winning these contracts through a bidding process. This practice made it possible for many state correctional systems to be run at a profit. Other companies, however, objected to the use of cheap prison labor, arguing that it created unfair competition. The practice also generated protests because it involved brutality and corruption of prison officials and politicians via bribes. In 1929 the United States government passed the Hawes-Cooper Act banning interstate shipment of prison-made goods, and by 1940 all of the states had passed legislation restricting commerce in such goods.)

In 1919 Cunningham wrote *Kate O'Hare's Prison Letters*, followed by *In Prison*, which was first published in 1920, while she was in prison, then reissued in 1923.

She and Francis O'Hare were divorced in 1928. That same year she married Charles Cunningham, a California lawyer. From 1939 until 1940 she was assistant director of the California Department of Penology. One of her accomplishments in that position was the development of an extensive reform of California's prison system.

Doris Malkin Curtis

First woman president of the American Geological Institute (1981); first woman president of the Geological Society of America (GSA) (1990).

Born Brooklyn, New York, January 12, 1914; died Houston, Texas, May 26, 1991.

A geologist at Shell Oil Company from 1942 to 1979, Curtis also served as president of the Society of Economic Paleontologists and Mineralogists. In 1981 she became the first woman president of the American Geological Institute, a federation (founded in 1848) of national scientific and technical societies in the earth sciences. She also became, in 1990, the first woman to be elected president of the Geological Society of America, a professional society of geologists.

Curtis earned a B.S. degree from Brooklyn College (Brooklyn, New York) and a Ph.D. degree from Columbia University (New York, New York).

Curtis formed a geological consulting firm in 1990. She died at age seventy-seven in the midst of her presidential term at the Geological Society of America.

Mary Leiter Curzon

First U.S. woman to be vicereine of India (1898).

Born Chicago, Illinois, May 27, 1870; died London, England, July 18, 1906.

Curzon, daughter of a partner of Marshall Field's store in Chicago, Illinois, met George Curzon at a ball in London in 1890; they were married in 1895.

George Curzon was undersecretary of state for Foreign Affairs from 1895 to 1898. In 1898 he was named viceroy of India with the title, Baron Curzon of Kedleston. After he served six years in the post, the couple returned to England, and George Curzon was appointed warden of the Cinque Ports. (The Cinque, or Five, Ports—Dover, Sandwich, Hythe, Romney, and Hastings—were created by William the Conqueror and granted special privileges in exchange for furnishing warships for the king when he needed them. Winchelsea and Rye were added before the time of Henry III. The warden of the Cinque Ports acts as their superintendent.) The following year he was reappointed viceroy, but after a conflict with Lord Kitchener, his superior, he resigned.

Eleanor D'Antuono

First person to be invited to perform as a special guest artist with the Kirov Ballet of Leningrad (now St. Petersburg) (1978).

Born Cambridge, Massachusetts, 1939.

She danced in *Giselle* and performed the role of Odille in *Swan Lake,* when the Kirov Ballet was on tour in the Soviet Union in 1978. In January, 1979, she again danced with the troupe in performances of *Giselle* and *Swan Lake* in Leningrad and four other cities in the U.S.S.R.

D'Antuono, who has been a principal dancer with the American Ballet Theater since 1961, toured the Soviet Union with her troupe in 1966.

She has gained wide recognition, especially for her roles in *Giselle, Swan Lake,* and *Petrouchka.* Choreographer Alvin Ailey created "Giggling Rapids," a section of his ballet, *The River,* for her in 1970. "Giggling Rapids" is one of eleven sections of the ballet—plus prologue and epilogue—during which the dancer must execute particularly challenging movements.

DAR *(see Daughters of the American Revolution)*

Virginia Dare

First child born to English parents on American soil (1587).

Born Roanoke Island, Virginia (later North Carolina), August 18, 1587.

Named after the early colony, Virginia Dare, daughter of Ellinor White and Ananias Dare, was born on the Roanoke Plantation on August 18, 1587. Nine days later, her grandfather, John White, governor of the colony of Virginia, boarded a ship to sail back to England. When he returned three years later, nothing remained of the settlement but its fortifications.

Linda Darnell

First woman to sell securities on the New York Curb Exchange (1941); first to act as a specialist in any exchange in the world; first to make a speech on the floor of an open securities market.

Born Dallas, Texas, October 16, 1921; died Chicago, Illinois, April 10, 1965.

On November 18, 1941, Darnell, appearing on the floor for only one day, sold $875 worth of U.S. bonds and $146.75 worth of savings stamps in thirty minutes. She sold the bonds and savings stamps as part of a fund-raising effort.

Pushed by her mother to study dancing, acting, and modeling, Darnell chose acting. She made her film debut in *Hotel for Women* when she was only fifteen years old. Darnell was very popular in the 1940s. Two of her major films were *Forever Amber* (1947) and *A Letter to Three Wives* (1949).

She died in a fire while visiting her former secretary in Chicago.

Lydia Barrington Darragh

Reportedly the first woman to spy on behalf of the colonists (1777).

Born Dublin, Ireland, 1729; died Philadelphia, Pennsylvania, December 28, 1789.

Darragh and her husband immigrated to Philadelphia, Pennsylvania, in 1754, where she undertook a career as a midwife and nurse.

One story tells that on December 2, 1777, Darragh overheard British officers (who had taken over one of her rooms) plotting a surprise raid on George Washington's encampment at Whitemarsh, near Chestnut Hill, Pennsylvania. Darragh left her house on the morning of December 4, got beyond the British lines, and gave the message to her friend Col. Thomas Craig. He warned Washington, and the attack was unsuccessful.

There is disagreement about the historical accuracy of this story. Contemporary histories do not mention her feat, but an 1827 magazine story quotes several people who reported getting the account from Darragh herself.

Daughters of the American Revolution (DAR)

First women's patriotic group based on heredity (1890).

Sons of the American Revolution (SAR), founded in 1889, decided at its first congress (1890) not to admit women's auxiliaries. In July, 1890 Mary Smith Lockwood wrote a letter to the *Washington Post* announcing a meeting to form a women's group. The president of SAR suggested the name Daughters of the American Revolution for the new order. Lockwood, who was a resident of Washing-

Daughters of the American Revolution National Board of Management

ton, D.C., is thus credited with being the organization's "Literary Founder."

In August, 1890, the three founders of the DAR, Lockwood, Ellen Hardin Walworth, and Eugenia Washington met at the home of Walworth, in Washington, D.C. Because of a rainstorm, attendance was low at this first organizational meeting of the DAR.

Caroline Harrison (see entry), wife of President Benjamin Harrison, was the organization's first president. Walworth was the first secretary-general.

Daughters of St. Crispin

First women's national labor organization (1869).

Daughters of St. Crispin (DOSC) held its founding convention as a national union in Lynn, Massachusetts, on July 28, 1869. Thirty delegates from twelve lodges located in Massachusetts, Maine, New York, San Francisco, Chicago, and Philadelphia attended. Carrie Wilson was elected as the first president.

The organization, patterned after the Knights of St. Crispin (KOSC), the national union of male shoe workers, was instrumental in convincing KOSC to recognize them and support them in their battle for equal pay for equal work. In 1870 KOSC passed a resolution calling for equal pay for equal work. The following year, the men's union successfully struck the shoe factories in Baltimore, Maryland, demanding that the DOSC women who had struck be rehired.

As a result of the financial depression of 1873, the power of the Daughters of St. Crispin was weakened, and the organization went out of existence in 1876.

Bette (Ruth Elizabeth) Davis

*First woman to head the Academy
of Motion Picture Arts and
Sciences (1941); first to receive
the American Film Institute's
highest honor, the Life
Achievement Award (1977).*

Born Lowell, Massachusetts,
April 5, 1908; died Neuilly-sur-Seine,
France, October 6, 1989.

Best known for dramatic roles in
such films as *All About Eve* (1950),
Davis—veteran of more than eighty
films—began her acting career on
the stage. Right after attending
Cushing Academy, a finishing school
in Ashburnham, Massachusetts, already set on becoming an actress,
she wished to study with stage actress Eva Le Galliene, but was rejected. Instead she enrolled in the
John Murray Anderson Dramatic
School in New York City in 1927.
After her work with a stock company,
Davis made her Broadway debut in
Broken Dishes, a comedy (1928). Two
years later, after she appeared on
Broadway in *Solid South,* she had a
successful screen test and went to
work for Universal Studios. In 1931,
the first year she worked there, she
appeared in two movies, *Bad Sister*
and *Seed.*

Her first major role, however, was
as leading lady opposite George Ar-
liss in *The Man Who Played God*
(1932)—the first of a long series of
movies she made under contract with
Warner Brothers. Some of the films
were pretty lackluster, however, and
she had a protracted struggle with
Warner Brothers to get quality
scripts. One outstanding role at that
time was that of Mildred in *Of
Human Bondage,* for which Warner
Brothers loaned Davis to RKO.

The first Academy Award of
Davis's career came in 1935 for *Dan-
gerous;* the second was awarded in
1938 for *Jezebel.* She received the
New York Film Critics' Best Actress
Award for her performance in *All
About Eve,* marking a high point in
her career. Davis garnered ten Oscar
nominations and won a television
Emmy award for her performance in
*Strangers: The Story of a Mother and
a Daughter* (1979).

In 1962 Davis published her autobiography, *The Lonely Life.*

Katharine Bement Davis

*First person to conduct a
national survey of sexual
attitudes and experiences (1929).*

Born Buffalo, New York, January
15, 1860; died Pacific Grove, California, December 10, 1935.

Davis took the names of over
2,000 middle-class women, primarily
college graduates, from the member-

ship lists of women's clubs and college alumnae groups. Most were born around 1880. Her findings were published in her book, *Factors in the Sex Life of Twenty-two Hundred Women*, published in 1929.

The survey revealed that more than fifty percent of the unmarried women, and thirty percent of the married women, had "intense emotional relationships" with women; that twenty percent of the entire sample had had homosexual experiences; that few women in the sample had had premarital heterosexual experiences; that most of the married women used contraceptives and described sex in positive terms.

Davis graduated from Rochester Free Academy (Rochester, New York) in 1879, taught for a time, then entered Vassar College (Poughkeepsie, New York) as a junior in 1890—graduating with honors in 1892. She resumed her teaching career, then moved into social work: she took charge of a settlement house in Philadelphia. Returning to academe, she earned a Ph.D. degree in political economy from the University of Chicago (Chicago, Illinois) (1900).

From 1901 to 1914 Davis served as superintendent of the newly opened Reformatory for Women at Bedford Hills, New York. In 1914 she became the first woman to be named New York City commissioner of corrections, and from 1917 to 1928 she served as general secretary of the Bureau of Social Hygiene, a branch of the Rockefeller Foundation.

Eleonora de Cisneros *(born Eleanor Broadfoot)*

First woman opera singer trained in the United States to be hired by the Metropolitan Opera (1899).

Born New York, New York, October 31, 1878; died New York, New York, February 3, 1934.

Educated at St. Agnes Seminary in Brooklyn, New York, de Cisneros studied music first with Francesco Fanciulli. She then studied the Italian method of singing under Mme. Adeline Murio-Celli. In 1899 tenor Jean de Reszke took her to Maurice Grau, manager of the Metropolitan Opera; he hired her immediately.

De Cisneros (born Eleonora Broadfoot and billed on the stage as Eleanor Broadfoot) made her U.S. debut with the Metropolitan Opera Company in Chicago on November 24, 1899. She sang the role of Rossweise in Wagner's *Die Walküre*. She debuted in New York City at the Metropolitan Opera House on January 5, 1900, singing the same role. Standing 6'2" tall, de Cisneros was an imposing figure on the stage and had a strong mezzo-soprano voice.

After one season, she left the Metropolitan Opera, married Cuban journalist Count François de Cisneros, and went to Italy to study. She made her Italian debut at Teatro Regio Ducal, Turin, in 1902, then toured the major houses of Europe. De Cisneros sang in the Bayreuth Wagner festival, said to be the first American singer to perform a major role there.

In 1906 Oscar Hammerstein brought her back to New York City to sing at his Manhattan Opera House; she performed there for two seasons.

During World War I, de Cisneros was chair of the Artists and Musical Committee of the New York Catholic War Fund's Women's Committee. She is reputed to have sold $30 million in liberty bonds—more than any other individual.

Vaughan DeLeath

First woman to croon on a regular radio broadcast (1920).

Born Mt. Pulaski, Illinois, September 26, 1900; died Buffalo, New York, May 28, 1943.

DeLeath, a young concert singer from the Pacific Coast who had studied music at Mills College in Oakland, California, had moved to New York City in 1919 to advance her career. In an attempt to convince inventor and radio station owner Lee DeForest to hire her, she climbed the stairs to the top of the World Tower building, where the DeForest station was housed in a tiny nine-foot square room. She sang "Swanee River" into a microphone with a huge horn. Crooning, singing softly, and/or murmuring, was necessary because there was a danger that a strong high note might shatter a transmitter tube. DeForest broadcast her crooning in December, 1920, calling her the "first lady of radio" and the "original radio girl." (In 1932, as part of an anniversary broadcast at the station, her original programs were reaired.)

In 1921 DeLeath became one of the first performers on WJZ, in New York City, which gained recognition as a key station. She composed more than 500 songs and sang in the Broadway shows *Laugh Clown Laugh* (1923) and *Easy Come, Easy Go* (1925).

In 1939 she sang and played the piano in the TV studio at Radio City in New York City, on a program being aired on W2XBS. Phone requests for favorite songs began to come in, which she would then sing. Because of its intimate nature, the show was well received.

Annetta Del Mar

First woman to regularly freeze her body (except head) in ice (1939).

Dates unknown.
During the New York World's Fair

(1939–40), Del Mar froze her body thirty to forty times each day.

Ellen Curtis Demorest

First person to create and distribute accurate patterns for home dressmaking (1860).

Born Schuylerville, New York, November 15, 1824; died New York, New York, August 10, 1898.

Demorest had established a millinery business when she was very young. Soon after graduating from Schuylerville Academy, in Schuylerville, New York, she opened shops in Philadelphia, Pennsylvania; Troy, New York; and New York City. She married William Demorest, a dry goods merchant, in 1858. In 1860 they opened a new shop in New York City, called Mme. Demorest's Emporium of Fashions. He decided to publish a fashion magazine after she had come up with the inventive idea of creating accurate patterns that could be copied and used for dressmaking in the home. They stapled a tissue-paper dressmaking pattern to each of the magazines. The magazine, *Mme. Demorest's Mirror of Fashions,* also featured the standard colored fashion plates. This innovative means of distributing accurate patterns proved to be an extremely successful enterprise: the magazine evolved from a quarterly into a monthly, and in 1876, the peak sales year, 3 million patterns were sold.

Demorest, a supporter of the women's cause, hired large numbers of women to work for her in her pattern business. She also pointed women toward fields that were uncommon for them at the time, such as bookkeeping, typesetting, and telegraphy. Active in women's service organizations, she was one of the founders of Sorosis (see entry) and its vice president and treasurer.

Mary Andrews Denison

First woman to write a murder mystery (1860).

Born Cambridge, Massachusetts, May 26, c. 1826; died Cambridge, Massachusetts, October 15, 1911.

A prolific writer, Denison wrote nonfiction, short stories, sketches, and novels, often under the pen names N. I. Edson and Clara Vance. She wrote her first book, *Edna Etheril, the Boston Seamstress,* in 1847. During the 1860s she wrote eight or nine "dime" novels, including *The Mad Hunter* (1860), a murder mystery. (See also Anna K. Green.)

Cora Dennison

First woman to get married on television (1928).

Dates unknown.

Dennison, a citizen of Kansas City, Missouri, was married to James Fowlkes as a special television event broadcast from Des Plaines, Illinois.

Maya Deren *(born Eleanora Derenkowsky)*

First woman to receive a Guggenheim Fellowship for creative work in the field of motion pictures (1946); first to receive the Cannes Grand Prix Internationale for Avant-Garde Film (1947).

Born Kiev, Ukraine, April 29, 1917; died Queens, New York, October 13, 1961.

Deren immigrated to the United States with her family in 1922. Upon arriving, the family shortened its name from Derenkowsky to Deren. She attended Syracuse University, Syracuse, New York (1933–35), and earned an A.B. degree from New York University (New York, New York) in 1936. She attended the New School for Social Research (New York, New York) (1937–38), and earned an M.A. degree in literature from Smith College (Northampton, Massachusetts) in 1939.

Soon after receiving her M.A., Deren began to study and write about dance. She directed several films, including *Witch's Cradle* (1943), *At Land* (1944), *Study in Choreography for Camera* (1945), and *Ritual in Transfigured Time* (1946), for which she received the Avant-Garde Film Award at Cannes. Six of her experimental films focused on dance, and members of the Metropolitan Ballet School appeared in her last film, *The Very Eye of Night* (1959).

She was one of the founders of Creative Film Foundation, established to promote the production of avant-garde films. She also lectured and wrote about film, her most notable work being *An Anagram of Ideas on Art, Form and Film* (1946), a significant theoretical treatise.

Elsie de Wolfe (Lady Mendl)

First woman interior decorator (1905).

Born New York, New York, December 20, 1865; died Versailles, France, July 12, 1950.

De Wolfe, who had gained some reputation during the late 1800s as an actress, a set designer, and a socialite of markedly good taste, left the theater and decided to turn to interior decorating. She received her first commission in 1905, to decorate the Colony Club, New York City's first club for women. The job being a noted success, she made her debut as an interior decorator, a term that was created to describe her around 1910.

She was especially innovative in her use of multimirrors, table lamps instead of hanging ones, and brightly colored fabrics. In addition, it was her practice to conceal electrical cords by putting them inside the walls of the places she decorated.

De Wolfe wrote many articles on interior decorating, which ran in such magazines as *Good Housekeeping.* Several of her articles were compiled in what became a significant book on interior design, *The House in Good Taste,* published in 1913.

She married Sir Charles Mendl, attaché at Bristol Embassy, Paris, France, in 1926. She died at the Villa Trianon, Versailles, France, which she and a close friend had bought and restored in the early 1900s.

Gladys Dick

Founder of what is thought to be the first professional organization for the adoption of children in the United States (1918).

Born Pawnee City, Nebraska, December 18, 1881; died Menlo Park, California, August 21, 1963.

After earning a B.S. degree at the University of Nebraska, Lincoln, Nebraska, Dick received a medical degree from the Johns Hopkins University School of Medicine in Bal-

timore, Maryland, where she also interned and completed her residency. She went to the University of Chicago in 1911, where she conducted research on scarlet fever and kidney function. Three years later she joined the medical staff at John R. McCormick Memorial Institute for Infectious Diseases in Chicago, Illinois.

She married George Dick in 1914. They worked as a team in the area of prevention for infectious diseases. In 1923 they isolated the streptococcus that causes scarlet fever. The following year they introduced the Dick Test, a skin test for detecting susceptibility to the disease.

Dick was a founder of the Cradle Society of Evanston, Illinois, the first American adoption agency, which opened in 1918. When she was forty-nine, after having been married twenty-three years, she and her husband adopted two infants. She remained associated with the society until 1953.

Anna Elizabeth Dickinson

Probably the first woman to speak in the U.S. House of Representatives (1864).

Born Philadelphia, Pennsylvania, October 28, 1842; died Goshen, New York, October 22, 1932.

Dickinson began speaking in behalf of women's rights and abolition as early as 1860, when she was only eighteen. In 1863 she continued to make effective political speeches on behalf of some of the Republican candidates.

She gained a reputation as a successful political public speaker, due to a speaking tour of New England and addresses in Pennsylvania and New York City. In 1864 she spoke before the House of Representatives at the invitation of a Republican congressman for whom she had campaigned. President Abraham Lincoln was in the audience.

After the Civil War, Dickinson continued to speak and give lectures, averaging about 150 each season. Her popularity and that of such lectures finally waned, however, and she was forced to retire from the speaking circuit. In 1876 she debuted in Boston as an actress, playing the role of Anne Boleyn in a play she wrote, *A Crown of Thorns*. In 1888 she made her final attempt at political speaking, a tour for the Republicans, which was aborted.

She spent the last two decades of her life living quietly with a couple who were her friends.

Frances Dickinson

Cofounder of first Roman Catholic convent in the United States (1790) (see also Ann Teresa Mathews).

Born London, England, 1755; died Port Tobacco, Maryland, 1830.

In 1773 Dickinson took her final vows at a Carmelite convent in Belgium and assumed the name Clare Joseph of the Sacred Heart of Jesus. Along with Ann Teresa Mathews, she cofounded the Carmelite convent in Port Tobacco, Maryland, in 1790. Mathews (Mother Bernardina Teresa Xavier of St. Joseph) served as its first prioress, and Dickinson was assistant to the prioress. When Mathews died in 1800, Dickinson succeeded her, serving as prioress until her death.

(Mildred) Babe Didrikson (family prefers Didriksen) *(see (Mildred) Babe Didrikson Zaharias)*

Darlene Dietrich

First woman to catch a bullet in her mouth (1980).

Dates unknown.

One of the featured shows at the International Brotherhood of Magicians Convention in Pittsburgh, Pennsylvania, was Dietrich's act. She caught a bullet in a special cup that she held in her mouth. The bullet was fired through a glass pane. The producers of the television show, "You Asked for It," invited her to perform the trick on television, and she accepted. The trick is considered an extremely dangerous one. Houdini once said he would attempt it, but he changed his mind. Several people have died while trying to catch bullets.

Shirley Dinsdale

First woman to win an Emmy Award (1949).

Born c. 1928.

Dinsdale and her puppet, Judy Splinters, starred in a show called "Judy Splinters." The show, which ran for fifteen minutes a day five times a week from June 13, 1949, until June 30, 1950, on KTLA television (Los Angeles, California), was designed for a young audience. Noted for her "savvy ad-libbing dialogue," Dinsdale won the Emmy for "most outstanding television personality."

Starting in show business when she was only fifteen, Dinsdale trained with Edgar Bergen, a famous radio and stage ventriloquist. By 1945, she had her own radio show.

Dorothea Lynde Dix

First woman to organize the Army Nursing Corps (1861); first person to issue a report on prison conditions (1844–45).

Born Hampden, Maine (then part of Massachusetts), April 4, 1802; died Trenton, New Jersey, July 17, 1887.

Dix taught a Sunday school class for women in a Massachusetts prison, the East Cambridge House of Correction, in 1841. She was astonished by the poor conditions in the institution and the harsh treatment of the inmates, especially those who were mentally ill. Mentally ill women were imprisoned with male criminals. Seeing such inequities prompted her to travel throughout the state and observe the conditions at other correctional institutions, as well as institutions for mental patients. Her circuit culminated with a report on state institutions that she presented to the Massachusetts legislature. In 1843 the state of Massachusetts passed a bill to enlarge an insane asylum in the town of Worcester.

Dix, who had run away from home to live with her grandmother when she was only twelve, traveled extensively in Massachusetts and other parts of New England. She was instrumental in bringing about reform in insane asylums in such places as Providence, Rhode Island, and Utica, New York. Gaining a following, she traveled to other parts of the country, investigating the conditions of various public institutions. Her observations and reports led directly to the opening of thirty-two new institutions throughout the United States, including new hospitals in Trenton, New Jersey, and Harrisburg, Pennsylvania. A further result of her campaigning was that the number of asylums in the country increased from 13 in 1843 to 123 by 1880.

In 1845 Dix collaborated with Horace Mann on the book *Remarks on Prisons and Prison Discipline in the United States*, a work that advocated many of the reforms later adopted by penologists. In addition, between the years 1845 and 1852, Dix was instrumental in the passage of federal bills to establish or enlarge eleven state hospitals.

Early in the Civil War, in 1861, Secretary of War Edwin Stanton appointed Dix head of the army nurses. Her supervision was criticized, however. Among the reasons for the criticism was that she refused to accept women, even though they were qualified, if she did not approve of their religious affiliations. She also declared that the nurses had to be of high moral character, thirty or older, and plain. Approximately 10,000 women served in the corps, including 1,000 from the South. The total number included nuns, emergency workers, volunteers for various kinds of work, relief organization workers, and camp followers. Dix served as head of the Army Nursing Corps until 1866. She died in one of the hospitals she had founded.

Carol Doda

First woman to be a "topless" entertainer (1964); first to be a "bottomless" entertainer (1969).

Dates unknown.

Doda first performed as a "topless" (breasts uncovered) and "bottomless" (totally nude) entertainer at the Condor Night Club, San Francisco, California. She performed there from 1964 to 1985. (Although the nightclub stopped having topless and bottomless shows in 1988, it continued to display a giant neon likeness of her outside the building, modified so that the figure appeared to be dressed in a cancan outfit.)

In 1964, the year she first danced topless, she underwent twenty weeks of silicone injections that increased her breast size to forty-four inches. In 1965 she and other topless entertainers were arrested for "lewd conduct." However, after deliberating for only nineteen minutes, the jury acquitted them. By 1972 Doda was earning $700 per week for her nude shows.

California enacted a law in 1969 which held that local communities could ban topless dancing and topless establishments. In addition, the Supreme Court upheld a 1970 California regulation that allowed revoking liquor licenses of establishments that featured performers imitating acts of "gross sexuality."

In 1988 Doda initiated a sexual fantasy telephone service. She also sings with a band.

Sarah Read Adamson Dolley

First woman intern (1851); first president of a dispensary for needy women and children (1886).

Born Schuylkill Meeting, Pennsylvania, March 11, 1829; died Rochester, New York, December 27, 1909.

In 1847 Dolley's uncle, Dr. Hiram Corson, took her into his office to study medicine as his apprentice. She then applied to several medical schools in Philadelphia but was rejected. Finally, she was admitted to Central Medical College, Rochester, New York, and graduated after attending only two series of lectures. At twenty-two she began her internship as a physician at Blockley Hospital, Philadelphia, Pennsylvania, under the sponsorship of her uncle and his colleague, Dr. Isaac Pennypacker, thus becoming the first woman to intern at a hospital.

In 1852 Dolley set up a practice, primarily for women and children. She maintained an active medical practice for several years, part of the time with her husband, Dr. Lester C. Dolley, who was a professor of surgery and anatomy. From 1886 until 1894 she was the president of a dispensary to accommodate needy women and children.

The Women's Society of the state of New York elected her president in 1907.

Margaret Donahue

First woman executive in major league baseball (1926).

Born c. 1893; died Crystal Lake, Illinois, January 30, 1978.

Donahue joined the Chicago Cubs in 1919 as a clerk and typist. By 1926 she had moved considerably higher up the ladder to corporate secretary, thus becoming the first woman executive in major league baseball. Finally, in 1950, she became vice president.

Mary H. Donlon

First woman to be editor-in-chief of a law review (1919); first to be appointed to the federal bench from New York State (1955).

Born Utica, New York, 1894; died Tucson, Arizona, March 5, 1977.

After Donlon graduated from the Utica Free Academy, she attended Cornell University Law School in Ithaca, New York. She edited three issues of the *Cornell Law Quarterly*

(November, 1919; January, 1920; March, 1920). In 1921 she earned an LL.B. degree and was admitted to the bar the same year.

In 1928 she began practicing law in New York City as a partner in the firm Burke and Burke. In 1940, running on the Republican ticket, she was defeated in a race for the U.S. congressman-at-large from New York State. After that, she became active in national as well as state Republican campaigns. In 1944 she became the first woman to head a resolutions subcommittee at a Republican National Convention. She was given a lifetime appointment as a U.S. Customs Court judge in 1955, thus becoming the first woman from New York named to the federal bench. (See also Genevieve Cline.)

Donlon received an honorary doctor of laws degree in 1947 from Skidmore College, Saratoga Springs, New York. And in 1961, Cornell University, where she served as a trustee for twenty-nine years, named a dormitory in her honor.

Susan Miller Dorsey

First woman to be made honorary life president of the National Education Association (1934); first to be an assistant superintendent of the Los Angeles, California, city schools (1913).

Born Penn Yan, New York, February 16, 1857; died Los Angeles, California, February 5, 1946.

Dorsey was named honary life president of the National Education Association in recognition of her forty-year career in education. She began her teaching career soon after her graduation from Vassar College, Poughkeepsie, New York, where she earned a B.A. degree in classics (1877). She taught until she married Patrick W. Dorsey in 1881. They moved to Los Angeles, California, where she became a social welfare worker, then a teacher (1893).

Dorsey's husband deserted her in 1894, taking their only child, a son, with him. She continued her teaching career, now at Los Angeles High School, where she rose to vice principal in 1902. She served in that position until 1913, when she was appointed the assistant superintendent of the Los Angeles school system, the first woman to hold that position. In 1920 she was appointed superintendent of the Los Angeles school system, thus becoming the second woman in the United States to head a metropolitan school system. (See also Ella Flagg Young.)

Mother Mary Katharine Drexel

Founder of Sisters of the Blessed Sacrament for Indians and Colored People (1891).

Born Philadelphia, Pennsylvania, November 26, 1858; died Cornwells Heights, Pennsylvania, March 3, 1955.

Born Katharine Mary Drexel, she was a member of a wealthy, altruistic family. After her parents died, Drexel and her two sisters inherited $14 million. Following a suggestion made to her by Pope Leo XIII, with whom she had a personal audience in 1887, she decided to devote her life to missions. She also decided to use part of her fortune to found a new religious order. In 1889 she entered the novitiate of the Sisters of Mercy (Pittsburgh, Pennsylvania) and, after taking her final vows, founded the Sister of the Blessed Sacrament for Indians and Colored People in 1891. A year later the motherhouse was established at Cornwells Heights, Pennsylvania. Drexel received formal approval for the order in 1913.

She directed all aspects of the order's work for forty years. At the time of her death, the order had grown to 501 sisters living in fifty-one convents. Three houses of social service and sixty-one schools had been established, including a boarding school for Pueblos (Santa Fe, New Mexico), where four of the first sisters of the order went to teach in 1894, and a school for black girls (Rock Castle, Virginia), instituted in 1899. In 1915 the order founded Xavier University (New Orleans, Louisiana).

In 1964 the first stage of Mother Mary Katharine's beatification process began. In 1973 her religious writings were approved, the next step in the process. At the time of this writing, there is no evidence that she has been proclaimed blessed by papal decree.

Florence West Duckering

One of the first two women to be admitted to the American College of Surgeons (ACS) (1914).

Born Sussex, England, August 22, 1869; died Peterborough, New Hampshire, October 25, 1951.

Duckering graduated from Tufts College Medical School (Boston, Massachusetts) in 1901. She and Alice Gertrude Bryant (see entry) were the first two women admitted to the American College of Surgeons (1914). They were among approximately 1,000 candidates to be admitted to the ACS, which was organized the previous year.

Alene B. Duerk

First woman to be appointed admiral in the U.S. Navy (1972).

Born Defiance, Ohio, March 29, 1920.

Duerk graduated from the Toledo Hospital School of Nursing, Toledo, Ohio, in 1941 and earned a B.S. degree from the Frances Payne Bolton School of Nursing at Western Reserve University (now Case Western Reserve University), Cleveland, Ohio, in 1948. Commissioned as an ensign in the U.S. Navy in 1943, Duerk served both stateside and on a hospital ship in the Pacific. Following that service she moved to reserve status. In 1951, during the Korean War, her reserve unit was called back to active duty. Two years later, she transferred from the reserves to the regular Navy. There she taught nursing classes and served in various nursing roles.

In 1965 she became director of nursing at the San Diego Naval Hospital Corps School, San Diego, California. Following her service in San Diego, she was the chief of nursing services at Great Lakes Naval Hospital (1968–70).

Duerk became head of the Navy Nurse Corps in 1970 and was promoted from captain to rear admiral in 1972. She retired in 1975.

Marjorie Dumont

First woman to wed in an airplane (1919).

Born Yorkville, Indiana, date unknown.

On May 31, 1919, Dumont and U.S. Army Lieutenant R. W. Meade of Cincinnati, Ohio, were married in a giant Handley-Page bomber cruising at 2,000 feet over 10,000 spectators at Ellington Field, Houston, Texas. The wedding party of twelve cruised for twenty minutes after the ceremony.

Natalie Dunn

First woman world champion in figure roller skating (1976).

Born San Antonio, Texas, 1956.

At the age of twenty, Dunn became the first U.S. woman to win the world championship in figure roller skating in Rome, Italy, in 1976.

She won her first figure skating event when she was seven years old; by the time she was sixteen she held the national singles title. Dunn was one of only a few women skaters who could do the triple Salchow jump and triple Mapes, two of the most intricate and difficult maneuvers. After winning the world championship in Rome, Dunn was able to defend her crown successfully the following year in Montreal, Canada. By 1979 she had won the world championship title three times and the U.S. national championship title nine times.

Jean (Gilligan) Dunne

First woman stock specialist on any U.S. stock exchange (1973).

Born 1951.

Dunne, who works for Gilligan, Will and Company, where her father is a senior partner, joins other stock specialists in buying and selling orders in an attempt to stabilize the market in their stocks. She has to risk her firm's funds as part of the process. Dunne has worked as a wire clerk on the stock exchange floor of the American Stock Exchange (AMEX) and in the back office of Gilligan, Will and Company.

Loula Dunne

First woman director of the American Public Welfare Association (APWA) (1950).

Born Grove Hill, Alabama, date unknown.

Dunn started her career in the realm of public welfare even before she studied social work. From 1916 to 1917 she taught illiterate children living in the rural areas of Alabama. She studied social work at Alabama Polytechnical Institute in 1917 and, after a hiatus in 1923 during which she worked, continued her studies in that field at the University of North Carolina, Wilmington. From 1923 to 1933 she was a caseworker, assisting the director of the Alabama State Child Welfare Department. After that, she worked in various public welfare positions, including that of regional social worker and director of employment in six southern states.

She became director of the American Public Welfare Association in 1950, after serving as the commissioner of the Alabama State Department of Public Welfare from 1937 to 1950. She was vice president of three organizations: the American Association of Social Workers (1935–36), the Child Welfare League (1940–50), and the American Society for Public Administration (1946–47). In 1959 she was appointed one of only twelve members of a federal advisory panel on coordination of federal and state welfare benefits.

Emily Dunning (Barringer)

First woman ambulance surgeon (1903).

Born Scarsdale, New York, September 27, 1876; died New Milford, Connecticut, April 8, 1961.

Dunning, after earning a medical degree from Cornell University Medical School (New York, New York) and graduating second in her class, became an ambulance surgeon for Gouverneur Hospital in New York City, where she was also the first woman to do emergency work. Upon learning of her appointment, medical interns throughout the city petitioned against it. However, when she answered her first emergency call in a horse-drawn ambulance on June 29, 1903, the doctors and others at Gouverneur Hospital cheered her.

She had made an earlier attempt to join the staff at Gouverneur Hospital, scoring the second-highest grade on the qualifying exam, but had been turned down because she was a woman. She then became an assistant to Mary C. Putnam Jacobi, M.D. (see entry).

Her second attempt to join the Gouverneur Hospital staff was successful, and she served a two-year internship and residency there. In 1905 she became a member of the hospital staff, acting as a house surgeon, the first woman to serve in that position in a New York City hospital.

After marrying Benjamin S. Barringer, M.D., she retired from her private practice in New York City, but took up medical practice again later. In all, she practiced medicine for fifty years, including clinical work in Vienna and Austria.

Dunning chaired a special commission of the American Medical Women's Association (1943). The group was successful in its lobbying for legislation to allow women medical doctors to secure commissions in the U.S. Army and Navy.

Doriot Anthony Dwyer

First woman appointed to the first chair in a major orchestra (1952).

Born Streator, Illinois, date unknown.

Dwyer, who began playing the flute when she was eight years old, graduated from the Eastman School of Music, Rochester, New York, with a B.S. in music in 1943. She joined the Washington National Symphony Orchestra; two years later she joined the Los Angeles Philharmonic as the second flutist. She played with that orchestra until 1952, when she became the Boston Symphony Orchestra's first-chair flutist.

Dwyer has also performed as a solo recitalist, including a notable performance at the Berkshire Music Festival, at Tanglewood, Massachusetts, in 1972. She also gave concert recitals at New York City's Alice Tully Hall in 1980 and again in 1982.

The great-grandniece of Susan B. Anthony, founder of the National Council for Women, Dwyer was named to the Women's Hall of Fame of the Seneca Falls Historical Society, Seneca Falls, New York, in 1974.

Amelia (Mary) Earhart (Putnam)

First woman to fly solo across the Atlantic Ocean (1932); first to be a transatlantic plane passenger (1928); first to set an altitude record in an autogiro (a rotary-wing aircraft) (18,451 feet, on April 8, 1931); first to pilot an autogiro carrying passengers (1930); first to make a solo transcontinental round trip flight (1928); participant in the first Women's Air Derby (1929); founder of the Ninety-nines, an organization of women flyers (see entry) (1929); first to fly from Hawaii to the United States mainland, Oakland, California (1935); first to receive the Distinguished Flying Cross (1932).

Born Atchison, Kansas, July 24, 1897; presumed dead in the Pacific Ocean near Howland Island, July 2, 1937.

Earhart's first job was as a nurse in Toronto, Canada, caring for casualties of World War I. After the war she was briefly a premedical student at Columbia University (New York, New York), and was taught to fly by Neta Snook—a trailblazing woman pilot. Earhart soloed for the first time in southern California, June, 1921, in a Kinner Airster, and a year later—on her twenty-fifth birthday—she bought her first plane, a Kinner Canary.

After moving back to New England to be with her mother, Earhart continued to fly. On June 17, 1928—flying with pilot Wilmer Stultz and mechanic Lou Gordon—she took off from Trepassey Bay, Newfoundland, on the flight that would bring her into

the public spotlight: the first flight of a woman across the Atlantic Ocean. She returned to gala receptions and ticker-tape parades. Earhart became aviation editor of *Cosmopolitan* magazine and a vice president of Ludington Airlines.

In 1929 Earhart became a cofounder and first president of the Ninety-nines, an international organization of women pilots. She married publisher George Putnam on February 7, 1931, and thereafter he became her manager and publicist. In May, 1932, piloting a Lockheed Vega monoplane, Earhart became the first woman to fly solo across the Atlantic.

Purdue University, Lafayette, Indiana, hired Earhart as a counselor for young women and an aviation consultant. The university trustees also bought her a Lockheed Electra, with twin Pratt & Whitney Wasp engines.

It was in the Electra that Earhart and Freddie Noonan, her navigator and a veteran Pan American World Airways pilot, took off from Miami, Florida, on June 1, 1937, to attempt their round-the-world flight. On June 29, Earhart and Noonan landed their silver monoplane at Lae, New Guinea, after a flight from Port Darwin on the northern coast of Australia. Two days later, the pair took off for tiny Howland Island, 2,550 miles away in the middle of the

Pacific. The Coast Guard cutter *Itasca* reported contact with Earhart at 3:20 P.M. Eastern Daylight Time on July 2; she reported approximately thirty minutes of fuel remaining, and she had not sighted land. It was the last contact with Earhart and Noonan. The Coast Guard estimated that she had been within 100 miles of Howland Island and was forced down into the Pacific—perhaps because she had overshot the island or run out of fuel.

No trace of the plane or its passengers was found, and they were presumed dead, but rumors and theories about their disappearance circulated for years afterward. One popular theory held that Earhart and Noonan had been taken prisoner and killed by the Japanese. The story apparently came from some U.S. veterans of the war in the Pacific and from natives of Saipan—under Japanese control at the time—who said the pair had been imprisoned there.

Among the awards Earhart won in her lifetime were the Distinguished Flying Cross, the Harmon International Trophy, the Gold Medal of the National Geographic Society, and a $10,000 award for flying from Hawaii to the United States mainland. In July, 1963, a commemorative postage stamp bearing her picture was issued by the U.S. Post Office.

Earhart appeared in the first *New York Times* crossword puzzle on February 15, 1942. Her name, in 21 Across, was the answer to the clue, "Flier lost in Pacific, 1937." (See also Theodosia Burr.)

Penny Ann Early

First woman to play professional basketball (1969).

Dates unknown.

She played a promotional game as a member of the Kentucky Colonels of the American Basketball Association, making a "cameo" appearance as a public relations stunt in her only game.

Early, an aspiring jockey on the thoroughbred racing circuit, was scheduled to be the first woman to ride in a professional thoroughbred race at Churchill Downs in Louisville, Kentucky, in November, 1968—but her horse was scratched from the race. Two days later she was scheduled to ride again, but was replaced when the male jockeys threatened a boycott. The following year, on April 19, 1969, Early rode the favorite, Royal Fillet, to a four and three-quarter length victory (in horse racing, a "length" refers to the length of the horse) in the Lady Godiva Handicap at Suffolk Downs, Massachusetts. It was the first parimutuel thoroughbred race open only to female jockeys.

Crystal Eastman

First woman to draft workers' compensation legislation (c. 1910).

Born Marlborough, Massachusetts, June 25, 1881; died Erie, Pennsylvania, July 8, 1928.

As secretary and only woman member of the New York State Employers' Liability Commission, and also as author of *Work Accidents and the Law* (1910), Eastman was a powerful force behind the drafting of the early workers' compensations laws.

Eastman, who graduated from Vassar College, Poughkeepsie, New York (1903), earned a master's degree in sociology at Columbia University, New York, New York (1904) and an LL.B. degree from the New York University Law School, New York, New York (1907).

Sister of Max Eastman, a prominent writer, editor, and socialist, she was cofounder of the Congressional Union for Woman Suffrage, predecessor of the National Woman's party (1913). From 1917 to 1921 Eastman was editor of the *Liberator,* a radical journal previously called the *Masses.* Her interests in workers and socialist causes continued after she and her family moved to England in 1921.

Linda A. Eastman

*First woman to head a
metropolitan library system in
the United States (1918).*

Born Oberlin, Ohio, July 17,
1867; died Cleveland, Ohio, April 5,
1963.

Also a cofounder of the Ohio Library Association (1895) and its first
woman president (1903), Eastman
was in 1918 unanimously elected director of the Cleveland Public Library.

Eastman grew up in Cleveland,
Ohio, where she attended the Cleveland Normal School and graduated
from public high school. She became
a teacher, staying with that career
until 1892. While she was teaching,
the second library in Cleveland was
set up in her schoolroom.

In 1892 she began her career in
the library system by working for the
Cleveland Public Library. In part, she
resumed her role as teacher when
she organized and became an instructor in library administration at
the School of Library Science at Western Reserve University, Cleveland,
Ohio.

Eastman became president of the
American Library Association in
1928.

Peggy (Margaret) O'Neale (or O'Neill) Eaton

*First and only woman whose
virtue was the subject of a
Cabinet meeting (1829).*

Born Washington, D.C., December
3, 1799; died Washington, D.C., November 8, 1879.

The daughter of a tavern keeper,
Peggy O'Neale became the wife of
John Henry Eaton, secretary of war
and a member of President Andrew
Jackson's cabinet. She became the
object of gossip in Washington, D.C.,
as early as 1821; at that time she was
married to John Timberlake, but she
was linked romantically with John
Eaton, then senator from Tennessee.
Many wives in the higher social circles vowed not to associate with a
woman whose reputation was as besmeared as hers. Timberlake died in
1828, and Peggy and Eaton were
married in January, 1829. After more
rumors spread, the cabinet members
held a session in September, 1829, to
discuss the issue of Peggy Eaton's
virtue. After the session, President
Jackson—whose own wife, Rachel,
had been what he vowed was an innocent target of slander—declared
Eaton innocent. In January, 1830, he
mandated that members of the cabinet who disapproved of her resign.
His mandate, and the squabbling

among the cabinet members, became public knowledge; there were several cabinet resignations, including that of John Eaton.

The Eatons lived in Florida from 1834 to 1836, during which time he was governor of the state. He was ambassador to Spain from 1836 to 1840. Afterwards they returned to Washington, D.C., where he practiced law until his death in 1856.

The Eatons had two daughters, both of whom married into Washington society and had children. One of the daughters and her husband died young, leaving grandmother Peggy with four grandchildren to raise. Peggy, who had attended dancing school when she was young, and whom Dolley Madison had declared the best dancer at a dancing students' ball, hired an Italian dancing teacher for her grandchildren. In 1859 she became the topic of Washington society gossip once more when she married the dancing teacher, Antonio Buchignani, who was only nineteen years old. Buchignani cheated her out of the fortune that John Eaton had left to her, and in 1866 he ran away with Peggy's youngest granddaughter. Peggy and Buchignani were divorced in 1868, and he married the granddaughter the same year.

Elsie Eaves

First woman admitted to full membership in the American Society of Civil Engineers (ASCE) (1927); first to be admitted to the American Association of Cost Engineers (AACE) (1957); first to receive AACE's Award of Merit (1967); first to be made an honorary lifetime member of ASCE (1979).

Born Idaho Springs, Colorado, 1898; died Roslyn, Long Island, March 27, 1983.

Eaves graduated from the University of Colorado, Boulder, in 1920, with a B.S. degree in civil engineering. She then followed a career with the U.S. Bureau of Public Roads, the Colorado State Highway Department, and the Denver and Rio Grande Railroad.

In 1927 she held the position of

assistant manager of market surveys for *Engineering News-Record,* a weekly publication, and in 1945 she became the manager of *Business News.* She retired in 1963, having spent nearly thirty-seven years in the publications field. After her retirement from publishing, she was adviser on housing costs to the National Commission on Urban Affairs and on construction cost reporting in Iran to the International Executive Service Corps.

Eaves, who was a charter member of the Society of Women Engineers, was given honorary lifetime membership in the American Society of Civil Engineers, the society's highest honor (1979). The University of Colorado gave Eaves its highest alumni award, the George Norlin Silver Medal, in 1974.

Mabelle E. Ebert

First woman whose marriage ceremony was broadcast over the wireless (1920).

Dates unknown.

In 1920 U.S. Navy Seaman John R. Wichman was stationed aboard the U.S.S. *Birmingham,* on duty in the Pacific Ocean. Ebert was in a Detroit, Michigan, church. The marriage ceremony was telephoned to a local telegraph office, which transmitted it to the Great Lakes Naval Training Station, which in turn sent it via wireless to Wichman's ship.

Mary (Morse) Baker Eddy

Founder of the Christian Science Association (1876) and the Church of Christ (Scientist) (1879).

Born Bow, New Hampshire, July 16, 1821; died Chestnut Hill, Massachusetts, December 3, 1910.

Eddy was deeply influenced by the teachings of Phineas Parkhurst Quimby (1802–66), a blacksmith's son, clockmaker, itinerant "mesmerist" (hypnotist), and healer from Lebanon, New Hampshire. Eddy came to believe that she had been chosen to carry to the world Quimby's message—as she modified it—that disease was really a false *belief,* and that its cure therefore lay in *mental* prescriptions. Quimby also believed that one could cure illness by means of "telepathic magnetism," even if the healer were separated from the patient by great distances.

Eddy believed that Quimby's ministry actually relieved some of her illnesses and ailments. Inspired by his actions and left to spread the word alone after Quimby's death in 1866, Eddy wrote *The Science of Man* (1870). In the fall of 1875, two of her disciples published the first edition of *Science and Health*—the book which was to become the gospel of the Christian Science religion. It went through 382 editions in her lifetime alone.

After the Christian Science Association and the Church of Christ (Scientist) had been established, Eddy obtained a charter for her Massachusetts Metaphysical College (Lynn, Massachusetts) as an institution that could grant degrees in Christian Science. The school surrendered its charter in 1889, but during the period of its existence, Eddy personally and virtually alone instructed over 600 students in Christian Science.

In 1883 she founded the monthly *Christian Science Journal,* in 1898 the weekly *Christian Science Sentinel,* and in 1908 the Christian Science Church's daily newspaper, *The Christian Science Monitor.*

Marian Wright Edelman

Founder and president of the Children's Defense Fund (1973).

Born Bennettsville, South Carolina, June 6, 1939.

Edelman, who is best known as a leading advocate for children's rights, founded and became president of the Children's Defense Fund, which addresses such issues as teen-

age pregnancy, early death among infants, and child abuse.

Having earned a B.A. degree from Spelman College, Atlanta, Georgia (1960), Edelman decided to continue her education. She won a John Hay Whitney Fellowship to attend Yale Law School, New Haven, Connecticut, and earned an LL.B. degree there (1963).

After finishing law school, she served an internship in a program set up by the National Association for the Advancement of Colored People (NAACP) Legal Defense and Education Fund, Inc. She received training for one year and then was paid a salary to set up a practice in the South. She opened a law office in Jackson, Mississippi, where she focused on civil rights efforts. She applied for admission to the Mississippi bar and became the first black woman to be admitted (1965).

Edelman was active in the Head Start program in Mississippi, defending it against political attack. Head Start launched a project called the Child Development Group of Mississippi (CDGM), which received a $500,000 grant; it created more than 2,000 jobs in the state of Mississippi and reportedly benefited approximately 12,000 children in its first year.

The daughter of a Baptist minister, Edelman and her husband, Peter, who teaches at the Georgetown University Law Center, Washington, D.C., have three children. Among other awards, she received the Black Women's Forum Award (1980), the Albert Schweitzer Humanitarian Prize (1987), and the Hubert Humphrey Civil Rights Award (1989). She has received honorary degrees from several colleges and universities, including Yale University, New Haven, Connecticut (1963); Smith College, Northampton, Massachusetts (1969); and the University of Miami, Miami, Florida (1989).

Gertrude Ederle

First woman to swim the English Channel (1926).

Born New York, New York, October 23, 1906.

Ederle was always a fast swimmer—at the age of twelve she set a new 800-yard freestyle record of thirteen minutes, nineteen seconds. She and other members of the New York Women's Swimming Association that year introduced the six-beat crawl stroke, replacing the old four-beat crawl. In 1922, competing against fifty-one other women, Ederle won a three-and-one-half-mile race across New York Bay. In the 1924 Olympics, she was a member of the winning 400-meter freestyle relay team. She also placed third in the 100-meter and 400-meter freestyle events. In 1924 alone, Ederle set eighteen world records; between 1921 and 1925 she held twenty-nine national and world records before she became a professional swimmer.

On August 6, 1926, Ederle set out to swim across the English Channel. Although the channel's width is twenty-one miles, stormy weather and turbulent waters forced Ederle to traverse a much greater distance of thirty-five miles, from Cap Gris-Nez, France, to Dover, England. Her time was fourteen hours and thirty-one minutes—one hour and fifty-nine minutes faster than any man had swum it before her. Unfortunately, Ederle's hearing was permanently and severely impaired by the stormy waves that she navigated during her long swim.

When Ederle returned to New York

City after the channel swim, she was greeted by a crowd of 2 million people who cheered her in a ticker-tape parade up Broadway. Afterwards, she earned $2,000 weekly on the vaudeville circuit, giving swimming exhibitions and answering questions about her feat.

In 1953 Ederle was presented the Helms Foundation Hall of Fame Award, and in 1965 she became one of the first twenty-one inductees into the International Swimming Hall of Fame.

Sarah Emma Edmonds

First and only woman officially inducted into the Grand Army of the Republic (1897), an organization of Civil War veterans.

Born New Brunswick, Canada, December, 1841; died La Porte, Texas, September 5, 1898.

Edmonds, whose father was known as a tyrant, ran away from home, dressed as a man, adopted the name Franklin Thompson, and became a Bible peddler. When the Civil War broke out, Edmonds/Thompson was living in Michigan. In 1861 she enlisted in the Second Michigan Regiment of the Volunteer Infantry. She saw active duty in Virginia, which included the first Bull Run battle and the first peninsular campaign of 1862. She also served in a hospital for the wounded, was a mail carrier, and became a colonel's aide. She spied behind the Confederate lines at least twice, one of the times being asked to disguise herself as a woman! In 1863 she deserted the infantry, but returned as a *female* nurse with the U.S. Christian Commission.

In 1882 she applied for a pension due her as a veteran, writing to her former infantry comrades to confirm her military history. The veterans invited her to their reunion in 1884, where they testified in her behalf. In 1884 Congress granted her a pension of twelve dollars per month.

She wrote her memoirs, *Nurse and Spy in the Union Army,* in 1865.

Sister Elizabeth M. Edmunds

First nun to be commissioned as a U.S. Navy officer (1973).

Born Shamokin, Pennsylvania, c. 1941.

A member of the order of the Sisters of Mercy, she was commissioned as a navy lieutenant upon her graduation from Pennsylvania University Medical School (Philadelphia). In 1975 she interned, and from 1976 to 1978 was a resident, at the Good Samaritan Hospital, Dayton, Ohio. Later, Edmunds established, and still maintains, a practice in family medicine in Reading, Pennsylvania.

Katherine Philips Edson

First woman on the executive committee of the National Municipal League (1912).

Born Kenton, Ohio, January 12, 1870; died Pasadena, California, November 5, 1933.

In 1890 Edson traveled to Illinois to study voice at the music conservatory in Chicago. While training there, she married. A few years later, she and her husband moved to California, where she became active in public health matters, as well as woman suffrage, which had gained some success in that state.

In 1912 she became an agent for the State Bureau of Labor Statistics, where she spent most of her time concentrating on minimum-wage legislation and workday length for student nurses. She also became the first woman named to the executive committee of the National Municipal League (founded in 1894, and now called the National Civil League), a consortium made up of organizations and individuals working to improve state and local governments and to develop techniques for effective citizen action. From 1913 to 1931 she was a member of the State Industrial Welfare Commission. Four years of that time (1920–24) she was one of eight members of the Republican party's National Executive Committee.

From 1932 until her death she was a member of the board of directors of the National League of Women Voters.

Rosa Smith Eigenmann

First woman ichthyologist to gain prominence (1888).

Born Monmouth, Illinois, October 7, 1858; died San Diego, California, January 12, 1947.

In 1880 Eigenmann published a paper on fish in the San Diego area, marking the first of more than twenty papers she would publish in the field of ichthyology and cryptogamic botany.

She attended a business college in San Francisco, then Indiana University in Bloomington (1880–82), and finally Harvard University in Cambridge, Massachusetts (1887–88), where she studied cryptogamic botany. She also reported for the *San Diego Union* (1886).

During some of her travels, she met Carl H. Eigenmann, whom she married in 1887. After 1893 she all but abandoned her profession, limiting herself to editing her husband's manuscripts; she concentrated on raising their five children, while her husband continued his career as a professor of zoology at Stanford University, Palo Alto, California.

Amy Eilberg

First woman ordained as a rabbi in Conservative Judaism (1985).

Born Philadelphia, Pennsylvania, October 12, 1954.

At the time of her ordination, Eilberg lived in Bloomington, Indiana. She held two master's degrees: one from the Jewish Theological Seminary (New York, New York) (1978), and the other from the Smith College

School for Social Work (Northampton, Massachusetts) (1984).

In February, 1985, the Rabbinical Assembly of the century-old Conservative movement amended its constitution to permit the ordination of female rabbis, and the following May Eilberg was ordained along with eighteen new male rabbis from the Jewish Theological Seminary.

She said that she intended to exercise all ritual privileges and obligations as a rabbi. For example, she would wear the prayer shawl and phylacteries (leather boxes containing scriptures)—practices previously reserved for men.

Eilberg, whose husband was professor of religious studies at Indiana University (Bloomington) at the time of her ordination, served as chaplain at Methodist Hospital, Indianapolis, Indiana. At the time of this writing she is a chaplain in the department of chaplaincy services at Stanford

University Hospital, Palo Alto, California.

Ruth Eisemann-Schier

First woman on the Federal Bureau of Investigation's Ten Most Wanted list of fugitives (1968–69).

Born Honduras, c. 1942.

On December 17, 1968, Eisemann-Schier and her partner in crime, Gary Krist, kidnapped Barbara Jean Mackle, a student at Emory University in Atlanta, Georgia. The abduction occurred at a motel in Georgia. Eighty hours later, Mackle was discovered alive, buried in a box about twenty miles northeast of Atlanta. Joint warrants for the arrest of Krist and Eisemann-Schier were then issued. The kidnappers had received a $500,000 ransom, most of which was recovered later.

Krist was captured on December 22 in Florida, apparently having deserted Eisemann-Schier. Eisemann-Schier was put on the FBI's Ten Most Wanted list in January. She was arrested on March 5, 1969, in Norman, Oklahoma, where she was working as a carhop. The FBI traced her there by fingerprints taken when she had applied for a nursing position in a Norman hospital in February.

On May 29, 1969, she was sentenced to seven years in prison. Krist received a life sentence. After serving three years of her sentence, Eisemann-Schier was released from prison in April, 1972. She was immediately deported to Honduras.

Gertrude B. Elion

First woman to achieve the twofold distinction of a Nobel Prize for physiology or medicine (1988) and induction into the National Inventors Hall of Fame (1991).

Born New York, New York, January 23, 1918.

In 1944, when a shortage of men caused by World War II created more job opportunities for women, Elion found employment at Burroughs Wellcome, a pharmaceutical company in Tuckahoe, New York. Initially, she worked as laboratory assistant to Dr. George H. Hitchings but soon became his colleague. Over the next forty years this team was credited with developing many major drugs used to combat a broad spectrum of ailments, including gout, heart disease, leukemia, malaria, and peptic ulcers. Their research also led to the development of acyclovir, effective in treating herpes virus infections, and AZT, the drug often used to combat AIDS. For their work they were awarded the Nobel Prize for physiology or medicine in 1988, an award they shared with British pharmacologist Sir James Whyte Black.

Elion had graduated summa cum laude from Hunter College (New York, New York) with a major in biochemistry (1937); she also earned an M.S. degree from New York University (New York, New York) in 1941. After a period of employment as a high school teacher and food analyst, and then as a research assistant at Johnson & Johnson, Elion was hired by Burroughs Wellcome and began her long association with Hitchings.

Their work together over the years focused on the ways the biochemistry of normal human cells differs from that of cancer cells, parasites, bacteria, and viruses.

Elion officially retired from Burroughs Wellcome in 1983, but continued to work as a research professor of pharmacology at Duke University (Durham, North Carolina) and as a member of the National Cancer Advisory Board and the World Health Organization.

She was awarded honorary doctorates by many colleges and universities, including Hunter College and New York University. In 1968 the American Chemical Society awarded Elion its Garvan Medal.

Since patents are issued for drugs, the developers of new drugs are considered inventors. In recognition of her lifetime of achievements in creating new drugs, Elion was inducted into the National Inventors Hall of Fame in 1991.

Martha May Eliot

First woman to be elected president of the American Public Health Association (1947).

Born Dorchester, Massachusetts, 1891; died Cambridge, Massachusetts, February 14, 1978.

Eliot, a 1913 Phi Beta Kappa graduate of Radcliffe College (Cambridge, Massachusetts), received her M.S. degree from Johns Hopkins University (Baltimore, Maryland) in 1918. She taught at Yale University (New Haven, Connecticut) from 1921 to 1946, and from 1924 to 1956 was an official of the U.S. Children's Bureau. Eliot was on the Harvard University (Cambridge, Massachusetts) faculty from 1956 until her retirement in 1960.

From 1923 to 1926, Eliot and Dr. Edward Park of Yale University developed a cure for rickets: cod-liver oil and sunshine. She introduced the use of social workers in public health programs, and in World War II she headed a federal program called Emergency Maternity and Infant Care, which provided health care and assistance for wives and infants of armed forces personnel. In 1946 Eliot won the Lasker award for her outstanding contributions to medicine in this program.

After serving as president of the American Public Health Association for one term, Eliot was assistant director general of the World Health Organization from 1949 to 1951. In 1964 the American Public Health Association established an annual award in her name to recognize her achievement in maternal and child health.

Elizabeth Lummis Ellet

First woman writer to emphasize the role of women in the development of their country (1848).

Born Sodus Point, New York, c. 1812; died New York, New York, June 3, 1877.

Ellet wrote a three-volume work, *The Women of the American Revolution* (1848–1850), containing 160 biographical sketches of notable women of the revolutionary period.

After attendingd a girls' school in Aurora, New York, she made her publishing debut as a translator at the age of twenty-two. She continued writing and publishing after her marriage in 1835. In addition to the three-volume work, she published at least two more significant works, *Domestic History of the American Revolution* (1850) and *Pioneer Women of the West* (1852).

Maud Howe Elliott

First woman, with her sister Laura Richards (see entry), to win a Pulitzer Prize for biography (1916).

Born South Boston, Massachusetts, November 9, 1854; died Newport, Rhode Island, March 19, 1948.

Elliott, the daughter of Julia Ward Howe (see entry) and Samuel Gridley Howe, studied art and drama in the United States and Europe. She published anonymously a romance novel, *A Newport Aquarelle,* in 1883. Later, she began to write newspaper columns on art, travel narratives, and biographies.

In 1912 she was a leader in the Progressive party, under whose sponsorship President Theodore Roosevelt unsuccessfully sought a third term in office.

Elliott and her sister wrote a biography of their mother, *Julia Ward Howe, 1819–1910* (1915), for which they shared the 1916 Pulitzer Prize for biography. In 1923 Elliott wrote her autobiography, *Three Generations.*

Betty Ellis

First woman to officiate at a professional soccer match (1981).

Born c. 1941.

Ellis served as a linesman in a match on May 10, 1981, between the San Jose Earthquakes from California and the Edmonton Drillers from Alberta, Canada. At that time she was the only woman among 163 North American Soccer League officials. She had started refereeing about 1971 at local matches, then moved up to college and semiprofessional levels.

Theresa West Elmendorf

First woman to be president of the American Library Association (1911).

Born Pardeeville, Wisconsin, 1855; died Buffalo, New York, September 4, 1932.

Also one of the first to be inducted into *Library Journal*'s Library Hall of Fame (1951), Elmendorf graduated from the Milwaukee, Wisconsin, public school system and began her career as an assistant at the library of the Young Men's Association of Milwaukee—which later evolved into a new municipal library.

She became deputy librarian, then head librarian of the Milwaukee Public Library, resigning in 1896 to marry Henry L. Elmendorf of St. Joseph, Missouri, a vice president of the American Library Association (ALA). They moved to Buffalo, New York, where he headed the new Buffalo Public Library; she was his partner and associate but never received public acknowledgment.

Theresa Elmendorf was president of the New York Library Association in 1903/4, vice librarian of the Buffalo Public Library from her husband's death in 1906 until 1926, and in 1911/12 served her history-making term as president of the American Library Association.

Her greatest contribution was in the area of bibliography; her *Classroom Libraries for Public Schools* was published in 1923.

Equal Rights Association, American

First national suffrage association (1866).

The constitution of the American Equal Rights Association (AERA), the first national suffrage association, was adopted on May 10, 1866, in New York City. At the time, the Fourteenth Amendment to the U.S. Constitution was in the process of being

"Election Day" cartoon c. 1909

ratified by the United States; the association decided to support suffrage regardless of color, race, or sex. The group lost in its cause, because woman suffrage did not become part of the amendment.

The president of the association was Lucretia Mott (see entry), and the secretary was Susan B. Anthony (see entry).

In 1869 the AERA split over the question of equal suffrage for blacks. As a result, the National Woman Suffrage Association (NWSA) and the American Woman Suffrage Association (AWSA) formed the National American Woman Suffrage Association (NAWSA) (see Woman Sufrrage Associations).

Carol Esserman

First woman police officer to kill a suspect in the line of duty (1981).

Born c. 1945.

Esserman, a plainclothes officer with the New York City Police Department, fatally shot alleged numbers runner Robert L. Greene in the back as he attempted to escape capture. She and her partner, members of a special anticrime unit, were indicted by the Bronx district attorney, who charged that there had been no evidence that Greene had a gun or that a shot had been fired at the police officers. He also claimed that money allegedly in the victim's possession had disappeared.

The two officers were suspended without pay pending trial, but were acquitted on February 1, 1983. Esserman testified that she fired because Greene had pointed a pistol at her, and that earlier he had fired at her partner.

Susan R. Estrich

First woman to be president of the Harvard Law Review ***(1976); first to manage a major presidential campaign (1987).***

Born Cambridge, Massachusetts, 1952.

Estrich was named president of the *Harvard Law Review* in 1976. The *Review,* founded in 1887, publishes legal news monthly from November to June.

In October, 1987, Estrich was appointed manager of Democratic candidate Michael Dukakis's campaign for the presidency. In order to manage the campaign, she was granted a leave of absence from Harvard University (Cambridge, Massachusetts), where she was a professor in the law school.

Prior to the Dukakis campaign, Estrich had been senior policy advisor to Walter F. Mondale (1984); deputy national issues director for the Edward F. Kennedy presidential campaign (1980); executive director of the Democratic National Platform Committee; special counsel to the Senate Judiciary Committee; and special assistant to Massachusetts Senator Edward F. Kennedy.

A graduate of Wellesley College (Wellesley, Massachusetts) with a major in political science, Estrich is a co-author of *Dangerous Offenders: The Elusive Target of Justice* (1985), and the author of *Real Rape* (1987). Estrich herself was a rape victim.

Dorothy Harrison Wood Eustis

Founder of The Seeing Eye in the United States (1930).

Born Philadelphia, Pennsylvania, May 30, 1886; died New York, New York, September 8, 1946.

Eustis and her first husband, Walter Wood, were successful breeders of dairy cattle. In 1921, six years after Wood's death, she moved to Vevey, Switzerland, where she set up a breeding kennel for dogs. In 1923 she and her second husband, George Eustis, participated in a program that produced a special class of German shepherds. The dogs were exceptionally intelligent, obedient, alert, handsome, and forgiving; they were later trained for police and military duty.

During this period, the Eustises learned of a school in Potsdam, Germany, that trained dogs to serve as guides for blind war veterans. As a result of her excitement about the dogs, Dorothy Eustis wrote an article, "The Seeing Eye," which was published in the *Saturday Evening Post* in 1927.

Eustis and her husband were divorced, and she returned alone to the United States. In 1930 she founded and was the first president of The Seeing Eye in Morristown, New Jersey, a training school for guide dogs for the blind. She participated in the training of the dogs and remained president of the school until 1940, when she was named honorary president. At the time of her death, the school had trained more than 1,300 guide dogs.

Eustis received an honorary degree from the University of Pennsylvania (Philadelphia) (1933) and a gold medal from the National Institute of Social Sciences (1936).

Alice Evans

First woman to be president of the Society of American Bacteriologists (1928); first woman scientist to hold a permanent appointment in the U.S. Dairy Division of the Bureau of Animal Industry (1913).

Born Neath, Pennsylvania, January 29, 1881; died Alexandria, Virginia, September 5, 1975.

Evans is best known for her discovery of the danger of unpasteurized milk, and particularly her study of the role of pasteurization in killing the undulant fever-causing bacterium *Bacillus abortus*. She initially encountered skepticism from other scientists—in part because of her gender and because she had no Ph.D. degree—but in time her theories were confirmed by the scientific community, and in the 1930s the pasteurization of all milk was mandated for the entire U.S. dairy industry.

Evans had contracted undulant fever herself while working as an assistant bacteriologist in the hygienic laboratory of the U.S. Public Health Service (later the National Institutes of Health). The illness ravaged her for seven years.

Evans attended Susquehanna Collegiate Institute (Towanda, Pennsylvania) from 1898 to 1901. She taught for four years before completing her B.S. degree in bacteriology at Cornell University (Ithaca, New York) in 1909. She then went to the University of Wisconsin (Madison), where she was granted an M.S. degree in bacteriology in 1910. She did additional graduate work at George Washington University (Washington, D.C.) and the University of Chicago (Chicago, Illinois).

Employed in 1910 by the Dairy Division of the U.S. Department of Agriculture to study the bacteriology of milk and cheese, she was appointed an assistant bacteriologist with the U.S. Public Health Service in 1918, remaining there until her retirement as a senior bacteriologist in 1945.

In 1928 Evans became the first woman to be president of the Society of American Bacteriologists (founded 1899, now the American Society for Microbiology). The society promotes improved education in microbiology and encourages the highest professional and ethical standards. It also lobbies for sound regulatory policies with regard to microbiology.

Evans served from 1925 to 1931 as a member of the Committee on Infectious Abortion. In 1930 she was a delegate to the International Microbiological Congress in Paris, France, and from 1945 to 1957 she served as honorary president of the Inter-American Committee on Brucellosis. In 1975 Evans was named an honorary member of the American Society for Microbiology. She was awarded an honorary degree in medicine from the Woman's Medical College of Pennsylvania (Philadelphia) in 1934, and an honorary doctorate of science from both the University of Wisconsin in 1936 and Wilson College (Chambersburg, Pennsylvania) in 1936.

(Baby) Evans

First child to be born in an airplane (1929).

Mrs. T. W. Evans gave birth to her daughter in an airplane flying over Miami, Florida.

Beatrix Fairfax *(see Marie Manning)*

Phoebe Fairgrave *(see Phoebe Fairgrave Omlie)*

Harriet Farley (Donlevy)

First woman editor of a woman's labor magazine (1842).

Born Claremont, New Hampshire, February 18, 1813; died New York, New York, November 12, 1907.

Farley was teaching at an academy in Atkinson, New Hampshire, where her father, a clergyman, was the principal, when she decided to go to work in a textile mill. She said she wanted a liberating experience, so in 1837 she began working at a mill in Lowell, New Hampshire, where most of the workers were female.

Three years later, she wrote an article for *The Lowell Offering,* a magazine written for, and by, women who worked in a textile mill. She defended the mill owners against the charge that they were causing the female workers to suffer. In 1842 a local newspaper began to publish *The Lowell Offering* on a monthly basis, and Farley left the mill to become full-time editor of it. She chose to eschew all controversy and, appearing to ignore the widely publicized disputes over wages and working conditions in places such as the textile mills, concentrated on things of a literary and inspirational nature. The magazine went under in 1845.

Farley also published a compilation of her writings, *Shells from the Strand of the Sea of Genius* (1847), *Happy Nights at Hazel Nook,* a book for children (1852), and her last book, *Fancy's Frolics* (1880).

Farley married John I. Donlevy in 1854, and they had one child. Donlevy disapproved of his wife's working, which is reportedly the reason she spent the following fifty years or more quietly tucked away.

Margaret Petherbridge Farrar

First woman to produce a crossword-puzzle book (1924); first to be editor of **The New York Times** *crossword puzzles (1942).*

Born Brooklyn, New York, March 23, 1897; died New York, New York, June 11, 1984.

In 1924 Farrar and two colleagues at the New York *World*—F. G. Hartswick and Prosper Buranelli—produced the first crossword-puzzle book ever published. (The publisher was Simon & Schuster in New York City.) The book was an instant success and sold approximately 400,000 copies the first year it was in print.

Farrar had begun working for the New York *World* in 1919. As a secretary in the Sunday department, she was in charge of the weekly crossword puzzles.

In 1942, after several years of experience with crosswords, she pioneered and edited the Sunday *New York Times Magazine* crossword puzzles, the first to be offered by that newspaper. The *Times* Sunday editor at that time, Lester Markel, held several meetings with Farrar, during which they considered the launching of crossword puzzles. Apparently one reason for inaugurating the puzzles was to give the reading audience some relaxation during the gloomy wartime. Farrar designed the number and layout of the puzzles, hoping to enlist the interest of a wide variety of readers and puzzle solvers. The first puzzle, published on February 15, 1942, was a huge success. Its subject matter was timely. For example, one answer to a clue was "Wavell," referring to a famous British general who for some months in 1942 was the supreme commander of the Allies in the Far East. Another answer was "Amelia"—the famous woman pilot, Amelia Earhart, who had disappeared in her airplane in 1937 (see entry).

Farrar, who graduated from Smith College, Northampton, Massachusetts (1919), married John Farrar, cofounder of Farrar, Straus & Giroux, publishers, in 1926. She remained at the *Times,* and in 1950 the newspaper began offering daily crossword puzzles, also under her editorship. She retired in 1968.

Rebecca Ann Latimer Felton

First woman to serve in the U.S. Senate (1922).

Born Decatur, Georgia, June 10, 1835; died Atlanta, Georgia, January 24, 1930.

Rebecca Ann Latimer graduated first in her class from Madison Female College (Madison, Georgia) in 1852. A year later, on October 11, 1853, she married the commencement speaker, William Harrell Felton, a physician and Methodist clergyman. The couple bought a farm near Cartersville, Georgia. Felton gave birth to two sons and a daughter. The daughter died in infancy and, tragically, both sons died of diseases during the Civil War.

After the war, Felton helped her husband rebuild the farm and run a school. She was active in a local temperance club and helped provide aid

for Confederate widows and orphans. She also was successful as her husband's campaign manager and press secretary when he served in the U.S. Congress and in the Georgia state legislature between 1874 and 1894.

Felton acquired a reputation as a formidable woman and substantial public figure. She worked as a newspaper editor, lectured around the state on behalf of women's interests and against the practice of leasing convicts for work, and campaigned with the Woman's Christian Temperance Union in opposition to the liquor trade. She campaigned for prison reform as well. In 1908 both convict leasing and liquor sales were outlawed in Georgia.

Felton also worked on behalf of vocational training for poor white girls. As a result, she was given much of the credit for the establishment in 1915 of the Georgia Training School for Girls (Atlanta).

For thirty years, writing in the *Atlanta Journal* and other newspapers, Felton spoke out in support of various causes, particularly those involving the interests of women. Her columns also carried suggestions about farming and household management. Less palatable were her endorsements of some of the prejudices of her day, as she inveighed against Catholics, Jews, evolution, and child labor laws. She once suggested the mass lynching of black males as a way of discouraging rape.

In 1920, in a series of pieces for the *Atlanta Sunday American,* Felton advocated isolationism, opposing President Wilson and the League of Nations. Her articles helped get Thomas E. Watson elected senator and fellow isolationist Thomas Hardwick elected governor.

Senator Watson, a Democrat, died in 1922; Felton, also a Democrat, was appointed for one day by the governor to fill Watson's unexpired term. The appointment was a transparent gesture by Hardwick to curry favor with women—since he had opposed suffrage. Congress was not in session, and would not meet again until Watson's successor was elected, so there would be no opportunity for Felton to actually function as senator. Appointed on October 30, she persuaded Senator-elect Walter George to delay presenting his credentials so she could take the oath of office and serve one day—November 21, 1922. Felton was eighty-seven years old. She made one lighthearted speech and gave up her seat, returning to Georgia amid much national publicity.

Hallie (Flanagan) Ferguson *(see Hallie Flanagan)*

Ma (Miriam Amanda) Ferguson

First woman to be elected governor of a U.S. state (1924).

Born Bell County, Texas, June 13, 1875; died Austin, Texas, June 25, 1961.

In 1899 she married James E. Fer-

guson, who later became governor of Texas. During his second term (1917), however, he was impeached and removed from office for misuse of state funds.

At her husband's urging, Ma Ferguson ran for office in 1924. Her platform: to exonerate her husband, to vitiate Ku Klux Klan power, and to bring the state budget under control. She and her husband were nonsmokers and strong Prohibitionists; neither was active on behalf of women's suffrage. She won the Democratic primary in a runoff election, which was tantamount to election in the gubernatorial race.

Once installed, she influenced the Texas legislature into granting her husband "legislative amnesty." Such amnesty was later declared unconstitutional. Thereafter, it was widely said in Texas that Ma Ferguson signed the papers, but "Farmer Jim" was the governor. She granted executive clemency to 3,500 prisoners and pushed through a law forbidding the wearing of masks in public—legislation obviously targeting the Ku Klux Klan. She was not successful, however, in reducing state spending.

After losing in the Democratic primaries of 1926 and 1930, Ferguson was narrowly elected to a second term as governor in 1932. In 1940 she lost in a third bid for the governor's chair.

Ferguson, whose nickname "Ma" was an acronym of her given names, Miriam Amanda, attended a preparatory school called Salado College (Salado, Texas), and Baylor Female College (Belton, Texas), but did not graduate from either school.

Geraldine Anne Ferraro

First woman to be nominated by a major political party as candidate for vice president of the United States (1984); first to be chair of the Democratic Platform Committee (1984).

Born Newburgh, New York, August 26, 1935.

Ferraro, whose mother had moved the family to New York City after their father died in 1943, received a B.A. degree from Marymount Manhattan College (New York, New York) in 1956. From 1956 until 1960 she taught grade school in public schools in Queens, New York, while attending evening law classes at Fordham University (New York, New York), where she received the J.D. degree in 1960. Just after her graduation from law school, she married John Vaccaro, a New York real estate developer, on July 16, 1960.

Ferraro was admitted to the New York State bar in 1961 and worked in private practice in New York City from 1961 until 1974. She served as assistant district attorney for Queens County, New York, from 1974 until 1978, leaving that position in part because her boss paid her less than male colleagues because she was married. Ferraro was admitted to practice before the U.S. Supreme Court in 1978; she also made a successful run, in 1978, for the U.S. House of Representatives as representative from the Ninth District of New York (Queens) and was reelected in 1980 and 1982.

In 1984 Ferraro became the first woman to be named chair of the National Platform Committee of the Democratic party, and a few months later was selected by Walter F. Mondale, the party's presidential candidate, as his running mate and nominee for vice president. During the campaign, Ferraro had to contend with many questions and harsh criticism about her family's finances. The Democratic ticket was defeated by Ronald Reagan, who amassed the highest electoral vote total in the nation's history. Ferraro had not attracted as many women's votes as expected, but women contributed more than $4 million to her campaign.

As a politician, Ferraro is known as a strong proponent of women's rights. She supports federal funding for abortions, especially in cases of rape or incest, despite the fact that her stand has been attacked by Cardinal John J. O'Connor, archbishop of New York. Ferraro argues that although she is a Roman Catholic, it is not right for her to impose her moral views on others. She fought for economic parity for women; in 1981 she cosponsored the Economic Equity Act, intended to accomplish many of the goals of the defeated Equal Rights Amendment.

After her vice-presidential defeat, Ferraro wrote *Ferraro: My Story* (1985). Since 1988 she has been a fellow of the Harvard Institute of Politics, Cambridge, Massachusetts. At the time of this writing, she is in a race for the U.S. Senate, hoping to unseat New York's Republican incumbent Alfonse D'Amato.

Jessie Field (Shambaugh)

Founder of organizations that became the 4-H Club (1901).

Born Shenandoah, Iowa, June 26, 1881; died Clarinda, Iowa, January 15, 1971.

While studying at Western Normal College in Shenandoah, Iowa, Field (born Celestia Josephine Field) taught at a local one-room schoolhouse. There she helped her students form a Boys Corn Club and a Girls Home Club, whose goals were to teach the boys better farming techniques and the girls better home management skills.

When Field became superintendent of schools for Page County, Iowa, in 1906, she set up Corn Clubs and Home Clubs in all 130 of the county's schools. To publicize the clubs, she created a three-leaf clover pin with the letter "H"—standing for Head, Heart, and Hands—on each leaf. As the organization evolved, a fourth "H" was added (1913). It originally represented Home, then later Health. In 1914 the clubs became a national organization—under sponsorship of the Federal Extension Service of the U.S. Department of Agriculture—now known as the 4-H Club.

The club motto is "To make the

best better," and members take a pledge to devote "my Head to clearer thinking, my Heart to greater loyalty, my Hands to larger service, and my Health to better living, for my club, my community, and my country." The 4-H movement has now spread to over fifty countries.

In 1912 Field resigned as school superintendent to take a position in New York City as the YWCA's national secretary for rural and small town activities, remaining until 1917 when she returned to Iowa and married. In her later years, Field served as a national adviser to 4-H groups.

Throughout her career, Field advocated the addition of agriculture to the three R's. She wrote *Farm Arithmetic* (1909), which sought to make rural education relevant. Field also wrote two autobiographies: *The Corn Lady: The Story of a Country Teacher's Life* (1911) and *A Real Country Teacher: The Story of Her Work* (1922).

Pattie Field

First woman in the U.S. consular service (1925).

Born Denver, Colorado, c. 1902.

A graduate of Radcliffe College (Cambridge, Massachusetts), Field was one of seventeen people to pass the State Department competitive exam for consular service in 1925, on her second attempt. Hundreds of people took the exam. She was appointed vice consul in Amsterdam, the Netherlands, on September 2, 1925. As vice consul she assisted the American consul, working to further the commercial interests of the United States and looking after the welfare of U.S. citizens in the Netherlands. Field resigned her position in July, 1929, and left the consular service.

Crystal Fields

First girl to win the national Pitch, Hit, and Run Championship (1980).

Born Cumberland, Maryland, 1969.

The Pitch, Hit, and Run competition, open to children of both sexes and divided by age groups, features three events: hitting for distance, running a base path for speed, and pitching at a target. Winners advance from local to district to divisional matches, then to the final playoff which is held as one of the preliminary events to the annual major league all-star baseball game. On July 18, 1980, at the stadium of the Seattle Mariners baseball team in Seattle, Washington, Fields, eleven years old, defeated seven boys in the nine-to-twelve-year-old age group. An all-star shortstop and outfielder for her Little League team in Cumberland, Maryland, Fields batted .528 in 1979.

Dorothy Fields

First woman to win an Oscar for songwriting (1937); first to be elected to the Songwriters' Hall of Fame (1971).

Born Allenhurst, New Jersey, July 15, 1905; died New York, New York, March 28, 1974.

Fields wrote the Oscar-winning lyrics to Jerome Kern's tune "The Way You Look Tonight," one of the songs in the movie *Swing Time* with Ginger Rogers and Fred Astaire (1936). She had started writing lyrics for Broadway shows in 1928, and over the next forty years she wrote more than 400 songs.

Daughter of Lew Fields of the vaudeville comedy team of Weber and Fields, Dorothy Fields collaborated with her brother, Herbert, as well as with Jimmy McHugh and Arthur Schwartz, composers. She and McHugh wrote songs for the 1928 musical *Blackbirds of 1928*. Performed 518 times, it was the longest-running all-black revue in the history of Broadway, with a cast that included Bill "Bojangles" Robinson. Among their most popular songs

were "I Can't Give You Anything but Love," and "I Must Have That Man."

Fields turned to Hollywood in 1930, writing songs for such movies as *Love in the Rough* (1930), *Dinner at Eight* (1933), and Jerome Kern's *Roberta* (1935). She and her brother wrote songs and libretti for stage musicals by Cole Porter (*Let's Face It, Something for the Boys*), Sigmund Romberg (*Up in Central Park*), and for the 1946 smash hit by Irving Berlin—*Annie Get Your Gun*. Screenwriter Sidney Sheldon joined them to create the screenplay for the film version of *Annie Get Your Gun*, and the three shared the 1950 Screenwriters' Guild Award for their work.

Fields's final work was *Seesaw*, her nineteenth Broadway musical, for which Cy Coleman wrote the music. Her legacy includes a long list of classic songs: "On the Sunny Side of the Street," "I'm in the Mood for Love," "Don't Blame Me," "Lovely to Look At," "Big Spender," and many others. When the first election of the Songwriters' Hall of Fame was held in 1971, Fields was the only woman among the ten writers selected.

Mary Ann Fischer

First U.S. woman to successfully give birth to quintuplets (1963).

Born Hecla, South Dakota, 1933. On September 14, 1963, Fischer, age thirty, gave birth to four girls and a boy in Aberdeen, South Dakota. She and her husband, Andrew, had five other children; he was a shipping clerk with a weekly take-home pay of seventy-six dollars. They lived on a small farm at the edge of town and owned two milking cows—which helped to feed the family.

On December 1, the first of the quintuplets went home from the hospital. The Internal Revenue Service assured the Fischers that they would not have to pay taxes on more than $70,000 of the gifts that had been sent to the babies.

Anna L. Fisher

One of the first women to be selected for the U.S. space shuttle program (1978) (see also National Aeronautics and Space Administration).

Born St. Albans, New York, August 24, 1949.

The first women astronauts, a group of six, were selected in 1978 and admitted to a training program in scientific, engineering, and medical duties. None, however, was to be trained in piloting the space shuttle. After Fisher—already an M.D.—completed her training and evaluation period in August, 1979. Her assignments as an astronaut included: development and testing of the Remote Manipulator System, verification of flight software, and medical backup in rescue helicopters. She was also on-orbit capsule communicator for the *STS-9* mission. Her first space flight came on November 8, 1984, on the second flight of the orbiter *Discovery*. On this mission, the orbiter crew accomplished the first space salvage in history, retrieving the *Palapa B-2* and *Westar VI* satellites. At the end of the mission, Fisher had made 127 orbits of the earth and logged eight days in space.

As of April, 1990, Fisher was assigned to the Space Station Support Office in Houston, Texas. She became the crew representative for space station development in the areas of training, operations concepts, and health maintenance.

Fisher graduated from San Pedro High School, San Pedro, California (1967). From the University of California–Los Angeles, she earned a

B.S. degree in chemistry (1971), an M.D. degree (1976), and an M.S. degree in chemistry (1987). She completed her medical internship at Harbor General Hospital, Torrance, California (1977). In 1978, just before her selection as an astronaut candidate, Fisher was working as a specialist in emergency medicine in hospitals in the Los Angeles area.

Eugenia Tucker Fitzgerald

First woman to found a secret college society for women (1851).

Dates unknown.

Tucker founded the Adelphean Society at Wesleyan College, Macon, Georgia, a social and service group. The secret society later became Alpha Delta Phi (1904), then Alpha Delta Pi (1913).

Hallie Flanagan (Ferguson)

Director and organizer of the Federal Theatre Project (1935); first person to receive the annual citation of the National Theatre Conference (1968).

Born Redfield, South Dakota, August 27, 1890; died Old Tappan, New Jersey, 1969.

The Federal Theatre Project was a program of the Works Progress Administration during the Depression. Producing live performances ranging from Shakespeare and contemporary plays to circuses and vaudeville, the project brought 1,200 productions to over 25 million people between 1935 and 1938.

Flanagan, a Phi Beta Kappa graduate of Grinnell College (Grinnell, Iowa), wrote a play—*The Curtain*—that brought her to the attention of Prof. George Pierce Baker of Harvard University (Cambridge, Massachusetts) and won her a place in his workshop for playwrights. After earning an M.A. degree from Vassar College (Poughkeepsie, New York) and teaching for a year at Grinnell, Flanagan founded the Vassar Experimental Theater in 1925 and was a Vassar professor until 1942.

In 1928, as a result of a Guggenheim-sponsored tour of European theaters and her investigation of government subsidies for the arts, Flanagan published *Shifting Scenes of the Modern European Theatre*. Three years later she wrote, with Margaret and Ellen Clifford, *Can You Hear Their Voices?*—a documentary drama about poor Arkansas farmers, based on a story by Whittaker Chambers.

Harry Hopkins, administrative aide to President Franklin D. Roosevelt and one of Flanagan's contemporaries at Grinnell, met with Flanagan in 1935 to discuss means of providing work for theater people. That discussion gave birth to the Federal Theatre Project, the relief program organized by Flanagan that resulted in a national network of regional theaters turning out stage productions of every genre: musicals, drama, social commentary, documentaries, etc. As administrator, Flanagan had to balance artistic, political, union, and social concerns. The experiences of the Federal Theatre Project were chronicled in *Arena: The Story of the Federal Theatre* (1940), written by Flanagan and her project staff.

From 1942 to 1946 Flanagan was dean of Smith College (Northhampton, Massachusetts), then held a position as professor in Smith's new theater department until her retirement in 1955.

Mina (Williamina) Stevens Fleming

First U.S. woman elected to the Royal Astronomical Society (1906); first to be officially appointed by Harvard Corporation as curator of astronomical photographs at Harvard University (Cambridge, Massachusetts) (1898); first to discover "white dwarfs," stars of extremely high density (1910).

Born Dundee, Scotland, May 15, 1857; died Boston, Massachusetts, May 21, 1911.

Fleming, educated in public schools in Dundee, taught in Dundee until she was married in 1877. In 1881 she became an assistant to Prof. Edward Pickering of Harvard College. For thirty years she worked as Pickering's assistant, first in his household and later in the college observatory. Her most notable scientific feat was a classification of stars based upon the special study of stellar spectra—the pattern they produced when their light was refracted by passing it through a prism. In 1890 she wrote a book called the *Draper Catalogue of Stellar Spectra*, a work classifying more than 10,000 stars according to her new system. (See also Annie Jump Cannon.)

She was elected to the Royal Astronomical Society (RAS) in 1906— the first woman to be so honored. The RAS, a professional society that supports and publishes astronomical research, has since the eighteenth century shared the directorship of the Royal Observatory at Greenwich.

In 1910 Fleming published her discovery of "white dwarfs"—hot, dense compact stars, usually white or bluish in color, which are in what is believed to be their final evolutionary stage.

Alice Fletcher

Founder and charter member of the American Anthropological Association (1902); first and only ethnologist ever to produce a complete description—including musical notations—of a Plains Indian ceremony (1904).

Born Havana, Cuba, March 15, 1838; died Washington, D.C., April 6, 1923.

A member of the Archaeological Institute of America from 1879 until she died, Fletcher went in 1881 to visit and live among the Omaha tribe in Nebraska. On their behalf, she went to Washington and participated in the drafting of congressional legislation to apportion common tribal lands to individual members of the tribe. The legislation was passed in 1882, and the following year Fletcher was appointed to oversee the execution of its provisions. She was instrumental in the enactment of similar legislation for the Winnebago of Nebraska (1887) and the Nez Percé of Idaho (1889–93).

Her pioneering attempts to assess the needs of Native Americans led to her 1885 book, *Indian Education and Civilization.* In 1896 she was elected vice president of the American Association for the Advancement of Science, and in 1905 served as president of the American Folk-Lore Society.

In 1902 Fletcher founded the American Anthropological Association, a professional society of anthropologists and others interested in biological and cultural origins and in the development of the human race.

Fletcher's encyclopedic observations of the Pawnee rituals were published in her 1904 book, *The Hako: A Pawnee Ceremony.* The first detailed documentation of a Plains Indian ceremony, Fletcher's book included careful descriptions of the words (spoken and chanted), songs, and possibly dances that comprised the ritual.

Also active in the burgeoning women's movement, Fletcher joined Sorosis (see entry), and became the organization's secretary in 1873.

Elizabeth Gurley Flynn

First woman to chair the national committee of the American Communist party (1961); first to be convicted of sedition under the Smith Act (1952).

Born Concord, New Hampshire, August 1890; died Moscow, U.S.S.R., September 5, 1964.

Her family moved to the Bronx, New York, when she was ten. In 1906, at the Harlem Socialist Club,

Flynn made her first speech, called "The Subjection of Women under Socialism." The following year she left Morris High School in the Bronx for full-time work with the Industrial Workers of the World (IWW).

Married in 1908—and divorced in 1920—she worked for the IWW in the Far West between 1908 and 1910. She was arrested several times. With nationalistic feelings and suspicion of radicals running high after World War I, Flynn formed the Worker's Defense Union to help immigrants threatened with deportation. In 1920 she was a founding member of the American Civil Liberties Union (ACLU). She was also involved in the efforts (1920–27) to free Bartolomeo Vanzetti and Nicola Sacco, a pair of Italian-born anarchists who were tried for murder in Massachusetts and eventually executed.

In 1926 Flynn retired from almost all labor activities for about ten years due to a heart ailment. She returned to politics in 1936, however, and in 1937 joined the Communist party. She organized lectures and wrote on women's issues—including equal pay and protective legislation—in the *Daily Worker*. Flynn gained a widespread reputation as a successful reformist and activist for the Communist party, and on March 12, 1961, after the death of the current chair, Eugene Dennis, she became the first woman to chair the party's national committee.

The ACLU asked her to resign in 1940 because of her Communist ties. She was convicted of sedition under the Smith Act in 1952, at the peak of the McCarthy era; she served three years in prison, beginning in 1955. When she died in Moscow in 1964 she was given a state funeral. Her ashes are buried in Chicago, Illinois.

Football League, Women's Professional

First women's professional football league (1974).

The league consisted of seven teams—the Dallas Bluebonnets (Texas), Los Angeles Dandelions (California), Toledo Troopers (Ohio), Detroit Demons (Michigan), Columbus Pacesetters (Ohio), Fort Worth Shamrocks (Texas), and the California Mustangs. The teams played ten games each year under male coaching staffs. Each player earned twenty-five dollars per game.

Esther Forbes

First woman to be an elected member of the American Antiquarian Society (1960).

Born Westborough, Massachusetts, June 28, 1891; died Worcester, Massachusetts, 1967.

The American Antiquarian Society (AAS), which collects, processes, and preserves records for public use had been in existence for 148 years at the time Forbes became a member. Her election reflected her many years of work as a writer, editor, and historian.

Forbes graduated from Bradford Academy, Haverhill, Massachusetts, in 1912. She then took writing courses at the University of Wisconsin (Madison) from 1916 to 1918. In 1919 she was hired as an editorial assistant at Houghton Mifflin publishing house in Boston, Massachusetts, where she remained until 1926.

She then devoted her time to writing. Among her novels are *O Genteel Lady!* (1926), *A Mirror for Witches* (1928), *The General's Lady* (1938), and *Rainbow on the Road* (1954). The work that brought her the most attention was *Johnny Tremain* (1943), a children's novel, which earned her the Newbery Award in 1944. Her historical novel, *The Running of the Tide* (1948), which is set in New England during the period between the Revolutionary War and the War of 1812, won the Metro-Goldwyn-Mayer Novel Award.

In 1942 she became the second woman to win the Pulitzer Prize for history (see also Margaret Leech) for her historical work, *Paul Revere and the World He Lived In*.

Juliana Rieser (or Reiser) Force

First director of the Whitney Museum of American Art (1930).

Born Doylestown, Pennsylvania, December 25, 1876; died New York, New York, August 28, 1948.

In 1914 Gertrude Vanderbilt Whitney asked Force to assist her in the running of Whitney Studio, a gallery in New York City with a reputation for showing works by avant-garde American artists. Whitney later decided to open a museum devoted entirely to American art, particularly emphasizing contemporary works. As director of the museum, Force instituted an extensive exhibition program. She bought many works by living artists. Since she was a collector of American primitive art herself, she included primitive works in the Whitney collection. Though Force was already directing the museum in 1930, it did not open officially until 1931.

Force was a pioneer in many areas related to art. In her role as director of the museum, she arranged lectures by historians and art critics. She also initiated a series of publications that included biographies and monographs of American artists.

Recognized as an expert in her field, Force was appointed as chair of the newly organized American Art Research Council in 1942. It was the first organization of its kind to sponsor research in the field of American art. She remained the director of the Whitney Museum until she died.

Dian Fossey

First woman primatologist to be accepted by mountain gorillas in their natural environment (1967).

Born San Francisco, California, January 16, 1932; died December 27, 1985, Karisoke Research Centre, Rwanda.

In 1967 Dian Fossey left Louisville, Kentucky, where she had been working as a therapist in a hospital for crippled children, to go to the volcanic mountains on the Rwanda-

Zaire-Uganda border in central Africa in order to study the rapidly disappearing mountain gorillas. She went under the sponsorship of Louis Leakey, the famous naturalist and paleontologist, whom she had met during her first trip to Africa, in 1963.

Her work there resulted in a cover story in *National Geographic* magazine (January, 1970) that won many converts to the cause of saving the gorillas, who were being driven out by the encroachment of civilization and killed or captured by poachers.

In her early years in the high rain forests of Rwanda, Fossey concentrated on scientific studies, getting close to the gorillas in their natural habitat so she could observe their behavior and culture. Within three years she had gotten the big primates to accept her presence among them—a feat achieved by no scientist before her. Mainly through imitating their gestures, she was able to win their confidence to the extent that the gorillas would let her touch them on a regular basis, and they finally allowed her to be part of their family gatherings.

As time went on, her focus shifted from science to preservation. When she began her studies in 1967, there were about 600 of the great apes. By the time of her death, their number had dwindled to about 400. Fossey became obsessed with protecting these creatures that she considered to be her family, to the point of waging open warfare with poachers.

Fossey, who had thoroughly enjoyed her first real association with animals when she rented a farm cottage near Louisville many years before, now lived like a recluse among the gorillas, having minimal contact with other researchers, and leaving Africa only briefly on a few occasions: periods while she earned a Ph.D. at Cambridge University and time spent in the United States working with her publishers on *Gorillas in the Mist* (1983).

On December 27, 1985, after nineteen years of living among the gorillas, Fossey was found dead at her mountain camp. A guest researcher was charged by Rwandan authorities with her murder. But the considerable mystery surrounding Fossey's death has never been solved.

One consequence of Fossey's work and writings, and of the movie based on *Gorillas in the Mist,* was an outpouring of contributions to the Digit Fund, established by Fossey to provide support for antipoaching activities and to finance the research of the Karisoke Centre. The fund was named for Fossey's favorite gorilla, Digit, who was killed by poachers.

Fossey was buried in the gorilla graveyard at her mountain camp—next to Digit.

(Ann) Leah Fox

First woman to receive the Purple Heart medal (1942).

Born Canada, c. 1918.

Fox was head nurse at Hickam Field, Hawaii, at the time of the attack on Pearl Harbor, December 7, 1941. She received the Purple Heart for being wounded.

Margaret and Kate (Catherine) Fox

Reportedly the first persons to be spiritualist mediums (1848).

Margaret: Born Canada, c. 1833; died Brooklyn, New York, March 8, 1893. Kate: Born Canada, c. 1839; died New York, New York, July 2, 1892.

In 1848 the two Fox sisters, living with their parents in Hydesville, New York, reported strange rappings in their bedroom. They then related that they had been in contact with the spirit world—the first such report in recorded U.S. history (1848). They identified their spirit contact as Charles B. Rosma, an itinerant peddler who, the girls said, told them he had been murdered five years previously and buried below their house. The following day the family's cellar was excavated; the diggers found human hair and pieces of bone.

When their parents sent them away—Margaret to Rochester, New York, and Kate to Auburn, New York—the mysterious rappings followed them.

The following year, 1849, the two girls went professional, taking their public demonstrations of spirit world communications on tour. Their success spawned hundreds of imitators, and their followers were numerous, including such celebrities as William Cullen Bryant, James Fenimore Cooper, and Horace Greeley. Spirit circles formed all across the United States.

The sisters both became alcoholics and neither lived to be older than sixty.

Nance Frank

First woman skipper to enter an ocean sailboat race with an all-woman crew (1991).

Dates unknown.

In a fifty-foot sailboat called *Ichiban,* Frank and her crew of twelve sailed a 475-mile race from Annapolis, Maryland, to Newport, Rhode Island in June, 1991. They weren't first, but they weren't last either, coming in eighth out of a fleet of nine. This was the first time the thirteen women had been to sea as a crew.

Lucinda Franks

First woman to receive the Pulitzer Prize for national reporting (1971).

Born Chicago, Illinois, 1946.

Franks, a freelance writer, shared the 1971 Pulitzer Prize with journalist Thomas Powers for *The Making of a Terrorist,* five articles written for United Press International (UPI). The series was about Diana Oughton, the radical activist who was killed in an explosion in a private house in Greenwich Village, New York City. At the time Franks received the prize, she was the youngest person ever to win it.

In addition to the terrorist articles, she is also known for *Waiting Out a War: The Exile of Private John*

Picciano. The nonfiction work is based on a U.S. soldier who refused to fight during the Vietnam War (1974).

Franks graduated from Vassar College, Poughkeepsie, New York, in 1968. She immediately got her first reporting job on a trial basis at UPI's London bureau. She later reported for *The New York Times*. From 1977 to 1982 she taught writing at Vassar College. In 1983 she was the Ferris Professor of Journalism at Princeton University, Princeton, New Jersey.

Gretchen Fraser

First U.S. skier to win an Olympic gold medal in special slalom; first to win an Olympic medal in skiing (1948).

Born Tacoma, Washington, 1919.

Prior to 1948, the best Olympic performance by a U.S. skier was an eleventh-place finish in the 1938 winter games. At the Winter Olympics in St. Moritz, Switzerland, in 1948, Fraser, of Vancouver, Washington, placed second in the women's alpine combined event. (The two-part event includes a downhill race and a slalom.) The twenty-eight-year old, 115-pound skier received her silver medal on February 4th—the first ever won by a U.S. skier. The following day she went on to win the special slalom

event—another U.S. first—with a time of 1 minute, 57.2 seconds.

The first woman to receive the Silver Belt Trophy (1940), Fraser was selected for the U.S. Olympic team in 1940, but the games were cancelled because of World War II. In 1941 she won the National Women's Alpine Combined and the National Women's Downhill titles; the following year she won the National Women's Slalom Championship.

After Fraser retired from competition, she was named an officer of the National Ski Association and a member of the board of directors of the U.S. Equestrian Team. In 1960 she was named to the National Ski Hall of Fame. A founder of the first U.S. amputee ski club, Fraser was selected as chair of the Special Winter Olympics in 1983.

Marcia Frederick

First U.S. woman to win a gold medal at the world gymnastic championships (1978).

Born Springfield, Massachusetts, c. 1963.

Frederick, a fifteen-year-old from Springfield, Massachusetts, won a gold medal in what was her second international gymnastic competition. She won on uneven bars, executing a Stalder shoot with a full pirouette, which is a circle swing with legs apart straddling the bar, followed by a shooting pirouette, resulting in a handstand. This was the first time a gymnast had ever been able to complete such a maneuver. She scored 9.95, with two of the judges of the competition giving her the perfect score of 10. Before this, the world's best record was held by Cathy Rigby, from the United States, who had won a silver medal in 1971.

Pauline Frederick

First woman network news analyst and diplomatic correspondent in American radio (1939); first to anchor network radio's convention coverage (1960); first to moderate a presidential debate (1976, between Gerald R. Ford and Jimmy Carter); first to be elected president of the United Nations Correspondents Association.

Born Gallitzin, Pennsylvania, 1906; died Lake Forest, Illinois, May 9, 1990.

Starting her career as a newspaper journalist in high school, Frederick then received a master's degree in international law from George Washington University in Washington, D.C. Although she disliked the concept of "women's news," to which many women journalists were assigned, Frederick came up with a novel way to get the attention of newspaper editors: she interviewed the wives of Washington diplomats and sold the stories to the *Washington Star.* She wrote for *United States Daily* (predecessor of *U.S. News and World Report*), then for the North American Newspaper Alliance. She became a war correspondent for the alliance in 1945.

Frederick's first network broadcast came from Washington, D.C., in 1939, her first overseas broadcast from China in 1945, and her first network television broadcast from the national political conventions in Philadelphia in 1948. She covered the Nuremberg trials of Nazi war criminals, the Korean War, wars in the Middle East, the turmoil in the Congo, and the Cuban missile affair. She was correspondent at the United Nations for NBC for twenty-one years. Later in her career, she was international affairs analyst for National Public Radio.

For her contributions to journalism, Frederick received the Paul White Award from the Radio-Television News Directors' Association and the George Foster Peabody Award in 1954. In 1975 she was named to the Hall of Fame of Sigma Delta Chi, the journalists' society. She received honorary doctorate degrees in journalism, law, and the humanities from twenty-three colleges and universities.

Betty Goldstein Friedan

Cofounder, organizer, and first president of the National Organization for Women (NOW) (1966–70) (see also National Organization for Women).

Born Peoria, Illinois, 1921.

Friedan is a cofounder of the National Conference for Repeal of Abortion Laws (1968), which became the National Abortion Rights Action League (NARAL) after the U.S. Supreme Court's *Roe* v. *Wade* decision. In 1970 she founded the National Women's Political Caucus and led the nationwide Women's Strike for Equality. She was an organizer and early director of the First Women's Bank and Trust Company, and an organizer of the first International Feminist Congress (1973).

Friedan burst upon the national consciousness in 1963 with her book *The Feminine Mystique,* which describes the pressures that U.S. women are under to perform the roles of traditional wife and mother, and the concomitant notion that straying from this hallowed path is deviant and suspect behavior.

In 1981 Friedan brought out *The Second Stage,* a book presenting a reformist view of feminism. The following year she was named Author of the Year by the American Society of Journalists and Authors.

Educated at Smith College (Northampton, Massachusetts), where she graduated summa cum laude in 1942, and at the University of California–Berkeley, where she was a 1943 research fellow, Friedan trained in journalism and psychology.

In 1988 Friedan was named Distinguished Visiting Professor at the University of Southern California and its Institute for the Study of Men and Women.

Carrie Fuld

Cofounder of the Institute for Advanced Study (1930).

Born Baltimore, Maryland, March 16, 1864; died Lake Placid, New York, July 18, 1944.

Fuld and her brother, Louis Bamberger, members of a philanthropic family, founded the Institute for Advanced Study in Princeton, New Jersey. Formally opened in 1933, it was designed to provide a base for a community of scholars to do advanced research. The institution is staffed by professors and postdoctoral students who are primarily involved in research and imaginative scholarship.

Ida Fuller

*First person to receive a Social
Security check (1940).*

Born Ludlow, Vermont, September 6, 1874; died Brattleboro, Vermont, January 27, 1975.

Fuller, who was a classmate of President Calvin Coolidge in Ludlow, Vermont, received a Social Security check in the amount of $22.54 in January, 1940. She was the first of 3,700 women and men to receive social security checks at that time.

When she reached her ninety-first birthday, she was the first person to receive one of the many retroactive checks to be issued to people under an amendment signed by President Lyndon B. Johnson (1965). This check was made out for $60.90.

Fuller worked as a clerk for John G. Sargent, who later became President Calvin Coolidge's attorney general. She had her footprints preserved in concrete at the Social Security Administration headquarters in Washington, D.C.

Lucia Fuller

*Cofounder of the American
Society of Miniature Painters
(1899).*

Born Boston, Massachusetts, December 6, 1870; died Madison, Wisconsin, May 20, 1924.

Fuller studied art at Cowles Art School, Boston, Massachusetts, and at the Art Students League, New York, New York. In 1893 she was one of several women painters asked to execute murals for the Women's Building at the World's Columbian Exposition in Chicago, Illinois. In 1899 she became the first treasurer of the American Society of Painters.

That same year, Fuller also became a founding member of the American Society of Miniature Painters. She painted miniature portraits of many prominent people, including J. P. Morgan. Her most frequent medium was watercolor, often on ivory.

Among her awards for excellence in painting were the bronze medal at the Paris, France, Exposition (1900); the gold medal at the St. Louis, Missouri, Exposition (1904); and the silver medal at the Buffalo, New York, Exposition (1911).

(Sarah) Margaret Fuller (Ossoli)

*First woman to publish
significant art criticism (1840);
first to be a foreign
correspondent (1846); first
person to be a book review editor
(1844).*

Born Cambridgeport (now part of Cambridge), Massachusetts, May 23, 1810; died in a shipwreck off Fire Island, New York, July 19, 1850.

Fuller wrote the first important piece of art criticism written in the United States. She covered an exhibition of paintings executed by Washington Allston; the article appeared in the first issue of *The Dial*. She went on to become editor of *The Dial* from 1840 to 1842, in which she wrote numerous articles of criticism on paintings. In 1844 she became a literary critic for the *New York Tribune*, having been hired by Horace Greeley to review books. She determined which books were to be reviewed and regularly critiqued the work of leading authors of the day. In addition, Fuller reviewed classic works. It was during that time that her reputation as a leading American critic crystallized. She maintained that position on the *Tribune* until 1846, when Greeley appointed her foreign correspondent, the first U.S. woman to hold such a position.

In addition to her articles of criticism, she published a book in 1845 titled *Woman in the 19th Century and Kindred Papers Relating to the Sphere, Condition and Duties of Woman,* one of the most influential feminist works of the time. She also wrote *Papers on Literature and Art,* a seminal work that greatly contributed to the establishment of a standard of practical criticism in the United States.

Fuller was educated at home in the classical tradition and then attended a private school for two years. As a young girl she gave evidence of an intellectual maturity beyond her age. However, she went through gloomy periods during which she suffered from nightmares and sleepwalking.

She was a member of the Ralph Waldo Emerson and Bronson Alcott circle, a New England intellectual group. She and Elizabeth Peabody (see entry) were charter members of the Transcendental Club formed around 1937.

In 1849 she was married secretly to an indigent aristocrat, Giovanni Angelo, Marchese d'Ossoli, whom she had met in Rome while working there as a correspondent for the *Tribune*. When the couple and their only child were sailing from Europe to New York, their ship was wrecked off Fire Island, New York, and all three were killed. Only the child's body was recovered.

Zona Gale

First woman to receive the
Pulitzer Prize for drama (1921).

Born Portage, Wisconsin, August 26, 1874; died Chicago, Illinois, December 27, 1938.

A dramatization of her novel, *Miss Lulu Bett*, opened on Broadway in New York, New York, in 1920, and she received the Pulitzer Prize the following year.

A prolific writer, Gale wrote numerous biographies, essays, and plays as well as novels. In *Miss Lulu Bett* and much of her other writing, she focused on everyday life in small towns, such as Portage, where she grew up. By 1919 she had written four volumes of stories about a fictitious small town called Friendship Village.

In addition to her literary activities, Gale was a reporter for the *Milwaukee Journal* (1895–1901) and the New York *Evening World* (1901). Along with her friend Jane Addams (see entry) she became involved in various humane causes.

Juliane Gallina

First woman to be named brigade
commander by the U.S. Naval
Academy (USNA) (1991).

Born Pelham, New York, August 3, 1970.

Gallina, whose current rank is midshipman captain, is the leader of 4,300 members of the brigade. She presides over ceremonies, daily formations, and parades. Commander Gallina is the second woman ever to hold such a position in a military ser-

vice academy—the first was at the U.S. Military Academy at West Point. Gallina acts as the key liaison between midshipmen and the academy officers.

The 146-year-old U.S. Naval Academy first admitted women in 1976, despite the fact that a "considerable segment" of the midshipmen, faculty, and class indicated that women had no place there. The academy's treatment of women has been attacked during recent years, and just six months before Gallina was named commander, an internal academy review was held in response to several incidents of sexual harassment and violence.

During Gallina's first two years at the academy, she was the coxswain of the women's crew team and a member of the track and lacrosse teams. She is a graduate of Pelham Memorial High School, Pelham, New York.

Mary Garden

First woman to direct a major opera company (1921).

Born Aberdeen, Scotland, February 20, 1874; died Aberdeen, Scotland, January 3, 1967.

After being a member of the Chicago Opera Company (Chicago, Illinois) for eleven years, Garden became its director during the 1921/22 season.

When she was six years old, Garden came to the United States with her family. They lived first in Brooklyn, New York, then in Chicopee, Massachusetts, finally settling in Chicago, Illinois, in 1888, when Garden was fourteen years old. She soon began taking singing lessons. She showed considerable potential, so she went to Paris, France, for more voice training. There she gained a reputation as a singer, although she was not yet performing in public. While attending a performance at the Opéra-Comique, however, Garden was asked to replace a soprano in the opera who suddenly became ill after the first two acts. The opera was Gustave Charpentier's *Louise,* and Garden and the opera were an overnight success. Following this surprising debut, she sang the soprano role more than a hundred times.

Garden became best known for her role as Mélisande in Claude Debussy's opera, *Pelléas et Mélisande,* which she sang for the first time in 1902.

She made her American debut in 1907 when she sang the title role in Jules Massenet's opera, *Thaïs.* The performance took place at Oscar Hammerstein's Manhattan Opera House in New York City.

Garden joined the Chicago Opera Company in 1910, remaining a part of the company until the 1930/31 season, after which she retired.

Helen Hamilton Gardener *(born Alice Chenoweth)*

First woman member of the U.S. Civil Service Commission (1920); first to serve on any federal commission (1920).

Born Winchester, Virginia, January 21, 1853; died Washington, D.C., July 26, 1925.

Gardener graduated from the Cincinnati Normal School in Ohio in 1873. Following her graduation, she taught and became a lecturer. Early in her career, she demonstrated a strong belief in the equality of the sexes. Writing under the pen name of Helen Hamilton Gardener—a name she legally adopted—she published a compilation called *Men, Women and Gods and Other Lectures* (1885).

In 1890 Gardener wrote a novel titled *Is This Your Son, My Lord?*, whose central theme attacked legalized prostitution. The novel was very popular. In 1895 she joined Elizabeth Cady Stanton in preparing Stanton's *Woman's Bible*.

Gardener married Charles Smart in 1875. After he died in 1901, she married again and moved to Washington, D.C. She decided to become a woman suffrage lobbyist, and in 1917 she became vice president of the National American Woman Suffrage Association. She also became the chief liaison to President Woodrow Wilson's administration.

In 1920 President Wilson appointed Gardener to serve on the U.S. Civil Service Commission. She remained there for five years, helping with policy making, reforming procedures, and advocating redress of inequities in the system.

Lucy McKim Garrison

First woman to collect and notate slave songs (1861–67).

Born Philadelphia, Pennsylvania, October 30, 1842; died West Orange, New Jersey, May 11, 1877.

Garrison, who grew up as part of an aristocratic society in Philadelphia, attended a school in New Jersey run by the Grimké sisters and the husband of Angelina Grimké, Theodore Weld. She studied piano and violin at the school, which was part of a utopian colony. After studying for a few months in 1857, she began to teach piano while continuing her study of music. Garrison continued teaching and studying until she married in 1865, after which she began to assist her husband in editorial work and reviewing books for *The Nation*.

In 1861, after Union forces had captured the Sea Islands off the

South Carolina coast, Garrison's father was named general secretary of a Union relief committee, which went there to assist the slaves that were being freed. Lucy Garrison accompanied him and, while there, made musical notations of the songs of the slaves. Two of the songs, arranged for voice and piano, were published but did not sell well.

She married Wendell Phillips Garrison in 1865, and they gathered the first collection of slave songs to be published, *Slave Songs of the United States,* published in 1867. William Francis Allen, a well-known writer of the day, and Charles Ware, a song collector, were collaborators.

Mary Gartside

First person to undergo a successful appendectomy (1885).

Born c. 1863; died 1919.

The operation was performed by Dr. William West Grant in Davenport, Iowa, when Gartside was twenty-two years old.

Janet Gaynor *(born Laura Gainor)*

First woman to win an Academy Award for best acting (1927–28).

Born Philadelphia, Pennsylvania, October 6, 1906; died Palm Springs, California, September 14, 1984.

Gaynor won the first Academy

Award for cumulative work in three films: *Seventh Heaven* (1927), *Sunrise* (1927), and *Street Angel* (1928). (Early in the history of the Oscar, awards were given for cumulative work.)

She began her movie career as an extra. Later, she appeared in comedy shorts by Hal Roach. Her first role of substance was in *The Johnstown Flood,* produced by Fox in 1926. In 1927, with the release of *Seventh Heaven* and *Sunrise,* Gaynor became Fox Studio's top star.

By 1934 she had become Hollywood's most popular woman actor and a number one box office appeal. She and her frequent costar, Charles Farrell, appeared to the public as archetypes of good-looking, wholesome, likable Americans. Throughout the 1930s, they were loved as a team and labeled "America's favorite lovebirds."

Gaynor was nominated for an

Oscar in 1937 for her role in *A Star is Born* and was a success in *The Young in Heart* in 1938. Thereafter she did little in Hollywood. Gaynor died in 1984 as a result of critical injuries she received in an automobile accident in 1982.

Lois Gibbs

Founder of the Citizen's Clearinghouse for Hazardous Wastes (CCHW) (1981); first president of the Love Canal Homeowners Association (1978).

Born c. 1951.

In 1979 Gibbs attacked both the U.S. government and the New York State government for not finding a solution to the contamination problem in the Love Canal section of Niagara Falls, New York, where she and her family lived. Approximately 20,000 tons of toxic chemical wastes from the Hooker Chemicals and Plastics Corporation were dumped in that area. About 1,000 families had to be evacuated from their homes as a result of a sharp rise in birth defects and health problems. Gibbs's two young children were among those who suffered multiple health problems. She contends that the ailments disappeared after she moved her family out of the Love Canal area. Eventually, Gibbs won the fight to close the hazardous dump.

Gibbs now lives in Washington, D.C. As a lobbyist and head of the the Citizen's Clearinghouse for Hazardous Wastes, she has acted as adviser to other people troubled by toxic waste and its problems. For example, she advised the citizens of Times Beach, Missouri, how to organize and deal with the dioxin crisis (1983).

In 1981 she published an autobiographical work, *Lois Gibbs: My Story*, and in 1981 CBS aired the made-for-TV film, *Lois Gibbs and the Love Canal*.

She was the North American winner of the first Goldman Environmental Prize in 1991. The prize awards $60,000 each year to each of six outstanding environmentalists from six continents.

Mildred E. Gillars *(see Axis Sally)*

Mabel Gillespie

Organizer and first president of the Stenographers' Union (1917); first woman on the executive board of the Massachusetts State Federation of Labor (1918).

Born St. Paul, Minnesota, 1877; died Boston, Massachusetts, 1923.

Gillespie attended Radcliffe College (Cambridge, Massachusetts) from 1898 until 1900. She then pursued social settlement work. After the founding of the National Women's Trade Union League (NWTUL), she became interested in its work and decided to concentrate on the problems of women and their working conditions. She was an executive board member of the league from 1919 until 1922.

She was the only person to serve on the Minimum Wage Commission throughout its existence—1913–19. The commission came into existence after Massachusetts became the first state to pass a minimum wage law in 1912.

Lucy Giovinco

First U.S. bowler to win the Women's Bowling World Cup (1976).

Dates unknown.

Giovinco, a bowler from Tampa, Florida, bowled 620, to win the three-game round final by 116 pins. Doris Gradin of Sweden was her contender at the event, held in Teheran, Iran, in 1976.

Girl Scouts of the U.S.A.

First voluntary organization for girls (1912).

The Girl Scouts of the U.S.A. (GSA) was founded by Juliette Gordon Low (see entry) of Savannah, Georgia, on March 12, 1912. The organization, originally called the Girl Guides, changed its name to Girl Scouts in 1915 and opened its headquarters in Washington, D.C. In 1950 the organization was finally chartered by a special act of Congress.

The GSA promotes people and their well-being, the arts, and the outdoors. The largest voluntary organization for girls in the world, it has more than 300 Girl Scout councils, open to girls between the ages of six and seventeen. Since its inception, forty million young women have joined. (See also Daisy Gordon.)

Kate Gleason

First woman to be president of a national bank (1917); first to be a member of the American Society of Mechanical Engineers (ASME) (1918).

Born Rochester, New York, November 25, 1865; died Rochester, New York, January 9, 1933.

Gleason became president of the First National Bank of Rochester, Rochester, New York, after the male president of the bank resigned to join the military services during World War I. She served as president until 1919. During her tenure as president of the bank, she promoted the large-scale development of low-cost housing.

Cornell University, Ithaca, New York, admitted Gleason as a special student in 1884. Her field of study was mechanical arts. She also attended Sibley College of Engraving and Mechanics Institute (now the Rochester Institute of Technology), Rochester, New York, part time during that school year.

Gleason's father, the owner of Gleason Works, a machine-tool factory, designed a machine that would cut automobile gears. After working for her father as a sales representative and marketing the machine for some time, she became a director of the company. As secretary and treasurer of the company, she initiated a business promotion strategy that changed Gleason Works from a small machine-tool factory into the leading U.S. producer of gear-cutting machinery. Having brought the company to this kind of success by 1913, she decided to branch out on her own. She then restored another machine-tool company to financial solvency.

Pursuing the low-cost construction approach to housing that she had promoted when she was president of the bank in Rochester, she traveled to California where she examined adobe buildings and drafted plans that were used to begin development of low-cost homes in Sausalito. Unfortunately, the project was abandoned shortly after its start because the state of California condemned part of the tract of land. In 1920 she bought land on the Sea Islands off South Carolina, where con-struction was begun on what she planned to develop into an artists' and writers' colony. The resort colony was not completed, however, until after her death. It was Gleason's younger sister who oversaw the completion of the building.

Gleason never claimed that she made a special contribution to the field of mechanical engineering, and reportedly she had little technical ability. However, she gained a wide reputation in housing construction and the machine-tool business. She was not only accepted as a member of the American Society of Mechanical Engineers, but was also the society's representative to the World Power Conference in Germany in 1930.

Gleason left a large estate—$1,400,000—a large portion of which was used to set up the Kate Gleason Fund for charity and education.

Mary Katherine Goddard

First woman postmaster (1775); first person to print the Declaration of Independence with all signers' names included (1777).

Born Groton or New London, Connecticut, June 16, 1738; died Baltimore, Maryland, August 12, 1816.

After the death of her father in

1762, Goddard worked in the family printing shop in Providence, Rhode Island, along with her mother and brother. In 1765 they began publishing the *Providence Gazette*, a Providence, Rhode Island, weekly newspaper. She and her brother ran a new shop in Philadelphia, Pennsylvania, from 1768 to 1773. Then her brother opened yet another shop in Baltimore, Maryland, where she joined him in 1774. While there, she took over the publishing of the *Maryland Journal*. She printed the Declaration of Independence in the *Journal*. She gave up the printing business after a severe argument with her brother.

Goddard served as postmaster in Baltimore, Maryland, from 1775 until 1789. She then ran a bookshop for twenty years.

Maria Goeppert-Mayer

First U.S. woman to win the Nobel Prize for physics (1963).

Born Katowice, Poland (then Kattowitz, Germany), June 28, 1906; died San Diego, California, February 20, 1972.

. Goeppert-Mayer shared the prize with the German scientist J.H.D. Jensen and Eugene Wigner of Princeton University, New Jersey. She became the first U.S. woman to win a Nobel Prize for physics, and the second woman ever to win it. Marie Curie was the first, in 1903. She and Jensen received the award for their work (carried out separately) promoting the theory that the stability of atomic nuclei is due to the arrangement of the protons and neutrons in relatively fixed shells or orbits.

Her long history in the field of science began in 1930, when she earned a doctorate in physics from the University of Göttingen, Germany. She married Joseph Mayer, an American physical chemist, that year, and they moved to the United States the following year to work at Johns Hopkins University in Baltimore, Maryland. For several years the two of them collaborated with a colleague in the study of organic molecules. They also studied the separation of uranium isotopes.

In 1939 the couple joined the chemistry department at Columbia University, New York, New York. They accepted positions at the University of Chicago in 1946, and she achieved the rank of full professor in 1959. While there she was affiliated with the Argonne National Laboratory as a senior physicist.

Goeppert-Mayer, who was known for her wide-ranging work in quantum electrodynamics, spectroscopy, and crystal physics, also collaborated with Jensen on the publication of *Elementary Theory of Nuclear Shell Structure* (1955).

Hetty Goldman

First woman to direct an archeological excavation (1911); first to be appointed professor at the Institute for Advanced Study (1936).

Born New York, New York, December 19, 1881; died Princeton, New Jersey, 1972.

Goldman's first excavation at Halae, Greece, in 1911, was the basis for her dissertation, which helped her earn a Ph.D. degree from Radcliffe College, Cambridge, Massachusetts, in 1916. Several excavations followed this pioneering one.

In 1921 she directed the beginning stages of an excavation at Colophon in Ionia, Asia Minor, but the Greco-Turkish War halted the work the following year. She conducted excavations in Yugoslavia in 1932. Between 1934 and 1939 she headed an excavation at Cilicia Tarsus, Turkey; World War II interrupted these digs.

She wrote *Excavations at Eutresis in Boetia* (1931), a classic work in the field of archeology, and three volumes (published in 1950, 1956, and 1963) on her excavations at Gözlü Kule, Tarsus.

Goldman had an educational background that prepared her well for archeological work. She earned a B.A. degree in Greek and English from Bryn Mawr College, Bryn Mawr, Pennsylvania, in 1903; she received her M.A. and Ph.D. degrees from Radcliffe in 1911 and 1916, respectively. On the basis of an article she published in 1910, she received the Charles Eliot Norton Fellowship to attend the American School of Classical Studies in Athens, Greece, from 1910 to 1912.

She was appointed to the staff of the School of Humanistic Studies at the Institute for Advanced Study, Princeton, New Jersey, in 1936. While she was there, she was active in sponsoring many refugees who fled the Nazis to come to the United States. By this time, Goldman had a history of humane activities. During the Balkan wars and World War I, she had worked for the Red Cross in New York City, and in 1918 she had returned to Greece, the country of her first excavation, in order to help Jewish refugees and Jewish communities that were established there.

Goldman was an elected fellow of the American Academy of Arts and Sciences (1950); the recipient of a gold medal for Distinguished Archaeological Achievement, awarded by the Archaeological Institute of America (1966); and, on her seventy-fifth birthday, the honored guest at the Institute for Advanced Study (1956). At her death in 1972, Goldman was still the only woman to have been appointed professor at the institute.

Winifred Goldring

First woman president of the
Paleontological Society (1949).

Born Kenwood, New York, February 1, 1888; died Albany, New York, January 30, 1971.

Goldring, who was the valedictorian of her graduating class in high school, earned a B.A. degree from Wellesley College, Wellesley, Massachusetts (1909), after which she served as an assistant to one of the geology professors at the college. She earned an M.A. degree from Wellesley in 1912. She also did graduate work in paleontology, paleobotany, and geography at Columbia University, New York, New York; Harvard University, Cambridge, Massachusetts; and Johns Hopkins University, Baltimore, Maryland.

Goldring taught at the Teachers School of Science, Boston, Massachusetts, and at Wellesley. She became affiliated with the New York State Museum, Albany, New York, in 1914, and was appointed associate paleontologist in 1920. In 1939 she became the first woman to be named the New York State paleontologist, a position she held until her retirement in 1954.

In 1949 Goldring became the first woman ever to be elected president of the Paleontological Society. She was vice president of the Geological Society of American in 1951 and was given an honorary doctorate degree by Smith College, Northampton, Massachusetts, in 1957.

Grace Goldsmith

First woman to head a graduate
school of public health and
tropical medicine (1967).

Born St. Paul, Minnesota, April 8, 1904; died New Orleans, Louisiana, April 28, 1975.

Having both studied and taught medicine, and having been aggressive in helping to found the Tulane School of Public Health and Tropical Medicine (New Orleans, Louisiana), Goldsmith had the right background to qualify as dean of the school.

She graduated first in her class at the Tulane University School of Medicine and went on to earn an M.S. degree in medicine at the University of Minnesota (Minneapolis) in 1936. She began her medical teaching career back at Tulane, where she helped institute the first nutrition training program. Having a special interest in internal medicine, she wrote several articles on vitamin deficiencies and nutrition. Goldsmith became dean of the School of Public Health and Tropical Medicine in 1967.

In recognition of her outstanding contributions to the field of medicine, she received an honorary degree from the Woman's Medical College of Pennsylvania (Philadelphia) in 1962, and the American Medical Association presented her with the Goldberger Award in Clinical Nutrition in 1964.

Daisy Gordon

First Girl Guide in the United States (1912).

Dates unknown.

Gordon was the niece of Mrs. Juliette Gordon Low (see entry), founder of the Girl Scouts of the U.S.A.

Gale Ann Gordon

First woman to fly solo as a navy pilot (1966).

Born Ohio, 1943.

Ensign Gordon was assigned to the Pensacola Naval Air Station in Florida as a member of the Medical Service Corps. The twenty-three-year-old pilot from Stow, Ohio, made her historic solo flight on March 29, 1966, in a propeller-driven T-34 trainer; she had begun flight training on February 23, 1966—the only woman in a squadron of 999 men.

Gale, who earned a master's degree from Michigan State University (East Lansing), was particularly interested in aviation experimental psychology, the study of mental states and reactions to various types of flight experiences and phenomena.

Margaret Gorman

First woman to be chosen as Miss America (1921).

Born Washington, D.C., 1906.

When Gorman was fifteen years old and a pupil at a Washington, D.C., high school, she entered and won the Natural Beauty Tournament, the first incarnation of the annual Atlantic City, New Jersey, event that was later to be known as the Miss America Beauty Pageant. Conceived by the Atlantic City Business Men's League as a way of keeping tourists in town after Labor Day, the tournament featured young women from locations close to Atlantic City. Some were sponsored by newspapers and some were unsponsored walk-ons.

Gorman represented the *Washington Herald,* having been chosen as Miss Washington from among 1,500 Washington contestants. Petite (5'1", 108 pounds, measurements 30-25-32), she was the smallest and youngest contestant ever to win the Miss America contest. The competitors all wore conservative swimming costumes; Gorman's was knee-length and somewhat baggy.

Blonde and blue-eyed, she won

what were then the symbols of Miss America—a tiara replication of Lady Liberty's headpiece and a huge American flag fashioned into a coronation robe. She was also given an oversized $5,000 trophy, sporting a gilded mermaid reclining on a base of teak wood, which she would eventually pass on to the next Miss America.

Katharine Meyer Graham

First woman member of the board of the Associated Press (1974); first to receive the John Peter Zenger Award (1973).

Born New York, New York, June 16, 1917.

After Graham's husband, Philip Graham, long-time publisher of the *Washington Post,* committed suicide in 1963, she became the president of

Washington Post Company, which publishes the *Washington Post* and *Newsweek* magazine. In 1973 she became the publisher, chief executive officer, and chair of the board. That same year, she received the John Peter Zenger Award, named for the famous colonial printer and awarded for distinguished service in behalf of freedom of the press and the people's right to know.

In 1974 Graham was named to the board of the Associated Press, a news cooperative that disseminates news to member newspapers.

Graham attended Vassar College (Poughkeepsie, New York) and earned a B.A. degree at the University of Chicago (Chicago, Illinois) in 1938. That same year, she started reporting for the San Francisco *News.* In 1939 she went to work for the *Washington Post,* which was then owned by her father. She married Philip Graham in 1940. She and her husband bought the *Post* from her father in 1948 for $1 million.

Graham is a fellow of the American Academy of Arts and Sciences.

Martha Graham

First woman to receive the Samuel H. Scripps American Dance Festival Award (1981).

Born Allegany, Pennsylvania, May 11, 1894; died New York, New York, April 1, 1991.

Graham began her dance training in 1910 at the Denishawn School (Los Angeles, California)—founded by Ruth St. Denis (see entry) and Ted Shawn—and danced with that company until 1923, the year she joined the *Greenwich Village Follies of 1923* as a specialty dancer. She then taught two years at the Eastman School of Music, Rochester, New York, giving her first solo recital there in the spring of 1926.

Graham pioneered the practice of presenting modern dance seasons in legitimate houses. Starting as a concert and recital dancer, she went on to form her own school and company, which lasted until her death. She was a major influence on two generations of dancers; more than three-fourths of the performing members of her company went on to be choreographers and company directors themselves. She choreographed over 160 ballets in her lifetime.

The Scripps American Dance Festival Award—presented to her in Durham, North Carolina, in 1981 by Betty Ford, wife of former U.S. President Gerald Ford and a former dancer who studied with Graham in the 1930s—was the largest grant ever awarded to anyone in the field of dance. Recognizing her lifelong contributions to American modern dance, the award citation hailed Graham for "creating a dance technique that has become the basis of the education of hundreds of thousands of dancers around the world and establishing a new form for dance and twentieth-century theater."

Grand Jury, First Sexually Integrated

In 1870 Wyoming became the first state to have a sexually integrated grand jury. (See also First Sexually Integrated Jury.)

Chief Justice Dome of Wyoming stopped a motion to prohibit the integration of the jury, stating: "It seems to be eminently proper for women to sit upon Grand Juries, which will give them the best possible opportunities to aid in suppressing the dens of infamy which curse the country."

Ella Tambussi Grasso

First woman elected governor in the United States who did not follow her husband into office (1975); first to be reelected (1978).

Born Windsor Locks, Connecticut, May 10, 1919; died Hartford, Connecticut, February 5, 1981.

Grasso, who had served in Congress from 1971 to 1974, became governor of Connecticut in a landslide victory in 1975. When she ran again in 1978 she received more than seventy-five percent of the town votes in the state.

Grasso earned a B.A. degree

(1940) and an M.A. degree (1942) from Mount Holyoke College, South Hadley, Massachusetts. She married Thomas Grasso, a teacher, and they had two children.

From 1943 to 1946 she was assistant state director of research for the Federal War Manpower Commission, Connecticut. In 1952 she held a Democratic seat in the Connecticut legislature. From 1959 to 1970 she was Connecticut's secretary of state.

Two months before she died of cancer, Grasso resigned as governor.

Rebecca Gratz

Founder of the first Hebrew Sunday School Society (1838).

Born Philadelphia, Pennsylvania, March 4, 1781; died Philadelphia, Pennsylvania, August 27, 1869.

Gratz, who founded the society in Philadelphia, Pennsylvania, gave early evidence of her interest in both charity work and religion. For example, at the age of twenty, she helped organize the Female Association for the Relief of Women and Children in Reduced Circumstances (1801). In 1815 she founded the Philadelphia Orphan Asylum, and for part of 1818, she ran a religious school for Jewish children. In 1838 she opened the first Hebrew Sunday School Society for boys and girls, with no tuition. She was its president for twenty-six years.

Gratz was thought to be the prototype for the character of Rebecca in the novel *Ivanhoe,* by Sir Walter Scott.

Hanna Holborn Gray

First woman president of a major U.S. university (1978); first to be a provost at Yale University (1974); first to be an acting president at Yale University (1977).

Born Heidelberg, Germany, October 25, 1930.

In 1978 Gray was named the first woman president of the University of Chicago (Chicago, Illinois), a private research university. She battled successfully the problems of reduced enrollment, student protesters, and the university's reputation of being gloomy.

When Hanna Holborn was four years old, her family immigrated to the United States. She grew up in New Haven, Connecticut, graduated from Bryn Mawr College, Bryn Mawr, Pennsylvania (1950), and earned a Ph.D. degree from Harvard University, Cambridge, Massachusetts (1957). She taught history at Harvard for three years. In 1961 Gray went to the University of Chicago, remaining a member of the history department faculty for eleven years.

She married Charles M. Gray in 1954. From 1965 to 1970 she and her husband, also a scholar and teacher in the field of history, edited the *Journal of Modern History*.

Gray was named dean of the College of Arts and Sciences at Northwestern University, Evanston, Illinois, in 1972. In 1974 she became provost of Yale University, the first woman to hold that position. When Kingman Brewster, Jr., then president of Yale, was appointed U.S. ambassador to Great Britain in 1977, she became the acting president. Before the Yale search committee arrived at its choice for a new president, however, she was invited by the University of Chicago to be its president—and she accepted. She resigned as president of the University of Chicago in 1992.

Anna K. Green

First woman to write a detective story (1878).

Born Brooklyn, New York, November 11, 1846; died Buffalo, New York, April 11, 1935.

Green wrote *The Leavenworth Case*, a detective story with an intriguing plot. The work, which was a bestseller, was adapted for the stage and filmed twice—in 1923 and 1936. The central character, a detective named Ebenezer Gryce, and his assistant, Amelia Butterworth, would appear again in many of Green's later stories.

A prolific writer, Green wrote approximately forty mysteries, a verse drama, and two volumes of poetry. Critics maintained that her plots were well executed, but her language was at times euphemistic, her dialogue unrealistic.

She received a B.A. degree from Ripley Female College, Poultney, Vermont, in 1866. (See also Mary Andrews Denison.)

Edith Greenwood

First woman to receive the Soldier's Medal (1943).

Dates unknown.

Greenwood, a nurse from North Dartmouth, Massachusetts, was

cited for heroism in saving the lives of patients in a Yuma, Arizona, hospital fire that occurred on April 17, 1943. She and a ward attendant, Pvt. James Ford, were able to evacuate all the patients. No one was injured.

Ethel V. Gressang

First woman to be married in a dirigible balloon—the **Mayflower** *(1930).*

Dates unknown.

On December 27, 1930, floating over the Gulf of Mexico near St. Petersburg, Florida, Gressang, a resident of Chicago, Illinois, was married to Frank H. Johnston of Shanghai, China, by Lieut. Comdr. Karl Lange of the United States Naval Reserve.

Denny Griswold

Founder and editor of first public relations weekly in the world (1944).

Born New York, New York, 1914.

Griswold began editing and publishing *Public Relations News,* the first public relations weekly, in 1944. At the time she founded the paper, only twenty-five corporations had what were termed "formal" departments; approximately 100 firms were involved in public relations.

She grew up in New York City, where she received a B.A. degree from Hunter College in 1932. She earned an M.A. degree at Radcliffe College (Cambridge, Massachusetts), and attended Columbia University (New York, New York). Griswold has held a variety of positions in public relations and journalism, including that of managing editor for *Forbes* and editorial staff member at *Business Week.* She was also a member of the public relations department at J. Walter Thompson advertising agency. She wrote *The Public Relations Handbook* (1948). At the time of this writing she is still editing and publishing *Public Relations News.*

Griswold is the widow of Dr. Glenn Griswold, who was a co-editor of *Public Relations News* and an editor of *Business Week.* She married J. L. Sullivan in 1951.

She has received more than 100 honors and awards. A founder of Women Executives in Public Relations and the International Women's Forum, she is listed in *Who's Who* and *Who's Who of American Women.*

Charlotte Vetter Gulick

Cofounder of the Camp Fire Girls (1910).

Born Oberlin, Ohio, c. 1866; died South Casco, Maine, July 28, 1928.

Gulick, along with her husband

Luther Halsey Gulick and William Chauncey Langdon, founded the Camp Fire Girls (see entry) in 1910. The national, nonsectarian, interracial organization stresses character development and the importance of good mental and physical health. She was also the first president of the Association of Directors of Girls' Camps.

After graduating from Drury College (Springfield, Missouri), she spent a year at Wellesley College (Wellesley, Massachusetts). Following her year at Wellesley, she studied medicine for another year before setting up a summer camp to practice what was called the husband/wife theory of the harmonious development of body, mind, and spirit.

Gulick married in 1887. Her husband, an authority on hygiene and physical training, and an author of works on those subjects, died in 1918.

Janet Guthrie

First woman to drive in the Indianapolis 500 auto race (1977).

Born Iowa City, Iowa, March 7, 1938.

In 1977 Guthrie became the first female entrant in the famous race, qualifying at 188.404 miles per hour. She was the first woman to drive around the track in a practice session, and the first woman to complete the mandatory driving test for rookies. In the Indianapolis 500 race, however, the Lightning-Offenhauser that she was driving broke a valve seat after twenty-six laps, and she had to quit.

A year later Guthrie made another attempt, and on May 29, 1978, she became the first woman to complete the event, finishing eighth. She drove the race with a broken right wrist. The injury, incurred when Guthrie fell during a charity tennis match, forced her to reach across her body to shift gears with her left hand. A clandestine shot of Novocain suppressed the pain somewhat. She conceded to her crew at one point in the race that her arm was feeling rather "mediocre." In this race she piloted a more stable Wildcat-SGD. After the race, her crew acted as a team of bodyguards to prevent her enthusiastic fans and well-wishers from shaking her hand.

Before entering the 500, Guthrie had been driving her own Jaguar in road races since 1963. She decided to make racing a full-time pursuit in 1967, and won the under-two-liter prototype class in 1970 and the North Atlantic Road Racing Championship 8 sedan class in 1973.

In 1976 and 1977 Guthrie was sponsored by Rolla Vollstedt, a major builder of Indianapolis-type racers.

In 1978 she was sponsored by Kelly Girl, the temporary-employment service.

Guthrie is a physicist and aerospace engineer; she graduated from the University of Michigan (Ann Arbor) in 1960.

Gymnastics, Women's

The first women's gymnastics instruction was given at Mount Holyoke College (South Hadley, Massachusetts) in 1862. Miss Evans taught the class.

Helene Hahn

First woman to head the business and legal areas of a major motion picture studio (1984).

Born New York, New York, date unknown.

Hahn is senior vice president of business and legal affairs for Walt Disney Pictures, where she has supervised the studio's cofinance deals with several other motion picture companies, including Silver Screen Partners and Touchwood Pacific Partners. She also oversees the stu-

dio's long-term executive contracts and agreements with directors Steven Spielberg and Dawn Steel, producer Simpson-Bruckheimer, and others.

Raised in New York, Hahn earned a B.A. degree at Hofstra University, Hempstead, New York, and received her J.D. degree from Loyola University of Los Angeles (now Loyola Marymount University), Los Angeles, California in 1975. She was admitted to the bar in 1975 and was an instructor in entertainment law at Loyola before accepting a position as attorney with the American Broadcasting Company.

Before joining Disney, Hahn served for seven years at Paramount Pictures. In 1977 she began as a staff attorney in the legal department; by the time she left the company in 1983, she had become senior vice president.

Ruth Hale

Founder of the Lucy Stone League (1921), whose goal was the establishment of a woman's legal

*right to be officially known by
her maiden name after marriage.*

Born Rogersville, Tennessee, c.
1886; died New York, New York, September 18, 1934.

Hale, after establishing her reputation as a journalist, critic, and
press representative, married journalist Heywood Broun in 1917. When
he went to Europe to cover World War
I for the *New York Tribune,* Hale got
a job on the staff of the Paris edition
of the *Chicago Tribune.* Four years
later, in 1921, she demanded that
the State Department issue a passport in her birthname. After a considerable struggle with bureaucratic
paperwork, Hale was told by the
State Department that she had been
issued a passport in the name of
"Miss Ruth Hale;" she returned it,
however, because it had been made
out to "Mrs. Heywood Broun."

Hale became active in the effort to
ensure a married woman's right to
elect to use her birthname. An early
success came in May, 1921, when a
married woman's birthname was
used in a real estate deed—reportedly for the first time. Shortly after
this victory, Hale was elected president of the new Lucy Stone League.
One of her actions in this capacity
was to denounce a U.S. ruling that
married women working for the federal government be required to use
their husbands' names.

In 1926 the league was successful
in obtaining a ruling that a married
woman could take out a copyright in
her birthname; other efforts met with
less success.

Ruth Hale was educated at the Hollins Institute (Hollins, Virginia) and
the Drexel Academy of Fine Arts (Philadelphia, Pennsylvania), where she
studied painting and sculpture. At
eighteen she began her career as a
professional journalist, working for
the Hearst bureau in Washington,
D.C. (The Hearst bureau is part of the
vast publishing network that was
headed by William Randolph Hearst.)
Shortly afterwards, Hale became
drama critic for *The Philadelphia Public Ledger;* she is believed to have been
one of the first women in that field.

In 1915/16 Hale wrote for *The
New York Times;* after her marriage
to Heywood Broun she wrote for the
Chicago Tribune in Paris, then
worked for a period as a press agent
for theatrical producers, and as a
writer for magazines such as *Vogue*
and *Vanity Fair.* She had a brief but
unsuccessful career as a Broadway
lyricist.

Sarah Josepha Hale

*First woman to be editor of a
major magazine for women
(1828).*

Born Newport, New Hampshire,
October 24, 1788; died Philadelphia,
Pennsylvania, April 30, 1879.

Hale was hired as editor of the then-new *Ladies Magazine* of Boston, Massachusetts, first published in January, 1828. The magazine, which had as its mission "to make females better acquainted with their duties and privileges," initially had fifty pages and went to 600 subscribers. Its first issue contained articles praising patriotism, motherhood, and charity for widows and orphans, along with a piece attacking the practice of dueling. An editorial advocated a complete education for women—one of Hale's favorite causes. In the magazine's early days, Hale wrote most of its material.

In 1834 the magazine's name was changed to *American Ladies Magazine,* and in 1837 it was acquired by Louis Godey of Philadelphia, Pennsylvania, owner of *Godey's Lady's Book.* The two publications merged, retaining the title of *Godey's Lady's Book.* By 1837 it had 10,000 subscribers, and by 1860, with 160,000 subscribers, it was the largest magazine of its kind in the United States.

Educated at home, Hale started her working life as a schoolteacher, writer of newspaper articles and poetry, and milliner. Her publications include *The Genius of Oblivion* (1823), a book of poetry; *Northwood* (1827), a novel; and *Poems for Our Children* (1830)—which includes "Mary's Lamb," better known as "Mary Had a Little Lamb."

She moved to Philadelphia in 1841. In 1851 she was one of the organizers of the Ladies' Medical Missionary Society of Philadelphia. Her own ambitious book about the achievements of women—*Woman's Record: or sketches of all distinguished Women, from the Creation to A.D. 1654*—contains biographies of some 2,500 women; it was published in 1853. A frequent theme in her writing was that "the secret, silent, influence of woman" can be a major influence in a man's life, and that the minds and morals of children are shaped by their mothers.

Hale retired in December 1877—in her ninetieth year.

Margaret Haley

First woman to speak from the floor of the National Education Association annual meeting (1901).

Born Joliet, Illinois, November 15, 1861; died Chicago, Illinois, January 5, 1939.

Haley got her high school education at St. Angela's Convent in Morris, Illinois. She began teaching at Chicago area county schools in 1876, while taking college courses at the State Normal University (now Illinois State University) in Bloomington, Illinois, and also at Cook County Normal School (now Chicago State University) in Chicago.

She became an early member of the Chicago Teachers' Federation when it was formed in March, 1897. Her first successful battle for that organization came in 1899, when the Chicago Board of Education refused to honor a salary increase that had been promised to the city's teachers. The board claimed that it didn't have the funds to meet the salary commitments. Haley and the union president, Catharine Goggin, audited city tax revenues and found that they were substantially less than they should be because of the underassessment of some major utility firms. The union fought the issue to the Supreme Court, which affirmed in 1907 that the utilities had to be reassessed. The city then refused to apply the increased tax monies to teacher salaries, so Haley and the union went to court again. Once again, Haley and the union prevailed.

In 1900 Haley was elected district vice president of the Chicago Teachers' Federation, and in 1901 she resigned to become a full-time paid business agent for the CTF, continuing a career as an advocate of teachers' rights that was to last for more than thirty years. The following year she led the CTF into the Chicago Federation of Labor. Soon afterwards, she became the president of the nearly defunct National Federation of Teachers, reorganizing and revitalizing that organization. In 1901 Haley became the first woman to speak from the floor of the National Education Association's annual convention, and as a spokesman for the NFT, she made the NEA pay attention to the needs of grade school teachers. The NFT championed the classroom teacher and became a major voice in the NEA at a time when that organization was dominated by college presidents, professors of education, and school administrators.

In 1907 Haley secured enactment by the Illinois legislature of a state pension plan for teachers; she also enlisted her unions in the support of such causes as woman suffrage and child labor legislation.

She led, in 1910, the successful battle to get Ella Flagg Young (see entry), superintendent of Chicago schools, elected president of NEA.

Around 1916 Haley joined the Women's Trade Union League, becoming its national vice president; she also became a charter member and organizer of the newly organized American Federation of Teachers. Haley battled with the Chicago Board of Education over the Chicago Teachers' Federation's affiliation with the labor movement. That issue was resolved when, in 1917, the CTF secured passage of a state tenure law for teachers; Haley, in return, agreed that the CTF would withdraw from the Chicago Federation of Labor.

She edited and wrote much of the Chicago Teachers' Federation *Bulletin* from 1901 to 1908; she also wrote and edited *Margaret Haley's Bulletin* from 1915 until 1916 and again from 1925 until 1931. Haley went into semiretirement in the 1930s, but remained active in the teachers' movement until her death.

Anne Hall

First woman elected to full membership in the National Academy of Design (NAD) (1833).

Born Pomfret, Connecticut, 1792; died New York, New York, 1863.

In 1827 Hall became the first woman artist elected to the National Academy of Design, which had been founded the previous year. She rose to the position of associate member in 1828, then became a full member in 1833—the first woman to do so. In 1846 she became vice president of the academy.

Hall was best known for her miniatures. Her first art instructor was Samuel King, who taught such artists as Gilbert Stuart and Washington Allston. Under his tutelage she learned the technique of miniature painting on ivory. Hall's first exhibition of her miniatures was held at the American Academy of Fine Arts, New York City, in 1817.

Mary Agnes Hallaren

First nonmedical woman to be a regular army officer (1948).

Dates unknown.

Hallaren, a colonel, was sworn in as director of the Women's Army Corps (WAC) on December 3, 1948. Since the WAC had been incorporated into the regular army on June 12, 1948, as a full-fledged corps, they were no longer an auxiliary organization and Hallaren—from Lowell, Massachusetts—became a regular army officer.

Alice Hamilton

First woman to receive the Lasker Award of the U.S. Public Health Association (1947); first to be a professor on the faculty of Harvard University Medical School (1919).

Born New York, New York, 1869; died Hadlyme, Connecticut, 1970.

The Lasker Award, the most prestigious in the field of public health, is presented to pioneers in the field of hygienic and industrial disease research and to those who develop methods for preventing occupation-related ailments. The award carried a cash stipend of $1,000; its greatest honor, however, was that it said of the recipient: no one has achieved more in this field.

Younger sister of classicist Edith Hamilton, Alice Hamilton attended Miss Porter's School (Farmington, Connecticut), then the Fort Wayne College of Medicine (Fort Wayne, Indiana), finally receiving an M.D. degree from the medical department of the University of Michigan (Ann Arbor) in 1893. She completed her medical internship, then went to Germany for further work in bacteriology and pathology.

Hamilton served for a time as professor of pathology at the Woman's Medical School of Northwestern University (Evanston, Illinois), then accepted a post as bacteriologist with Chicago's new Memorial Institute for Infectious Diseases (1902). During the same year there was an epidemic of typhoid fever in Chicago; Hamilton's investigations caused the city of Chicago to reorganize its health department.

She began to focus on industrial diseases, and in 1908 was appointed to the Illinois Commission on Occupational Diseases. For the next nine years she served in various capacities for the state of Illinois and the federal government, studying industrial poisons, toxic substances, and con-taminants, as well as visiting mills, mines, and smelters in her investigations of workplace abuses. Her work led to legislation setting standards for control of industrial poisons.

In 1919, as assistant professor of industrial medicine at Harvard Medical School (Cambridge, Massachusetts), Hamilton became Harvard University's first woman professor. After 1925, she was on the faculty of Harvard's School of Public Health.

A member of the Health Committee of the League of Nations from 1924 to 1930, Hamilton retired from Harvard in 1935, accepting a consultancy in the U.S. Labor Department's Division of Labor Standards. From 1944 to 1949 Hamilton was president of the National Consumers League.

Her autobiography, *Exploring the Dangerous Trades,* was published in 1943.

Mary Hammon *(see Goodwife Norman and Mary Hammon)*

Penny Harrington

First woman to be appointed police chief of a major U.S. city (1985).

Born Lansing, Michigan, c. 1943.

Harrington was for three years the commander of one of three police precincts in Portland, Oregon, before becoming the city's police chief in 1985.

Her path to police chief was not an easy one. She first applied (along with her husband) for a job as police officer in Portland in 1964. She was turned down; he was hired. In 1965 she joined the staff of the Woman's Protective Division of the Police Bureau, where she worked with juveniles. In 1971 Harrington filed a civil rights complaint against the city, citing the sexist language on such documents as the police department competitive exams. One specific complaint was against the word "policeman." She was successful in her suit, and the wording was changed to "police officer."

Harrington sought a job as police officer and was successful this time. She moved up the ranks, becoming a detective, then first sergeant, lieutenant, captain, commander, and finally police chief, after having filed forty-two complaints. She was the first woman to achieve any of these positions in a major U.S. metropolitan police department.

In 1986 Harrington had disputes with the mayor and with union heads, who charged her with nepotism for the hiring and/or special treatment of family members, such as her husband and sister. In April of that year she also had conflicts with the city commission which charged that police efforts to suppress the trafficking of narcotics in Portland had been ineffectual. Finally, on June 2, 1986, Harrington resigned as police chief after a special investigating committee declared that she had shown "defects of leadership."

Beverly Messenger Harris *(see Beverly Messenger-Harris)*

Patricia Roberts Harris

First woman to hold two U.S. cabinet positions (1977 and 1979).

Born Mattoon, Illinois, May 31, 1924; died Washington, D.C., March 23, 1985.

Harris attended Howard University in Washington, D.C., where she was an activist student and vice chairman of the student chapter of the National Association for the Advancement of Colored People (NAACP). She graduated summa cum laude and Phi Beta Kappa in 1945, with a B.A. degree.

Harris pursued graduate study in industrial relations for two years at the University of Chicago (Illinois), and also served as program director for the Young Women's Christian Association in Chicago from 1946 to 1949.

From 1949 to 1953 she was assistant director for the American Council on Human Rights and, from 1953 to 1959, executive director of the national headquarters of Delta Sigma Theta, a black sorority.

She married William Beasley Harris, a professor of law at Howard University, in September, 1955.

Harris earned a doctor of jurisprudence degree from George Washington University Law School (Washington, D.C.) in 1960, graduating first in her class of ninety-four students; she had also been associate editor of the *Law Review*. She was admitted to the District of Columbia bar the same year.

In 1961, after working for one year as an attorney in the criminal division of the U.S. Department of Justice, Harris was named associate dean of students and law lecturer at Howard University. She became an assistant professor in 1963 and was promoted to associate professor in 1965.

Between 1962 and 1965 she was also vice chairman of the National Capitol Area Civil Liberties Union, and in July 1963 President John F. Kennedy named her cochairman, with Mildred McAfee Horton, of the National Women's Committee for Civil Rights.

President Lyndon B. Johnson appointed her in March, 1964 to the Commission on the Status of Puerto Rico; that same year she seconded his presidential nomination at the Democratic National Convention, and in May, 1965, Johnson named her U.S. ambassador to Luxembourg—the first black woman to hold ambassadorial rank.

While ambassador, Harris also served in 1966 and 1967 as alternate U.S. delegate to the United Nations General Assembly.

In August, 1967, she rejoined the Howard University law faculty as a full professor. Two years later she was named dean of the law school and remained in that position until she left to go into private practice.

Harris served from 1968 to 1969 on the National Commission on the Causes and Prevention of Violence, and from 1969 to 1973 as a member of the Carnegie Commission on the

Future of Higher Education. In 1972 she was temporary chair of the Democratic party's credential committee.

Chosen in December, 1976, by President-elect Jimmy Carter to be Secretary of Housing and Urban Development, she served in that position from January, 1977 to August, 1979, when she became secretary of the Department of Health, Education and Welfare. Harris occupied that post from 1979 to 1981; during her tenure, the department was renamed the Department of Health and Human Services (1980).

In 1982 Harris ran for mayor of Washington, D.C., losing to Marion S. Barry, Jr.

Her husband died in 1984; at the time of her own death in 1985, Harris was a professor at the George Washington National Law Center in Washington, D.C.

Caroline Scott Harrison

First president-general of the Daughters of the American Revolution (DAR) (1890); first first lady to install electricity in the White House (1889).

Born Oxford, Ohio, October 1, 1832; died Washington, D.C., October, 1892.

Harrison was married to President Benjamin Harrison (1853). They had one daughter and several grandchildren. She was a creative artist and enjoyed playing the piano. Although she appeared to care a great deal for her family and home, she was also active in charity and social work, and she assumed a leadership position in the Daughters of the American Revolution. (See also Harriet Stone Lothrop and Daughters of the American Revolution.)

She graduated from the Oxford Female Institute, Oxford, Ohio, where her father was the principal. She then taught music briefly at a school in Carrollton, Kentucky, just before marrying Benjamin Harrison. An invalid for the last few months of her life, Harrison died at the White House.

Harriet Boyd Hawes

First archeologist to discover and completely excavate a Minoan town (1901–04).

Born Boston, Massachusetts, October 11, 1871; died Washington, D.C., March 31, 1945.

Hawes discovered a Minoan town of the Early Bronze Age at Gournia, Crete, in 1901 and continued to work there until 1904. In 1908 the American Exploration Society published her report on her findings—it is still considered the definitive one.

After graduating from Smith College, Northampton, Massachusetts, in 1882, Hawes taught for four years before beginning graduate work at the American School of Classical Studies, Athens, Greece. She returned to the states in 1900 and taught modern Greek and Greek archeology at Smith. It was during a leave of absence from Smith that she discovered the Minoan city at Crete. In 1910 Hawes received an honorary degree from her alma mater.

Between 1920 and 1936 she gave lectures at Wellesley College, Wellesley, Massachusetts, on the topic of pre-Christian art. She retired in 1936.

Lucy Webb Hayes

First first lady to ban liquor in the White House (1877).

Born Chillicothe, Ohio, 1831; died Fremont, Ohio, 1889.

Hayes and President Rutherford B. Hayes hosted many social gatherings at the White House, but she insisted that liquor not be served, even at state functions. Her maternal grandfather, Judge Isaac Cook of Connecticut, was an advocate of temperance and had asked members of his family to espouse the cause.

Hayes's father, James Webb, a physician from Kentucky, died of cholera in Lexington, Kentucky, while on a trip there to free slaves whom he had inherited. She and her two brothers were young when he died. Mrs. Webb, who had inherited enough money to support the family and finance the children's college education, later moved to Ohio in order for them to attend Ohio Wesleyan University, Delaware, Ohio. Lucy was probably the first female to enroll there. The family moved again, and Hayes enrolled at Wesleyan Female College, Cincinnati, Ohio, graduating in 1850. While in Cincinnati, she renewed her acquaintance with Rutherford B. Hayes and married him in 1852.

Hayes became known as a woman of strong beliefs and character and as a philanthropist. She was the first president of the Woman's Home Missionary Society of the Methodist Episcopal Church (1880), a position she held until she died.

Ann Hayward

First woman to be married in a parachute (1940).

Dates unknown.

At the site of the parachute jump attraction at the 1940 World's Fair in Flushing Meadow Park, New York City, Hayward and her groom, Arno Rudolphi, sat side by side, in harnesses, suspended fifty feet in the air from parachutes. The minister who married them, the maid of honor, best man, and four musicians were also suspended from parachutes.

Edith Head

*First woman to head the design
department of a major motion
picture studio (1938).*

Born Los Angeles, California, October 28, 1907; died Hollywood, California, October 24, 1981.

Head, who was first hired by Paramount Studios to sketch fashion designs, became their chief designer in 1923 and then head of the entire designing department fifteen years later.

Also a designer of uniforms for Pan American World Airways and United Nations (New York, New York) guides, Head received thirty-five nominations for Oscars for best costumes. She won her first Academy Award in 1949 for the costumes in *The Heiress*—in which Olivia de Havilland won the Oscar for best actress. She won other Oscars for such movies as *All About Eve* (1951); *A Place in the Sun* (1951); *Roman Holiday* (1953); *Sabrina* (1954); and *The Sting* (1973). Head, who went to work for Universal Studios in 1967, received more than 1,000 screen credits.

She earned a B.A. degree at the University of California–Los Angeles, and an M.A. degree at Stanford University, Palo Alto, California, where she specialized in languages. She also studied art in Los Angeles. Before joining Paramount Studios, she taught art and languages in private schools.

Barbara Ruckle Heck

*Cofounder of the Methodist
Church in the United States
(1766).*

Born Ballingrane, Ireland, 1734; died Ontario, Canada, August 17, 1804.

Heck and her cousin, Phillip Embury, established a Methodist Society in New York City. She organized its first meetings and was responsible for the erection of the first church building—the John Street Methodist Church, which still exists.

Public records show that a daughter was born to the Hecks in Camden, New York, in 1772. The next available record, from 1774, shows them living at Sorel, near Montreal, Canada, where Heck's husband was serving in the British army and Heck once again organized a Methodist Society.

Alma Heflin

*First woman test pilot for a
commercial aircraft company
(1941).*

Born Lock Haven, Pennsylvania, date unknown.

Heflin, a teacher, began her flying lessons in Spokane, Washington, in 1934, and in 1938 she became the first woman to lead an annual light plane cavalcade to Florida. The Piper Aircraft Corporation, where Heflin had been publicity director, hired her as a test pilot on November 12, 1941, the first woman to be hired for such a job.

Flying a Piper Cub Coupé, she bush piloted in Alaska for five months in 1942. Following her flights in Alaska, the U.S. Army hired her to test planes used for their "Grasshopper Squadron"—a group of pilots who spotted artillery fire and scouted in enemy territory. She spent 120 hours monthly testing the planes, which is approximately thirty-five hours more than airline pilots fly each month. During one training maneuver, her parachute fouled; she was injured when she hit the ground and had to spend six months in the hospital. This was the only accident she had during her test piloting career.

While she was the publicity director at Piper, she edited the corporation's house organ, *Cub Flier*, raising the circulation of the magazine from 7,500 to 85,000 in only ten issues. She published an account of her flying experiences, *Adventure Was the Compass*, in 1942.

Rachel Henderlite

First woman to be ordained as a U.S. Presbyterian minister (1965).

Born North Carolina, 1905.

After being approved unanimously by 125 commissioners in the Richmond, Virginia, presbytery, Henderlite became minister of the All Souls Presbyterian Church, Richmond, in 1965. She was also the first woman professor of Christian education at the Austin Theological Seminary in Texas (1966) and the first woman president of the Presbyterial Council of Church Union (1976).

In 1980 she became president of the Consultation on Church Union, in which ten leading Protestant denominations participated. The group took significant steps toward ecumenical unity by approving a proposed form of the ministry that would include bishops and recognized lay ministers.

Henderlite earned a B.A. degree from Agnes Scott College (Decatur, Georgia); an M.A. degree from the Biblical Seminary at New York University (New York, New York); and a Ph.D. degree from Yale Divinity School (New Haven, Connecticut).

Annie W. Henmyer

First president of the U.S. Woman's Christian Temperance Union (WCTU) (1874).

Born Sandy Spring, Ohio, 1827; died 1900.

The national WCTU was organized at a meeting in Cleveland, Ohio, in 1874. Henmyer was elected president and Frances Willard (see entry) was elected corresponding secretary. (In the 1879 election for president, Henmyer lost to Willard.)

Much of Henmyer's life was devoted to the sick and needy. During the Civil War, for example, she comforted and nursed the wounded. She also opened a public kitchen in Nashville, Tennessee, to provide wounded patients with food other than the usual army rations. She was one of the organizers of the Ladies' and Pastors' Christian Union (1868). Women members of this organization, under the supervision of their pastors, visited and assisted the sick and needy.

After the Civil War, Henmyer was the publisher of a successful periodical, *Christian Woman*, from 1871 to 1882.

She was president of the Iowa State Sanitary Commission in 1863. She also became the president of the Woman's Relief Corps (1889–90), the women's auxiliary of the Grand Army of the Republic, an organization consisting mainly of Civil War veterans.

Frieda B. Hennock

First woman appointed to the Federal Communications Commission (FCC) (1948).

Born Kovel, Poland, September 27, 1904; died Washington, D.C., June 20, 1960.

Hennock's appointment to the FCC was seen as a reward for her strong support of the Democratic party. Her major accomplishment with the FCC was to persuade the commission to reserve some 242 television channels for educational and noncommercial objectives.

Hennock immigrated with her family to the United States in 1910. She worked while attending Brooklyn Law School, Brooklyn, New York, as an evening student. She graduated in 1924, then had to wait a year—until she reached the age of twenty-one— to be admitted to the bar. Beginning her law practice in 1926, she was the youngest woman lawyer in New York City.

After she achieved a great deal of success first as a criminal lawyer, then as a corporate lawyer in New York City, President Harry S. Truman nominated her for a federal judge seat in 1951, but the Senate refused to support her, allegedly because she was having an affair with a married judge. Hennock withdrew her name from the nominations.

Hennock, who had served on the FCC since 1948, left when President Dwight D. Eisenhower refused to reappoint her in 1955.

Barbara Herman

First woman cantor in U.S. Reform Judaism (1975).

Born c. 1952.

Herman became a cantor at Beth Sholom Temple of Clifton-Passaic, New Jersey, in 1975. She had served there as a student cantor before her investiture from Hebrew Union College–Jewish Institute of Religion (New York, New York).

Married to a cantor, Herman completed a five-year program at the School of Sacred Music, Hebrew Union College–Jewish Institute of Religion.

Herman was the trailblazer for a slowly but steadily increasing number of women cantors, particularly in the Conservative and Reconstructionist branches of Judaism.

Robin Herman

One of the first two women reporters to enter a male players' dressing room (1975).

Born c. 1952.

Herman, a *New York Times* reporter, regularly covered the New York Islander hockey team games. On January 21, 1975, she was in Montreal, Canada, covering an all-star game of the National Hockey League, between the Islanders and the Montreal Canadiens. She and Marcelle St. Cyr of Radio CKLM, Montreal, were invited by the coaches of both teams to interview the players in their dressing room. The players were not notified of the visit in advance, however.

As a result of this event with the Islanders, the wives of the New York Rangers asked their husbands to petition to bar women from the players' locker room, and the team members complied.

Maggie (Marguerite) Higgins

First woman to win the Pulitzer Prize for international reporting (1951).

Born Hong Kong, September 3, 1920; died Washington, D.C., January 3, 1966.

Higgins earned an M.S. degree in journalism from Columbia University, New York, New York, in 1942, then went to work for the New York *Herald Tribune*. She witnessed the liberation of Dachau by the Allies and covered the trials of the Nazi war criminals at Nuremberg. She was named Berlin bureau chief in 1947 and Tokyo bureau chief in 1950.

Having become one of the United States's most famous war correspondents, Higgins won the Pulitzer Prize in 1951 for twenty-three months of reporting from Korean war zones—the only woman correspondent reporting from the battlefront.

She had previously distinguished herself with interviews of Nikita Khrushchev, Jawaharlal Nehru, Chiang Kai-shek, and other national leaders. The wife and daughter of soldiers, in the course of her career Higgins reported from the battlefields of World War II, Korea, and Vietnam.

Higgins is buried in Arlington National Cemetery.

Carla Anderson Hills

First woman to be secretary of the Department of Housing and Urban Development (1975).

Born Los Angeles, California, January 3, 1934.

After attending Stanford University (Stanford, California), where she graduated cum laude in 1955, Hills earned an LL.B. degree from Yale Law School (New Haven, Connecticut) in 1958.

From 1958 to 1961 she was assistant district attorney for Los Angeles, California, then from 1962 to 1974 she worked as a lawyer with a private firm in Los Angeles. Hills served as assistant attorney general, U.S. De-

partment of Justice, Civil Division, from 1974 to 1975.

In 1975 President Gerald Ford named Hills to be the first woman secretary of the Department of Housing and Urban Development (HUD), a post she held until 1977. Some of the most notorious publicity about her relationship with HUD came after she left the department and went to work for a law firm in Washington, D.C. One of the firm's clients hired Hills to lobby Samuel Pierce, her successor at HUD, in connection with a housing project that the client wanted to build with HUD funding in Beverly Hills, California. The project caused a scandal about the need for providing subsidized housing in such an affluent setting as Beverly Hills.

In 1989, after receiving unanimous confirmation by the U.S. Senate, Hills was named U.S. trade representative, executive office of the president, and was charged with carrying out four main tasks: to successfully conclude the Uruguay Round of multilateral trade negotiations; to protect U.S. interests as Europe moves toward integration in 1992; to effectively implement free trade agreements with Canada and Israel; and to substantially increase U.S. access to Japan and other markets.

Hills has been a director of IBM, Corning Glass Works, American Airlines, Federal National Mortgage Association, and the Chevron Corporation. She has been awarded honorary degrees from Pepperdine University (Malibu, California), Washington University (St. Louis, Missouri), Mills College (Oakland, California), Williams College (Williamstown, Massachusetts), and Lake Forest College (Lake Forest, Illinois).

Tina (Argentina) Schifano (Ramos) Hills

First woman president of the Inter American Press Association (1977).

Born Pola, Istria Province, Italy, October 4, 1921.

Before becoming the first woman president of the Inter American Press Association (IPA) (1977), an organization that fights for freedom of the press, Hills was the second vice

president of the association, having been elected unanimously. IPA is especially active in its fight for freedom of the press in Latin America.

Hills and her Italian parents immigrated to the United States when she was fourteen. She became a U.S. citizen and attended New York University (New York, New York). When she was only eighteen she began her career with the Buitoni-Perugina Company, an Italian food and candy concern; she quickly rose to manager of their Fifth Avenue store and then to an executive position.

Hills became an officer in El Mundo enterprises, San Juan, Puerto Rico, after marrying Angel Ramos, who owned the newspaper, *El Mundo*. He also headed radio and television enterprises. When Ramos died in 1960, she took over the running of El Mundo, including the newspaper, two leading radio stations, and the highest-rated television station in San Juan.

Under her direction, the San Juan *El Mundo* had by 1976 grown to an afternoon and evening daily, with a circulation of 140,000. She moved the site of the paper from an outdated building in Old San Juan to a modern facility in Hato Rey. Hills was also instrumental in developing a typeface that made the newspaper easier to read and oversaw the distribution of the paper into classroom programs. She was editor and publisher of *El Mundo* from 1961 to 1987. She also ran a film company that distributed English-speaking films dubbed in Spanish throughout Latin America, her aim being to educate young people about various ways of life.

As a result of Hills's policies, women comprised half of the work force at El Mundo enterprises. In accordance with Puerto Rican law protecting pregnant working women, pregnant women at El Mundo received leave with half pay for four weeks before and after giving birth.

Tina Ramos married Lee Hills, a newspaperman, in 1963. He was the recipient of the 1955 Pulitzer Prize for behind-the-scenes reporting. Tina and Lee Hills were the first couple to receive individually the Maria Moors Cabot Award, presented by Columbia University (New York, New York) to citizens who make outstanding contributions to inter-American relations. Lee Hills received the award in 1946, Tina in 1967. Hills donated her award honorarium to a scholarship fund for a Spanish-speaking student.

Tina Hills, who was the director of the Red Cross in San Juan for a time, has received several honorary degrees. Among them are an honorary degree in law from the Inter-American University of Puerto Rico (San Juan) in 1969; an honorary doctorate in humanities from both Queens College (Charlotte, North Carolina) in

1972 and the University of Miami (Miami, Florida) in 1978; and an honorary doctorate in philosophy and letters from the Universidad Metropolitana (Puerto Rico) in 1990.

At the time of this writing, Hills presides over The Angel Ramos Foundation, which came into being in 1966. The largest private foundation in Puerto Rico, it provides support and scholarship money for bright and economically deprived young people. The foundation also promotes freedom of the press.

Himalayan Expedition

First all-woman expedition to climb Annapurna in the Himalayas (1978).

The group of women, all but one from the United States, climbed Annapurna in Nepal. Reaching 26,545 feet, it is the world's tenth-highest mountain.

This expedition was especially enticing to climbers because the Nepalese government grants very few permits for climbing the Himalayas. Headed by Arlene Blum, the expedition included Vera Watson, Irene Miller, Wanda Rutkiewicz, Vera Komarkova, Margi Rusmore, Elizabeth Klobusieky-Mailaender, Annie Whitehouse, Piro Kramar, Joan Firey, Christy Tews, Marie Ashton, Dyanna Taylor, and Alison Chadwick-Onyszkiewicz.

Rusmore, from a family of hikers and backpackers, was at twenty the youngest member. Blum, holder of a Ph.D. degree in physical chemistry, had been part of the first all-woman climb of the Denali summit of Mount McKinley (Alaska), the highest peak in North America, in 1970. Rusmore had also scaled Mount McKinley prior to her climb of Annapurna.

Two women—Vera Watson and Alison Chadwick-Onyszkiewicz—died in their attempt on Annapurna. They were the first American women to die on that peak.

Lois E. Hinson

First woman president of the National Association of Federal Veterinarians (NAFV) (1973).

Born Hazlehurst, Georgia, 1926.

Serving as the first woman president of the NAFV from 1973 to 1974, Hinson was also the first woman inspector in charge of the U.S. Department of Agriculture (USDA) Federal Meat Inspection Division. In 1973 she also became the first woman chief staff veterinarian for horse protection in the USDA.

Hinson earned her degree from the University of Georgia College of Veterinary Medicine (Athens,

Georgia) in 1950, becoming the first woman to graduate from that college.

Judith Hird

First woman to be a parish pastor in the the Lutheran Church in America (1972).

Born c. 1946.

Hird, a graduate of Thiel College (Greenville, Pennsylvania) and Gettysburg Lutheran Theological Seminary (Gettysburg, Pennsylvania), was named parish pastor of the Holy Cross Lutheran Church, Toms River, New Jersey, in 1972. She was twenty-six years old at the time.

Mary Hirsch

First woman licensed to train thoroughbred horses (1934).

Born c. 1913.

Hirsch worked for three years as an assistant trainer with her father, Max Hirsch, a famous trainer of thoroughbreds. In July, 1934, the racing authorities of Illinois licensed her to train horses.

In April, 1936, she was one of seventy-five trainers granted a trainer's license by the state of New York.

In 1937, Hirsch became the first woman trainer of a horse that ran in the Kentucky Derby; the horse, No Sir, ran thirteenth.

Lucy Hobbs (Taylor)

First woman to graduate from dental school (1866).

Born Franklin City, New York, March 14, 1833; died Lawrence, Kansas, October 3, 1910.

After graduating from Franklin Academy, Malone, New York, in 1849, Hobbs began teaching school and studying medicine under a local physician. In 1859 she applied—but was refused admission—to the Eclectic Medical College in Cincinnati, Ohio. College officials advised her to study dentistry.

She applied to the Ohio College of Dental Surgery (Cincinnati) and was refused, but a graduate accepted her as an apprentice. She opened an office in Cincinnati, moving to Iowa when the Civil War broke out.

In 1865 Hobbs was elected to membership in the Iowa State Dental Society and named delegate to the American Dental Association convention. The Iowa Society supported her reapplication to the Ohio College of Dental Surgery, where she was admitted, graduating in 1866 with the highest final examination grades in her class. She practiced in Chicago, then married and moved to Lawrence, Kansas, where she and her husband (whom she had instructed in dentistry) opened a practice.

Oveta Culp Hobby

First director of the Women's Army Auxiliary Corps (WAAC) (1941); first woman to receive the U.S. Army Distinguished Service Medal (1945); first secretary of Health, Education and Welfare (1953).

Born Killeen, Texas, January 19, 1905.

Privately educated, Hobby was for a time a student at Mary Hardin–Baylor College (Belton, Texas) and the University of Texas Law School (Austin). From 1925 to 1931 she served as parliamentarian for the Texas House of Representatives, and in 1930 was also assistant to the city attorney of Houston.

In 1931 she married William Pettus Hobby, former Texas governor

(1917–21) and publisher of the *Houston Post*. Hobby went to work for the *Post*, where she was book editor from 1933 to 1936 and assistant editor from 1936 to 1938. She was named executive vice president in 1938.

With war imminent, Hobby joined the Bureau of Public Relations of the U.S. War Department, and in July, 1941, was appointed chief of the women's division, where she helped make plans for a women's auxiliary branch of the U.S. Army: the Women's Army Auxiliary Corps (WAAC). When the WAAC was created on May 14, 1942, Hobby was appointed director, with the equivalent army rank of major (later raised to colonel). She held this position until July, 1945. The Women's Army Auxiliary Corps was changed to Women's Army Corps (WAC) on July 1, 1943, and it was made a part of the regular army. Under her direction, the WAC grew to a maximum strength of about 100,000 during World War II, with about 17,000 members serving overseas. For her services, at the end of the war Hobby became the first woman to be awarded the U.S. Army Distinguished Service Medal (1945).

After the war, Hobby became coeditor and publisher of the *Houston Post*. She also became the president of the Southern Newspaper Publishers organization (1949), and a director of the KPRC radio and television stations in Houston.

Increasingly active in national politics, Hobby helped organize the Democrats for Eisenhower during Dwight D. Eisenhower's presidential campaign in 1952. After he took office in January, 1953, President Eisenhower named her director of the Federal Security Administration. When the FSA was elevated to cabinet status in April, 1953 as the U.S. Department of Health, Education and Welfare, Hobby became its first secretary and the second woman (after Frances Perkins—see entry) in the U.S. cabinet.

After her resignation as secretary of HEW in July, 1955, Hobby became president and editor of the *Houston Post*. Her husband died in 1964, and she was named chairman of the board in 1965. She also served as chairman of the board of Channel Two TV Company (elected 1970) and as a director of the Corporation for Public Broadcasting from 1968.

From 1978 to 1983 Hobby was chairman of the board of H & C Communications, Inc., and since 1983 has chaired its executive committee.

Hockey Association, U.S. Field

First organization to establish standards for women hockey players (1922).

The U.S. Field Hockey Association, founded in 1922, governs the standards of play for women hockey players in schools, clubs, and colleges. It also sponsors sectional and national tournaments, as well as foreign tours.

The United States sent its first field hockey team to the Olympics in 1984, winning a bronze medal for third place.

Ethel Ann Hoefly

First air force nurse to achieve rank of brigadier general (1972).

Born c. 1920.

Hoefly, who had served with the U.S. Army Nurse Corps during World War II, transferred to the U.S. Air Force Nurse Corps (USAFNC) in 1949, when it was first established. The recipient of an M.A. degree from Columbia University (New York, New York), she was named chief of the USAFNC in 1968.

Hoefly retired in 1974.

Jane Hoey

First director of the Bureau of Public Assistance, Social Security Board (1936).

Born Greeley County, Nebraska, January 15, 1892; died New York, New York, October 6, 1968.

Hoey worked on the New York City Board of Child Welfare, for the Home Service of the American Red Cross, and for the New York Tuberculosis and Health Association from 1916 to 1926. In 1926 she received an honorary LL.D. degree from Holy Cross College (Worcester, Massachusetts), and was appointed assistant director and secretary of the newly organized Welfare Council of New York City, where she worked until 1936.

Following her tenure on the council, she became the first director of the Bureau of Public Assistance, where she was responsible for providing help for the aged, the blind, and dependent children. In 1953 President Dwight D. Eisenhower appointed Oveta Culp Hobby (see entry) as the secretary of Health, Education and Welfare. Hobby forced Hoey out of her position with the Bureau of Public Assistance, saying that Hoey held a policy-making position that should be filled by an appointee of the Republican administration. Hoey's response: "There is nothing political about poverty."

Returning to the National Tuberculosis Association in 1953, she served as director of social research until 1957.

Hoey graduated from Trinity College (Washington, D.C.) in 1914, where she was president of the student government during her senior year, and in 1916 earned an M.A. degree at Columbia University (New York, New York), where she majored in political science.

She served as president of both the William J. Kerby Foundation, which gives assistance to the underprivileged, and the Council on Social Work Education.

Claire Giannini Hoffman

First woman director of the world's largest bank—the Bank of America (1949); first to serve on the executive committee of the Bank of America (1952); first to serve on the board of trustees of the Employees' Profit Sharing Pension Fund of Sears, Roebuck and Co. (1962); first to serve on the board of directors of Sears, Roebuck and Co. (1963).

Born San Francisco, California, 1904.

After attending Mills College (Oakland, California), Hoffman became the traveling companion and aide of her father, Amadeo Peter Giannini, who was the founder of the Bank of America. Shortly after his death in 1949, she succeeded him as a director of the bank. When her brother died in 1952, she succeeded him on the executive committee of the bank.

In 1985 Hoffman resigned from the board of the bank—now called Bank America—because she was outraged at what had happened to her father's company. She charged that the bank's leaders were "more and more reluctant to be held accountable for their actions." Among those actions was the sale of the bank's headquarters, which she considered a monument to her father. As a further form of protest, in 1987 she boycotted the annual meeting of the board of directors of the bank. (Early in 1988 Bank America, once a pacesetter in banking, had the weakest balance sheet of any sizable commercial bank.)

Hoffman was the only woman guest at the annual conferences of the International Bank for Reconstruction and Development, the International Finance Corporation, the International Development Association, and the International Monetary Fund for two decades. In 1977 she was the only honorary member of the American Institute of Banking. She was the first woman appointed to the board of regents of St. Mary's College of California (Moraga, California), and is a trustee of Rosemary Hall, a preparatory school in Greenwich, Connecticut.

She is the widow of Clifford P. Hoffman, a former Stanford University football captain who became an investment banker.

Wilhelmina Cole Holladay

Founder and president of the board of directors of the National Museum of Women in the Arts (1981).

Born October 10, 1922, Elmira, New York.

The National Museum of Women in the Arts, Washington, D.C., a forum for honoring women's contributions to the history of art and a vehicle for creating a greater awareness of their aesthetic achievements throughout history, is the first such repository of the art and archives of women's art in the world.

When the museum formally opened in April, 1987, its inaugural exhibition was *American Women Artists, 1830–1930,* a comprehensive survey of the first century of work by women artists in the United States. The museum also commissioned— with support from the National Endowment for the Arts—*Concerto for Two Pianos and Orchestra* from Ellen Taaffe Zwilich (see entry), who was awarded the Pulitzer Prize for music in 1983.

Holladay, who did postgraduate work in history of art at the University of Paris (Paris, France), earned a B.A. degree from Elmira College (Elmira, New York) in 1944. She also took courses in art history at Cornell University (Ithaca, New York) and studied at the University of Virginia (Charlottesville).

From 1945 to 1948 she worked for the Chinese nationalist government. During this period her duties included serving as social secretary to Madame Chiang Kai-shek. Her career was interrupted when she married Wallace F. Holladay, an architect and engineer, and began to raise a family. In 1957, however, she took up her career again, working part-time at the National Gallery of Art in Washington, D.C.

After working at the gallery for two years, Holladay traveled to Europe, where she toured art galleries and museums. She noted that women artists were essentially unrecognized by the art establishment. Among her findings were paintings by the seventeenth-century Flemish artist Clara Peters, whose name was conspicuously missing from all the standard art books Holladay consulted. This discovery gave her the impetus to begin her collection. With the assistance of her husband, she began the first major gathering of works by women artists in the world, approximately 300 works by 150 artists from

nineteen countries. Spanning three and a half centuries, these works became the nucleus of the collection for the national museum.

In 1982 the collection, first housed in the Holladay home in Georgetown, Washington, D.C., was moved to its present site two blocks from the White House at New York Avenue and 13th Street. Holladay led the fund-raising drive and promotion of the museum (1982–87). There was, however, some opposition to the museum. Some people felt the museum would isolate women's art, not promote it; others maintained that it could end up fostering mediocre works. The praise outweighed the criticism. Many people felt that talent, which had been overlooked, had been found and that more works of art by women that needed recognition would be added to the collection. In 1987 the museum and its library formally opened. By then the museum housed 500 works, and its membership had grown to 67,000. At the time of this writing, the museum has in its private collection more than 1,200 works of art dating from the Renaissance to the present, and the museum's library, which includes more than 12,000 archival files on women from all periods and countries, is the most comprehensive source of information on women artists available anywhere.

Holladay is listed in *Who's Who in*

American Art and *Who's Who in the World*. A former chair of the board of the Adams National Bank, she is a trustee of the U.S. Capitol Historical Society, a recipient of the Distinguished Woman Award from the Northwood Institute, Midland, Michigan (1987), and the Distinguished Achievement Award from the National League of American Pen Women (1988). A member of the National Women's Forum, she received an honorary doctoral degree in humanities from Elmira College, Elmira, New York (1989) and the Woman of Distinction award from Birmingham Southern College, Birmingham, Alabama (1991).

Elise Holloway

First woman "special peace agent" of the American Society for the Prevention of Cruelty to Animals (ASPCA) (1974).

Born Florida, c. 1950.

Holloway patrolled New York City's Central Park as a member of the Auxiliary Mounted Police. Then in 1974 she became the first woman to be named "special peace agent" in a group of eighteen male ASPCA agents. Her duties included using a revolver to humanely kill doomed, injured animals and issuing citations to people who were discovered mistreating animals.

Jeanne M. Holm

First woman general officer in the U.S. Air Force (USAF) (1971).

Born Portland, Oregon, 1921.

Holm enlisted in the Women's Army Auxiliary Corps (WAAC) in 1942, and was commissioned second lieutenant in 1943. She retired after the end of World War II and began studies at Lewis and Clark College in Portland, Oregon. Her studies were interrupted when she was recalled to active duty in 1948, at which time she transferred to the air force.

She supervised manpower needs for the Allied air forces from 1957 to 1965; served as director of women in the air force from 1965 to 1972, and was director of the Secretariat of Air Force Personnel from 1973 to 1975. In 1971 she was appointed brigadier general of the USAF, and ultimately became a major general, the highest rank attained by any woman in the U.S. armed forces.

Holm, a founder and first chair of the organization Women in Government, retired from the air force in 1975. President Gerald Ford appointed her as special assistant for women for the last year of his term (1976–77). Following her retirement, in 1977 she served on the Defense Advisory Committee on Women in the U.S. services.

Winifred Holt

Founder of Lighthouses for the Blind (1913).

Born New York, New York, November 17, 1870; died Pittsfield, Massachusetts, June 14, 1945.

In 1903 Holt established the Ticket Bureau for the Blind, which provided tickets to concerts for blind people. Ten years later, Holt and her sister, Edith, founded the New York Association for the Blind at their home in New York City. Winifred Holt was secretary and a leading fundraiser. The purpose of the organization was twofold: to educate the public about the possibility of making the blind self-supporting, and to find ways to prevent blindness.

In 1915 France asked Holt to establish the first foreign Lighthouses for those blinded in the battles of World War I. She was named Chevalier of the French Legion of Honor in 1921.

Holt also founded *Searchlight,* the first Braille magazine for children, and was responsible for the practice of training blind children in public school classes along with children with normal sight.

Grace Brewster Murray Hopper

First woman to develop operating programs for the first

automatically sequenced digital computer (c. 1945); first to develop the concept of automatic programming (1951) that led to the Common Business Oriented Language (COBOL) programming language; first person to receive the computer sciences Man of the Year award from the Data Processing Management Association (1969); first to receive, as an individual, the U.S. Medal of Technology, awarded by President George Bush (1991).

Born New York, New York, December 9, 1906; died Arlington, Virginia, January 1, 1992.

Hopper graduated from Vassar College (Poughkeepsie, New York) in 1928; she earned an M.A. degree (1930) and a Ph.D. degree (1934) from Yale University (New Haven,

Connecticut). After teaching at Vassar from 1931 to 1944, she enlisted in the WAVES (Women Accepted for Voluntary Emergency Service) branch of the navy in World War II (1944). She was assigned to work at the Bureau of Ordnance Computation Project, programming an early version of the electronic computer called the Mark I. Leaving the navy in 1946, Hopper retained her naval reserve status while remaining a faculty member at Harvard's applied physics computation laboratory. She left Harvard in 1949.

In 1966 the navy recalled Hopper as a commander to supervise the standardization of the navy's computer languages and programs. One consequence of Hopper's work was the first computer language compiler—a program that translates programming language into "machine language" that can be understood by the computer.

Known to her colleagues and subordinates as "Amazing Grace," Hopper was one of two women to be named a fellow of the Institute of Electrical and Electronics Engineers, winning the IEEE's McDowell Award in 1979. She was the first woman to be promoted to captain in the navy while on the retired reserve list (1973).

In 1983 Hopper was appointed rear admiral by President Ronald Reagan. When she retired from the navy in 1986, at the age of eighty, she was the oldest officer on active duty in all of the armed services. Following her retirement, she became a senior consultant to the Digital Equipment Corporation, a position she held until her death.

Olive Hoskins

First woman to be a U.S. Army warrant officer (1926).

Dates unknown.

Hoskins, of Pasadena, California, entered the army as a civilian grade headquarters clerk in 1907. In 1916 she was appointed army field clerk, and when that grade was abolished in 1926, she became a warrant officer. An army warrant officer, holding a rank between enlisted persons and commissioned officers, is usually a skilled technician with a specific area of expertise.

During World War I, Hoskins was in charge of personnel at the Judge Advocate's Office in San Francisco, California. She served in the Philippines from 1919 to 1922; in Omaha, Nebraska, at the Seventh Corps Area Headquarters from 1922 to 1933; in the Philippines again from 1933 to 1936; and at the Ninth Corps Area Headquarters in San Francisco, California, until her retirement in 1937.

Harriet Goodhue Hosmer

First successful woman sculptor in the United States (1853).

Born Watertown, Massachusetts, October 9, 1830; died Watertown, Massachusetts, February 21, 1908.

As a teenager, Hosmer decided to become a sculptor and established a studio at her home. She studied technique, and was taught by a physician who gave her anatomy lessons similar to his lectures at a local medical school. She passed an examination and received a diploma.

In 1852 Hosmer went to Rome to study, and began selling busts based on figures from classic mythology. Her first original work was a bust of Daphne. Her *Puck* figure, executed in 1856, was a great success, selling fifty replicas at $1,000 each.

In 1864 she published an article in the *Atlantic Monthly* titled "The Process of Sculpture," a response to those who asserted that much of her success was due to the skills of her workmen.

Hosmer continued to live and work in Europe, remaining there until 1900, when she returned to Watertown.

She was also an avid mountain climber, and Mount Hosmer in Missouri is named for her.

Hospital, Woman's

First hospital for treatment of women's diseases (1855).

On February 10, 1855, thirty women met to plan the organization of the Woman's Hospital. Opening on May 4 in New York City, it was the first institute in the world established by women "for the treatment of diseases peculiar to women and for the maintenance of a lying-in hospital."

The original hospital, located at East 29th Street and Madison Avenue, had a forty-patient capacity, with some wards set aside for poor patients. Wealthy patients were charged according to the location of their rooms. The staff was comprised of one surgeon, J. Marion Sims (male), a nurse, and two matrons—

one who administered to the sick and one who supervised domestic arrangements.

The hospital, known as the "birthplace of gynecology," moved to East 49th Street, between Lexington and Park Avenues, and finally to West 114th Street, between Amsterdam and Columbus Avenues. The hospital is now part of St. Luke's hospital complex.

Hazel Hotchkiss (Wightman)

Member of the first U.S. women's doubles team to win a gold medal in Olympic tennis (1924); first woman to win an Olympic gold medal in mixed doubles tennis (1924).

Born Healdsburg, California, December 20, 1886; died Boston, Massachusetts, December 5, 1974.

Hotchkiss and Helen Wills (see entry) defeated Great Britain's Edith Covell and Kitty McKane, 7–5, 8–6, to win the Olympic gold medal in women's doubles in 1924. Hotchkiss and R. Norris Williams defeated Marion Jessup and Vincent Richards, another U.S. team, 6–2, 6–3, to win the Olympic gold medal in mixed doubles in 1924. That same year, she and Wills won the women's doubles at Wimbledon.

From 1909 to 1911, then again in 1919, she won the U.S. women's singles championship. She was one of the winners in the U.S. women's doubles championship from 1909 to 1911; she won again in 1915, 1924, and 1928 with Wills as her partner.

Hotchkiss established the Wightman Cup (see entry) in 1923. She was elected to the International Tennis Hall of Fame in 1957.

Edith Houghton

First woman to be hired as a scout for a major league baseball team (1946).

Dates unknown.

Houghton was a star player (shortstop) for the Philadelphia Bobbies, a women's team, which eventually folded. The Philadelphia Phillies of the National League hired her as the team's scout in 1946. Less than a week later, she was appointed to the 1946 All-American Board of the National Baseball Congress. The board, comprised of major league scouts, chooses the best major league prospects in the United States.

Houghton had played against Nippon College (Japan) baseball players when she was only thirteen. Later she became a member of the Women Accepted for Voluntary Emergency Service (WAVES).

Julia Ward Howe

***First woman elected to the
American Academy of Arts and
Letters (1908).***

Born New York, New York, May
27, 1819; died Newport, Rhode Island, October 17, 1910.

Educated by governesses and private schools, she married Samuel
Gridley Howe, head of the Perkins Institute for the Blind, in 1843. They
settled in South Boston, Massachusetts. The marriage was a troubled
one, however, because her husband
vehemently opposed the appearance
of married women in public life.

In 1854 Howe published anony-
mously two books of poetry: *Passion
Flowers* and *Words for the Honor*.
Two plays followed in 1857: *Lenora,*

or the World's Own, which was not a
commercial success, and *Hippolytus,*
which was not produced. In 1862,
with the Civil War in progress, the
Atlantic Monthly published her "Battle Hymn of the Republic." It was
soon sung to the melody of "John
Brown's Body," and within two years
had achieved massive popularity in
the North.

In 1868 Howe founded the New
England Woman Suffrage Association, serving as its president from
1868 to 1877 and from 1893 to her
death.

She published *Sex and Education,*
a book advocating coeducation, in
1874, and a biography of Margaret
Fuller (see entry) in 1883. In 1881
she had been elected president of the
Association for the Advancement of
Women; during this period, she gave
numerous public speeches encouraging a return to established ancestral
values which, in her opinion, were
being forgotten in the greediness that
characterized the Gilded Age.

After Howe was elected to the
American Academy of Arts and Letters, she remained the only female
member until 1930.

Howe's daughters, Laura Howe
Richards (see entry) and Maud Howe
Elliott (see entry), wrote a biography
of their mother, which won a Pulitzer
Prize for biography in 1915.

"Lady Clerks Leaving the Treasury Department in Washington"

Mary F. Hoyt

First woman to be a Civil Service appointee (1883).

Born Southport, Connecticut, June 17, 1858; died New York, New York, October 20, 1958.

The Civil Service Act, or the Pendleton Act, which created a system of federal employment based on merit and examination scores rather than political patronage, was signed by President Chester A. Arthur early in 1883. The first Civil Service examination was administered on July 12, 1883. Hoyt received the highest score, and on September 5 she became the first woman (and the second person) to be appointed to a federal position under the provisions of the Civil Service Act.

Hoyt was appointed to a clerkship in the Bank Redemption Agency of the Treasury Department, a position she held for five years. She later worked for the U.S. Census Bureau.

An 1880 graduate of Vassar College (Poughkeepsie, New York), Hoyt received a letter from President Dwight D. Eisenhower on her 100th birthday. In the letter, he said, "A door was opened to a new world of careers for women in our land and you were the first to enter it."

Winnifred Huck

Established the precedent of seeking to fill the unexpired term of a relative in public office (1921).

Born Chicago, Illinois, September 14, 1882; died Chicago, Illinois, August 24, 1936.

Huck, whose father was a congressman from Illinois, asked to fill his unexpired term when he died in

Winnifred Huck (right) with Mary Nolan (center) and Alice Robertson (left)

1921. The governor of Illinois took no action at the time, but Huck was elected to her father's seat in the regularly scheduled Illinois election in 1922—the only one of ten women running for congressional seats in the United States to be elected.

As a result of her precedent, almost fifty percent of the women who attained congressional office during the next forty years did so as replacements for husbands or fathers who had died in office.

Huck served from November, 1922, to March, 1923. In her later years, as a newspaper columnist, she posed as an ex-convict seeking employment, writing stories whose intent was to create job opportunities for ex-prisoners.

Shirley Mount Hufstedler

First person to be named secretary of the U.S. Office of Education (1979).

Born Denver, Colorado, August 24, 1925.

When President Jimmy Carter appointed her to the post in 1979, she was serving on the U.S. Court of Appeals for the Ninth Circuit, and was the senior female judge in the United States. At that time, over 900 constitutional lawyers polled by the *National Law Review* picked her as their first choice for the next Supreme Court vacancy.

Hufstedler graduated from the University of New Mexico (Albuquerque) and from Stanford Law School (Palo Alto, California). From 1949 to 1959 she was a member of the law firm of Beardsley, Hufstedler & Kemble in Los Angeles. She served on the Los Angeles County Superior Court, the California Court of Appeals, and was named by President Lyndon Johnson to the federal court in 1968.

Adella Hughes

First woman to serve as manager of a major symphony orchestra (1918).

Born Cleveland, Ohio, November

29, 1869; died Cleveland Heights, Ohio, August 23, 1950.

Hughes, who graduated from Vassar College, Poughkeepsie, New York, in 1890, went on to become a professional accompanist. During the next few years she successfully organized major performances and concert series, taking care of the contracts, the engagement of performers, and most other associated details.

In 1901 she was a leader in the establishment of a regular concert series in Cleveland, and she sponsored a Musical Arts Association that brought ballet, opera, and other performances to the city.

She introduced Cleveland to the young conductor Nikolai Sokoloff in 1918. He organized the Cleveland Orchestra, with Hughes as manager. She held the position for the next fifteen years, during which time she was responsible for such innovations as children's concerts, radio broadcasts, summer "pops" concerts, and music-appreciation programs in the public schools.

Sarah Tilghman Hughes

First woman federal judge to swear in a U.S. president (1963).

Born Baltimore, Maryland, 1896; died Dallas, Texas, April 22, 1985.

Hughes was appointed a federal judge by President John F. Kennedy in 1961. After Kennedy was assassinated in 1963, Hughes, who was a friend of both Kennedy and Lyndon B. Johnson, swore Johnson in as president of the United States on November 22, 1963. Jacqueline B. Kennedy, now widow of President John F. Kennedy, stood by Johnson's side on board *Air Force One* as Hughes led the ceremony.

Hughes was a graduate of the George Washington Law School, Washington, D.C. While attending classes there, she also worked as a Washington police officer. She later became a women's rights activist and wrote a bill which would allow women to serve on Texas juries.

In 1930 she was elected to serve in the Texas House of Representatives, and was reelected twice. After being appointed a state district judge in 1935, she was reelected seven times.

As part of her special recognition, she was elected president of the National Federation of Business and Professional Women's Clubs.

Harriot Kezia Hunt

First woman to practice medicine in the United States (1835).

Born Boston, Massachusetts, November 9, 1805; died Boston, Massachusetts, January 2, 1875.

Privately educated in Boston, Hunt taught school from 1827 to

1833, then studied anatomy and physiology with a physician in 1833. In 1835 she and her sister set up a medical practice primarily for women and children, advocating a regimen of good nursing, diet, regular bathing, exercise, and rest. Five years later her sister married and withdrew from the practice.

Hunt applied repeatedly to Harvard Medical School (Cambridge, Massachusetts). She was eventually accepted by Dean Oliver Wendell Holmes in 1850, at the same time that he admitted black students for the first time. The male medical school students rioted in protest, and Hunt was forced to withdraw. (The first woman to earn a medical degree in the United States was Elizabeth Blackwell, see entry.)

In 1843 Hunt organized the Ladies' Physiological Society and gave lectures. In 1849 she gave a free course of public lectures in Boston on physiology and hygiene, and in 1853 she was awarded an honorary degree from the Female Medical College of Pennsylvania.

Hurricanes

The National Weather Service first used women's names for hurricanes in the Atlantic, Caribbean, and Gulf of Mexico in 1953. Prior to 1953, the Weather Service had designated hurricanes either by date or by the army phonetic alphabet (Able, Baker, Charlie, etc.). The first hurricane to receive a woman's name was Alice, in 1953.

Anne M. Hutchinson

First woman to start a religious sect (1635); first to dissent against Puritan orthodoxy (1635); first woman to preach to women (1635); and possibly the first woman to be excommunicated (1638).

Born Alford, Lincolnshire, England, 1591; died Pelham Bay Park (now The Bronx), New York, August, 1643.

Hutchinson immigrated with her family to Boston, Massachusetts, in 1634; she became a nurse and mid-

wife. Described by John Winthrop as "a woman of fierce and haughty carriage," she led meetings in protest against the power and authority of the clergy and the Massachusetts Puritans. She founded the Antinomian party and held weekly meetings at her home (often attended by about seventy-five Puritans, men and women) to discuss secular and theological matters. The party attacked basic tenets of Puritanism, particularly the doctrine of salvation through works.

Hutchinson was tried and convicted of heresy and sedition before the General Court of the Massachusetts Colony; she was excommunicated by the Boston Anglican Church and banished in 1638. At the end of her trial Hutchinson claimed to have experienced divine revelation; consequently, the judge said that she had assumed postures to which only men were entitled: dominating her husband, exerting authority over the community, attacking the sanctity of ministers, and in general showing insufficient respect for the "fathers" of the community.

She settled in Rhode Island with her husband, children, and seventy followers. After challenging the authority of the Rhode Island magistrates, she and her family moved to Bronx, New York, where she and all but one of her children were killed by Native Americans in 1643.

The Hutchinson River and the Hutchinson River Parkway in the Bronx and Westchester County, New York, are named for Anne Hutchinson.

Ada Louise Huxtable

First person to receive the Pulitzer Prize for criticism (1970).

Born New York, New York, 1921.

Huxtable was the assistant curator of architecture and design at the Museum of Modern Art from 1946 to 1950. From 1950 to 1963 she was a freelance writer and contributing editor for *Progressive Architecture* and *Art in America*. She was architecture

critic for *The New York Times* from 1963 to 1982 and served on its editorial board from 1973 to 1982. Her books on architecture include *Classic New York* (1964), *Kicked a Building Lately?* (1976), and *Architecture Anyone?* (1986).

Huxtable, who was a Fulbright fellow in architectural study in Italy in 1950 and again in 1952, was instrumental in the establishment of the Landmarks Preservation Commission for New York City in 1965. A Phi Beta Kappa key holder and magna cum laude graduate of Hunter College (New York, New York), she is a fellow in the American Academy of Arts and Sciences and is an honorary member of the Royal Institution of British Architects.

The first Pulitzer Prize for criticism was awarded to Huxtable in 1970, in recognition of her efforts to promote and preserve quality in architecture. Among her many other awards is the Woman of the Year award, 1974, presented to her by the American Association of University Women.

Ida Hyde

First woman elected to the American Physiological Society (1902); first to conduct research at Harvard Medical School (1896).

Born Davenport, Iowa, September 8, 1857; died Berkeley, California, August 22, 1945.

Hyde earned a B.S. degree from Cornell University in Ithaca, New York, in 1891. She then attended Bryn Mawr College, Bryn Mawr, Pennsylvania, where she did research for two years in the fields of physiology and biology.

In 1893 she was invited to study at the University of Strassburg, Germany. Following advanced study there, she earned a Ph.D. degree with honors in physiology from the University of Heidelberg, Germany. She was the first woman to receive a Ph.D. degree at that university.

She conducted research at Harvard Medical School from 1896 to 1897, the first woman to do so. Following her research there, she taught at the University of Kansas in Lawrence, Kansas, where she was named professor of physiology in 1905. In 1902 she was made the first female member of the American Physiological Society. She studied at the medical college of Rush University (Chicago, Illinois), from 1908 to 1912.

Hyde, who also wrote textbooks in her field, retired in 1920.

Indiana University

First state college to grant equal privileges to women (1860s).

Sarah Parke Morrison was the first woman to enroll at—and receive a degree from—Indiana University.

Laura Ingalls

First woman to fly nonstop east to west across North America (1935).

Dates unknown.

Ingalls was also the first to fly solo around South America (1934), and the first to graduate from a government-approved flying school (Parks Air College of St. Louis, Missouri, 1930). But all of these accomplishments were eclipsed by the notoriety she achieved by being the first to be accused, tried, and convicted as a Nazi espionage agent during World War II (1942).

She first attracted public attention as a stunt flyer. In Muskogee, Oklahoma, on May 26, 1930, the twenty-five-year-old New Yorker performed 980 consecutive loop-the-loops in three hours and forty minutes to win $1,036 in prize money. In St. Louis, on August 13, she performed 714 barrel rolls (a complete rotation of the plane on its longitudinal axis) to best the men's record by 297 and the women's by 647.

Ingalls's record-breaking east-to-west flight—from Roosevelt Field, Long Island, New York, to Glendale, California—took thirty hours and twenty-seven minutes flying time. Flying a Moth biplane, she left New York on October 5, 1930, made nine stops, and arrived at Glendale on October 9. She made the return trip in twenty-five hours, thirty-five minutes flying time, landing in New York on October 18.

Her most notable flight came when she left Miami, Florida, on March 8, 1934, and flew alone for 22,000 miles over the West Indies, Central America, and around South America—with a flight across the

Andes. The trip took forty-nine days, and she returned on April 25. For her extraordinary achievement, Ingalls received the Claude B. Harmon Trophy for U.S. women pilots and the award of the Ligue Internationale des Aviateurs.

Flying a 190-mile-per-hour Lockheed Orion monoplane, Ingalls became the first woman to fly nonstop east to west across the United States. Her transcontinental time was eighteen hours, nineteen minutes, and thirty seconds from Floyd Bennett Field, Brooklyn, New York, to Burbank, California—where she arrived on July 10, 1935. Two months later, on September 12, she broke Amelia Earhart's record by flying nonstop from Los Angeles to New York in thirteen hours, thirty-four minutes.

A few months later, Ingalls's political self began to emerge. On June 24, 1936, she flew over the convention hall in Philadelphia, where the Democratic National Committee was meeting, and released six homing pigeons for the Emergency Peace Campaign in an appeal to President Franklin D. Roosevelt to make the Democrats the "American Peace Party."

On September 26, 1939, she flew over the White House and dropped pamphlets supporting the Women's National Committee to Keep the United States Out of the War. This act violated two Civil Aeronautic Board regulations, and Ingalls's pilot license was suspended. The pamphlets called on Congress to withstand President Roosevelt's pressure to repeal the arms embargo provisions of the Neutrality Act.

Arrested by the FBI on December 18, 1941, for failing to register as a German agent under the Foreign Agents Registration Act, Ingalls claimed that she was actually carrying out counterespionage against Germany. It was proven, however, that since August 1, 1941, she had received a salary from the Germans via the Gestapo chief in the United States.

Ingalls was indicted by a federal grand jury on December 23 and pleaded no defense on January 2, 1942; on January 16 she changed her plea to innocent. On February 13, 1942, the jury found her guilty. At her sentencing, Ingalls said, "I felt that I had a right to follow the dictates of my conscience. My motives were born of a burning patriotism and a high idealism." One witness had testified that she regularly wore a swastika pendant and referred to Hitler as "a marvelous man." She was sentenced to eight months to two years in prison, and was released on October 4, 1943.

Mary Shotwell Ingraham

First woman to receive a U.S. Medal for Merit (1946); a founder of the United Service Organizations (USO) (1941).

Born Brooklyn, New York, January 5, 1887; died Huntington, Long Island, New York, April 16, 1981.

As a founder and former vice president of the USO (an organization that supplies social, recreational, and welfare facilities for the armed services), Ingraham was awarded the Medal for Merit by President Harry S. Truman. Her citation noted her service to the country, and recognized her actions on a committee of the U.S. War Department that selected the first women for officers' training in the Women's Auxiliary Army Corps.

A 1908 graduate of Vassar College (Poughkeepsie, New York), Ingraham worked for the Brooklyn (New York) YWCA and served as its president from 1922 to 1939. From 1940 to 1945 she was president of the national board of the YWCA. She also served from 1938 to 1968 as an unsalaried member of the New York City Board of Higher Education. In 1959 she headed a committee of the board whose 1960 report led to the establishment of the City University of New York in 1961.

Ingraham was the mother of Mary Ingraham Bunting, first woman to serve on the Atomic Energy Commission.

May Irwin

First movie actress to kiss on-screen (1896).

Born Whitby, Ontario, Canada, June 27, 1862; died New York, New York, October 22, 1938.

Born Georgia Campbell, she moved with her family to Buffalo, New York, in 1875, and soon she and her sister, Ada, were on stage as the singing team of May and Flo Irwin. From 1883 she sang and played light stage comedy and farce until she retired in 1920.

The celebrated kiss was shared by her costar, John Rice, in a short scene from *The Widow Jones* (1896). It led to demands for screen censorship.

Mary Putnam Jacobi

First woman to be accepted at the École de Médecin of Paris, France (1868); first to be elected to the New York Academy of Medicine (1880); founder of the Association for Advancement of the Medical Education of Women (later the Women's Medical Association of New York City) (1872).

Born London, England, August 31, 1842; died New York, New York, June 10, 1906.

Jacobi was born in England to American parents. Her father was George Putnam, the publisher. The family moved to Staten Island, New York, in 1848. Jacobi studied chemistry and pharmacy, and in 1863 she graduated from the New York School of Pharmacy (New York, New York). The following year she graduated from the Female Medical College of Philadelphia (Pennsylvania) (later Woman's Medical College). In 1868 she entered the École de Médecin of

Paris, graduating with high honors in 1871.

From 1871 to 1896 Jacobi was an instructor and eventually professor of materia medica and therapeutics for the Woman's Medical College of New York Infirmary. She also founded, in 1872, the Association for Advancement of the Medical Education of Women (later the Women's Medical Association of New York City), whose mission was to promote and improve the education of women in the field of medicine.

Also interested in social causes, Jacobi helped organize the Working Woman's Society, which later became the National Consumers League. The organization worked to abolish sweatshops.

An essayist and woman of letters, Jacobi wrote throughout her career. Her first essay was published in the *Atlantic Monthly* in 1860. She also wrote over 100 medical papers; in 1876 she won the Boyleston Prize, sponsored by Harvard University (Cambridge, Massachusetts), for her paper "The Question of Rest for Women during Menstruation."

Anna M. Jarvis

Initiator of Mother's Day (see entry) (1908, 1914).

Born Grafton, West Virginia, May 1, 1864; died West Chester, Pennsylvania, November 24, 1948.

Jarvis began her campaign for the establishment of a day honoring mothers in 1907, after the death of her own mother. The first observances of the day were held in 1908, on the second Sunday in May, when various churches in Grafton, West Virginia, and Philadelphia, Pennsylvania, honored mothers. The custom of wearing carnations on Mother's Day also began at that time. Jarvis's intensive letter-writing campaign was so successful that by 1913 there were Mother's Day observances in almost every state. In 1914 President Woodrow Wilson signed a joint resolution of Congress recommending the observance of Mother's Day by government offices, and the following year the president was given authorization to proclaim the second Sunday of each May as national Mother's Day.

Eventually, as a result of Jarvis's efforts, there were mother's day observances in at least forty-three countries. However, she spent much of the latter part of her life in an attempt—largely unsuccessful—to prevent the commercialization of the day.

Jazz Festival, Women's

First jazz festival exclusively for women musicians (1978).

The festival, held in Kansas City, Missouri, in March, 1978, featured such women musicians and recording artists as Mary Lou Williams, Marian McPartland, Betty Carter, Toshiko Akiyoshi (see entry), and Mary Osborne.

Emma R. H. Jentzer

First woman special agent of the Bureau of Investigation (predecessor of the Federal Bureau of Investigation) (1911).

Born c. 1883; died Brooklyn, New York, May 4, 1972.

The bureau was formed in 1908, and Harry R. Jentzer—Emma Jentzer's husband—was appointed the first agent. Emma Jentzer was working as an interpreter at the Ellis Island immigrant station in New York City. She herself became a member of the bureau after her husband's death. She was a special agent from 1911 to 1919.

Johns Hopkins Medical School

First medical college to admit women on an equal basis with men (1893).

The start-up funds of Johns Hopkins Medical School (Baltimore, Maryland) were invested in the Baltimore and Ohio Railroad (B & O) stocks, which were not profitable in the early 1890s. As a result, the school was in financial straits and threatened not to open. Mary Garrett, daughter of the president of the B & O, donated $300,000 to the school, on the condition that women be admitted. The school opened and women were admitted in 1893.

By 1903, fourteen of the seventeen women's medical schools that were in operation in 1893 had closed as a result of drives to make medical schools coeducational.

Opha M. Johnson

First woman member of the U.S. Marine Corps Reserve (1918).

Dates unknown.

On August 12, 1918 the secretary of the navy authorized the commandant of the Marine Corps to enroll women as reservists. Johnson enlisted the following day. She held the rank of private and served as a clerk in the headquarters of the Quartermasters Corps in Washington, D.C. She was discharged in 1919.

"Marinettes" on the White House Lawn c. 1919

During World War I, 277 women served as enlisted marines.

Harriet Lane Johnston (see Harriet Lane)

Henrietta Deering Johnston

First woman to be recognized as a pastel artist (c. 1709).

Born probably Ireland, before 1670; died Charleston, South Carolina, March, 1728 or 1729.

She arrived in the colonies at Charles Town, South Carolina, in 1707. When her husband had serious health problems and financial difficulties, Henrietta Johnston helped support the family by working as a painter of portraits, executing at least forty between 1707 and 1720. Most of her works were done with dry, colored chalk on paper. (Pastel was a rare medium in the American colonies at the time.) Johnston is best known for her study of Governor Robert Johnson.

Elizabeth Jones

First woman to be chief sculptor-engraver of the U.S. Mint (1981).

Born Montclair, New Jersey, c. 1935.

The eleventh person to hold the position since the U.S. Mint was established in 1792, Jones is responsible for designing and preparing new mint medals, designing new U.S. coin issues, and preparing dies for continuing production of existing U.S. coins.

One of her first designs for the mint was the George Washington commemorative half dollar in 1982. She also designed the presidential medal for President Ronald Reagan and the Olympic silver dollar (1983).

A 1957 graduate of Vassar College (Poughkeepsie, New York) with a B.A. degree in art, Jones studied for two years at the Art Students League, New York City, then resided, studied, and worked for the next two decades in Rome, Italy. While in Italy, Jones designed a gold medal in honor of Pope John Paul II for the Italian government (1979).

In 1988 she designed the figure of Nike, Greek goddess of victory, which is seen on the obverse of the Olympic five-dollar gold piece—the half eagle.

In 1972 the American Numismatic Association named her Outstanding Sculptor of the Year.

Sara Jordan

First woman president of the American Gastroenterological Association (1942–44); first to be a member of the board of directors of the Boston Chamber of Commerce (1948).

Born Newton, Massachusetts, 1884; died Boston, Massachusetts, November 21, 1959.

Jordan joined the Lahey Clinic, Burlington, Massachusetts, in 1921, where she specialized in diseases possibly deriving from the tensions of daily life, especially illnesses of the gastrointestinal tract. From 1922 to 1958, she was head of the gastroenterology department at the clinic, and from 1942 to 1944 served as president of the American Gastroenterological Association, elected to this position in recognition of her contributions to medicine.

She earned an A.B. degree in classics from Radcliffe College (Cambridge, Massachusetts), in 1904, and her doctorate in philology from the University of Munich (Germany), in 1908. She graduated first in her class from Tufts College Medical School (Medford, Massachusetts), in 1921.

Jordan held various offices, including that of chair of the American Medical Association Section on Gastroenterology (1941–48). She was a member of the Boston Chamber of Commerce board of directors, where she served for three years.

Her honors and special recognition include the Elizabeth Blackwell Citation for the Teaching and Practice of Medicine (1951) and the Julius Friedenwald Medal for Outstanding Achievement in Gastroenterology (1952).

Ann Hasseltine Judson

One of the first two U.S. women to serve as overseas missionaries (1812) (see also Harriet Newell).

Born Bradford, Massachusetts, December 22, 1789; died Rangoon, Burma, October 24, 1826.

Born Nancy Hasseltine, she was educated at Bradford Academy (Bradford, Massachusetts), and taught school in nearby towns. In 1812 she married Adoniram Judson, a Congregational missionary. Accompanied by Nancy's childhood friend, Harriet Newell, and Newell's husband, the Judsons sailed to India, where they converted to the Baptist faith. After only a few months, however, the East India Company, opposed to missionary activities, decided to deport them—so they sailed to the Isle of France (now Mauritius) in the Indian Ocean. From there, Judson and her husband decided that Burma (now Myanmar) was a fertile field for their missionary work.

In July, 1813, they came to Rangoon, Burma, but had little success with converts for the first few years. Ann Judson was forced by illness to leave Burma in 1821 and return to the United States. She went back to Burma in 1823, though, and shortly thereafter the British captured Rangoon. Suspecting that the American missionaries were spies, the emperor put Judson's husband into prison. He was released in November, 1825; about a year later, Ann Judson died of tropical fever.

Dorothy Misener Jurney

First woman to become a board member of the Associated Press Managing Editors (APME) association (1972).

Born Michigan City, Indiana, May 8, 1909.

Among the many newspaper jobs Jurney held were:

- reporter for the *Michigan City News* (1938) and *News Dispatch* (1938–39)
- reporter for the Gary, Indiana, *Post-Tribune* (1939–41)

- editor in the women's department, *Miami News* (1943–44; 1946–49)
- women's editor, *Miami Herald* (1949–59)
- women's editor, *Detroit Free Press* (1959–72)
- assistant city editor (the first woman) and later acting city editor of the *Washington Daily News* (1944–46)
- assistant managing editor of the *Detroit Free Press* (1973)
- assistant managing editor for features of the *Philadelphia Inquirer* (1973–75).

In addition to dealing with normal matters that come before any board of directors, the board members of the Associated Press discuss specific problems of the newspaper industry and what the AP should be doing for newspapers throughout the country. Jurney says that when she was a member, the board particularly addressed what the AP might do for women readers.

As chair of the nominations committee of the American Society of Newspaper Editors, she was chosen as one of two women to accompany the delegation of the American Society of Newspaper Editors to the People's Republic of China in 1975. That same year, after retiring from the *Philadelphia Inquirer,* she founded the Women's Network, an executive placement agency for women journalists with management aptitude.

Jurney, who attended Western College for Women (Wayne, Pennsylvania) from 1926 to 1928, earned a B.S. degree in journalism from Northwestern University (Evanston, Illinois) in 1930. She founded the New Directions for News Program at the University of Missouri School of Journalism (Columbia) in 1987.

At the time of this writing, Jurney is one of only two women members of the Associated Press Managing Editors (APME) Regents, a group of retired newspaper people.

Jury, First Sexually Integrated

The first sexually integrated jury, consisting of six women and six men, was formed in Albany, New York, in 1701. (See also Grand Jury, First Sexually Integrated.)

In the early years of the United States, women were systematically excluded or exempted from jury service. In 1961 the U.S. Supreme Court, ruling on the appeal of a woman convicted by an all-male jury of murdering her husband, rejected her arguments, ruling that the right to an impartially selected jury "does not entitle one accused of crime to a jury tailored to the circumstances of the particular case, whether relating to the sex or other condition of the defendant, or the nature of the charges to be tried."

This ruling was overturned in *Taylor* v. *Louisiana* (1975), when the court ruled 8 to 1 that "it is untenable to suggest these days that it

"Studies in Expression When Women Are Jurors"

would be a special hardship for each and every woman to perform jury service or that society cannot spare *any* [Court's italics] women from their present duties.'' The Court said that the Louisiana law (allowing women to be automatically exempted from jury duty) was in violation of the Sixth Amendment, which stipulates that a defendant has the right to a jury drawn from a fair cross section of the community.

Roberta A. Kankus

First woman licensed to be a commercial nuclear power plant operator (1976).

Born Elmira, New York, 1953.

Kankus was trained on the job for fourteen months from 1975 until 1976, at the Peach Bottom Power Plant of the Philadelphia Electric Company. After this training, she passed a test required for licensing as a senior engineer and nuclear power plant operator. Prior to the training program, Kankus, twenty-three years old, had worked as an assistant mechanical engineer for the company, located sixty miles outside of Philadelphia.

She graduated from Rensselaer Polytechnic Institute (Troy, New York).

Kappa Alpha Theta

The first Greek-letter sorority was established at Indiana Asbury University (now De Pauw) in Greencastle, Indiana, in 1870.

Rhoda Hendrick Karpatkin

First woman executive director of the Consumers Union (1974).

Born New York, New York, June 7, 1930.

Karpatkin became the executive director of the Consumers Union of the U.S. Inc., after practicing law privately from 1954 to 1974.

She earned a B.A. degree from Brooklyn College (Brooklyn, New York) in 1951 and an LL.B. degree from Yale University (New Haven, Connecticut) in 1953.

Laura Keene

First woman to be a theater manager (1853).

Born London, England, c. 1820; died Montclair, New Jersey, November 4, 1873.

Keene arrived in New York City

from England in 1852, making her U.S. stage debut in September of that year. She became manager of the Charles Street Theatre in Baltimore, Maryland, on December 24, 1853—the same day that Catherine Sinclair (Forrest) also became a theater manager.

In 1855 she opened her own theater in New York City—Laura Keene's Varieties—where she was manager and leading lady. The following year she moved into a new theater, Laura Keene's Theater, again as manager and leading lady. She left there in 1863.

She was in Ford's Theatre, Washington, D.C., when President Lincoln was shot. She recognized John Wilkes Booth as the assassin, and held the president's head in her lap until he was taken from the theater.

Keene's innovations in the theater included the establishment of the matinee as a regular feature and the initiation of long runs for individual plays.

Mary Kimball Kehew

First president of the National Women's Trade Union League (1903); cofounder of the Union for Industrial Progress (1894) (see also Mary Kenney).

Born Boston, Massachusetts, September 8, 1859; died Boston, Massachusetts, February 13, 1918.

Kehew joined the Women's Educational and Industrial Union in 1886. She became a director in 1890, and was president from 1892 to 1913, and again from 1914 to 1918.

In the 1890s, Kehew and Mary Kenney founded the Union for Industrial Progress, an umbrella organization for bookbinders, laundry and tobacco workers, and women in the clothing trade.

First Convention of National Women's Trade Union League

Kehew was president of the National Women's Trade Union League for one year, 1903–04. As president of the league—a lobbying organization that strove to improve living and working conditions for women employed in the Boston area—she fostered trade unionism and sought labor and social reforms. The league also provided reports, surveys, and statistics, and drafted bills for state legislators.

Beverly Gwinn Kelley

First woman to command a U.S. Coast Guard vessel at sea (1979); one of the first two women to serve on an armed U.S. military ship (1977).

Born Bonita Springs, Florida, c. 1952.

For a period of twenty-seven months—April, 1979 to July, 1981—Kelley commanded the ninety-five-foot Coast Guard patrol boat, *Cape Newagen*. While she was skipper of the boat, Kelley and her crew won a Coast Guard citation for "professionalism" for their rescue work during a Hawaiian storm in 1980. Struggling with seventy-mile-per-hour winds and twenty-foot seas, they managed in four days to rescue twelve people from endangered or sinking boats.

As an ensign, Kelley, of Bonita Springs, Florida, and third-class petty officer Debra Lee Wilson, of San Jose, California, were the first women to serve alongside men on armed vessels. They were assigned to seagoing cutters with duties that included enforcement of the 200-mile fishing limit. (Foreign vessels are forbidden to fish within 200 miles of the U.S. coastline.)

Clara Louise Kellogg

First U.S.-trained prima donna (1861); first U.S. operatic singer to achieve a major reputation in Europe (1867).

Born Sumter, South Carolina, July 9, 1842; died New Hartford, Connecticut, May 13, 1916.

Brought up in Connecticut, Kellogg studied piano from the age of five while also studying voice in New York State. She made her debut as an operatic singer at the Academy of Music in New York City in 1861 when she sang the role of Gilda in Verdi's *Rigoletto*.

She experienced her first major success in 1863 when she was the first woman to sing the role of Marguerite in Gounod's *Faust* at a performance in the United States. She made her London debut in the same role in 1867 to similar acclaim, and that role was to be her most noteworthy for the next fifteen years.

Between 1873 and 1876 Kellogg

established and spent much of her time promoting an English-language opera company in the United States, serving as leading singer, wardrobe director, and coach to young singers. Her career declined in the early 1880s when she lost favor with opera audiences in metropolitan areas. Her concerts became limited to smaller towns in the South and West.

Suzanne Kennedy

First woman veterinarian at a U.S. national zoo (1976).

Born c. 1955.

In 1976 Kennedy became the first woman veterinarian to work at the National Zoological Park in Washington, D.C. She was responsible for treating the entire range of animals housed at the zoo.

A Michigan State University (East Lansing, Michigan) graduate in veterinary medicine, she did research in the fungal diseases of birds while practicing veterinary medicine at the zoo.

The first woman keeper at the national zoo was Brenda Hall, who joined the staff in 1971.

Mary Kenney (O'Sullivan)

First woman to be a general organizer for the American Federation of Labor (1892); cofounder of the Union for Industrial Progress (1894); cofounder of the National Women's Trade Union League (1903).

Born Hannibal, Missouri, January 8, 1864; died West Medford, Massachusetts, January 18, 1943.

Born of Irish immigrants, Kenney organized around 1899 the Women's Bindery Workers' Union, a unit of the Ladies' Federal Labor Union that was affiliated with the American Federation of Labor (AFL). Samuel Gompers hired her for the AFL, and she organized workers in New York City, Troy, New York, and several cities in Massachusetts. She was also elected to the Chicago Trades and Labor Assembly and became a friend of Jane Addams (see entry).

In 1894 Kenney married John O'Sullivan, labor editor of the *Boston Globe*. They moved to Boston; she bore four children and continued her organizing activities among the rubber, garment, and laundry workers.

In 1894, Kenney and Mary Kimbell Kehew (see entry) organized the Union for Industrial Progress in Boston; the UIP made pioneering studies of factory and workshop conditions. A few years later (1903), at the AFL convention in Boston, Kenney and William E. Walling cofounded the National Women's Trade Union League; Kenney was named its first secretary, and later became its first vice president.

After her husband's accidental death in 1912, Kenney worked as a factory inspector in the Massachusetts Division of Industrial Safety. As a supporter of the textile workers' strike in Lawrence, Massachusetts (1912), she broke with the Boston Women's Trade Union League and the AFL, and served as a liaison between the Industrial Workers of the World—organizers of the strike—and the president of the American Woolen Company. Her activities led to a settlement of the strike with major wage increases for the textile workers.

Kenney continued to work as a factory inspector until her retirement in 1934.

Marion E. Kenworthy

First woman to be elected president of the American Psychoanalytic Association (1958); first director of the first mental hygiene clinic of the YWCA (1919); first woman to be professor of psychiatry at Columbia University, New York, New York (1930).

Born Hampden, Massachusetts, c. 1891; died New York, New York, June 26, 1980.

Kenworthy was a pioneer educator in psychiatric social work, mental health, and child guidance. A descendant of Mayflower settlers, she graduated with honors from Tufts University Medical School (Medford, Massachusetts) at the age of twenty-two. She was the first female physician at the Gardner State Colony for Chronic Mental Patients in Massachusetts, where she was in charge of 2,400 female patients. After moving to New York City she entered public service, heading the first mental hygiene clinic of the YWCA, where she worked with juvenile delinquents and researched causes of suicide among young people. Known as the "mother of psychiatric social work," Kenworthy joined the faculty of the Columbia University School of Social Work (New York, N.Y.) in 1921 and was named professor of psychiatry there in 1930—the first woman to achieve this rank. She retired from Columbia in 1957 and was named professor emeritus. Her friends, colleagues, and former students contributed more than $400,000 to establish the Marion E. Kenworthy Chair in Psychiatry at Columbia's School of Social Work. In 1958 she was elected president of the American Psychoanalytic Association;

founded in 1911, the APA was established to set standards for the training and practice of psychoanalysts.

Carrie (Caroline) Kilgore

Believed to be the first U.S. woman to ascend in a balloon (1908).

Born Craftsbury, Vermont, January 20, 1838; died Swarthmore, Pennsylvania, June 29, 1909.

At seventy years of age, Kilgore was the only woman passenger in the first balloon flight of the Philadelphia Aeronautical Recreation Society (Philadelphia, Pennsylvania). She was a member of the society, which was made up of balloon hobbyists and enthusiasts. On the first flight, Kilgore and the other (male) passengers stayed aloft for several hours.

In 1863 Kilgore was a member of the first class of women of the Hygeio-Therapeutic College to be admitted to Bellevue Hospital clinics in New York City. Women in the Bellevue program served a medical apprenticeship; they did not receive a formal medical education. Two years later, Kilgore earned a medical degree, and also began to read law. After repeated attempts to take the bar examination were rebuffed, she was admitted to the Central Pennsylvania Law School in 1881, becoming

its first female graduate in 1883. In 1890 Kilgore was admitted to practice before the Supreme Court of the United States.

Billie Jean Moffitt King

Founder of World Team Tennis (1976); founder of the Women's Professional Softball League (1975); first woman athlete to earn $100,000 in a single year (1971).

Born Long Beach, California, November 22, 1943.

On September 20, 1973, at the Houston (Texas) Astrodome, in front of a live audience of 30,400, the largest ever to watch a tennis match, and an international TV audience estimated at 60 million, Billie Jean King defeated male professional Bobby Riggs to win the largest purse ever paid for a single tennis match: $100,000. The match—billed as "The Battle of the Sexes"—was just one more pinnacle in a tennis career that already had many.

When she was eleven years old, King quit softball (although she was reputed to be an excellent shortstop) to concentrate on tennis. Three years later, at fourteen, she won the southern California girls fifteen-and-under championship. In 1961, at eighteen, King and partner Karen Hantze were the youngest pair ever to win the Wimbledon women's doubles. King went on to win more Wimbledon titles—an impressive twenty—than any woman ever before: six singles, ten doubles, and four mixed doubles between 1961 and 1975. In 1973, the year of her victory over Riggs, she was named top woman athlete of the year.

Perhaps the single most influential figure in the successful battle for equality—including pay parity—for women athletes, King founded two leagues for professional women athletes and participated in the establishment of *WomenSports* magazine (1974). She wrote *Tennis to Win* (1970) and, with Kim Chapin, *Billie Jean* (1974).

Louisa King

First president of the Woman's National Farm and Garden Association (1914).

Born Washington, New Jersey, 1863; died Milton, Massachusetts, 1948.

Her mother's garden had included over 200 varieties of herbs, inspiring Louisa King's lifelong dedication to gardening. She was one of the founders of the Garden Club of America (1913). Serving as president of the Woman's National Farm and Garden Association from 1914 to 1921, King

published *The Well-Considered Garden* in 1915, followed by several other gardening books. She favored artistic over practical considerations, advocating sound planning and careful use of color.

In 1921 King was awarded the George White Medal of the Massachusetts Horticultural Society. She was the first woman to receive the medal, the highest gardening honor in the United States.

King was also a fellow of the Royal Horticultural Society of Great Britain.

Elizabeth Kingsley

Creator of the double-crostic puzzle (1934).

Born Brooklyn, New York, 1871; died New York, New York, 1957.

Kingsley's double-crostic puzzle was the first ever to appear in print. Beginning in 1934, she published a puzzle weekly in the *Saturday Review of Literature*. (Double-crostics are part crossword, part acrostic literary puzzles, the completed pattern/answer to which yields a quotation from an author.) She said she created the puzzle to heighten the appreciation of "classical English and American poet and prose masters." During the seventeen years that she created the puzzles, she used more than 50,000 words for the answers to the clues.

A graduate of Wellesley College (Wellesley, Massachusetts) in 1898, she taught English at a girls' high school in Brooklyn, New York, from 1900 to 1914. In 1925 a niece taught her how to do crossword puzzles, which were a very popular form of entertainment at the time. Kingsley created a crossword puzzle and sold it to the *Chicago Daily News* for ten dollars. At this time, she worked for Houghton Mifflin (Boston, Massachusetts) and Babson Institute (Wellesley Hills, Massachusetts).

Kingsley was one of the founders of the Brooklyn and Boston Ethical Culture Societies.

Rose Markward Knox

First woman elected to the board of directors of the American Grocery Manufacturers' Association (1929).

Born Mansfield, Ohio, November 18, 1857; died Johnstown, New York, September 27, 1950.

In 1890 she and her husband combined their savings and started a company later known as the Knox Company, a manufacturer of gelatin. Her husband died in 1908, after which she ran the company, overseeing its growth and development to a leading position in the industry. An enlightened manager, Rose Knox instituted the five-day week at her company in 1913 (employees had previously been working half-days on Saturday). Later she also established two-week vacation and sick-leave policies for her employees.

Susan G. Komen Foundation

First foundation to solely support breast-cancer research (1982).

The foundation was established by Nancy G. Brinker in Dallas, Texas, in memory of her sister, Susan, who died of breast cancer in 1980. By the end of 1985, over $1 million had been donated to the foundation.

The Goodman sisters grew up in Peoria, Illinois. Nancy moved to Dallas in 1968 after graduating from the University of Illinois (Urbana, Illinois). She has been a department store executive, a public relations

Susan Goodman Komen (left) and Nancy Goodman Brinker (right)

specialist, and a talk-show hostess.

In 1984, when she was thirty-seven, Nancy underwent a mastectomy.

Doris Kopsky

First woman champion of the National Amateur Bicycle Association (1937).

Dates unknown

During a 1937 Buffalo, New York, tournament, Kopsky, from Belleville, New Jersey, covered one mile in 4 minutes, 22.4 seconds, to win the championship.

Juanita Morris Kreps

First woman to be appointed secretary of commerce (1977); first to be director of the New York Stock Exchange Board of Directors (1972).

Born Lynch, Kentucky, January 11, 1921.

During the early 1970s, Kreps gained a widespread reputation in the field of economics, which led her to high-level positions with such companies as Eastman Kodak, R. J. Reynolds, J. C. Penny Co., and Western Electric. In most cases, she became the first woman director of the companies.

In 1976 she came to the attention of President Jimmy Carter, who nominated her for the position of secretary of commerce, and she was sworn in during the month of January, 1977. She served in that position until 1979.

Having earned a B.A. degree from Berea College (Berea, Kentucky) in 1942, Kreps earned M.A. and Ph. D. degrees in economics from Duke University (Durham, North Carolina) in 1944 and 1948, respectively. While attending Duke, she married Clifton H. Kreps, a fellow economist, and they had three children.

She taught economics at Denison University (Granville, Ohio); Hofstra College (now Hofstra University, Hempstead, New York); and Queens College (Queens, New York) from 1945 to 1955. Returning to Duke University as an assistant professor in 1955, she advanced through the professorial ranks, and in 1972 was named to the James B. Duke Professorship, the university's most prestigious chair.

Among the most popular of the

many books she wrote are *Sex in the Marketplace: American Women at Work* (1972) and *Sex, Age and Work: The Changing Composition of the Labor Force* (1975).

After resigning from her position as secretary of commerce in 1979, she was appointed to the Commission for a National Agenda.

Kathy Kusner

First woman to be granted a jockey's license to race thoroughbred horses at major tracks (1968).

Born c. 1940.

A champion equestrian who began riding when she was ten years old, Kusner was a member of three U.S. Olympic equestrian jumping teams, winning sixth place at the 1964 Olympics, fourth place at the 1968 Olympics, and second place in 1972. In 1958, at the age of eighteen, she set a world record in women's equestrian jumping, clearing a height of seven feet, three inches.

In 1967 Kusner applied for a jockey's license with the Maryland Racing Commission. It originally rejected her application, but Kusner took the matter to court and the commission was compelled to issue the license. She received her license on October 30, 1968.

Kusner made her racing debut in September, 1969, finishing third in a race at Pocono Downs, Pennsylvania. The following year she won several races in South Africa, and in 1972 she won the international puissance class at the Pennsylvania National Horse Show.

Labor Reform Association, Lowell Female

First major women's union (1845).

The first major women's union was the Lowell Female Labor Reform Association, established in the state of Massachusetts in 1845. The first president of the union was Sarah Bagley (see entry).

Ladies' Day

First Ladies' Day (1867).

The Knickerbocker Base Ball Club of New York offered free admission to wives, daughters, and girlfriends on the last Tuesday of each month. Arrangements for "suitable seats or settees" were made by a committee of the club.

Janna Lambine

First woman U.S. Coast Guard (USCG) pilot (1977).

Dates unknown.

Lambine, who had earned a B.S. degree in geology, became a pilot for the USCG after graduating from naval aviation training school at the Naval Air Station, Whiting Field, Milton, Florida. Her duties as a USCG pilot involved search-and-rescue missions and surveillance for pollution of fisheries.

Bertha Knight Landes

First woman to be elected mayor of a sizable U.S. city (Seattle, Washington, 1926).

Born Ware, Massachusetts, October 19, 1868; died Ann Arbor, Michigan, November 29, 1943.

After her graduation from Indiana University (Bloomington) in 1891, Bertha Landes became a schoolteacher, got married, brought up a family, and moved to Seattle. She became involved in the woman's club movement and won a Seattle city council election in 1922. Reelected in 1924, Landes was named president of the city council. One of her responsibilities in that position was to act as mayor when the elected mayor was out of town. On one such occasion, Landes fired the chief of police, a dramatic gesture intended to show that Seattle, a den of gambling and vice, had to be cleansed and reformed. The mayor made a hasty return and reinstated the police chief.

Landes was elected mayor in 1926, but was soundly defeated in a bid for reelection.

Harriet Lane (Johnston)

First woman to have a federal steamship named for her (1857).

Born Mercersburg, Pennsylvania, 1830; died Narragansett Pier, Rhode Island, 1903.

The first federal steamship, a revenue cutter belonging to the U.S. Treasury Department, at President James Buchanan's request, named the *Harriet Lane* in honor of the young woman who was President Buchanan's favorite niece and his White House hostess.

Lane, who was educated at the Academy of the Visitation Convent, Georgetown, D.C., served her bachelor uncle as White House hostess from 1857 to 1861.

In 1861 the cutter *Harriet Lane* fired the first shot from any vessel in the Civil War.

Julia Clifford Lathrop

First woman to head an important U.S. government bureau—she was the first director of the U.S. Children's Bureau (1912).

Born Rockford, Illinois, June 29, 1858; died Rockford, Illinois, June 29, 1932.

The daughter of an Illinois con-

Harriet Lane at President Buchanan's inaugural ball

Julia Lathrop (left) with Jane Addams (center) and Mary McDowell (right)

gressman and an advocate of women's suffrage, Lathrop was appointed to the Children's Bureau by President William Howard Taft; she was the bureau's first director, serving from 1912 to 1921. Originally a part of the Department of Commerce, the Children's Bureau was moved to the Department of Labor in 1915. Its mission was to investigate and report on the welfare of children and to enforce child labor laws.

An 1880 graduate of Vassar College (Poughkeepsie, New York), Lathrop was an early resident of Hull House, a settlement house in Chicago. She moved there in 1890 and stayed for twenty years. In 1893 she became the first woman appointed to the Illinois Board of Charities, where she helped to establish the nation's first juvenile court (1899).

After illness forced her retirement from the Children's Bureau, she served from 1922 to 1924 as president of the Illinois League of Women Voters, and from 1925 to 1931 on the Child Welfare Committee of the League of Nations.

Sister Mary Alphonsa (Lathrop)
(born Rose Hawthorne)

Founded the first U.S. free home or hospice for the care of the terminally ill (1900).

Born Lenox, Massachusetts, 1851; died Hawthorne, New York, 1926.

Daughter of author Nathaniel Hawthorne and Sophia Peabody Hawthorne, Rose Hawthorne married George Lathrop in 1871. A writer like her father, she published short stories in *St. Nicholas* magazine and the *Atlantic Monthly,* and a volume of her poetry was published in 1888.

In 1891 she and her husband converted to Catholicism. They separated in 1895, and he died in 1898.

Lathrop began work with cancer sufferers in 1896. She took a three-month nursing course, and set up three rooms on the Lower East Side of New York City for the care of cancer victims. The facility was expanded in 1898.

In 1899 Lathrop joined the lay sisters of the Dominican third order, becoming Sister Mary Alphonsa. Sister Mary took her first vows in 1900 and her final vows in 1909. Along with her associate, Alice Huber, Lathrop founded in New York City the Dominican Congregation of St. Rose of Lima (1900), the Servants of Relief for Incurable Cancer.

Law School, St. Louis

First law school to admit women (1869).

St. Louis Law School (Missouri) (now Washington University School of Law) graduated Phoebe W. Couzins (see entry) in 1871. She and another woman had matriculated in 1869.

Florence Bridgewood Lawrence

First woman movie star (1910).

Born Hamilton, Ontario, Canada, January 2, 1886; died West Hollywood, California, December 28, 1938.

Born Florence Bridgewood, daughter of a British father and an American mother, she became part of her parents' traveling tent show. In 1907 she began her film career with Thomas Edison, then joined Vitagraph. Later, she joined D. W. Griffith's Biograph, first playing as "The Biograph Girl." In 1910 she was per-

suaded to join the Independent Moving Picture Company.

Lawrence played the first Juliet from *Romeo and Juliet* on the U.S. screen. By 1910 her name was on movie posters, set in larger type than the name of the film.

In 1915 an injury on a movie set resulted in four years of partial paralysis, and Lawrence's career went into decline. She committed suicide in 1938.

Ann Lee

Leader of the first Shaker group to come to the United States (1774); first leader of conscientious objectors (1780).

Born Manchester, England, February 29, 1736; died near Albany, New York, September 8, 1784.

Born Ann Lees in Manchester, England, she shortened her name to

Lee. In her early twenties she joined the "Shaking Quakers," or Shakers. When the Shakers received a revelation that the opening of the gospel would take place in *New* England—not in her homeland—Lee and a group of Shakers immigrated to New York, sailing on May 19, 1774.

They made many converts in the colonies, and Lee and eight others founded a "family" in Niskeyuna (later Watervliet), New York, near Albany (1776).

The Shakers, whose official name is the United Society of Believers in Christ's Second Appearing, believed that since Christ first appeared as a man, the second appearance would be as a woman, redeeming the character of women, which had been blemished through the fall of Eve.

Consequently, the Shakers were the first Christian group that tried to free women from the subjection they had endured at the hands of all other religious societies. They advocated equal rights for women.

Since Lee was a pacifist, she publicly proclaimed her views as a conscientious objector during the Revolutionary War. She was accused of aiding the British, and was jailed as a traitor (1780). She was transferred to the Poughkeepsie, New York, jail, then released.

Margaret Leech

First woman to receive the Pulitzer Prize for history (1942); only woman to win the Pulitzer Prize for history twice (1942, 1960).

Born Newburgh, New York, November 7, 1893; died New York, New York, February 24, 1974.

Leech's first Pulitzer came for *Reveille in Washington,* her book on the nation's capital during the Civil War period. Her second prize winner was *In the Days of McKinley,* described as "a first-rate book about a second-rate president." This book also won Columbia University's coveted Bancroft Prize (1960).

A 1915 graduate of Vassar College (Poughkeepsie, New York), Leech also wrote novels—*The Back of the Book* (1924), *Tin Wedding* (1926), and *The Feathered Nest* (1928). She is also the author of *Divided by Three* (1934), a play which she wrote with Beatrice Kaufman.

Ethel Leginska

First woman to conduct a leading U.S. orchestra (1925); organizer of women's symphony orchestras (1925–30); first woman to write an opera (1932).

Born Hull, England, April 13, 1886; died Los Angeles, California, February 26, 1970.

Born Ethel Liggins, she was considered a prodigy as a child pianist. She studied in Germany and Austria, and at some early point in her career adopted the name Leginska. Her U.S. concert debut came in 1913; critics wrote that her playing displayed "masculine vigor, dashing brilliance and a great variety of tonal color." Leginska's career as a concert pianist continued until 1926, when she abandoned the concert stage after a series of nervous breakdowns and devoted her time to composing and conducting. By then she had already led orchestras in England, France, and Germany as guest conductor.

Her U.S. debut on the podium with the New York Symphony in 1925 marked the first time a woman ever conducted a major U.S. orchestra. She was also the first U.S. woman conductor/composer to conduct at the Boston Opera House (1927).

Living in Boston from 1925 to 1930, Leginska founded and conducted the Boston Philharmonic, the Woman's Symphony Orchestra, and the Boston English Opera Company. In 1932 she organized the National Women's Symphony (New York City), which was short-lived.

Leginska was the first U.S. woman to write an opera—*The Rose and the Ring* (1932), based on a story by William Thackeray. Her first opera to be performed was the one-act *Gale* (1935), which was first presented by the Chicago City Opera in 1935 under Leginska's baton. In Los Angeles, California, she conducted the premiere of *The Rose and the Ring* in 1957.

Some of the most memorable compositions by Leginska include the symphonic poem *Beyond the Fields We Know* (1922); *Quatre sujets barbares* (1924), a suite for orchestra; and *Triptych for 11 Instruments* (1928).

After 1938, Leginska was active primarily as a piano teacher.

Augusta Lewis (Troup)

First woman to be an elected executive of any nationwide labor union (1870).

Born New York, New York, c. 1848; died New Haven, Connecticut, September 14, 1920.

Lewis became the first woman executive of a national labor union when she was elected corresponding secretary of the International Typographical Union (ITU) in 1870. She had been founder and first president of the Women's Typographical Union No. One in 1868; the following year she addressed a national convention of the ITU and secured a charter for her women's union. Shortly afterwards, however, the ITU began admitting women to regular locals with full membership rights.

A graduate of the Convent School of the Sacred Heart (Manhattanville, New York), Lewis became a reporter and journalist when she was about nineteen. After learning the typesetting trade, she joined the staff of Joseph Pulitzer's New York *World*. Following an ITU strike settlement, which resulted in the firing of most of the nonunion women typesetters, Lewis resigned in sympathy with the fired women.

In 1874 Lewis married a New Haven newspaper owner (and former typographers' union executive), raised a family, and continued her career as a journalist.

Ida (Idawalley) Zoradia Lewis

First woman to be an official U.S. lighthouse keeper (1879).

Born Newport, Rhode Island, February 25, 1842; died Limerock, Rhode Island, October 24, 1911.

Lewis became de facto lighthouse keeper in 1857 when her father, the official keeper, suffered a stroke. From then until her death in 1911 she manned the lighthouse; in 1879 the federal government named her the official keeper.

Lewis saved numerous people and animals from drowning, and newspaper accounts of these rescues made her famous throughout the country. Her last recorded rescue came when, at sixty-four years of age, she saved a vacationer from drowning. On another occasion she rescued three shepherds trying to retrieve a valuable sheep from the water; she then rescued the sheep.

Lewis won many honors and awards during her lifetime, including an award from the Carnegie Hero Fund in 1906 (which provided a pension), and a gold medal from the American Cross of Honor Society (1906).

Nancy Lieberman

First woman athlete to play in a men's professional league basketball game (1986).

Born Brooklyn, New York, July 1, 1958.

As a member of the Springfield Fame, a Massachusetts team of the U.S. Basketball League, Lieberman scored ten points in her team's 135–115 victory over the Westchester Golden Apples.

She is a graduate of Old Dominion College (now University) in Norfolk, Virginia, where she was a star player on the women's basketball team. In 1979, after propelling her team to the women's national collegiate basketball championship, she became the second woman to receive the Margaret Wade Trophy as outstanding woman player of the year. (Carol Blazejowski [see entry] was the first woman to win the trophy.) In 1980 Lieberman won it a second time.

After graduating from Old Dominion in 1980, Lieberman became a first draft choice of the Dallas Diamonds in the last season of the Women's Basketball League. She was also a first draft choice of Dallas in the newly organized Women's American Basketball Association (1984). In 1987 she joined the Washington Generals, the touring opponents of the Harlem Globetrotters, one of whose stars was Lynette Woodard (see entry).

The 5'10" Lieberman learned to play basketball at a public school in Far Rockaway, Queens, New York, and on the playgrounds in Brooklyn and Harlem, New York.

Mary Todd Lincoln

First widow of a U.S. president to receive a pension (1870).

Born Lexington, Kentucky, December 13, 1818; died Springfield, Illinois, July 16, 1882.

Married to Abraham Lincoln in 1842, she became the first lady at the White House in March, 1861. She was seated at the president's side when he was assassinated in Ford's Theatre in April, 1865. She was awarded a pension of $3,000 yearly, later increased to $5,000.

Mary Todd met Abraham Lincoln when she went to Springfield, Illinois, the state capital, to visit her sister, Elizabeth Todd Edwards. Her sister, an influential woman in her own right, had married Ninian W. Edwards when he was attending Transylvania College in Lexington, Kentucky.

After the president's death, Mary Lincoln lived in Germany and England from 1868 to 1871, returned to the United States for a period, then lived in Europe from 1876 to 1880. She returned to Springfield, Illinois, where she died.

Anne Spencer Morrow Lindbergh

First woman to qualify for a glider's license (1930); first to receive the National Geographic Society Hubbard Gold Medal (1934).

Born Englewood, New Jersey, 1906.

Lindbergh first began gliding in California, where she also took her qualifying flight exam. She earned a first-class glider pilot's license after successfully completing a six-minute flight over the Soledad Mountains, San Diego, California.

She married Charles Lindbergh in 1929. They had met when he visited her father, Dwight Whitney Morrow, who was the U.S. ambassador to Mexico at the time. Charles taught

her to operate the radio, copilot, and navigate. She also learned how to read Morse code and navigational charts. The year of their marriage, they pioneered a Transcontinental Air Transport (TAT) route across the United States, from New York to Los Angeles.

In April, 1930, the Lindberghs broke the transcontinental speed record while flying together. Piloting a Lockheed Sirius and making one stop in Wichita, Kansas, they made the flight from Glendale, California to Roosevelt Field, Long Island, New York in total air time of fourteen hours, twenty-three minutes. The flight covered approximately 2,700 miles, and the Lindberghs flew at altitudes of between 14,000 and 15,500 feet, at an average speed of just over 180 miles per hour. She earned a private pilot's license the following year.

Lindbergh, who graduated from Smith College, Northampton, Massachusetts, in 1928, has gained a considerable reputation as a writer. Among her works are: her first book, *North to the Orient* (1935), an account of the Lindberghs' Arctic-Asian trip; *Gift From the Sea* (1955), a collection of essays, which is probably her best-known book; *The Unicorn & Other Poems* (1956); and *Bring Me a Unicorn* (1972), diaries and letters.

In 1934 the National Geographic

Society awarded Lindbergh its Hubbard Gold Medal for her 40,000-mile flight as copilot and radio operator (along with her pilot husband) over five continents to survey transoceanic air routes.

Estelle Lawton Lindsey

First acting mayor of a major city (1915).

Dates unknown.

Lindsey was elected in June, 1915, as the only woman on the city council of Los Angeles. In the absence of both the mayor and president of the council, who traveled to San Francisco, Lindsey was selected as president pro tempore, which automatically made her the acting mayor ex officio.

Lindsey averred that if she had full powers she would establish a single tax system, which would include the identification of all property owners. She also declared that she would organize a school for mothers and assure that drunkards were publicly listed.

Berenice Lipson-Gruzen

First Western pianist (of either sex) to make a recording in China (1981).

Dates unknown.

In September, 1981, she recorded Chopin's Piano Concerto No. 2 with the Beijing Central Philharmonic. She also taught master classes at the new Central Philharmonic Conservatory and appeared with the Peking Central Philharmonic.

Nancy Littlefield

First woman accepted into the Directors Guild of America (DGA) (1952).

Born Bronx, New York, c. 1929.

Littlefield had to take a stiff battery of tests, including an oral exam, to be accepted by the DGA in 1952. For fourteen years following her acceptance, she was the only assistant director in the guild.

From 1978 to 1983 she was the director of the New York City Office for Motion Pictures and Television. In 1983 she became the president of (212) Studios in Long Island City, Queens, New York, a film and videotape studio.

Littlefield worked on various television series, including some episodes of "Naked City" and "The Defenders." In 1979 she won an Emmy for her production of *And Baby Makes Two,* a documentary about pregnancy among teenagers.

A former student at City College of New York (New York, New York), in 1980 Littlefield taught a film course at Columbia University (New York, New York).

Little League

First girls in Little League baseball (1974).

The Little League baseball program was officially opened to girls on December 26, 1974, when President Gerald Ford signed the legislation.

The charter was amended to refer to "young people" rather than "boys," and a reference to the promotion of "manhood" among Little League players was removed. The Little League had sought changes in its membership and charter after being involved in numerous lawsuits seeking to open the program to girls.

Mary (Rice) Livermore

First woman news reporter at a political convention (1860); first president of the Association for the Advancement of Women (1873).

Born Boston, Massachusetts, December 19, 1820; died Melrose, Massachusetts, May 23, 1905.

Livermore graduated from a female seminary in Charlestown, Massachusetts, in 1836. After teaching languages for two years, she tutored in the South for three years, returning to Massachusetts to head a co-

educational school in Duxbury, Massachusetts.

In 1845 she married a minister, and while raising a family she continued to work as a writer and editor. She was associate editor of *The New Covenant,* a Universalist monthly that her husband had purchased in 1858 and edited until 1869.

In 1860 she was a reporter at the Republican National Convention in Chicago, Illinois, that nominated Abraham Lincoln.

During the Civil War, Livermore went to work for the Chicago Sanitary Commission, and in 1862 she and her friend, Jane Hoge, were named heads of the commission. Their responsibilities included fund-raising, supply allocation, and oversight of military hospitals.

She convened the first women's suffrage convention in Illinois in 1868, and in 1870 became the editor of *Woman's Journal,* the official publication of the American Woman Suffrage Association. She resigned as editor in 1872, at which time Lucy Stone (see entry) and her husband became editors. Livermore served the AWSA as president from 1875 to 1878. She also became a well-known temperance speaker.

Belva Ann Bennett McNall Lockwood

First woman lawyer admitted to practice before the U.S. Supreme Court (1879); first woman to receive votes in a presidential election (1884).

Born Royalton, New York, October 24, 1830; died Washington, D.C., May 19, 1917.

In 1871 Lockwood was admitted to the newly established National

University Law School, Washington, D.C. (later part of George Washington University). Since she was a woman, she was not able to get her 1873 diploma until she wrote a letter to President Ulysses S. Grant, ex officio president of the school. In 1873 she was admitted to the bar in Washington, D.C.

In 1876 Lockwood was refused admission to the U.S. Supreme Court. Her personal lobbying led to a bill in Congress that enabled women to plead before the Supreme Court, stipulating that "any woman member of the bar of good moral character who had three years' practice before a state supreme court was eligible for admittance to practice before the United States Supreme Court." President Hayes signed the bill on February 15, 1879, and in March Lockwood was admitted to practice before the Court.

A fervent suffragist known nationally as a speaker on women's rights in 1884, Lockwood ran for president as a candidate of the National Equal Rights party, receiving less than one-tenth of one percent of the vote (approximately 4,000 votes in six states). She was opposed by other suffragists, including Susan B. Anthony (see entry). She ran for president again in 1888, garnering fewer votes.

In one of her historic cases, Lockwood entered a successful motion to allow Samuel Lowey, a southern black lawyer, to practice before the U.S. Supreme Court—a precedent-setting victory that was important to black attorneys.

As a child, Lockwood attended country schools and started teaching when she was fifteen. She got married at eighteen and was widowed at twenty-three. After the death of her husband, she resumed her studies at Genesee College (later Syracuse University), Lima, New York, and graduated with honors in 1857. She resumed teaching and in 1869, after studying law informally, applied to the law school at Columbian College (later George Washington University). She was turned down, and was later rejected by Georgetown University (Georgetown, D.C.) and Howard University (Washington, D.C.) as well. In 1909, however, she received an honorary LL.D. degree from Syracuse University.

Hannah E. Myers Longshore

First woman to hold a faculty position in a U.S. medical school (1851).

Born Sandy Spring, Maryland, May 30, 1819; died Philadelphia, Pennsylvania, October 18, 1901.

Also Philadelphia's first woman physician, Longshore received her M.D. degree from the Female Medical College (later the Woman's Medical College) of Pennsylvania (Philadelphia). She had enrolled in October, 1850, for a four-month session (the college's first class), then attended a second session in September–December, 1851, during which she also served as a demonstrator. Her M.D. degree was awarded on December 31, 1851. In 1852 she went to the New England Female Medical College (Boston, Massachusetts) as the first woman demonstrator of anatomy. When Longshore returned to Philadelphia to practice medicine, she inaugurated a series of public lectures for women on the subjects of hygiene and physiology.

Educated at Quaker schools until she was fourteen, Longshore was apprenticed to Joseph Longshore, a graduate of the University of Pennsylvania Medical School (Philadelphia) and a cofounder of the Female Medical College. On March 26, 1841, she married his brother, Thomas E. Longshore. Longshore retired from the practice of medicine in 1892.

Nancy Lopez

First woman to win five straight Ladies Professional Golf Association tournaments (1978).

Born Torrance, California, January 6, 1957.

In the most meteoric debut in the history of professional women golfers, Nancy Lopez exploded onto the professional scene in mid-1977, and by the end of the 1978 season had tallied an unprecedented series of accomplishments. She had won nine Ladies Professional Golf Association (LPGA) tournaments, including an unprecedented five straight, and the LPGA championship tournament. She also won more money—$189,814—in her rookie year than any other player of either sex. In 1978, 1979, 1985, and 1988 she was named Player of the Year as well as being the Vare Trophy winner, awarded for the lowest average score per round for the year (1978). Lopez won LPGA championships again in 1985 and 1989. By the end of the 1980s, she had won over forty tournaments and some $2.7 million.

Harriett Stone Lothrop

First president of Children of the American Revolution (1895).

Born New Haven, Connecticut, June 23, 1844; died San Francisco, California, August 2, 1924.

The Children of the American Revolution is an offshoot of the Daughters of the American Revolution, of which Lothrop was also a member. The organization is dedicated to helping young people become useful citizens as a result of knowing about the past and their American heritage. Lothrop served as CAR president for six years.

Publishing under the pen name Margaret Sidney, she produced short stories and poetry, which began to appear in 1870. One story, "Polly Pepper's Chicken Pie" (1877), became the first part of *Five Little Peppers,* a children's narrative published in monthly serials in 1880. She went on to write many "Pepper" books, millions of copies of which have been sold; they are still in print. Lothrop was a prolific writer, producing over forty books.

Nancy Lotsey

First girl to play in organized baseball competition with boys (1963).

Born Morristown, New Jersey, c. 1955.

Lotsey was admitted to play in the New Jersey Small-Fry League; in her first game she was the winning pitcher and hit a home run. Her team won the league championship, with a 10–1 won-lost record.

She applied to be batboy of the New York Yankees under the name "James Lotsey." She was subsequently declared ineligible by the team, but the attempt did give her the opportunity to meet the Yankee players.

At Morristown High School, Lotsey played all-girl basketball, softball, and volleyball. She graduated in 1972.

Elsie S. Lott

First woman to receive the U.S. Air Medal (1943).

Dates unknown.

Lott, a second lieutenant in the Army Nurse Corps, received the U.S. Air Medal for meritorious achievement as a nurse in June, 1943. She had nursed five patients who were evacuated by air from India to Washington, D.C.

Nancy Harkness Love

First woman to command the Women's Auxiliary Ferrying Squadron, part of the Army Air Force's Transport Command (1942).

Born 1914.

At Avenger Field, Texas, site of the first all-female cadet air base, she was the first to fly a P-51 Mustang, a fighter plane (1943). The Women's Auxiliary Ferrying Squadron, established on September 10, 1942, was assigned to fly all kinds of aircraft to any bases in the noncombat zone. Its members had civilian, not military, status, and earned $3,000 per year. Love commanded the squadron in 1942, until it was merged (in November, 1942) with the Women's Air Force Service Pilots (WASPs, see entry), headed by Jacqueline Cochran.

Wife of the deputy chief of staff for the air transport command, Love had been flying for twelve years prior to her appointment as commander. She had been an air marker (someone who determines the location of signs and symbols that are put on roofs to guide pilots over unfamiliar terrain) for the Bureau of Commerce, a test pilot at a flying school she helped run, and had contributed to the development of the tricycle landing gear on medium and heavy bombers. She was also one of the original group of pilots who ferried airplanes manufactured for Britain to the Canadian border early in World War II.

In her days as a student at Vassar College (Poughkeepsie, New York), Love had organized student flying clubs.

Esther Pohl Clayson Lovejoy

First woman to be director of the board of health of a leading U.S. city (1907).

Born Seabeck, Washington Territory, November 16, 1869; died New York, New York, August 17, 1967.

Lovejoy went to the University of Oregon Medical School (Eugene) in 1890, earning her M.D. degree in

1894—the second woman to graduate from the school, and the first woman actually to practice medicine in the state of Oregon.

Lovejoy lived for some time in Alaska, but after Emil Pohl, her first husband, died, she returned to Oregon. She became a member of the Portland, Oregon, Board of Health, and in 1907 was elected director of the board. Under her supervision, the city acquired a national reputation for its high sanitation standards.

When World War I broke out, Lovejoy tried as a member of the American Medical Women's Association to secure for U.S. women doctors the right to serve overseas. Her attempts were unsuccessful; however, she herself went with the American Red Cross to try to help the people of Paris. This experience resulted in her book, *The House of the Good Neighbor* (1919).

In 1919 Lovejoy was named director of American Women's Hospitals—later American Women's Hospital Service—a post she held for forty-eight years. Also a founder and first president of the Medical Women's International Association (1919), she served as president of the American Medical Women's Association in 1932/33.

Lovejoy was the only person to receive twice the Elizabeth Blackwell Medal of the American Medical Women's Association. She was also honored by the governments of France, Yugoslavia, and Greece.

After running unsuccessfully for a seat in Congress in 1920—as Democratic representative from Oregon—Lovejoy worked in Smyrna, Turkey, in the wake of the Turkish attacks on the Greek and Armenian sections (1922).

Her last two books were about the achievements of women physicians: *Women Physicians and Surgeons* (1939) and *Women Doctors of the World* (1957).

Juliette Gordon Low

Founder of the Girl Scouts of the U.S.A. (1912) (see also Daisy Gordon).

Born Savannah, Georgia, October 31, 1860; died Savannah, Georgia, January 18, 1927.

Low attended schools in Georgia, Virginia, and New York City. In 1886 she married a Georgian, who was a member of the select set of the Prince of Wales. She traveled extensively, spending a great deal of time in England, where in 1911 she met Sir Robert Baden Powell, founder of the Boy Scouts of America. With his encouragement, she organized three girl guide troops in Scotland and two in England. She organized the first American unit of Girl Guides in Savannah, Georgia, on March 12, 1912. There were two patrols—the

Pink Carnation and the White Rose—each with about sixteen girls. In order to pass the "tenderfoot" test, members were required to learn to tie knots, make peppermint drops, blaze a trail, and light a fire with only one match.

In 1912 Low's work resulted in the establishment of a national organization called the Girl Guides. In 1915 it was renamed the Girl Scouts of the U.S.A., with Low as its first president. She held the office until 1920.

Florence Lowe (see Pancho (Florence) Lowe Barnes)

Josephine Shaw Lowell

First president and a cofounder, with Maud Nathan (see entry), of the Consumers League of New York, the first organization of its kind (1890).

Born West Roxbury, Massachusetts, December 16, 1843; died New York, New York, October 12, 1905.

Lowell was also the first woman commissioner of the New York State Board of Charities, a position she held for thirteen years starting in 1876. She was appointed as a result of her reports on jail and almshouse conditions. During her term as commissioner, the first custodial asylum for feebleminded women was established in Newark, New York, in 1887. She was also responsible for install-

ing matrons, staff in charge of women prisoners and suspects, in all police stations (1888).

In 1884 Lowell wrote *Public Relief and Private Charity,* advocating a state-administered philanthropy. She said the community should "refuse to support any except those whom it can control." Later, Lowell decided that the improvement of poor working conditions and the payment of adequate wages should be her own cause. To help attain her goals, she and Maud Nathan organized the Consumers League, which strove to better factory and shop working conditions for New York women and girls.

Lowell served as president of the Consumers League from 1890 to 1896. In the contrast between some of her writings and her personal activities, Lowell tried to balance the theoretical and the practical. Theoretically, she believed that the function of charity was to reform people morally and thereby make them more productive. On the other hand, her practical day-to-day observation of poor people in prisons and almshouses impressed on her the immediate need for increasing salaries and improving working conditions so that families would be intact and mothers could stay at home.

In 1893 Lowell wrote *Industrial Arbitration and Conciliation,* and in 1894 she organized the Women's Municipal League as a political lobby group.

A member of an ardent abolitionist family, Lowell was educated in New York, Boston, and Europe. Her brother, Robert Gould Shaw, led the black regiment from Boston until his death in 1863. (The movie *Glory* tells the story.) She was married in 1863, but her husband was killed in battle the next year, just before their daughter was born. Soon after, she turned to welfare work and fund-raising, including supporting the National Freedman's Relief Association of New York.

Lucky (Joy) Piles Lucas

First woman to be certified as a professional ski instructor (1941).

Born Spokane, Washington, February 15, 1917.

One of the first professional ski instructors in the Pacific Northwest, Lucas passed her certification examination in April, 1941. She reports, "Even much later after [World War II], the Pacific Northwest was very far ahead of the other Ski Instructor Divisions in that women were accepted equally out here as instructors, where elsewhere, they were only used as 'baby sitters' and not allowed to actually teach classes."

Always an athlete, she excelled in hiking, dancing, swimming, diving, roller skating, ice skating, baseball, basketball, and all school intramural sports. She met her husband on her first ski trip, when she was twenty-one. They were married the following year.

Lucas attended the Professional Ski Instructors of America (PSIA) National Ski Academy and National Race Camp. She is the author of "Teaching Children of All Ages to Ski," published in the *PSIA Professional Journal,* and many other instructional articles. As of February, 1992, Lucas, age seventy-five, was still running training clinics for new ski instructors and teaching skiing one day a week.

Shannon W. Lucid

One of the first women to be selected for the U.S. space shuttle

*program (1978) (see also
National Aeronautics and Space
Administration).*

Born Shanghai, China, January 14, 1943.

The first women astronauts, a group of six, were selected for a training program in scientific, engineering, and medical duties. None, however, was to be trained in piloting the space shuttle.

At the time of her selection by NASA in 1978, Lucid was a research associate with the Oklahoma Medical Research Foundation, Oklahoma City, Oklahoma. After she became an astronaut in August, 1979, she was assigned to the Flight Software Labo-

ratory in Downey, California, and the Astronaut Office interface at the Kennedy Space Center, Florida, working on payload testing, shuttle testing, and launch countdowns.

Lucid's first space flight was launched on June 17, 1985; on the mission, the crew deployed communications satellites for Mexico, the Arab League, and the United States. Her second flight, on the orbiter *Atlantis,* was launched on October 18, 1989. It orbited the earth seventy-nine times, and the crew deployed the spacecraft *Galileo* on its voyage to explore the planet Jupiter. Flying once again with the *Atlantis* crew on her third mission, Lucid made 142 orbits of the earth before the shuttle landed at the Kennedy Space Center on August 11, 1991. With the completion of her third mission, Lucid had logged twenty-one days in space.

After graduating from Bethany High School, Bethany, Oklahoma (1960), Lucid earned a B.S. degree in chemistry from the University of Oklahoma, Norman, (1963), and M.S. and Ph.D. degrees in biochemistry from the University of Oklahoma (1970, 1973).

Lucid is a private pilot with commercial, instrument, and multi-engine ratings.

Olga Madar

First woman vice president of the United Automobile Workers (UAW) (1970).

Born Sykesville, Pennsylvania, May 17, 1915.

Madar joined the UAW staff in 1944, having been an employee in the Willow Run, Michigan, bomber plant. She was elected member at large to the UAW national board in 1966. She became the first woman to be elected vice president in 1970.

Helen Magill (White)

First woman to receive a Ph.D. degree (1877).

Born Providence, Rhode Island, November 28, 1853; died Kittery Point, Maine, October 28, 1944.

Magill graduated from Swarthmore College (Swarthmore, Pennsylvania), where her father was president, in 1873. In 1877 she earned a Ph.D. degree from Boston University Massachusetts, having written a dissertation titled "The Greek Drama."

She pursued postdoctoral studies in the classics at Cambridge University (England) from 1877 to 1881.

After serving as principal of a private school in Pennsylvania, she became the director of Howard Collegiate Institute (West Bridgewater, Massachusetts), resigning in 1887.

Magill married Andrew D. White, a former president of Cornell University (Ithaca, New York), in 1890. White was minister to Russia from 1892 to 1894 and ambassador to Germany from 1897 to 1903.

Bertha Mahony (Miller)

Cofounder of the first magazine devoted exclusively to reviews and criticism of children's literature (1924).

Born Rockport, Massachusetts, 1882; died Ashburnham, Massachusetts, 1969.

With Elinor Whitney, Mahony founded the *Horn Book Magazine,* an outgrowth of the Bookshop for Boys and Girls, a children's reading room that Mahony had established in 1916. Later, in 1936, Mahony and her husband William Davis Miller, along with Whitney and her husband William Keld, formed Horn Book, Inc., an award-winning publishing company specializing in books for children.

After completing a one-year secretarial course as a member of the first class of Simmons College for Women (Boston, Massachusetts, 1903), Mahony took a job in a Boston bookstore. In 1906 she became assistant secretary of the Women's Educational and Industrial Union (WEIU)—a Boston, Massachusetts, social service agency. Under the aegis of the WEIU, Mahony organized a children's theater group. She later organized the Bookshop for Boys and Girls, which broke new ground for organizations of its type, including the publication of suggested reading lists and the introduction of an early version of a summer bookmobile.

Mary Mandame

First woman to be compelled to wear a distinctive mark on her clothing for a sexual offense (1639).

Dates unknown.

In 1639, in Plymouth, Massachusetts, Mandame was convicted of a "dallyance" with a Native American and was sentenced to be publicly whipped. The sentence also required her to wear a badge of shame on her left sleeve. Her co-felon, Tinsion, was also whipped at the pillory.

Wilma P. Mankiller

First woman to be installed as principal chief of a major Native American tribe (1985).

Born Rocky Mountain, Oklahoma, 1945.

Mankiller, the daughter of a full-blooded Cherokee and a white mother, was named to the post in 1985. Two years later she ran for a four-year term and won in a runoff election.

The Cherokee in Oklahoma constitute the second-largest U.S. tribe, with 67,000 registered members. Prior to her election, Mankiller had been deputy principal chief. She said that her main concern was the tribe's economic development, noting that Cherokee "are worried about jobs and education, not whether the tribe is run by a woman or not."

Mann Act

The Mann Act, passed in 1910, made it illegal for anyone to transport women across state lines, or to import women for immoral purposes. The fines for breaking the law ranged from $200 to $2,000.

Shelley Mann

*First woman to win the
100-meter butterfly competition
in Olympic swimming (1956).*

Born Virginia, c. 1938.

The first time the 100-meter butterfly event was held in women's Olympic swimming was at the games in Melbourne, Australia, in 1956. Mann won the event with a time of one minute, eleven seconds.

Mann began swimming as therapy to strengthen her arms and legs, which were crippled by a polio attack when she was six years old. At twelve she started training for competition, and two years later was U.S. national champion. From Arlington, Virginia, Mann trained at the Walter Reed Swim Club of Washington, D.C. At various times, she held records for backstroke, freestyle, individual medley, and butterfly. She was elected a member of both the International Swimming Hall of Fame, and the Swimming and Diving Hall of Fame in 1966.

Marie Manning

*First journalist to write an
advice-to-the-lovelorn column
(1898).*

Born Washington, D.C., c. 1873; died Washington, D.C., November 28, 1945.

Under the name Beatrice Fairfax, Manning wrote a column for W. R. Hearst's newspaper the *New York Evening Journal* from 1898 until her marriage in 1905. She resumed the column in 1930 and continued writing it into the 1940s. In her columns, which were very successful, Manning preached the virtue of common sense: "Dry your eyes, roll up your sleeves, and dig for a practical solution." The question most frequently asked by her readers (usually by young men) was, "What can I do to be more popular?"

Educated in the United States and England, and a graduate of a Washington, D.C., finishing school, Manning began her journalism career with Joseph Pulitzer's New York *World* in 1897. That same year she moved to the *Evening Journal,* writing for the woman's page.

Author of novels and short stories, Manning published *Personal Reply* (1943), a book of advice to World War II servicemen and their families, and *Ladies Now and Then* (1944) her autobiography.

Arabella (Belle Aurelia) Mansfield Babb

*First woman to be admitted to
the bar (1869).*

Born Sperry Station, Iowa, May 23, 1846; died Aurora, Illinois, August 2, 1911.

A graduate of Iowa Wesleyan University (Mount Pleasant, Iowa) (1866), Mansfield (first called Belle and then Arabella) read for the law instead of attending law school, which was an acceptable practice at the time. She applied for admission to the bar and passed the bar exam with high honors. At that time, an Iowa law stated that admission to the bar was open to "any white male person"; an Iowa judge interpreted this law to the effect that it also did not deny the right of a female to be admitted. The judge's interpretation and Mansfield's admission to the bar were noted with approval by the *Revolution,* a magazine published by the suffragists.

Although she never practiced law, Mansfield continued her studies in that field. She earned an M.A. degree and then an LL.B. degree from Iowa Wesleyan in 1870 and 1872, respectively. From 1872 to 1873 she studied law in Paris, France.

She joined her husband, John Mansfield, on the faculy at Iowa Wesleyan for a short time, both then taking positions at Indiana Asbury University (later DePauw, Greencastle, Indiana) (1879). After a hiatus, during which she cared for her husband who had become mentally ill, she resumed her teaching at DePauw, where she was later named dean of the school of art and dean of the school of music.

Frances Marion

First woman to win an Academy Award for writing (1931); first to win an Academy Award for an original story (1932).

Born San Francisco, California, November 18, 1888; died Los Angeles, California, May 12, 1973.

Born Marion Benson Owens, she changed her name to Frances Marion about 1910 while a student and advertisement model. Her first Oscar, for writing, was awarded for her work on *The Big House* (1930), one of her early "talkies." She received the second Oscar for an original story, *The Champ* (1931).

Marion began her movie industry career with Bosworth Studios as an extra, script reader, stunt woman, and film editor. Her first scenario, written in 1916, was for *The Foundling,* starring Mary Pickford. She then wrote a series of movie scripts; in some cases, such as *Just Around the Corner* (1922), she directed as well. She also directed Pickford in *The Love Light* (1921).

At least seventy of her films were westerns, written for—and in conjunction with—her husband Fred Thomson, a popular cowboy star of the silent era.

In 1925 Marion formed her own company—Frances Marion Pictures.

Its productions included *Love* (1927), with Greta Garbo, and *The Lady* (1925), with Norma Talmadge.

When sound came to Hollywood, Marion wrote for the "talkies": *Anna Christie* (1930), first sound film for Greta Garbo; *Dinner at Eight* (1933); and others, including her Oscar winners.

Overall, Marion saw at least 136 of her screenplays produced in her lifetime. Her book, *How to Write and Sell Film Stories,* was published in 1937.

Anne Henrietta Martin

First woman to run for the U.S. Senate (1918).

Born Empire City, Nevada, September 30, 1875; died Carmel, California, April 15, 1951.

Active on the national scene as a suffragist, Martin was vice chair and legislative chair of the National Woman's party when a Nevada senator's seat was vacated by his death. Martin ran for the seat as an independent, but as a pacifist and suffragist she held some unpopular views and was defeated. She was defeated again in 1920, although on both occasions she polled twenty percent of the vote.

A woman of many talents, Martin earned an A.B. degree from the University of Nevada (Reno) in 1894, where she also won the state women's championship in tennis. She received a second A.B. degree (1896) and an A.M. degree in history (1897) from Stanford University (Palo Alto, California). She then founded and headed the history department of the University of Nevada, remaining there until 1903 when she left for extensive world travels.

In England about 1910, Martin became active in the suffrage movement; on one occasion, she was one of thirty women arrested for disturbing the peace—by order of Home Secretary Winston Churchill. During the same period, she began writing about social issues under the name of Anne O'Hara.

Returning to Nevada in 1911, Martin was elected president of the state suffragists; under her leadership, Nevada women won the vote in 1914.

After Martin's unsuccessful bids for the Senate, she moved to Carmel, California, working with the Women's International League for Peace and Freedom, opposing U.S. involvement in World War II just as she had in World War I. (She had received a short workhouse sentence after being arrested for picketing the White House in 1917.)

Martin parted company with the National Woman's party in the 1920s and 1930s; she exhorted women to vote together as a bloc and to shun the male-dominated political parties.

Lillien Jane Martin

Probably the first woman to start a mental hygiene clinic—also called a child guidance clinic— for preschool children; first to start an old age counseling center (1929).

Born Olean, New York, July 7, 1851; died San Francisco, California, March 26, 1943.

After she graduated from Vassar College (Poughkeepsie, New York) in 1880, Martin taught physics and chemistry at an Indianapolis, Indiana, high school. She moved to San Francisco, California, where in 1889 she was named vice principal and head of the department of science at Girls' High School.

In 1894 Martin left the United States for the University of Göttingen, in Germany, where she was awarded a Ph.D. degree in psychology in 1898. Returning to California, she was hired by Stanford University (Palo Alto, California) as an assistant professor of psychology. Martin became a full professor in 1911, and in 1915 was named head of the psychology department—a first for a woman.

Retiring from Stanford in 1916 at the age of sixty-five, Martin moved to San Francisco and set up a practice as a consulting psychologist. During these San Francisco years she set up the mental hygiene clinic for preschool children and the counseling center for the elderly.

Martin believed that one did not have to grow old. At seventy she was elected president of the California Society of Mental Hygiene, holding the post from 1917 through 1921. She was psychopathologist and chief of the mental hygiene clinic at San Francisco Polyclinic Hospital and Mount Zion Hospital. At the age of eighty-one she embarked on a coast-to-coast automobile trip. Martin worked regularly at her office as a consulting psychologist until a week before her death at ninety-two.

In 1913 Martin received an honorary Ph.D. degree from the University of Bonn in Germany—the first American psychologist to be so honored.

Patricia J. Martin

First woman chair of the American Advertising Federation (AAF) (1981).

Born Croton-on-Hudson, New York, June 25, 1928.

In 1959 Martin joined the Advertising Women of New York, one of AAF's organizations, serving as president from 1969 to 1971. In 1975 AAF, with 25,000 members—advertisers, media professionals, and photographers—in more than 200 clubs throughout the country, honored her as one of their chosen women of the year. She became the first woman to be named chair of the AAF in 1981, and since 1982 she has been an honorary member of the board of directors.

She received a B.A. degree from the College of New Rochelle, New Rochelle, New York, after which she became an editor at Warner-Hudnut in New York City, remaining there until 1958. From 1959 to 1985 she was director of marketing support for the Parke-Davis division of Warner-Lambert. Following her tenure there, she and Joan Lipton formed Martin and Lipton Advertising, Inc., an advertising agency specializing in health and personal-care products.

Among the honors and awards Martin has received are the 1980 Leadership Award given by the International Organization of Women Executives and the 1982 Matrix Award for women in communications.

May Massee

First woman member of the American Institute of Graphic Arts (AIGA) and first to receive its gold medal (1959).

Born Chicago, Illinois, May 1, 1881; died New York, New York, December 24, 1966.

A champion of quality color printing and high standards in illustrations, Massee was editor of *The Booklist,* a publication of the American Library Association, from 1913 to 1922. She then joined Doubleday Page publishers as head of the children's book department, the second such department in the United States. In 1922 she founded the children's book department at Viking Press, where she served as editor and director for twenty-seven years.

Before becoming involved in publishing, Massee attended the Normal School in Milwaukee, Wisconsin (1897–99), taught for a while, and then organized the Wisconsin Library School (Madison, Wisconsin) around 1900. Later, at the urging of Theresa W. Elmendorf (see entry), she became a librarian in the children's room at the Buffalo Public Library (Buffalo, New York).

Ten children's books that Massee edited won Newbery Medals, a prize awarded annually by the American Library Association for the "most distinguished contribution to American literature for children." The association also honored four books that she edited with the Caldecott Medal for the "most distinguished American picture book for children." In 1950 she received the Constance Lindsay Skinner Award from the Women's National Book Association, awarded for distinguished leadership in the publication of children's books, and in 1959 Massee became the first woman to receive the gold medal of the American Institute of Graphic Arts, an organization (founded 1914) of graphic designers, art directors, illustrators, and craftsman in printing and allied graphic fields.

Sybilla Masters

First woman inventor whose invention was patented (1715).

Birth date and place unknown; died Philadelphia, Pennsylvania, 1720.

The patent office in London, England, has an entry dated November 25, 1715, granting a patent to Thomas Masters for his wife Sybilla's invention of a device for cleaning and curing Indian corn. The device was innovative in that the corn was pulverized by a stamping method rather than by the usual grinding method.

Corn meal made by this process was called "Tuscarora Rice." It was sold in Philadelphia, Pennsylvania, as "a cure for consumption" and was thus called "the first American patent medicine." Sales of the "cure" were disappointing, however.

On February 18, 1716, a second patent was entered in the London office, again under the name of Thomas Masters, for a process of staining and working palmetto leaves for covering and decorating bonnets and hats.

Although the patents were taken out in the London patent office, they were also recorded and published in Pennsylvania.

Masters's place of birth is not known, but it is possible that she was born in Bermuda. There is evidence that her father emigrated from there to New Jersey in 1687.

Ann Teresa Mathews

Cofounder of first Roman Catholic convent in the United States (1790) (see also Frances Dickinson).

Born Charles County, Maryland, 1732; died Port Tobacco, Maryland, June 12, 1800.

Because Maryland didn't permit public mass in the eighteenth century, Mathews traveled to Belgium to enter the Discalced (barefoot) Carmelites—a contemplative working order, influenced by St. Teresa of Spain. She took her vows in 1755, taking the name Bernardina Teresa Xavier of St. Joseph. In 1774 she became a prioress (Mother Bernardina).

Maryland removed its restrictions on Roman Catholic worship after the American Revolution. Mother Bernardina therefore returned to the

United States to cofound (with Frances Dickinson) the Carmel convent in Port Tobacco, Maryland, on October 15, 1790. Mathews became its first prioress. The convent moved to Baltimore in 1830.

Susie Mathieu

First woman public relations director in major league professional hockey (1977).

Dates unknown.

Formerly assistant sports information director for St. Louis University (St. Louis, Missouri), Mathieu became public relations director for the St. Louis Blues of the National Hockey League.

Burnita S. Matthews

First woman to serve as a federal district judge (1949).

Born Burnell, Mississippi, 1894; died Washington, D.C., April 25, 1988.

Matthews was appointed to the federal District Court for the District of Columbia by President Harry S. Truman in 1949. In 1968 she became a senior judge, which allowed her to reduce her court workload without having to retire.

Having earned both LL.B. and LL.M. degrees from the National University Law School (now part of George Washington University, Washington, D.C.) in 1920, she applied to the Veterans Administration for a law-related position and was told that women were not hired. Thus, in 1920, she opened a private law practice. Upon requesting to join the local law association, she was refused membership because she was a woman. That same year, after women got the vote, she became the lawyer for the National Woman's party. While representing the party, she drafted several laws expanding women's rights.

One of the most interesting cases Matthews presided over was the 1957 bribery trial of James R. (Jimmy) Hoffa, the teamster union chief.

Geraldine Pratt May

First director of Women in the Air Force (WAF) (1948).

Born Albany, New York, April 21, 1895.

The Women's Armed Services Integration Act of 1948 declared Women in the Air Force (WAF) to be a formal component of the U.S. Air Force. May, who had risen to the rank of lieutenant colonel in the Women's Army Corps (WAC) and had been named staff director with the Army Ground Forces, was promoted that year to full colonel and appointed the director of the WAF.

After graduating from the University of California–Berkeley in 1920, May became a social worker and an administrator with the Camp Fire Girls organization.

She married Albert May in 1928, and they moved to Oklahoma. After living there for several years, the Mays returned to California in 1942, when she joined the Women's Army Auxiliary Corps (WAAC). She was commissioned second lieutenant upon graduating from the WAAC (later WAC) officers' training school in Iowa. In 1943 she became the staff director for the Air Transport Command. She quickly moved up the ranks from second lieutenant to major and then to lieutenant colonel. By 1947 she had been promoted to staff director with the Army Ground Forces.

Diana K. Mayer

First woman to be vice president of Citicorp (1974).

Born c. 1947.

Mayer was hired by Citicorp's corporate development department in 1971. By 1974 she was the director of three Citicorp subsidiaries.

A graduate of Wellesley College (Wellesley, Massachusetts) and the Harvard Graduate School of Business (Cambridge, Massachusetts), she was a portfolio analyst with a brokerage house.

In 1981 Mayer was first named administrative vice president in the money management division of the Marine Midland Bank of New York, then appointed a senior vice president.

Mary Maynard

First woman president of a local union of the United Mine Workers of America (1977).

Born c. 1938.

Maynard, the only woman in a local union of ninety-eight men in Rum Creek, West Virginia, was elected president in 1977. She was a truck driver for Pittston Coal Company, not a coal miner.

Divorced, she had two sons to support. She had earned a degree in dietetics after attending college for two years, but the salary she received as a truck driver—fifty-six dollars per day—was considerably more than she could earn as a dietician.

Before taking the job at Pittston, Maynard drove a truck for a construction company and a school bus.

Augusta Maywood

First U.S. woman to win international fame as a dancer;

first to form a traveling dance troupe (for tours in Italy) (1850).

Born New York, New York, 1825; died Lemberg, Austrian Galicia (now Lwów, Poland), November 3, 1876.

Born Augusta Williams, she took her stepfather's name (Maywood) after her mother divorced and remarried.

Maywood made her Philadelphia debut in 1837 at the age of twelve; her fame spread immediately to New York as well. She went to study at the Paris Opéra, was engaged there in 1838, and in 1839 gave her first performance to glowing critical reviews.

She danced in Vienna in 1846 and 1847, then in Italy in 1848, becoming the darling of the Italian public for ten years. Her traveling company staged the ballet version of *Uncle Tom's Cabin* shortly after its first stage dramatization.

In 1849 Maywood was named *prima donna assoluta* at La Scala in Milan. She retired from the stage in 1858 when she married Carlo Gardini, a physician. They moved to Vienna, where she opened a ballet school. Gardini left her in 1864 when she bore her second illegitimate child. The child, a son, died the day it was born.

Maywood continued her teaching and choreography in Vienna until 1873; she died in obscurity.

Mildred Helen McAfee (Horton)

First director of Women Accepted for Volunteer Emergency Service (WAVES) (1942).

Born Parkville, Missouri, May 12, 1900.

Having served on a wartime committee to establish a naval reserve program for women, McAfee was named director of the new organization—WAVES—on July 30, 1942. A full-fledged naval reserve branch, WAVES grew to a corps of 86,000 officers and enlisted women by 1945, and McAfee held the naval rank of captain.

A 1920 graduate of Vassar College (Poughkeepsie, New York), McAfee taught at Tusculum College (Greeneville, Tennessee) (1923–26); was dean of women at Centre College (Danville, Kentucky) (1927); earned an M.A. degree at the University of Chicago (Illinois) (1928); served as executive secretary for the Vassar College Alumnae Association (1932–34); and as dean of women, Oberlin College (Oberlin, Ohio), 1934–36.

In 1936 McAfee became the seventh president of Wellesley College (Wellesley, Massachusetts), serving until she accepted the WAVES post in 1943. After World War II she returned to the post of president at Wellesley, a position she held until 1949.

From 1950 to 1953 McAfee was president of the National Social Welfare Assembly; from 1959 to 1961 she was president of the American Board of Commissioners of Foreign Missions; and in 1962 she was a U.S. delegate to the United Nations Educational, Scientific, and Cultural Organization (UNESCO).

McAfee was cochair, with Patricia Roberts Harris (see entry), of the National Women's Committee for Civil Rights (1963–64). She also served on several corporate boards of directors.

(Sharon) Christa McAuliffe

First citizen passenger on a space mission (1986); first woman to die in a space accident (1986).

Born Boston, Massachusetts, September 2, 1948; died Cape Canaveral, Florida, January 28, 1986.

McAuliffe was chosen as the only citizen passenger on the *Challenger* space shuttle on July 19, 1985, after President Ronald Reagan specified that he wanted to send a teacher in order to signify the importance of the teaching profession. One of 11,000 applicants for the space mission, McAuliffe was a social studies teacher at Concord High School (Concord, New Hampshire), where she developed a course titled "The

American Women." During the flight of the *Challenger,* she was to have taught science lessons over PBS television to school groups across the country.

McAuliffe, a mother of two, had been an all-star softball player in high school. She earned an M.A. degree in American history and secondary education from Framingham State College (Framingham, Massachusetts) in 1970, and an M.Ed. degree from Bowie State College (Bowie, Maryland) in 1978.

On January 28, 1986, the space shuttle *Challenger* exploded shortly after launching at Cape Canaveral, killing all seven on board.

Susan McBeth

First major compiler of a Nez Percé dictionary (1873–75).

Born Doune, Scotland, 1830; died Mt. Idaho, Idaho, 1893.

McBeth began missionary work among the Nez Percé of Idaho in 1873; her goal was to help raise their educational level and increase their sense of individual identity and responsibility by reducing the influence of the chiefs and tribal bonds. Ultimately, she wanted to see the Native Americans assimilated into the dominant society. During this period she carried out her compilation of the

Nez Percé dictionary, the first major work of its kind.

After emigrating from Scotland to Ohio with her parents in 1832, McBeth attended the Steubenville Female Seminary (Steubenville, Ohio), graduating in 1854. She began a teaching career, and within a short time joined the staff of Fairfield University, a branch of the State University of Iowa (Iowa City).

In 1860 McBeth went to Native American territory near the Texas border (now Oklahoma) to teach Native American girls of elementary through high school age. Returning to Fairfield University when the Civil War broke out, McBeth became in 1863 one of the first women to be an agent of the U.S. Christian Commission, a Protestant relief organization. McBeth's job was to work with sick and injured soldiers in a St. Louis, Missouri, military hospital.

Mary McCauley

First woman to receive a military pension from a state government (1822).

Born Trenton, New Jersey, October 13, 1754; died Carlisle, Pennsylvania, January 22, 1832.

The famous "Molly Pitcher" of Revolutionary War fame, McCauley got her nickname as a result of carrying pitchers of water to soldiers of the Continental army in the battle of Monmouth. In the course of the battle, which took place on June 28, 1778, her first husband, John C. Hays, a soldier in the Seventh Pennsylvania Regiment, was either wounded or overcome by the heat. One story tells that McCauley took his place at the battery and loaded the cannon for the rest of the battle, which was eventually won by the Continental troops.

The Seventh Pennsylvania was commanded by Dr. William Irvine, in whose household McCauley had worked as a domestic before her 1769 marriage to John C. Hays. When her husband joined Irvine's regiment, she followed him to the army camp in New Jersey, where she took care of kitchen, laundry, and nursing chores—a common practice at that time. After the war, Mary and John Hays returned to Carlisle, Pennsylvania, where John died. In 1792 Mary Hays married John

Molly Pitcher (Mary McCauley)

McCauley, another Revolutionary War veteran. Thirty years later, in 1822, the legislature of Pennsylvania voted to acknowledge Mary McCauley's wartime service by granting her an immediate payment of forty dollars plus an annual pension of forty dollars for the rest of her life.

Mary McCauley is often confused with Margaret Corbin (see entry); both were called "Captain Molly."

Anne O'Hare McCormick

First woman to be on the editorial board of **The New York Times** *(1936); first to win the Pulitzer Prize for distinguished correspondence (1937).*

Born Wakefield, Yorkshire, England, May 16, 1880; died New York, New York, May 29, 1954.

McCormick's first association with *The New York Times* was as a free-lance writer for the newspaper's Sunday magazine. A frequent traveler with her husband, whom she had married in 1916, she wrote several foreign dispatches, which were published in the *Times* in 1920. Two years later she was hired as a regular *Times* correspondent, with a bylined column, "Abroad," which ran three times a week. As one of the few writers who refused to dismiss Mussolini, she drew special attention. She became the first woman on the editorial board of the *Times* in 1936. Her responsibilities included writing a minimum of two unsigned editorial pieces each week. She became a respected authority on international affairs, and in 1937 she won the Pulitzer Prize for foreign correspondence.

McCormick's family emigrated from England to the United States when she was an infant. She grew up in Ohio and graduated from the College of St. Mary of the Springs (Columbus, Ohio), now The Dominican College. Although she had no professional training for newspaper writing, she very early developed an interest in that field. Before joining *The New York Times,* she had become an associate editor of the weekly *Catholic Universe Bulletin* (Cleveland, Ohio) and contributed articles and poems to *Atlantic Monthly* and *Smart Set.*

Among the international stories that she covered were the establishment of the state of Israel (1948) and the Korean War (1950–52). *The Hammer and the Scythe: Communist Russia Enters the Second Decade* (1928) was her most noted book. Two volumes of her *Times* pieces, titled *The World at Home* and *Vatican Journal,* were edited by Marion T. Sheehan and published posthumously.

McCormick, a recipient of several honorary degrees, was presented with the American Woman's Association Medal in 1936 and received the Woman's National Press Club Achievement Award in 1945. In 1947 she was elected to the National Institute of Arts and Letters.

Catharine W. McCulloch

First woman to be nominated as a presidential elector (1916).

Born Ransomville, New York, 1862; died Evanston, Illinois, 1945.

McCulloch, an attorney, writer, suffragist, and president of the Women's Bar Association of Illinois, was nominated as a Democratic elector in 1916. The Illinois Democratic platform supported equal suffrage and an eight-hour day for male and female farm workers. She was defeated in her bid, but continued to work for women's issues, serving from 1920 to 1923 as chair of the League of Women Voters' Committee on Uniform Laws Concerning Women.

A graduate of the Rockford Female Seminary, Rockford, Illinois (1885) and the Union College of Law, Chicago, Illinois (later the Northwestern University Law School) (1886), she married Union classmate Frank H. McCulloch. She joined his law firm, which they renamed McCulloch and McCulloch. In 1898 she was admitted to practice before the U.S. Supreme Court.

From 1890 to 1912 McCulloch was legislative superintendent of the Illinois Equal Suffrage Association, and she served as the first vice president of the National American Woman Suffrage Association from 1910 to 1911.

Her writings included *Bridget's Daughters,* a feminist play (1911), and *Mr. Lex* (1899), a fictionalized treatment of the legal disadvantages at which married women and mothers find themselves.

Marilyn Wehrle McCusker

First woman to be killed in an underground mine in the United States (1979).

Born Utica, New York, February 2, 1944; died October 2, 1979, Osceola Mills, Pennsylvania.

To get her job in the mine of the Rushton Mining Company at Osceola Mills, Pennsylvania, McCusker hired a lawyer and sued the company. In May, 1977, the company—a subsidiary of the Pennsylvania Coal Company, owned by the Pennsylvania Power and Light Company—settled by hiring its first female miners. Bernice Dombroski, of Osceola Mills, was the first to be hired, and Marilyn McCusker got her job as well, along with a cash settlement of $30,000.

McCusker worked as a general laborer, serving on all three shifts. She put bolts in the tunnel roofs to support them, installed fireproof curtains, and laid track. Her regular pay was $9.46 per hour, with overtime pay for the second and third shifts.

On Tuesday, October 2, 1979, just before her shift was to end at 4 P.M., McCusker was installing roof bolts when the roof of the tunnel above her gave way. A huge piece of shale—about twenty feet long, sixteen feet wide, and three feet thick—came down, pinning McCusker to the floor of the mine. Other workers raised the piece of shale with a jack, but McCusker was dead when they got her body free.

At the time of the accident, it was estimated that over 2,000 women were employed in underground mines in the United States.

Anne E. McDowell

First woman to publish a newspaper, the weekly Woman's Advocate, *that was wholly operated by women (1855).*

Born Smyrna, Delaware, 1826; died Philadelphia, Pennsylvania, 1901.

In 1855 McDowell launched the *Woman's Advocate* in Philadelphia, Pennsylvania. The entire newspaper staff was women—not only the editors but the typesetters and printers as well, and they received the same wages as men working in the same fields.

The paper was especially concerned with the lives and working conditions of blue-collar women, and even served as an informal employment agency for them. It included literary material as well.

The *Woman's Advocate* went out of business in 1860. The Philadelphia *Sunday Dispatch* then made McDowell editor of the women's department. She stayed at that post until 1871, when she took a similar job at the Philadelphia *Sunday Republic*.

In 1884 McDowell was instrumental in establishing an organization to provide sickness and death benefits for the employees of John Wanamaker's department store; she also instituted the McDowell Free Library for the women who worked for Wanamaker's.

Irene McFarland

First woman to save her own life by jumping with a parachute (1925) (see also Tiny (Georgia) Broadwick).

Dates unknown.

As a result of her life-saving jump in Cincinnati, Ohio, McFarland became the first woman member of the Caterpillar Club, whose members made forced parachute leaps from balloons, dirigibles, and airplanes. The club chose its name because of the way some caterpillars float to the ground suspended by a fine web-like thread.

Anita Newcomb McGee

Founder of the Army Nurse Corps (1901); first woman appointed assistant surgeon general in the U.S. Army (1898).

Born Washington, D.C., 1864; died Washington, D.C., 1940.

McGee, who received an M.D. degree from Columbian (later George Washington) University, Washington, D.C., drafted the section of the Army Reorganization Act of 1901 that established the Nursing Corps as a permanent part of the U.S. Army.

She had been assigned to screen and train nurses for the army and navy during the Spanish-American War of 1898. When the war ended, she organized those nurses who wanted to remain into a corps under the aegis of the U.S. Surgeon General. In August, 1898, McGee was appointed first director of the corps and the first woman assistant surgeon general, a position she held until the end of 1900. In 1901 her opponents—who included the American Red Cross—forced the insertion of a provision requiring that the director of the new Army Nurse Corps be a graduate nurse, thus McGee was prevented from serving as director after the 1901 act took effect.

The Red Cross had opposed McGee because it saw procurement of nurses as part of its Geneva Treaty functions and resented McGee's initiative. Also, her effective recruiting methods caused the Red Cross to receive less in government funding than it would have if the organization had not had to compete with the new nurse corps. McGee had also made an enemy of Elisabeth M. Reid, who was politically connected and headed the American Red Cross committee to procure nurses.

Organizer of the Society of Spanish-American War Nurses, she served as its president from 1898 to 1904. In 1904/05, McGee and a group of the society's nurses assisted Japanese nurses in the Russo-Japanese War.

She was a member of the American Association for the Advancement of Science, the Women's Anthropological Society of America, and the Daughters of the American Revolution.

Mary McGrory

First woman to receive the Pulitzer Prize for commentary (1975).

Born Boston, Massachusetts, 1918.

McGrory, the author of a nationally syndicated column appearing in the *Washington Post* and some fifty other newspapers, received the Pulitzer Prize after twenty years of graphic and riveting writing on a national level.

Among her most famous pieces are those covering the Senator Joseph McCarthy hearings, and later the Watergate scandal.

McGrory attended the Girls' Latin School (Boston, Massachusetts) and earned a B.A. degree in English from

Emmanuel College (Boston, Massachusetts) in 1939. She worked for Houghton Mifflin publishers right after her graduation. In 1942 she joined the *Boston Herald* as a secretary but began writing feature stories and book reviews. She became a book reviewer for the *Washington Star* (D.C.) in 1947.

She is the annual host for a Christmas party held for infants and orphans in Washington, D.C.

Ann McKim

First woman to have a clipper ship named for her (1832).

Born Baltimore, Maryland, date unknown; died 1875.

Born Ann Bowly, she married Isaac McKim (1775–1838) on December 21, 1808. He built and named in her honor the fastest merchant ship of its era, *Ann McKim*. The first vessel of the "three-skysail-yarder" type, it was built with the finest fittings: mahogany hatches and rails, and a cannon of the best grade of brass. The ship was a forerunner of the Yankee clippers that began to appear in the 1840s.

Mary McLaren

First woman to be a barber for men aboard a U.S. ship (1967).

Born c. 1947.

McLaren, a graduate of a barber school in Newton, Connecticut, was a barber on board a Moore-McCormack cruise ship, *Brasil* (1967).

Edith Eleanor McLean

First premature infant to be placed in an incubator (1888).

Born New York, New York, September 7, 1888.

McLean weighed two pounds, seven ounces when she was born two months prematurely in the maternity ward of the State Emigrant Hospital at Ward's Island, New York City.

Neysa McMein

First woman artist to be invited to the White House, where she painted portraits of Presidents Harding (c. 1922) and Hoover (c. 1931); possibly the first U.S. woman to make a flight in Count Ferdinand von Zeppelin's dirigible (c. 1916).

Born Quincy, Illinois, January 24, 1888; died New York, New York, May 12, 1949.

Born Margary Edna McMein, she arrived in New York in 1913 seeking a career as an artist. One of her first steps was to adopt the name Neysa at the advice of a numerologist. She found success in fashion design and fashion sketching, which in turn led to work in commercial illustration. She specialized in portraits and cover designs for magazines such as *The Saturday Evening Post, Woman's Home Companion,* and *Collier's.* Her covers featured attractive, smart-looking American women—not the "baby doll" type.

Between 1923 and 1937 McMein designed all of the covers for *McCall's* magazine. As a "serious" artist, she painted portraits of Presidents Harding and Hoover; literary figures like Anne Lindbergh, Dorothy Parker, and Edna St. Vincent Millay; entertainers such as Beatrice Lillie and Charlie Chaplin; and political personages such as Charles Evans Hughes.

She created posters in both world wars for both the United States and France. During World War I she was a YMCA entertainer and lecturer for the troops in France.

McMein's reputation as an adventurous sort and a lover of travel led to her invitation to make a flight in one of Count Ferdinand von Zeppelin's dirigibles. She also once rode 100 miles on a camel in North Africa.

Aimee Semple McPherson

Probably the first woman to give a sermon over the radio (1922).

Born Ingersoll, Ontario, Canada, October 9, 1890; died Oakland, California, September 27, 1944.

McPherson was a magnetizing preacher, whose hallmark was a striking costume of white dress, white shoes, and flowing blue cape. In the early 1920s she drew audiences of 5,000 to her Angelus Temple in Los Angeles, California, for her dramatized Pentecostal sermons, which she delivered about nine times a week. Her first radio sermon was aired by a San Francisco radio in 1922.

Married at eighteen to a traveling evangelist, Robert Semple, she was ordained as a preacher in a Pentecostal ceremony of the Full Gospel Assembly in 1909. The two of them then traveled to China to preach. Their tour lasted only three months, however; her husband died and she then returned to the United States and joined the Salvation Army. While working with the organization in New York City in 1912, she married Harold McPherson. In 1916 she began her traveling revival tours. Held in tents across the country, her meetings were characterized by faith healing and speaking in tongues. They were run and attended by fundamentalists.

In 1921, after being divorced from Harold McPherson, she initiated the building of the Angelus Temple of the Church of the Foursquare Gospel, which was dedicated in 1923. Thousands of people, running the gamut from itinerant workers from various parts of the country to well-known members of Los Angeles society, flocked to her highly stylized, orchestrated services.

In 1923 McPherson also founded a Bible college, which in the succeeding two decades graduated more than 3,000 ordained missionaries and evangelists.

McPherson suffered a nervous breakdown in 1930, followed by a series of unpleasant courtroom cases, in which she was the defendant in many libel suits involving questionable financial transactions. In 1944 she died of an overdose of sleeping pills. Her death was ruled accidental, however.

After her death, her son Rolf McPherson assumed responsibility for running the church. It then had over 400 branches in the United States and Canada and some 200 branches abroad.

McPhetridge, Louise *(see Louise McPhetridge Thaden)*

Madeline H. McWhinney

First president of the First Women's Bank and Trust

*Company, New York, New York
(1974); first woman to be an
officer of the Federal Reserve
Bank of New York (1960).*

Born Denver, Colorado, 1922.

The First Women's Bank, incorporated and chartered in 1975, was established to provide an antidote to years of sexist practices in the banking industry. Plans for the bank were drawn in 1972, when feminist Betty Friedan (see entry), New York City Council member Carol Greitzer, and others began work to create the first full-service commercial bank to be owned and operated chiefly by women. The bank encountered difficulties shortly after it opened, however, and McWhinney left in 1976; she was replaced by Lynn Salvage.

McWhinney was a Phi Beta Kappa, magna cum laude graduate of Smith College (Northampton, Massachusetts) (1943). She then began a thirty-year career as an economist with the Federal Reserve Bank, serving as chief of the Financial and Trade Statistics Division (1955–59); chief of the Market Statistics Department (1960); and first woman to be named an assistant vice president in the Federal Reserve System (1965). She also received an M.B.A. degree from New York University (New York, New York) in 1947, winning the Key

Award for highest academic achievement. From 1957 to 1959 she served as the first woman president of the New York University Graduate School of Business.

McWhinney became a member of the Woman's Economic Round Table in 1978, serving as its chair in 1987/88. She also served on the board of governors of the American Stock Exchange in 1977/78. In 1980, she was appointed a permanent member of the New Jersey Casino Control Commission.

Jacqueline Means

---

*First woman to be ordained into
the U.S. Episcopal priesthood
(1974).*

Born Peoria, Illinois, c. 1937.

A high school dropout and daughter of alcoholic parents, Means married at sixteen and became the mother of four. She earned a high school equivalency diploma and a license as a practical nurse.

In 1974 Means and fourteen other women were ordained in defiance of church law. In September, 1976, however, the General Convention of the Episcopal Church opened its priesthood to women and ruled that the group ordained with Means in

1974 would be accepted into the Episcopal priesthood without official ordination. Some 1,700 participants, opposed to this decision, voted to secede and form a new body: the Anglican Church of North America.

Means was ordained as a deacon; her functions included assisting the parish rector in a number of ways, including offering the chalice of communion and making hospital calls.

At Means's ordination, which took place at All Saints' Church, Indianapolis, Indiana, forty-five priests took part in the service, which was attended by a large audience of her supporters. A handful of people left the church in protest.

Her first assignment was to All Saints' Church, an inner-city parish of about 150 members.

Marianne Means

First woman reporter to be assigned full-time coverage of the White House (1961–65).

Born Sioux City, Iowa, June 13, 1934.

Means began covering Washington politics in 1959 for the Washington bureau of the Hearst newspapers. She was assigned full time to the White House in 1961. The following year she won the New York Newspaper Women's Club Front Page Award.

A Phi Beta Kappa student with a B.A. degree from the University of Nebraska (Lincoln) (1956), Means was copy editor of the Lincoln *Journal* from 1955 to 1957. After her four-year assignment to the White House, she joined King Features as a syndicated political columnist in 1965. In 1977 Means earned a law degree (J.D.) from the George Washington University Law Center (Washington, D.C.).

In 1974 she reported that President Lyndon B. Johnson had told her in confidence that Lee Harvey Oswald had acted alone in the assassination of President John F. Kennedy—but that he had been working under the orders or influence of Cuban dictator Fidel Castro.

During her White House years, Means published a book titled *The Woman in the White House* (1963).

Leila Mechlin

First woman to be recognized as an important art critic/editor (1900).

Born Washington, D.C., 1874; died Washington, D.C., 1949.

Mechlin, one of the founders of the

American Federation of Arts (1909), became art critic for the *Washington Evening Star* and *Sunday Star* in 1900, a position that was to establish her as the first major woman art critic in the United States. She remained art critic for the two newspapers until 1945.

She also established and was editor of the *American Magazine of Fine Arts*, the first major twentieth-century periodical devoted exclusively to art. The periodical, originally titled *Art and Progress*, was first published in 1909. Mechlin remained involved with the magazine until 1931. In 1932 she helped select and assemble the art exhibition for the Olympic Games in Los Angeles, California. She was also one of the early champions of the establishment of the National Art Gallery in Washington, D.C., advocating it as early as 1908. From that point on, Mechlin made a national art gallery one of her main goals, writing about it in her editorials and articles for *Art and Progress*, the official magazine of the American Federation of Arts. Her dream was finally realized when the National Gallery of Art was officially installed in its completed building on March 17, 1941.

Mechlin, who received honorary degrees from George Washington University (Washington, D.C.) (1921) and the University of Nebraska (Lincoln) (1927), was the secretary of the American Federation of Arts (1912–33) and was elected a fellow of the Royal Society of Arts, London, England, in 1940.

Medical College, Boston Female

First institution to teach medicine to women (1848).

The Boston Female Medical College (Boston, Massachusetts) moved from home to home during the year after it opened on November 1, 1848. Led by male doctors, the school was incorporated as New England Female Medical College on May 24, 1856. The college merged with the homeopathic medicine department of the Boston University School of Medicine in 1874, thus making the Boston University School of Medicine the first coeducational medical school in the United States.

Medical Society, New England Hospital

First women's medical society in the world (1878).

The society was organized in 1878 by Dr. Marie E. Zakrzewska, who became the first president.

In 1910 the organization's name was changed to the New England Women's Medical Society, and in

1950 it became a branch of the American Medical Women's Association. Its purposes were to promote opportunities for women doctors, to ensure that they were treated fairly and equitably vis-à-vis male doctors, and to provide a means for exchanging scientific and professional information.

Dorothy Reed Mendenhall (see Dorothy Reed)

Merchant Marine Academy (see United States Merchant Marine Academy)

Fayvelle Mermey

Probably the first woman to be the president of a synagogue (1960).

Born 1916; died Larchmont, New York, 1977.

Mermey was elected president of the Reform Synagogue in Larchmont, New York, for two terms: 1960–62 and 1972–74. She was also the founder of the Women's Interfaith Seminary in Larchmont.

Her 1960 election demonstrated that Reform Judaism was achieving its goal of making women equal to men in the administration of synagogues.

Mermey graduated from New Jersey State College and attended the Columbia University School of Journalism (New York, New York). From 1964 to 1970 she was a columnist and feature writer for the *Mamaroneck Daily Times* of Mamaroneck, New York.

Beverly Messenger-Harris

First woman to be rector of an Episcopal church (1977).

Born Buffalo, New York, April 29, 1947.

By the late seventies, a few women had been ordained Episcopal priests (see also Jacqueline Means); Messenger-Harris's own ordination took place on January 8, 1977. However, attaining the position of rector—the person in charge of the parish—was still seen as the biggest obstacle for women. In addition to managing the fiscal and other administrative affairs of the parish, the rector exercises considerable influence in the selection of other clergy. Messenger-Harris became the first American woman to attain this position when she was named rector of Gethsemane Episcopal Church in Sherrill, New York, a community of about 3,000 residents with about 100 members in the Episcopal parish. She stayed at Gethsemane from June, 1977, to June, 1981; then she served at other churches before returning to her original parish.

Declining membership at three

churches—Gethsemane, St. John's (Oneida, New York), and Trinity (Canastota, New York)—led to the forming of a three-part consortium. Messenger-Harris served as vicar at all three churches from 1987 to 1991.

Baptized a Roman Catholic, she began attending an Episcopal church with her father when she was three after her mother died in 1949. She earned a B.A. degree in religion at William Smith College (Geneva, New York) in 1972, then graduated from Bexley-Hall Seminary in Rochester, New York (1975).

Messenger-Harris is now a writer, living in Sherrill, New York. Still acting as a priest from time to time, she wishes to remain a part of the church but no longer wants to make it her profession.

Debbie (Deborah) Meyer

First woman to win three individual Olympic gold medals at one competition (1968); first to win the 800-meter freestyle Olympic swimming event (1968); first to win the 200-meter freestyle Olympic swimming event (1968).

Born Annapolis, Maryland, August 14, 1952.

The 800-meter freestyle and 200-meter freestyle events for women were first held at the 1968 Olympics. Meyer won the 800-meter with a time of 9 minutes, 24.0 seconds—more than 11 seconds better than second-place finisher, Pam Kruse, of the United States. She won the 200-meter with a time of 2 minutes, 10.5 seconds; the second- and third-place finishers, both of the United States, were Jan Henne (2 minutes, 11.0 seconds) and Jane Barkman (2 minutes, 22.2 seconds).

Meyer won her third gold medal in 1968 in the 400-meter freestyle, which she swam in 4 minutes, 31.8 seconds.

Between 1967 and 1969 she set fifteen freestyle records. In 1967 she was the Pan American champion in the 400- and 800-meter events, and from 1967 to 1970 she held the 400-meter and 1,500-meter freestyle titles. She was also the U.S. 400-meter medley champion in 1969.

Meyer won the James E. Sullivan Award as top amateur athlete in 1968, and in 1977 was inducted into the International Swimming Hall of Fame. During her career, she set twenty-four U.S. records and won nineteen Amateur Athletic Union (AAU) championships.

Lucy Rider Meyer

Cofounder of the first U.S. deaconess home (1887).

Born New Haven, Vermont, September 9, 1849; died Chicago, Illinois, March 16, 1922.

An 1867 graduate of the New Hampton Literary Institution in Fairfax, Vermont, Meyer taught at Oberlin (Oberlin, Ohio) before graduating from that college in 1872. Between 1873 and 1875 she studied at the Woman's Medical College of Pennsylvania (Philadelphia); she then resumed her teaching career as professor of chemistry at McKendree College (Lebanon, Illinois).

In 1885 she started, with her husband, the Chicago Training School for City, Home, and Foreign Missions in Chicago, Illinois. She resumed her medical studies at the Woman's Medical College of Chicago, receiving her M.D. degree there in 1887.

The Methodist Church in Germany had begun work with deaconesses in 1836. In the United States, however, the use of deaconesses was not successful until Meyer's pioneering efforts. Methodist deaconesses took no vows and earned no salary; they did receive, however, room, board, and a small allowance. Their function was to perform social work in the cities.

In 1908 Meyer formed the Methodist Deaconess Association, a more liberal house than some of the sister establishments.

She published a social protest novel, *Mary North*, in 1905.

Military Academy (see United States Military Academy)

Military Band, Women's

First band in the U.S. armed forces to be composed entirely of women (1942).

The band was a Women's Army Auxiliary Corps unit organized at Fort Des Moines, Iowa. Originally comprised of eleven recruits, it grew to forty—its maximum size—by 1943. Because their rehearsal facility was in a borrowed basement, they were known as the "Lost Battalion."

Edna St. Vincent Millay

First woman to receive a Pulitzer Prize in poetry (1923).

Born Rockland, Maine, February 22, 1892; died Austerlitz, New York, October 19, 1950.

Millay won the 1923 Pulitzer Prize for her fourth book of verse, *The Ballad of the Harp-Weaver*.

Vincent Millay, as she was called, published her first poem in *St. Nicholas* magazine for children when she was only fourteen. After graduating from high school, she lived with her family and wrote poetry. In 1912 her poem "Renascence" was published in a poetry anthology, *The Lyric Year*.

The poem was well received, and she was asked to give readings of it. Caroline Dow, the executive secretary of the Young Women's Christian Association's (YWCA) national training school in New York, attended one of the readings. Dow became Millay's sponsor and sent her to Vassar College (Poughkeepsie, New York).

After graduating from Vassar in 1917, Millay published her first book of poetry, *Renascence and Other Poems*. At that same time she was developing an interest in the theater, and wrote and acted in *Aria da Capo*, a one-act play staged by the Provincetown Players of Greenwich Village, New York. After a brief association with the Players, she once again concentrated on her writing. *A Few Figs from Thistles*, a poetry anthology, was published in 1920 and *Second April*, her third book of verse, was published in 1921. She also wrote two more plays, *Two Slatterns and a King* and *The Lamp and the Bell* (1921). *Eight Sonnets in American Poetry: A Miscellany* was published in 1922.

In 1927 Millay wrote the libretto for Deems Taylor's opera *The King's Henchman*. The opera was first performed at the Metropolitan Opera House, New York City, in 1927 with Lawrence Tibbett singing the leading role; it was highly acclaimed.

She continued to write poetry, but the critical reaction became less favorable. Her early poems, many of them popular sonnets, were lyrical and personal in nature; many of them were about women and liberation. Later poems, on the other hand, demonstrated Millay's interest in political and social issues, and were not as well received.

An anthology of her poems, *Mine the Harvest*, was published posthumously.

Bertha Mahony Miller *(see Bertha Mahony)*

Elizabeth Smith Miller

First woman to come to the attention of the public by wearing the "Bloomer Costume" (1850/51).

Born Hampton, New York, September 20, 1822; died Geneva, New York, May 22, 1911.

The costume, consisting of a loosely belted tunic, a skirt that came to just below the knees, and Turkish pantaloons, was named for Amelia Bloomer (see entry), who introduced the outfit in her newspaper *The Lily* in 1851. The costume had been designed by Elizabeth Smith Miller (daughter of noted reformer Gerrit Smith), and Bloomer saw it when Miller wore it on a visit to her cousin, Elizabeth Cady Stanton (see entry), in Seneca Falls, New York, in the winter of 1850/51.

With time, the skirt became longer and the trousers disappeared.

Miller was educated at a private school in New York and at a Quaker school in Philadelphia, Pennsylvania. In 1875 she published a popular recipe book, *In the Kitchen*.

Frieda Segelke Miller

First woman to represent the United States in the International Labor Organization (ILO) (1946).

Born La Crosse, Wisconsin, April 16, 1890; died New York, New York, July 21, 1973.

Miller was the second director of the Women's Bureau at the U.S. Department of Labor (1944–53), and the second female commissioner of labor of New York State (see also Frances Perkins). Prior to that, she was director of the Division of Women in the New York State Department of Labor (1929–39) and a New York City factory inspector (1924–26).

She earned a B.A. degree at Milwaukee-Downer College (Milwaukee, Wisconsin), then went to the University of Chicago (Chicago, Illinois) as a fellow to study economics, sociology, political science, and law. In 1916 she was a research assistant and social economy teacher at Bryn Mawr College (Bryn Mawr, Pennsylvania). Miller also helped found the Workers' Education Bureau of America.

As substitute representative for Assistant Secretary of Labor David A. Morse, Miller became the first woman to represent the United States in the International Labor Organization, an agency of the United Nations that reports on labor practices worldwide. In her role with the ILO, Miller worked for improvement of conditions in both the economic and social aspects of labor.

Joyce D. Miller

First woman to be elected to the AFL-CIO executive council (1980).

Born Chicago, Illinois, 1928.

A leading spokesperson for women trade unionists and a champion of issues concerning working women, Miller was elected to the post after the council waived a rule that limited membership to just one person from each of the unions represented. The waiver, made in February, 1980, was designed to pave the way for greater representation of women and minorities within the AFL-CIO leadership.

At the time she was named to the

thirty-five-seat council, Miller was vice president of the Amalgamated Clothing and Textile Workers. She had also been president of the 12,000-member Coalition of Labor Union Women; their program advocated a national health insurance plan, child care, and support for the Equal Rights Amendment.

During her student days, Miller worked on a factory assembly line that produced gumballs for vending machines. After she graduated from the University of Chicago (Chicago, Illinois), with a bachelor's degree in 1950 and a master's degree in 1951, she held a variety of teaching and labor positions.

The Amalgamated Clothing and Textile Workers union made her the education director in Pittsburgh, Pennsylvania, and Chicago, Illinois; she then held the post of social services director, running programs involving treatment for alcoholism, day care, and services for retirees.

Mary P. Miller

First woman to be a passenger on an airship (1906).

Dates unknown.

The 40-horsepower, 22,500-cubic-foot dirigible was owned by her husband, Major Charles J. S. Miller, and piloted by Leo Stevens. On the eve-ning of August 11, 1906, Mary Miller and Stevens took off in it from Franklin, Pennsylvania. Her husband had planned to go too, but the ship was losing gas from the airbag, and Major Miller could not go because of his weight. Miller volunteered to replace her husband. It rose 600 feet into the air and flew ⅛ mile before the engine stopped. Unfortunately, Miller had thrown out the sparking crank when she cast off the drag line, so the airship came down.

Mill Owner

First woman to run a mill (1644).

According to Plymouth Colony records of 1644, "Mistress Jenny" was identified as the person who promised to tend to the grinding at the mill and to keep bags of "corn" (grain) from spoiling and "loosening."

Lorna Mills

First woman to be named president of a federally chartered savings and loan company (1957).

Born Long Beach, California, February 5, 1916.

In 1936 Mills went to work for the

Laguna Beach, California, Federal Savings & Loan as a stenographer and clerk. She was one of three employees at the time; the bank had $300,000 in assets. By the mid-1970s that figure had grown to over $200 million.

Mills served as president and manager from 1957 to 1982, when the bank merged with the Great American First Savings Bank. She retained her post after the merger.

Mississippi State College for Women

First state college for women (1884).

The original name of the Mississippi State College for Women, Columbus, Mississippi, was Mississippi Industrial Institute and College for the Education of White Girls of the State of Mississippi. It was established in 1884 and graduated its first students in 1885. By 1889 there were ten graduates.

In the 1980s when many women's colleges across the country began admitting men, Mississippi State College for Women was the last state women's college to enroll a male student. This event came about as a result of a decision by the U.S. Supreme Court in *Mississippi University for Women* v. *Hogan* (1982), when the Court ruled by a five-to-four margin that the school's "policy of excluding males from admission to the School of Nursing tends to perpetuate the stereotyped view of nursing as an exclusively woman's job," saying that Hogan's exclusion amounted to unconstitutional sexual bias. (The school's name was changed to Mississippi University for Women in 1982.)

Maria Mitchell

First woman elected to the American Academy of Arts and Sciences (1848); first to have a comet named for her (1847); first to be elected to the American Philosophical Society (1869).

Born Nantucket, Massachusetts, August 1, 1818; died Lynn, Massachusetts, June 28, 1889.

Using a two-inch telescope, Mitchell discovered a new comet in 1847. The discovery made her instantly famous. The comet was named "Miss Mitchell's Comet," and the king of Denmark awarded her a gold medal. Her finding also led to her election in 1848 as the first woman member of the American Academy of Arts and Sciences.

Mitchell's father, an educator and astronomer, was responsible for most of her education. In her early years, she assisted him with chronometer ratings of Nantucket whaling ships.

In 1836 Mitchell was appointed librarian of the Nantucket Athenaeum, a position she occupied for twenty years. From 1849 to 1868 she also worked for the U.S. Nautical Almanac Office. Elected in 1850 to the American Association for the Advancement of Science, she was the only woman member until 1843.

When Vassar Female College (Poughkeepsie, New York) was founded in 1865, Mitchell was named professor of astronomy and director of the college observatory, where Matthew Vassar offered her the use of a twelve-inch telescope— third largest in the United States.

Mitchell was a founder of the American Association for the Advancement of Women (1873), a group whose purpose was to promote the work and achievements of women and confront the problems they encountered. She served as its president from 1875 to 1876.

In 1905 Mitchell was elected to the Hall of Fame of Great Americans, which was then at New York University, now at Bronx Community College (Bronx, New York) of the City University of New York.

Jerrie Mock (born Geraldine Fredritz)

First woman to fly solo around the world (1964).

Born Newark, Ohio, 1925.

When she landed her single-engine Cessna 180 at Port Columbus, Ohio, on April 17, 1964, she had flown 22,858.8 miles in twenty-nine days, eleven hours, fifty-nine minutes, with twenty-one stopovers, since her flight began on March 19. The thirty-eight-year-old Columbus, Ohio, pilot set three other records during the flight: first to fly alone across the Pacific Ocean from west to east, first to fly a single-engine plane in either direction across the Pacific, and first woman to fly solo from coast to coast by going around the world. On May 4, 1964, President Lyndon Johnson presented Mock with the Federal Aviation Agency's Gold Medal Award. She was also named vice chair of the Women's Aviation Advisory Committee of the Federal Aviation Agency.

Mock, the mother of three, attended Ohio State University (Columbus), where she majored in aeronautical engineering. She began her flying lessons in 1957, and received her private pilot's license in 1958. After earning her pilot's license, she became manager of the Logan County Airport in Lincoln County, Illinois. In 1960 she was hired to manage Price Field, a small general aviation port in Columbus, Ohio.

In November, 1969, after achieving twenty-one world records in aviation, Mock retired from flying, delivering her plane to a missionary priest in the jungles of New Guinea.

At the time of this writing, Mock spends much of her time lecturing on flying and world travel.

Models' Training School

First school for mannequins (1928).

The school, called L'Ecole de Mannequins and located in Chicago, Illinois, trained young women to be models and mannequins. In 1928 mannequins, who were earning one dollar an hour, were often asked to pose for two hours at a time. Six thousand models working in Chicago formed a union and demanded shorter hours and higher pay.

Karen Moe (Thornton)

First U.S. woman to win the Olympic 200-meter butterfly event (1972).

Born Santa Clara, California, c. 1952.

Moe won the Olympic 200-meter butterfly swimming event the second time it was held (1972) in a time of 2 minutes, 15.57 seconds, which was her record time in the event. The United States swept the event with Lynn Colella taking the silver medal and Ellie Daniel the bronze.

The first time the 200-meter butterfly was held as an Olympic event was in 1968.

In 1976 Karen Moe Thornton finished the Olympic 200-meter butterfly event in a time of 2 minutes, 12.90 seconds. Although she swam nearly 3 seconds faster than she did in 1972, she only placed fourth.

Harriet Monroe

Founder of the first magazine devoted solely to modern poetry (1912).

Born Chicago, Illinois, December 23, 1860; died Arequipa, Peru, September 26, 1936.

In October, 1912, Monroe published the first issue of *Poetry: A Magazine of Verse,* now called *Poetry.* The poet Ezra Pound was its first foreign correspondent, sending literary letters about poets and poetry in France and other parts of Europe. She continued to edit it until her death in 1936.

Monroe attended the Visitation Convent School in Georgetown, D.C., 1876–79. For the next two decades, she was a correspondent and cultural reviewer for various Chicago and New York City newspapers.

Her own poetry career began about 1888; her first book of verse, *Valeria and Other Poems,* was published in 1891. She was honored by the selection of her poem, "Columbian Ode," for the program dedicating Chicago's World Columbian Exposition in 1892.

Maria Hester Monroe

First daughter of a president to be married in the White House (1820).

Born Paris, France, 1803; died Oak Hill, Albemarle County, Virginia, 1850.

Monroe, daughter of James Monroe, fifth president of the United States, married Samuel L. Gouverneur. The ceremony was held in the White House on March 9, 1820.

Helen (Nellie) Barrett Montgomery

First woman president of the Northern Baptist Convention (1921).

Born Kingsville, Ohio, 1861; died Summit, New Jersey, 1934.

Reportedly the first woman to hold such a position in any large Christian denomination, Montgomery became the president of the convention after a history of involvement in the Baptist Church.

As early as 1888, for example, she was teaching a large Bible class. In 1913 she became the first president of the newly formed Woman's American Baptist Foreign Mission Society, a position she held until 1924. In 1915 she cofounded the World Wide Guild, an organization that recruits young women for Baptist missionary service.

Montgomery, a graduate of Wellesley College, Wellesley, Massachusetts (1884), wrote *The King's Highway* (1915), a popular book about missions throughout the world, and *The Centenary Translation of the New Testament* (1924), which she translated from Greek.

Deborah Moody

First woman to receive a colonial land grant (1645); first to cast a vote (1655).

Born Avebury, England, c. 1580; died Gravesend, Long Island, New York, c. 1659.

After a rift with the government of England, Moody sailed to the colonies in 1639. She gained a group of followers who went with her to Gravesend, Long Island, where they planned a town, held town meetings, bought land from the Native Americans, and established what became the first colonial settlement to be run by a woman.

Moody was given a land grant by the Dutch government in Kings

County, New York (now Brooklyn), in 1645. Entitled to a vote by virtue of that grant, she cast her first vote in 1655. She was the first woman to receive such a grant and to exercise the right to vote.

Helen Wills Moody *(see Helen Wills)*

Anna Carroll Moore

First person to chair the Children's Services Division of the American Library Association (1900).

Born Limerick, Maine, July 12, 1871; died New York, New York, January 20, 1961.

The function of the Children's Services Division was to give advice on book collection, and to produce reports on library innovations or activities such as storytelling, puppetry, preschool programs, and exhibits. When Moore chaired the organization in 1900, it was known as the Club of Children's Librarians.

In 1895 Moore had entered the Library School of Pratt Institute (Brooklyn, New York). From 1897 to 1906, she served as the head of its new children's department—also known as the Pratt Institute Free Library.

In 1903 Moore published *A List of Books Recommended for a Children's Library*.

In 1906 Moore became supervisor of the children's division of the New York Public Library. She held the position until 1940 when, at the age of seventy, she was forced to retire. During this period she was also known as an author, critic, and columnist. Her reputation and influence were felt even abroad. In 1911, when what is now the main branch of the New York Public Library opened at Forty-second Street and Fifth Avenue, there was a Central Children's Room. The same year Stockholm, Sweden, opened the first children's library in Europe, motivated in part by her contributions to the field.

Moore was also known for her support of Leo Frank, a Jewish man convicted in 1913 for the Atlanta, Georgia, murder of Mary Phagan. She had known him when he visited Pratt Library as a child, and they later kept up a correspondence. Certain of his innocence, she visited him and spoke out in his support. Frank was lynched in 1915. Most think he was wrongly convicted, victim of a contemporary surge of antisemitism.

Ellie (Eleanor) Durall (Brown) Moore

First woman head of an all-woman governors board of a professional basketball team (1973).

Born Central City, Kentucky, February 11, 1940.

Woman of the Year Award in 1973 and is listed in *Who's Who in America* (1976).

Cathleen Synge Morawetz

First woman to head a mathematical institute in the United States (1984).

Born Toronto, Canada, 1923.

Morawetz came to the United States in 1945 and became a naturalized citizen in 1950. After earning degrees from the University of Toronto (Toronto, Canada) and the Massachusetts Institute of Technology (Cambridge), she was awarded a Ph.D. degree in mathematics from New York University (New York, New York) in 1951. She joined New York University's Courant Institute of Mathematical Sciences as a research associate in 1952, and was named professor in 1965. She became director of the institute in 1984.

In 1986 Morawetz was awarded an honorary doctor of science degree from Princeton University for her work as "an ingenious problem solver." She is a member of the American Association for Advancement of the Sciences and the American Academy of Arts and Sciences, as well as a trustee of the American Mathematical Society.

On July 8, 1973, Moore paid more than $1 million for majority ownership of the stock in the Kentucky Colonels team of the American Basketball Association and became the head of the team's five-woman governors board.

Once married to former Kentucky Governor John Y. Brown, Jr., she earned a degree in commerce at the University of Kentucky (Lexington) and taught English at Barrett Junior High School (Louisville, Kentucky). The mother of three children, she is now married to Robert Moore of Louisville, Kentucky. When she was a teenager, she played center for the girls' basketball team in Central City, Kentucky.

Moore has been a member of the board of directors of the Kentucky Repertory Theater and a member of the Louisville Chamber of Commerce Club. She received the Kentucky

Esther McQuigg Slack Morris

First woman justice of the peace (1870).

Born Spencer, New York, August 8, 1814; died Cheyenne, Wyoming, April 2, 1902.

Morris was appointed justice of the peace of a Wyoming settlement called South Pass City, which had a population of 460. She herself had only lived in the settlement for a year. Her term in office lasted less than a year, during which she tried approximately seventy cases.

Morris's first husband, Artemus Slack, died and left her an estate in Illinois. She then married John Morris, a merchant, and went with him to Wyoming, where she soon gained a

reputation as a woman suffragist. One of her sons, Edward Slack, a newspaper editor, described her in the *Daily Leader* as the "Mother of Woman Suffrage." During the Wyoming statehood celebration, the former justice of the peace was credited with being a pioneer in that cause. In 1895 she was selected as a Wyoming delegate to the national suffrage convention held in Cleveland, Ohio.

Emma Sadler Moss

First woman to be elected president of a major medical society (1955).

Born c. 1898.

Moss was elected president of the American Society of Clinical Pathologists (ASCP).

A New Orleans pathologist, Moss began her career as a medical technologist in 1910 at New Orleans' Charity Hospital of Louisiana. She began the study of medicine in 1930 and became head of Charity Hospital's department of pathology in 1940. She was still holding that position in 1955, when she was named president of the ASCP. Her specializations included parasitology, fungus diseases, and the training of medical technologists.

Mother-in-law's Day

First celebrated on March 5, 1934, in Amarillo, Texas.

The innovator was a local newspaper editor, Gene Howe. The first guest of honor was Mrs. W. F. Donald, his mother-in-law. Now called Mother-in-law's Day and celebrated on the fourth Sunday in October, the occasion is still observed only in Amarillo, Texas.

Mother's Day

First celebrated on May 10, 1908, in some parts of West Virginia and Pennsylvania; the first national observance was on May 10, 1914.

A day of observance for mothers had first been suggested by Anna Jarvis (see entry) in 1907. She campaigned with letters to state governors, members of Congress, and the press at the White House, and within six years most of the states were celebrating Mother's Day on the second Sunday in May.

In 1914 observance of the day was enacted into law. President Woodrow Wilson issued a proclamation that directed all government officials to display the U.S. flag and invited all the citizens of the country to join him and the officials in doing the same, "as a public expression of our love and reverence for the mothers of our country."

Motoring Club, Woman's

First all-woman auto race (1909).

The club sponsored an all-woman auto race that left New York City for Philadelphia on January 12, 1909, and returned to New York a couple of days later. Participants boarded their vehicles outside New York's Plaza Hotel, where the Woman's Motoring Club held its meetings. The passengers, as well as the drivers, were women, but each entry could be accompanied by a chase car with a male mechanic. Cars could be powered by gasoline, steam, or electricity.

Twelve competitors entered the race, and several prizes were awarded, including the Benjamin Briscoe Trophy for Mrs. John R. Ramsay of Hackensack, New Jersey, in a Maxwell Runabout with one passenger; the Hugh Chalmers Trophy, for Mrs. John Newton Cuneo of Richmond Hill, Queens, New York, in a Lancia Lampo with one passenger; and the Woman's Motoring Club Cup to Alice DiHeyes of Brielle, New Jersey, driving a new customized Cadillac with four passengers.

Lucretia Coffin Mott

First president of the American Equal Rights Association (1866).

Born Nantucket, Massachusetts, January 3, 1793; died Philadelphia, Pennsylvania, November 11, 1880.

Mott, a Quaker minister who had lectured across the country on such topics as abolition of slavery, temperance, peace, and women's rights, gained a widespread reputation as a social reformist. She and Elizabeth Cady Stanton (see entry) organized a women's convention in Seneca Falls, New York, in July, 1848. Although the convention was presided over by James Mott, Lucretia's husband, she and Stanton led the discussion on women's rights. The convention's "Declaration of Sentiments" began "We hold these truths to be self-evi-

dent, that all men *and women* are created equal." In 1852 Mott was elected president of the annual women's rights convention, and in 1866 she became the first president of the American Equal Rights Association.

Linking organized women's rights and suffrage movements with the convention held at Seneca Falls, many Americans labeled Mott the "mother" of the feminist movement. Among the many first rights that were called for at the convention was the right of women to vote.

A zealous abolitionist—one of the organizers of the Anti-slavery Convention of American Women, 1937— Mott campaigned for Negro suffrage until she died.

Throughout the later years of her life, she wrote and gave lectures (the last one six months before she died) on such topics as the injustices endured by women, abolition of slavery, peace, and the positive aspects of liberal religion.

Pauline Moyd

First woman to conduct a symposium of the American Institute of Mining, Metallurgical and Petroleum Engineers (AIMMPE) (1957).

Dates unknown.
The symposium was convened to

discuss the topic "Alumina Source Materials in Glass." Women had previously chaired small sessions of the AIMMPE, but Moyd was the first to lead a major symposium. As a geologist, she had spent years exploring mineral deposits in the United States and Canada, prospecting for aluminum and uranium. She had also done research in the area of concrete materials. In 1960, when she was one of three women speakers among 400 specialists who presented papers at an AIMMPE convention, Moyd lobbied for greater efforts to interest female students in mining and metallurgy.

Shirley Muldowney

First person to win the National Hot Rod Association's World Championship three times—in 1977, 1980, and 1982.

Born New York State, c. 1940.

First woman drag racer to exceed 250 miles per hour, Muldowney started racing the family car on the local drag strip in Schenectady, New York, working her way up through the stock, modified, semipro, and professional classes of drag racing. In 1977 Muldowney became the first woman to win the Winston World Championship, drag racing's most coveted

award. The same year, she was the first woman named to the ten-member all-American auto-racing team. In 1980 she won the Winston World Championship again, becoming the first person to win it twice, and in 1982 she won the National Hot Rod Association's World Championship for the third time.

Judith Sargent Murray

Reportedly the first woman to be a regularly published essayist (1792).

Born Gloucester, Massachusetts, May 1, 1751; died Natchez, Mississippi, July 6, 1820.

Writing essays under the pen name Constantia, on themes such as women's equality and better education for young females, Murray was a regular contributor to the *Massachusetts Magazine*. A series of essays titled "The Gleaner," written from the point of view of a male persona named Mr. Vigillius, was popular and ran from 1792 to 1794. Murray used the male persona to express her views on such topics as education, politics, and religion.

Among her other publications were her first essay, "Desultory Thoughts upon the Utility of Encouraging a Degree of Self-Complacency, Especially in Female Bosoms," published in *Gentleman's and Lady's Town and Country Magazine,* Boston, Massachusetts (1784); a play, *The Medium,* which was performed one time in Boston (1795); *The Traveller Returned* (1796); and *The Gleaner,* a three-volume compilation of her essays (1798). She also wrote "On the Equality of the Sexes," published in *Massachusetts Magazine.* The essay was published in 1790, but Murray claimed that it was written in 1779, thus predating Mary Wollstonecraft's *Vindication of the Rights of Woman* (1792), widely considered the first great feminist document.

Caroline Clark Myers

First woman employed by the U.S. Army as a teacher (1917).

Born c. 1888; died Boyds Mill, Pennsylvania, July 3, 1980.

During World War I, Myers and Gary C. Myers, her husband, developed materials and methods of teaching illiterate soldiers to read.

Myers was named a Laura Spellman Rockefeller Scholar in 1930. She became the chair of the board of the *Highlights for Children* magazine in 1971, after the death of her husband. Prior to that, she had been managing editor.

Maud Nathan

Probably the first woman to give a speech in a synagogue in place of the rabbi's sermon (1897).

Born New York, New York, October 20, 1862; died New York, New York, December 15, 1946.

Speaking at New York City's Temple Beth-El, Nathan's talk was titled "The Heart of Judaism." She said that Judaism embodied a love of righteousness, including social justice.

Sister of Annie Nathan Meyer, who founded Barnard College (New York, New York) in 1889, and a cousin of U.S. Supreme Court Justice Benjamin Cardozo, Nathan began working with charities after her marriage to her cousin, Frederick Nathan (1880). In 1890 she helped Josephine Shaw Lowell (see entry) form the Consumers' League of New York, becoming president of the New York branch in 1897. She held that post for about twenty years.

In 1898, when the National Consumers League was founded, Nathan was named to the executive committee and later became a vice president.

Unlike her sister, Nathan supported the women's suffrage movement, and was a first vice president of the Equal Suffrage League of New York.

National Aeronautics and Space Administration (NASA)

First women astronauts in the U.S. space program.

On January 16, 1978, NASA named thirty-five candidates for the space shuttle program, including six women. These first women to be chosen for the U.S. space effort were: Anna L. Fisher, M.D., from California; Shannon W. Lucid, a biochemist (Ph.D.) from Oklahoma; Judith A. Resnik, an electrical engineer (Ph.D.) from California; Sally K. Ride, researcher in physics (Ph.D) from California; Margaret Seddon, M.D., from Tennessee; and Kathryn D. Sullivan, who was finishing her Ph.D. in geology at the time she was chosen. (See entries for each of the six astronauts.)

NASA's two astronaut categories are pilot and mission specialist. Pilot astronauts serve as both space shuttle commanders and pilots. Mission specialists, working with the commander and pilot, have responsibility for the coordination of shuttle operations in the areas of crew activity planning, inventory of consumable items, and experiment and payload operations.

Astronaut candidates, chosen from the civilian and military populations, have to meet certain physical requirements and have both a bachelor's degree and some work experience, or they may substitute higher degrees for the work experience. Pilot astronaut candidates must have had, in addition, at least 1,000 hours of jet aircraft pilot-in-command time.

The program includes training in engineering, medical, and scientific duties. Astronaut candidates are assigned to the Astronaut Office at the Johnson Space Center, Houston, Texas. In addition to the training, there is an evaluation period.

A spokesperson for NASA noted that the agency had not found a fully qualified woman in the first eighteen years of the space program, but "In the last few years, because of the women's movement, frankly, more women have been qualified."

National Amateur Athletic Federation

First woman's division of the National Amateur Athletic Federation (1923).

Lou Henry Hoover, wife of Herbert C. Hoover, who later became the thirty-first president of the United States, organized the woman's division of the National Amateur Athletic Federation in 1923. The slogan that the organization chose was: "A sport for every girl and every girl for a sport."

National Organization for Women (NOW)

First modern feminist organization in the United States.

Betty Goldstein Friedan (see entry) founded and became the first president of NOW in October, 1966. It is the largest of the contemporary organizations dedicated to insuring civil rights and equality for women. Its membership consists of men and women who support "full equality for women in truly equal partnership with men." The organization supports passage of the Equal Rights Amendment and enforcement of federal legislation prohibiting sexual discrimination. Among the small group that met with Friedan to form the organization was Dorothy Haener, who was appointed the international representative of the United Auto Workers Women's Department (1961) and Aileen Hernandez, who succeeded Friedan as president (1970), becoming the first black president.

In 1977 Eleanor Cutri Smeal became the first housewife to be president of NOW. Smeal, holder of a Phi Beta Kappa key, earned a B.A. degree from the University of Florida (Gainesville) in 1963 and joined NOW in 1970. She was also the first president to be paid a salary—$17,500 per year.

Divisions within NOW include the Legal Defense and Education Fund, Sexual Assault Task Force, and Task Force on Older Women (TFOW). Laurie Shields and Tish Sommers, coordinators of the TFOW in 1975, lobbied to secure passage of California's Displaced Homemaker Act, the first of its kind in the United States (1975). The act provided for the establishment of centers which prepare displaced homemakers to support themselves and their families. The centers, the first of which was opened in California in 1975, provide counseling, training in marketable skills, basic education, job placement, financial support for transportation, child care and living expenses, and emotional support.

Nellie Neilson

First woman to be president of the American Historical Association (1943).

Born Philadelphia, Pennsylvania, 1873; died South Hadley, Massachusetts, May 26, 1947.

Neilson has a host of other first-time accomplishments to her name. She was the first woman to have a volume published in the Oxford Studies in Social and Legal History; first woman to edit a yearbook of the Selden Society (Yearbook 10: *The Reign of Edward IV of England*); first woman to have an article published in the *Harvard Law Review;* and the first woman to be elected a fellow of the Mediaeval Society of America.

In 1893 Neilson graduated from Bryn Mawr College (Bryn Mawr, Pennsylvania), where she also earned M.A. and Ph.D degrees (1899). From 1900 to 1902 she was a reader at Bryn Mawr, leaving there to go to Mount Holyoke College (South Hadley, Massachusetts), as a history instructor. She was named chair of the history department in 1903, holding the post until she retired in 1939. In

1905 Neilson was promoted to professor of history.

Before her election to the presidency of the American Historical Association, Neilson had served as second vice president (1941), and as first vice president (1942). She was also a fellow of the Royal Historical Society.

Dorothy Nepper-Marshall (see Patricia McGowan Wald)

Agnes Nestor

First woman to be elected president of an international labor union (1903).

Born Grand Rapids, Michigan, June 24, 1880; died Chicago, Illinois, December 28, 1948.

Nestor began working in a factory when she was fourteen years old; she worked ten hours a day, six days a week. In 1897 her family moved to Chicago, and the following year—when she was eighteen—she led a successful strike at the Eisendrath Glove factory in Chicago. The workers picketed for ten days, after which the Eisendrath management met all of their demands.

As a delegate of her local union, Nestor helped organize the International Glove Workers Union (affiliated with the American Federation of Labor) in 1902, and the same year she founded Operators Local #1 of the International Glove Workers Union (IGWU). She and Elizabeth Christman led female workers out of the men's union, and Nestor was elected president of the new women's local.

From 1907 she was a member of the executive board of the National Women's Trade Union League, and from 1913 until her death in 1948 she was president of the Chicago chapter. From 1906 to 1948 she was on the executive board of the IGWU; she served as national vice president from 1903 to 1906; secretary-treasurer from 1906 to 1913; president from 1913 to 1915; vice president from 1915 to 1938; then director of research and education until her death.

Nestor helped organize unions in other industries—particularly the needle trades—and she participated in strikes by garment workers from 1909 to 1911. She was appointed to a federal commission by President Woodrow Wilson to consider aid for vocational education, and during World War I, as a member of an advisory council serving Secretary of Labor William Born Wilson, she represented the interests of U.S. women in war labor legislation.

Agnes Nestor was awarded an honorary doctorate by Loyola University, Chicago, Illinois, in 1929.

Judy Neuffer

First woman assigned to U.S. Navy pilot training (1973).

Born 1949.

Neuffer was also the first pilot in the history of the U.S. Navy to fly into the eye of a hurricane; her assignment was to measure wind speeds and plot the exact location of the eye. She was monitoring Hurricane Carmen, with winds of 150 miles per hour, in a navy reconaissance four-engine P-3 Orion plane during Labor Day weekend, August 30 to September 1, 1974.

Lieutenant junior grade Neuffer, a fighter pilot's daughter, graduated from Ohio State University (Columbus) with a B.S. degree in computer science. After completing the navy's Officer Candidate School for Women at Newport, Rhode Island, she was assigned as a computer programmer in the naval installation in San Diego, California.

On the same day in 1973 that she was assigned to pilot training, the navy announced that seven other women (including four civilians) had been chosen to take the eighteen-month pilot training course at Pensacola, Florida. The navy was the first branch to train women pilots to fly transport aircraft or helicopters. None was given aircraft carrier assignments.

Anna A. Nevins

Said to be the only woman wireless operator in the world (1909).

Born New York, New York, c. 1886.

Nevins, whose fiancé was a wireless operator on a large ocean liner, learned to operate a telegraph key in 1907. Her job, in 1909, was to send and receive telegraph messages in her office atop the Waldorf-Astoria Hotel in New York City, communicating with ships at sea. During her 8 A.M. to 4 P.M. work day, she was kept busy with commercial messages from various types of people in business. There were also occasional messages of a more romantic sort.

Josephine LeMounier Newcomb

Founder of the first self-sufficient women's college connected to a men's college (1887).

Born Baltimore, Maryland, October 31, 1816; died New York, New York, April 7, 1901.

In 1845 she married Warren Newcomb, a grocery wholesaler from Kentucky. Their daughter, Harriott Sophie Newcomb, was born in 1855, and in 1863 Warren Newcomb retired from business to devote his life to the education of their daughter. He died in 1866, and Sophie died of diphtheria in 1870 at the age of fifteen.

Searching for a suitable memorial for her daughter, Josephine Newcomb became a philanthropist: in 1886 she donated $100,000 to Tulane University in New Orleans, Louisiana, for the creation of the H. Sophie Newcomb Memorial College for Women. The new college opened in September, 1887. Newcomb later made gifts to the college totalling $3.5 million.

Harriet Newell

One of the first two U.S. women to go overseas as missionaries (see also Ann Judson); the first woman missionary from the United States to die on foreign soil (1812).

Born Haverhill, Massachusetts, 1793; died Isle of France (now Mauritius), November 30, 1812.

In February, 1812, Harriet married Samuel Newell, a student at Andover Theological Seminary (Andover, Massachusetts). Together they planned to serve as missionaries in India, a country previously unvisited by American missionaries. They reached India in June of that year and spent some time with British missionaries, but the British East India Company—opposed to any attempts to convert Indians to Christianity—forced them to leave the country on August 4. After a long and difficult voyage, they were brought ashore on the Isle of France (now Mauritius) in October.

While the Newells were en route, an infant daughter was born to them prematurely. The infant died five days later and was buried at sea. Newell, weakened by tuberculosis and the rigors of childbirth, died a month after they arrived at the Isle of France.

New Jersey

First colony/state to grant women the right to vote (1776).

The constitution of the new state of New Jersey granting women the right to vote was passed by the legislature on July 2, 1776.

In 1807 the law was revoked, mainly because the women were not voting for the state legislators who were in power.

Mary Nichols

Believed to be the first woman to found a school whose purpose was to teach scientific topics to women (1837).

Born Goffstown, New Hampshire, August 10, 1810; died London, England, May 30, 1884.

Although her formal education was not extensive, Nichols was teaching by the time she was eighteen. In Lynn, Massachusetts, she started a girls' school, where she lectured on hygiene, physiology, and anatomy.

This teaching led to a career in health education, including lectures in which she advocated the regimen of Sylvester Graham. To achieve good health, people were advised to bathe daily, get plenty of exercise and fresh air, avoid meat, tea, coffee, and alcohol, and eat whole wheat bread.

In 1842 Nichols published her *Lectures to Ladies on Anatomy and Physiology*. She became a proponent of the water-cure (hydropathy) system, the treatment of pain or illness by immersing parts of the body in water, and in 1845 opened her own water-cure house in New York City.

As a writer, she presented in *Six-Penny Magazine* her own eye-witness story of the death of Edgar Allen Poe's wife.

In 1853 Nichols and her second husband planned a utopian community that would espouse total freedom—including free love. It never opened. But in 1856, apparently having undergone a spiritual transformation, she made confession, penance, and chastity the hallmarks of a similar community. Towards the end of her life, Nichols claimed that by the laying on of hands she could heal people.

Ruth Nichols

First woman in the world to receive an international hydroplane license (1924); first to fly nonstop from New York, New York, to Miami, Florida (1928); first to be a pilot for a commercial passenger airline (1932).

Born New York, New York, February 23, 1901; died New York, New York, September 25, 1960.

Nichols, who began flying in 1922, made the pioneering New York–Miami flight with copilot Harry Rogers on January 3, 1928, in twelve hours.

When Nichols graduated from Miss Masters' School (Dobbs Ferry, New York) in 1919, she got a plane ride as a graduation present. Her pilot was World War I ace Eddie Stinson, brother of Katherine Stinson (Otero) and Marjorie Stinson (see entries) of the renowned Stinson aviation family. Nichols's life was never the same again.

In 1924 Nichols graduated from Wellesley College (Wellesley, Massachusetts). She had started flying in 1922, and in 1927 she was granted a pilot's license. When the U.S. Department of Commerce published its list of licensed pilots in August, 1927, Nichols was the only woman on a list of thirty-seven New York pilots. She was the second woman to be granted a transport pilot's license by the Department of Commerce (1927) (see also Phoebe Fairgrave Omlie).

After flying in the Women's Air Derby (see entry) in 1929, she went on to make two transcontinental flights—breaking the women's speed records in both directions.

On the westbound flight, Nichols arrived in Burbank, California on December 1, 1930. Her flying time was sixteen hours, fifty-nine and one-half minutes, lowering the record for women by three hours, forty-four and one-half minutes. Flying in a 450 horsepower large-cabin monoplane, Nichols took eight days for the entire trip. Her average speed on the last leg from Kingman, Arizona, to Burbank was 161 miles per hour.

Returning to the East Coast, Nichols landed at Roosevelt Field, Long Island, New York, on December 10. Her flying time was thirteen hours, twenty-two minutes. Total elapsed time for the trip was twenty-nine hours, one minute, forty-three seconds; her average speed was just under 200 miles per hour.

In very short order, she established a long list of flying records:

- women's altitude record: 20,000 feet (1930)
- first woman to land in forty-six of the then forty-eight states (1929)
- first woman to fly from Los Angeles, California, to New York, New York, in thirteen hours, twenty-one minutes—one hour less than Charles Lindbergh (1930)
- women's altitude record: 28,743 feet (1931)
- women's speed record: 210.754 miles per hour (1931)
- women's world distance record: Oakland, California, to Louisville, Kentucky (1931)
- world altitude record (men and women) for diesel-engine plane: 19,928 feet (1932)
- first woman to pilot a twin engine executive jet (1955)
- women's speed record: greater than 1,000 miles per hour (1958)
- women's altitude record: 51,000 feet (1958).

Nichols's forty-six-state tour, which covered ninety-eight cities and 12,000 miles, was mounted to promote a new venture called Aviation Country Clubs, which crashed with the stock market in 1929.

In 1932 Nichols was hired as a pilot by New York and New England Airways; she is the first woman to work as a commercial pilot (see Helen Richey). She started a flying school for women at Adelphi College (Garden City, New York) in 1939.

In 1940 Nichols organized Relief Wings, a civilian air ambulance service, and made the assets of the organization available to the U.S. government when the United States entered World War II in 1941. Those assets financed the establishment of the Civil Air Patrol, of which Nichols was a director from 1940 until 1949.

During the war, she earned a flight instructor's rating, qualifying to fly multi-engine aircraft. In 1948/49 she was the pilot for a worldwide UNICEF tour. Nichols worked for several charitable organizations in the 1950s, including the White Plains Hospital (White Plains, New York), Save the Children Federation (New York, New York), United Hospital Fund, and the National Nephrosis Foundation.

Nineteenth Amendment

The amendment to the United States Constitution that first guaranteed women the right to vote (1919).

The 1878 resolution in favor of woman suffrage introduced by Republican Senator Aaron Augustus Sargent (California), at the request of Susan B. Anthony (see entry), failed to pass. On June 4, 1919, the Nineteenth Amendment, guaranteeing suffrage for women, was passed by the Sixty-sixth Congress. The follow-

ing day it was proposed to the legislatures of several states. Alabama, Florida, and North Carolina took no action; Delaware, Georgia, Louisiana, Maryland, Mississippi, South Carolina, and Virginia rejected it.

On August 18, 1920, Tennessee voted to ratify the amendment, thus making three-fourths of the states necessary for ratification. Later, the Tennessee House of Representatives rescinded its ratification.

On August 26, 1920, the U.S. secretary of state declared the amendment ratified. On September 14, 1920, it was ratified by Connecticut and on February 8, 1921, by Vermont; both states had delayed action while the ratification process was proceeding.

The Ninety-nines

First U.S. organization of licensed women pilots (1929).

The organization got its name because 99 out of a total of 126 women who were licensed pilots joined. Amelia Earhart served as its first president (see entry).

At the suggestion of Phoebe Fairgrave Omlie (see entry), the group introduced the practice of placing markings on buildings and other ground objects to assist pilots in visual navigation.

Kathleen Nolan

First woman president of the Screen Actors Guild (1975).

Born St. Louis, Missouri, September 27, 1933.

Despite a nominating committee that favored a man as president of the guild, Nolan, petitioning independently as a candidate, won the seat with a two-to-one victory margin out of the 8,000 votes cast. Three other women were elected to three other offices of the guild, which was founded in 1933.

Nolan, who began her acting career on her parents' Mississippi river showboat when she was a baby, played Kate, a lead role, in the television series, "The Real McCoys," which ran from 1957 to 1963. She also played Wendy in *Peter Pan*, a role made famous by Mary Martin who starred in the show on Broadway.

Mae Ella Nolan

First woman to be elected to Congress to serve in her husband's place (1923); first to chair a congressional committee (1924).

Born San Francisco, California, September 20, 1886; died Sacramento, California, July 9, 1973.

The wife of Republican Representative John Nolan of California, Mae Ella Nolan ran for his seat after he died in office. In a special election, she ran against six male opponents, defeating the closest one by over 4,000 votes. Nolan was elected to complete her late husband's unexpired term and the subsequent regular term—during which she was the only woman in Congress.

John Nolan had been the leader of the prolabor faction in the Republican party, and when she was assigned to the Labor Committee, Nolan vowed to carry forward her husband's mission. She opposed the Equal Rights Amendment, which the American Federation of Labor had condemned for eradicating safeguards that had been won for women through years of legislative battles.

In December, 1923, Nolan chaired the House Committee on Expenditures in the Post Office Department. She retired after serving only one term—and she hadn't made a single speech in the house.

Martha Norelius

First woman to win successive Olympic gold medals (1924, 1928).

Born Stockholm, Sweden, January 29, 1908; died 1955.

In 1924 Norelius won the 400-

meter freestyle event, defeating Gertrude Ederle (see entry). In 1928 she won the 400-meter freestyle event and won a gold medal as one of the four members of the 4 × 100-meter freestyle relay.

Norelius was raised in the United States. She turned professional after the Amateur Athletic Union (AAU) suspended her in 1924 for swimming an exhibition in the same pool with professional swimmers. As a professional, she won the $10,000 ten-mile William Wrigley Marathon in Toronto, Canada in 1920.

Norelius was reportedly the first competitive woman swimmer to use what had been the traditional male style—high head and elbow position, arched back, and heavy six-beat leg kick. Between 1926 and 1928 she set some thirty world records in events ranging from fifty meters to marathons.

In 1967 she was inducted into the International Swimming Hall of Fame.

Goodwife Norman and Mary Hammon

First women to be tried for lesbianism (1649).

Dates unknown.

Both women were citizens of the Massachusetts Bay Colony. In 1649 Norman was found guilty of lesbianism and sentenced to "public acknowledgment"; Hammon was acquitted.

Eleanor Holmes Norton

First woman to chair the Equal Employment Opportunities Commission (1977).

Born Washington, D.C., June 13, 1937.

A graduate of Dunbar High School in Washington, D.C., Norton received a B.A. degree from Antioch College (Yellow Springs, Ohio) in 1960, an M.A. degree in American studies from Yale University (New Haven, Connecticut) in 1963, and a J.D. degree from Yale in 1964—thereby becoming one of the handful of black women in the legal profession in the 1960s.

After clerking for a federal judge

in Philadelphia, Pennsylvania, Norton became assistant legal director of the American Civil Liberties Union (ACLU) in New York City, beginning her five-year association with that organization. While with the ACLU Norton specialized in First Amendment (freedom of speech) cases; in fact, the first case that she won before the U.S. Supreme Court was argued in behalf of a white supremacist group that had been denied permission to stage a rally.

In 1970 Norton was appointed chair of the New York City Commission on Human Rights, where she campaigned against segregationist housing bills, sex discrimination in the workplace, and the lack of minority representation in advertising. In the early 1970s, she was one of the advocates for the use of Ms. rather than Miss or Mrs., arguing that "a person's performance, character and personality should not be judged on whether she is married or not."

As a champion of twenty-four-hour day-care centers, Norton argued that it did no good to rescue women from gender discrimination on the job if they had no place to leave their children while they worked.

She became a cofounder of the Black Feminist Organization in 1973 and, in March, 1977, President Jimmy Carter named Norton chair of the Equal Employment Opportunities Commission (EEOC), a post she held until the Reagan administration came into power in 1981.

After leaving the EEOC, Norton became a tenured law professor at the Georgetown University Law Center (Washington, D.C.) and a director on several corporate boards, including the Metropolitan Life Insurance Company. She gave up these positions to run for public office as a Democrat, and was elected in 1990 to represent the District of Columbia as a nonvoting delegate to the U.S. House of Representatives. Holmes pointed out that although the D.C. delegate does not vote in Congress, the delegate's position is neither impotent nor passive. That delegate may become Speaker of the House, accrue seniority, head a committee, introduce legislation, and speak on the House floor.

"I ran for Congress," Norton said "because I am a policy junkie. That is to say, I enjoy the business of thinking through public policy."

Mary T. Hopkins Norton

First woman Democrat elected to Congress without being preceded by her husband (1925); first to head a state political party organization (1932).

Born Jersey City, New Jersey, March 17, 1875; died Greenwich, Connecticut, August 2, 1959.

Mary Norton (right) with Mrs. Julius Kahn and John Phillip Hill

Norton, who had attended a business college when she was young and worked as a secretary for some years, was elected to Congress by New Jersey Democrats in 1925. She was the first woman Democrat elected to that assemblage without being preceded by her husband. She was also the first woman elected to Congress from the East.

Norton was the second woman to chair a congressional committee (see also Mae Ella Nolan). She served as chair of the House Labor Committee from 1932 to 1947, and is credited with the enactment of the Fair Labor Standards Act, which was passed during President Franklin D. Roosevelt's administration. One of the major aspects of the act was that it outlawed sex-based salary distinctions.

A staunch member of the Democratic Party and protégé of Frank Hague, the Jersey City, New Jersey, political boss, Norton was the first woman to head the Democratic party in New Jersey, beginning in 1932 (and the first to be a state chair of *any* national political party). She finished her first term in 1935 and served again from 1940 to 1944. She was a member of the Democratic State Committee of New Jersey from 1921 to 1944.

In 1944 she became a member of the Democratic National Committee, chaired the national party Platform Committee and Credentials Committee at the Democratic National Convention in 1948, and headed the Administration Committee in 1949. After she retired from Congress in 1951, she headed the Woman's Advisory Committee of the Defense Manpower Administration of the U.S. Department of Labor.

Antonia C. Novello

First woman to be appointed Surgeon General of the United States Public Health Service (1990).

Born August 23, 1944, Fajardo, Puerto Rico.

Novello, who was sworn into the office of U.S. Surgeon General by the first woman Supreme Court Justice, Sandra Day O'Connor, graduated from the University of Puerto Rico (San Juan), with a B.S. degree in 1965 and an M.D. degree in 1970. She earned a master's degree in public health from Johns Hopkins University (Baltimore, Maryland) in

1982, and in 1987 was selected to attend the Program for Senior Managers in Government at the John F. Kennedy School of Government at Harvard University (Cambridge, Massachusetts). She served her pediatric internship and residency at the University of Michigan (Ann Arbor), where she was selected Intern of the Year (1970).

From 1978 until her appointment as Surgeon General in 1990, Novello worked in the U.S. Public Health Service at the National Institutes of Health. A board-certified pediatrician, she has been a clinical professor of pediatrics at the Georgetown University School of Medicine (Washington, D.C.). She is the author (and co-author) of over seventy-five scientific articles and chapters pertaining to pediatrics, nephrology, and public health policy.

Novello was the first woman president of the Pan American Medical Society, and the first Hispanic to be appointed Surgeon General. She is married to Joseph Novello, M.D., a Washington psychiatrist and medical journalist.

Her many honors and awards include the Public Health Service Surgeon General's Exemplary Service Medal and Medallion, the Public Health Service Meritorious Service Medal, the Achievement Award of the National Conference of Puerto Rican Women, and the 1991 Women's History Month Recognition Award, presented by Bronx Community College (Bronx, New York) of the City University of New York.

NOW *(see National Organization for Women)*

Clara Dutton Noyes

Founder of the first U.S. school for midwives, Bellevue Hospital, New York, New York (1911).

Born Port Deposit, Maryland, October 3, 1869; died Washington, D.C., June 3, 1936.

Noyes graduated from the Johns

Hopkins Hospital School for Nursing (Baltimore, Maryland) in 1896, then stayed on for a year as head nurse. From 1897 to 1901 she was superintendent of the nurses' training school of the New England Hospital for Women and Children in Boston, Massachusetts. From there, she went to New Bedford, Massachusetts, where she was superintendent of St. Luke's Hospital and its nursing school (1901–10). Between 1910 and 1916 Noyes served as the general superintendent of nurse training schools for Bellevue and Allied Hospitals in New York City.

In 1911, in New York, New York, Noyes founded the Bellevue (Hospital) School for Midwives. The first school for midwives in the United States, and the only one to be publicly funded, the school was established because midwives in the United States generally received little training, in contrast to the European practice of having midwives serve a long apprenticeship. Despite the lack of trained midwives, the first U.S. statistics on attended births showed that in 1910, fifty percent of all births were attended by midwives (undoubtedly a reflection of the European immigrant tradition). The Bellevue school closed in 1938.

During World War I, Noyes headed the Bureau of Nursing of the American Red Cross's Department of Military Relief, which included 19,000 nurses—more than 10,000 of them overseas. From 1919 until her death, Noyes was director of the American Red Cross Department of Nursing, and from 1918 to 1922 she was president of the American Nurses Association.

Noyes won the Patriotic Service Medal of the American Science Association and the National Institute of Social Sciences (1919), the Florence Nightingale Medal of the International Red Cross (1923), and the French Medal of Honor (1929).

Nunnery, Trappist

First Trappist Nunnery in the United States (1949).

The nunnery was established at Wrentham, Massachusetts, by a group of nuns, some of whom were Americans, who had returned from Ireland after taking their vows. They ranged in age from nineteen to thirty-five. They built thirty-seven cells and kept forty cows on their 500 acres of land.

The nuns of the order are vegetarians who have chosen a life of poverty and chastity. A typical day at the nunnery begins at 2 A.M. and, depending on the season, ends at 7 P.M. or 8 P.M.

Nurse-Midwives, American Association of

First nurse-midwife organization (1928).

The American Association of Nurse-Midwives was established in Kentucky in 1928. It was the only practicing group of nurse-midwives in the United States at that time. It was made up of sixteen members, all of whom were from the Frontier Nursing Service (see Mary Breckinridge).

In 1939 a graduate school of midwifery was established in Hyden, Kentucky.

In 1968, the AAN-M was merged into the American College of Nurse-Midwives, whose members are registered nurses certified to provide gynecological services and care for mothers and babies throughout the maternity period. Members of the AAN-M have completed an accredited program of study and clinical experience in midwifery and have passed a national certification examination.

Nursing, School of, New England Hospital for Women and Children

First permanent school of nursing (1872).

Described as the "first general training school for nurses in Amer-ica" the school opened on September 1, 1872 at the New England Hospital for Women and Children. The hospital was staffed entirely by women doctors—they controlled the hospital and trained the nurses. The founders of the nursing school were Dr. Susan Dimock and Dr. Marie E. Zakrzewska; the school offered a complete staff of physician-instructors in all areas of medicine and nursing. Student nurses were able to participate in a program that included training in medicine, obstetrics, and surgery.

The first group of five probationary nurses was offered a one-year graded course in scientific nursing. Working from 5:30 A.M. to 9:00 P.M. and sleeping in rooms near the hospital wards so they could help with night emergencies, they also attended lectures presented by the staff doctors on obstetric, medical, and surgical nursing. Linda Richards, one of the five probationary nurses, was awarded the first diploma from the school in 1873.

Emma M. Nutt

First woman telephone operator (1878).

Born c. 1849; died June 4, 1926.

Nutt worked for Telephone Despatch Company, the first such company in Boston, Massachusetts, from September 1, 1878, until 1911, when she retired.

Early Telephone Exchange—Women Operators

At the time she joined the business, regular exchange service was established for the first time; there were approximately sixty subscribers.

(Mary) Adelaide Nutting

First U.S. nurse to become a university professor (1906).

Born Frost Village, Quebec, Canada, November 1, 1858; died White Plains, New York, October 3, 1948.

In 1889 Nutting entered the Johns Hopkins Hospital School for Nurses (Baltimore, Maryland), graduating in 1891. In 1894 she became its principal; she set up a three-year course of training and study, instituted scholarships for needy students, and established tuition fees so that the school would not have to be dependent on free lectures by doctors.

From 1891 to 1893 Nutting was a head nurse at Johns Hopkins; in 1894 she was named superintendent of nurses. At her urging, Teachers College of Columbia University (New York, New York) established a nursing education program in 1899, with Nutting as its director. Co-author, with Lavinia L. Dock, of the four-volume *History of Nursing* (1907–12), Nutting was also an early member of the American Society of Superintendents of Training Schools for Nurses of the U.S. and Canada (later called the National League of Nursing Education), serving as its president in 1896 and 1909.

In 1944 the National League of Nursing Education created the Mary Adelaide Nutting Medal in her honor and awarded it to her for that year.

Annie Oakley (born Phoebe Ann Moses)

First woman whose name became a slang expression (popular from the 1890s).

Born Darke County, Ohio, August 13, 1860; died Greenville, Ohio, November 3, 1926.

"Annie Oakley" was a slang name given to free tickets that had been

punched several times to identify them as complimentary; with all their holes, they reminded people of one of Oakley's tricks: tossing a playing card into the air and shooting it full of holes.

After her father died in 1870, Oakley—known then as Phoebe Ann Moses or Mozer—became a skilled hunter, bringing home game to help support her family. When she was fifteen, she won a shooting match with a vaudeville marksman named Frank Butler. She married Butler in 1876; for the next few years they toured as "Butler and Oakley," with Annie Oakley apparently taking her name from a suburb of Cincinnati.

In 1885, with her husband as manager, Oakley joined Buffalo Bill Cody's Wild West Show and stayed with the show for sixteen years. She was a great success in Europe, and from 1902 to 1904 she played the lead in *The Western Girl*, a stage melodrama. In 1917 Oakley rejoined Buffalo Bill for his farewell season.

Sandra Day O'Connor

First woman associate justice of the U.S. Supreme Court (1981)

Born El Paso, Texas, March 26, 1930.

President Ronald Reagan introduced his first nominee to the U.S. Supreme Court on July 7, 1981, describing her as a person with "unique qualities of temperament, fairness and intellectual capacity." Three months later Sandra Day O'Connor took the seat of retiring Associate Justice Potter Stewart as the first and only woman on the Court. Her nomination was a significant event for the Supreme Court, which early in its history had barred women from even practicing law.

The eldest child of Mr. and Mrs. Harry Day of Duncan, Arizona, San-

dra grew up on a cattle ranch on the Arizona–New Mexico border. She completed her undergraduate and law studies at Stanford University (Palo Alto, California) in five years, graduating magna cum laude with a B.A. degree in 1950, then receiving her law degree in 1952. She was third in her law class and an editor of the *Stanford Law Review.* (The valedictorian was William H. Rehnquist, an associate justice when O'Connor was named.) In 1952 she met fellow law student John Jay O'Connor III, whom she married.

After her graduation, O'Connor couldn't get a job offer in the male-dominated world of private legal practice. "I interviewed with law firms in Los Angeles and San Francisco, but none had ever hired a woman before me as a lawyer, and they were not prepared to do so," O'Connor said. She received one offer: a position as a legal secretary.

Choosing to enter public service, O'Connor, the mother of three sons, served first as a deputy county attorney in San Mateo, California, and later as assistant attorney general in Arizona.

Between 1954 and 1957 she was in Frankfurt, Germany, where her husband was stationed in the U.S. Army, and she worked as a civilian lawyer for the Quartermaster Corps.

When they returned to the United

States, O'Connor ran her own law firm for six years. She also worked on behalf of the Republican party as a county precinct committee person (1960–65). From 1965 to 1969 she served as assistant attorney general in Arizona.

One of Arizona's leading role models for women, O'Connor was appointed to the Arizona State Senate in 1969, then was elected for two subsequent terms. She was named majority leader in the Arizona Senate in 1973, the first woman to hold that position. While in the Senate she was an author of a law providing for the death penalty in Arizona, and in 1972 she served as state cochair of the committee to reelect Richard M. Nixon as president.

In 1975 O'Connor was elected Maricopa City, Arizona, Superior Court judge; four years later Governor Bruce Babbitt appointed her to the Arizona Court of Appeals, Arizona's second-highest court.

Considered a moderate-to-conservative Republican, Justice O'Connor had strongly supported the federal Equal Rights Amendment as an Arizona senator, and was reported to be personally opposed to abortion. In practice, however, she had opposed various measures designed to limit abortion, and her nomination to the Supreme Court was opposed by anti-abortion groups.

Phoebe Fairgrave Omlie

First to win a cross-country Women's Air Derby in the lighter-planes class (1929); first woman to be granted a transport pilot's license by the Department of Commerce (1927); first to get an aircraft mechanic's license (1927).

Born Des Moines, Iowa, November 21, 1902; died Indianapolis, Indiana, July 17, 1975.

Omlie, from Memphis, Tennessee, flew a Monocoupe in the Women's Air Derby, which began on August 18, 1929. She completed the 2,350 miles from Santa Monica, California, to Cleveland, Ohio, in twenty-four hours and twelve minutes. Louise Thaden (see entry) won the heavier-planes class.

Born Phoebe Fairgrave, she made her first parachute jump at the age of seventeen. In 1921, as a member of the Glenn Messer Flying Circus, she set an altitude record for a parachute jump of 15,200 feet. She also developed a double parachute jump and was the first woman to perform it. In this trick, she jumped, deployed one chute, cut loose from it, and went into free fall, then released a second chute.

Before she was twenty she married Vernon Omlie, her chief pilot. He taught her to fly, and together they ran a flying school. Omlie and her husband also worked as aerial forest-fire spotters. When the Mississippi River flooded Little Rock, Arkansas, in 1928, Omlie flew in medicine and supplies, rescued stranded people, and ferried the mail.

In 1928 Omlie became the first woman to complete a National Air Reliability Tour, covering 5,000 miles and visiting thirteen states in a month. During the 1920s, she received the first federal pilot's license and the first aircraft and mechanic's licenses to be issued to a woman. She was also issued, in 1927, the first transport pilot's license granted to a woman by the Department of Commerce (see also Ruth Nichols).

In 1931, at the National Air Races in Cleveland, Ohio, women competed against men for the first time. Omlie accrued the highest number of points overall, winning $2,500 and an automobile.

During Franklin D. Roosevelt's presidential campaign in 1932, Omlie suggested that he use a plane to move speakers around the country. She got the job, and flew over 5,000 miles in the campaign. After Roosevelt's election, he appointed her technical adviser to serve as liaison between the National Advisory Committee for Aeronautics and the Bureau of Air Commerce.

Omlie headed a 1942 project, sponsored jointly by the Works Progress Administration and the Office of Education, to train 5,000 people as airport ground workers. The following year she joined the Civil Aeronautics Administration, working there in several capacities until her retirement in 1952.

Kitty O'Neil

First woman to be accepted into Stunts Unlimited—an organization of Hollywood's top stunt people (1976).

Born Corpus Christi, Texas, c. 1947.

A stunt performer who debuted in the 1970s in such TV series as "Policewoman," "Bionic Woman," and "Baretta," O'Neil was both a stunt-person and athlete.

When she was four months old, concurrent attacks of measles, mumps, and chicken pox left her totally deaf. Determined that O'Neil would lead a normal life, her mother—a full-blooded Cherokee—went to the University of Texas (Austin) to learn how to teach the girl to read lips, speak, respond to directions, and generally communicate successfully with those around her. Her mother's success was spectacular: after becoming a fine music student, learning to play both piano and cello, O'Neil won several awards.

O'Neil was equally successful at sports. She won the Southwest District Junior Olympic Diving title; this brought her to the attention of Sammy Lee, a two-time Olympic diving champion. She then moved to Anaheim, California, where she attended high school and trained with Lee. She won more than thirty blue ribbons, numerous first-place trophies, and gold medals in a diving career that included a twelfth-place finish in the U.S. team trials for the Tokyo Olympics in 1964, and a first-place finish in the women's ten-meter diving championship. O'Neil then went on to race boats, drag cars, production sports cars, dune buggies, and motorcycles.

O'Neil married Duffy Hambleton, a movie stunt man, and persuaded him to teach her his profession. She was a good student, accomplishing a string of record-breaking achievements:

- official waterskiing speed record: 104.85 miles per hour (1970)
- world land speed record for women (in a thirty-eight-foot, three-wheeled, rocket-powered land missile): 322 miles per hour (1976)
- only woman ever to do a cannon-car rollover, in which a moving vehicle is flipped over by an explosive device

In November, 1977, O'Neil performed a stunt for a television special that set two records for women: the longest fall (112 feet) and the highest (112 feet) attempted while afire in a protective suit.

In 1977 she was the only woman in the world qualified for international motorcycle competition; she held a professional license granted by the Fédération Internationale Motorcycliste.

In 1979 O'Neil's story was told in a made-for-TV movie, *Silent Victory: The Kitty O'Neil Story,* aired by CBS.

Anna O'Neill

First woman appointed to a professional position in the U.S. Government Service (1912).

Dates unknown.

O'Neill was appointed assistant to the legal adviser in 1912. She retired after thirty-five years in the State Department.

Mary Kenney (O'Sullivan) *(see Mary Kenney)*

Katherine Stinson (Otero) *(See Katherine Stinson)*

Ruth Bryan Owen (Rohde)

First woman diplomat to represent the United States in a foreign country (1933).

Born Jacksonville, Illinois, October 2, 1885; died Copenhagen, Denmark, July 26, 1954.

In 1933 President Franklin D. Roosevelt appointed the first woman diplomat, Ruth Bryan Owen, as envoy extraordinary and minister plenipotentiary to Denmark and Iceland.

Daughter of William Jennings Bryan (three-time presidential candidate), Owen attended the University of Nebraska (Lincoln) for two years, and in 1903 married William Homer Leavitt. They were divorced in 1910. That same year she married Maj. Reginald A. Owen of the British army. Maj. Owen died in 1927. From 1915 to 1918 she worked as a volunteer operating-room nurse with British forces in the Middle East. She was also secretary-treasurer of the American Woman's War Relief Fund. When she returned to the United States, she took up residence in Florida, where she became (1926) a successful public speaker and a public-speaking instructor at the new University of Miami (Miami, Florida). In 1925 she was made vice chair of the Florida Board of Regents.

Owen was the first woman to be elected to the U.S. House of Representatives from the Deep South. She served as Democratic representative from Florida from 1929 to 1933, when she was defeated in her bid for reelection because of her pro-Prohibition views. Owen served as minister from 1933 to 1936, when she married Borge Rohde, a Danish national—which made her a Danish citizen.

In 1949 Owen was named alternate U.S. representative to the General Assembly of the United Nations. She was awarded Denmark's Distinguished Service Medal in 1954.

A prolific author, she wrote books about her career, Scandinavian tales, and numerous other subjects.

Fanny (Frances) Bond Palmer

First woman to gain recognition as a lithographer (1840s).

Born Leicester, England, June 26, 1812; died Brooklyn, New York, August 20, 1876.

Palmer didn't gain wide recognition as an artist until 1849, when she became a staff artist of Nathaniel Currier's firm (known as Currier & Ives after James Ives joined the firm in 1857). They published her two views of Manhattan (New York): one from Brooklyn Heights and the other from Weehawken, New Jersey. Her watercolor painting, *The High Bridge at Harlem New York* (1849), is thought to be her most important original work of art.

The daughter of Robert Bond, a successful and wealthy attorney in London, Fanny was educated in private schools in England in the fields of art, music, and lithography. She married Edmund S. Palmer in the 1830s. Evidently some financial problems made it difficult for the Palmers to remain in England, so they decided to move to the United States. Fanny, her husband, and their twin children arrived in the United States during the early 1840s. The Palmers established a lithography printing and publishing house in New York City. In spite of the fact that her lithographic work gained the sanction of such renowned artists as William H. Ranlett, the business failed.

Later, Palmer gained the reputation of being one of the most prolific artists of the Currier firm. In the 1850s she produced large numbers of landscapes, including rural settings, directly on stone. It was especially difficult to capture the atmosphere of a rural setting on stone, and few of her fellow lithographers were able to do it. One of the perfecters of the lithographic crayon, she probably introduced to American printers the art of printing a background tint.

Sophia Palmer

First editor in chief of the American Journal of Nursing (1900).

Born Milton, Massachusetts, 1853; died Forest Lawn, New York, 1920.

Palmer was an 1878 graduate of the Boston Training School for Nurses (now the Massachusetts General Hospital School of Nursing), when it was under Superintendent Linda Richards. In 1889 she founded and was one of the first administrators of the Garfield Memorial Hospital (Washington, D.C.) training school for nurses. She was a founding member of the American Society of Superintendents of Training Schools for Nurses (1893), and the first chair of the New York State Board of Nurse Examiners (1903).

From 1893 to 1895 Palmer was one of the editors of *Trained Nurse and Hospital Review,* published by the Buffalo General Hospital, Buffalo, New York.

Maud Wood Park

First national president of the League of Women Voters (1919).

Born Boston, Massachusetts, January 25, 1871; died Reading, Massachusetts, May 8, 1955.

An 1898 graduate of Radcliffe College, Cambridge, Massachusetts, Park chaired the Massachusetts Woman Suffrage Association from 1900 to 1907. She also helped organize the Massachusetts College

Equal Suffrage League in 1901, and was vice president from 1907 until it was dissolved in 1916.

As a member of the Congressional Committee of the National American Woman Suffrage Association, Park lobbied for passage of the Nineteenth Amendment, the suffrage amendment. In 1919, just before the Nineteenth Amendment became law in 1920, Park became the first president of the League of Women Voters, a nonpartisan organization dedicated to the support of labor reforms. It worked to protect working women and children, improve public health, extend the Children's Bureau, and so on. Park served the league as president until 1924.

Park helped organize the first Parent-Teacher Association (see also Alice McLellan Birney), and arranged for Boston school buildings to be used as community centers.

Park was married twice—to Charles E. Park (1897–1904) and to Robert Hunter (1908–28). Both marriages were kept secret, perhaps because of her public activities.

Louella (Oettinger) Parsons

First woman to write a movie column for the newspapers (1914).

Born Freeport, Illinois, August 6, 1893; died Santa Monica, California, December 9, 1972.

Parsons wrote a movie column, featuring information and gossip about the young industry, for the Chicago *Record-Herald* from 1914 to 1918.

She moved to the New York *Morning Telegraph* in 1918 as movie critic, but before the year was out she was rehired by the William Randolph Hearst syndicate to write a gossip column, which she continued to produce until her retirement in 1965. In the 1930s and 1940s her daily column was carried by about 400 newspapers.

In 1934 Parsons had a radio interview show called "Hollywood Hotel." She wrote two volumes of memoirs, *The Gay Illiterate* (1944) and *Tell It to Louella* (1961).

Mary Ann Patten

First woman to navigate a clipper ship (1856).

Born Boston, Massachusetts, 1837; died Boston, Massachusetts, March 17, 1861.

Patten made her first clipper voyage aboard the *Neptune's Car*, a 1,616-ton, 216-foot clipper, in 1855; her husband, Joshua, was captain. They sailed from New York around Cape Horn (at the southern tip of South America) to San Francisco, California—a distance of 15,000 miles—in 101 days, then on to Foochow, China, to pick up tea. From China, the *Neptune's Car* sailed around the Cape of Good Hope (at the southern tip of Africa) to London, England—a voyage of 116 days—then back to New York. Patten learned to navigate on this voyage.

On July 1, 1856, Patten and her husband embarked in the *Neptune's Car* from New York City on another voyage around Cape Horn to San Francisco. Joshua Patten, already suffering from tuberculosis, became seriously ill on the voyage, reportedly lapsing into delirium and then a coma. Mary Patten—pregnant with their first child—took command, plotting the ship's course with the navigational skills she had learned on the 1855 voyage.

After a stormy voyage, the *Neptune's Car* arrived in San Francisco on November 15, 1856. Patten took her husband, still in a coma, to the Isthmus of Panama, where she arranged for him to be transported overland to the east coast where he was put aboard a steamer bound for New York. From New York he was taken to Boston.

On March 10, 1857, Patten gave birth to a son. Her husband died on July 25, still in a coma.

The insurers of the *Neptune's Car* sent Patten a check for $1,000, generally considered at the time to be insufficient compensation for her feat. Friends and well-wishers in Boston collected another $1,400 in tribute to her achievement and heroism. In 1861 Mary Patten, too, succumbed to tuberculosis.

The Mary Patten Infirmary at the U.S. Merchant Marine Academy at King's Point, New York, was named to honor her memory.

Cissy (Eleanor) Medill Patterson

First woman to publish a large metropolitan daily newspaper (1934).

Born Chicago, Illinois, November 7, 1881; died Marlboro, Maryland, July 24, 1948.

A socially prominent woman, Patterson persuaded her friend William Randolph Hearst to let her run the floundering Washington *Herald* in the early 1930s. In a few years she raised its circulation from under 60,000 to 115,000. In 1937 she took over another Hearst paper, the Washington *Times,* and in 1939 she bought both papers herself and merged them into the Washington *Times-Herald*. That paper was bought in 1954 by the *Washington Post*.

Although Patterson's family had no prior experience in the newspaper business, they founded the *Chicago Tribune,* her brother founded the New York *Daily News,* and her niece founded New York *Newsday*.

Alice Paul

First chair of the National Woman's party (1942); author of the original draft of the Equal Rights Amendment (1923).

Born Moorestown, New Jersey, January 11, 1885; died Moorestown, New Jersey, July 9, 1977.

A Quaker whose secondary education was in private schools, Paul graduated from Swarthmore College (Swarthmore, Pennsylvania) in 1905. Following a year of graduate work at the New York School of Social Work (New York, New York), she went to England in 1906, where she spent

Alice Paul raising suffrage flag over National Woman's Party headquarters

the NAWSA were too passive, and left to found her own, more militant organization: the Congressional Union for Woman Suffrage (1913). The CUWS merged in 1917 with the Woman's party to form the National Woman's party.

Paul succeeded in arranging a méeting with President Woodrow Wilson to urge him to support suffrage. She went to jail three more times before the Nineteenth Amendment, which granted women the vote, was passed by Congress in 1919 and ratified by the states in 1920. She later said that the ratification of the Nineteenth Amendment was the high point of her life.

After that victory, Paul studied law, earning a degree from the Washington College of Law (1922) and master's and doctorate degrees from the American University (Washington, D.C.) in 1927 and 1928.

She drafted and succeeded in getting introduced into Congress the first Equal Rights Amendment on behalf of women (1923). It failed then, and on numerous successive attempts. Paul took her campaign to an international audience, getting support for women's rights from the League of Nations.

In the 1920s Paul founded and represented at the League of Nations the World Party for Equal Rights for Women, known as the World Women's party.

three years doing settlement work and becoming involved in the feminist movement. While in England, Paul was arrested seven times and jailed at least three times for suffragist agitation. On one occasion she went on a hunger strike in prison, and was force-fed for four weeks.

She also continued graduate study at the University of Birmingham and the University of London, receiving an M.A. in absentia from the University of Pennsylvania (Philadelphia) in 1907. After her return to the States, she earned a Ph.D. at the University of Pennsylvania (1912).

In 1912 Paul was named chair of the congressional committee of the National American Woman Suffrage Association (NAWSA) (see Woman Suffrage Associations); she soon decided, however, that the politics of

Believing that many of world's troubles were caused by the inability of women to exert political power, Paul argued that World War II would not have occurred if women had been represented at the Versailles Peace Conference at the end of World War I.

Elected chair of the National Woman's Party in 1942, she was instrumental in getting the United Nations Charter to affirm the rights of women as equal to those of men.

Paul's influence helped in finally getting the Equal Rights Amendment through Congress in 1970—but the amendment fell just short of the number of states needed for ratification.

Cecelia Payne-Gaposhkin

First woman to receive a tenured professorship at Harvard University (Cambridge, Massachusetts) (1956); first to be chair of the department of astronomy (1956).

Born Wendover, England, May 10, 1900; died Cambridge, Massachusetts, December 6, 1979.

After studying at Cambridge, England, under Dr. Edward A. Milne, Payne-Gaposhkin came to the United States in 1923 to work toward her doctorate, earning a Ph.D. degree in astronomy at Radcliffe College (Cam-

bridge, Massachusetts) in 1925. The *Astronomical Union* described her Ph.D. dissertation as "undoubtedly the most brilliant ever written in astronomy." She became a naturalized citizen in 1931. One of the first women professors at Harvard University, Payne-Gaposhkin was tenured in 1956 and served as head of the astronomy department there from 1956 to 1960.

Along with Sergei I. Gaposhkin, her Russian-born husband, she made a special study of novae, a type of variable star that suddenly increases in brilliance by thousands of times its original intensity and then decreases in brightness over a period of months. In the 1930s, they made millions of observations of several thousand variable stars. Their published findings became standard source material for researchers.

In 1965 Payne-Gaposhkin joined the Smithsonian Astrophysical Observatory to carry on further research.

The American Astronomical Society awarded her its highest honor—the Russell Lectureship—in 1977.

Elizabeth Palmer Peabody

First woman to be a professional speaker (1827); founder of the first formally organized private U.S. kindergarten (1860);

believed to be the first woman publisher in the United States (c. 1841).

Born Billerica, Massachusetts, May 16, 1804; died Jamaica Plain, Massachusetts, January 3, 1894.

In 1827 Peabody launched a series of history lectures in public schools, teachers' colleges, and lecture halls, promoting the chronological history charts invented by Polish general Józef Bem.

Peabody and Margaret Fuller (see entry) were the two women charter members of the Transcendentalist Club (1837). The club's members included Ralph Waldo Emerson, A. Bronson Alcott, W. E. Channing, Jones Very, and other members of the New England literati who shared an almost mystical belief in romantic individualism and the harmony of all things in nature. Around 1841 Peabody opened a Boston, Massachusetts, bookstore and became a publisher.

Peabody and her sister Mary Peabody Mann founded and headed the U.S. kindergarten movement. Elizabeth Peabody was inspired by the principles of Friedrich Froebel, the German educator (1782–1852) who founded the kindergarten system. Froebel had designed a system to help children make the transition from home to school by providing an environment in which they play and learn and become accustomed to a life of greater structure and socialization. In 1877 Peabody became president of the newly organized American Froebel Union.

Anna Claypoole Peale

First woman painter of miniatures to paint a U.S. president (1818).

Born Philadelphia, Pennsylvania, March 6, 1791; died Philadelphia, Pennsylvania, December 25, 1878.

Peale painted a miniature of President James Monroe in 1818. She also painted miniatures of Presidents Andrew Jackson and James Monroe, and statesman Henry Clay.

Early in the 1800s, Peale and her sister Sarah (Sally) (1800–85) were already becoming two of the first women in the United States to gain widespread recognition as professional artists. One of Anna Peale's miniatures was shown in the first exhibit of the Pennsylvania Academy of the Fine Arts (Philadelphia) in 1811. Another was exhibited there in 1814. A few years later, Sally's portraits and still lifes were exhibited at the academy.

Henrietta Johnston (see entry) preceded the Peale sisters as an artist, having sold several pastel portraits from 1707 to 1720, including a portrait of Governor Robert Johnson of South Carolina. However, she did not enjoy the widespread recognition that the Peale sisters received.

The daughters of a painter, the Peale sisters had one other sister, Margaretta (1795–1882), who was also a painter, although lesser known. Anna and Sally, who worked together for many years, were elected to the Pennsylvania Academy of Fine Arts in 1824. Sally, who outlived Anna by seven years, became known as a leading portraitist in St. Louis, Missouri.

Ruth Stafford Peale

First woman president of the National Board of North American Missions (NBNAM) (1967); first to chair the program and planning committee of the National Council of Churches General Assembly (1966).

Born Fonda, Iowa, September 10, 1906.

Peale became a member of the NBNAM in 1960, became its president in 1967, and served in that capacity until 1969. The NBNAM is the evangelical branch of the Reformed Church in America.

After earning an A.B. degree from Syracuse University, Syracuse, New York (1928), she taught high school math for three years. Later, she became active in various church organizations. From 1936 to 1946, and again from 1955 to 1956, she was the national president of the women's board of domestic missions of the Reformed Church of America. She was also the national president of the Home Missions Council (1942–44). In 1940 she served as president, general secretary, and editor in chief of the Foundation for Christian Linguistics.

In 1945 she and her husband, Norman Vincent Peale, began to edit and publish *Guideposts*, an interfaith monthly magazine, which is the largest nonprofit magazine of an inspirational nature published in the United States.

A delegate to the General Assembly of the National Council of Churches, Peale was in 1966 named chair of the program and planning committee—the first woman to hold the position. The General Assembly is the highest policy-making body of the council, composed of delegates from most major Protestant and Orthodox denominations in the United States.

Along with her husband, she received a medallion from the Society for the Family of Man (1981). She is an honorary life member of the National League of American Pen Women.

Annie Smith Peck

The first person to climb the north peak of Mount Huascarán (Peru), altitude 21,812 feet, the highest altitude ever reached in the Western Hemisphere (1908); a founder of the American Alpine Club (1902).

Born Providence, Rhode Island, October 19, 1850; died New York, New York, July 18, 1935.

A teacher by profession, Peck first saw the Matterhorn mountain in Switzerland during a trip she made while pursuing classical studies in Germany and Greece. It was then that she decided to try mountain climbing. Her first real success came in 1888 when she climbed Mount Shasta in California, with an altitude of 14,380 feet.

In 1895 she climbed the Matterhorn, 14,780 feet, and then two mountains in Mexico: Mount Popocatepetl, 17,887 feet, and Mount Orizaba, 18,314 feet, in 1897. The Orizaba ascent made her the first woman in the Americas to climb a mountain over 18,000 feet. By 1900 she had climbed twenty major mountains.

Peck went to Europe to represent the United States at the Paris Congrès Internationale de l'Alpinisme in 1900. She also climbed the Jungfrau in Switzerland, 13,642 feet. After helping found the Alpine Club in 1902, Peck climbed the Illampu peak of Mount Sorata, Bolivia, 21,300 feet, achieving success with the second attempt in 1904. In 1908 she climbed the north peak of the twin-peaked Mount Huascarán, Peruvian Andes, 21,812 feet. With the completion of this climb, Peck reached the highest point any person had ever attained in the Western Hemisphere. Nineteen years later, the Lima Geographical Society named the north peak Cumbre Aña Peck in her honor (1927).

Peck was a woman of many firsts, and at least one of them was not related to mountain climbing. An honors graduate of the University of Michigan (Ann Arbor), where she majored in Greek, she continued her studies and received an M.A. degree from Michigan in 1881. She decided to pursue her studies in the classics and applied to the American School of Classical Studies, Athens, Greece, where she was the first woman to be admitted (1885).

Throughout her years as an educator, she taught in schools in a variety of geographical locations, including Cincinnati, Ohio; Montclair, New Jersey; Providence, Rhode Island; and Saginaw, Michigan. She taught Latin at Purdue University (West Lafayette, Indiana) from 1881 to 1883. Following her tenure there, she traveled to Germany to begin advanced study in the classics.

Peck wrote numerous chronicles, guidebooks, and handbooks, including *A Search for the Apex of South America* (1911); *The South American Tour* (1913); and *Industrial and Commercial South America* (1922).

When she was sixty-one, she climbed Mount Coropuna in Peru, 21,250 feet, the first person ever to climb it (1911). After she reached the top, she drove in a pennant that said, "Votes for women." The last mountain Peck climbed was Mount Madison in New Hampshire, 5,380 feet; she was eighty-two.

Ellen Fitz Pendleton

First woman to serve as juror to award the American Peace Prize (1923).

Born Westerly, Rhode Island, August 7, 1864; died Newton, Massachusetts, July 26, 1936.

When the American Peace Prize jury was selected in 1923, the year of the founding of the prize, Pendleton was the only woman named to be a juror.

After graduating from Wellesley College (Wellesley, Massachusetts) in 1886, she remained there and taught, first as a tutor, then as an instructor. She earned an M.A. de-

gree from Wellesley in 1891. She moved up the academic ranks to associate professor of mathematics, then became dean.

Pendleton was a strong advocate of academic freedom. In 1911 she became the first alumna to be elected president of Wellesley College, a position she held for twenty-five years. Under her administration, the college's offerings and endowment grew several times over. She retired from Wellesley in 1936.

Sophie Penkinson

Reportedly the first woman blacksmith (late 1890s).

Dates unknown.

When she was just a bride, Penkinson assisted her husband in blacksmithing in Odessa, Russia. Just before the turn of the century the couple immigrated to the United States. They became U.S. citizens and settled in New York City, where her husband died in 1919. She continued to work as a blacksmith at a shop on Pike Street until 1933.

Mary Engle Pennington

First woman member of the American Society of Refrigerating Engineers.

Born Nashville, Tennessee, October 8, 1872; died New York, New York, December 27, 1952.

Three years after receiving a Ph.D. degree in chemistry from the University of Pennsylvania (Philadelphia) in 1895, Pennington opened her own clinical laboratories in Philadelphia. Specializing in bacteriological analysis, she became noted for developing procedures to ensure the purity of milk. While running her own laboratories, she also headed Philadelphia's bacteriological laboratory, where she developed standards of milk inspection that were adopted throughout the country. As early as 1905 she had begun her investigative work in refrigeration.

From 1898 to 1906 she lectured at the Woman's Medical College of Pennsylvania (Philadelphia). In 1907 she was appointed bacteriological chemist for the Department of Agriculture. The following year she headed the new food research laboratory of the Bureau of Chemistry, Department of Agriculture. In order to observe firsthand the storage and handling of food, she rode freight trains, checking the temperatures and conditions of the refrigerator cars. Continuing her work into the years of World War I, she established standards for refrigeration cars that were in effect for many years.

In 1919 Pennington moved into private industry. She became a pioneer in the safe techniques of freezing foods, gaining worldwide recognition as a perishable-foods expert. Later, she became an independent consultant on foods.

A 1940 winner of the Garvan Medal of the American Chemical Society, she was the first woman elected to the American Poultry Historical Society's Hall of Fame. At the time of her death, Pennington was the president of the American Institute of Refrigeration.

Frances Perkins *(born Fannie Coralie Perkins)*

First woman to be secretary of labor and a cabinet member (1933–45).

Born Boston, Massachusetts, April 10, 1882; died New York, New York, May 14, 1965.

Perkins championed social secu-

rity, federal public works and relief, minimum wages, maximum hours, and the abolition of child labor. She was responsible for unemployment insurance and the U.S. Employment Service. Named to the New York State Industrial Commission by Governor Alfred E. Smith (1919), she was the first woman in this position and, at an annual salary of $8,000, the highest-paid state employee. Perkins was appointed again in 1923 when the commission was called the New York State Industrial Board; she chaired it from 1926 to 1929. Smith named her state industrial commissioner in 1928, and she kept the same post under Governor Franklin D. Roosevelt from 1929 to 1933.

When Governor Roosevelt became president in 1933, he named Perkins secretary of labor and a member of his cabinet. As such, she had a major role in drafting much of the New Deal's prolabor legislation: the Na-

tional Industrial Recovery Act, the Civilian Conservation Corps Act, the national Labor Relations Act, the Social Security Act, the Fair Labor Standards Act, and more. But for all her efforts on behalf of American labor, Frances Perkins (Miss Perkins, she called herself, though a married woman) was reviled by labor leaders such as William L. Green of the American Federation of Labor and John L. Lewis of the United Mine Workers, because she was "an outsider," not a part of the organized labor movement. She was threatened with impeachment but managed to defuse the opposition with an appearance before the House Judiciary Committee in 1939. U.S. Senator Martin Dies put her on his list of dangerous villains—along with Joseph Stalin and Adolf Hitler. Even Rexford G. Tugwell, confidant of President Franklin D. Roosevelt, charged that she suffered from a "passion for veracity."

The President and Eleanor Roosevelt stood by her and she survived the epithets, surviving longer—until 1945—than any other member of Roosevelt's original cabinet except one (Harold Ickes). Her vision, which changed the lives of working men and women in the United States, was probably inspired by a tragedy she witnessed as a young woman: the Triangle Shirtwaist Factory fire in 1911. As Frances Perkins watched, young girls leaped or fell from the burning ten-story loft building near New York's Washington Square, trapped because the factory's owner had locked the exits to the roof for fear his employees might steal the shirt-waists, carry them to the roof, and drop them to accomplices below. The fire claimed 146 lives—and Frances Perkins never forgot it.

A 1902 graduate of Mount Holyoke College (South Hadley, Massachusetts), Perkins taught for a time in Lake Forest, Illinois, before accepting a position as executive secretary of the Philadelphia Research and Protective Association in Pennsylvania.

After receiving an A.M. degree in economics and sociology from Columbia University, (New York, New York) in 1910, she worked for two years as secretary of the New York Consumers' League (see also Josephine Lowell), working for industrial reform and the improvement of sweatshop conditions.

Antoinette Perry

First woman to have an award named after her (1947).

Born Denver, Colorado, June 27, 1888; died New York, New York, June 28, 1946.

The award named after Perry is called, in full, the American Theatre Wing Institute Antoinette Perry Award. However, it is more commonly known by Perry's nickname— the Tony. Perry was an actress, a theatrical director, and was active in professional theater organizations.

Perry directed her first play, *Hotbed,* in 1928. Other plays under her direction included *Strictly Dishonorable* (1929), *Personal Appearance* (1934), *Ceiling Zero* (1935), *Kiss the Boys Goodbye* (1938), and *Harvey* (1944). She also wrote the play *Lady in Waiting* (1940).

Sarah Worthington Peter

Founder of the first school for industrial art (1848).

Born Chillicothe, Ohio, May 10, 1800; died Cincinnati, Ohio, February 6, 1877.

Named the Philadelphia School of Design (Philadelphia, Pennsylvania), the institution provided women with skills they needed to secure employment in commercial art at reasonable pay. In 1850 the school was linked to the Franklin Institute, and in 1932 it was integrated into the Moore Institute of Art, Science and Industry (now Moore College of Art and Design).

Peter was educated in private schools in Frankfort, Kentucky, and Baltimore, Maryland. She married Edward King in 1816. Both during her marriage and after her husband's death, she continued independent study of French, German, medieval art, and the sciences.

The daughter of a wealthy Ohio governor, she became active in charitable institutions, organizing in Philadelphia an association for the protection of seamstresses. Having converted to Catholicism in 1855, she also worked for church organizations, including sisterhoods. She was the first president of the Woman's Museum Association in Cincinnati, Ohio, in 1853. In 1876 the association became the Cincinnati Academy of Fine Arts.

Esther Peterson

First person to be special assistant to the president for consumer affairs (1964–67).

Born Provo, Utah, December 6, 1906.

A woman with a distinguished career in the field of consumer affairs, Peterson became the first special assistant to the president for consumer affairs when she assumed that position under President Lyndon B. Johnson. Also from 1964 to 1967, she was chair of the President's Committee on Consumer Interests. As special assistant, she was a consumer spokesperson and adviser to the president on consumer-related matters.

Peterson held notable posts under two other presidents. She was reappointed as special assistant for consumer affairs by President Jimmy Carter, under whose administration she also chaired the Consumer Affairs Council, designed to give consumers a voice in federal policy making; earlier, in 1961, she had been appointed director of the Women's Bureau in the labor department, assistant secretary of labor for labor standards, and executive vice chair of the President's Commission on the Status of Women (see entry) by President John F. Kennedy.

Among her many honors is an award from the Food Marketing Institute, which is particularly notable because the institute named an annual award after her—the Esther Peterson Award—for the person who does the most for consumers. President Jimmy Carter awarded her the Presidential Medal of Freedom in 1979.

She was also elected to Utah's Beehive Hall of Fame in 1982.

Peterson has also had a distinguished career—beginning in the 1930s—in the field of labor. She was assistant director of education of the Amalgamated Clothing Workers (1939–44), served as the union's legislative representative (1945–48), and was legislative representative of the Industrial Union Department of the AFL-CIO (1957–61).

From 1970 to 1977 Peterson was vice president of consumer programs and consumer adviser to the president of Giant Food Corporation, where she spearheaded numerous innovative consumer-related projects. She had her own consumer radio talk show and appeared on various television news and talk shows speaking about contemporary consumer issues.

Beginning in 1984, Peterson served as representative to the Economic and Social Council (ECOSOC) of the United Nations for the International Organization of Consumers Unions (IOCU). In that capacity, she helped secure passage of the *Guidelines for Consumer Protection* by the U.N. General Assembly.

In her work with senior citizens, Peterson serves as a member of the board of directors of the United Seniors Health Cooperative (formed 1986), which helps the elderly get information and assistance they need and supports legislative initiatives that serve their interests.

Chair of the Consumer Insurance Interest Group from 1987, Peterson also represents consumer interests related to insurance matters.

Jane Cahill Pfeiffer

First woman to be a White House fellow (1966); first to be chairman of the board of directors of NBC (1978).

Born Washington, D.C., September 29, 1932.

After Pfeiffer graduated from the University of Maryland (College Park) in 1954, she spent six months as a novice nun. In an abrupt turnabout, she joined IBM in 1955. In charge of the company's space-tracking system in Bermuda, her job was to interpret a radar screen in the Mercury space program.

In 1966 Pfeiffer took a leave of absence to serve as the first woman White House fellow under President Lyndon B. Johnson. As White House fellow, Pfeiffer worked with Robert Wood, undersecretary of the Department of Housing and Urban Development. Their project was to streamline and upgrade the old Housing and Home Finance Agency.

Returning to IBM, Pfeiffer was promoted in 1972 to vice president of communications and government relations. She left the company in 1976, however, after she married Ralph A. Pfeiffer, Jr., a senior vice president at IBM and father of ten children. A year later, President Jimmy Carter offered her an opportunity to be the first woman secretary of commerce, but she turned it down because of the difficulties it might present for her marriage, and because of a recent operation for thyroid cancer.

In November, 1977, RCA hired her as a consultant. At the time, she was also consulting for such clients as the Bank of America; Bethlehem Steel; Yankelovich, Skelly, and White; and Yale University. A year later, she was named NBC board chairman, reporting to Fred Silverman, the president. As chairman, she worked on all aspects of NBC's operations, with central involvement in the areas of government relations, news, corporate planning, and personnel. She held the post until 1980, then left to return to private consulting.

Pfeiffer was a member of the President's General Advisory Committee on Arms Control and Disarmament, 1977–80, and of the President's Committee on Military Compensation. She has been a director of Chesebrough-Ponds, Inc., International Paper Company, J. C. Penney Company, the Overseas Development Council, Ashland Oil Company, and MONY Financial Services.

Awards won by Pfeiffer include the Eleanor Roosevelt Humanitarian Award, 1980; the Distinguished Alumna Award, University of Maryland, 1975; and the Humanitarian Award of the National Organization for Women, 1980.

Irna Phillips

First writer of what is considered to be radio's first soap opera (1930).

Born Chicago, Illinois, July 1, 1901; died Chicago, Illinois, December 22, 1973.

Working at WGN Radio, Chicago, Illinois, in 1930, Phillips wrote and performed in a daily ten-minute serial, "Painted Dreams."

In 1932 she switched to NBC, and for the next six years she wrote what became radio's most popular daytime serial, "Today's Children." For a brief period, she also starred in this serial, which was virtually a carbon copy of "Painted Dreams." In 1937 NBC launched "The Guiding Light," which Phillips coauthored. The soap opera serial enjoyed the longest run in broadcast history, having begun on radio in 1937 then moving to television in 1952. It is still one of television's most popular soap opera serials.

During the 1940s, Phillips had five soap opera serials running concurrently on radio. She made a successful move to television soap operas, where she created such hits as "The Guiding Light" (1952), "As the World Turns" (1956), and "Another World" (1964). In 1964 she also acted as consultant for the first successful evening television soap opera serial, "Peyton Place."

The innovator of "tease" endings and dramatic organ music in the background, she recommended that the serials focus on themes of self-preservation, the importance of family, sex, or a combination of all three.

Having received a B.S. degree in education from the University of Illinois (Urbana), she taught for one year before continuing her studies and earning an M.A. degree at the University of Wisconsin (Madison), after which she taught English and public speaking for four more years.

Julia Miller Phillips

First woman to win an Academy Award as a producer (1974).

Born New York, New York, April 7, 1944.

Julia Miller graduated from Mount Holyoke College (South Hadley, Massachusetts) in 1965.

From 1965 to 1969 she was an editorial assistant at the *Ladies Home Journal*. In 1969 she was associate editor and East Coast story editor for Paramount Pictures (New York, New York). The following year Phillips was head of Mirisch Produc-

tions (New York, New York), and in 1971 she held the post of creative executive with First Artists Productions (New York, New York). She also founded in 1971, along with her husband Michael Phillips and actor/producer Tony Bill, Bill/Phillips Productions. Moving to Los Angeles the same year, Phillips became a producer for Ruthless Productions (Los Angeles, California), a position she still holds.

With her husband and partner, Phillips produced some of the big hits of the 1970s: *The Sting* (won an Oscar as the best movie), *Taxi Driver*, and *Close Encounters of the Third Kind*. She and Michael Phillips were later divorced.

In 1990 her book *You'll Never Eat Lunch in This Town Again* was published. A behind-the-scenes tale of filmmaking, deals, and stars, the book angered a number of Hollywood stars; it was also very successful.

Lena Madeson Phillips

Founder of the National Federation of Business and Professional Women's Clubs, Inc. (BPW) (1919).

Born Nicholasville, Kentucky, September 15, 1881; died Marseilles, France, May 21, 1955.

In 1918 Phillips was asked by the Young Women's Christian Association (YWCA) to organize the National

Business Women's Committee for women running businesses involved in war work. The war ended before the group was able to function, but she and the other members decided to remain a committee, working on behalf of business and professional women. Thus was born the National Federation of Business and Professional Women's Clubs. She served first as executive secretary and then president of the organization from 1926 to 1929.

Phillips attended the Peabody Institute of Music (Baltimore, Maryland) and graduated from the Law School of the University of Kentucky (Lexington) in 1917. She earned an M.A. degree from New York University (New York, New York) in 1923. She then opened a private office in New York City, where she practiced law until 1935.

She was the president of the International Federation of Business and Professional Women from 1930 to 1947.

Margaret Philipse

Believed to be the first female business agent in the colonies (1660).

Born Elberfeld (now the North Rhine–Westphalia region of Germany); died c. 1690.

Philipse arrived in New Nether-land (now part of New York state) from Holland in the 1650s as a merchant and trader. (Interestingly, under Dutch law, married women could receive grants of feme sole trader privileges, allowing them to conduct their own business.) She established a shipping line between Amsterdam and New Amsterdam (now New York City), probably in the early 1660s. In 1660 she was a business agent for Dutch merchants trading with New Netherland.

When her husband died in 1661, she took over his business as a merchant and trader, shipping furs to Holland in exchange for Dutch merchandise, which she then sold in New Amsterdam. Philipse retired about 1680.

Joan Phipps *(see Mary Bacon)*

Mary Pickford *(born Gladys Smith)*

First movie star to form and own her own film company (1916); first woman movie star to have her name in marquee lights (1914); first woman movie star to fly in a movie (1915).

Born Toronto, Ontario, Canada, April 8, 1893; died Santa Monica, California, May 29, 1979.

Pickford began her acting career on the stage. Famed producer David

year was 1917: she made *Poor Little Rich Girl* and *Rebecca of Sunnybrook Farm*.

Pickford was the first star to be paid thousands of dollars per week. By 1932 her fortune was estimated at $32 million, and at her death in 1979 it was estimated at $50 million.

Joanne E. Pierce and Susan Lynn Roley

First women special agents of the Federal Bureau of Investigation (1972).

Belasco named her Mary Pickford for a play, *The Warrens of Virginia*, which ran at his Times Square theater in New York City, in 1907. She began her film career in 1909 as an extra working for the American Motoscope & Biograph Company. In 1909 and 1910, her first two years in motion pictures, Pickford appeared in seventy-four films—mostly one-reelers. Her billing as "America's Sweetheart" came in 1914 with the film *Tess of the Storm Country*, when her name appeared in marquee lights. Eventually she had over 200 silent films and four "talkies" to her credit.

In the 1915 movie, *A Girl of Yesterday*, Pickford flew in a plane for the first time, also becoming the first actress to fly in a film.

In 1916 she created the Mary Pickford Film Corporation, and in 1919 Pickford, D. W. Griffith, Charles Chaplin, and Douglas Fairbanks formed United Artists. Her biggest

Pierce, thirty-one, a former Roman Catholic nun from Niagara Falls, New York, and Roley, twenty-five, a former U.S. marine lieutenant from Long Beach, California, completed a fourteen-week course at Quantico, Virginia, where they underwent training in hand-to-hand combat and weaponry. Out of the first thirty women who had applied to be agents, they were the first two to succeed.

J. Edgar Hoover, who headed the FBI for forty-eight years, had forbidden women to be agents. After he died, however, the acting director of the FBI, L. Patrick Gray, III, changed the policy. From the spring of 1972, women were allowed to apply for positions as agents.

The Bureau of Investigation, which had preceded the Federal Bureau of Investigation, hired its first woman agent in 1911 (see Emma R. H. Jentzer).

Molly Pitcher (see Mary McCauley and Margaret Corbin)

Pocahontas

The first Native American woman to inspire literary works (1767).

Born probably Jamestown, Virginia, c. 1595; died Kent, England, c. 1617.

Daughter of Powhatan, chief of the Algonquin tribes in Virginia, Pocahontas (whose real name was Matoaka) rescued John Smith, head of the Jamestown settlement, from captivity by pleading with her father (1607). Believed to be the first Native American woman to marry a Virginia colonist (1609), she was married about 1609 to a "private Captaine called Kocoum." In 1613 she was captured by the English and exchanged for prisoners and stolen goods.

The following year Pocahontas married colonist John Rolfe, and they had a son, Thomas. In 1616 they sailed together for England, where she was presented to King James I and Queen Anne. She was never to return to her native country, dying in England.

Pocahontas was the inspiration for a 1767 novel called *The Female American* by "Unca Eliza Winfield" (otherwise unidentified), and for an 1808 play, *The Indian Princess,* which James Nelson Barker produced in Philadelphia, Pennsylvania.

Police Officers

The first women to be appointed as regular police officers were in Los Angeles, California, in 1910. (See also Alice Stebbins Wells.)

Sarah Childress Polk

First first lady to institute strict Sabbath observance and ban dancing at presidential functions (1845).

Born Murfreesboro, Tennessee, September 4, 1803; died Nashville, Tennessee, August 14, 1891.

A Presbyterian fundamentalist, Polk was the wife of James K. Polk, the eleventh U.S. president, whom she had married in 1824. The severity of her fundamentalist beliefs caused her to oppose many worldly entertainments such as horse racing and the theater, and her ban on White House dancing was unpopular. Nevertheless, she was a widely re-

"Pocahontas Saving Capt. John Smith from Execution"

spected first lady, praised even by her husband's political opponents.

After her husband's death, she continued to command respect. She lived in Nashville, Tennessee, a city controlled alternately by northern and southern forces during the Civil War. Despite the continually shifting tides of war, Union and Confederate commanders alike presented themselves to Mrs. Polk, who had gained the reputation of being a powerful woman.

Postal Service

First two women to be appointed as inspectors for the U.S. postal service (1971).

Jane W. Currie and Janene E. Gordon became the first two women inspectors of the 234-year-old U.S. Postal Service in 1971. At that time, twenty-four inspectors were sworn in after completing a twelve-week training period. The course of study included training in karate and the use of firearms.

Ann Preston

First dean of the first women's medical college in the United States (1866).

Born West Grove, Pennsylvania, December 1, 1813; died Philadelphia, Pennsylvania, April 18, 1872.

After attending Quaker schools, Preston began lecturing on physiology and hygiene to classes of women and girls from her local community. (See also Mary Nichols.)

In 1847 she was apprenticed to Dr. Nathaniel R. Moseley; after two years with him, she applied for admission to medical schools, only to meet with rejections because of her sex. She enrolled in 1850 in the first class of seven students at the Female Medical College (later named Woman's Medical College) of Philadelphia, Pennsylvania, graduating in 1851. In 1853 she was appointed professor of physiology and hygiene, and in 1866 was named dean of the college. She remained at the college until her death.

Sally Priesand

First U.S. woman ordained as a rabbi in Reform Judaism (1972).

Born Cleveland, Ohio, June 27, 1946.

Priesand earned a B.A. degree in English at the University of Cincinnati (Cincinnati, Ohio) in 1968, a B.A. degree in Hebrew letters in 1971, and an M.A. degree in Hebrew letters (1972) from the Hebrew Union College–Jewish Institute of Religion (Cincinnati, Ohio).

In 1972, in Cincinnati, she became the first woman in Reform Judaism to be ordained as a rabbi. She served as assistant and associate rabbi to Rabbi Stephen Wise at the Free Synagogue, New York, New York, from 1972 to 1978, then as rabbi at Temple Beth El, Elizabeth, New Jersey, from 1979 to 1981. She also served as chaplain at Lenox Hill Hospital, New York, New York, from 1979 to 1981.

Since 1981, Priesand has been spiritual leader at Monmouth Reform Temple, Tinton Falls, New Jersey.

In 1975 Priesand's book *Judaism and the New Woman* was published.

Among many other activities, she was chairman of the Task Force on Women in the Rabbinate from 1977 to 1983, and she serves as a trustee of Planned Parenthood of Monmouth County, New Jersey.

Priesand was named Man of the Year for 1972 by Temple Israel, Columbus, Ohio, and in 1973 was awarded an honorary doctorate of Hebrew Letters by Florida International University (Miami).

Elizabeth Primrose-Smith

First woman and first athlete to run the U.S. Olympic Festival (1991).

Born c. 1948.

Primrose-Smith is the president and executive director of the Olympic Festival, the nation's largest multisport competition, which is held every summer except during Olympic Game years. About 4,000 athletes and trainers participate in the festival, and some thirty-seven sports are represented. She became head of the festival in 1991, when it was held in Los Angeles, California.

In 1981 she was a primary executive, working with Peter Ueberroth in setting up the 1984 Olympic Games in Los Angeles. She has also been a member of a consulting team at McKinsey & Company (Los Angeles).

Primrose-Smith is an athlete as well as an executive. An excellent swimmer, she nearly made the 1964 Olympics when she was sixteen. She won a Pan American Games gold medal for a 4 × 100-meter freestyle swimming event in 1963.

Property Law, Married Woman's

The first married woman's property law was passed in Mississippi in 1839. Before women began to have the support of the property laws, married women and widows had few, if any, rights to hold property—including income from their employment—in their own names.

A similar bill was introduced in New York in 1836, but it failed.

Eve Queler (Rabin)

---

*First woman to conduct at a
major European opera house
(1974); first to be associate
conductor of the U.S.
Metropolitan Orchestra (1965);
the first to conduct at
Philharmonic Hall (New York,
New York) (1971); first
woman signed to conduct the
Philadelphia Orchestra
(Pennsylvania) (1976); and
first director of the Opera
Orchestra of New York, which
she founded in 1967.*

Born New York, New York, January 1, 1936.

As a very young child, Queler demonstrated a special talent in music. She received a scholarship to a Bronx music school when she was only five. She graduated from the High School of Music and Art (New York, New York), where she learned to play the French horn (1954). She then attended City College of New York (CCNY), Mannes College of Music (New York, New York), and Hebrew Union School of Education and Sacred Music (New York, New York).

Queler made her operatic conducting debut in 1966 at an outdoor performance of Mascagni's *Cavalleria Rusticana* in Fair Lawn, New Jersey. She conducted the Opera Orchestra's performance of Puccini's *Tosca* at Alice Tully Hall (New York, New York) in 1969.

Queler was the assistant conductor of the Ft. Wayne Philharmonic (Ft. Wayne, Indiana) for one year (1970/71). The following year she was the conductor at the Mostly Mozart Festival at Lincoln Center in New York City. As the first woman to conduct at a large European opera house, she conducted Verdi's opera *I Vespri Siciliani* at the Teatro del Liceo, Barcelona, Spain, in 1974.

Queler has been the assistant conductor of the New York City Opera since 1965, and is still the director of the Opera Orchestra of New York.

Queler prefers rare works to those more commonly performed, and she often does première performances of lesser-known works.

Harriet Quimby

First U.S. woman to qualify for a pilot's license (1911); first to fly across the English Channel (1912); first to be authorized to fly U.S. mail (1912).

Born Coldwater, Michigan, May 1, 1875, or Arroyo Grande, California, 1884; died Boston, Massachusetts, July 1, 1912.

Word had gotten around that something unusual was going on at Moisant Aviation School in Garden City, Long Island, New York, in May of 1911. Hundreds of curious onlookers would turn up at 4:30 A.M. to

Harriet Quimby (right) with Matilde Moisant

watch her training as she flew a monoplane about fifty feet above the ground. Wearing an aviation cap with a heavy veil, she couldn't be recognized, until one morning after about two weeks of training when a gust of wind lifted the veil and revealed the pilot to be Harriet Quimby, twenty-seven, editor, drama critic and feature writer for *Leslie's Weekly* in New York City.

On May 12, 1911, as her thirty-horsepower Blériot monoplane moved across the field in preparation for a takeoff, the wheels of the running gear broke off and one wing fell away. Quimby calmly shut off the power and jumped from the plane.

After failing to pass her flight test on the first attempt (her landing was unsatisfactory), she passed it the next day, August 1, 1911, and became the second woman in the world to receive a pilot's license. (The first was Hélène Dutrieu of France.) Quimby was flying a Moisant monoplane.

On September 23, 1911, Quimby was the sole competitor in a twenty-mile cross-country race for women at an International Aviation Meet at Nassau Boulevard, Long Island, New York, winning $600. Her fame grew, heightened by her own articles in *Leslie's Weekly*. She flew at the inauguration of President Francisco

Madero in Mexico City. On April 16, 1912, she took off from the Dover, England, aerodrome in a Blériot monoplane and, after circling Boulogne twice, landed near the village of Hardelot. The first woman to fly across the English Channel, she had flown for thirty minutes at 1,500 feet. Of her flight, *The New York Times* commented: "It still proves ability and capacity, but it doesn't prove equality."

Quimby was authorized by Postmaster General Hitchcock to deliver mail from Squantum Airfield near Boston, Massachusetts, on July 7, 1912. But on July 1, during the third annual Boston aviation meet, 5,000 spectators watched horrified as a Blériot monoplane piloted by Quimby with passenger William A. P. Willard, manager of the meet, suddenly turned almost perpendicular at a height of 6,000 feet (higher than any woman had previously flown) and hurled the unstrapped Quimby and Willard from their seats.

They plummeted into Dorchester Bay, where their crushed bodies were retrieved from the mud at the bottom of the bay. The plane landed in the water on its back, intact except for minor damage to wires and struts. At the time of Quimby's death, pilot Blanche Scott (see entry) was circling the area at 500 feet. She landed and collapsed in her grief.

Mary Ann Quinn

Probably the first licensed woman steeplejack (1946).

Born c. 1928.

Quinn worked for Aerial Engineering, a firm in Los Gatos, California, started by her late husband. One of her assignments required her to climb 300 feet and paint a tower owned by the National Broadcasting Company. She has painted more than 2,000 municipal and school flagpoles annually.

Cornelia B. Sage Quinton

First woman to head an art museum (1910).

Born Buffalo, New York, c. 1879; died Hollywood, California, 1936.

From 1905 to 1909 Quinton was the assistant to the director of the Albright Art Museum/Gallery, Buffalo, New York. When Charles M. Kurtz, the director, died in 1909, she was chosen unanimously to head the museum. She directed the gallery (later known as Albright-Knox Art Gallery) from 1910 to 1924. In 1910 Quinton was curator of the Alfred Stieglitz Photosecession exhibit at the Albright Gallery. She was also overseer of the gallery's contemporary American sculpture exhibition of over 700 pieces in 1916. That same year she became the first secretary-treasurer of the Association of Art Museum Directors. Also a member of the Buffalo Fine Arts Academy, she served as its art director for twenty years—from 1905 to 1924.

In 1924 Quinton became director of a new museum of fine arts in San Francisco, California, endowed by Mr. and Mrs. Adolph Spreckles, and known as the California Palace of the Legion of Honor. In 1972 the California Palace merged with the M. H. de Young Memorial Museum to form the organization now known as The Fine Arts Museums of San Francisco.

Quinton attended at least two art schools: the Art Students' League of Buffalo (later Albright Art School) (Buffalo, New York) and the Art Students' League of New York (New York, New York).

She received an honorary doctorate degree from Syracuse University (Syracuse, New York) in 1910, and the Cross of the Legion of Honor from France (1920) as a result of organizing several traveling exhibitions of French art during World War I.

Quinton believed that war memorials should be entrusted to the best artists, but she questioned, "Must we suffer not only war but the commemoration of war?"

Bessica Raiche

First U.S. woman to fly solo (1910).

Born c. 1874, Beloit, Wisconsin; died Balboa, California, April 10, 1932.

Raiche, flying a pusher-type plane that she had designed and built with her husband in their Mineola, Long Island, New York, home, made her first solo flight in mid-September, 1910. The plane was constructed of bamboo, wire, and silk. Blanche Scott (see entry) had attempted a solo flight on September 2, 1910, but the Aero Club of America had ruled it "accidental."

Raiche made twenty-five flights in a single week in her plane. A brush with danger on her fifth flight, when she caught her long skirt in the airplane's controls, convinced her that long skirts were dangerous, so she switched to riding breeches. (She had already been branded eccentric for wearing bloomers and participating in "masculine" sports like swimming, diving, and shooting.) She re-ceived from the Aeronautical Society a gold medal inscribed to "the first woman aviator of America."

She and her husband formed the French-American Aeroplane Company; their planes featured piano wire to reduce weight.

When she was compelled to give up flying because of poor health, Raiche and her husband moved to California, where she became a physician. She was active in many other fields as well, including painting, music (she studied in France), and languages.

Barbara Allen Rainey

First woman U.S. Navy pilot (1974).

Born Long Beach, California, 1948; died Milton, Florida, July 13, 1982.

Rainey completed her flight training in one year and became the first woman pilot in the history of the U.S. Navy and the first to receive the U.S. Navy's Wings of Gold, an insignia of distinction.

Lieutenant Commander Rainey, who had served with the Pacific Fleet Squadron in California, was on active duty with Training Squadron Three at the naval air station, Whiting Field, Milton, Florida, when she suddenly died at the age of thirty-four—no cause of death was given. Her remains were flown to Arlington National Cemetery, where she was accorded full military honors: a horse-drawn caisson, a band and marching escort, pallbearers, a firing party, and a bugler.

Rainey graduated from Lakewood High School, Long Beach, California, and earned a B.A. degree at Whittier College (Whittier, California).

Alice Huyler Ramsey

First woman to make a transcontinental auto trip (1909).

Born Hackensack, New Jersey, c. 1887; died Covina, California, September 10, 1983.

On June 6, 1909, accompanied by three female passengers, Ramsey began a 3,800-mile trip from New York City to San Francisco, driving a Maxwell-Briscoe open car. The trip, sponsored for promotional purposes by the Maxwell-Briscoe Company, was an eventful one: the touring group was bogged down for twelve rainy days in Iowa; the front wheels

of the thirty-horsepower automobile collapsed when they hit a prairie dog hole in Utah; and eleven sets of fabric tires were worn out. The women accompanying Ramsey were Margaret Atwood, Hermione Johns, and Nettie R. Powell. They completed the trip in forty-one days, on August 8, 1909.

A graduate of Vassar College (Poughkeepsie, New York), Ramsey was president of the Women's Motoring Club of New York. During her later years she lived in Covina, California, where at the age of ninety she was still driving an automobile, having had no accidents in her lifetime.

Shulamit Ran

First woman to be appointed composer-in-residence by a major U.S. orchestra (1991).

Born Israel, 1949.

The two-year appointment with the Chicago Symphony (Chicago, Illinois) includes a commitment to compose a full-length work and responsibility for the orchestra's con-

temporary-music programming. The composer is also involved in the orchestra's educational programs.

Born in Israel, Ran came to the United States at fourteen as a result of winning a scholarship to the Mannes School of Music in New York City. During the same year (1963) the young pianist performed her own work, *Capriccio*, with the New York Philharmonic conducted by Leonard Bernstein.

In 1991 Ran won the Pulitzer Prize for her *Symphony*, commissioned by the Philadelphia Orchestra and premiered in 1990.

(Marie) Gertrude Rand

First woman to be a fellow of the Illuminating Engineering Society of North America (1952); first to win the Edgar D. Tillyer Medal of the Optical Society of America (1959).

Born Brooklyn, New York, October 29, 1886; died Stony Brook, New York, June 30, 1970.

Rand was a 1908 graduate of Cornell University (Ithaca, New York), with an A.B. degree in experimental psychology. She continued at Bryn Mawr College (Bryn Mawr, Pennsylvania), earning A.M. and Ph.D. degrees in psychology in 1911. She remained at Bryn Mawr as a teacher and researcher until 1927; in the meantime, she married Clarence Ferree (1918), and together they researched the way color perception is affected by illumination.

From 1924 to 1927 Rand served on the National Research Council's committee on industrial lighting, and in 1928 she and her husband accepted positions at the Wilmer Ophthalmological Institute of Johns Hopkins University School of Medicine (Baltimore, Maryland), remaining there until his death in 1943. One of the projects Rand and her husband were responsible for was the lighting of the Holland Tunnel under the Hudson River (New York City–Jersey City, New Jersey). During World War II they developed standards of visual health and acuity for airplane pilots and ship lookouts. They also held numerous patents for lighting devices and instruments. At the Wilmer Institute, Rand held the positions of associate professor of research ophthalmology, associate professor of physiological optics, and finally associate director of the research laboratory in physiological optics.

From 1943 until her retirement in 1957, Rand was a research associate at the Knapp Foundation of the College of Physicians and Surgeons, Columbia University (New York, New York), where she did research on color blindness—its assessment and detection.

In 1952 Rand became the first

woman to be named a fellow of the Illuminating Engineering Society of North America. The society, founded in 1906, is a technical association whose members include electrical and mechanical engineers, architects, designers, educators, students, contractors, distributors, utility personnel, scientists, and manufacturers dealing with the art, science, or practice of illumination. The society provides speakers, technical assistance, lighting exhibitions, and competitions for its members. In 1963 Rand was awarded the society's Gold Medal.

Claire Randall

First woman secretary of the
National Council of the
Churches of Christ (1974).

Born Dallas, Texas, October 15, 1919.

Randall became secretary of the National Council of the Churches of Christ in the U.S.A., one of the highest and most prestigious religious posts in the United States, in 1974. While in office, she worked toward ecumenism and achievement of better ties between the council, a federation of thirty Protestant and Eastern Orthodox denominations in the United States, and the Roman Catholic Church. Before that, she was director of the Christian World Mission and program director and associate director of Church Women United (1962–73). In 1988 she was named national president of Church Women United.

Randall earned a B.A. degree from Scarritt College for Christian Workers (Nashville, Tennessee) in 1950. She went on to receive several honorary degrees, including a D.D. degree from both Berkeley Seminary (Berkeley, California) and Yale University (New Haven, Connecticut) in 1974, and an L.H.D. degree from Austin College (Sherman, Texas) in 1982.

She served on the National Commission on International Women's Year (1975–77) and the Martin Luther King, Jr. Federal Holiday Commission (1985).

Randall received the Woman of the Year in Religion Award presented by the Heritage Society (1977) and was awarded the Order of St. Vladimir, Russian Orthodox Church (1984).

Mimi (Marian) Randolph

First woman floor clerk on the
New York Cotton Exchange
(1968).

Dates unknown.

Employed by Wells Brothers, Wall Street cotton merchants, Randolph's job was to transmit orders from the Wells company office to the broker on the floor of the exchange.

She also had a career as an actress. Making her debut as Mimi Randolph, she appeared in a number of Broadway shows including *Partition* in 1948 and *All for Love,* a 1961 musical in which she played the role of Mrs. Malaprop.

Jeannette Rankin

First female member of Congress (1917).

Born Missoula, Montana, June 1, 1880; died Carmel, California, May 18, 1973.

Elected for the first time to the House of Representatives in 1916 as a Republican from Montana, she became the first and only member of the House to vote against United States entry into World War I.

Defeated in her bid for reelection in 1919, Rankin continued to lobby for consumers and antiwar causes.

She returned to Congress in 1941 to serve a second term in the House of Representatives.

On December 8, 1941, the day after the Japanese bombing of Pearl Harbor, Congress voted to mobilize the armed forces and enter World War II. Rankin voted against entering the war, becoming the first and only member of Congress to cast a dissenting vote on the issue—and ending her political career.

One of her final, major antiwar gestures came when she led the Jeannette Rankin Brigade to the Capitol in Washington, D.C., in a 1968 protest against the Vietnam War.

Betsy (Elizabeth) Rawls

First woman to serve as a rules official for a U.S. Open men's golf championship (1980).

Born Spartanburg, South Carolina, May 4, 1928.

Before Rawls became a rules official in 1980, no woman had ever served in that role, even on the professional golf tour.

Herself an outstanding golfer, Rawls won the U.S. Women's Open four times during the 1950s and 1960s and the Ladies Professional Golf Association (LPGA) Championship twice. When she was only eighteen, she won the Trans-Mississippi and Texas Amateur titles.

In 1951 she turned professional, winning the U.S. Open in 1951, 1953, 1957, and 1960, a record of four wins which she shares with Mickey Wright. She was the LPGA president for the 1961/62 term.

Rawls was named to the LPGA Hall of Fame and the Golf Hall of Fame in 1960. After enjoying a career of fifty-five wins, she retired in 1975.

Katherine Rawls

Probably the first person to do the flip turn in swimming competition (1936).

Born Florida, c. 1917.

Rawls, of Fort Lauderdale, Florida, swam the leadoff leg when her team won the bronze medal for the 4 × 100-meter freestyle event at the 1936 Olympics in Berlin. She also finished second in springboard diving and seventh in the 100-meter freestyle event.

Gail Reals

First woman promoted to brigadier general in direct competition with men (1985).

Born near Syracuse, New York, c. 1937.

Reals joined the marines fifteen months after graduating from high school, attended officer candidate school, and was commissioned a second lieutenant (1961). In 1968 she became the personnel officer in the marine security guard battalion in Beirut, Lebanon. She spent most of the 1970s as the commanding officer of the Woman Recruit Training Battalion, Parris Island, South Carolina.

From 1988 to 1990 Reals was commanding general at the Quantico, Virginia, base, where she was in charge of 9,000 people. In 1990 she retired from the U.S. Marine Corps.

Vinnie Ream

First woman to win a federal commission for sculpting (1866).

Born Madison, Wisconsin, September 25, 1847; died Washington, D.C., November 20, 1914.

A clerk in the U.S. Post Office De-

partment during the Civil War, Ream became an avid student of sculptor Clark Mills in a wing of the Capitol in 1863.

Within a short time, Ream began sculpting busts of congressmen and other notables, including Senator John Sherman, General George Custer, and newspaper editor Horace Greeley. Some of her distinguished friends brought her to the attention of President Abraham Lincoln, who agreed to sit for her—because she was an independent woman of meager means—so she could model a bust of him. The president reportedly sat for thirty minutes a day for five months. Ream's bust of Lincoln was so successful with the president's Washington colleagues and admirers that after his assassination, Congress authorized $10,000 for Ream to produce a full-scale marble sculpture of the slain president. While studying in Rome in 1869, Ream chose Carrara marble for the Lincoln statue. It was unveiled on January 25, 1871, in the rotunda of the U.S. Capitol.

Ream won a $20,000 commission in 1875 to sculpt Admiral David Farragut; the statue was unveiled in 1881 in Farragut Square, Washington, D.C.

Ream married in 1878 and, in response to her husband's wishes, gave up her career as a professional sculptor. She resumed it in 1906, however, and completed her last work—a statue of Sequoyah, the Cherokee—for the state of Oklahoma shortly before she died in 1914.

Dorothy Reed (Mendenhall)

One of the first two women to be employed by a U.S. Navy hospital (1898).

Born Columbus, Ohio, September 22, 1874; died Chester, Connecticut, July 31, 1964.

Reed made navy history when she and fellow medical student Margaret Long worked in the operating room and the bacteriological laboratories at the Brooklyn Navy Yard Hospital in New York City.

Reed never attended high school. Instead she was educated entirely by private tutors in Germany and the United States. However, she was accepted as a student at Smith College (Northampton, Massachusetts), where she earned a B.L. degree in 1895. In 1900 she received an M.D. degree from Johns Hopkins University (Baltimore, Maryland). She was awarded a fellowship in pathology and interned at Johns Hopkins Hospital. In her research as a pathology fellow, she made important advances in the study of Hodgkin's disease, proving that it was not—as was generally believed at the time—a form of tuberculosis. She demonstrated that a definite diagnosis of the disease was possible because a specific type of blood cell was always present.

Offered reappointment at Johns Hopkins, Reed declined as a way of protesting because the opportunities for women were so few there. In 1902 she became a resident at the New York Infirmary for Women and Children (New York, New York), and in 1903 became the first physician in residence at Babies Hospital (New York, New York).

After her 1906 marriage to physicist Charles E. Mendenhall and their subsequent move to the University of Wisconsin (Madison), Reed joined the department of home economics at the university as a field lecturer. In 1915 she organized the first clinic for infants in the state; she also became the chair of the Visiting Nurse Association—a position she was to hold for twenty-one years. During the same period she also served periodically as medical officer for the U.S. Children's Bureau.

Reed wrote part of *Child Care and Child Welfare: Outlines for Study* (1921), a famous publication of the Children's Bureau. She also wrote *Midwifery in Denmark* (1929), a book arguing that the United States should follow the Danish model of educating midwives in order to lower the infant mortality rate.

In 1959 Reed and Florence R. Sabin (see entry) left their papers to Smith College; the pair was honored by the college in 1965, when the new science center building was named for them.

Esther Reed

Cofounder of the first relief organization of the American Revolution (1780).

Born London, England, 1746; died Philadelphia, Pennsylvania, 1780.

In 1771 Reed left England for the American colonies with her new husband. She soon became active in the revolutionary movement, and in 1774 was hostess to many of the delegates to the First Continental Congress. She and Sarah Franklin Bache (daughter of Benjamin Franklin)—formed a committee of about thirty-five women whose mission was to raise money (in gold) to purchase clothing and supplies for Continental army soldiers. Their efforts were centered in Philadelphia and Germantown, Pennsylvania.

Reed died suddenly from acute dysentery.

Reformatories for Women

First state reformatory to be established exclusively for women (1877).

The first state reformatory for women was opened in 1877 in Sherborn (now Framingham), Massachusetts. In 1911 it was renamed the Reformatory for Women.

The first superintendent was Eudora Clark Atkinson.

Aurelia Henry Reinhardt

First woman moderator of the American Unitarian Association (1940).

Born San Francisco, California, April 1, 1877; died Palo Alto, California, January 28, 1948.

Having graduated from the University of California at Berkeley in 1898, she began to teach at the University of Idaho (Moscow) that same year. In addition to teaching, she coached dramatics.

Several years later, Reinhardt returned to her studies and earned a Ph.D. degree at Yale University (New Haven, Connecticut) in 1905, where she wrote her dissertation on Ben Jonson's *Epicoene*. While at Yale, she also completed her translation of Dante's *De Monarchia*. The translation was published in 1904.

Reinhardt, married in 1909 to George F. Reinhardt, was a wife and mother for only five years before becoming a widow. After the death of her husband, she resumed her teaching career. In 1916 she was appointed president of Mills College (Oakland, California), serving in that position until 1943.

From 1923 to 1927 Reinhardt was the president of the American Association of University Women. From 1928 to 1930 she served as chair of the General Federation of Women's Clubs, and was the moderator of the American Unitarian Association from 1940 to 1942. As an unpaid moderator, Reinhardt represented the Unitarian churches on official occasions. She was also an adviser on policy to the various boards of directors.

Judith A. Resnik

First woman astronaut to die on a space flight (1986); one of the first six women to be selected for the U.S. space shuttle program (1978) (see also National Aeronautics and Space Administration).

Born Akron, Ohio, April 5, 1949; died on the space orbiter *Challenger*

above Cape Canaveral, Florida, January 28, 1986.

Resnik and all other members of the *Challenger* crew, including Sharon Christa McAuliffe (see entry)—first civilian woman in space—died when *Challenger* exploded one minute and thirteen seconds after being launched from the Kennedy Space Center in Florida.

A 1966 graduate of Firestone High School, Akron, Ohio, Resnik earned a B.S. degree in electronical engineering from Carnegie-Mellon University, Pittsburgh, Pennsylvania, in 1970, and a Ph. D. degree in electrical engineering from the University of Maryland (College Park) in 1977. She worked for RCA in Moorestown, New Jersey, and Springfield, Virginia, then was a biomedical engineer and staff fellow in the Laboratory of Neurophysiology at the National Institutes of Health in Bethesda, Maryland (1974–77), experimenting in the physiology of visual systems.

Resnik was working as a senior systems engineer in product development with Xerox Corporation at El Segundo, California, at the time she was selected by NASA for a space shuttle program. The group of six first women astronauts was selected for a program that included training in scientific, engineering, and medical duties. None, however, was trained in piloting the space shuttle. Resnik flew as a mission specialist

on the initial flight of the earth orbiter *Discovery*, August 30, 1984. On this mission, the *Discovery* crew was nicknamed "Icebusters" for their success in removing hazardous ice particles from the orbiter using the Remote Manipulator System. Resnik logged six days, fifty-seven minutes in space on this flight.

Resnik was awarded the NASA Space Flight Medal in 1984.

The Revolution

First regularly published women's newspaper to cover the entire spectrum of news (1868).

The newspaper, a sixteen-page weekly published in New York City from January, 1868 until May, 1870, was financed by George F. Train and David Melliss.

Susan B. Anthony (see entry) was the publisher and business manager of the paper, and Elizabeth Cady Stanton (see entry) was co-editor, along with Parker Pillsbury.

Rhodes Scholars

First women permitted to be Rhodes Scholars (1977).

When Cecil Rhodes died in 1902, he left a will with stipulations for establishing scholarships at Oxford University for male college graduates from the (onetime) British Colonies who display "outstanding capacities for scholarship and leadership." The 1975 Sex Discrimination Act (Great Britain) allowed Rhodes trustees to modify the will, which they did in 1976.

In 1977 twenty-four of the seventy-two Rhodes scholars were women, including thirteen from the United States: Maura J. Abeln, Caroline E. Alexander, Katherine Lynn Burke, Nancy Lee Coiner, Diane L. Coutu, Sarah Jane Deutsch, Laura Garwin, Sue M. Halpern, Daryl Koehn, Allison Muscatine, Mary Cargill Norton, Suzanne Perles, and Denise Thal.

Eileen Lach, a student at the University of Minnesota (Minneapolis), was endorsed as a Rhodes candidate by the selection committee in 1972, but the state interviewing committee turned her down.

Karen Riale

First woman member of the U.S. Air Force Band (1972).

Born c. 1949.

In 1972, Riale, holding the rank of airman, became a clarinetist in the U.S. Air Force Band, of which her husband was also a member.

When the band was asked to per- form at President Richard Nixon's inauguration in 1973, she refused because the air force hadn't "finished tailoring the band's specially designed black uniform with white pinstripes for women."

Ellen Swallow Richards

Founder of the science of home economics (1899); first president of the American Home Economics Association from its founding in 1908; first woman to graduate from the Massachusetts Institute of Technology (Cambridge) (1873); first elected to the American Institute of Mining and Metallurgical Engineers (c. 1881); founder of the Association of Collegiate Alumnae (later the American Association of University Women) (1881).

Born Dunstable, Massachusetts, December 3, 1842; died Boston, Massachusetts, March 30, 1911.

After graduating from Vassar College, Poughkeepsie, New York (1870), Richards was accepted as a special student in chemistry at the Massachusetts Institute of Technology (MIT) Cambridge, graduating with a B.S. degree in 1873, while achieving an M.A. degree in chemistry that same year. She continued her studies at MIT for two more years, then claimed that her professors did not want a woman to get the first doctorate in chemistry. She began teaching sanitary chemistry, which deals with the purity of air, water, and food. In 1876 she persuaded MIT to open a women's laboratory for the study of chemistry, and in 1884 was instrumental in setting up the world's first laboratory for studying sanitary chemistry. She was assistant to William Nichols, head of the laboratory.

In the 1880s Massachusetts passed the first Food and Drug Act, in part a response to her report on sanitary conditions in the state (1878–79).

The Association of Collegiate Alumnae (later the American Association of University Women), founded by Richards in 1881, places emphasis on the importance of lifelong learning and achievement by women.

After 1890 she increasingly concentrated on what was coming to be known as the home economics movement. At the World's Fair in Chicago, Illinois, in 1893, Richards was director of the model kitchen sponsored by the U.S. Department of Agriculture. The primary activity was food analysis. During this period she was also working as a dietary consultant to hospitals.

In 1899 Richards organized a series of summer conferences whose purpose was to define courses of study and standards for teacher training and certification in home economics. At these conferences, staged in Lake Placid, New York, the term "home economics" was used for the first time. After she founded the American Home Economics Association in 1908, she served as its president until 1910.

Laura Howe Richards

*First woman, along with her sister, Maud Howe Elliott (see entry), to win a Pulitzer Prize for biography (1915); first person to write a book of nonsense rhymes published in the United States—*Sketches and Scraps *(1881).*

Born Boston, Massachusetts, February 27, 1850; died Gardiner, Maine, January 14, 1943.

The two sisters won the Pulitzer Prize for a biography of their mother, *Julia Ward Howe* (see entry).

Laura Howe married Henry Richards in 1871. The marriage lasted seventy-one years and produced seven children. She wrote jingles in the *St. Nicholas Magazine* (1873), children's books, and books for young girls. In 1890 Richards wrote *Captain January,* a book for young girls that became her most famous; it sold 300,000 copies. She was also involved in charitable and community activities throughout her life.

Helen Richey

First woman to fly airmail transport (1934); first to be awarded an instructor's license by the Civil Aeronautics Authority (1940).

Born 1910, McKeesport, Pennsylvania; died 1947.

Flying for Central Airlines, Richey made her first airmail transport flight on December 31, 1934, on a route that went from Washington, D.C., to Detroit, Michigan via Pittsburgh, Pennsylvania and Cleveland, Ohio. In 1940 she received the first instructor's license ever awarded to a woman by the Civil Aeronautics Authority.

Stating that she was not merely a "fair-weather flier," Richey resigned her position at Central Airlines after Department of Commerce officials suggested that she was not strong enough to fly trimotor, twelve-passenger Ford transport planes in adverse weather conditions. She had flown about a dozen round-trips during her ten-month period of employment.

"The pilots' union refused to take her in, not because of lack of ability, but because she was a female," Amelia Earhart (see entry) said in support of Richey. Other female pilots, however, such as Ruth Nichols (see entry) and Ruth Haviland, thought Richey might not have had the physical ability to handle the heavy, trimotor airplane in bad weather.

The first woman from her Pennsylvania county to earn a pilot's license, Richey obtained her transport pilot's license in August 1933 after having completed the necessary 1,000 hours of solo flying.

On December 30, 1933, Richey and Frances H. Marsalis, in their plane *The Outdoor Girl,* set a world endurance record of nine days, twenty-one hours, and forty-two minutes for continuous flying (with refueling). Richey set two world records in 1936: fastest time for a Class C light plane over a 100 kilometer course (February 1, Langley Field, Virginia, fifty-five minutes), and highest altitude in a midget plane (May 2, between Washington, D.C., and New Market, Virginia, 18,448 feet).

She went to England in 1942 as a member of the Aviation Transport Auxiliary, an organization of American women supporting the British Women's Ferry Command. One of her assignments was to fly planeloads of bombs from munitions factories to air bases. Later during World War II she served as flying instructor for the U.S. Army. She was discharged with the rank of major in 1944.

Richey was never in a crash.

Julia Richman

First president of the Young Women's Hebrew Association (1886).

Born New York City, 1855; died Neuilly, France, June 24, 1912.

Graduating in 1872 from New York Normal College in New York City (later Hunter College of the City University of New York), Richman became a public school teacher and, from 1884 to 1903, a school principal. She served as president of the Young Women's Hebrew Association from 1886 to 1890. She was a member of the board of directors of the Educational Alliance (founded in 1889), whose mission was to aid in the Americanization of Jewish immigrants—men, women, and children.

From 1903 until her resignation in 1912, Richman was New York City district superintendent for Lower East Side schools. A high school in New York City is named for her.

Marilla Ricker

Believed to be the first woman to assert her constitutional right to vote (1870).

Born New Durham, New Hamp-shire, 1840; died Dover, New Hampshire, November 12, 1920.

Her ballot was refused, but she did vote in 1871—apparently the first U.S. woman to have a vote officially acknowledged. After Ricker had paid her taxes in 1870, she claimed the right to vote, saying that the Fourteenth Amendment's reference to a qualified "elector" should be construed to include a woman.

Educated in local schools, Ricker began teaching at the age of sixteen. She married in 1863 and was widowed in 1868. After beginning to read law in 1876, she was admitted to the District of Columbia bar in 1882. Her practice there consisted primarily of criminal law and labor reform. In 1884 she was appointed U.S. commissioner, and in 1891 was admitted to practice before the U.S. Supreme Court.

Ricker announced her candidacy for governor of New Hampshire in 1910, but her filing fee was refused by the state attorney general on the basis that since Ricker did not have the right to vote, elective office was forbidden to her.

Libby Riddles

First woman to win the Iditarod Trail Sled Dog Race (1985).

Born Minnesota c. 1957.

The grueling sled-dog race, run annually in March, follows the route of the old Iditarod Trail, a turn-of-the-century overland mail and cargo route. It crosses over 1,100 miles of Alaskan wilderness from Anchorage northwest to Nome, crossing numerous rivers, two mountain ranges, and part of the frozen Bering Sea. Temperatures can range from 40°F. to −50°F, and winds have been recorded at velocities up to 140 miles per hour. There are twenty-seven checkpoints.

Contestants may take as many as eighteen dogs; Riddles used thirteen. Competing in the race for the third time, she completed the course in just over seventeen days—about three hours ahead of the second-place finisher. She won $50,000, and was voted Professional Sportswoman of the Year for 1985 by the Women's Sports Foundation.

Riddles makes her home in the small Seward Peninsula town of Teller, just northwest of Nome.

After Riddles's victory in 1985, the Iditarod was won by another woman—Susan Butcher—for four of the next five years.

Sally K. Ride

One of the first women to be selected for the U.S. space shuttle program (1978) (see also National Aeronautics and Space Administration).

Born Los Angeles, California, May 26, 1951.

The first women astronauts, a group of six, were selected for a training program in scientific, engineering, and medical duties. None, however, was to be trained in piloting the space shuttle.

At the time she was selected by NASA as an astronaut candidate, Ride was completing a Ph.D. degree in physics at Stanford University, (Palo Alto, California), where she had carried out research assignments in the areas of general relativity, astrophysics, and free-electron laser physics.

After serving as on-orbit capsule

communicator for the *STS-2* and *STS-3* missions, Ride made her first space flight aboard the orbiter *Challenger*, which was launched on June 18, 1983.

Ride also flew as a mission specialist on *STS 41-G*, launched from the Kennedy Space Center, Florida, on October 5, 1984. On this mission the crew deployed the *Earth Radiation Budget Satellite* and carried out an extra-vehicular activity to demonstrate potential satellite refueling. After this mission, Ride had logged 14.3 days in space.

After the space shuttle *Challenger* exploded, Ride was appointed to the Presidential Commission on the Space Shuttle *Challenger* Accident. Following the investigation, she was assigned to NASA headquarters as special assistant to the administrator for long-range and strategic planning. She left NASA in the autumn of 1987 to accept the position of science fellow at the Stanford University Center for International Security and Arms Control, working as a physicist.

Ride graduated from Westlake High School, Los Angeles, California (1968); earned a B.S. degree in physics and a B.A. degree in English (1973); M.S. and Ph.D. degrees in physics (1975, 1978), all from Stanford University, Palo Alto, California.

Aileen Riggin

First woman to win an Olympic springboard diving event (1920); first Olympic competitor to win medals in both swimming and diving events (1924).

Born Newport, Rhode Island, May 2, 1906.

At the 1920 games, the first time an Olympic springboard diving competition was held, Riggin won the gold medal at the age of fourteen. At the time, she was the youngest athlete ever to win a gold medal in any event. (The distinction was taken from her at the 1936 games by thirteen-year-old Marjorie Gestring (from Los Angeles, California) who

Aileen Riggin (left) with Gertrude Ederle (center) and Helen Wainright (right), Olympic team

also won a diving event.) Four years later, in the 1924 Olympics, Riggin won the silver medal in springboard diving, and a bronze medal in the 100-meter backstroke (time: 1 minute, 28.2 seconds).

In 1922 Riggin made the first slow-motion and underwater diving and swimming movies for sports columnist Grantland Rice. Two years later she turned professional: she gave diving and swimming exhibitions at the Hippodrome, the famed New York City show arena, made movie appearances, and toured with swimmer Gertrude Ederle (see entry) after Ederle's historic swim across the English Channel. In 1930 Riggin also helped fabled showman Billy Rose mount his first aquacade—an aquatic exhibition.

Holder of four springboard diving titles—three outdoor and one indoor—Riggin was inducted into the Swimming Hall of Fame in 1967.

Mary Roberts Rinehart

First U.S. correspondent to report from the front lines in World War I (1915); first reporter to interview Queen Mary of England (1915).

Born Pittsburgh, Pennsylvania, August 12, 1876; died New York, New York, September 22, 1958.

A news correspondent for the *Sat-urday Evening Post,* Rinehart reported from the front lines in France and Belgium during the month of January, 1915. That same year, she became the first reporter ever to interview Queen Mary. She had sailed to Europe in early January, and witnessed a night attack at Dunkirk, France, during which Zeppelin dirigibles dropped more than sixty bombs. She visited the Belgian frontline trenches, and also saw French troops under the command of General Foch. On the same trip Rinehart interviewed the King and Queen of Belgium and Britain's Queen Mary, gaining access because she was a famous writer and had firsthand knowledge of action at the front. Her interview with Queen Mary was originally published (with the Queen's consent) in the *Saturday Evening Post;* when it was published in Rinehart's book *Kings, Queens and Pawns* (1915), however, it was censored in Britain. In response, Rinehart observed that in England there was "the general feeling that no member of the royal family should ever talk for publication."

Writer par excellence, Rinehart averaged one book per year for more than forty years. Among the genres in which she established herself was the detective story. Her works, *The Circular Staircase* and *The Man in Lower Ten,* were published in 1908 and 1909 respectively. The novels offered a combination of humor, love, mystery, and murder. She also gained a widespread reputation for a series of light-hearted novels and stories about an unmarried older woman and her two middle-aged female friends. The novel that gained the most recognition was *Tish*, which was serialized in the *Saturday Evening Post*, and then published in book form in 1916.

Rinehart's autobiography, *My Story*, was published in 1931 (revised in 1948). She collaborated on four plays, the most notable one being *The Bat* (1920), based on her novel, *The Circular Staircase*.

By the time she was seventy-five, her books all together had sold over 10 million copies.

Isabel Hampton Robb

Organizer and first president of the American Nurses' Association (1897).

Born Welland, Ontario, Canada, 1860; died Cleveland, Ohio, April 15, 1910.

After her graduation from Collegiate Institute in St. Catherine's, Ontario, she taught school briefly, then decided to enter nursing. In 1883 she completed the two-year course at the newly established Bellevue Hospital Training School for Nurses in New York City.

Robb's nursing career began in Rome, Italy, and advanced rapidly. In 1886 she became superintendent of nurses at Cook County Hospital (Chicago, Illinois). Just three years later she became superintendent of nurses and principal of the nurses' training school at the new Johns Hopkins Hospital (Baltimore, Maryland). She founded the Society of Superintendents of Training Schools for Nurses of the U.S. and Canada in 1894, which later was called the National League of Nursing Education. She became its president in 1908. Robb was a major figure in the founding of the Nurses' Associated Alumnae of the U.S. and Canada in 1897 and served as its first president from 1897 to 1901. The association became known as the American Nurses' Association in 1911; it is still the recognized bargaining agent for registered nurses in the United States.

Robb died on April 15, 1910, when she was crushed between two streetcars.

Alice M. Robertson

First woman to preside over the U.S. House of Representatives (1921).

Born Tullahassee, Oklahoma (then Native American territory), January 2, 1854; died Muskogee, Oklahoma, July 1, 1931.

The daughter of missionary educators, Robertson (born Mary Alice Robertson) was elected to the House of Representatives from Oklahoma in 1920. At that time she was the only woman member of the house. Jeannette Rankin (see entry) the first woman member of Congress, had served from 1917 to 1919. Robertson had been given the position of president pro tem as a ceremonial gesture. Her single act in that capacity was to announce the vote on a minor appropriations bill for funding a U.S. delegation to the centennial celebrations of Peru's independence.

After studying for two years at Elmira College (Elmira, New York), Robertson was employed by the Office of Indian Affairs in Washington, D.C. In 1879 she resigned to teach school in Tullahassee, Oklahoma. In 1885 she was named to head a girls' boarding school at Muskogee, Oklahoma, remaining there until 1899. (The school later became a coeducational college and, eventually, the University of Tulsa.)

Robertson was named federal supervisor of Creek Indian schools in 1900—a post she held until her retirement in 1913. After her election to the House of Representatives, she was assigned to the House Committee on Indian Affairs. She was defeated in her bid for reelection.

Betty (Elizabeth) Robinson

First woman to win the 100-meter dash at the Olympic Games (1928).

Born Riverdale, Illinois, c. 1912.

Robinson, a sixteen-year-old high school student from Riverdale, Illinois, won the event the first time it was ever held at the Olympics. Her time was 12.2 seconds.

She was badly injured in a plane crash three years later and had difficulty walking for two years afterwards.

A young woman of many talents, Robinson was also named captain of the Northwestern University Rifle Team in 1931.

In 1936 she came back to win an Olympic gold medal as a member of the 4 × 100-meter relay team. Dur-

ing her career, she set a number of records for sprint distances.

Julia B. Robinson

First woman mathematician elected to the National Academy of Science (1976).

Born St. Louis, Missouri, c. 1920; died Oakland, California, July 30, 1985.

Robinson, a mathematics researcher, concentrated on solving logic problems with number theories. One of her best-known projects showed that there was no automatic method of deciding which equations have integer solutions, i.e., solutions expressed in whole numbers rather than fractions.

After receiving a Ph.D. degree in mathematics at the University of California–Berkeley in 1948, she joined the Berkeley faculty and remained there throughout her teaching career.

Elizabeth Rodgers

First woman to be appointed master workman (president) of a Knights of Labor District Assembly (1886).

Born Woodford, Ireland, 1847; died Milwaukee, Wisconsin, August 27, 1939.

Her family moved from Ireland to Canada when she was a young child. After her marriage, she and her husband settled in Chicago, Illinois, around 1876.

The Knights of Labor wanted to organize all labor in the United States into a single national body. In 1881 Rodgers was named head of an all-woman local assembly, then rose to her 1886 position as head of all of the Knights of Labor assemblies in the greater Chicago area.

The Knights of Labor began declining in 1887, and Rodgers left the movement, becoming chief executive officer of the Women's Catholic Order of Foresters—an organization she had helped found in the 1890's. She held this position until 1908.

Edith Nourse Rogers

First woman to officially deliver the votes of the electoral college (1925).

Born Saco, Maine, March 19, 1881; died Boston, Massachusetts, September 10, 1960.

Rogers was a Calvin Coolidge presidential elector in 1924 who became secretary of the electors, delivering (as required by an 1887 law) their ballots to be counted by a joint session of Congress early in January following the election.

During World War I, as a representative of the Women's Overseas Service League, she inspected military field hospitals. In 1922 Rogers was appointed as a dollar-a-year inspector of veterans' hospitals.

Her husband, John Jacob Rogers, was a Republican Congressman from Massachusetts. When he died in 1925, she won his seat, becoming the first woman from New England to hold a seat in Congress. She was re-elected to the seat seventeen times.

In 1942 she wrote a bill to establish the Women's Army Corps, and in 1944 she was one of the major drafters of the G.I. Bill of Rights (officially named Servicemen's Readjustment Act).

Rogers was educated privately at home and then at a boarding school and a French finishing school. Among the honors she received were the Distinguished Service Medal of the American Legion (1950).

Harriet Burbank Rogers

First woman to teach the deaf exclusively by speech and lip reading (1867).

Born North Billerica, Massachusetts, April 12, 1834; died North Billerica, Massachusetts, December 12, 1919.

After graduation from Massachusetts State Normal School (West Newton, Massachusetts) in 1851, Rogers became a schoolteacher. In 1863 she began giving private instruction to a young deaf girl, and by 1866 had opened her own school in Chelmsford, Massachusetts, with five students. A year later she moved with her pupils to the Clarke Institution for Deaf Mutes (later Clarke School for the Deaf) in Northampton, Massachusetts. She became the first director of the institution, and remained in that position until 1886, when she resigned because of ill health.

Rogers rejected the finger alphabet method of teaching the deaf, preferring the German oral method of lip reading and speaking. The finger alphabet method, widely used in the United States, relied upon the use of a manual alphabet or sign language. With the German method, deaf children learn to reproduce sounds by touching the throats and chests of their teachers, feeling the vibrations and breathing patterns and trying to reproduce those patterns themselves.

Mother Mary Joseph Rogers *(born Mary Josephine Rogers)*

Founder of the Maryknoll Sisters of St. Dominic (1920).

Born Roxbury, Massachusetts, October 27, 1882; died New York, New York, October 9, 1955.

Rogers earned an A.B. degree from Smith College (Northampton, Massachusetts) in 1905. She demonstrated her interest in foreign missions in 1906 when, as an assistant in zoology at Smith College, she started a mission-study class. Two years later she resigned from Smith, and by 1909 had earned a teaching diploma at Boston Normal School (Boston, Massachusetts).

After three years of teaching, Rogers moved to Ossining, New York, where the Reverend James Anthony Walsh had started the Maryknoll Seminary—officially, the Catholic Foreign Mission Society of America. Rogers's goal was to set up a program for training women for missionary service, and in 1914 her organization at Ossining was called the Pious Society of Women for the Foreign Missions.

In 1920 a papal decree was issued directing the formation of a new order: The Foreign Mission Sisters of St. Dominic. The first group of twenty-one novices took their vows. Rogers was named superior general in 1925—a post she held until 1947, when she declined to be reelected.

In 1954 the name of the Foreign Mission Sisters was officially changed to the Maryknoll Sisters of St. Dominic—and at the time of Rogers's death in 1955, the Maryknoll Sisters had grown to 1,160 sisters in eighty-four missions around the world—the first and largest order devoted exclusively to foreign missions.

Ruth Bryan Owen (Rohde) *(see Ruth Bryan Owen)*

Susan Lynn Roley *(see Joanne E. Pierce and Susan Lynn Roley)*

Janice Lee York Romary

First woman to carry the U.S. flag at the Olympic Games (1968).

Born California, c. 1928.

Romary, a forty-year-old from San Mateo, California, and winner of ten national fencing championships, carried the flag as the leader of the 392-member U.S. contingent at the 1968 Olympiad in Mexico City.

A graduate of the University of Southern California (Los Angeles), she competed in her first Olympics in 1948.

Edith Ronne

One of the first two women to land on Antarctica (1947); the first to take an Antarctic-based flight (1947).

Dates unknown.

In 1944 she married Finn Ronne, who led the Ronne Antarctic research expedition in 1947. The expedition's chief pilot was Harry Darlington.

Both men and their wives traveled on the *Port of Beaumont,* a 1,200-ton diesel driven ship, which sailed from Beaumont, Texas on January 25, 1947. It sailed into Marguerite Bay, Antarctica, on March 12, 1947. The ship was then docked for the winter on Stonington Island. Edith Ronne and Jenny Darlington, a scientist, became the first two women to land on Antarctica. The two women also became the first to winter at Antarctica, staying until June, 1948. Finn Ronne named part of Antarctica Edith Ronne Land. When he was not at base, she wrote newspaper articles for him.

On August 21, 1947, Ronne was on board a single-engine, ski-equipped L-5 plane, piloted by Capt. James Lassiter. She served as an observer to check flying approaches to a weather station on a 6,000-foot-high plateau.

Florence Rood

First woman president of the American Federation of Teachers (AFT) (1924).

Dates unknown.

Four unions—three from Chicago, Illinois, and one from Gary, Indiana—met in April, 1924, and founded the American Federation of Teachers. Although Margaret Haley (see entry) had been anticipated as the first president, Charles Stillman, representing the Chicago Federation of Men Teachers (high school) was chosen. As a result, the AFT became primarily a high school teachers' union. Rood, the second president and the first woman to hold the position, served from 1924 to 1926.

A union-affiliated leader from St. Paul, Minnesota, Rood had been elected leader of the Department of Classroom Teachers of the National Education Association (NEA) in 1910.

(Anna) Eleanor Roosevelt

First first lady to take stands on controversial issues and become an advocate for human rights (1939); first to hold a press conference (1933); first to travel by air to a foreign country (1934); first former first lady to be appointed delegate to the United Nations (1945).

Born New York, New York, October 11, 1884; died New York, New York, November 7, 1962.

On March 6, 1933, Roosevelt hosted a press conference in the Red Room of the White House—a groundbreaking event for a first lady. Held for a small group of women reporters, the press conference dealt with

Eleanor Roosevelt in a studio portrait, May 3, 1924

Eleanor Roosevelt giving address at housewarming of new headquarters of the Democratic Women's Workshop in New York City, January 5, 1956

the economic crisis in the United States and its effect on women. Roosevelt also discussed her husband's inaugural address and its message to the American people.

Roosevelt, known during her own lifetime for setting new precedents, embarked on a flying trip on March 6, 1934, that took her to Haiti, Puerto Rico, and the Virgin Islands. The trip, undertaken to allow Roosevelt to study social conditions in those Caribbean islands, covered 2,836 air miles.

The first lady had taken her first airplane flight on April 20, 1933, when she and Amelia Earhart (see entry), her dinner guest at the White House, decided on the spur of the moment to fly to Baltimore.

A major national and political figure in her own right during the years that her husband, Franklin Delano Roosevelt, was governor of

New York and then president of the United States, she was especially known for her advocacy of human rights. In 1939 she announced in her newspaper column that she was resigning from the Daughters of the American Revolution (DAR) because that organization had refused to allow black singer Marian Anderson to give a concert in its Constitution Hall. As U.S. delegate to the United Nations, Roosevelt chaired the United Nations Commission on Human Rights in 1946, and played a major role in the drafting of the Universal Declaration of Human Rights that was adopted by the U.N. in 1948.

Roosevelt was a prolific writer; her published books include *This Is My Story* (1937); *The Moral Basis of Democracy* (1940); *This I Remember* (1949); and *The Autobiography of Eleanor Roosevelt* (1961).

Ernestine Rose

Author of the first petition for a law granting married women the right to own property (1840).

Born Piotrków, Russo-Poland, 1810; died Brighton, England, August 4, 1892.

The petition, which went to the New York State Legislature, led to the passage of an 1848 law safeguarding the property of married women.

As an unmarried woman in Poland in 1827, she fought successfully to keep her inheritance rather than have it automatically become part of her dowry. She lived for a time in Germany, Holland, and France, then went in 1830 to England—where she came into contact with social reformers such as Robert Owen.

In 1836 she married William E. Rose, one of Owen's disciples, and they moved to the United States. With other utopian socialists, they established a short-lived colony in Skaneateles, New York, in 1843.

From the 1850s on, Rose was active in woman's rights, temperance, and antislavery movements.

Ethel Greenglass Rosenberg

First and only woman to be executed in peacetime for treason (1953).

Born New York, New York, September 28, 1915; died Sing Sing Prison, Ossining, New York, June 19, 1953.

Along with her husband, Julius, she was executed in the electric chair at Sing Sing Prison, Ossining, New York, for conspiracy to commit wartime espionage.

She met Julius Rosenberg in 1936; they married in 1939. He was a Communist, and they turned their attention to anti-Fascist and labor activities. Ethel had been fired from her job in 1935 for being on the strike committee of the Ladies' Apparel Shipping Clerks' Union.

Ethel Rosenberg's brother, David Greenglass, confessed to passing atomic secrets to Julius Rosenberg, who was arrested in July, 1950. In August Ethel was also arrested, accused of having been the typist in the transactions.

The following March, after a two-week trial, the Rosenbergs were convicted of treason and sentenced by Judge Irving Kaufman to die in the electric chair. David Greenglass was sentenced to fifteen years in prison.

As their convictions were appealed, Ethel Rosenberg spent the next two years as the only female prisoner in the Condemned Cells at Sing Sing Prison. Numerous articles appeared in periodicals claiming the Rosenbergs' innocence, and the National Committee to Secure Justice in the Rosenberg Case was established.

When the U.S. Circuit Court of Appeals unanimously upheld the conviction, the Rosenbergs' attorneys took the case to the U.S. Supreme Court—which refused to review it. Ethel's mother, Tessie Greenglass, tried to persuade Ethel to confess and back her brother's story; she refused. After a series of appeals and stays of execution, including two refusals by President Dwight D. Eisenhower to grant clemency, the Rosenbegs were executed on June 19, 1953.

Betsy Ross

Reputed to be the first U.S. flagmaker (1776 or 1777).

Born Philadelphia, Pennsylvania, January 1, 1752; died Philadelphia, Pennsylvania, January 30, 1836.

Born Elizabeth Griscom, she married John Ross in 1773. When he died, she continued their upholstery business and added to her income by fashioning flags for the state of Pennsylvania.

The traditional tale, first related publicly by her grandson in 1870, is that George Washington, Robert Morris, and Col. George Ross, members of a secret committee of the Continental Congress, commissioned Ross to design a flag for the fledgling nation. They suggested six-pointed stars, but Ross urged them to adopt five-pointed stars because they could be cut with a single snip of the scissors.

Historical records cast considerable doubt upon this traditional story.

Betsy Ross Bridge

First bridge named for a woman (1976).

The bridge spanning Philadelphia, Pennsylvania, and Pennsauken, New Jersey, opened on April 30, 1976.

Mary White Rowlandson

First woman to be released from Native American captivity (1676); first to write and publish a book in the colonies (1682).

Born South Petherton, England, c. 1635; died after 1682 (place unknown).

On February 10, 1676, Narragansett (native name Metacom) Indians attacked a settlement at Lancaster, Massachusetts. They took twenty-four hostages, primarily women and children, including forty-year-old Mary Rowlandson and three of her children. After eighty-three days, during which she traveled over 150 miles on foot and witnessed the death of one of her daughters, Rowlandson was ransomed on May 2, 1676.

She wrote a book about her experience. It was published anonymously in Cambridge, Massachusetts, in 1682, with an editorial apology for bringing a woman into "publick view." Titled *The Narrative of the Captivity and Restoration of Mrs. Mary Rowlandson,* the book went through fifteen editions by 1800.

In 1678, the town of Wethersfield, Connecticut, where her husband had been pastor of a local church before his death, voted her an annual pension of thirty pounds.

Susanna Haswell Rowson

First best-selling novelist in the United States (1794).

Born Portsmouth, England, c. 1762; died Boston, Massachusetts, March 2, 1824.

Her novel *Charlotte, A Tale of Truth,* first published in London in 1791 and then in Philadelphia in 1794, went into 200 editions. It told a supposedly true morality tale about how evil befalls a young English girl seduced by an English military officer. *Charlotte* was Rowson's second novel; The first, *Victoria,* was published in 1786.

Rowson had come to the United States in 1768 with her father, who had remarried after her mother died in childbirth. Because of his Loyalist stand, he and the family were interned during the early days of the

Revolutionary War. In 1778 they were granted the right to depart for England, where they settled in London.

Rowson married; she and her husband were actors in England. They came to the United States in 1793, and in 1796 settled in Boston, Massachusetts.

In 1797 Rowson started one of the first schools in the United States to provide girls with an education beyond the elementary school level. She ran the school until 1822. During this period, she continued to write novels and magazine articles.

Julie Roy

First woman to successfully sue her psychiatrist for inducing her to have sex as part of the therapy (1975).

Born Port Huron, Michigan, c. 1938.

In March, 1969, Roy began seeing psychiatrist Renatus Hartogs in New York City, sometime after the breakup of her marriage and a subsequent sexual relationship with a woman. In August, Hartogs convinced Roy to have sex with him as part of the therapy program. They had a sexual relationship that lasted for more than a year.

In 1971 Roy sued the psychiatrist for $1.25 million in malpractice damages. The jury handed down a verdict in her favor in March, 1975. The compensatory damages were set at $250,000 and the punitive at $100,000. Hartogs appealed the verdict, but the appeal was turned down in January, 1976.

Anne Newport Royall

First woman to have an exclusive interview with a U.S. president (1825); reputedly the first woman newspaper reporter (1831).

Born Baltimore, Maryland, June 11, 1769; died Washington, D.C., October 1, 1854.

Her reputation is based on a popular story that she was trying to get President John Quincy Adams to answer questions about the Bank of America, and that she once followed him when he went for his morning dip in the Potomac River, sitting on his clothes until he agreed to answer her questions.

In 1831 she published a weekly newspaper, *Paul Pry,* in Washington, D.C. Renowned for its gossip and caustic editorial comment, it lasted until 1836.

Between 1836 and 1854 Royall published another newspaper, *The Huntress,* which became famous for its ability to uncover graft in high places. She also wrote, in the 1820s, ten travel books on U.S. settlements.

At some point in her later years Royall was convicted in Washington, D.C., of being a "common scold," i.e., a woman whose customary rudeness and physical assaults made her subject to common law punishment as a public nuisance.

Barbara Jo Rubin

First woman jockey to win a regular parimutuel thoroughbred race (1969).

Born Miami, Florida, c. 1949.

The nineteen-year-old Rubin passed the first test required for her to qualify as a jockey on January 13, 1969. Two days later, with Rubin scheduled for her first mount, the male jockeys at Tropical Park in Coral Gables, Florida, staged a boycott, and Rubin was replaced with a male jockey. The boycotting jockeys were fined. Two weeks later, on January 28, Rubin—the only woman jockey in the field—won her first race at Hobby Horse Hall racetrack in Nassau in the Bahamas, riding Fly Away.

On February 22, 1969, Rubin made history when she rode home her first United States winner atop Cohesian at the Charles Town track in West Virginia. She was welcomed by a group of the male jockeys at the end of the race.

Forced to retire in January, 1970,

because of knee problems, Rubin placed first, second, or third in forty-two out of eighty-nine races, including twenty-two wins.

Wilma Rudolph

First woman runner to win three gold medals at a single Olympic Games (1960); first to win both Olympic sprint events (1960); first to win an Olympic 200-meter dash event (1960).

Born St. Bethlehem, Tennessee, June 23, 1940.

Rudolph overcame severe physical disabilities on her way to becoming a championship runner. At four she was attacked by double pneumonia and scarlet fever. The illnesses left her without the use of her left leg. Members of her family massaged the leg four times a day, and when she

was eight she began walking with the aid of a special shoe. She discarded the special shoe when she was eleven, and by the time she reached high school Rudolph had become an outstanding athlete.

In her sophomore year at Burt High School (Clarksville, Tennessee) Rudolph set a state basketball record by scoring 803 points in twenty-five games. While still a high school student, she won a bronze medal at the 1956 Olympic Games as a member of the U.S. 4 × 100-meter relay team.

Rudolph was a student at Tennessee State University (Nashville) when she won three gold medals at the 1960 Olympic Games, taking the 100-meter sprint in 11.0 seconds (a world record), the 200-meter dash in 24.0 seconds, and contributing to a team time of 44.5 seconds in the 4 × 100-meter relay. She was named Associate Press Athlete of the Year in 1960 and 1961, and received the James E. Sullivan Award as the top amateur athlete. During the same period, she was the Amateur Athletic Union 100-yard dash champion from 1959 to 1962, and in 1961 she set world indoor records in the 60-yard dash.

Her life and athletic career were documented in *Wilma*, a 1977 television movie. In 1980 Rudolph was named to the Women's Sports Hall of Fame, and she was accorded the honor of lighting the torch to open the 1987 Pan American Games.

Tracie Ruiz

First person to win an Olympic synchronized swimming event (1984).

Born Honolulu, Hawaii, 1963.

Synchronized swimming, an event in which competitors perform compulsory figures and dance-like routines, was certified as an Olympic event just three months before Ruiz won it for the first time in 1984. She won the solo category, then teamed with Candy Costie—her partner since 1975—to win the duet category. Ruiz scored 99.467 in the compulsory figures section of the solo competition, the highest score ever recorded in that portion of the event. She scored 99 on her final routine, a four-minute performance that began with a fifty-second underwater sequence.

Ruiz had won the world solo championship in 1982; Ruiz and Costie together had placed second in the duet category. In 1983 Ruiz won the solo event at both the America Cup and the Pan American Games, and Ruiz and Costie won the duet event at both competitions. Ruiz—now Tracie Ruiz-Conforte—took second place for a silver medal at the 1988 Olympic Games.

Aline B. (Louchheim) Saarinen

First woman to head an overseas television news bureau (1971).

Born New York, New York, March 25, 1914; died New York, New York, July 13, 1972.

A noted art and architecture critic, Saarinen became art and architecture editor for NBC television early in the 1960s. In 1964 she became a correspondent on women's matters for NBC and the moderator of a panel show called "For Women Only." Saarinen was named chief of the Paris (France) bureau of NBC television in 1971—a position she held until her death.

She graduated Phi Beta Kappa with an A.B. degree from Vassar College (Poughkeepsie, New York) in 1935, then earned an A.M. degree in history of architecture from the Institute of Fine Arts at New York University (New York, New York) in 1941. During the 1940s, Saarinen (then Louchheim) was an art editor for *Art News* (1944–48), then associate art editor and art critic for the *New York Times* (1947).

Saarinen won an international award for art criticism (1951) and the American Federation of Arts Award for best newspaper criticism (1953). Her books include *5,000 Years of Art* (1946) and *The Proud Possessors* (1958).

In 1954 she married renowned Finnish architect Eero Saarinen and changed her byline to Aline B. Saarinen. After her husband's unexpected death in 1961, she wrote *Eero Saarinen on His Work* (1962).

The only woman member of the U.S. Fine Arts Commission in Washington, D.C., Saarinen was offered the post of ambassador to Finland in 1964, but she declined the position.

Florence R. Sabin

First woman member of the National Academy of Sciences (1925); first woman to graduate from the Johns Hopkins University School of Medicine (1900); first to be elected president of the American Association of Anatomists (1924).

Born Central City, Colorado, November 9, 1871; died Denver, Colorado, October 3, 1953.

Accepting a position as an assistant in anatomy, Sabin became, in 1902, the first woman to join the medical faculty of Johns Hopkins University (Baltimore, Maryland). She achieved the rank of full professor of histology in 1917. She studied the lymphatic system, blood cells, and blood vessels for several years. By 1919 she had determined the origin of red corpuscles. The first woman elected president of the American Association of Anatomists (1924), she became the first woman member of the National Academy of Sciences in 1925.

After graduating from Smith College (Northampton, Massachusetts), Sabin received a medical degree from Johns Hopkins University Medical School (Baltimore, Maryland) in 1900, the first woman graduate. She interned at Johns Hopkins Hospital, following which she returned to the medical school to begin research. Another first for Sabin was her membership at the Rockefeller Institute for Medical Studies (1925), where she established and headed a department of cellular studies, conducting research on tuberculosis.

As a result of her work, the state of Colorado passed the Sabin Health Bills, which led to a tremendous drop in the death rate from tuberculosis and a ninety percent drop in the number of cases of syphilis. Among the awards Sabin received were the Jane Addams Medal for distinguished service by an American woman, the Lasker Foundation Award for achievement in the field of public health, and the Trudeau Medal of the National Tuberculosis Association (1945).

Ruth St. Denis *(born Ruth Dennis)*

Cofounder of the first major dance school in the United States (1915).

Born Newark, New Jersey, January 20, 1879; died Hollywood, California, July 21, 1968.

In 1914 St. Denis married Ted Shawn, her dance partner. Together, they founded Denishawn, a school of dance in Los Angeles, California (1915), and then a dance company that made national tours. Their stu-

dents included Martha Graham (see entry) and Doris Humphrey, who became a major dancer and choreographer. The company enjoyed considerable success through the 1920s, but closed in 1932 after the Depression hit. St. Denis and Shawn were separated in 1931—they never divorced.

At fourteen, St. Denis starred in a show produced by her mother. The following year she made her New York City dance debut, appearing in vaudeville and musical comedy—including productions by David Belasco, director and playwright, who reportedly gave her the name St. Denis. Her own first dance work, *Radha*, inspired by Hindu dance movements, was presented in 1906. A successful European tour followed.

After the breakup of the Denishawn school and company, St. Denis experimented with religious dance forms, then in the early 1940s resumed public performances, dancing at the Jacob's Pillow dance festival on a farm in Lee, Massachusetts. Shawn established the farm dance site in 1933. Men dancers performed there until 1939. In 1940 he built a theater to accommodate an audience of 500. The repertory of the dance festival included ballet, ethnic, and modern dance. She continued to perform there every year until 1955.

Considered a major force and influence in modern American dance,

St. Denis wrote *Lotus Lights* (1932) and *Ruth St. Denis: An Unfinished Life* (1939).

St. Mary's College

First Catholic graduate theology program open to women (1943).

The president of St. Mary's College (South Bend, Indiana) was Sister Madeleva, born Mary Evaline Wolff (1887–1964). She was a noted poet and medieval scholar.

Prior to the college's initiation of the program, which was designed to train women to teach religion at college level, there was no Catholic university that admitted women as graduate theology students.

It closed in 1969, after nearby Marquette University (Milwaukee, Wisconsin) and the University of Notre Dame (Notre Dame, Indiana) had begun admitting women. By then, St. Mary's had awarded 76 doctorates and over 300 master's degrees.

Suzanna Madora Salter

First woman mayor (1887).

Born Kansas, March 1, 1860; died Norman, Oklahoma, March 17, 1961.

When Salter was twenty-seven years old, she was elected mayor of Argonia, Kansas, population 500, in

1887, the first year women were allowed to vote in the Kansas local elections. An official of the Women's Christian Temperance Union, she was nominated for the post by "Wets" as a prank. When she went to her polling place to vote, Salter discovered she had been nominated. She received a two-thirds majority vote in the election.

Salter served one year, receiving a salary of only one dollar.

Deborah Sampson (Gannett)

First woman to impersonate a man in battle (1782); first to lecture on military experience (1802).

Born Plympton, Massachusetts, December 17, 1760; died Sharon, Massachusetts, April 29, 1827.

Sampson enlisted in the Fourth Massachusetts Regiment under the name of Robert Shurtleff (also listed as Shirtliff) in May, 1782. It was discovered that she was a woman when she developed a fever and had to be hospitalized in Pennsylvania. She was discharged from the army in 1783.

A year earlier, she had been wounded in a battle near Tarrytown, New York, but did not have to be hospitalized. Thus, her true sex remained a secret. That same year, however, she was excommunicated from the First Baptist Church of Middleborough, Massachusetts, because of a strong suspicion that she was "dressing in men's clothes, and enlisting as a Soldier in the Army."

After she was discharged from the army, she made public appearances—in uniform dress—at various theaters, lecturing on her military experiences (1802).

In 1792 she received a pension of thirty-four pounds from the state of Massachusetts and four dollars per month from the United States, after Paul Revere appealed on her behalf (1805).

Joan Benoit (Samuelson) *(see Joan Benoit)*

Marlene Sanders

First woman to anchor a television network evening newscast (1964); first to be vice president of a television network news division (1976).

Born Cleveland, Ohio, 1931.

Sanders became the first woman to serve as anchor on a network evening newscast when regular anchor Ron Cochran lost his voice. At the time, Sanders had her own daily newscast, "Marlene Sanders with the Woman's Touch."

After getting her first television job as a production assistant for a news program on a local New York City station, Sanders became the associate producer of "Night Beat," a celebrity interview show featuring Mike Wallace (1956). In 1962 she went to New York City radio station WNEW as assistant director of news and public affairs, where she wrote "The Battle of the Warsaw Ghetto," a radio documentary that won for her the 1964 Writers Guild of America Award. In 1964 she joined ABC-TV News.

For three months in 1966, Sanders was the only woman television correspondent covering the Vietnam War. She worked as a general correspondent, then in 1971 served once more as a fill-in anchor for Sam Donaldson's Saturday evening newscast. During this period at ABC, Sanders also produced the first network television documentary on women's liberation.

Her success as a producer of television documentaries—including *Children in Peril, The Hand That Rocks the Ballot Box,* and *Woman's Place*—led to her 1976 promotion by ABC to vice president and director of television documentaries. She resigned from ABC in 1978, and was hired by CBS News as a producer and correspondent. Sanders left CBS in 1987 rather than accept a transfer to CBS radio.

She joined WNET, New York City's public television station, in 1989. The same year, Sanders and Marcia Rock wrote *Waiting for Prime Time,* a book about television newswomen.

Sanders's documentaries garnered numerous awards, including the *McCall's* magazine Golden Mike Award (1964), the Women in Communications Award (1973), the Broadcast Woman of the Year Award given by American Women in Radio and Television (1975), and the Deadline Club Award (1977).

Mary Sandmann *(see Mrs. Cornell Deeny)*

Alice B. Sanger

First woman to be employed in the executive offices of a U.S. president (1890).

Born Indiana, date unknown.

Sanger was the White House stenographer for President Benjamin Harrison. Her salary was $1,400 per year.

Margaret Sanger

First woman to open a birth control clinic (1916).

Born Corning, New York, September 14, 1883; died Tucson, Arizona, September 6, 1966.

Sanger had a special interest in birth control because her mother, who died at forty-nine, had endured eighteen pregnancies. Having been a nurse in the slums of New York City, she was aware of the poverty and illness that resulted from repeated pregnancies. Before Sanger opened her clinic in 1916, even doctors would not give out birth control information. (Congress had passed legislation in 1873 declaring information and devices related to contraception to be obscene materials.)

In 1914 Sanger launched a monthly magazine called *Woman Rebel,* which lasted for seven months. When the phrase "birth control" appeared in the magazine for the first time, the U.S. Post Office refused to mail the magazine, and Sanger was indicted. She went to Europe until the indictment was dismissed in 1916. Returning to the United States, Sanger then printed and distributed a pamphlet of contraceptive advice called *Family Limitation.* By 1917, 160,000 copies of the pamphlet were in circulation.

Sanger's first birth control clinic was opened in the Brownsville section of Brooklyn, New York, on Octo-

Margaret Sanger at Birth Control Trial, Court of Special Sessions, Brooklyn, New York, 1915

ber 16, 1916. It occupied two rooms on the ground floor at 46 Amboy Street, and announced its services with handbills printed in English, Yiddish, and Italian. The staff consisted of Sanger, her sister Ethel Byrne, and Fania Mindell, a Yiddish-speaking woman. There were no doctors. In the first ten days, 500 women came to get information and contraceptive devices. They signed statements declaring themselves to be married women. The clinic's clients paid for the devices and for a copy of an article titled "What Every Girl Should Know." They were not charged for "hygienic advice."

Mindell was fined for selling books; Byrne was given a thirty-day sentence (later reversed), and went on a hunger strike until she had to be carried out on a stretcher; Sanger was sentenced to thirty days in prison, and although the New York Court of Appeals refused to reverse her conviction, they did interpret the law in such a way that doctors were permitted to give women assistance and advice under the guise of preventing venereal disease.

After her release from prison, Sanger began publication of *The Birth Control Review*.

Sanger's efforts began to bear fruit: during World War I, the U.S. government distributed condoms to soldiers, along with copies of "What Every Girl Should Know." In 1921

Sanger founded the American Birth Control League, serving as its president until 1928. The League's membership peaked in 1926 at 37,000. In 1925 the American Medical Association first gave its support to contraception.

In 1927 Sanger organized and addressed the First World Population Conference in Geneva, Switzerland. Almost a generation later, in 1953, she was to be a founder and first president of the International Planned Parenthood Federation.

Believing that children should be born only if they are wanted, Sanger's fight for birth control lasted fifty years. She was put in jail at least nine times as a result of aggressively fighting for the right of women to practice birth control.

The sixth of eleven children, Sanger attended Claverack College (Hudson, New York), then trained as a nurse at White Plains Hospital (White Plains, New York)—although she never completed her nursing studies. About 1911 she became a member of the Socialist Party, leaving after a year to join the Industrial Workers of the World (IWW). When she decided that her primary concern lay in the area of birth control and contraception, she left the IWW to become a writer and lecturer.

Sanger wrote several books, including *Women, Morality and Birth Control* (1922); *My Fight for Birth*

Control (1931); and *Margaret Sanger: An Autobiography* (1938).

Kathleen Saville

Member of the first woman and man team to row across the Atlantic (1981).

Date unknown.

Saville and her husband, Curtis, left the Canary Islands off the western coast of Africa on March 18, 1981. They rowed to Antigua in the West Indies, arriving there on June 10. The couple, who live in Providence, Rhode Island, were aboard their twenty-five-foot sailboat for forty-seven days and twenty hours.

Saville became the first woman of any nation to row the Atlantic.

Hope Skillman Schary

Probably the first woman to become a cotton fabric manufacturer/converter (1942); founder and president of Skillmill, Inc., a cotton manufacturing and textile firm (1942).

Born Grand Rapids, Michigan, c. 1908; died New Milford, Connecticut, May 23, 1981.

During the 1930s Schary worked as a creative stylist for various textile firms. She went on to form her own textile company, Skillmill, Inc., and employed only women for many years. She headed the company until she retired in the early 1960s. She became the president of Fashion Group, Inc., an organization made up of approximately 5,000 women who were in the fashion industry, an office she held from 1958 to 1960.

Schary, who gained a wide reputation as a leader in the women's rights movement, served two terms as president of the National Council of Women of the United States (1970–72 and 1976–78). At the time of her death, she was vice president of the International Council of Women (1981).

She graduated from Goucher College, (Towson, Maryland), and married Saul Schary, an artist.

Virginia M. Schau

First woman to receive the Pulitzer Prize for spot news photography (1954).

Born c. 1915; died Santa Rosa, California, May 28, 1989.

Schau, an amateur photographer from San Anselmo, California, was the second person to win the Pulitzer in this class. She won the prize for two pictures of her husband rescuing a truck driver when the cab of his semitrailer went over the side of the Pit River Bridge near Redding, California, on May 3, 1953.

Schau and family members were behind the truck in the Mount Shasta, California, area when the truck's steering mechanism failed. The truck went through a guardrail and stopped, partially over the edge of the bridge with the cab suspended from its rear wheels and the engine on fire. While some other people held him, Schau's husband, Walter, hung over the edge and rescued the truck driver with a rope. Virginia Schau photographed the rescue. The photographs, distributed by the Associated Press, appeared in the Akron, Ohio, *Beacon-Journal* in May, 1953.

Dacie Schileru

First woman to compete in a National Collegiate Athletic Association (NCAA) event (1973).

Born Rumania, date unknown.

Schileru, a student at Wayne University (Detroit, Michigan), who had immigrated to the United States when she was eighteen, qualified for the diving competition in the college division swimming championships.

Prior to 1973, the NCAA had been an all-male domain. In 1972, however, Congress passed the Title IX legislation which outlawed sex discrimination and guaranteed equal access and opportunities for women in education, including sports. Therefore, 1973 was the first year in which women participated in NCAA events.

Before the federal legislation, there had been an organization for collegiate women athletes parallel to the NCAA—the Association of Intercollegiate Athletics for Women (AIAW). In 1980 the NCAA perpetrated what came to be known as the "rape" of the AIAW by unilaterally establishing a number of championships for women's sports, setting up competing events on the same dates as the AIAW and securing exclusive television contracts. Consequently, the number of member schools participating in AIAW events dropped to a handful, and the organization collapsed.

Gretchen Schoenleber

First woman to be elected a member of the New York Cocoa Exchange (1935); first to be a member of any commodity exchange (1935).

Dates unknown.

In 1927 Schoenleber succeeded her father as president of Ambrosia Chocolate Company (Milwaukee, Wisconsin), a business established in 1884. Nearly a decade later, she was elected to the New York Cocoa Exchange (1935). The Cocoa Exchange is a commodity exchange in New York City dealing in futures and futures options on cocoa. (A future is a commitment to buy or sell a specified amount of a commodity at an agreed-upon price during a specified month.) Members of the exchange trade for their own accounts and for the accounts of customers.

Schoenleber graduated from the University of Wisconsin (Madison) in 1913.

Margarethe Meyer Schurz

First person to operate a private kindergarten (1857).

Born Hamburg, Germany, August 27, 1833; died New York, New York, March 15, 1876.

As a teenager in Hamburg, Schurz had attended lectures by Friedrich Froebel, known as the father of the international kindergarten movement. Inspired by his theories, she opened a kindergarten in one room of her home in Watertown, Wisconsin, where she followed the Froebelian principles of providing students with pleasant surroundings, self-activity, and physical training. She taught her daughter and several children of relatives for a few months during 1857. Thereafter she and her family left Watertown, and moved around considerably, so she never organized another kindergarten.

Schurz married in 1852; she and her husband, Carl, immigrated to the United States that same year, settling in Watertown in 1856. In 1859 the Schurz family moved to Boston, Massachusetts, where Margarethe became acquainted with Elizabeth Peabody (see entry), an advocate of the kindergarten movement in the United States, who founded a Boston school in 1860.

Schurz's husband became a Civil War general and then a U.S. senator from Missouri (1869–75). Shortly after her death, he was named secretary of the interior, serving in that post until 1881.

Marcy Schwam

First woman to run up the stairs of the Empire State Building, New York City (1978).

Born New York, date unknown.

Schwam, a physical fitness instructor from Ossining, New York, competed in the first Annual Empire State Building Run-Up, a course involving the ascent of 1,575 stairs to the observation deck on the eighty sixth floor.

She finished in 16 minutes and 3.2 seconds, placing tenth overall among fifteen competitors, only three of whom were women. Gary Muhrcke won the competition in 12 minutes and 32 seconds.

Arlette Rafferty Schweitzer

First woman to give birth to her own grandchildren (1991).

Born Lemmon, South Dakota, November 8, 1948.

Schweitzer was a surrogate mother for her daughter, Christa Schweitzer Uchytil, who was born without a uterus—a problem occurring in about 1 in 5,000 women. Arlette Schweitzer gave birth to twins on October 12, 1991: Chad Daniel was born first, at 1:21 A.M., followed by Chelsea Arlette at 1:22 A.M. She said she bore the children as an act of love for her daughter and son-in-law, Kevin Uchytil. Eggs were taken from Christa Uchytil's ovaries, fertilized with her husband's sperm, and implanted in the grandmother's womb. The official document of birth of the twins lists Kevin and Christa Uchytil as the parents, based upon a sworn statement from Dr. William Phipps of the University of Minnesota (Minneapolis), who performed the in-vitro fertilization and implantation.

Arlette Schweitzer is the only woman in the United States to give birth to her own grandchildren. The only other similar case is a woman in South Africa who gave birth to her daughter's triplets (1987).

After she married Daniel Schweitzer, a sales representative for Keebler Company, Arlette Schweitzer graduated from Northern State University (Aberdeen, South Dakota) with a B.A. degree in education and library media.

Blanche Scott

First U.S. woman to fly (1910).

Born probably Rochester, New York, c. 1885; died Rochester, New York, January 12, 1970.

After attending Fort Edward College (Fort Edward, New York), Scott made several pioneering ventures. In 1910 she became the second woman to drive overland in an automobile from New York to San Francisco. Shortly after that trip, Glenn Curtiss trained her to fly. Her first solo flight, in September, 1910, in Hammondsport, New York, occurred by accident: her instructor had put a throttle block in her tricycle-gear Curtiss plane to permit her to taxi without leaving the ground, but a sudden wind lifted her to forty feet. "In those days," she said, "they didn't take you up in the air to teach you. They gave you a bit of preliminary ground training. They told you this and that. You got in. They kissed you goodbye and trusted to luck you'd get back."

In 1912, Scott made her first cross-country flight; it lasted sixty-nine days. She joined Glen Curtiss's exhibition team as a stunt pilot on the barnstorming circuit, earning as much as $5,000 per week for "death dives" (dropping from 4,000 feet to level out at 200 feet) and other daredevil maneuvers such as flying upside down 20 feet above the ground. She retired from barnstorming in 1916.

After World War I Scott worked for several years as a screenwriter, radio commentator, and assistant manager of a radio station.

In 1948 Scott flew as a guest of the U.S. Air Force in a training version of the Shooting Star jet fighter, thus becoming the first woman to ride in a jet.

For some time she was special consultant for the United States Air Force Museum at Wright-Patterson Air Force Base in Ohio, resigning in 1956.

Scott was honored by the Antique Airplane Association on the fiftieth anniversary of her first flight.

Charlotte Scott

First woman elected to the council of the American Mathematical Society (AMS) (1894–95).

Born Lincoln, England, June 8, 1858; died Cambridge, England, November 8, 1931.

Scott, a successful scholar and teacher in the field of mathematics, was a supporter of the New York Mathematical Society and a contributor to its *Bulletin*. When the society reorganized and became the Ameri-

can Mathematical Society in 1894/95, she was elected to the society's council.

Scott attended Cambridge University (England) in 1880, where her record was excellent, but she was not allowed to get a formal degree. However, she was permitted to earn both a bachelor's degree and a doctor of science degree from the University of London in 1882 and 1885 respectively.

In 1885 Bryn Mawr College (Bryn Mawr, Pennsylvania), which had recently been established, invited Scott to set up undergraduate and graduate mathematics programs. She was one woman among six of the first faculty members.

She was elected vice president of the American Mathematical Society in 1906, and in 1922 seventy members of the society gathered with seventy of Scott's former students to pay homage to her.

She retired from the mathematics department at Bryn Mawr in 1925.

Elizabeth Cochrane Seaman (see Nellie Bly)

Eleonora R. Sears

First woman to play against men in a polo match (1910); first to win the U.S. national squash racquets championship (1928).

Born Boston, Massachusetts, September 28, 1881; died West Palm Beach, Florida, March 26, 1968.

On August 13, 1910, at Narragansett Pier, Rhode Island, Sears—a wealthy, athletic member of the social elite—became the first woman to play in a polo match against men when she, a Miss Handy, and two other women played a four-chukker match against four men. (A chukker is a seven and one-half minute period of play.) The women played two chukkers riding astride their ponies, and two riding sidesaddle. Two days later, Sears and Emily Randolph played against a two-man team. The matches, according to *The New York Times,* "caused a sensation."

The first women's squash racquets tournament was held in Greenwich, Connecticut, in January, 1928. Forty women competed, including tennis great Hazel Hotchkiss (Wightman) (see entry), who lost in an early round. In the final match, on January 19, Sears defeated Miss A. Boyden of Boston, Massachusetts, three sets to one.

Secret Service Agents, First Women

First women recruited as Secret Service agents (1971).

In 1970 President Richard M. Nixon issued a directive urging the appointment of more women to responsible government positions. The Treasury Department, in compliance with that directive, recruited the first women Secret Service agents in 1971. They were: Laurie B. Anderson, twenty-four, Jersey City, New Jersey; Sue A. Baker, twenty-five, Oak Ridge, Tennessee; Kathryn I. Clark, twenty-four, Salt Lake City, Utah; Holly A. Hofschmidt, twenty-eight, Milwaukee, Wisconsin; and Phyllis F. Shantz, twenty-five, Rome, New York. College graduates all, they were sworn in with their backs to the photographers and television cameras.

The Secret Service is a 127-year-old agency. The main duties of the agents are protecting the president, vice president, and their immediate families, and guarding U.S. currency against counterfeiters.

Margaret Rhea Seddon

First woman to achieve the full rank of astronaut (1979); one of the first women to be selected for the U.S. space shuttle program (1978) (see also National Aeronautics and Space Administration).

Born Murfreesboro, Tennessee, November 8, 1947.

The first women astronauts, a group of six, were selected for a training program in scientific, engineering, and medical duties. None, however, was to be trained in piloting the space shuttle.

Prior to her selection by NASA as an astronaut candidate, Seddon had served a surgical internship and three years of a general surgery residency in Memphis, Tennessee. She had done clinical research into the effects of radiation therapy on nutrition in cancer patients.

Seddon became the first woman to achieve the full rank of astronaut when she completed her astronaut training and evaluation period in August, 1979. She then worked on orbiter and payload software, served as launch and landing rescue helicopter physician, and as technical assistant to the director of Flight Crew Operations.

She flew her first space mission aboard the *Discovery*, launched from the Kennedy Space Center in Florida on April 12, 1985. This mission saw the first unscheduled extra-vehicular

activity as a result of the malfunction in the *Syncom* spacecraft and subsequent attempt to activate the satellite. Its duration was 168 hours.

Her next space flight, a nine-day mission on board the *Spacelab Life Sciences (SLS-1)*—the *Columbia,* was launched on June 5, 1991. Among other experiments, this mission explored the response of humans, animals, and cells to microgravity and the return to earth's gravity. Seddon had logged sixteen days in space when the *Columbia* touched down at Edwards Air Force Base, California, on June 14, 1991.

Kathryn Sellers

First woman to be head judge of a juvenile court (1918).

Born Marysville, Ohio, c. 1871.

At age eighteen, Sellers went to Washington, D.C., and applied to take a civil service examination for a job as a meteorological clerk in the Weather Bureau—the first woman to take such an examination. She passed the examination and was awarded the job, at a salary of fifty dollars per month. She described the salary as "opulent."

Sellers then passed the examination for a librarian's position in the U.S. State Department. She learned several languages as part of her job, and reclassified over 85,000 books.

In 1910 she began law studies, attending evening classes at the Washington College of Law (Washington, D.C.), graduating in 1914 with B.L. and M.L. degrees. Sellers worked from 1914 to 1917 for the U.S. Neutrality Board doing reference work, then in 1917 was hired as a law clerk by the U.S. State Department's Division of Foreign Intelligence to index its confidential information records.

President Woodrow Wilson nominated Sellers as head judge of the Washington, D.C., juvenile court in 1918. She served in that position until 1934.

Ellen Semple

First woman president of the Association of American Geographers (1921).

Born Louisville, Kentucky, January 8, 1863; died West Palm Beach, Florida, May 8, 1932.

Semple, who taught at Oxford University (England), Wellesley College (Wellesley, Massachusetts), and Columbia University (New York, New York), was one of the educators who helped establish geography as a university discipline.

After earning an M.A. degree from Vassar College (Poughkeepsie, New York) in 1891, she traveled to Germany to study anthropogeography.

Since she was a woman, she was not allowed to enroll at the University of Leipzig. However, she attended classes and sat next to the platform of her mentor, Friedrich Ratzel, where she could listen to his lectures. Ratzel maintained that environment determines human development. Semple espoused this theory and went on to teach it herself. She opened a girls' school in Louisville, Kentucky (1893), where she taught history and Ratzel's environmental theory. She also wrote articles developing his theory. Two longer works, *American History and Its Geographic Conditions* (1903) and *Influences of Geographic Environment on the Basis of Ratzel's System of Anthropo-Geography* (1911), were deemed significant.

From 1923 to 1932 Semple was professor of anthropogeography at Clark University (Worcester, Massachusetts).

Kate Sessions

First woman to receive the Meyer Medal from the American Genetic Association (1939).

Born San Francisco, California, November 8, 1857; died La Jolla, California, March 24, 1940.

Sessions, a horticulturalist, won the Meyer Medal in 1939 for distinguished service in the introduction of foreign plants to the United States. She had traveled throughout the world, collecting many new plants, such as the Erythea palm, flame eucalyptus, Chinese twisted juniper, and a variety of acacias to be planted at Balboa Park, which she created in San Diego, California, in 1892.

Before leasing the land to establish Balboa Park, she had earned a Ph.B. degree in chemistry from the University of California–Berkeley in 1881, taught primary school, and then opened a plant nursery in Coronado, California, in 1885.

Sessions was one of the founders of the San Diego Floral Association (1909), where she served as an officer and board member for more than twenty years.

Elizabeth Ann Bayley Seton

First U.S. woman to be a saint in the Roman Catholic Church (1975); founder of the first U.S. Catholic order (1809).

Born New York, New York, August 28, 1774; died Emmitsburg, Maryland, January 4, 1821.

Seton, who grew up in New York City and New Rochelle, New York, was primarily concerned with problems of the poor. In 1779 she helped found the Society for the Relief of Poor Widows with Small Children, reportedly the first charitable institu-

tion in New York City. She served as treasurer of the institution for several years.

In 1803 her husband, William Seton, became ill. She sailed with him to Italy, hoping the voyage might help him recover. He died in December of that year, however, and she returned to New York.

Seton joined the Roman Catholic Church in 1805 and was confirmed in 1806. In 1808 she taught school in Baltimore, Maryland. The following year Seton took her vows, and she and a small group of followers moved to Emmitsburg, Maryland, where they established the first U.S. sisterhood, the Sisters of Charity of St. Joseph (1809). They also opened there, in 1810, the first tuition-free girls' parochial school in the United States. The new order spread to Philadelphia, Pennsylvania, in 1814 and New York City in 1817.

Mother Seton was beatified in 1963 and canonized in 1975.

Seven Sister Colleges

The first time all seven sister colleges were headed by women (1978).

In March, 1978, when Mary Patterson McPherson became president of Bryn Mawr College (Bryn Mawr, Pennsylvania), it marked the first time all of the seven sister colleges were headed by women. The six other sister colleges and their presidents at that time were:

Barnard (New York, New York)
  Jacqueline Mattfeld

Mount Holyoke (South Hadley, Massachusetts)
  Elizabeth Topham Kennan

Radcliffe (Cambridge, Massachusetts)
  Matina Horner

Smith (Northampton, Massachusetts)
  Jill Conway

Vassar (Poughkeepsie, New York)
  Virginia B. Smith

Wellesley (Wellesley, Massachusetts)
  Barbara W. Newell

Edna Sewell

First director of the Associated Women of the American Farm

Bureau Federation (AFBF) (1927).

Born Ambia, Indiana, 1881; died Lafayette, Indiana, 1967.

Married in 1897, Sewell began a public-speaking career in farm communities a few years afterwards. In 1916, in connection with Purdue University (West Lafayette, Indiana), she organized and then directed the first three home-improvement tours ever conducted in the United States. One of the main purposes of the tour was to demonstrate to farm wives new and more efficient ways of caring for their homes and families.

From 1921 to 1927 she held various executive positions in the Indiana Farm Bureau. In 1927 the Associated Women of the American Farm Bureau Federation established its Home and Community Department and named Sewell as its head. In 1934 the department was renamed Associated Women of the AFBF. Sewell directed it until she retired in 1950. She remained active in the affairs of the AFBF throughout her lifetime.

Sexual Harassment

First class-action sexual harrassment case (1991).

Federal District Judge James Rosenbaum of Minneapolis, Minnesota, ruled on December 16, 1991, that a group of women iron workers would be allowed to bring a sexual harassment suit against the Eveleth Taconite Company as a class action. This was the first time a federal court permitted a class-action sexual harassment suit.

The suit is to be filed by approximately 100 women iron miners who work for the company, which first hired women in 1975.

The miners have alleged that the company is prejudicial in its compensation, hiring, and promoting, and that their male coworkers have abused them verbally and have touched them.

Mary Foot Seymour

Founder of the first all-woman secretary school in the United States (1879).

Born Aurora, Illinois, 1846; died New York, New York, March 21, 1893.

Seymour went to school in New York City and then became a teacher. In 1879 she opened the Union School of Stenography in New York City. At that time the typewriter was already widely used, and she assumed a new field of employment would be available to women. Within a short period of time, she had branched out with four schools, a business employing twenty-five stenographers, and an employment bureau.

In 1889 she began publication of the *Business Woman's Journal* and established the Mary F. Seymour Publishing Company, with only women officers. She sold stock in the company, which had a capital value of $50,000.

Eva Shain

First woman to judge a world heavyweight fight (1977).

Born c. 1929.

New York State licensed Shain as a boxing judge on March 21, 1975, along with Carol Castellano. They were the second and third women to be licensed, Carol Polis having been the first (1974). Shain was a judge at the Muhammad Ali vs. Ernie Shavers match at Madison Square Garden (New York, New York) on September 29, 1977. She voted nine to six in favor of Ali, who won a unanimous fifteen-round decision.

Shain, who studied accounting at New York University (New York, New York) and worked for eight years as a bookkeeper in New Jersey, attended her first fight in 1963. After being licensed, she judged nearly 3,000 amateur fights.

Jessie Field Shambaugh *(see Jessie Field)*

Mary Driscoll Shane

First woman to do play-by-play broadcasts of baseball games (1977).

Born c. 1949.

Shane joined WMAQ radio, an all-news NBC affiliate in Chicago, Illinois, specializing in sports, in 1975. In 1977 she was assigned to do play-by-play broadcasts of Chicago White Sox games.

After graduating from the University of Wisconsin (Madison), where she majored in history and broadcasting and earned a teaching certificate, Shane taught high school history.

In 1972 she was a Milwaukee representative of the Women's Political Caucus at the Democratic National Convention.

Susie M. Sharp

First woman elected chief justice of a state supreme court in a popular election (1975).

Born Reidsville, North Carolina, July 7, 1907.

Sharp was the first woman elected chief justice of the North Carolina Supreme Court, an office she assumed on January 2, 1975. She was also the first woman supreme court judge in North Carolina (appointed by Governor Kerr Scott in 1949) and the first appointed to the state's supreme court as an associate justice (1972).

Sharp graduated from the University of North Carolina Law School (Chapel Hill) in 1926—the only woman in her class. She practiced law in Reidsville from 1929 to 1949 and was the first woman city attorney in North Carolina.

She upheld the state's right to use funds for busing schoolchildren in urban areas. She ruled against reinstating a mandatory state death penalty and the use of state bonds for private investment.

Anna Shaw

First woman to be ordained as minister in the Methodist Protestant church (1880).

Born Newcastle-on-Tyne, England, February 14, 1847; died Moylan, Pennsylvania, July 2, 1919.

Shaw, who had immigrated to New Bedford, Massachusetts, in 1851, delivered her first sermon in 1870, received a license to preach in 1871, and was ordained in the Methodist Protestant church in 1880.

She began teaching when she was only fifteen. After the Civil War, having decided to become a preacher, she studied at Albion College (Albion,

Michigan), a Methodist coeducational institution. Following her studies there, she graduated from the Boston University Divinity School (Boston, Massachusetts) in 1878, the only woman in her class.

Directly after her graduation Shaw became the pastor at a Methodist Episcopal church in East Dennis, Cape Cod, Massachusetts (1878). Since only ordained ministers were allowed to administer sacraments, she applied to the New England Conference of the Methodist Episcopal church to become ordained. Because she was a woman, her request was denied. Upon appealing to the General Conference to override the New England Conference's decision, she was told her license to preach was revoked. The Methodist Protestant church later agreed to ordain her. Thus, she became the first woman ordained in that denomination.

In 1883, while still in the ministry, she enrolled at Boston University Medical School, graduating with an M.D. degree in 1886.

She then became heavily involved in the woman's suffrage and temperance movements, lecturing and serving as a national officer. From 1892 to 1904, most of which time Susan B. Anthony (see entry) was president of the National American Woman Suffrage Association, she was vice president. Shaw served as president of the association from 1904 to 1915.

Anna Shaw (left) with Carrie Chapman Catt

The suffrage amendment (see Nineteenth Amendment) was passed by the House of Representatives on January 10, 1918, and by the Senate on June 4, 1919, a month before Shaw died.

Jean Shiley

First U.S. woman to win the Olympic high jump (1932).

Born Harrisburg, Pennsylvania, November 20, 1911.

Shiley's Olympic win set a world record: she jumped five feet, five and three-quarter inches. She won a jump-off with Babe Didrikson Zaharias (see entry) who also leaped five feet, five and three-quarter inches. Zaharias' jumping style caused her head to clear the bar before her body, which was called "diving" and ruled illegal. However, she did receive the bronze medal and a share of the world record. (Shortly afterwards, her jumping style was ruled legal.)

Shiley placed fourth at the 1928 Olympics with a four-foot, eleven and one-half-inch jump. From 1929 to 1932 she was the American Athletic Union (AAU) high-jump champion.

Ruth Shipley

First woman to head a major section of the U.S. Department of State (1928).

Born Montgomery County, Maryland, 1885; died Washington, D.C., 1966.

Shipley became chief of the Passport Division of the U.S. Department of State in 1928. She had worked her way up to that position after first being a clerk in the Records Division of the State Department—a job she took in 1914 when she was forced to support her child and invalid husband. She then became assistant chief of the Office of Coordination and Review.

In 1939, at the start of World War II, all passports were invalidated for security reasons. Shipley directed the replacement procedure on a worldwide scale.

Shipley helped draft the McCarran Internal Security Act of 1950, which gave the secretary of state the authority to deny passports to suspected Communists. While serving as chief of the Passport Division, she was criticized for espousing antiliberal politics and accused of denying passports arbitrarily.

Muriel Siebert

First woman to own a seat on the New York Stock Exchange (1967); founding member of the National Women's Forum (1987).

Born Cleveland, Ohio, c. 1932.

Named to the *Working Woman* magazine Hall of Fame as "one who has made a difference," Siebert earned a reputation as a top airlines securities analyst before she founded her own firm and bought a seat on the New York Stock Exchange for a reported $445,000. Her company, Muriel Siebert and Company, works exclusively for corporate and institutional clients.

Siebert was appointed New York State banking commissioner in 1974 by Governor Hugh Carey. She was also the first woman to be a trustee of the Manhattan Savings Bank (1975–77). From 1981 to 1984 Siebert served on the Advisory Committee of the Financial Accounting Standards Board, and in 1982 was a candidate for the U.S. Senate. A director of the New York Council of the Boy Scouts of America, Siebert became in 1986 the first woman to chair the Boy Scouts' General Campaign.

Siebert helped found the National Women's Forum in 1987. The organization is now part of the International Women's Forum (founded in 1980), which is composed of nineteen domestic and ten international women's networks of women of influence and achievement. Their purpose is to share ideas, experiences, and resources and thereby enhance their effectiveness.

Honors awarded to Siebert include the Women's Equity Action League Award (1978), the first national Emily Warren Roebling Award, Women's Hall of Fame (1984), and the Women on the Move Award of the Anti-Defamation League (1990).

She attended Western Reserve

University (Cleveland, Ohio) from 1949 to 1952, and has received honorary doctorate degrees from numerous colleges and universities, including St. John's University (Queens, New York), St. Bonaventure University (St. Bonaventure, New York), and Adelphi University (Garden City, New York).

Gayle Sierens

First woman to do play-by-play coverage of National Football League games (1987).

Born 1954.

The first game Sierens covered was for NBC; it was between the Kansas City Chiefs and the Seattle Seahawks on December 27, 1987.

For nine years prior to the National League coverage, she had been news anchor and sportscaster for WXFL, Tampa, Florida, covering such events as the North American Soccer League games and an equestrian meet.

Sigma Delta Chi

First women journalists admitted into Sigma Delta Chi (1969).

Sigma Delta Chi, a national honorary society dedicated to promoting excellence in journalism, voted to accept women into its membership for the first time in November, 1969—thereby breaking its sixty-year men-only tradition. The resolution to admit women had been introduced every year starting in 1964; when it was passed in 1969, only 8 of 160 delegates voted against it. In the first week after the resolution passed, sixteen women were initiated into the society, and on November 21—on a vote by the University of Georgia's chapter—Sigma Delta Chi initiated its first black woman member: Charlayne Hunter, reporter for *The New York Times*.

Mary Michael Simpson

First ordained woman to preach in Westminster Abbey (1978); first U.S. Episcopal nun to be ordained as a priest (1977); first woman to become a canon in the American Episcopal church (1977).

Born Texas City, Texas, 1926.

At the time Simpson, a deacon, was ordained (1977), she became one of approximately 100 Episcopal priests in the United States. She was named canon at the Cathedral of St. John the Divine, New York, New York, a position she held from 1977 to 1987. (A canon in the Episcopal church is a member of the clergy and the cathedral staff, performing special services and assisting the dean.) Although not the first woman to speak at Westminster Abbey, she was the first ordained woman to preach at this British shrine, where all but two of England's monarchs have been crowned since 1065. The sermon, given to an audience of 700, was at the invitation of one of the four canons of the abbey. It was part of a tour to help British champions of sexual equality promote the ordination of women by the Anglican church.

Before her ordination, Simpson attended an Episcopalian training school for deaconesses. She became a member of the Order of St. Helena and was the academic head of Margaret Hall, a girl's school in Kentucky. She also spent several years in Liberia as a missionary.

Caroline Smith

First woman to win the Olympic platform diving event (1924).

Born Illinois, date unknown.

Smith, from Cairo, Illinois, won the platform diving event the first time it was ever held at the Olympics. She won by a half point over Elizabeth Becker (also from the United States) who that year won the springboard diving gold medal.

Emma Hale Smith

First scribe for Joseph Smith, the prophet of Mormonism (c. 1829).

Born Harmony, Pennsylvania, July 10, 1804; died Nauvoo, Illinois, April 30, 1879.

Smith was married to the prophet, Joseph Smith, and although she was his scribe, he would not allow her to look at the "reformed Egyptian" characters in which the golden plates were written; she had to feel them through a cloth.

In addition to her role as scribe, she was president of the Female Relief Society, the leading women's organization of the Mormon church (1842).

The Smiths settled in Nauvoo, Illinois, in 1843, where the prophet secretly began to practice polygamy, which he proclaimed to be a law of God. He was murdered the following year by an anti-Mormon mob. Thereafter, Emma Smith remained in Nauvoo instead of joining the Mormon exodus to the Great Salt Lake Valley.

Smith married a non-Mormon but remained a Mormon by religion and raised her four sons, by Joseph Smith, as Mormons. One of her sons, Joseph III, organized the antipolygamous Mormon sect, the Reorganized Church of the Latter-Day Saints (1860).

Erminnie A. Platt Smith

First woman to engage in field ethnography (1880); first to be an officer for the American Association for the Advancement of Science (AAAS) (1885).

Born Marcellus, New York, April 26, 1836; died June 9, 1886.

Smith began her studies of the Iroquois at the Tuscarora reservation near Lewiston, New York, in 1880. Three years later she recorded the legends of these Native Americans in *Myths of the Iroquois*. She also compiled an Iroquois dictionary.

The same year that she became the first woman to be elected a fellow of the New York Academy of Sciences (1885), Smith was named secretary of the anthropology section of the AAAS, the first woman officer of the association. In 1879 she had read a monograph on jade before the group.

Smith, who graduated from Troy Female Seminary (Troy, New York) in 1853, conducted studies of crystallography and mineralogy in Germany. She was a member of the London Scientific Society.

Hazel Brannon Smith

First woman to win the Pulitzer Prize for editorial writing (1964).

Born Gadsden, Alabama, c. 1914.

Smith won the 1964 Pulitzer Prize for her editorial writing in the *Lexington Advertiser* (Lexington, Mississippi). A citation that commended her for "steadfast adherence to her editorial duty in the face of great pressure and opposition" and a cash award of $1,000 accompanied the prize. That year she also received an award for her editorials from the National Council of Women of the U.S., an organization that has withstood various kinds of harassment, including racial attacks and bombings.

Smith graduated from the University of Alabama (Tuscaloosa) in 1935 with a major in journalism. She then borrowed some money and in 1936 bought the *Durant News* (Durant, Mississippi), a weekly paper. In 1943 she bought the *Lexington Advertiser*, a larger weekly, and later two additional weeklies.

Smith used the *Lexington Advertiser* as a vehicle to launch her editorial attacks against the corrupt local politicians and racketeers in Holmes County, Mississippi. In 1946, partly as a result of her editorials, a grand jury voted sixty-four indictments against the county offenders.

In 1954 Smith was convicted in a libel suit that awarded a local white sheriff $10,000 because she had rebuked him editorially for shooting a black person in the back. Upon appeal to the Mississippi Supreme Court in 1955, her conviction was overruled on the grounds that her editorial comments were "substantially true." As a result of her writings, her husband, Walter Dyer Smith, was fired as administrator of the Holmes County Hospital in 1956, although the entire medical staff had passed a resolution to retain him.

In 1958 the *Lexington Advertiser* and the *Durant News* were boycotted by white citizens who opposed Smith's racial views. They had been spurred to action by the White Citizens Council, which went on to establish a rival newspaper.

Smith sought nomination for the Mississippi State Senate in 1967, but was defeated.

Among the many awards Smith has received are the Elijah Lovejoy Award "for demonstrating the ability to perform under great stress"; the Golden Quill Editorial Award for her editorial that protested the arrest of a bomb victim; and an award from the International Conference of Weekly Newspaper Editors (1963).

In 1982 the *Lexington Advertiser* folded and Smith went into debt. Four years later, when she was seventy-two, she was both sick and bankrupt, An ad hoc committee of Lexington citizens—black and white—formed to aid her.

Margaret Chase Smith

Only woman to be elected and serve in both houses of Congress (1940–73); first to be elected to the Senate without completing another senator's term (1948) (see also Mary Hopkins Norton).

Born Skowhegan, Maine, December 14, 1897.

After a special election held in June, 1940, Smith completed the unexpired term of her late husband,

Clyde H. Smith, in the House of Representatives. At the next regular election in September, 1940, Smith was voted to a full term in the House, and held her seat for three more terms after that.

In 1948 Smith was elected to the Senate after defeating her Democratic opponent, Adrian Scolten, on September 18. She was reelected to the Senate in 1954, 1960, and 1966, each time by a large majority. The only other woman ever before elected to a full term in the Senate was Hattie Caraway (see entry), but she had first obtained the seat in 1931 to complete the unexpired term of her late husband.

Having a special interest in the status of women in the armed forces, Smith was instrumental in getting the Women's Armed Services Integration Act passed in 1948. One of the stipulations of the act was that women were to receive equal pay, privileges, and rank.

At the Republican National Convention in 1964 she was placed in nomination for the presidency. Representative William V. Hathaway defeated Smith in the 1972 Senate election.

Sophia Smith

First woman to found and endow a women's college (1875).

Born Hatfield, Massachusetts, August 27, 1796; died Hatfield, Massachusetts, June 12, 1870.

Smith, an heiress and philanthropist, helped make plans for a women's college, which she endowed through her will. The college, named after Smith and located in Northampton, Massachusetts (as Smith had specified) was chartered in 1871 and opened in 1875, five years after her death.

Her will, drawn up by two Amherst College professors and Smith's pastor, declared that one result of educating women is that "as teachers, as writers, as mothers, as members of society, their power for good will be incalculably enlarged."

Smith became deaf at forty and she originally planned to bequeath money to found an institution for deaf mutes. However, the Clarke School for the Deaf (see also Harriet Rogers) was founded in 1868, so Smith decided to endow a college for women instead. She outlived six other siblings in her prosperous family, becoming the sole heir to the accumulated fortune.

Smith College was the first women's college to insist on the same standards for entrance as the best men's colleges.

Jill K. Conway became the first woman president of Smith in 1975, the year of the college's 100th anniversary.

Soccer World Championship, Women's

First team to win the Women's World Soccer Championship (1991).

On November 30, 1991, in Guangzhov, China, the U.S. team won the championship by a 2–1 victory over the Norwegian team. Coached by Anson Dorrance (male), the U.S. women had won six matches without a defeat, outscoring opponents 25–5. In the championship match, watched by 65,000 spectators, both U.S. goals were scored by Michelle Akers-Stahl—who chalked up ten goals in the tournament. Carin Jennings of the United States was named the tournament's most valuable player.

Although women's soccer is just beginning its third decade, sixty-five nations now field a women's soccer team.

Hannah Greenebaum Solomon

Organizer of the first assembly of Jewish women in the United States (1893).

Born Chicago, Illinois, January 14, 1858; died Chicago, Illinois, December 7, 1942.

In 1890 the producers of the 1892 World Columbian Exposition asked Solomon to organize a national Jewish Women's Congress in the United States to participate in the exposition's planned Parliament of Religions. Solomon assembled a group of women for this purpose; at their first meeting, they resolved to create the National Council of Jewish Women as a permanent organization.

A member of many Jewish social and cultural clubs, and one of the first Jewish members of the Chicago Woman's Club, Solomon became the first president of the council, serving until 1905, when she was named honorary president for life.

In addition to her involvement in various women's organizations, she gave legal advice to immigrants and worked to improve the lives of underprivileged young women.

Among her writings is *Fabric of My Life,* an autobiography.

Gale Sondergaard

First woman to receive the Academy Award for best supporting actress (1937).

Born Litchfield, Minnesota, February 15, 1899; died Woodland Hills, California, 1985.

Born Edith Holm Sondergaard, she won the Academy Award for best supporting actress in 1937, the first time that particular award was ever presented. She received the award for her role in *Anthony Adverse,* her first film. In 1946 she was nominated as best supporting actress for her role as Lady Thiang in *Anna and the King of Siam*.

A graduate of the Minneapolis School of Dramatic Arts (Minneapolis, Minnesota) (1921), Sondergaard performed on the stage before beginning her movie career. She made her New York City debut in *What's Your Wife Doing?* (1923) and performed with the Theater Guild as Sarah Undershaft in *Major Barbara* (1928) and as the lead, Nina Leeds, in *Strange Interlude* (1928). By the early 1940s Sondergaard had established her reputation as a villain, after playing that role in such movies as *The Little Princess* (1939) with Shirley Temple, and *The Letter* (1940) with Bette Davis. She also played in *Sherlock Holmes and the Spider Woman* (1944) and its sequel, *The Spider Woman Strikes Back* (1946).

Sondergaard was one of many members of the Hollywood community summoned before the House Committee on Un-American Activities in the post-World War II period. Refusing to answer the committee's questions, she took the Fifth Amendment and was subsequently blacklisted. Her second husband, director Herbert Biberman, was both blacklisted and jailed.

After being blacklisted, she toured in a one-woman show called *Woman* (1955–58), which also ran off-Broadway, and played in a production of *The Visit* in Minneapolis in 1967. She finally returned to Hollywood, playing in the films *Slaves* (1969), written by Biberman, and *The Return of a Man Called Horse* (1976).

Sondergaard's last performance on the New York stage was in *Goodbye Fidel* in 1980.

Sorosis

First women's professional club (1868)

The first women's professional club, conceived by journalists and other career women, was established in New York City in 1868.

The creed of Sorosis stated that the club was "an order which shall render the female sex helpful to each other [sic] and actively benevolent in the world."

Jane Croly, the major organizer, was a newspaper columnist who wrote under the pen name "Jennie Jones." The first president was Alice Carey.

The anecdote regarding the group's origins: Charles Dickens was making his second tour of the United States in 1868. There was a great demand for tickets to the New York Press Club Dinner, at which Dickens was a guest. Women were not allowed to attend. Upset by this treatment, the women got together and formed Sorosis, an organization that would help them support each other and counter similar slights that might occur in the future.

Caroline White Soule

First president of the Woman's Centenary Association (1871).

Born Albany, New York, September 3, 1824; died Glasgow, Scotland, December 6, 1903.

The function of the Woman's Centenary Association, the first national organization of church women in the United States, was to assist disabled preachers and their families, engage in home and foreign missionary work, and help educate women students in ministry. Soule became the first president of the association, serving from 1871 to 1880.

After graduating from the Albany Female Academy (Albany, New York) in 1841, she served for two terms as principal of a school established by Universalists in Clinton, New York. Married to a Universalist minister for nine years, she began a writing career after he died in 1852. In order to support her children, she wrote articles for Universalist magazines, moral tales, and novels. Later in her life, she wrote mostly about the church. She ran and edited a Sunday school paper, the *Guiding Star,* for several years.

Soule became the minister of St. Paul's Universalist Church, Glasgow, Scotland, and was ordained in 1880. She retired in 1892, but remained in Glasgow until her death.

Catherine Spalding

First Mother Superior of the Sisters of Charity of Nazareth (1813).

Born Charles County, Maryland, December 23, 1793; died Nazareth, Kentucky, March 20, 1858.

Spalding and two older women established a sisterhood near Bardstown, Kentucky. She was chosen as mother superior in 1813 and was elected again after her first vows in 1816. This sisterhood's rule became the model for others, including the community headed by Mother Elizabeth Seton (see entry). The sisterhood moved to Nazareth, Kentucky, in 1824 and became the Sisters of Charity of Nazareth.

In 1814 the sisterhood opened Nazareth Academy and in 1818 a convent. Mother Catherine and her society opened several schools: one in Bardstown (1819); a school in Scott County, Kentucky, which was relocated to Lexington, Kentucky (1823) and named St. Catherine's Academy; and the first Catholic school in Louisville, Kentucky, now named Presentation Academy (1831). The order also opened the first Catholic Infirmary in Kentucky, which became St. Joseph's Hospital (1833). Spalding divided her time between various institutions in Louisville and the convent of the Sisters of Nazareth.

Eliza Spalding

One of the first two U.S. women to cross the Continental Divide (1836).

Born Berlin, Connecticut, 1807; died Brownsville, Oregon, 1851.

Intending to establish missions among the northwestern tribes of Native Americans, Spalding and her husband, Henry, along with Dr. Marcus Whitman and his wife, Narcissa, set out from Liberty, Missouri, for the Oregon territory with an American Fur Company caravan. On July 4, 1836, they crossed the Continental Divide at South Pass, Wyoming.

Spalding and her husband established a mission among the Nez Percé near Lewiston, Idaho. Spalding learned the native language and taught in the mission school. As the number of white settlers grew, the Native Americans became more hostile. In 1847 the Whitmans and a number of other missionaries were killed by a group of Cayuse Indians. Spalding, whose husband was away at the time, was protected by the Nez Percé.

The Spaldings moved to Brownsville, Oregon, where Spalding died a short time later. When the situation became less volatile, Henry Spalding returned to the Nez Percé and led a massive religious revival that resulted in approximately 1,000 converts among the Nez Percé and the Spokane.

Louise Stanley

First woman director of the U.S. Bureau of Home Economics (1923).

Born Nashville, Tennessee, June 8, 1883; died Washington, D.C., July 15, 1954.

Stanley became director of the U.S. Bureau of Home Economics in 1923, a few years after having chaired the Legislative Committee of the American Home Economics Association.

She earned an A.B. degree from Peabody College at the University of Nashville (Nashville, Tennessee) in 1903; a B.Ed. degree from the University of Chicago (Illinois) in 1906;

an A.M. degree from Columbia University (New York, New York) in 1907; and a Ph.D. degree from Yale University (New Haven, Connecticut) in 1911.

Directly after she received her Ph.D., Secretary of Agriculture Henry C. Wallace appointed Stanley chief of the newly established Federal Board of Vocational Education (1911–12). She was instrumental in nutritional research that led to four basic diet plans. She was also responsible for surveys of rural housing and strategies for consumer purchasing. Stanley chaired the home economics department at the University of Missouri (Columbia) from 1917 to 1923, when she became director of the U.S. Bureau of Home Economics.

In 1943 she became assistant director of the newly formed Human Nutrition and Home Economics Bureau, a division of the Agricultural Research Administration. This position as special assistant to the administrator of agricultural research, which she held until 1950, enabled her to develop the home economics program internationally, with a concentration in Latin America. Between 1950 and 1953 Stanley was a consultant for home economics in the office of Foreign Agriculture Relations of the Department of Agriculture.

In 1953 the American Home Economics Association established the Louise Stanley Latin American Scholarship in her honor.

Elizabeth Cady Stanton

Cofounder of the National Woman Suffrage Association (NWSA) (1869); first woman to be a witness at a congressional hearing (1869).

Born Johnstown, New York, November 12, 1815; died New York, New York, October 26, 1902.

Stanton gave congressional testimony before the District Committee of the U.S. Senate to plead with senators not to bar women in the District of Columbia from voting.

In 1848 Stanton and Lucretia Mott (see entry) were driving forces behind the first women's rights convention. Using the Declaration of Independence, they drafted a Declaration of Sentiments, paraphrasing the original document to say, "men and women are created equal." Although Mott objected, Stanton became the first to publicly demand the vote for women when she put forward a resolution in favor of suffrage.

With Susan B. Anthony (see entry), Stanton organized the Women's Loyal National League to fight for the abolition of slavery (1863). They collected over 300,000 signatures in favor of a constitutional amendment to end slavery.

In 1868 Stanton was named coeditor of *The Revolution* (see entry), a weekly woman's suffrage newspaper. The following year, she and Susan B. Anthony founded the National Woman Suffrage Association, and Stanton became president. Their goal was to create "a movement controlled and defined by women."

After graduating from the Troy Female Seminary (Troy, New York) in 1832, Elizabeth Cady married abolitionist Henry Stanton (1840). She insisted that the word "obey" be stricken from the marriage ceremony. She became a lawyer, and in 1854 addressed the New York State Senate—the first woman to do so—in behalf of giving married women greater property rights.

When the U.S. Congress enacted the Fourteenth and Fifteenth Amendments that extended civil rights protection and the right to vote to African-American males, Stanton and Anthony opposed the amendments because women were omitted and did not receive these rights.

In a test of the constitutional right of women to hold elective office, Stanton ran for Congress in 1866 as an Independent. She was defeated, receiving only 24 of the approximately 12,000 votes that were cast.

At Stanton's urging, Senator Aaron A. Sargent of California introduced a woman suffrage amendment to the United States Constitution in 1878. The amendment, following the wording of the Fifteenth Amendment, was repeatedly introduced and defeated until it finally passed in 1920.

Working with Anthony and Matilda Gage, Stanton gathered many of the primary documents and source materials that led to the massive *History of Woman Suffrage,* a four-volume work. One volume per year was published in 1881, 1882, 1886, and 1902.

In 1895 Stanton published *The Woman's Bible*—a commentary on the Bible's disparaging references to women.

Stanton's autobiography, *Eighty Years and More,* a collection of remembrances and reflections, was published in 1898.

Nora Stanton (Barney)

First woman junior member of the American Society of Civil Engineers (ASCE) (1905).

Born Basingstoke, England, September 30, 1883; died Greenwich, Connecticut, January 18, 1971.

Stanton, granddaughter of Elizabeth Cady Stanton (see entry), received a B.C.E. degree from Cornell University (Ithaca, New York) in 1905, becoming the first woman in the United States to receive a degree in civil engineering.

In 1906 Stanton became an assistant to Lee De Forest, inventor of the radio vacuum tube and a pioneer in television. They were married in 1908 and divorced in 1912. She then married Morgan Barney, a marine architect, in 1919.

In 1909 she joined the staff of Radley Steel Construction Company as an assistant engineer and chief drafter. For several years, beginning in 1912, she was an assistant engineer for the New York Public Service Commission.

Stanton became a member of the ASCE in 1905 (see also Elsie Eaves), but she was only accorded junior status. Nearly twelve years later, she filed for associate membership but was refused. She then filed suit for reinstatement as a junior member, but the suit failed.

From 1909 to 1917 Stanton was active in the New York State woman's suffrage movement.

A person of many abilities and talents, Stanton was an architect, engineering inspector for the Public Works Administration in Connecticut and Rhode Island, and a structural-steel designer. From 1944 to her death in 1971, she was primarily a real estate developer. She was also actively involved in world peace and equal rights for women. She wrote *World Peace Through a Peoples Parliament* in 1944.

Status of Women

First Presidential Commission on the Status of Women (1961).

The Presidential Commission on the Status of Women was the first of its kind. It was proposed by Esther Peterson (see entry), whom President John F. Kennedy had appointed director of the Women's Bureau in the Labor Department, in 1961. Eleanor Roosevelt (see entry) chaired the commission and Peterson served as executive vice chair.

The commission's actions led to two announcements made by President Kennedy in 1962: that women were to be on an equal basis with men for Civil Service promotion, and that all executive department promotions were to be based on merit.

In June, 1963, President Kennedy signed the Equal Pay Act, sponsored by Representative Edith Green of Oregon, one of the most influential members of Congress at the time. In November, 1963, shortly before his assassination, President Kennedy created the Interdepartmental Committee on the Status of Women.

Sally Stearns

First woman coxswain of a men's college varsity crew (1936).

Born c. 1915.

Stearns served as coxswain for the varsity scull team of all-male Rollins College (Winter Park, Florida) when they defeated Manhattan College (Bronx, New York) in a match on the Harlem River in New York City on May 31, 1936. In Stearns's other race that year, the Rollins crew lost to Marietta College (Marietta, Ohio).

Ann Winterbotham Stephens

First woman to become a successful serial writer (1839).

Born Humphreysville (now Seymour), Connecticut, March 30, 1810; died Newport, Rhode Island, August 20, 1886.

Stephens was a prolific serial writer who became one of the most widely read novelists before 1900.

In 1831 she moved from Connecticut to Portland, Maine, after marrying Edward Stephens, a merchant and publisher. There she edited the *Portland Magazine* and the *Portland Sketch Book*. Her two books of poetry, *The Tradesman's Boast* and *The Polish Boy*, were published in 1834. Stephens and her husband moved to New York in 1837, at which time she became a writer and editor for popular women's magazines. Among them was *Ladies' Companion*, which achieved a circulation of 17,000 within a few years after she became associated with it. She also edited *Peterson's Magazine* and *Godey's Lady's Book*.

While editing and writing for the *Ladies' Companion*, in 1839 Stephens wrote a three-part serial called "Maleska," which later became the first Beadle Dime Novel (1860): *Maleska: the Indian Wife of The White Hunter*. A work with a tragic plot, "Maleska" concerns a powerful Indian mother who tries to fit in with her husband's white family. After his death, she finds his parents, who accept their grandson, but reject her. After twists and turns in a suspenseful plot, the serial novel ends with the tragic suicidal deaths of both mother and son.

Stephens wrote thirty books, many of them serials. As was the case with many of her serial narratives, "Maleska" was published as a novel after the last magazine installment of the serial. Counting its various reprints, the work probably sold close to 500,000 copies here and abroad.

Elizabeth Stern

First person to publish a report linking a specific virus to a specific cancer (1963); one of the first specialists in cytopathology.

Born Cobalt, Ontario, Canada, 1915; died Los Angeles, California, August 9, 1980.

Working with Herbert Traut, Stern conducted studies in cytopathology, the study of diseased cells. Her research, conducted in San Francisco and Los Angeles, led her to the study of the virus, herpes simplex, and in 1963 she published the first case report linking that specific virus to cervical cancer.

Stern was also responsible for another first: the discovery that prolonged use of birth control pills may cause cervical cancer. After conducting a study of 11,000 women in the Los Angeles area, she discovered a link between birth control pills and cervical dysplasia, a precursor of cervical cancer. In 1973 she wrote an article for *Science,* reporting her findings.

In 1968 the University of California (Los Angeles) Medical Center Auxiliary awarded Stern its Woman of Science Award. By 1979 she had made a substantial contribution to studies reporting the specific progression of cells from normal to advanced cervical cancer. These studies enabled medical laboratories to develop improved techniques of screening for cervical cancer.

A graduate of the University of Toronto (Toronto, Ontario), where she earned an M.D. degree, Stern conducted studies in the field of cervical cancer for more than thirty years.

Florine Stettheimer

First noted professional artist to work in the legitimate theater (1934).

Born Rochester, New York, August 19, 1871; died New York, New York, May 11, 1944.

Stettheimer designed the sets and costumes for the Virgil Thomson–Gertrude Stein opera, *Four Saints in Three Acts,* performed in 1934. Her work gained the praise of critics and audiences.

Knoedler's Gallery in New York City produced a one-woman exhibit for her in 1916. Although the show was not a success, she continued to pursue a painting career, teaching herself for the most part. Reluctant to exhibit her work, she allowed only a few pieces to be shown, and those were in group shows at museums.

In the 1920s Stettheimer and her two sisters, Carrie and Ettie, established an art-literary salon in New York City. Members of the group included Sherwood Anderson, Marcel Duchamp, Gaston Lachaise, H. L. Mencken, Elie Nadelman, Georgia O'Keeffe, and Leo Stein.

By the time she died, Stettheimer had created more than 100 paintings. The Museum of Modern Art (New York City), which owns her work, *Family Portrait No. 2*, held a memorial show in her honor in 1946.

Alzina Parsons Stevens

Probably the first person to be a probation officer (1899); first president of the Working Woman's Union Number 1 (1877).

Born Parsonsfield, Maine, May 27, 1849; died Chicago, Illinois, June 3, 1900.

Stevens, who learned the printing trade when she was only eighteen, joined a typographical union in 1872. In 1877 she organized and was the first president of the Working Woman's Union Number 1, and in 1890 she was elected district master workman of District Assembly 72 (Toledo, Ohio) of the Knights of Labor.

In the early 1890s Stevens was a resident of Hull House (see also Jane Addams), where she worked for economic and industrial reform. In 1893 she was appointed an assistant factory inspector in Illinois. She was a leader in lobbying that resulted in an improved child labor law (1897), and in 1899 she became the first proba-

tion officer at Cook County Juvenile Court, Chicago. Her duties included counseling and helping people on probation get jobs.

Nettie Stevens

First woman to demonstrate that sex is determined by a particular chromosome (c. 1903).

Born Cavendish, Vermont, July 7, 1861; died Baltimore, Maryland, May 4, 1912.

Stevens, a biologist and geneticist, shared the discovery with Edmund Beecher Wilson, also a biologist, although they were working independently of each other. In 1903 they discovered that an egg fertilized by an X-carrying sperm produced a female embryo, whereas a Y-carrying sperm produced a male.

After attending Normal School (Westfield, Massachusetts), she earned a B.A. degree (1899) and an M.A. degree (1900) both from Stanford University (Palo Alto, California). Immediately afterwards, she entered Bryn Mawr College (Bryn Mawr, Pennsylvania), earning a Ph.D. degree in biology in 1903. Stevens remained at Bryn Mawr until she died, teaching and carrying out research in major fields of biology, finally specializing in experimental morphology.

Matilda Evans Stevenson

Founder and first president of the Women's Anthropological Society of America (WAS) (1885).

Born St. Augustine, Texas, May 12, 1849; died Oxon Hill, Maryland, June 24, 1915.

Stevenson married James Stevenson in 1872. He became the executive officer of the U.S. Geological Survey, a division of the newly founded Bureau of Ethnology, and in 1879 he was assigned to report on archeological remains in the western territories. Matilda Stevenson accompanied him on that trip, and decided to make ethnology her vocation.

Her paper on Zuñi Indians and their children was highly commended, and she became known as the first U.S. ethnologist to consider children worthy of note.

In 1885 Stevenson helped found and became the first president of the Women's Anthropological Society of America, a society dedicated to supporting the careers of professional women anthropologists through exchange of information, data, news of job opportunities, and pressure on the (until then) all-male anthropological establishment to grant women full and equal status in the profession.

In 1888, the year her husband died, Stevenson was appointed to the staff of the Bureau of American Ethnology. By 1899 women were receiving unqualified acceptance into the field of anthropology, and the Women's Anthropological Society of America was absorbed into the previously all-male Anthropological Society of Washington.

Stevenson's most outstanding account of her work, *The Zuñi Indians: Their Mythology, Esoteric Fraternities, and Ceremonies,* was incorporated in the *Twenty-third Annual Report of the Bureau of American Ethnology* (1901–02), which was published in 1904.

Sarah Stevenson

First woman member of the American Medical Association (AMA) (1876).

Born Buffalo Grove (now Polo), Illinois, February 2, 1841; died Chicago, Illinois, August 14, 1909.

The Illinois State Medical Society chose Stevenson as its delegate to the American Medical Association meeting in Philadelphia (1876), at which time she was admitted to the convention. She was also the first woman appointed to the staff of the Cook County Hospital (Chicago, Illinois) in 1881 and the first to be on the Illinois Board of Health (1893).

Stevenson graduated from the State Normal University (Normal, Illinois) in 1863. After graduating, she taught in Illinois for four years. She then studied at Woman's Hospital Medical College (Chicago, Illinois), earning an M.D. degree in 1874. Prior to receiving her M.D., she spent a year studying with Thomas Huxley at the South Kensington Science School (London, England).

In 1875 Stevenson set up a medical practice in Chicago, and from 1875 until 1880, she was a professor of physiology and histology at her alma mater, which after 1879 was called Woman's Medical College. From 1880 to 1894 she was a professor of obstetrics.

Stevenson was also one of the founders of the Illinois Training School for Nurses (1880). That same year, her popular work, *The Physiology of Woman,* was published.

Stewardesses, First *(see Ellen Church)*

Eliza Daniel Stewart

Founded the first Woman's Temperance League, a forerunner of the Woman's Christian Temperance Union (WCTU) (1873).

Born Piketon, Ohio, April 25, 1816; died Hicksville, Ohio, August 6, 1908.

In 1858 Stewart helped organize a lodge of the temperance order of Good Templars in Athens, Ohio, and lectured on behalf of temperance. The Good Templars were a quasi-religious group inspired by the tales of the medieval Knights Templars, or holy warriors. The Good Templars were going forth to crusade on behalf of the Christian life and to do battle against the liquor dragon. She then branched out and founded the first woman's temperance league in Osborn, Ohio, in 1873. In 1874 she directed a county temperance union, which was probably the first organization of its kind in the United States. That same year, at a convention in Cleveland that organized the National WCTU, she was elected chairman of the resolutions committee.

Stewart, who had attended seminaries and taught in Ohio, made the opening speech at the World's WCTU Convention in London, England, in 1895.

Katherine Stinson (Otero)

First woman pilot to skywrite (1915); first to fly at night (1915); first to tour China and Japan (1917).

Marjorie (left) and Katherine Stinson just after flight in Katherine's biplane, 1913

Born Jackson, Mississippi, 1891; died Santa Fe, New Mexico, July 8, 1977.

Known throughout her flying career as Katherine Stinson, she became in 1912 the fourth woman worldwide to qualify for a pilot's license—then issued by the Fédération Aéronautique Internationale. (See also Harriet Quimby.) The next year she and her mother, Emma Beavers Stinson, incorporated the Stinson Aircraft Company, and in 1915 they opened Stinson Field, which is now part of the San Antonio, Texas Municipal Airport.

In 1915, with torches on her plane's wingtips, she wrote "CAL" in the sky in celebration of California. In 1917 she became the first woman pilot to tour China and Japan; a crowd of 25,000 watched her first flight exhibition in Tokyo. The tour was ended prematurely, however, by World War I.

For the next few years, billed as the "flying schoolgirl," Stinson barnstormed, appeared in air shows, and performed stunts. She was barred from serving in the air service during World War I, and instead joined a Red Cross ambulance service. In 1918 she piloted an airmail flight from Chicago to New York for the U.S. government. In order be able to make the flight, she was sworn in as a post office clerk.

In 1928 she married Miguel A. Otero, Jr., a World War I aviator, and because of a love pact they made never to be separated, they vowed never to fly a plane again. Living in New Mexico, she won an architectural award for her design for her own home.

Marjorie Stinson

First woman to fly as a passenger over the Panama Canal (1928).

Born c. 1895; died Washington, D.C., April 15, 1975.

A member of one of America's outstanding aeronautical families, she was the daughter of Emma Beavers Stinson and the sister of Katherine Stinson (see entry). Her brothers were Eddie Stinson, an airplane designer, and Jack Stinson, a pilot.

Marjorie Stinson got her pilot's license in 1913, just after her sister Katherine. She worked as chief flying instructor in her family's flying school (1915). By the time she was twenty she had trained over 100 student pilots.

When the U.S. Army refused to let Marjorie and Katherine join as pilots, and the ban on civilian flying shut down the family flying school, Marjorie went to work in the offices of the Aeronautical Division of the U.S. Navy in Washington, D.C.

In 1928 she flew as a passenger over the Panama Canal in a U.S. Army plane with a male pilot. She had to sign a form releasing the United States from any damages in case of accident.

Grace Zaring Stone

First woman to write a novel that was made into the first movie to be shown at Radio City Music Hall (New York, New York) (1933).

Born New York, New York, January 9, 1896; died Mystic, Connecticut, September 29, 1991.

The first movie to be shown at Radio City Music Hall in New York City was *The Bitter Tea of General Yen* in 1933. The film, based upon Stone's novel by the same name, starred Barbara Stanwyck and Nils Asther, and was directed by Frank Capra. The plot of the novel and film centered around a New England woman who traveled to China with the hope of marrying a missionary, but became the prisoner of a Chinese warlord with whom she fell in love.

Among the other novels Stone wrote was a bestseller, *Escape*, an anti-Nazi thriller that she wrote in 1939 under her pen name, Ethel Vance. Stone said she used the pen name to protect her daughter, who was still living in occupied Europe. This novel was also made into a movie, which starred Norma Shearer, Robert Taylor, and Conrad Veidt.

Stone, the great-great-granddaughter of Robert Owen, the British socialist, wrote several other books under her pen name, including *Reprisal* (1942) and *Winter Meeting* (1946). In 1948 *Winter Meeting* was made into a film starring Bette Davis.

A prolific author, she also wrote *The Heaven and Earth of Doña Elena* (1929); *The Almond Tree* (1931); *The Cold Journey* (1934); *The Secret Thread* (1949); *The Grotto* (1951) and *Althea* (1962).

Stone, who was educated at Catholic schools and the Isadora Duncan School of Dancing in Paris, France, was named a fellow of the Royal Society of Literature (Great Britain), and was elected to the council of the Authors League of America in 1956.

Lucy Stone

First woman arrested for an act of civil disobedience (1858); first to keep birth name and lend it to a political movement (1855).

Born West Brookfield, Massachusetts, August 13, 1818; died Boston, Massachusetts, October 18, 1893.

One of the major political figures of her time, Stone was a strong crusader for the rights of women. When she married Henry Blackwell in 1855, she insisted on keeping her birth name. She called herself Mrs. Stone. Thus, the phrase "Lucy Stoner" was adopted to signify a woman who kept her own name after marriage. (See also Ruth Hale.) During their May wedding ceremony, she and Blackwell, brother of Elizabeth Blackwell (see entry), also read a protest against the marriage laws.

Woman suffrage and abolition were two of her main concerns. In 1859 she led the call for the first national woman's rights convention, which was held in Worcester, Massachusetts, with Paulina Wright Davis chairing. In 1858, as a protest against the denial of women's right

to vote, she refused to pay property taxes in Orange, New Jersey. As a consequence, she was arrested and her household goods were sold to raise the tax money.

In 1847 Stone was appointed as lecturer by the American Anti-Slavery Society. In 1863 she gave her support to the Women's Loyal National League, an organization newly established by Susan B. Anthony (see entry) and Elizabeth Cady Stanton (see entry) to muster support for the abolition of slavery. In 1866 she helped organize—then served on the executive committee of—the American Equal Rights Association, whose goal was to secure the right to vote for both blacks and women.

This goal was the major cause of a split between Stone and Anthony/Stanton: they disagreed about the stand they should take on the Fifteenth Amendment. The amendment—designed to give the vote to blacks—said that the right to vote could not be refused a person on the grounds of race, color, or previous condition of servitude. All three women wanted the scope of the amendment broadened to include guaranteeing the vote to women; Stone, however, wanted to support the amendment whether it included women or not. Anthony and Stanton wanted to defeat the amendment if women were not included. Thus, in May, 1869, Anthony and Stanton established the National Woman Suffrage Association, while Stone and Julia Ward Howe, president of the New England Woman Suffrage Association, formed the American Woman Suffrage Association in November of the same year.

In 1870 Stone established and helped finance the *Woman's Journal,* the AWSA's weekly newspaper. Published for nearly fifty years without interruption, it became known as "the voice of the woman's movement."

Nadine Strossen

First woman to be president of the American Civil Liberties Union (ACLU) (1991).

Born Jersey City, New Jersey, August 18, 1950.

A graduate of Harvard University and the Harvard University Law School (Cambridge, Massachusetts), Strossen was general counsel to the ACLU from 1986 to 1991. In 1991 she was teaching constitutional law at New York University Law School (New York, New York) and was a member of the board of directors of the Human Rights Watch and the National Coalition Against Censorship.

Suffragist Newsstand

The first suffragist newsstand was opened in front of the headquarters of the Equality League of Self-Supporting Women, on East 22nd St in New York City in 1910. The stand sold suffragist pamphlets and magazines, as well as suffragist ribbons, buttons, postcards, and copies of addresses made by Susan B. Anthony (see entry). Elizabeth Dock was in charge of the newsstand, and on opening day, she was assisted by Mrs. Lee De Forest, wife of the radio and television trailblazer, and Leonora O'Reilly. The stand was open from 11:00 A.M. to 1:00 P.M. daily.

Kathryn D. Sullivan

One of the first women to be selected for the U.S. space shuttle program (1978) (see also National Aeronautics and Space Administration); first U.S. woman to perform an extra-vehicular activity in space (1984).

Born Paterson, New Jersey, October 3, 1951.

The first women astronauts, a group of six, were selected for a training program in scientific, engineering, and medical duties. None, however, was to be trained in piloting the space shuttle.

Just prior to her selection by NASA, Dr. Sullivan was completing her doctorate in geology at Dalhousie University, Halifax, Nova Scotia, Canada, where her work included participation in several oceanographic expeditions under the auspices of the U.S. Geological Survey, Wood's Hole Oceanographic Institute, and the Bedford Institute.

After she became an astronaut in August, 1979, Sullivan's shuttle assignments included software development, lead chase photography of launches and landings, and orbiter and cargo testing. She was a member of the spacesuit monitoring and extra-vehicular activity (EVA) crew, and served as a capsule communicator in mission control for numerous shuttle missions.

Her first space mission was launched from the Kennedy Space Center in Florida on October 5, 1984, and lasted eight days. During this mission, Sullivan and Orbiter Commander Leetsma carried out a successful EVA, demonstrating the feasibility of in-flight satellite refueling.

On Sullivan's second mission, launched on April 24, 1990, the Hubble Space Telescope was deployed. With the completion of that mission, Sullivan had logged 13.3 days in space. As of January, 1992, Sullivan was slated to be aboard flight *STS-45*—scheduled for launch in spring, 1992—as a mission specialist and payload commander.

After graduating from Taft High School, Woodland Hills, California (1969), Sullivan received a B.S. degree in earth sciences from the University of California–Santa Cruz (1973), then spent a year as an exchange student at the University of Bergen, Norway, before going to Dalhousie University for her doctorate.

Dalhousie awarded Sullivan an honorary doctorate in 1985. She also received the NASA Exceptional Service Medal (1988, 1991); National Air and Space Museum Trophy, Smithsonian Institution (1985); NASA Space Flight Medal (1984, 1990); American Institute of Aeronautics and Astronautics Haley Space Flight Award (1991); and the American Aeronautic Society Space Achievement Award (1991).

Mary E. Jenkins Surratt

First woman to be accused as an accomplice in the assassination of a U.S. president (1865).

Born Waterloo, Maryland, c. 1820; died Washington, D.C., July 7, 1865.

President Abraham Lincoln was assassinated on April 14, 1865. His assassin, John Wilkes Booth, was a friend of Surratt's son John, a Confederate courier. Booth and his fellow conspirators, Lewis Payne and George Atzerodt, had met in her boarding house.

Shortly after Lincoln's death, police searched Surratt's boarding-house, and on April 17 she was arrested. Her trial, which convened on May 12, 1865, was held before a nine-member commission. The de-

fendants were Payne, Atzerodt, and three others; Booth had been killed as he tried to flee after the assassination.

At the trial, all defendants were found guilty; Surratt and three others were sentenced to hang, and on July 7, 1865, they were hanged at the Old Penitentiary (later Fort McNair), in the southwestern part of Washington, D.C.

Surratt proclaimed her innocence to the end, and many have come to believe her. Her son had apparently abandoned Booth after learning of the assassination plan, and it seems possible that witnesses against her were coerced by the War Department. Some evidence may have been suppressed, including Booth's diary and the existence of two separate plots: one to assassinate the president and the other to kidnap him.

After the trial, five of the nine

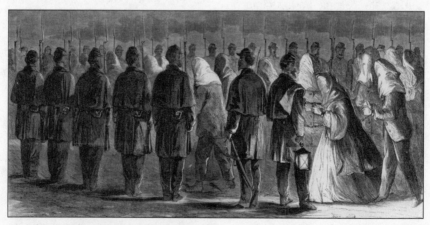

"Mary Surratt with conspirators and assassins . . ."

commissioners recommended that Surratt's sentence be commuted to life imprisonment; these recommendations were apparently suppressed when the findings were presented to President Andrew Johnson.

Carol Sutton

First woman to head the news staff of a major U.S. daily newspaper (1974).

Born St. Louis, Missouri, June 29, 1933; died Louisville, Kentucky, February 19, 1985.

After growing up in St. Louis, Missouri, Sutton graduated from the University of Missouri School of Journalism (Columbia) in 1955. The same year, she was hired by the *Courier-Journal* of Louisville, Kentucky, as a secretary. Within a year she was promoted to reporter, writing about

fires, floods, politics, corruption in city government, and public affairs.

Sutton was named editor of the *Courier-Journal*'s "Women's World" section in 1963. In 1974 she became managing editor of the paper, and shortly thereafter her photograph appeared on the cover of *Time*. In 1976 she was promoted to assistant to the publisher of the jointly operated *Courier-Journal* and *Louisville Times*. From 1979 until her death in 1985, Sutton was senior editor of the two newspapers, which have separate editorial staffs.

In 1975 and 1976 Sutton served on the Pulitzer Prize juries.

May Sutton (Bundy)

First woman to win the women's singles title at the Wimbledon Lawn Tennis Championships (England) (1905).

Born Plymouth, England, September 25, 1887; died Santa Monica, California, October 4, 1975.

The 1904 U.S. women's singles champion, Sutton won the Wimbledon title in 1905 and again in 1907. She had also won the U.S. women's doubles title, with partner Miriam Hall, in 1904.

Sutton won her first southern California tennis championship when she was twelve, and dominated that event until the last year she played in it—when she was forty-one years old.

The year after her second Wimbledon victory, Sutton was crowned queen of the Tournament of Roses (Pasadena, California).

After retiring from competition, Sutton was a tennis instructor until the 1950s. She was inducted into the International Tennis Hall of Fame in 1956.

Mary Swindler

First woman editor in chief of the **American Journal of Archaeology** *(1932).*

Born Bloomington, Indiana, January 3, 1884; died Haverford, Pennsylvania, January 16, 1967.

Having gained recognition for her major work, *Ancient Painting* (1929), Swindler was named editor in chief of the *American Journal of Archaeology* in 1932, a position she held until 1946.

Swindler earned A.B. (1905) and A.M. (1906) degrees from Indiana University (Bloomington), where her major field was Greek. She won a Greek fellowship at Bryn Mawr College (Bryn Mawr, Pennsylvania) in 1906, and in 1912 she earned a Ph.D. degree there.

Deciding to make Bryn Mawr her home base, she remained affiliated with the college for fifty years. She was professor of classical archaeology from 1931 until 1949, at which time she left Bryn Mawr to teach at the University of Pennsylvania (Philadelphia) (1949–50). She taught at the University of Michigan (Ann Arbor) from 1950 to 1953, then returned to Bryn Mawr. She also participated in excavations at Tarsus, Turkey, sponsored by Bryn Mawr (1934–38).

Swindler was one of only three scholars to receive the prize of the American Council of Learned Scholars (1959) and named a fellow of both the Royal Society of Arts, London, and the German Archaeological Institute.

Kathrine Switzer

First woman with a number to finish the Boston Marathon (1967).

Born Amberg, Germany, January 5, 1947.

In 1967 she clandestinely secured an entry in the marathon under the name K. Switzer. When an official discovered that the K stood for Kathrine, he tried to rip the cardboard number from her sweatshirt. She escaped, and went on to finish the race.

Switzer was later manager of

sports promotions (1977–80), and director of media affairs and sports programs (1980–85) for Avon Products, Inc.

Switzer was named Outstanding Female Runner of 1975 by the Road Runners Club of America and Runner of the Decade by the Road Runners Club of America (1976). In 1984 she won a national honorary award from the President's Council on Physical Fitness and Sports.

Margery Ann Tabankin

First woman president of the National Student Association (NSA) (1971).

Born Newark, New Jersey, c. 1948.

Tabankin graduated from the University of Wisconsin (Madison) in 1971, where she studied the politics of urban poverty.

After serving one year as the president of the National Student Association in 1972, she became the executive director of Youth Project, a privately funded charitable organization established to develop leadership among young people in community self-help programs. That year, after meeting with thirty college student leaders, Tabankin called for a nationwide college campus strike to protest the Vietnam War. She was arrested five times for her anti-Vietnam war demonstrations. In 1972, when she was chosen as the president of the NSA, she received an invitation to visit Hanoi.

In 1977 Tabankin was chosen to head Volunteers in Service to America (VISTA). Her responsibilities included running the educational programs of ACTION, the parent organization of VISTA, and overseeing the work of VISTA's 5,000 volunteers working in poverty programs. She resigned from VISTA after the election of President Ronald Reagan.

Irene Barnes Taeuber

First woman president of the Population Association of America (1953).

Born Meadville, Missouri, December 25, 1906; died Hyattsville, Maryland, February 24, 1974.

When the Population Association of America (PAA) was first established (1935), Taeuber launched her career as a demographer by helping the association prepare a bibliography. The following year she joined the staff of the Office of Population Research at Princeton University (Princeton, New Jersey) and became co-editor of *Population Index,* a bibliographical journal. While remaining affiliated with Princeton, she was a visiting professor at Johns Hopkins University (Baltimore, Maryland) from 1961 to 1965. She retired from Princeton in 1973, after being promoted to senior research demographer in 1961.

Taeuber joined the Library of Congress as director of its census library project (1941–44). In 1944 she became head of the social demography section of the American Sociological Association and, in 1961, the first woman vice president of the International Union for the Scientific Study of Population.

She received three degrees in the field of sociology: an A.B. degree from the University of Missouri (Columbia) (1927); an A.M. degree from Northwestern University (Evanston, Illinois) (1928); and a Ph.D degree from the University of Minnesota (Minneapolis) (1931).

During her many years of experience as a demographer, Taeuber wrote some 250 articles and was co-author of more than a dozen books, including *The Changing Population of the U.S.* (1958) and *People of the U.S. in the Twentieth Century* (1971), both written with her husband, Conrad Taeuber. In 1958 she wrote *Population in Japan,* a culmination of twenty years of work, in which she explained that education in birth control was helping Japan solve its population problems.

Mrs. Josiah Taft

First woman to have her vote recorded (1756).

Dates unknown.

Taft, a citizen of Uxbridge, Massachusetts, taking the place of her son, a minor, voted in favor of levying a town tax (1756).

Nellie (Helen) Herron Taft

Only first lady to be buried in Arlington National Cemetery (1943).

Born Cincinnati, Ohio, June 2, 1861; died Washington, D.C., May 22, 1943.

Taft, educated in private schools in Cincinnati, Ohio, was primarily interested in music. After teaching for some time, she established a salon devoted to intellectual pursuits. William H. Taft joined the group, and, after several years of dating, they married in 1886.

After President Taft died in 1930, Nellie Taft remained in Washington and was buried beside her husband in Arlington National Cemetery when she died in 1943.

Tailoresses, United Society of New York

First women's labor organization (1825).

The United Tailoresses Society of New York was founded by Lavinia Waight and Louise Mitchell in 1825. Approximately 600 women members of the organization went on strike for four or five weeks in 1831. The union was dissolved later in the decade.

Marion Talley

First woman to sing in a movie (1926).

Born Nevada, Missouri, December 20, 1907; died Beverly Hills, California, January 3, 1983.

Talley, who studied piano and violin as a child, sang "Caro Nome"

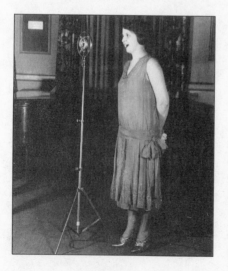

from Verdi's *Rigoletto* in a film of the New York Philharmonic Symphony Orchestra shown at the Warner Theater, New York City, in 1926.

She debuted as a Metropolitan Opera performer when she sang the role of Gilda in *Rigoletto* in 1926. Talley, who sang with the Metropolitan until 1929, was a featured singer in a 1936 movie, *Follow Your Heart*.

Ida Tarbell

First woman to be a muckraking writer (1902).

Born Erie County, Pennsylvania, November 5, 1857; died Bridgeport, Connecticut, January 6, 1944.

The term "muckraker" came from President Theodore Roosevelt; he compared writers such as Tarbell, Lincoln Steffens, and Upton Sinclair—who were concerned with exposing political and commercial corruption—with the "man with a Muck-rake" in John Bunyan's *Pilgrim's Progress*. From 1894 to 1906 Tarbell (known to her enemies as "Miss Tarbarrel") was assistant editor of *McClure's Magazine;* the articles she wrote attacking John D. Rockefeller and the oil monopoly were published in book form as *The History of the Standard Oil Company* (1904). They spurred federal investigations into the company and its practices, which ultimately led to the breaking up of the Standard Oil Company of New Jersey in 1911, under the provisions of the Sherman Antitrust Act of 1902.

In 1906 Tarbell, Steffens, and others purchased *American Magazine;* Tarbell was associate editor until 1915, when she left to go on the lecture circuit.

President Woodrow Wilson made Tarbell a member of his Industrial Conference in 1919; she later served on President Warren Harding's Unemployment Conference. From 1933 to 1938 Tarbell was a member of the National Women's Mobilization Committee for Human Needs.

Tarbell was educated at Allegheny College (Meadville, Pennsylvania), graduating in 1880 as one of only five women students. After two years as a teacher, she was hired by the *Chautauquan* magazine (a home study guide), for which she wrote from 1883 to 1891. She studied in Paris,

France, from 1891 to 1894 and to help meet her expenses there she also wrote articles for *McClure's.* Her articles on Napoleon—published in book form in 1895 as *A Short Life of Napoleon Bonaparte*—were particularly outstanding.

Tarbell's autobiography, *All in the Day's Work,* was published in 1939.

Helen Brooke Taussig

First woman president of the American Heart Association (1965).

Born Cambridge, Massachusetts, May 24, 1898; died Kennett Square, Pennsylvania, May 20, 1986.

A pediatrician for more than thirty years, in the later years of her life Taussig specialized in heart problems and wrote a noted work in that field, *Congenital Malfunctions of the Heart* (1947).

After earning an A.B. degree at the University of California–Berkeley— where she was also a top tennis player—she studied at Harvard Medical School (Cambridge, Massachusetts) with an unofficial status; there she did research on the heart. (When Taussig applied to Harvard to take a two-year course in her chosen field of public health, she was told that she would first have to study medicine for two years. She agreed, but since Harvard Medical School did not formally admit women at that time, she enrolled for a half-course as a special student.) Later she attended Boston University Medical School (Boston, Massachusetts), and ultimately earned an M.D. degree from Johns Hopkins Medical School (Baltimore, Maryland) in 1927. There she became the first woman to attain the rank of full professor (1959).

During the period that she was concentrating on pediatrics, Taussig developed a surgical method for replacing a constricted pulmonary artery that caused cyanosis in what were labeled "blue babies." The first successful surgery using her method was performed in 1945 by Alfred Blalock, M.D., a prominent surgeon whom Taussig had interested in her findings.

Taussig was awarded the Presidential Medal of Freedom (1964) and became the first woman president of the American Heart Association in 1965. Her other first achievements include becoming a master in the American College of Physicians (1972) and an elected member of the National Academy of Sciences (1973).

Tax

First women to pay a poll tax (1695).

In 1695 the province laws of Massachusetts required that self-supporting women, as well as men, must pay a poll tax, but women paid at half the rate of men.

Anna Edson Taylor

First woman to survive going over Niagara Falls alone in a barrel (1901) (see also Sadie Allen).

Dates unknown.

On October 24, 1901, wearing a leather harness, Taylor went over Horseshoe Falls in a four and one-half foot by three foot barrel, which had cushions inside to protect her against injury. Horseshoe Falls, which is 167 feet high, is the Canadian side of Niagara Falls. Taylor went over the falls for a cash reward to put toward a loan that was due on her Texas ranch.

Lucy Hobbs Taylor *(see Lucy Hobbs)*

Nancy Hays Teeters

First woman appointed to the board of governors of the Federal Reserve Bank (1978).

Born Marion, Indiana, July 29, 1930.

Named to the Federal Reserve Board of Governors during the administration of President Jimmy Carter in 1978, Teeters served until 1984, when she left to become vice president and chief economist with IBM.

Teeters was educated at Oberlin College (Oberlin, Ohio), where she earned an A.B. degree in economics in 1952, and at the University of Michigan (Ann Arbor), where she received an M.A. degree in economics in 1954. She worked from 1957 to 1966 as staff economist for the government finance section of the Board of Governors of the Federal Reserve System (Washington, D.C.). After five years as economist for the Bureau of the Budget (1966–70), she was named senior fellow of the Brookings Institute, serving from 1970 to 1973. From 1974 to 1978 Teeters was chief economist for the House of Representatives Committee on the Budget. While at the Brookings Institute, Teeters and three other authors wrote *Setting National Priorities: The 1972 Budget* (1971) and similar works for the 1973 and 1975 budgets.

From 1974 to 1975 Teeters was president of the National Economists Club.

Kateri (Catherine) Tekakwitha

First woman for whom a Roman Catholic mass was celebrated in the vernacular (1676).

Born Auriesville, New York, 1656; died Sault St. Louis, Canada, April 17, 1680.

When Tekakwitha, the daughter of an Algonquin Indian mother and a Mohawk Indian father, was baptized on Easter Sunday, April 18, 1676, in St. Peter's Chapel, Caughnawaga (near what is now Fonda, New York), the rite was celebrated in the vernacular. She was christened Catherine.

After the Mohawk Indians and the French signed a peace treaty, Jesuit missionaries arrived in New York in 1667 and began to build a community. Influenced by the Jesuits, Tekakwitha, whose mother was Christian, decided to join the Roman Catholic church. Her response to the hostility that she experienced from members of her Native American community was to escape and seek refuge at the mission of St. Francis Xavier, Sault

St. Louis, on the shore of the St. Lawrence River in Canada.

Recognized as a person of outstanding religious character, one who had adopted a life of chastity and prayer, she was proposed for sainthood in 1932, becoming the first Native American to receive such praise.

Tennis

First national women's tennis championships (1896)

The first national women's tennis championships were held at the Philadelphia, Pennsylvania, Country Club in 1896. Ellen Hansell Allardice, who took up tennis after watching a match at John Wanamaker's estate, won the singles championship.

Louise McPhetridge Thaden

First to win a cross-country women's air derby (the first "Powder Puff" derby) in the heavier-planes class (1929). (See also Air Derby, Women's.)

Born Pennsylvania c. 1906.

Thaden, of Pittsburgh, Pennsylvania, covered the course from Santa Monica, California, to Cleveland, Ohio, in a Travelair in twenty hours, nineteen minutes, and ten seconds. The distance was 2,350 miles. The race began on August 18, 1929.

Thaden flew a Travelair biplane at an altitude of 25,400 feet in 1928, thereby establishing a women's altitude record.

In March, 1929, she set a record for consecutive flight, staying aloft for over twenty-two hours, but the record only lasted for a month. During 1929 she also set a women's speed record of 156 miles per hour.

With Mrs. F. H. Marsalis as copilot, Thaden set a new women's endurance flying record in 1932: the flight lasted eight days, four hours, and five minutes.

In 1936 Thaden and ex-actress Blanche Noyes, copilot, won the Bendix race from Los Angeles, California, to Cleveland, Ohio, taking away $7,000 in winnings. They flew a Beechcraft Staggerwing plane.

In 1937 Thaden received the Claude B. Harmon Trophy for the year's most outstanding woman flyer of 1936.

In 1938 her book *High, Wide and Frightened* was published.

Alice Thomas

Probably the first woman tavernkeeper and the first woman tavernkeeper to be arrested (1670s).

Dates unknown.

In the early 1670s Alice Thomas, a widow, ran a tavern in Boston, Massachusetts. After complaints were submitted against her, she was arrested and convicted of selling liquor without a license, profaning the Sabbath, receiving stolen goods, and promoting "frequent secret and unseasonable entertainment in her house to Lewd Lascivious and Notorious persons of both sexes, giving them opportunity to commit Carnale Wickedness." Thomas, who was probably the first tavernkeeper, and the first to be arrested, was fined, whipped, and sent to prison. However, she bought her peace with the authorities by giving a large financial contribution to the city of Boston.

Evylyn Thomas

First reported woman victim of an auto accident (1896).

Dates unknown.

While riding her bicycle in New York City, Thomas suffered a fractured leg when hit by Henry Wells of Springfield, Massachusetts, who was driving a Duryea Motor Wagon. Wells was held in jail overnight.

Helen A. Thomas

First woman to head the White House Bureau of a major news service (1974).

Born Winchester, Kentucky, August 4, 1920.

Thomas became the White House bureau chief for United Press International (UPI) in 1974, the first woman to achieve such a position. The following year she added two more first accomplishments to her list: she became the first woman to be elected president of the White House Correspondents Association and the first to head the Gridiron Club of Washington, D.C., a group of reporters, editors, columnists, and cartoonists that had limited its membership to men for nearly a century.

Thomas, who earned a B.A. degree from Wayne State University (Detroit, Michigan) in 1942, wrote *Dateline: White House*, a work that describes her experiences as a reporter during the administrations of Presidents John F. Kennedy, Lyndon B. Johnson,

Richard M. Nixon, and Gerald Ford. (See also Emily Briggs and Marianne Means.)

Martha Carey Thomas

First woman college faculty member to become a dean (1884).

Born Baltimore, Maryland, January 2, 1857; died Philadelphia, Pennsylvania, December 2, 1935.

Thomas was the first foreigner and first woman to earn a doctorate in Zurich, Switzerland (1882). She graduated with distinction. She had been allowed to be in the classroom at the Universities of Göttingen and Leipzig (Germany) but was refused degrees. She went abroad to study after having graduated from Cornell University (Ithaca, New York) in 1877. She had also studied Greek privately at Johns Hopkins University (Baltimore, Maryland), where she was not allowed to attend classes.

Thomas became a professor and dean at Bryn Mawr College for Women (Bryn Mawr, Pennsylvania) when it opened in 1885. She insisted that Bryn Mawr, unlike other women's colleges, enforce entrance examination requirements as rigid as those at top colleges for men, such as Harvard. She also instituted a rigid curriculum, which did not allow for free electives. An autocrat, she limited student freedom, but she established scholarships for European students to study at Bryn Mawr. The college was not integrated racially, and Jewish professors found it difficult to get promoted.

Thomas was an advocate of women's rights, however, and became the first president of the National College Women's Equal Suffrage League (1908). During World War I, she joined the League to Enforce Peace.

After inheriting a half-million dollars from a friend in 1915, she is said to have lived a profligate life, mainly abroad.

Elizabeth Thompson

First patron of the American Association for the Advancement of Science (AAAS) (1873).

Born Lyndon, Vermont, 1821; died Littleton, New Hampshire, July 20, 1899.

In 1873 Thompson donated $1,000 for scientific research, thus becoming the AAAS's first patron.

Educated in country schools, Thompson married a wealthy Harvard University graduate in 1843. He died in 1869, bequeathing her an annual income in excess of $50,000. After his death, she devoted her life to charitable work. Included in her projects was the Elizabeth Thompson Science Fund, which was one of the first U.S. endowments for research in science.

Gertrude Hickman Thompson

First woman to head the board of directors of a U.S. railroad (1930).

Born Virginia City, Montana, 1877; died Yonkers, New York, August 27, 1950.

Thompson's husband was director and president of the Magma Copper Company, which controlled the entire capital stock of the Magma Arizona Railroad. On June 27, 1930, Thompson's husband died. In October of the same year Thompson was made chair of the board of directors of the thirty-mile Magma Arizona Railroad, a division of the Southern Pacific System, and chair of the board of the Bryce Thompson Institute for Plant Research, Inc., in Yonkers, New York. She also was named a director of Newmont Mining Corporation, also founded by her husband.

A noted philanthropist, Thompson contributed to civilian relief in Belgium, Italy, and France during World War I, for which she received a citation from each government. During World War II, she established the Mrs. William Boyce Thompson Foundation for knitting and distributing woolen clothing to the armed services. She also funded and established a dispensary in Lille, France, for children with tuberculosis. She was honored by the Daughters of the American Revolution with a lifetime membership.

Mary Harris Thompson

First major woman surgeon (1870).

Born Fort Ann, New York, April 15, 1829; died Chicago, Illinois, May 21, 1895.

Like Elizabeth Blackwell (see entry), Thompson did not find an easy path into the medical profession. She taught herself math and Latin, then taught in order to pay her way through the Troy Conference Academy (West Poultney, Vermont) and Fort Edward Collegiate Institute (Fort Edward, New York). After briefly attending the New England Female Medical College (Boston, Massachusetts) and serving a one-year internship under Elizabeth Blackwell and her sister Emily, both practicing physicians, Thompson returned to the New England Female Medical College. She earned her first M.D. degree there in 1863.

Thompson decided to establish a medical practice in Chicago, Illinois. Since her M.D. degree from Boston was not acceptable in Chicago, she enrolled in 1869 at the Chicago Medical College, becoming the only woman to receive an M.D. degree there. (Soon after her graduation, the college stopped admitting women.)

In 1870 she cofounded the Woman's Hospital Medical College in Chicago. She also joined the instructional staff as professor of clinical obstetrics, diseases of women, and hygiene (1870–73). In 1874 she founded a nurses' training school. In 1879 the medical college and nurses' school were reorganized to form the Woman's Medical College. Two years later the hospital became connected with Northwestern University (Evanston, Illinois) and was renamed the Northwestern University Woman's Medical College. The woman's medical school closed when all Chicago medical schools became coeducational.

Thompson, who eventually specialized in abdominal and pelvic surgery, became one of the most well-known surgeons in the United States. She invented an abdominal needle that is still used by physicians.

Thompson was elected to the American Medical Association (AMA) in 1886.

Sarah Thompson

First U.S. woman to become a countess (1791).

Born Concord, New Hampshire, October 18, 1774; died Concord, New Hampshire, December 2, 1852.

Thompson's father, Benjamin Thompson, a physicist, had been dubbed count of the Holy Roman Empire, the Order of the White Eagle, by Charles Philip Frederick, duke of Bavaria in 1791. She then became countess of Rumford.

Thompson's parents separated in 1775 and never saw each other afterwards. Her father, however, continued to contribute money for Sarah's needs, and in 1790 he sent for his daughter, who joined him in England. She returned to the United States in the summer of 1799, but in 1811 she traveled to Auteuil, France (near Paris) to live with her father. After her father's death, Thompson returned to the United States, where she lived for the remainder of her life.

Jeanette Thurber

Founder of the only nationally chartered music school in the United States (1891).

Born New York, New York, 1851; died Bronxville, New York, January 2, 1946.

In 1885 Thurber (born Jeannette Meyer) founded the American School of Opera. It was to be the first element of a national conservatory of music, presenting complete operas in English and featuring U.S. singers. The school failed in 1887. Four years later, Thurber launched the National Conservatory of Music, and Congress granted the school a national charter, authorizing it to grant diplomas and award Doctor of Music and honorary degrees. In 1921 President Woodrow Wilson approved an amendment to the school's charter, permitting it to establish branches outside Washington, D.C., but the school failed.

For three years, from 1892 to 1895, noted composer Antonín Dvořák was director of the National Conservatory of Music. During that period, he composed his *New World* Symphony.

Thurber introduced to the United States the solfeggio method of music instruction, in which the notes of the scale are sung as do-re-mi-fa-sol, and so on.

Tracey Thurman

First woman to win a civil suit as a battered wife (1985).

Dates unknown.

Thurman was physically abused by her estranged husband, Charles Thurman, on several occasions. She filed a number of complaints at the Torrington, Connecticut, police station. The complaints, allegedly, were ignored.

On June 10, 1983, Charles Thurman came to her home and attacked her. A male police officer was on the scene when her ex-husband stabbed her thirteen times and repeatedly kicked her in the head. The police officer did nothing to stop the assault.

Scarred and partially paralyzed, Thurman filed a suit, and for the first time in history, a federal judge allowed a citizen to file a domestic violence suit against a police department. She charged the Torrington Police Department with violating her civil rights. In June, 1985, a federal jury, ruling that twenty-four past or present officers had violated the constitutional equal protection rights of Tracey Thurman, awarded her $2.3 million in damages. The jury also awarded $300,000 to Thurman's three-year-old son who had witnessed the brutal crime. The court's decision on behalf of Tracey Thurman was a landmark in that the police department was found guilty not only of negligence but of violating a citizen victim's civil rights.

In October, 1985, Thurman accepted $1.9 million in damages in exchange for the withdrawal of an appeal of the June decision, which had awarded her the $2.3 million.

Charles Thurman was sentenced to fifteen years imprisonment for assault.

Bonnie Tiburzi

First woman to be hired as a jet pilot by a major U.S. airline (1973).

Born 1948.

When she was only twelve years old, Tiburzi, a member of a family of pilots, received flying instructions from her father, a former U.S. airlines pilot. A resident of Pompano Beach, Florida, in 1973 she became a pilot (third officer) on a Boeing 727 jet operated by American Airlines.

Elizabeth Timothy

First woman to publish a newspaper (1738).

Born the Netherlands, date unknown; died Charleston, South Carolina, 1757.

Timothy and her family emigrated from Holland to the United States in 1731, living first in Philadelphia, Pennsylvania. In 1733 they moved to Charleston, South Carolina.

When her husband died in 1738, Timothy published their weekly newspaper, *South-Carolina Gazette*, until she turned it over to her son, Peter, in 1746.

Between 1739 and 1745, she also published some twenty books and pamphlets, most of which were historical in nature.

Benjamin Franklin praised Timothy for her business expertise and fortitude in raising her family alone.

Ana Tjohnlands

One of the first two women to serve as ambulance doctors (1914) (see also Helen Balliser).

Dates unknown.

Tjohnlands and Balliser passed the Cornell Medical School (New York, New York) examinations, which qualified them to serve as Bellevue Hospital ambulance doctors. They served in that function for eighteen months, beginning in 1914.

E. L. Todd

First woman to invent an airplane (1908).

Dates unknown.

A former stenographer at the U.S.

Patent Office in Washington, D.C., she announced on July 30, 1908, that she had invented a collapsible airplane. She exhibited a working model of it at an air show at the Brighton Beach racetrack in Brooklyn, New York.

Todd maintained that the plane, which was one-third its flying size when collapsed (thus simplifying the problem of transporting it) was perfect as far as current knowledge of aeronautics was concerned.

Sally Tompkins

First woman to be a commissioned officer in the Confederate army (1861).

Born Poplar Grove, Virginia, November 9, 1833; died Richmond, Virginia, July 25, 1916.

President Jefferson Davis commissioned Tompkins as captain of the cavalry in 1861, so that she could keep open a private hospital that she had established. At that time, all private hospitals were being abandoned.

She had set up her own infirmary, Robertson Hospital, in Richmond, Virginia, which had enough beds to accommodate at least twenty-five patients. Between 1861 and 1865 the record for healing patients at Robert-

son was unmatched by any other hospital: there were only seventy-three deaths out of 1,333 patients admitted for care. Tompkins's success was attributed in part to her insistence on maximum hygiene.

After the Civil War, Tompkins worked occasionally as a nurse; she also did church and charitable work.

Trade School for Girls

First public vocational high school for girls (1904).

The first public vocational high school for girls, which grew out of an experimental summer program, was established in Boston, Massachusetts, in 1904, with Florence M. Marshall acting as the first principal. The courses were designed to prepare young women for jobs in industry.

Janet Graeme Travell

First woman personal physician to a president of the United States (1961).

Born New York City, December 17, 1901.

After receiving her M.D. degree at Cornell University Medical College (New York, New York) in 1926, Travell served two years of internship-residency at New York Hospital (1927–29) and held a research fel-

lowship at Bellevue Hospital (New York, New York) for the study of pneumonia (1929). During the two-year period of residency and research, Travell was also an ambulance surgeon for the New York City Police Department, where she held the rank of lieutenant.

In 1929 she was appointed house physician at New York Hospital, the only woman physician on staff. At that time she also studied arterial disease at Beth Israel Hospital (New York, New York), which led to her studies of new pain-relieving techniques (1939–41).

Travell was an associate professor of clinical pharmacology at Cornell University Medical College from 1952 until her appointment to the White House in 1961. She was also an associate physician in Beth Israel's cardiovascular research unit.

A specialist in the relief of muscle spasms, Travell had first treated President Kennedy in 1955, following his spinal surgery. When she became his physician, she prescribed daily swims as part of his treatment program. Travell later became the physician for the entire Kennedy family, resigning as White House physician in 1965.

In 1961 she received a special achievement award from Albert Einstein Medical College (New York, New York) and an honorary degree from the Woman's Medical College of Pennsylvania (Philadelphia).

Travell was not the first woman invited to be White House physician. President Grover Cleveland (1885–89, 1893–97) had asked Anna Easton Lake to serve as White House physician and to treat his daughter, who had cerebral palsy, but Lake suffered a stroke and never reported to the White House.

Marietta Peabody Tree

First woman to serve the U.N. as a permanent ambassador (1964); first to serve as chief U.S. delegate to the U.N. (1961).

Born Lawrence, Massachusetts, April 12, 1917; died New York, New York, August 15, 1991.

Tree became active with the U.N. in 1961, when she became the U.S. representative to the Human Rights

Women's Triathlon competitors, June, 1990

Commission and a chief U.S. delegate. In 1964 she became the first woman to be a U.S. representative on the Trusteeship Council of the U.N., with the rank of ambassador. She was a member of Secretary General U Thant's staff at the U.N. Secretariat from 1966 to 1967.

Tree was one of the founders of Sydenham Hospital in New York City, the first interracial voluntary hospital in the United States (1943). She became a member of the Fair Housing Practices Panel (New York, New York) in 1958 and served on the board of commissioners of the New York City Commission on Human Rights from 1959 to 1961.

Tree, who majored in political science at the University of Pennsylvania (Philadelphia), became active in Democratic politics after World War II, and was a member of the New York State Democratic Committee from 1954 to 1960.

Tree's daughter, Frances Fitzgerald, is a Pulitzer Prize–winning author.

Triathlon, Women's

First women's only triathlon (1990).

The first women's only triathlon, introduced by Danskin, was held in Long Beach, California in June, 1990, with more than 2,000 women competing. The three events were a 2.4-mile ocean swim, a 112-mile bicycle race, and a marathon run (26.2 miles).

The triathlon was won by Lisa Lahti.

Virginia Yapp Trotter

First woman named to the highest education post in the U.S. government (1974).

Born Boise, Idaho, November 29, 1921.

Trotter received a B.A. degree (1943) and an M.A. degree (1947) at Kansas State University (Manhattan), and a doctorate at Ohio State University (Columbus) (1960).

As Assistant Secretary for Education, she headed the Education Division of Health, Education and Welfare (HEW). When she was named to that position in 1974, it gave her authority over the Office of Education and the new National Institute of Education, established to conduct and coordinate research. She left the position when President Jimmy Carter was elected.

Prior to her government position, Trotter taught and held administrative positions in home economics at the Universities of Nebraska, Utah, and Vermont. One of her specialties was the improvement of conditions for handicapped homemakers. Trotter became head of the University of Nebraska School of Economics (Omaha) (1963), where she led a successful fight to establish the School of Home Economics as a separate entity, removing it from the control of the College of Agriculture. She became vice chancellor of academic affairs at the University of Nebraska in 1972.

Trotter was appointed vice president of academic affairs at the University of Georgia (Athens), on September 1, 1977 and retired June 30, 1988.

In 1986 she was one of two university administrators sued by Jan Kemp, a professor whose contract had not been renewed. Kemp charged that student athletes who were not achieving passing grades in the remedial English program were being allowed to remain in the program beyond the allotted time, or were being placed prematurely in the university's core curriculum. Kemp, who had been coordinator of the remedial English program at the university, won the $2.5 million suit.

Augusta Lewis Troup *(see Augusta Lewis)*

Harriet Tubman

First woman to run an underground railroad to help slaves escape (1850).

Born Dorchester County, Maryland, c. 1820; died Auburn, New York, March 10, 1913.

Born to Benjamin Ross and Harriet Greene, whose parents had been brought from Africa in chains, Tubman was originally named Araminta Greene. She later adopted her mother's first name.

She was put to work at a very young age as a domestic servant and field hand; she also worked with her father as a woodcutter. A person of

great strength, she was able to overcome many physical adversities, such as the lingering aftereffects of a fractured skull she suffered as a teenager when a slave overseer struck her with a heavy object.

About 1844 she married John Tubman, a former slave, who was also from Maryland. They had no children. Five years later, in 1849, her owner died; rumors spread that his slaves were to be sold out of state. Tubman escaped, fleeing to Philadelphia, then on to Saint Catherines, Ontario, Canada.

In 1850 she began her underground railroad activities, returning to Maryland to help her sister and two children escape. The following year she first led one of her brothers and his family out of Maryland, then a second large group that included another brother and his family. It was her intention to bring out John Tubman as well, but he had remarried, and chose to stay in Maryland.

In a ten-year period preceding the Civil War, Tubman made about nineteen trips, helping as many as 300 people escape to Canada. An especially important event in her life occurred in June, 1857, when she managed to move her elderly parents out of Maryland to freedom.

Tubman won the admiration and respect of many prominent abolitionists of her day as she addressed numerous meetings and conventions. John Brown, the noted abolitionist and leader of the famous raid at Harper's Ferry (now in West Virginia), referred to her as "General Tubman."

Her underground activities caused consternation among Maryland slaveholders, who held conventions in 1858 to try to solve the problem of escaping slaves. The slaveholders offered rewards for her capture that ranged as high as $40,000.

For several years after her escape, Tubman lived at Saint Catherines; this was also the destination for many of the "passengers" on her underground railroad. About 1858, however, U.S. Senator William H. Seward, a member of the new Republican party and an enemy of slavery, sold her a small farm at Auburn, New York, which became her home.

When the Civil War broke out, Tubman served the Union forces as a spy and scout, collecting information from slaves behind Confederate lines. She also worked as a nurse.

After the war she continued to work for former slaves in the South, lobbying for schools for them and for their right to vote. She also opened her home in Auburn to poor and elderly blacks; it became formally known as the Harriet Tubman Home for Indigent Aged Negroes. Still in existence well after her death, it was supported in part by friends, former slaves, and Auburn citizens.

Tubman also struggled for many years to secure compensation and a pension for her Civil War service; about 1898, Congress finally voted her a twenty-dollar-a-month pension.

After she died of pneumonia in 1913, the town of Auburn installed a plaque in Tubman's honor in the town square; Booker T. Washington spoke at the installation ceremony.

Barbara Wertheim Tuchman

First woman to receive the Pulitzer Prize for general nonfiction (1963); first to be elected president of the American Academy and Institute of Arts and Letters (1979).

Born New York City, January 30, 1912; died Greenwich, Connecticut, February 6, 1989.

Tuchman won the Pulitzer Prize for *The Guns of August* (1962), a diplomatic and military history of the period leading up to and including the first weeks of World War I. In 1972 she won her second Pulitzer Prize for *Stilwell and the American Experience in China* (1971). Among her bestsellers of popular historical scholarship were *The Proud Tower* (1966); *A Distant Mirror* (1978); *Practicing History* (1981); and *The First Salute* (1988).

Tuchman earned a B.A. degree in history and literature from Radcliffe College, Cambridge, Massachusetts, in 1933. After working as a research assistant on the staffs of the Institute of Pacific Relations in New York and Tokyo (1934–35), she became an editorial assistant and writer for *The Nation,* owned by her father at the time. During the Spanish Civil War, she reported from Madrid and Valencia. From 1943 to 1945 she was an editor for the Office of War Information.

In 1979 she became the first woman president of the American Academy and Institute of Arts and Letters.

Esther Van Wagoner Tufty

First woman elected to the National Press Club (1971).

Born Kingston, Michigan, July 2, 1896; died Alexandria, Virginia, May 4, 1986.

In January, 1971, the National Press Club (NPC), which had banned women for forty years, voted to admit women—two days after the Women's National Press Club had voted unanimously to admit men. Tufty became the first woman member of the NPC that year. She also became, in later years, the only woman elected president of the American Women in Radio and Television, the American Newspaper Women's Club, and the Women's National Press Club (now Washington Press Club).

After graduating from high school, Tufty became assistant society editor for the *Pontiac Press* (Pontiac, Michigan). She later graduated from the University of Wisconsin (Madison).

In 1935 she established the Tufty News Service and acted as president, editor, and writer. She began covering Washington, D.C., during President Franklin Delano Roosevelt's first term (1935). She continued to head the news service, which eventually covered Washington for some two dozen Michigan newspapers, until she suffered a stroke in 1985.

In 1976 Tufty was inducted into Sigma Delta Chi's Hall of Fame for Journalists.

Florence Turner

First person in U.S. films to receive a contract (1907).

Born New York, New York, c. 1888; died Los Angeles, California, August 28, 1946.

Turner, first known as "The Vitagraph Girl," was hired by Vitagraph Studios (New York, New York) in 1907 to play the lead in a short comedy, *How to Cure a Cold.* She received a film contract from the company that same year. A very popular actress, her name appeared on the screen in 1910, making her one of the few film personalities of the period to gain that kind of recognition, since most screen actors did not receive billing. In 1911 she played in *A Tale of Two Cities,* the first multiple-reel film to be widely shown as a single feature film rather than a serial.

In 1913 Turner left Vitagraph, establishing her own film company in England in 1915. The first year the company opened she produced *My Old Dutch,* which became a very popular film. Voted England's most popular actress, she was nevertheless forced to close her studio in 1916. Most British studios closed during World War I.

She returned to the United States where she wrote, directed, and played character roles in films produced by the bigger studios, such as Metro-Goldwyn-Mayer. In 1920 she made one more attempt at establishing herself in England, but was not successful. However, while she was there she produced what was to be her last significant film, *Film Favou-*

rites (1924). She returned to the film industry in Los Angeles, but she never regained her star billing or her status as a moviemaker.

Louisa Huggins Tuthill

First person to write a history of architecture that was published in the United States (1848).

Born New Haven, Connecticut, July 6, 1799; died Princeton, New Jersey, June 1, 1879.

Tuthill's husband died in 1825, and she decided to become a writer. Her first book, *James Somers: The Pilgrim's Son*, was published anonymously, as were many of her early works. Two of her most widely read books were *I Will Be a Lady: A Book for Girls* (1845) and *I Will Be a Gentleman: A Book for Boys* (1846). After writing these and other books offering guidance in moral living, social amenities, child care, and housekeeping, Tuthill turned to work of a more academic nature and composed the *History of Architecture from the Earliest Times* (1848). The book, dedicated to "ladies," offered brief descriptions of attractive well-designed buildings found mostly in the United States and Europe.

Dorothy Tyler

First woman jockey (1907).

Born Joplin, Missouri, c. 1893.

In Joplin, where Tyler grew up, people said, "No boy in Joplin of her age is her equal in physical strength." The fourteen-year-old took advantage of her strength and trained to become a jockey. In 1907, riding Blackman, one of her own two horses, she won a quarter-mile race, competing against several seasoned jockeys, one of whom was considered a professional. The race, held in Joplin where her father was mayor, was her first.

Julia Gardiner Tyler

First woman to marry a U.S. president while he was in office (1844).

Born Gardiner's Island, New York, May 4, 1820; died Richmond, Virginia, July 10, 1889.

Tyler was the daughter of a New

York State senator, who was killed in a gun explosion aboard the U.S.S. *Princeton* in 1844. She married John Tyler, the tenth president of the United States, on June 26, 1844, just four months after her father's death. John Tyler was a widower and thirty years older than Julia. Their courtship having been the subject of gossip in Washington, they married quietly in an Episcopal church in New York City.

After John Tyler left the White House, the couple moved to his Virginia plantation, Sherwood Forest, where they raised seven children.

Julia Tyler, who had the reputation of being an outstanding hostess and once let her name and likeness be used for a commercial advertisement, became an outspoken champion of the Confederacy. During the Civil War, after the death of her husband, she fled with her children to her mother's home on Staten Island, New York. Her plantation was seized by the Union army during the war, but Tyler was able to recover it after the war.

Letitia Christian Tyler

First first lady to die while her husband was president (1842).

Born New Kent County, Virginia, November 12, 1790; died Washington, D.C., September 10, 1842.

A member of a wealthy and prominent family, Letitia married John Tyler in 1813, when he was a member of the Virginia House of Delegates. The Tylers had nine children, seven of whom survived infancy.

In 1839 Letitia suffered a paralytic stroke, which left her an invalid for the rest of her life.

John Tyler became president of the United States in 1841, succeeding William Henry Harrison who died in office. The first lady lived in seclusion at the White House until 1842, when she died of a second stroke.

Reba C. Tyler

First woman to command a NATO military unit (1973).

Dates unknown.

Tyler, a captain in the U.S. Army, was appointed commander of a NATO unit at Mannheim, West Germany, in 1973. Thirty-four male members of the Forty-eighth Adjutant General Postal Detachment were under her direction.

Mrs. W. C. Tyler

One of the first three women to sit in the Electoral College (1917).

Dates unknown.

The first three women to sit in the

Electoral College (1917) were suffragists from California: Mrs. Tyler (Los Angeles), Mrs. Spinks (San Francisco), and Mrs. Wylie (Fresno).

Tyler was a delegate to the National Democratic Convention in 1916. Following the convention, she toured Massachusetts, Missouri, New York, and Virginia, urging people to vote for the Democrats. She was also president of the Los Angeles Woman's County Democratic Committee.

Typing Training

First typing training course for women (1877).

The first typing training course was offered at a central branch of the YMCA in New York City in 1877. It was a six-month course attended by women students.

Typists, Advertisement for

First advertisement for typists (1875).

The first advertisement for typists appeared in *The Nation,* a New York City newspaper, on December 15, 1875. Bought by the Remington Company, the ad read:

"Mere girls are now earning from $10 to $20 a week with the 'Type-Writer', and we can secure good situations for one hundred expert writers on it in counting-rooms in this City."

Miriam O'Brien Underhill

First U.S. woman to be part of the first two-woman team to ascend the Matterhorn (Switzerland) (1932).

Born Forest Glen, Maryland, c. 1900; died Lancaster, New Hampshire, January 7, 1976.

Underhill first began mountain climbing in 1921, when she climbed the Alps. In 1929 she led the first traverse of the Aiguille de Grépon (France) without a man or a guide, and climbed the Jungfrau (Switzerland) in 1931. The following year Underhill and European climber Alice Damesme scaled the Matterhorn (14,780 feet).

In 1960 Underhill became the first person to make winter climbs of all of the 4,000-foot (or higher) peaks of the White Mountains in New Hampshire.

She was editor of *Appalachia,* the journal of the Appalachian Mountain Club (1956–61), and wrote her Amer-ican autobiography, *Give Me the Hills* (1971), an enlarged version of a 1956 edition published in Great Britain.

Agness Wilson Underwood

First woman city editor of a major daily newspaper (1947).

Born c. 1902.

In 1926 Underwood began her newspaper career at the Los Angeles, California, *Record* (which is now defunct), later becoming a police reporter. During her twelve years of police reporting, she once sequestered a woman murder suspect in her home for several hours in order to secure a scoop. Underwood became city editor of the *Los Angeles Evening Herald* (later the *Herald-Examiner*) in 1947.

In 1949 she received a "headliner" award from Theta Sigma Phi, the National Women's Journalism Fraternity.

Retiring in 1968, after nearly forty-two years in the newspaper business, she wrote her memoirs,

Newspaper Woman, published in 1969.

United States Air Force Academy, Women Cadets in

First women to register as cadets at the U.S. Air Force Academy (Colorado Springs, Colorado) (1976).

A United States law was passed in October, 1975, which ended the all-male tradition at U.S. service academies, and on June 28, 1976, 155 women registered at the Air Force Academy to begin training. Their training options were limited by a federal restriction that barred women from combat roles; the restriction was lifted in 1992, but at that time women could not train as fighter pilots, navigators, or missile-launch operators. (In the Persian Gulf War, women were attached to combat units and assigned to carry out support functions. None of the branches of the armed forces are forced to put women in combat roles, but may allow it. The United States Army, separately, bans women from such roles. The army's position is not affected by current Congressional action.)

The Air Force Academy also assigned thirteen women first- and second-lieutenants as training officers, who served as guidance counselors and role models.

In one of their first acts as trainees, the women joined the male cadets in formation, marching into the main cafeteria. As they ascended the ramp into the cafeteria, they marched under a large banner that read, "Bring Me Men."

United States Air Force Pilots

First women to earn wings as U.S. Air Force pilots (1977).

On September 2, 1977, the first ten women Air Force pilots received their wings, symbolizing their certification as official Air Force pilots, at a ceremony at Williams Air Force Base, Arizona. The women were assigned to tankers, cargo planes, and medical evacuation planes. Because of a federal restriction barring women from combat duty, they were barred from fighter or bomber assignments. That restriction was lifted in 1992.

Women (particularly the Women's Air Force Service Pilots) had flown in World War II, but not until December, 1977, did Congress pass a law granting them military status. (See also Jacqueline Cochran and Nancy Harkness Love.)

United States Coast Guard Academy

First women admitted to the U.S. Coast Guard Academy (1976).

The U.S. Coast Guard Academy (USCGA), founded in 1876, is located in New London, Connecticut. Unlike the other service academies that have senatorial nominees or regional quotas, the USCGA requires candidates to pass a competitive entrance exam. In 1976, the year that women were first admitted, 38 out of 227 women passed the exam and registered on June 28.

Since the U.S. Coast Guard is operated by the Department of Transportation, it was not affected by the October, 1975, law abolishing all-male traditions at the various service academies. Thus, the USCGA became coeducational voluntarily.

United States Merchant Marine Academy

First women admitted to the U.S. Merchant Marine Academy (1974)

The U.S. Merchant Marine Academy (USMMA) (Kings Point, New York) was established in 1943. In July, 1974, it became the first of the U.S. service academies to announce its acceptance of women candidates.

At that time, 15 women joined a class of 333 men. Eight of the first group of women graduated in 1978.

United States Military Academy

First women admitted to the U.S. Military Academy (1976)

The U.S. Military Academy (USMA) (West Point, New York) was founded in 1802. In 1976, 119 women were among the 1,480 newly admitted cadets. Sixty-one of those women were among the first to graduate from the academy in 1980.

United States Naval Academy *(see Juliane Gallina).*

University of Michigan

First state university to open its medical school to women students (1870).

Women were admitted to the medical school at the University of Michigan (Ann Arbor) in 1870, and the first diploma was awarded to Amanda Sanford in 1871. She was a graduate of the Woman's Medical College of Pennsylvania (Philadelphia), who had interned at the New England Hospital for Women and Children, located in Boston, Massachusetts.

Carolyn C. Van Blarcom

First woman nurse to become a licensed midwife (1913).

Born Alton, Illinois, June 12, 1879; died Arcadia, California, March 20, 1960.

After graduating from Johns Hopkins Hospital Training School for Nurses, Baltimore, Maryland (1901), Van Blarcom joined the school's faculty and became superintendent of nurses (1901–05). In 1905 she moved to St. Louis, Missouri, where she helped reorganize a nurses' training school.

She was named secretary of the New York State Committee for Prevention of Blindness. She instructed women who acted as midwives to use silver nitrate drops in babies' eyes; as a result, *ophthalmia neonatorum* (blindness in newborns) was virtually eliminated. In 1913 she went to England, where she studied and earned a license in midwifery. Upon returning to the United States, she wrote *The Midwife in England* (1913), which discussed the widespread training of midwives in England and pointed out that the United States was the only industrialized country that did not formally train and license midwives.

In 1914 Van Blarcom helped establish a school for midwives in affiliation with Bellevue Hospital (New York, New York) and publicized ways to prevent blindness caused by wood alcohol. During the 1920s she concentrated on assisting mothers and their infants through her writing. Health editor of a journal and a textbook writer on the subjects of prenatal, natal, and child care, she wrote popular books that included *Getting Ready to be a Mother* (1922) and *Building the Baby* (1929).

Chronically ill, Van Blarcom retired in the 1930s.

Adeline Van Buren

One of first two women to cross the continental United States on a motorcycle (1916).

Born 1894; died 1949.

On July 4, 1916, Van Buren, along with her sister Augusta, left Sheepshead Bay racetrack in Brooklyn, New York, on their motorcycles, arriving in San Francisco sixty days later on September 2. Their route, which included numerous side excursions, covered a total of 5,500 miles. And they became the first women in any motorized vehicle to ascend to the summit of Pike's Peak in Colorado.

The two women told the newspapers that the purpose of their trip was to convince the U.S. government that, in the event the country got involved in World War I, women as well as men were capable of serving in the armed forces. After the United States did enter the war, however, Adeline volunteered for the army and was rejected.

Augusta Van Buren *(see Adeline Van Buren)*

Venita Walker VanCaspel

First woman member of the Pacific Stock Exchange (1968).

Born Sweetwater, Oklahoma, October 3, 1922.

In 1968 VanCaspel founded and became president of VanCaspel & Co., Inc., a stock brokerage firm. One of her early goals was the education of as many people as possible in the area of financial planning. Thus, early in her career she held free seminars in department stores and later wrote several books on financial

planning. They include: *Money Dynamics for the 1980s, The Power of Money Dynamics* and *Money Dynamics for the 1990s*. At the time that VanCaspel opened her company, she became the first woman member of the Pacific Stock Exchange. The Exchange, headquartered in San Francisco, California, lists regional stocks as well as those on other exchanges.

In addition to founding VanCaspel & Co., she established the affiliate companies, VanCaspel Wealth Management, Inc. and VanCaspel Planning Service, an insurance company. Afterwards, she became a senior vice president of investments at Raymond James & Associates, a position she holds at the time of this writing. She has been a moderator on several national PBS shows, including "The Money Makers" and "Profiles of Success"; she is also listed in *Who's Who in Finance and Industry*.

VanCaspel began her studies at

Duke University, Durham, North Carolina (1944–46) and earned a B.A. degree at the University of Colorado, Boulder (1948), where she did postgraduate work (1948–51). Her major fields of study were economics and finance.

The YWCA named her Outstanding Woman of the Year in 1981. Her other awards include the University of Colorado Alumni Association Award (1987); the Northwood Institute (Midland, Michigan) Distinguished Woman Award (1986); and the Horatio Alger Award (1982). She is on the board of directors of Boy Scouts of America.

Ethel Vance (see Grace Zaring Stone)

Margaret Van Cott

First woman licensed to preach in the Methodist Episcopal church (1869).

Born New York, New York, March 25, 1830; died Catskill, New York, August 29, 1914.

Van Cott, a high school graduate, was an active participant in Episcopal church affairs during her married life, but when her husband died, she joined the Methodist Episcopal church (1866).

In 1868, after conducting revival meetings in such cities as Durham, New York, she received an "ex-

horter's license." The following year she was licensed to preach in the Methodist Episcopal church. Van Cott preached at revival meetings for over thirty years, often traveling as much as 7,000 miles during a given year.

Esther Van Deman

First woman Roman field archaeologist (1901).

Born South Salem, Ohio, October 1, 1862; died Rome, Italy, May 3, 1937.

Van Deman decided to specialize in Roman archaeology while studying on scholarship at the American School of Classical Studies in Rome, Italy (1901).

After earning an A.B. degree (1891) and an A.M. degree (1892) from the University of Michigan (Ann Arbor), Van Deman taught and studied until she began graduate study at the University of Chicago (Illinois), where she concentrated on the classics. She received her Ph.D. degree in 1898.

From 1899 until she left for Rome, Van Deman taught Latin at Mount Holyoke College (South Hadley, Massachusetts). After returning from Rome, she taught at Goucher College (Towson, Maryland) from 1903 to 1906.

In 1906 she became a fellow of the

Carnegie Institution of Washington, D.C., and went back to Rome. In 1910 she joined the Carnegie staff, working primarily in Rome.

During her career as an archaeologist, thirty years of which were spent in Rome, Van Deman established a reputation as the authority on ancient Roman building construction. In addition to being the first woman Roman field archaeologist, she was the first person to develop standards for dating the construction of the ancient buildings; she did this by focusing on both materials and construction methods. She was also a pioneer in the study of Roman aqueducts. Her book, *The Building of Roman Aqueducts,* was published in 1934.

From 1910 until she died, Van Deman worked primarily in Rome. At the time of her death, she was studying methods for perfecting the dating of brick and concrete buildings.

Mrs. Ralph Henry Van Deman

First woman to be an airplane passenger in the United States (1909).

Moments after she made her first flight (which lasted four minutes) at College Park, Maryland, on October 27, 1909, Van Deman said, "Now I know why birds sing. It was wonderful. There is no earthly sensation I can compare with it."

Her pilot was Wilbur Wright, who had been instructing Signal Corps officers when Van Deman, wife of an army captain, walked up to the plane and sat down beside him. He released the weight, and the plane was shot to the end of the monorail. On this first attempt, however, the plane stopped a few feet from the end of the rail. Van Deman, her skirt bound around her ankles with twine, remained in the plane as it was dragged back to the starting point. The second launch was successful, and Wright performed aerial maneuvers some sixty feet above the ground before landing the plane.

Wilbur Wright's sister, Katherine, and Edith Berg, wife of the European business manager for the Wright brothers, had ridden with Wilbur Wright on previous flights in France (see also Lena (Edith) Berg).

Bertha Van Hoosen

Cofounder and first president of the American Medical Women's Association (AMWA) (1915); first woman to head a medical division of a coeducational university (1918).

Born Stony Creek, Michigan, 1863; died Romeo, Michigan, 1952.

Van Hoosen, a graduate of the

medical department of the University of Michigan (Ann Arbor), gained a wide variety of medical experience as a resident doctor in hospitals in Massachusetts and Michigan, as a private physician in Chicago, and as an instructor of medicine at the Woman's Medical School of Northwestern University (Evanston, Illinois) (1888–1902).

When Northwestern's Woman's Medical School closed in 1902, Van Hoosen joined the instructional clinical gynecology staff at the University of Illinois College of Medicine (Chicago), where she remained until 1913, at which time she joined the Cook County Hospital (Chicago, Illinois) as chief of the gynecological staff. In 1920 she was appointed the hospital's chief of staff in obstetrics.

In 1915 Van Hoosen cofounded and served as the first president of the American Medical Women's Association. She felt that women in the medical field (including interns, residents, and students) needed a forum for discussing the difficulties they encountered and a support group to help them solve their problems.

In 1918, while still on staff at Cook County Hospital, Van Hoosen was appointed professor and head of obstetrics at Loyola University Medical School (Chicago, Illinois), thus becoming the first woman to head a medical division of a coeducational university. She remained at Loyola until 1937.

During her sixty-four years as a practicing physician, Van Hoosen delivered thousands of babies. When scopolamine-morphine ("twilight sleep") was a popular anesthesia, she administered it to women during delivery.

In the mid-1900s Van Hoosen gained fame as a surgeon by making appendectomy incisions that were only one-half inch in size, reportedly the smallest incisions ever made by any surgeon. She was later elected an honorary member of the International College of Surgeons. Her autobiography, *Petticoat Surgeon* (1947), was honored by the International Women's Council in 1949.

Mariana Griswold Van Rensselaer

First woman to be a professional art critic (1876).

Born New York, New York, February 21, 1851; died New York, New York, January 20, 1934.

Privately educated in the United States and Dresden, Germany, Van Rensselaer was a person of broad education and wide-ranging interests and accomplishments. She wrote many articles on art in the *American Architect and Building News* (1876). One of her popular works of art criticism was *Book of American Figure Painters* (1880). She continued to write some pieces on art after the turn of the century.

She also wrote a series of articles about English cathedrals that she had visited in 1884. The series appeared in *Century* magazine (1887–92), after which she expanded the text into a book titled *English Cathedrals* (1892).

Van Rensselaer was extremely interested in her home, New York City, and its colonial history. She wrote *History of the City of New York in the Seventeenth Century* (1909), a substantial two-volume work.

She was awarded an honorary degree by Columbia University (New York, New York) (1910) and received a gold medal from the American Academy of Arts and Letters (1923).

Lillian Wald

---

*First president of the National
Organization for Public Health
Nursing (1912).*

Born Cincinnati, Ohio, March 10,
1867; died Westport, Connecticut,
September 1, 1940.

One of the founders of the Department of Health and Nursing at Teachers College of Columbia University
(New York, New York) (1910), Wald
was named president of the National
Organization for Public Health Nursing in 1912. In 1918, during an influenza epidemic, she chaired the
Nurses' Emergency Council.

A worker among poor immigrant
families on the Lower East Side of
New York City, she founded the
Nurses' Settlement, which later became the Henry Street Settlement. In
1902 Wald sponsored Lina L. Rogers,
a nurse at the settlement, in a visit to
the New York City public schools. Rogers' demonstrations lasted about a
month, and at their completion the
New York City Board of Health
agreed with Wald's suggestion to establish the city's—and country's—
first public school nursing program.

Wald graduated from the New
York Hospital Training School for
Nurses (New York, New York) in
1891, and attended Woman's Medical College (New York, New York) in
1893.

Patricia McGowan Wald

---

*One of the first two women
trustees of the Ford Foundation
(1971).*

Born Torrington, Connecticut,
1928.

McGowan was a staff attorney
with the Center for Law and Social

Policy, a public interest law firm in Washington, D.C., when she and Dorothy Nepper-Marshall became in 1971 the first two women trustees of the Ford Foundation.

A graduate of Connecticut College for Women (New London) (1948) and Yale Law School (New Haven, Connecticut) (1951), she joined the Mental Health Law Project in 1972, remaining until 1977, when she became the assistant U.S. attorney general for legislative affairs (1977–79). McGowan, who holds a Phi Beta Kappa key, was appointed as judge in the Washington, D.C., circuit of the U.S. Court of Appeals in 1979 and chief judge in 1986.

Maggie Lena Walker

First woman to become a bank president (1903).

Born Richmond, Virginia, 1867; died Richmond, Virginia, 1934.

When Walker was a young girl she

joined the Grand United Order of St. Luke, an African-American fraternal society, founded in 1867 by a former slave. The order had been established to assure proper health care and burial arrangements for its members.

After serving in a minor office for five years, in 1899 Walker became secretary-treasurer of the organization, renamed the Independent Order of St. Luke. In 1902 she became the publisher of a newsletter, the *St. Luke Herald*. A year later she founded and became the president of St. Luke Penny Savings Bank (Richmond, Virginia). She served as president until 1929, when St. Luke Penny Savings and other African-American banks merged to become Consolidated Bank and Trust Company. She chaired the board of directors of Consolidated Bank until she died.

A graduate of Armstrong Normal School in Richmond, Walker taught for three years. During that time she became an agent for the Woman's Union, an insurance company. In 1912 she founded the Richmond Council of Colored Women.

Loretta Walsh

First woman to enlist in the U.S. Navy (1917); reportedly the first woman ever to enlist in a naval armed service (1917).

Born Philadelphia, Pennsylvania, c. 1898.

Walsh, from Philadelphia, Pennsylvania, was eighteen years old when she enlisted in the navy on March 22, 1917. She was accepted after having undergone the same examination as that given to male applicants.

The opportunity for women to enlist existed for a short time because naval district commandants had been ordered to hire women to have adequate staffing for World War I demands. Since their work was limited to stateside clerical duties, Walsh and the women who followed her encountered little resentment from navy men.

She became a chief yeoman in charge of recruiting for the Naval Coast Defense Reserve.

Mary Elizabeth Walsh

First woman to marry in a balloon (1874).

On October 19, 1874, Walsh and Charles M. Colton were married about a mile above Lincoln Park in Cincinnati, Ohio. The ceremony took place in the *P. T. Barnum;* its pilot, Washington H. Donaldson, worked for the master showman, as did Colton and Walsh. She was an equestrian with P. T. Barnum's Great Roman Hippodrome, which opened on October 13, 1874, in Cincinnati, Ohio.

A crowd of 50,000 people gathered in the park to watch the wedding ceremony in the balloon, a publicity stunt to draw attention to the hippodrome; Barnum's press agent was a member of the wedding party of six.

Barbara Walters

First woman to co-anchor a daily evening news program (ABC) (1976); first woman to be honored by the American Museum of the Moving Image (1992).

Born Boston, Massachusetts, September 25, 1931.

Walters joined NBC's "Today Show" in 1961, as a writer. Within a year she became a reporter and panel member. Between 1974 and 1976, she was a co-host on various television programs. From 1976 to 1978 she teamed with Harry Reasoner as a newscaster on the "ABC Evening News," for which she received a salary of $1 million per year. She became a host-interviewer on ABC's "The Barbara Walters Special" in 1976 and a co-host of "20/20" in 1979.

Walters' television personality, particularly her interviewing manner, underwent the typical under-the-microscope type of attention that is customary with celebrities—especially women celebrities who have ventured into previously all-male domains. She was the target of much commentary of the "pushy broad" variety; in a 1990 *Ladies Home Journal* interview Walters responded to a question about her aggressiveness: "When I first started out," she recalls, "there was a period when people called me pushy while a Mike Wallace [a male television journalist known for probing interviews] would be called authoritative. Or my questions were bitchy while someone else's were courageous; I was a nag while a man was inquisitive. But that's changed now. Women are much more accepted, even as anchors."

Walters graduated from Sarah Lawrence College (Bronxville, New York) in 1953.

In 1975 she received The International Radio and TV Society's Broadcaster of the Year Award and an Emmy from the National Academy of TV Arts and Sciences. In 1992 she became the first television personality to be honored by the American Museum of the Moving Image. The Museum, founded in 1977, features the evolution of the production, technology, and history of motion pictures and television. Walters was honored for outstanding contributions to the television medium.

Bernice R. Walters

First woman physician assigned to U.S. Navy shipboard duty (1950); first woman officer, other than nurses, to be ordered to a regular shipboard tour of duty (1950).

Dates unknown.

Walters, a lieutenant commander, was one of ten medical officers on board the navy hospital ship, U.S.S. *Consolation*. She was one of only five active-duty women doctors in the U.S. Navy's Bureau of Medicine and Surgery.

Walters, from New York City, earned an M.D. degree at Woman's Medical College of Pennsylvania (Philadelphia) in 1936.

Nancy Ward

Probably the first woman to sit on a Native American Council (1775).

Born Chota (now Monroe County) Tennessee, c. 1738; died Benton, Tennessee, 1822.

After Ward's husband was killed

in a skirmish between Cherokee and Creek, she took his place on the battle line, helping to rout the enemy. She was rewarded for her bravery by being placed at the head of the Cherokee Women's Council and given a seat in the Council of Chiefs. She was called "Beloved Woman" of the Cherokee tribe.

Ward married a white man who was pro-Cherokee after her first husband was killed, and she worked toward establishing peace between the Native Americans and whites. After the Cherokee had been subdued, Ward, the daughter of a Delaware father and Cherokee mother, pleaded on behalf of her tribe and crusaded for harmonious coexistence of the two races.

Anna Warner

First woman to write a do-it-yourself gardening book (1872).

Born New York, New York, August 31, 1827; died Highland Falls, New York, January 15, 1915.

A prolific writer of children's fiction and religious works, Warner was also a gardener. In 1872 she wrote *Gardening by Myself,* a detailed account of the planning, configuration, and tending of her garden on Constitution Island, New York, near West Point.

Warner and her sister Susan (see entry) were educated privately in the classics, music, and languages. They were taught by tutors as well as by their father, who had attended college. Bright and talented, they both pursued writing careers when their family needed money. Anna's first novel, *Dollars and Cents* (1852), was about a family that suffered financial loss and had to move from the city to the country. Anna, who wrote over twenty-five books, also collaborated with Susan on several works for children.

The sisters also taught Bible classes at West Point.

Susan Warner

First person to write a book that sold 1 million copies (1851).

Born New York, New York, July 11, 1819; died Highland Falls, New York, March 17, 1885.

The elder sister of Anna Warner (see entry), Susan became a prolific writer, publishing at least one book each year for almost thirty years. In 1851 her first book, *The Wide, Wide World,* was published under the pseudonym Elizabeth Wetherell. A work with a religious theme, the plot centers around a motherless child who is able to overcome many obstacles in life. Extremely popular in the United States and abroad, the novel sold over 1 million copies.

Warner's father, who had attended college, oversaw the private education of Susan and her sister Anna. He and tutors educated the sisters in music, languages, and the classics.

When the family suffered from financial difficulties, Susan and Anna began writing careers. Among the many books that Susan wrote after *The Wide, Wide World* were *Queechy* (1852), and *The Hills of the Shatemuc* (1856), both very popular. In addition to the books Susan wrote alone, she collaborated with Anna on several books for children.

The sisters also taught Bible classes at West Point.

Bennetta Washington

First person to head a Job Corps program for women (1964).

Born Winston-Salem, North Carolina, 1918; died Washington, D.C., May 28, 1991.

Washington served as principal of Cardozo High School, Washington, D.C., where she pioneered a work-study program that became a model for the National Teachers Corps (1961–64). At the same time, she directed the Cardozo Project in Urban Education, the President's Commission on Juvenile Delinquency, under Presidents John F. Kennedy and Lyndon B. Johnson (1961–64). In 1964 President Johnson asked her to launch the Job Corps program for women, which organized training centers throughout the United States.

Washington was the wife of Walter Washington, the first elected mayor of the District of Columbia. She served as the associate director of women's programs and education of the Job Corps, U.S. Labor Department (1970–73). She also represented the U.S. government on various diplomatic missions (1969–74). She remained with the Job Corps until 1980, becoming the special assistant to the assistant secretary for employment training in 1974.

Washington, who earned an A.B. degree (1937) and an M.A. degree (1938) from Howard University (Washington, D.C.) and a Ph.D. degree from Catholic University of America (Washington, D.C.) (1951), received an Alumni Achievement Award from Howard (1966) and Achievement Awards from American University (Washington, D.C.) (1974) and Catholic University of America (1974). She was awarded several honorary degrees and the Human

Rights and Fundamental Freedoms Award (1978).

Lucy Payne Washington

First woman to be wed in the White House (1812).

Born Hanover City, Virginia, c. 1772; died Megwillie, Virginia, January 29, 1846.

The widow of Major George S. Washington, nephew of George Washington, Lucy married U.S. Supreme Court Justice Thomas Todd in a White House ceremony on March 29, 1812. She was the sister of Dolley Madison, wife of incumbent President James Madison, fourth president of the United States.

Martha Dandridge Custis Washington

First woman to have her portrait appear on U.S. paper currency (1886); first to have her portrait on a postage stamp (1902).

Born New Kent County, Virginia, June 2, 1731; died Mount Vernon, Virginia, May 22, 1802.

Washington's portrait was on the front of a one-dollar silver certificate issued in 1886. Her image, modeled after a portrait by Gilbert Stuart, was

on an eight-cent dark lilac stamp, issued in 1902.

A member of a family of modest means, she was nonetheless accepted socially by the wealthy people who lived near Chestnut Grove Plantation where she grew up. In 1749, when she was eighteen, she married Daniel Custis, who inherited a large estate from his father. She had four children, two of whom died in infancy. Custis died in 1757.

Two years later, she married George Washington, and she and her two children moved to his plantation in Mount Vernon. Later she moved to New York, the site of the first capital, during the year of President Washington's inauguration (1789).

When President Washington retired, he and Martha returned to Mount Vernon where he died in 1799.

She then led a secluded life until her death in 1802.

Mary Ball Washington

First woman to have a monument dedicated to her (1893).

Born Virginia, 1706; died Fredericksburg, Virginia, 1793.

On October 20, 1893, Grover Cleveland, then the twenty-fourth U.S. president, dedicated a monument that was placed over the grave of Mary Ball Washington, the mother of President George Washington. The National Mary Washington Memorial Association, chartered in 1890, raised the necessary $11,500 (primarily donated by women) to erect the monument.

Previous attempts had been made to build a monument at the grave in Fredericksburg, Virginia, but they

had failed. In 1830, for example, a number of Fredericksburg women campaigned for a monument. They elicited the help of Silas E. Burrows, a wealthy New Yorker, who joined them in the campaign. The cornerstone was laid, followed by a ceremony at which President Andrew Jackson spoke, but the monument was not erected at that time due to the death of the stonemason.

Washington was the second wife of George Washington's father, Augustine (1694–1743), whom she married in 1730. They had two daughters and four sons.

Pokey (Lillian Debra) Watson

First woman to win the Olympic 200-meter backstroke event (1968).

Born Mineola, Long Island, New York, July 11, 1950.

Watson won the 200-meter backstroke event in 2 minutes 24.8 seconds in 1968, the first year the event was held.

In 1964, when Watson was only fourteen, she won an Olympic gold medal as part of a 4 × 100-meter freestyle relay team. She held the U.S. freestyle outdoor title in the 100-meter event (1965/66) and the 200-meter event (1966). In the Pan American Games (1967), she placed third in the 100-meter freestyle event and fourth in the 200-meter.

WAVES

First official U.S. Navy women's auxiliary (1942).

On July 30, 1942, a bill was signed establishing the WAVES. (Women Accepted for Volunteer Emergency Service). The first naval training was offered at Smith College (Northampton, Massachusetts), beginning in October of that year. Mildred McAfee (see entry) was the first commander of the auxiliary group.

At maximum strength in 1945, the WAVES numbered 86,000 women. In 1948 the organization was absorbed into the regular U.S. Navy and U.S. Navy Reserve.

Dorothy Weeks

First woman to earn a Ph.D. degree in mathematics from the Massachusetts Institute of Technology (M.I.T.) (1930).

Born 1893, Philadelphia, Pennsylvania; died June 4, 1990, Wellesley, Massachusetts.

After graduating Phi Beta Kappa from Wellesley College, Weeks worked for the U.S. Patent Office and the National Bureau of Standards. Between 1920 and 1924, she earned her master's degree while teaching and studying physics at M.I.T. in Cambridge, Massachusetts. After a brief career in retailing with Jordan Marsh in Boston, she returned to the academic world, teaching physics at Wellesley and studying for her Ph.D. at M.I.T. She was awarded the degree in mathematics in 1930.

For the next twenty-six years, Weeks was professor and head of the physics department at Wilson College in Chambersburg, Pennsylvania. After her retirement in 1956, she coordinated a program at the U.S. Army arsenal at Watertown, Massachusetts, developing radiological shielding materials for use against nuclear weapons, neutrons, and gamma rays. From 1964 until her retirement in 1976 she was a spectroscopist studying solar satellites at the Harvard College Observatory (Cambridge, Massachusetts).

Alice Stebbins Wells

First woman police officer to receive a regular appointment based on a civil service examination (1910).

Dates unknown.

Wells was appointed to the police force of Los Angeles, California, on September 2, 1910. By 1914 there were four women on the Los Angeles police force, carrying out regular patrol functions with full power of arrest; they were used especially for duty in skating rinks and movie theaters. Women police officers were also assigned to cases involving abandoned women.

In 1914 Wells spoke to the Consumers League in New York City on the necessity and desirability of having women on the police force. She also spoke before the New York State legislature, where a bill to put ten women on the New York City police force was passed without opposition.

Wells retired November 1, 1940.

Charlotte Wells

First woman to teach a regular class in phrenology (c. 1837).

Born Cohocton, New York, 1814; died West Orange, New Jersey, June 4, 1901.

After attending Franklin Academy (Prattsburg, New York), Wells began a teaching career. Her brothers established a phrenological center in New York City, where she joined them in 1837. She taught phrenology, a system in which a cranial examination is used to determine a person's character, and she gave phrenological "readings." Part of the premise of phrenology, a theory developed by Franz Joseph Gall around 1800, is that if a character profile can be determined through a cranial reading, the person being read can change his or her character. This theory had become a fad in the 1830s.

Wells was one of the founding members of the board of trustees of New York Medical College (Valhalla, New York).

Dottie (Dorothy) March West

First female vocalist to win a country-music Grammy award (1964).

Born McMinnville, Tennessee, October 11, 1932; died Nashville, Tennessee, September 4, 1991.

West, one of ten children, graduated from Tennessee Technological University (Cookeville) with a B.A. degree in music. She and her first husband, guitarist Bill West, toured as a singing duo, but she had no significant success until her 1963 recording of "Let Me Off at the Corner."

In 1964 she was a regular at the Nashville (Tennessee) Grand Ole Opry. She also won a country-music Grammy award—the first woman to reach this milestone—for her song "Here Comes My Baby."

West's biggest hit was her 1974 recording of "Country Sunshine." She also joined singer Kenny Rogers for two big hits: "Every Time Two Fools Collide" (1978) and "All I Ever Need Is You" (1979). During her lifetime she wrote more than 400 songs.

West died of injuries incurred in a Nashville automobile accident on August 30, 1991.

Mae West

First woman to have survival gear named after her (late 1930s).

Born Brooklyn, New York, August 17, 1893; died Los Angeles, California, November 22, 1980.

West, who became a popular comedian in the 1930s and early 1940s, developed and wrote most of her comic acts. She wore provocative clothes and did her own adaptation of popular dances of the day, such as the shimmy. During the 1920s she starred in *Sex,* a satiric show about investigations into sexuality by the pioneers in psychoanalysis.

In 1932 she made her first film,

Night After Night, for which she wrote her own dialogue. George Raft was the male star. By 1935, West was the highest-paid woman in the United States. She and W. C. Fields wrote and starred in *My Little Chickadee* (1940), probably West's most memorable film. She stopped making films in 1943, after moral crusaders managed to tame her work. She turned to stage and nightclub appearances instead. When she was sixty-two years old she performed with a group of musclemen in a very successful nightclub act. She appeared in one more notable film, *Myra Breckinridge* (1970), for which she once again wrote her own role.

West was famous for her double-entendres and provocative one-liners, such as that directed to Cary Grant in the film *She Done Him Wrong* (1933): "Come up and see me sometime."

Pilots and sailors named the vest-like life preserver after her. The inflatable jacket reminded them of the sexy star and her hourglass figure, so they named the preserver "Mae West," a term that became widely used during World War II.

Western Union Messenger Girls

First young women hired to deliver telegrams (1917).

The first Western Union messenger girls were Amie Ford, fourteen years old, and a second young woman who was a high school graduate. They were hired to carry telegrams in New Brunswick, New Jersey, in 1917.

The messenger girls made a hit, and a president of one of the largest banking institutions in the country called for more girls, saying they were quicker and brighter than male messengers. A big plus was that they did not smoke cigarettes.

When the young women were hired, they were not required to wear uniforms.

Edith Wharton

First woman to receive the Pulitzer Prize for fiction (1921); first to be grand officer in the Legion of Honor (1923); first to receive an honorary degree from Yale University (1923).

Born New York, New York, January 24, 1862; died near Paris, France, August 11, 1937.

Wharton received the Pulitzer Prize in 1921 for her novel, *The Age of Innocence* (1920), a superb portrayal of New York society in the 1870s. It concerns the moral dilemmas of a prudish man, who is eventually transformed by love and self-denial.

Wharton began writing in the late

1880s, her first works being mainly magazine stories and verse. Then in 1897 she and Ogden Codman wrote a guide to improving interior decoration, *The Decoration of Houses*. This book was followed by two compilations of short stories and her first novel, *The Valley of Decision*, published in 1902. Her first major novel, *The House of Mirth*, was published in 1905. She wrote a total of twenty novels, ten short story collections, and several travel books.

In 1923 Yale University (New Haven, Connecticut) awarded her an honorary L.H.D. degree, marking the first time Yale ever awarded a woman such a degree. In 1930 Wharton became a member of the American Academy of Arts and Letters.

During World War I she pursued humanitarian activities, including the organization of U.S. relief for refugees. In 1916 she received the Cross of the Legion d'Honneur. In 1923, as a result of her humanitarian work, she was named the first woman grand officer in the Legion of Honor of France.

Anne W. Wheaton

First woman to be a presidential spokeswoman (1957).

Born Utica, New York, c. 1893; died March, 1977.

Wheaton was a close friend of—and press representative for—Mamie Eisenhower. During President Dwight D. Eisenhower's administration (1957–61), she became the first woman to serve as a spokeswoman for a president when she was appointed White House associate press secretary. She served under Press Secretary James C. Hagerty.

After attending Simmons College (Boston, Massachusetts), she joined the staff of the Albany, New York, *Knickerbocker Press* in 1912 and later became one of the first women to be a political correspondent at the New York State capital. From 1924 to 1939 Wheaton was a public relations consultant for the National League of Women Voters and for several other women's organizations, including those favoring Prohibition reform.

In 1939 Wheaton became the director of women's publicity for the Republican National Committee. She was a public relations representative for the wives of Republican presidential candidates (1940; 1944; 1948) and a campaign aide for Nelson Rockefeller when he made his unsuccessful bid for the Republican nomination for president in 1964.

The Whirly Girls

First U.S. association of women helicopter pilots (1955).

When the Whirly Girls was founded in 1955, there were only thirteen licensed women helicopter pilots in the western world. The first woman to obtain a helicopter rating was Ann Shaw Carter (see entry). By 1959 twenty-four women belonged, one of whom was Janey Briggs Hart, wife of former Democratic Senator Philip A. Hart (Michigan).

Frances M. Berry Whitcher

First woman to be a satirical writer (1846).

Born Whitesboro, New York, November 1, 1811; died Whitesboro, New York, January 4, 1852.

Whitcher's special talent as a humorist went virtually unnoticed until some of her writing appeared in *Neal's Saturday Gazette* in 1846. Writing under the pen name "Frank," she satirized the styles of such writers as Reba Smith and Thomas C. Haliburton. A voracious reader with a unique talent for identifying styles and language that were easy to satirize, she also created a persona, "Widow Bedott," to imitate the rustic humor of the novels of the day. Some of the caricatures in the pieces were of country girls aspiring to become genteel and sophisticated. She also wrote a satiric serial, *Aunt Magwire's Experience,* for *Godey's Lady Book* (1847–49).

Her satires proved to be very popular. More than 100,000 copies of the *Widow Bedott Papers* (1856) were sold within a ten-year period.

Helen Magill White *(see Helen Magill)*

White House Honor Guard

First women to join the White House Honor Guard (1978).

Women made their debut as White House Honor Guards on May 17, 1978, during a welcoming ceremony for Zambian President Kenneth Kaunda. A break in the men-only tradition, the assignment of women guards came about primarily as a result of the efforts of First Lady Rosalynn Carter. Her campaigning was in part a response to a letter of complaint that she had received the previous year from Elizabeth Foreman of the U.S. Air Force. Foreman, of Medford, Oregon, had protested the barring of women as White House Guards.

The first guards chosen represented the five branches of U.S. military service: Air Force Sergeant Elizabeth Foreman, Army Specialist Fourth Class Christine L. Crews, Coast Guard Apprentice Edna Dunham, Marine Private First Class Myrna Jepson, and Navy Seaman Apprentice Catherine Behnke.

White House Police Force

First women to join the White House Police Force (1970).

In 1970 the Secret Service chose seven women—whose names were not given to the public—to join the Executive Protection Service. In addition to being attached to the White House, they were given assignments at diplomatic missions in the District of Columbia.

Most of the women who were chosen had served formerly with the Washington Metropolitan Police Department

Gertrude Vanderbilt Whitney

First woman to found a major art museum (1931).

Born New York, New York, January 9, 1875; died New York, New York, April 18, 1942.

The great-granddaughter of Commodore Cornelius Vanderbilt, who had accumulated one of the first great private fortunes in the United States, Gertrude expressed an interest in art when she was very young. After she married the wealthy and socially prominent Harry Payne Whitney, she studied sculpture under Hendrik Christian Anderson and Andrew O'Connor, and attended classes at the Art Students' League (New York, New York).

Whitney, who had been greatly influenced by sculptor Auguste Rodin, established an art studio in Greenwich Village, New York, where many contemporary artists such as Edward Hopper, George Luks, and John Sloan gathered. She began to buy works by these young artists, and began to supply space in her studio for the artists to exhibit their work (1908). The studio evolved into the Whitney Studio (1914) (see also Juliana Force). In 1929 she offered her collection, which numbered more than 500 pieces, to the Metropolitan Art Museum, along with a donation to pay for a new wing in which to house it. After the Metropolitan rejected her offer, Whitney established the Whitney Museum of Art in 1931, with Juliana Force as director. Throughout the years of her patronage, she continued her sculpting.

Among her many works are: *Aspiration,* her first commission, created for the Pan American Exposition in Buffalo, New York (1901); *Aztec Fountain* at the Pan American Union

Building in Washington, D.C. (1912); *Bill Cody,* in Cody, Wyoming (1922); the Columbus monument in Palos, Spain (1929); and *The Spirit of Flight,* exhibited at the New York World's Fair (1939).

In 1940 Whitney was elected an associate of the National Academy of Design.

Abigail Goodrich Whittelsey

First editor of the first U.S. magazine for mothers (1833).

Born Ridgefield, Connecticut, November 29, 1788; died Colchester, Connecticut, July 16, 1858.

Whittelsey and the Reverend Samuel Whittelsey, her husband, established a female seminary in Utica, New York, in 1828.

She joined the Utica Maternal Association—a voluntary organization whose mission was to foster ideals of Christian motherhood with the goal of raising pious children—and edited its newly formed magazine designed for an audience of mothers, reportedly the first magazine of its kind in the United States (1933). *Mother's Magazine,* highly didactic, instructed mothers in the care and discipline of children, dealt with school program issues, and encouraged the founding of other maternal associations.

The Whittelseys moved to New York City, where Abigail continued to edit and publish the magazine until she sold it in 1848. In 1850 she started and edited for two years another magazine, *Mrs. Whittelsey's Magazine for Mothers,* similar in makeup and tone to *Mother's Magazine.*

Sharon Wichman

First woman to win the Olympic 200-meter breaststroke (1968).

Born Indiana, c. 1952.

Wichman, from Fort Wayne, Indiana, won the women's 200-meter breaststroke at the Olympic Games in 1968. In a surprising victory, she swam the event in 2 minutes, 44.45 seconds.

Wightman Cup

First international women's tennis competition (1923).

Hazel Hotchkiss, who was married to George Wightman, established the Wightman Cup in 1923 when she donated a sterling vase to the U.S. Lawn Tennis Association as a prize in international women's team tennis. Great Britain challenged the United States for the cup, and the competition has continued to the present. The cup now goes to the victor of team matches between the United States and Great Britain. Playing doubles in the first cup match, held at Forest Hills, Queens, New York, Hotchkiss and her partner, Eleanor Goss, won 10–8, 5–7, 6–4. The United States won the cup by a score of seven matches to zero.

Hotchkiss (see entry) and Helen Wills (see entry) were never defeated when they played any official match. They won the Wimbledon women's doubles in 1924, and they won the U.S. women's doubles six times.

Hazel Hotchkiss Wightman (see Hazel Hotchkiss and Wightman Cup)

Doreen Wilber

First woman to win the Olympic individual archery championship (1972).

Born c. 1930.

The event, in which only women competed, was held for the first time at the Olympic Games in 1972. Wilber, a housewife from Jefferson, Iowa, shot two rounds of thirty-six arrows at each of four distances: seventy, sixty, fifty, and thirty meters. She scored 1,198 in the first round, and 1,226 in the second round, setting a world record of 2,424 points.

The rules for the women's archery event differ only in that the four rounds are from seventy, sixty, fifty, and thirty meters, whereas the men's rounds are from ninety, seventy, fifty, and thirty meters.

Emma Hart Willard

Organizer of the first higher education institution for women (1814).

Born Berlin, Connecticut, February 23, 1787; died Troy, New York, April 15, 1870.

After attending the Berlin Academy (Berlin, Connecticut) for two years, Willard was appointed a teacher there (1804). Two years later she was placed in charge of the academy. In 1807 she taught in an academy in Westfield, Massachusetts, and then became principal of a girls' academy in Middlebury, Vermont. Between 1807 and 1814 Willard also completed the Middlebury College

curriculum, but she was not allowed to attend classes or obtain a degree.

As an educational expert and observer, Willard recognized a substantial difference between the kind of education offered to men and women. Thus, when she and her husband, John Willard, a doctor, had financial difficulties, she decided to open her own boarding school. She wished to afford women an opportunity to study classical and scientific subjects. When she was twenty-seven years old she opened the Middlebury Female Seminary (1814).

In 1819 she applied to the New York legislature for endowment of her female institution of advanced study. She submitted her "Plan for Improving Female Education," which requested state aid for supplying equal educational opportunities to women. The plan was rejected. However, as a result of encouragement offered by Governor DeWitt Clinton, she opened the Waterford Academy (Waterford, New York).

In 1821, with the financial assistance of the town council of Troy, New York, she established the Troy Female Seminary, which was renamed the Emma Willard School in 1895. Educational offerings included moral and religious instruction and courses in literature, science, mathematics, and social studies. Before the first U.S. normal school—a secondary school for training teachers—was founded, 200 teachers had migrated from this school, which had a formidable curriculum. (In effect, this school was the first women's college.) By 1830 the enrollment of the college had risen to approximately 300 students, and it was one of the most influential schools in America. Willard remained head of it until 1838.

In 1854 she was one of only two U.S. representatives at the World's Educational Convention in London, England.

In her later years, she devoted most of her time to traveling and writing.

In 1905 Willard was elected to the Hall of Fame for Great Americans at Bronx Community College (Bronx, New York) of the City University of New York. Her sculpture, by Frances Grimes, was placed there in 1929.

Frances Elizabeth Willard

First woman to become a college president (1871); first to have her statue in the U.S. Capitol (1905).

Born Churchville, New York, September 28, 1839; died New York, New York, February 17, 1898.

A leader in the cause of woman suffrage, Willard was an organizer of the national Prohibition party (1882) and an early member of the Populist party. In 1871 she became the president of Evanston College for Ladies (Evanston, Illinois). The college merged with Northwestern University, becoming Woman's College of Northwestern University (Evanston) in 1873. She became dean of women there, a position she held until 1874.

Willard was the first vice president of the newly founded Association for the Advancement of Women (1873) and in 1888 became the first president of the National Council of Women. She was secretary of the U.S. National Woman's Christian Temperance Union (WCTU), for which she conceived the slogan, "For God and Home and Native Land," from 1874 to 1879, when she became president. She was the leader of the union for the remainder of her life.

A teacher for several years before becoming a college president, Willard had studied at Milwaukee Female College (Milwaukee, Wisconsin) in 1857 and graduated from North Western Female College (Evanston, Illinois) in 1859.

Willard wrote several books, including *Woman and Temperance* (1883); *Woman in the Pulpit* (1889); and an autobiography, *Glimpses of Fifty Years* (1889).

In 1905 a statue of Willard, sculpted by Helen Mears, was placed in Statuary Hall in the U.S. Capitol by the state of Illinois.

In 1910 she was elected to the

Hall of Fame for Great Americans at Bronx Community College (Bronx, New York) of the City University of New York. Her bust, displayed in the hall in 1923, was executed by Lorado Taft.

Sarah Eileen Williamson

First girl to be elected mayor of Boys Town (1991).

Born Portland, Oregon, September 22, 1974.

On May 2, 1991, Williamson was elected mayor of Boys Town, a non-sectarian municipality located ten miles west of Omaha, Nebraska. She is the first girl to be elected mayor in the seventy-four-year history of the village, which was founded by the Reverend Edward J. Flanagan. As part of her duties as mayor, she pre-

sides at numerous ceremonies and events, and acts as a positive role model for Boys Town's under-privileged, troubled boys and girls of all races and creeds.

Williamson attended the Nebraska Evangelical Lutheran High School (Waco, Nebraska) in 1988/89, then moved to Boys Town High School. After graduating from high school on May 17, 1992, Williamson plans to attend the University of Nebraska (Omaha) to begin her studies toward a profession in the medical field.

As part of her duties, she serves as Student Council president at Boys Town High School, where students attend regular classes. She has participated in basketball, taken lifeguard training, been a member of the flag corps, and conducted tours at the Boys Town Hall of History. Maintaining a 3.1 GPA, Williamson has worked part-time at a local pizza restaurant.

Frances L. Willoughby

First woman physician to hold a regular U.S. Navy commission (1948).

Born Harrisburg, Pennsylvania, c. 1906; died Woodbury, New Jersey, October 13, 1984.

During World War II, Willoughby, who had graduated from Dickinson

College (Carlisle, Pennsylvania) and the University of Arkansas School of Medicine (Little Rock), enlisted in the U.S. Navy, but was assigned to the naval reserve because of her sex. In 1948, however, as a result of the new Women's Armed Services Act of 1948, she was commissioned. The Women's Armed Services Act mandated that there were to be no separate women's branches in the armed forces, and that existing women's branches were to be absorbed into the regular armed forces. The army had already incorporated its Women's Army Corps (WAC) (see entry) into the regular army in 1943.

After retiring from the navy in 1964, Willoughby set up a private psychiatric practice in Glassboro, New Jersey.

She received the Benjamin Rush Award for achievement in psychiatry (1981).

Helen Wills (Moody)

First U.S. woman to win gold medals in both women's singles and doubles tennis at the same Olympic Games (1924).

Born Berkeley, California, October 6, 1905.

In 1924 Wills won the U.S. women's singles tennis tournament as well as the Olympic Women's singles. She and Hazel Hotchkiss (see

Helen Wills (Moody) (left) shaking hands with Elizabeth Ryan

entry) also defeated Great Britain's Edith Covell and Kitty McKane 7–5, 8–6 to win the Olympic gold medal in women's doubles. That same year, she and Hotchkiss won the women's doubles at Wimbledon. In 1928 she and Hotchkiss once again won the U.S. women's doubles.

A winner of eight Wimbledon singles titles (1927–30, 1932–33, 1935, and 1938), she also won seven U.S. singles titles (1923–25, 1927–29, 1931). She won the 1922 U.S. doubles with her partner, Mrs. J. B. Jessup, and the 1925 U.S. doubles with Mary Browne. She won the Wimbledon doubles in 1927 and 1930 with Elizabeth Ryan. The only woman ever to defeat Wills at Wimbledon was Kathleen ("Kitty") McKane (Godfree) of England in 1924.

She was inducted into the International Tennis Hall of Fame in 1958.

Debra Lee Wilson

*One of the first two women to
serve on an armed U.S. military
ship (1977) (see also Beverly
Gwinn Kelley).*

Sarah Wilson

*First "confidence" woman
(1771).*

Born Staffordshire, England,
1750; date of death unknown.

When Queen Charlotte of England's maid of honor discovered
that her twenty-one-year-old servant,
Sarah Wilson, had stolen a diamond
necklace, a miniature of the queen,
and a gown belonging to the queen,
she turned Wilson over to the palace
guards. Wilson was sentenced to
death in 1771, but her sentence was
commuted to indentured servitude in
the American colonies.

Upon reaching the colonies, Wilson escaped from her owner for eighteen months, sold the stolen items,
which she had managed somehow to
hide, and established herself in colonial society. Adopting the name of
the Marchioness de Waldegrave, the
sister of the queen of England, she
mingled with members of fashiona-
ble colonial society, promising government posts and commissions in
the army, for a substantial fee.

Jill Wine-Banks

*First woman to serve as executive
director of the American Bar
Association (1987).*

Born c. 1943.

A graduate of Columbia Law
School (New York, New York) Wine-
Banks was hired to head the
360,000-member American Bar Association in 1987. Her appointment
was a bold move for the association,
which was considered a conservative
male bastion. Her tenure was controversial, however, marked by criticism
of what some members felt to be her
abrasive personality and her alleged
misuse of power.

Wine-Banks, who had attained
prominence as an assistant Watergate special prosecutor and later as
general counsel to the United States
Army, resigned from the bar association position in 1990, saying that she
had achieved all of the major goals
she had set for the job.

Emma Carola Woerishoffer

*Founder of the first professional
school of social economy and
social research to be connected
with a college or university
(1915).*

Born New York, New York, 1885; died near Cannonsville, New York, September, 1911.

Woerishoffer became a millionaire when she was only one year old. Her father died in 1886, leaving his entire estate to her.

She graduated from Bryn Mawr College (Bryn Mawr, Pennsylvania) in 1907. Determined to battle social injustice, she chose social work as her profession. She began her career by joining the staff of a New York City neighborhood settlement house.

Woerishoffer was active in a number of social welfare projects and organizations, and in 1908 she became treasurer of the New York Women's Trade Union League. The following year, she went undercover to work in a number of laundries. She filed a report with the Consumer's League of New York City in which she described the horrendous conditions under which women were working. In 1910 she was appointed special investigator for the New York Bureau of Industries and Immigration.

Woerishoffer died in an automobile crash in 1911. She left a bequest of $750,000 to Bryn Mawr College. Part of the money was used to found the Carola Woerishoffer Graduate Department of Social Economy and Social Research (1915), the first such department to be connected with a college.

Martha Wollstein

First woman member of the American Pediatric Society (1930).

Born New York, New York, November 21, 1868; died New York, New York, September 30, 1939.

Wollstein, noted for her vital contributions to research in meningitis and mumps, also worked with Simon Flexner, M.D., at the Rockefeller Institute (New York, New York) in the first experimental analysis of polio in the United States.

A graduate of Woman's Medical College of the New York Infirmary (1889), she interned at Babies Hospital (New York, New York). In 1892 she began her career as a pathologist.

Wollstein wrote one of the first historical accounts of women's medical education in the United States (1908). In 1910 she and another colleague, Samuel Meltzer, a physiologist, began a study of pneumonia that lasted several years.

Woman Suffrage Associations

The first two woman suffrage associations were the National Woman Suffrage Association

Suffragette Night Paraders on roof of building in New York City, November 9, 1912

(NWSA) and the American Woman Suffrage Association (AWSA), both formed in 1869.

The NWSA was organized in May, 1869 by Susan B. Anthony (see entry) and Elizabeth Cady Stanton (see entry) to lobby for the passage of an amendment to the federal constitution giving the vote to women. Stanton was the organization's first president.

In November of the same year, representatives from twenty-one states met in Cleveland, Ohio, and formed the AWSA, whose purpose was to fight for suffrage bills by state legislatures. The AWSA was also created in reaction against the more activist stance of Anthony and Stanton

and the NWSA, which had favored opposition to the Fifteenth Amendment (giving the franchise to black males) unless it also gave the vote to white women as well. Lucy Stone (see entry) became chair of the AWSA executive committee, and Julia Ward Howe (see entry) was one of its prominent organizers and the principal speaker at the Cleveland meeting. Stone and her followers favored ratification of the Fifteenth Amendment, even if the franchise were not extended to women.

In 1890, having smoothed out their differences, the two organizations merged to form the National American Woman Suffrage Association (NAWSA), with Stone as chair of the executive committee. Once the merger took place, NAWSA concentrated on obtaining voting approval from each state. Elizabeth Cady Stanton was the first president (1890–92), and Susan B. Anthony was the second (1892–1900).

NAWSA espoused the concept that women were morally superior to men and would bring decency to politics. By 1910 there were 75,000 members and branches of the organization throughout the nation. However, the group's reluctance to become more militant in its strategies led to the establishment of the National Women's party. After women's failure to achieve suffrage in four states in 1915, the organization changed its tactics.

After ratification of the Nineteenth Amendment (the woman suffrage amendment) on August 26, 1920, the League of Women Voters became NAWSA's official replacement.

Woman Suffrage Law

First woman suffrage law in the United States (1869).

The first woman suffrage law was passed in Wyoming on December 10, 1869, by a twenty-one-member legislature, then signed by the governor. The same legislature also passed laws giving married women control of their own property and providing equal pay for women teachers.

Purportedly the motives of the legislature were to publicize the new territory of Wyoming and encourage women to migrate there.

Women in the Air Force (WAFs)

First women air force recruits (1949).

On June 12, 1949, by an act of legislature, Women in the Air Force (WAFs) became part of the regular U.S. Air Force. On September 27, 1949, in New York City, four former service women who had returned to civilian life were sworn in as WAFs: Helen Holmes (Roanoke, Virginia), Hatty Jenkins (Brooklyn, New York), Kay J. Madden (Bronx, New York), and Doris E. Stewart (New York, New York).

Women's Air Force Service Pilots (WASPs)

First group of women pilots to fly for the armed forces (1942); first women's ferrying squadron in the army's air force (1942).

During World War II, more than 1,000 women ferried fighter planes and bombers (between 1942 and

1944) to various points of embarkation in the United States. They also towed targets for practice shooting for combat pilots and performed other duties to free male pilots for combat.

Headquartered at New Castle Army Air Base, Wilmington, Delaware, the group—originally called the Women's Auxiliary Ferrying Squadron (WAFS)—was later known as the Women's Air Force Service Pilots (WASPs). The first commander of the group was Nancy H. Love (see entry). Among the first five pilots to pass the qualifying tests were Helen M. Clark and Cornelia Fort. Jacqueline Cochran (see entry) was named as director of women's flying training, with a concentration on cross-country flight to aid in WAFS qualification.

The WAFS/WASPs were assigned not only to ferry planes to combat areas, but also to tow targets for anti-aircraft gunner trainees, lay down smoke for ground maneuvers, carry out day and night training missions for radar and searchlight operators, and perform practice strafing runs.

The pilots, who drew a salary of $3,000 per year, had civilian rather than military status. Consequently, when the auxiliary was disbanded after the war, the women did not receive the benefits due to veterans.

They were accorded military status retroactively by a 1977 act of Congress.

Women's Army Auxiliary Corps (WAAC), (WAC)

First women's auxiliary group of the U.S. Army (1942).

On May 14, 1942, Congress authorized the Women's Army Auxiliary Corps (WAAC). Oveta Culp Hobby (see entry) became the director the following day. Performing duty as secretaries, medical technicians, cartography clerks, switchboard operators, and drivers, but not in combat, the WAACs served in the United States and overseas—in every theater of the war. About 40,000 WAACs were assigned to the U.S. Army Air Force.

The first detachment of WAACs began training at Fort Des Moines, Iowa, on July 20, 1942. They numbered 727 enlistees and one officer.

On September 30, 1943, the auxiliary became the Women's Army Corps (WAC), a regular contingent of the U.S. Army with the same status as other army service corps such as the quartermaster, signal, engineers, and chemical corps.

At peak strength in April, 1945, the WACs numbered 5,746 officers and 93,542 enlisted women.

Women's Rights Convention

First formal gathering to establish rights for women (1848).

The first Women's Rights Convention was held at Seneca Falls, New York, in 1848. Lucretia Mott (see entry) and Elizabeth Cady Stanton (see entry) initiated the call for the convention. The purpose of the convention was to organize women in the fight for equality. Twelve resolutions concerning the rights of women were placed before the group. All passed unanimously, except the one demanding suffrage. The group drew up a "Declaration of Sentiments," calling for the equality of women. The preamble echoed the words of the Declaration of Independence: "We hold these truths to be self-evident, that all men and women are created equal." Organized political campaigns immediately followed the convention.

Of the 260 women who attended only Charlotte Woodward lived to see the passage of the Nineteenth Amendment (see entry).

Women's Rights Convention, National

First national convention held to advocate women's rights (1850).

The first National Women's Rights Convention was held in Worcester, Massachusetts, on October 23/24, 1850. The convention, drew what was described as "a large audience" from nine states; attendees came in response to a national call sent out in May, 1850 by a committee of seven headed by Paulina W. Davis. The committee sent out letters signed by eighty-nine men and women; in return, they received endorsements from such notable citizens as William Lloyd Garrison, William Henry Channing, Elizabeth Cady Stanton, Ralph Waldo Emerson, Jane Swisshelm, A. Bronson Alcott, and Wendell and Ann Green Phillips. Attendees included Lucy Stone, Antoinette L. Brown, Harriot K. Hunt. Frederick Douglass, Sojourner Truth, Lucy Mott, Elizabeth Rose, and Abby Kelley.

The convention, called to order by Sarah H. Earl of Worcester, elected Paulina W. Davis as president. Attendees passed a resolution stating, "Women are clearly entitled to the right of suffrage, and to . . . equality before the law, without distinction of sex or color."

Women's Work Union

First union to establish a department of women's work (1885).

The Knights of Labor was the first union to establish a full-fledged department of women's work. Leonora Barry, a hosiery worker from Amsterdam, New York, was given the full-time job of general investigator and organizer.

The women's work department disbanded in 1890.

Women's World Fair

First fair devoted to the accomplishments of women (1925).

Grace Coolidge, wife of President Calvin Coolidge, exerted her influence and organized the first Women's World Fair: "The World Exposition of Women's Progress." It opened in Chicago, Illinois, on April 18, 1925. The fair was a panorama of what U.S. women had done for a quarter of a century—from 1900 to 1925. The exposition, housed on a two-acre site, included art and industrial exhibits.

President Coolidge made a radio address commemorating the fair. The opening was also announced by Judith Waller, the director of WMAQ radio (Chicago), which broadcast at the site during the fair's one-week run.

Edith Elmer Wood

First woman to chair a national committee on housing (1917).

Born Portsmouth, New Hampshire, September 24, 1871; died Greystone Park, New Jersey, April 29, 1945.

While living in Puerto Rico where her naval officer husband was stationed, Wood became actively involved in housing and public health issues. In 1906 she founded and became the first president of the Anti-Tuberculosis League of Puerto Rico. Between 1913 and 1915 she crusaded against slum housing in Washington, D.C.

Wood earned an M.A. degree from Columbia University (New York, New York), writing her thesis on European government financing and construction of low-income housing (1917).

From 1917 to 1929, Wood was chair of the national committee on housing of the American Association of University Women. She was a consultant to the housing division of the Public Works Administration (PWA) (1933–37) and to PWA's successor, the U.S. Housing Authority (1938–42).

Lynette Woodard

First woman to play on an all-male professional basketball team (1985).

Born Wichita, Kansas, August 12, 1959.

At the University of Kansas (Lawrence), Woodard set a national woman's record of 3,649 points (26.3-point average per game). She won the 1981 Wade Trophy for outstanding woman player of the year. After playing on a small-town team in Italy for a year and the U.S. national team for two summers, she was captain of the U.S. team that defeated the U.S.S.R. (1982) and co-captain of the U.S. team that won the Olympic gold medal (1984).

Woodard, chosen for the Harlem Globetrotters team at a tryout camp in July, 1985, made her debut with the team on November 13, 1985, in Seattle, Washington. She was the first woman ever to play basketball on an all-male professional team. She scored seven points during the Globetrotters' 81–65 victory over their touring rivals, the Washington Generals. The 5'11" guard usually played fifteen to eighteen minutes each game. She left the Globetrotters after two seasons because of a contract dispute.

In 1984 Woodard became the first free agent picked by a women's American basketball team (Columbus, Ohio). She was also named All-American four times in polls sponsored by Kodak.

Victoria Chaflin Woodhull

First woman to be a presidential candidate (1872); probably first woman to open a brokerage firm (1870).

Born Homer, Ohio, September 23, 1838; died Worcestershire, England, June 10, 1927.

Feminist, reformist, and orator, Woodhull and her sister, Tennessee Chaflin, became spiritual advisers to Cornelius Vanderbilt, the richest man in the United States at the time. He helped them establish the Woodhull, Chaflin & Company brokerage

firm in New York City in 1870. The firm became a thriving business.

Woodhull moved quickly from the business world to the world of politics. She campaigned for a single moral standard for women and men, tax reform, and woman suffrage. She joined the National Woman Suffrage Association headed by Susan B. Anthony (see entry), with whom Woodhull became a rival.

In 1871 Woodhull delivered a memorandum ("statement of facts") to the Judiciary Committee of the U.S. House of Representatives. The memorandum argued that woman suffrage should be granted under the terms of the Fourteenth Amendment—which, in Section 1, declares that all persons born or naturalized in the United States are American citizens and citizens of the state of their residence. It forbids the states to abridge the privileges and immunities of U.S. citizens, and to deny any person the equal protection of the laws. The committee tabled Woodhull's memorandum, but the National Woman Suffrage Association (NWSA) (see Woman Suffrage Associations entry) was pleased with her audacity and invited her to make a major speech at their 1871 convention. In the speech, Woodhull seemed to be vying for NWSA leadership, which put her in competition with Susan B. Anthony (see entry), the NWSA president. In 1872 Woodhull called for NWSA to set up a new political party; Anthony attacked this proposal and reasserted her own leadership. A woman with a powerful presence, Woodhull then held her own convention, and in May, 1872, she was named the presidential candidate of the newly formed Equal Rights party. Frederick Douglass, the black abolitionist leader, was named as her running mate. Woodhull was in jail on election day, having been arrested for sending obscene materials through the mail.

In 1866 Woodhull divorced her first husband and reportedly married James H. Blood, who had been a colonel in the Civil War. There was no record of the ceremony, however, and Woodhull kept her first husband's name. In 1876 she became religious and divorced Blood, citing adultery as the cause. In *Woodhull & Chaflin's Weekly,* a paper started by Woodhull and her sister in 1870, she declared that marriage was a divine institution.

Woodhull and Chaflin sailed to Europe in 1877 allegedly with money supplied by William Vanderbilt, son of Cornelius. William was defending his inheritance against attacks by other family members that his father was incompetent; they cited his spiritualism as the main grounds. It was rumored that Vanderbilt wanted the sisters—the commodore's spiritual mentors—out of the country so that they could not testify at the hearing on the will.

After a lengthy courtship, Woodhull married John B. Martin, a wealthy Englishman, in 1883. She lectured and continued to write, publishing *Humanitarian,* a journal dedicated to the study of eugenics, or hereditary improvement.

Mary Emma Woolley

First woman senator of Phi Beta Kappa (1907); first woman to represent the United States at a major diplomatic conference (1932).

Born South Norwalk, Connecticut, July 13, 1863; died Westport, New York, September 5, 1947.

Immediately after graduating from Wheaton Seminary (Norton, Massachusetts), Woolley joined its teaching staff, remaining there until 1890. In 1891 she became one of the first women to attend Brown University (Providence, Rhode Island), although her status was "guest" in classes with men. Later in the semester Brown opened separate courses for women. In 1894 she and Annie Weeden became the first two women to receive an A.B. degree from Brown. She earned an M.A. degree from Brown the following year.

Woolley taught biblical history and literature at Wellesley College (Wellesley, Massachusetts), where she became department chair (1895–99).

She was chosen as president of Mount Holyoke College (South Hadley, Massachusetts) in 1901. During her tenure there, she oversaw the development of a wider variety of courses and the expansion of the college's graduate program. She also became the first woman senator of Phi Beta Kappa in 1907. Phi Beta Kappa, founded at College of William And Mary (Williamsburg, Virginia) in 1776, was originally a secret literary society. It evolved into an honor society for outstanding junior and senior college and university students majoring in liberal arts and sciences. As part of her duties as senator, Woolley assisted the society's foundation in issuing awards and books to deserving students. Woolley retired from Mount Holyoke in 1937, the college's centennial year.

She was vice president of the American Peace Society from 1907 to 1913. President Herbert Hoover appointed her to the American delegation to the Geneva Conference on Reduction and Limitation of Armaments, (1932). Thus, she became the first woman to represent the United States at a major diplomatic function.

Fanny Bullock Workman

Reportedly the first U.S. woman to give a lecture at the Sorbonne (c. 1904).

Born Worcester, Massachusetts, January 8, 1859; died Cannes, France, January 22, 1925.

Workman, a member of a wealthy Massachusetts family, married William H. Hunter, a prominent physician whose practice was in Worcester, Massachusetts, in 1881. Five years after their marriage they began what became a lifelong series of travel and explorations.

They traveled throughout Europe in 1886. A few years later, when his health began to fail, William gave up his practice and the couple and their daughter moved to Europe, spending most of their time in Germany.

Explorers by nature, the couple decided to travel to more exotic places, such as Egypt, North Africa, and Palestine. They often bicycled on their trips. They also explored the Himalayas, making expeditions to lesser-known regions. Considering nearly every trip a scientific project, they studied the topography and atmosphere of the places they visited, recording and photographing what they experienced.

Fluent in several languages, Workman lectured on her explorations throughout Europe and the United States. When she lectured on her travels before the Sorbonne in Paris, she reportedly became the first U.S. woman to lecture there. In 1904 she also became an *officier de l'instruction publique* of France.

Among the mountains Workman climbed was Mount Koser Gunya, part of the Karakoram range of the Himalayas, north of Kashmir. She set an altitude record for women in 1903, when she reached its summit (21,000 feet). She also climbed the second highest of the Nunkum peaks in Kashmir (23,300 feet) in 1906, setting an altitude record that was not broken until 1934.

Goodwife (Goody) Wright

Reportedly the first person to be accused of witchcraft (1626).

Dates unknown.

The attitude of the Virginia colonists toward Wright was epitomized in their condescending name for her—"Goody." Brought before the general court, Wright was accused of casting a spell on the animals of the forest after a hunter had complained that he could never kill any animal he shot at. The hunter also accused her of bewitching his wife and child. Apparently the hunter's wife had refused to allow Wright to deliver their baby because, being left handed, she would have brought bad luck. Nevertheless, the child died after four months, and the mother was sick for three weeks. The hunter alleged that Wright had bewitched them out of spite.

Details of the disposition of Wright's case are sketchy, but she was not hanged. The only colonial woman legally hanged for witchcraft, outside of New England, was Rebecca Fowler of Maryland (1685).

Patience Lovell Wright

First professional woman wax sculptor (c. 1771).

Born Bordentown, New Jersey, 1725; died London, England, March 23, 1786.

In 1769, after the death of her husband Joseph, Wright began

sculpting in wax. Within two years, she had assembled an exhibit of her waxworks of famous living figures, which she took on tour.

Wright sailed to London, England, in 1772, where she created a new exhibit of famous people. Her wax sculpture, which became very popular, was innovative in its use of well-known living subjects and preceded Madame Tussaud's work by three decades.

Her rendition of Lord Chatham is among the wax figures in Westminster Abbey.

A friend of Benjamin Franklin, Wright offered refuge to American prisoners of war in her house in London.

Chien-Shiung Wu

First woman to receive the Comstock Prize from the National Academy of Sciences (1964).

Born Liuho, Chiangsu Province, China, May 31, 1912.

Wu, who immigrated to the United States after graduating from National Central University (Nanking, China) in 1936, became a naturalized citizen in 1954.

She gained a worldwide reputation as a physicist as a result of her research in the field of subatomic particles. One of her major accomplishments was to devise experi-

ments to confirm the theory, developed by Tsung-Dao Lee and Chen Ning Yang, that in certain reactions involving subatomic particles the principle of conservation of parity does not apply. (The conservation of parity principle, greatly simplified, says that in reactions atomic particles behave symmetrically.) Lee and Yang won a Nobel Prize for their part in this work.

Wu earned a Ph.D. degree in physics at the University of California–Berkeley. After teaching at Smith College (Northampton, Massachusetts) and Princeton University (Princeton, New Jersey), she joined the Division of War Research at Columbia University (New York, New York) (1944). She achieved the rank of full professor at Columbia in 1957.

In addition to being the first woman to receive the Comstock Prize, she was the first to receive the Research Corporation Award (1958), and the first to receive an honorary doctor of science degree from Princeton University. She was also elected to the National Academy of Sciences (1958).

She was honored as Woman of the Year (1962) by the American Association of University Women. Wu was president of the American Physical Society in 1975.

Joan Wyatt

First woman prison guard in a maximum security prison for men (1973).

Dates unknown.

Wyatt, from Burlington, Iowa, was appointed a guard at the Iowa State Penitentiary (Fort Madison) on February 1, 1973.

One convict immediately filed a suit, charging that her presence "inflames the passions of prisoners." On March 31, a federal district judge dismissed the suit.

Jeana Yeager

First woman to fly nonstop around the world without refueling (1986).

Born Ft. Worth, Texas, 1952.

The flight, which spanned nine days, three minutes and forty-four seconds, began at Edwards Air Force Base, Mojave Desert, California, on December 14, 1986, and ended safely (despite a damaged wing) at Edwards on December 23. Yeager's copilot was Dick Rutan; their plane was the *Voyager*, a featherweight aircraft designed by Dick's brother, Burt. Their record 26,000-mile flight without refueling beat the previous record of 12,532 miles, set in 1962 by a B-52 bomber.

Yeager, an engineer by training with ten years' flying experience, reported that the noise of their engines was deafening, and that they were buffeted about the tiny cabin—a mere seven feet long, four feet high— of their plane by turbulence. The *Voyager* was constructed of stiffened honeycomb paper and composite carbon-fiber materials; it weighed less than an automobile (1,860 pounds), but carried more fuel than a gasoline tank truck (9,400 pounds of 100-octane gasoline). Its wing span was 111 feet, greater than that of a Boeing 727. It employed the most up-to-date airfoil technology, navigational aids, and weather satellite links.

Yeager and Rutan's food consisted of prepacked meals, which they heated by sitting them on the radiator of the plane's engine.

Yeager and Rutan were awarded the Presidential Citizen's Medal by President Ronald Reagan. The *Voyager* was given a place of honor in the National Air and Space Museum in Washington, D.C.

Yeager grew up in Texas, where her hobbies were skydiving and helicopter flying.

Ella Flagg Young

First woman superintendent of a major public school system (1909) (see also Susan Dorsey); first woman president of the

National Education Association (1910).

Born Buffalo, New York, January 15, 1845; died Washington, D.C., October 26, 1918.

In 1865 Young became the first principal of the practice school of the Chicago Normal School (Chicago, Illinois), a position she held until she became a high school teacher and grammar school principal in 1871. In 1887 she became the assistant superintendent of the Chicago schools.

Young was an associate professor of pedagogy at the University of Chicago (Illinois), when she earned a doctorate there in 1900. She was then appointed professor of education. In 1905 she became principal of the Chicago Normal School. When she became the Chicago superintendent of schools in 1909, she introduced physical training and vocational courses. With the support of the Chicago Teachers' Federation throughout her tenure, she did not resign until 1915.

In 1910 Young became the first woman president of the National Education Association (NEA). The nominating committee of the NEA had voted 47–2 for a man for president. However, one of the two women on the committee obtained the floor and moved for acceptance of the minority proposal of Young for president. This parliamentary ploy came about when Young, who had been placed on the ballot by the NEA nominating committee as second vice president, was persuaded by a group of women teachers to decline the nomination. They then immediately nominated her for president. After a brief debate, Young was elected by a vote of 617 to 376. For its article reporting the event, *The New York Times* gave the headline "Women Outmanoeuvre Men." Young served for one year.

Young Women's Christian Association (YWCA)

First national nondenominational social service organization to provide a broad spectrum of activities and services specifically designed for young Christian women and girls (1886).

The YWCA was founded as a national group in 1886. The first president was Mrs. Henry Fowl Durant.

The YWCA movement had its origins in England in 1855, where it was composed of two separate groups, the Prayer Union and the General Female Training Institute.

In 1858 a Ladies Christian Association was established in New York City, and a local YWCA was organized in Boston in 1866.

Young Women's Hebrew Association (YWHA)

First national social service organization to provide a broad spectrum of activities and services specifically designed for young Jewish women and girls (1886).

The YWHA was founded in 1886 as an auxiliary of the Young Men's Hebrew Association (YMHA), with Julia Richman (see entry) serving as its first president. The YWHA became an independent unit in New York City in 1902. Mrs. Israel Unterberg was the first president of the independent association.

Eventually all YWHAs merged into Jewish Community Centers.

Marguerite Yourcenar *(pseudonym of Marguerite de Crayencour)*

First woman inducted into the French Academy (1980).

Born Brussels, Belgium, June 8, 1903; died Northeast Harbor, Maine, December 17, 1987.

Yourcenar moved to the United States in 1940, and eventually became a naturalized American citizen. She was a highly respected classicist, who translated ancient Greek poetry and wrote numerous historical works. Her best-known novel is *The Memoirs of Hadrian*, 1951.

The august French Academy, founded in 1635, elected her a member in 1980—not without some fervent opposition beforehand. One of its members indignantly characterized the event as "like putting a dove in a rabbit hutch." The secret vote went to Yourcenar on the first ballot, twenty to twelve, even though she had not conducted the usual campaign of intrigue and political maneuvering to win her seat. Her impeccable credentials made a strong case. Known as "The Immortals," members of the academy are elected for life. At the time of the vote, Yourcenar was in Central America doing research on the Mayan civilization.

Yourcenar's French nationality had been restored in 1979 through the efforts of Alain Peyrefitte, a member of the academy who was also French minister of justice. Yourcenar, however, who lived on Mount Desert Island, Maine, said that she intended to stay there and keep her American passport.

(Mildred) Babe Didrikson (family prefers Didriksen) Zaharias

First woman to win the Olympic eighty-meter hurdles (1932); first to win the Olympic javelin throw (1932); first U.S. woman to win the British Women's Amateur Golf Tournament (1947); first three-time winner of the Associated Press poll for Woman Athlete of the Year (1932, 1945, 1946).

Born Port Arthur, Texas, June 26, 1914; died Galveston, Texas, September 27, 1956.

Voted Outstanding Woman Athlete of the Century in an Associated Press poll in 1950, and inducted into the Women's Hall of Fame (Seneca Falls, New York) in 1976, Zaharias won, over a forty-year period, more medals and tournaments and set more records in more sports than any other twentieth-century athlete—of either sex.

She was the star of the girls' basketball team at her high school in Beaumont, Texas. She continued to star when she went to work for the Employers Casualty Insurance Company of Dallas and played on their championship basketball team, earning a place on the All-American teams in 1930, 1931, and 1932. In 1932 she went to the AAU women's national track and field meet, representing Employers Casualty as their entire team. At the meet, which also served as a qualifying event for the Olympics, she entered eight events and won five—the shotput, eighty-meter hurdles, javelin throw, broad

jump, and baseball throw—outscoring the entire twenty-two-member second-place team of the University of Illinois (Urbana).

After winning and setting world records in two events at the 1932 Olympic Games (Los Angeles), she toured the country giving exhibitions, even pitching an inning against the Brooklyn Dodgers for the Philadelphia Athletics without allowing a hit.

Zaharias took up golf in 1934. By 1945 she had won the Western Open three times. In 1946 she won the National Women's Amateur title, and in 1947 she won seventeen straight tournaments, including the British Women's Amateur.

Turning professional in 1948, she won the U.S. Open and most other tournaments she played in, losing only once in seven years. After she underwent surgery for cancer in 1953, Zaharias came back to win the U.S. Open and the All-American Open in 1954. After another operation in 1956, she succumbed to cancer in September of that year.

Her autobiography, *This Life I've Led,* was published in 1955.

Ellen Taaffe Zwilich

First woman to win a Pulitzer Prize for music (1983); first to earn a doctorate in composition from The Juilliard School (1975).

Born Miami, Florida, April 30, 1939.

In 1982 the American Composers Orchestra (ACO) commissioned the first orchestral work by Zwilich— Three Movements for Orchestra, her Symphony no. 1. The symphony, which is eighteen minutes long, won the 1983 Pulitzer Prize for music, making Zwilich the first woman to receive the prize in that category.

Another first for Zwilich came a few years earlier: in 1975 she became the first woman to receive her doctorate in composition from The Juilliard School (New York, New York). Before attending Juilliard, she earned both a B.A. degree (1960) and an M.A. degree (1962) from Florida State University (Tallahassee).

Zwilich, who had studied violin, trumpet, and piano, was a violinist for seven years with the American

Symphony Orchestra, conducted by Leopold Stokowski (1965–72).

Her compositions include three symphonies, eight concertos, and other orchestral works and chamber music. They have been performed by virtually every major orchestra in the United States, including the New York Philharmonic, the Clevland Or-chestra, and the Chicago Symphony.

In 1974 Zwilich's String Quartet won the Elizabeth Spraque Coolidge Chamber Music Prize. Her Sonata in Three Movements, composed in 1973, won an international gold medal in Italy in 1975, and she won the Arturo Toscanini Music Critics' Award in 1986.

INDEX

ABOUT THE AUTHORS

Phyllis J. Read is a co-author of *Strategies for Learning* (Kendall Hunt Publishers, 1991), and has served as a textbook editor and reviewer for major publishers, including Random House; D. C. Heath; Scott, Foresman; and Harcourt Brace Jovanovich. She has published critical articles in leading journals, including *Twentieth Century Fiction* and *Victorian Studies*, and her newspaper articles have appeared in local New York papers. She is a licensed private pilot with land and sea ratings. Read is the first woman to co-author a book on first achievements of women in the United States.

Bernard L. Witlieb is co-author of the McGraw-Hill text *Americas: A Multicultural Reader for Developmental Writers*. He was an editor of *The New York Times Book of the Environment 1965–1975*, assistant etymology editor of the *World Book Encyclopedia Dictionary*, and English language editor of the *Cuyas Spanish Dictionary*. His scholarly writings have appeared in the *Chaucer Newsletter*, *English Language Notes*, *Notes and Queries*, *The Ricardian*, and *Verbatim*. He has received three National Endowment for the Humanities grants and an Andrew Mellon fellowship.

Both authors are English professors at Bronx Community College of the City University of New York, and both reside in Westchester County, New York.